Lecture Notes in Artificial Intelligence   8861

Subseries of Lecture Notes in Computer Science

LNAI Series Editors

Randy Goebel
University of Alberta, Edmonton, Canada
Yuzuru Tanaka
Hokkaido University, Sapporo, Japan
Wolfgang Wahlster
DFKI and Saarland University, Saarbrücken, Germany

LNAI Founding Series Editor

Joerg Siekmann
DFKI and Saarland University, Saarbrücken, Germany

T0212806

Hoa Khanh Dam   Jeremy Pitt   Yang Xu
Guido Governatori   Takayuki Ito (Eds.)

PRIMA 2014: Principles and Practice of Multi-Agent Systems

17th International Conference
Gold Coast, QLD, Australia, December 1-5, 2014
Proceedings

Springer

Volume Editors

Hoa Khanh Dam
University of Wollongong
Northfields Avenue, Wollongong, NSW 2522, Australia
E-mail: hoa@uow.edu.au

Jeremy Pitt
Imperial College, London SW7 2BT, UK
E-mail: j.pitt@imperial.ac.uk

Yang Xu
University of Electronic Science and Technology of China
Chengdu, Sichuan 610051, China
E-mail: xuyang@uestc.edu.cn

Guido Governatori
NICTA Queensland Research Laboratory
GPO Box 2434, Brisbane, QLD 4001, Australia
E-mail: guido.governatori@nicta.com.au

Takayuki Ito
Nagoya Institute of Technology
Gokiso-cho, Showa-ku, Nagoya 466-8555, Japan
E-mail: ito.takayuki@nitech.ac.jp

ISSN 0302-9743   e-ISSN 1611-3349
ISBN 978-3-319-13190-0   e-ISBN 978-3-319-13191-7
DOI 10.1007/978-3-319-13191-7
Springer Cham Heidelberg New York Dordrecht London

Library of Congress Control Number: 2014953773

LNCS Sublibrary: SL 7 – Artificial Intelligence

Typesetting: Camera-ready by author, data conversion by Scientific Publishing Services, Chennai, India

Printed on acid-free paper

Springer is part of Springer Science+Business Media (www.springer.com)

Preface

Welcome to the proceedings of the the 17th International Conference on Principles and Practice of Multi-Agent Systems (PRIMA 2014) held in Gold Coast, Australia, during December 1–5, 2014. The proceedings feature high-quality, state-of-the-art research in multi-agent systems from all over the world.

PRIMA has emerged as one of the premier forums for bringing together researchers, developers, and academic and industry leaders who are active and interested in agents and multi-agent systems, their practices and related areas. PRIMA specifically offers an exceptional opportunity for showcasing work on foundations of agent systems and engineering agent systems as well as for promoting emerging areas of agent-research in other domains. PRIMA was originally a regional workshop on multi-agent systems held in Hanoi, Bangkok, Guilin, Kuala Lumpur, Auckland, Seoul, Tokyo, Taipei, Melbourne, Kyoto, and Singapore, which started in 1998. In 2009, PRIMA grew to become a high-quality international conference and was held in Nagoya, Japan (2009); Kolkata, India (2010); Wollongong, Australia (2011); Kuching, Malaysia (2012); and Dunedin, New Zealand (2013). PRIMA 2014 was a full-fledged conference for international researchers and practitioners to meet and share their work, built on the success of its predecessor workshops and conferences. PRIMA 2014 was co-located with the 13th Pacific Rim International Conference on Artificial Intelligence (PRICAI 2014).

PRIMA 2014 attracted 77 submissions from 24 countries, each of which was assigned to four Program Committee (PC) members, who were overseen by a senior PC (SPC) member. Each paper received at least three reviews. The review period was followed by an author response phase, and discussion among the PC, coordinated by the SPC member assigned to the paper. Of the 77 submissions, PRIMA 2014 accepted 21 full papers with an acceptance rate of 27.3%. In addition, 17 promising, but not fully mature contributions were accepted at reduced length as short papers; two of these were subsequently withdrawn by the authors. The papers that were submitted by one of the PC chairs were overseen by the other PC chairs in order to guarantee the integrity of the reviewing process.

The conference technical paper program covered a broad range of issues and topics in multi-agent systems, with sessions on:

- Self-Organization and Social Networks/Crowdsourcing
- Logic and Argumentation
- Simulation and Assurance
- Interaction and Applications
- Norms, Games and Social Choice
- Metrics, Optimization, Negotiation and Learning

The conference itself also included sessions to encourage interaction and networking, with lightning talks, an extended poster and demo session, and a panel, as well as an exciting set of invited talks, in conjunction with PRICAI.

We would like to thank all individuals, institutions, and sponsors that supported PRIMA 2014. We greatly appreciate the expertise and dedication of our SPC, PC, and external reviewers in providing timely detailed reviews. We are confident that this process has resulted in a high-quality diverse conference program. We are grateful to the substantial efforts of the local organization team led by Sankalp Khanna. We would also like to thank the senior advisors of PRIMA 2014: Aditya Ghose, Sandip Sen, and Makoto Yokoo. Finally, a special thanks goes to all who contributed with their submissions, presentations, questions, and active participation in the conference. We hope you enjoy the proceedings!

September 2014

Hoa Khanh Dam
Jeremy Pitt
Yang Xu
Guido Governatori
Takayuki Ito

Organization

General Co-chairs

Guido Governatori — NICTA, Australia
Takayuki Ito — Nagoya Institute of Technology, Japan

Program Co-chairs

Hoa Khanh Dam — University of Wollongong, Australia
Jeremy Pitt — Imperial College London, UK
Yang Xu — University of Electronic Science and Technology, China

Workshop and Tutorial Chairs

Charles Orgil Gretton — NICTA and Griffith University, Australia
Bastin Tony Roy Savarimuthu — University of Otago, New Zealand

Publicity Chairs

Vineet Padmanabhan — University of Hyderabad, India
Yuko Sakurai — Kyushu University, Japan
Minjie Zhang — University of Wollongong, Australia

Local Arrangements Chairs

Sankalp Khanna — CSIRO, Australia

Sponsorship Chair

Michael Blumenstein — Griffith University, Australia

Conference Secretary and Treasurer

Natalie Dunstan — Griffith University, Australia

Web Chair

Katsuhide Fujita — Tokyo University of Agriculture and Technology, Japan

Senior Advisors

Aditya Ghose	University of Wollongong, Australia
Sandip Sen	University of Tulsa, USA
Makoto Yokoo	Kyushu University, Japan

Senior Program Committee

Bo An	Chinese Academy of Sciences, China
Tina Balke	University of Surrey, UK
Paul Davidsson	Malmo University, Sweden
Yves Demazeau	CNRS - LIG, France
Frank Dignum	Utrecht University, The Netherlands
Guido Governatori	NICTA, Australia
Katsutoshi Hirayama	Kobe University, Japan
Takayuki Ito	Nagoya Institute of Technology, Japan
Zhi Jin	Peking University, China
Andrea Omicini	Università di Bologna, Italy
Julian Padget	University of Bath, UK
David Pynadath	USC Institute for Creative Technologies, USA
Bastin Tony Roy Savarimuthu	University of Otago, New Zealand
Paul Scerri	Carnegie Mellon University, USA
Paolo Torroni	University of Bologna, Italy
Pradeep Varakantham	Singapore Management University, Singapore
Harko Verhagen	Stockholm University, Sweden
Bo Yang	Jilin University, China
Jie Zhang	Nanyang Technological University, Singapore

Program Committee

Sathish Babu B.	Siddaganga Institute of Technology, India
Quan Bai	Auckland University of Technology, New Zealand
Francesco Belardinelli	Université d'Evry, France
Gauvain Bourgne	LIP6 - UPMC, France
Stefano Bromuri	University of Applied Sciences Western Switzerland, Switzerland
Nils Bulling	Clausthal University of Technology, Germany
Dídac Busquets	Imperial College London, UK
Arthur Carvalho	University of Waterloo, Canada
Shantanu Chakraborty	NEC Coporation, Japan
Xiaoping Chen	University of Science and Technology of China, China
Shih-Fen Cheng	Singapore Management University, Singapore
Amit Chopra	Lancaster University, UK
Mehdi Dastani	Utrecht University, The Netherlands

Franco Raimondi	Middlesex University, UK
Fenghui Ren	University of Wollongong, Australia
Alessandro Ricci	University of Bologna, Italy
Regis Riveret	Imperial College London, UK
Juan Antonio Rodriguez Aguilar	IIIA-CSIC, Spain
Antonino Rotolo	University of Bologna, Italy
Yuko Sakurai	Kyushu University, Japan
Guillermo Ricardo Simari	Universidad Nacional del Sur in Bahia Blanca, Argentina
Clara Smith	IRI, UNLP, Argentina
Insu Song	James Cook University, Australia
Jan-Philipp Steghöfer	University of Augsburg, Germany
Satoshi Takahashi	The University of Electro-Communication, Japan
John Thangarajah	RMIT University, Australia
Fujio Toriumi	The University of Tokyo, Japan
Wamberto Vasconcelos	University of Aberdeen, UK
Serena Villata	Inria Sophia Antipolis, France
Meritxell Vinyals	University of Southampton, UK
Xiaofeng Wang	Chinese Academy of Sciences, China
Brendon J. Woodford	University of Otago, New Zealand
Yanping Xiang	UESTC, China
Neil Yorke-Smith	American University of Beirut, Lebanon
Kun Yue	Yunnan University, China

Additional Reviewers

Ahlbrecht, Tobias	Morales, Javier
Airiau, Stéphane	Nguyen, Tung
Birje, Mahantesh	Niewiadomski, Artur
Dahlskog, Steve	Pujol-Gonzalez, Marc
Griffiths, Nathan	Qin, Kai
Hishiyama, Reiko	Ronald, Nicole
Hosseini, Hadi	S. Kakkasageri, Mahabaleshwar
Huang, Fan	Smyrnakis, Michalis
Ji, Jianmin	Testerink, Bas
Jing, Xiaoxin	Tsang, Alan
Kalia, Anup	Zambetta, Fabio
Kazar, Okba	Zbrzezny, Agnieszka
Knapik, Michał	Zhan, Jieyu
Knobbout, Max	Zhang, Dongxiang
Mohammed, Abdul-Wahid	Zhang, Haochong

Table of Contents

Simulation and Assurance

Interaction and Applications

Norms, Games and Social Choice

Metrics, Optimisation, Negotiation and Learning

PosoMAS: An Extensible, Modular SE Process for Open Self-organising Systems

Jan-Philipp Steghöfer, Hella Seebach, Benedikt Eberhardinger,
and Wolfgang Reif

Institute for Software & Systems Engineering, Augsburg University, Germany
{firstname.lastname}@informatik.uni-augsburg.de

Abstract. This paper introduces PosoMAS, the Process for open, self-organising Multi-Agent Systems. The process is composed of a number of practices, reusable and customisable building parts, and integrated into the lifecycle of the Open Unified Process to yield an iterative, incremental software engineering process tailored to open self-organising systems. The individual practices are introduced and their interplay described. We evaluate PosoMAS in two case studies and provide a qualitative comparison with existing AOSE processes.

1 Requirements for Agent-Oriented Software Engineering Processes

If a system has to be open and has to exhibit self-organisation, principled software engineering techniques become even more important. For instance, in such cases, the benevolence assumption, i.e., the assumption that the individual agents contribute to reaching an overall system goal, can no longer be maintained. The dynamics of self-organisation and the potential negative emergent effects are thus coupled with self-interested, erratic, and even potentially malevolent agents that still have to be integrated in the system. Examples for domains that exhibit such effects are energy management [1] and open grid computing [2].

Our previous scientific contributions (refer to, e.g., [1, 3–5]) have dealt with these issues without being embedded in a methodology for the principled design of such systems.

PosoMAS, the **P**rocess for **o**pen **s**elf-**o**rganising **M**ultiagent **S**ystems, has been designed to remedy this situation. It addresses a number of requirements outlined below that are motivated by the need to make multi-agent technology and self-organisation principles available to software engineers and by the specific characteristics of open, self-organising systems. We do not claim that the process is the be-all and end-all of agent-oriented software engineering approaches but addresses specific circumstances under which it is applicable. If a project does not adhere to the assumptions made by PosoMAS or requires additional aspects, other processes might be more suitable. However, due to its modular design, PosoMAS can be adapted to suit the needs of a specific product or development team. Based on an analysis of existing agent-oriented software engineer-

H.K. Dam et al. (Eds.): PRIMA 2014, LNAI 8861, pp. 1–17, 2014.

ing (AOSE) processes (cf. Section 2) and our own experience with self-organising systems, we identified the following requirements:

Extensibility and Customisability. The methodology must be extensible. It must be possible to combine it with different process models and to customise it for specific situations. This means that it must be possible to use the elements of the method in an agile context (e.g., in a specialised Scrum process) as well as in a heavy-weight context (e.g., the still pervasive waterfall method).

Independence from Architectures or Tools. The internal architecture of the agents (such as BDI) and the concrete implementation platform should play no role in the high-level design part of the process. Likewise, the modelling language should not be pre-determined to allow designers with a regular software engineering background to use tools that they know and understand.

Clear Separation of Different Architecture Domains. To accommodate open systems and separate design teams, the process has to provide aids that allow the separate definition of interfaces, data models, and interactions so that other development teams know how the agents should behave in the system, interact with other agents, and with the system as a whole.

Special Focus on Interactions between Agents and Agent Organisations. The dynamics of an open self-organising multi-agent system are defined by the interactions between agents within organisations. The behaviour of the individual agent within an organisation determines the fitness for purpose of the organisation and of its ability to reach its goal within the system. Organisational structure also affects scalability of the final system. In addition, self-organisation functionality is usually a result of bottom-up interactions that have to be consolidated with the top-down requirements [3].

We adopt the principles of standard software engineering methods such as the OpenUP (PosoMAS uses the Eclipse Process Framework (EPF) practices library that contains OpenUP building blocks), that promote, e.g., reuse, evolutionary design, shared vision. These principles are documented, e.g., in [6] for the Rational Unified Process (RUP), a commercial methodology that introduced many of the features present in modern processes. Arguably, the value of processes such as RUP stems mostly from their extensive documentation of SE practices and guidelines. These are used in a situational method engineering (SME) approach for the creation of a customised software engineering methodology from these reusable assets. Likewise, PosoMAS provides such assets containing a wealth of information on AOSE with a focus on self-organisation and adaptation which continues to grow as the process matures. These building blocks are collected in a *method library* or *method repository* [7] which is available at http://posomas.isse.de, along with the process description and an example.

This paper introduces PosoMAS, relates and compares it to existing AOSE methodologies in Section 2, describes the practices that make up the method content in Section 3 as well as the life cycle it uses in Section 4. Since the format of a paper is insufficient to describe a comprehensive methodology in full detail, the reader is advised to peruse the detailed process description at `http://posomas.isse.de`. The website also offers the process description for use in the EPF Composer. Finally, Section 5 compares PosoMAS with existing processes, discusses benefits and lessons learned in simulated development efforts. The paper closes with a discussion of future work.

2   Characteristics of Existing AOSE Methodologies

This section gives an overview of current AOSE methodologies, pointing out their unique characteristics. Apart from the original papers on the methodologies, we also use content provided by attempts to compare methodologies. Such comparative studies (e.g., [8]) are, however, to be taken with a grain of salt, since the set of evaluation criteria used are not necessarily agreed-upon standards. Since such standards are missing, however, such studies currently provide the only reference point for comparing AOSE methodologies. The processes selected below have been mainly chosen due to the currentness of the published method content. A recent overview of agent-oriented design processes is presented in [9] where a number of processes are cast in the IEEE FIPA Process Documentation Template but the book offers no *new* method content (e.g., for Gaia or Tropos) or a qualitative comparison of the methodologies.

The **Prometheus** methodology [10] combines specification, design, and implementation in a detailed process and is commonly accepted as one of the most mature AOSE approaches (cf. [11–13]). Prometheus uses a bottom-up approach for the development of multi-agent systems with BDI agents. While the focus on BDI is often lauded [12, 13], some authors criticise that this constitutes a restriction of application domains [11]. According to [10], however, only a subset of Prometheus is specific to BDI agents. Still, *independence* is thus limited. The process has no notion of agent organisation and focuses solely on *interactions* between the agents. This also limits the *separation of architecture domains*. A main feature are detailed and comprehensible guidelines that support the development steps, as well as support for validation, code generation, consistency checks, testing and debugging. These guidelines promote *extensibility* but it is unclear how the process can be adapted to different process lifecycles.

ADELFE has been specifically developed for the design of adaptive multi-agent systems (AMAS) with emergent functionality [14]. The methodology follows the Rational Unified Process (RUP) closely and uses UML and AUML, an extension of the UML meta-model with agent-specific concepts [15]. The method content for ADELFE is provided in the SPEM[1] format, making it *extensible* and reusable. It follows principles from the AMAS theory as well as classical object-oriented approaches. Adherence to the AMAS theory is also the main criteria when assessing the applicability of ADELFE for a specific system: it should have a certain complexity and should be open. Additionally, the development of algorithmic solutions to the core problems is an integral part of the process and therefore, the approach is mainly suitable when the algorithms are not known

---

[1] Software & Systems Process Engineering Metamodel (`http://www.omg.org/spec/SPEM/2.0/`), defined by the Object Management Group (OMG).

yet. This severely limits the methodology's *independence*. If an agent reaches a certain complexity in ADELFE, it is treated as a separate AMAS, thus providing a focus on *interaction* between agents and agent organisations. This also provides some separation of *architecture domains*, but the process does not provide guidelines on the separate, principled modelling of these domains.

ASPECS focuses on complex systems with an emphasis on holonic organisations [16] based on the PASSI methodology. A holon is here defined as "[...] self-similar structure composed of holons as sub-structures". The organisation into holons is captured in a meta-model that is used for the definition of the system structure. An important principle leveraged in ASPECS is the possibility of stepwise refinement of the holons. Like ADELFE, the methodology therefore has drawbacks w.r.t. *independence* and, in addition, relies on a specific meta-model. It is, however, extensible since the method content is available online. Both *separation of architecture domains* and a focus on *interactions* are ensured.

The *M*ulti*a*gent *S*ystems *E*ngineering methodology **MaSE** includes a development life cycle starting from the initial system specification and including implementation and deployment [12,13,17]. It has been applied in several research projects and has been lauded for its comprehensibility [11]. MaSE is *independent* of a specific agent architecture and can therefore be applied to heterogeneous systems [12]. A strength of the methodology is the way agent interactions and protocols are defined. Drawbacks are the complex description of concurrent tasks, the absence of models for the environment and agent behaviour, and missing specification tools for agent adaptivity [13,18]. In addition, the methodology was difficult to customise and organisational factors were not considered [19]. Based on this criticism, **O-MaSE** and "agentTool"[2] have been developed [19]. They provide a method engineering framework with which method fragments specified as SPEM[1] activities can be composed. The method content is based on a common meta-model and focuses mainly on analysis, design, and implementation. Organisations and the environment are now explicitly considered. *Extensibility* and *independence* are thus limited due to the specialised tool required and due to the meta-model. O-MaSE provides no overall system design activities, thus reducing the *separation of architecture domains.*

INGENIAS [20] aims at the development of organisational multi-agent systems and is the descendant of MESSAGE [21]. It uses meta-models to describe the relevant concepts in different aspects or "viewpoints" of a MAS, including organisation, agent, goals/tasks, interactions, and environment [20]. Relationships between the concepts for the different viewpoints are exploited to ensure consistency of the modelling. Meta-models are described in a specialised modelling language. The agents are based on BDI. INGENIAS is supported by specialised tools for modelling and process customisation. While this limits the *extensibility* and *independence* of the methodology, it offers full support for *separation of architecture domains* and for *interactions* between agents and agent organisations.

From the remarks above, it becomes clear that the other AOSE methodologies regarded do not fully support the particular set of requirements we identified.

---

[2] `http://agenttool.cis.ksu.edu/`

Table 1. Coverage of requirements for agent-oriented software engineering approaches

Requirement	Extensibility	Independence	Arch. Domains	Interaction
PosoMAS	Full	Full	Full	Full
OpenUP	Full	Full	No	No
Prometheus	Partial	No	Partial	Partial
ADELFE	Full	No	Partial	Full
ASPECS	Partial	No	Full	Full
O-MasE	Partial	Partial	Partial	Full
INGENIAS	No	No	Full	Full

The findings are summarised in Table 1. However, it must be noted that these requirements do not apply to all development situations. For some teams, it might be helpful to have a meta-model available or support by a dedicated tool. Others do not require support for agent organisations since the scale of the system under development is low or more complex organisational structures are not needed. In such situations, PosoMAS may not be an ideal candidate and one of the other methodologies may be better suited. It is thus important to consider the actual requirements of the development effort before choosing a process.

3   PosoMAS Practices

The practices for PosoMAS, compiled in a *practice library*, cover the disciplines requirements, architecture, and development. Testing and deployment are the focus of ongoing work (see, e.g., [22]) since both disciplines are very important in MAS and have not been dealt with sufficiently as of yet. The practices introduce techniques for the principled design of individual agents, organisations, their interactions, as well as the overall system and the environment. The categorisation of these techniques is an important aspect of the design of the process:

Agent Architecture. The design of the individual agents, separate for each distinct type of agent.

Agent Organisation. The specification of organisational paradigms that will structure the agent population at runtime.

Agent Interaction. The definition of interfaces and protocols used by agents to exchange information, delegate control, and change organisational structure.

System Architecture. The relationship between the different types of agents, the supporting infrastructure, external components, and the environment.

It is necessary to define common work products that can be used to exchange information between the activities and tasks specified for each of the areas. To structure these work products, respective SPEM domains (for work products) and disciplines (for tasks) have been introduced. The *agent system* and *individual agent* domains and disciplines complement the generic *architecture* domain and discipline. Agent interactions and agent organisations are captured in a respective domain and discipline as well.

3.1   Common Categories, Work Products, Roles, and Domains

The PosoMAS practices library introduces a number of work product slots, an additional role, changes in the interaction and responsibilities of the roles, and specialised domains. These elements allow the categorisation of artefacts within the development effort and provide a grouping of work products and tasks.

Work Products. They are used to exchange information between practices and capture the different architecture areas defined by PosoMAS. Work Product Slots are placeholders for concrete work products that allow interoperability between method content. Information about the agent architecture, e.g., is exchanged by a work product slot *[Agent Architecture]*. It serves as an abstraction of high-level artefacts that represent the documentation of the architecture of a single agent within a MAS.

Roles. A role fulfils certain tasks in the process, requires a certain skill set, and is usually assigned to one or more persons. To emphasise agile aspects, Poso-MAS puts focus on the *Product Owner* who represents the client in the process. PosoMAS includes it in the requirements elicitation process and in the aspects that relate to the system environment. This changes the responsibilities of the *Analyst*, who is the liaison between the development team and the customer, since the customer is now more directly involved in the process. Likewise, the *Architect* works closely with the product owner during requirements elicitation.

Domains. PosoMAS introduces or extends four domains—specialised categories for the classification of work products—that relate to the different areas of the development effort. Work products can be related to *Agent Interaction* and *System Organisation*. In addition, the *Requirements* and *Architecture* domains from the practices library included with the EPF are supplemented with domains that contribute content to them.

3.2   Overview of PosoMAS Practices

As PosoMAS is targeted at open systems, the architectural tasks are aimed at providing standardisation, separation of concerns, and interoperability. The applicability to a wide range of target systems has also been a concern. Therefore, even though some content of the practices is specific to open self-organising multi-agent systems, they do not require the use of a specific meta-model or agent architecture. The practice library provides the following practices:

Goal-Driven Requirements Elicitation. Operationalises the technique for requirements elicitation based on KAOS [23] and the work of Cheng et al. [24]. It provides an iterative process composed of the tasks *Identify System Goals, Refine System Goals to Requirements, Mitigate Uncertainty Factors, Define System Limitations and Constraints,* and *Validate Requirements*. By applying these actions, the goal model is successively refined until a complete model of the system requirements is gained. Beside the system goal model, a conceptual domain model as well as a glossary of the domain are outputs of this practice.

The approach is ideally suited for adaptive systems since uncertainties and their mitigation can be directly modelled in the requirements. This allows the stake-holders to reason about countermeasures and identify risks early on. The practice is easily embedded in iterative-incremental processes. System goals can be elaborated in different iterations, with a preference to elaborate those first that have the greatest potential impact and risk. Guidelines detail the application of the practice in an agile environment and how to capture process support requirements.

Pattern-Driven MAS Design. Provides guidance to design a multi-agent system based on existing architectural, behavioural, and interaction patterns and reference architectures. These three types of patterns correspond to the system architecture, agent architecture, and agent interaction areas. A design conscientious of existing work enables reuse, avoids making mistakes twice, and allows tapping into the knowledge that has been created elsewhere for a cleaner, leaner, and more flexible design. An architectural pattern can be applied in the development of the system architecture, while more fine-grained patterns and protocols can be used to create agent architectures and define interactions between agents. The use of patterns also facilitates communication between stakeholders and makes the architecture and the implementation more comprehensible. The practice lists a wealth of published work containing patterns for the design of agents and MAS (e.g., [25]), including the FIPA Interaction Protocols Specification (http://www.fipa.org/repository/ips.php3).

Evolutionary Agent Design. Describes an approach to design agents and their architecture in an evolutionary way that enhances the design over time while requirements become clearer and development progresses. During the development process, the agent types, their capabilities and behaviour, their internal architecture, and their interactions become clearer as the requirements mature and the system design progresses towards a shippable build. To allow the product to mature this way, the design of the agents has to adapt to new knowledge continuously and become more specific by refinement when necessary and incorporating changes in the requirements or the system environment. The practice defines three tasks for the design of the different agent elements. These are tightly interwoven with tasks from *Pattern-driven MAS Design* in the PosoMAS lifecycle. Special guidance on the design of modular agents and the intricacies of message-based MAS is provided. A specialised UML profile helps the designer to identify agents, operations that are available through messaging, and to define elements of the infrastructure the development team relies on.

Agent System Design. Outlines how the system the agents are embedded in is designed and how the agents interact with it. A multi-agent system not only consists of autonomous agents but also incorporates a multitude of additional infrastructure, external actors, interfaces, hardware, and environmental factors. These can have a significant impact on the overall system design and should be regarded early on. The practice provides tasks to identify these factors and incorporate them in the design of the overall system. This includes the identification and design of necessary interfaces between the agents and to external components in the system's environment as well as the identification of uncertainty factors in the environment. Additional guidance is provided with regard to the separation of concerns between system and agent level.

Agent Organisation Design. Describes the design of the organisation the agents will interact in. Multi-agent systems with many interacting agents require a form of structure or organisation imposed on the population. Sometimes, this structure is permanent, such as a hierarchy that determines the delegation of control and propagation of information, or transient, such as a coalition in which agents interact until a certain common goal is reached. The system designer has to decide which organisations are suitable for the system to reach the stated goals and implement mechanisms that allow the formation of these organisational structures at runtime. If this process is driven from within the system, "self-organisation" is present. This practice includes tasks, work products, and guidance that support the decision for a suitable system structure and the selection of a suitable self-organisation mechanism. If the system under development requires self-organisation, e.g., to be robust against agent failures or to adapt to a changing environment, these issues will have to be considered timely and thoroughly as the organisational structure and the algorithm to create it can have tremendous impact on the performance of the system. Introducing these concepts also influences the way the system is tested and deployed and has consequences for the operation of the deployed system. Possible system organisations and self-organisation approaches are, e.g., described in [26].

Model-Driven Observer Synthesis. Describes how observer implementations can be synthesized from constraints specified in the requirements documents as described in [4]. In adaptive systems, it is necessary to observe the system and react if the system enters an undesirable state or shows unwanted behaviour. For this purpose, feedback loops, operationalised as observer/controllers can be employed [27]. This practice describes an automatic transformation to observer/controller implementations from constraints defined during requirements analysis. A prerequisite of this practice is that constraints have been captured during requirements analysis. Ideally, these are expressed as OCL constraints that define the correct states of the system. If *Define System Limitations and Constraints* from the practice *Goal-driven Requirements Elicitation* is performed, constraints and a domain model should be available. At the same time, this ensures that a domain model containing the elements the constraints are defined on is available. Constraints can also be defined in a specialised document separate from the requirements model. The process can be repeated after the requirements or the domain model have changed, according to a model-driven design (MDD) approach. Changed parts of the system models and implementation will be re-generated while existing models and code are preserved.

Trust-Based Interaction Design. Guides the design of interactions in open systems that can be evaluated with trust models and agent decisions that use trust values to make the system more robust and efficient. Trust-based interaction design enables the agents in the system to determine and select trust-worthy interaction partners with a high likelihood of successful completion of an interaction. The added overhead of using trust is often justified if the interactions have a high risk or a high impact. Trust helps make the system more robust against unintentional and malevolent interaction behaviour and can even enable more efficient problem solving. To be effective, trust values need to be calculated using a trust model (see, e.g., [28]) that allows the quantification of an interaction's outcome. It is also helpful to define the intended outcomes with an implicit or explicit contract. The concept of an interaction can be regarded very generally. Not only are communications with other agents an interaction but also querying of sensors, the use of environmental data, and others. All these interactions are sources of uncertainties that can be mitigated by trust. The practice supports the design of the trust model, the decision making process of agents based on trust values, the design of an infrastructure to measure trust values, and the design of a reputation system.

Each practice is defined by an appropriate guidance in EPF that states the purpose of the practice, gives a description, and provides a brief instruction on how the elements of the practice relate to each other and in which order they should be read. The practice usually references a roadmap (another special type of guidance) for the adoption of the practice, a list of key concepts and white papers, and a set of guidances. A practice also takes one or several work products (or work product slots) as inputs and outputs. These work products are automatically derived from the respective relationships of the tasks. If the practices are combined into a process, the outputs of the practices can be used to instantiate the work product slots denoting the inputs of the other practices. The *Conceptual Domain Model* can, e.g., be used to fill the [Multi-Agent System Architecure] in early iterations of the process.

The detailed practice descriptions and the models for use in EPF are available at http://posomas.isse.de. We thus provide a repository for method content and make reusable assets available for combination with method content from other processes, fulfilling the appeal of the IEEE FIPA Design Process Documentation and Fragmentation Working Group and many authors (e.g., [29,30]).

4   The PosoMAS Life Cycle

The process life cycle determines the progression of a product under development in the context of the process, the stakeholders, and the environment. A well-defined life cycle provides guidance w.r.t. the order of activities the development team has to perform, the project milestones and deliverables, and the progress of the product. The advancement of a product development effort can thus be measured based on the planned and the actual progress within the life cycle. A methodology is created by embedding the activities and tasks defined in the practices into a life cycle. The structure the life cycle provides is often defined by phases (e.g., inception, elaboration, construction, and transition in the OpenUP as described below) that are executed sequentially. Each phase addresses different needs within the project and in general, a shift away from requirements, towards design and then implementation and testing is evident.

4.1   The Open Unified Process as a Method Template

The PosoMAS practices are embedded in the risk-value life cycle of the *Open Unified Process* (OpenUP) [31, 32]. It promotes an approach in which the most risky requirements and those that provide the greatest value are tackled first in an iterative-incremental way, in which each phase consists of a number of iterations. It is a lean, agile, process and towards an extensible process framework that provides a starting point for customisations and extensions.

The technical practices described in the OpenUP practice library deal with all disciplines of the development process. In general, they are described on a very high level of abstraction. Therefore, most of them are replaced by more specific practices defined by PosoMAS. For example, the practice *Evolutionary Design* is superseded by PosoMAS' *Evolutionary Agent Design*. However, the proposed process borrows a number of practices from testing and deployment as these areas are still under active development. The EPF practice library also contains a "core" area in which common elements are defined, including categories, roles, work products (and work product slots), and guidance, some of which are refined by the practices in the PosoMAS practices library.

4.2   The PosoMAS Life Cycle and Work Breakdown Structure

PosoMAS adds most of its method content in the design activities and replaces use cases with system goals as the main model to capture requirements. It also adopts the OpenUP project and iteration life cycle by incorporating the EPF practices *Risk-Value Life Cycle* and *Iterative Development* which divide the work in PosoMAS in four phases. In each phase, specialised activities are applied to accommodate open self-organising multi-agent systems. They are all specified in detail by activity diagrams such as the one in Figure 1.

The **inception phase** is often iterated only once and lays the foundational work for the project. The development team, the product owner, and the stakeholders have to come to an agreement about the scope of the project, including the features of the system and the final quality standards (task *Develop Technical Vision*, practice *Shared Vision*). For this purpose, extensive requirements elicitation is performed. PosoMAS uses goal-driven requirements elicitation from the practice of the same name. The requirements and the shared vision are also used to *Agree on a Technical Approach* (includes the task *Envision Architecture*, practice *Evolutionary Architecture*).

Notably, the activity *Plan and Manage Iteration* addresses *Prepare Environment* and *Project Process Tailoring* during inception. As in later phases, its outputs are an *Iteration Plan* and a *Work Items List* that describe the timetable and break down of work packages, as well as a *Risk List* containing critical points that need to be addressed. The inception phase ends with a *Life Cycle Objectives*

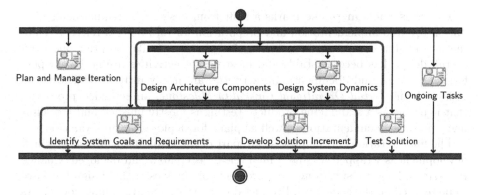

Fig. 1. Overview of the elaboration phase of the PosoMAS. Red frames indicate original PosoMAS content.

Milestone that determines the project scope and the objectives the project has to fulfil at the end of the inception phase.

The **elaboration phase** puts the focus of the development team on the design of the software and the realisation of the requirements. At the same time, first implemented features generate value for the customer and are the basis for further elaboration of the requirements. The activity diagram in Figure 1 shows the most important activities. System design activities are now added. Early implementation and testing are also performed, along with change management.

Design activities include *Design Architecture Components*, *Design System Dynamics*, and *Develop Solution Increment*. Requirements are selected and design and subsequent implementation are then performed to develop an increment that provides value to the customer and reduces the risk inherent in the project. *Design Architecture Components* deals with the static parts of the system design and the trust infrastructure and includes sub-activities for system architecture, agent architecture, and trust-based interaction design. It also includes a task from *Model-driven Observer Synthesis* for the definition of the observation model. The use of patterns and re-usable architectural elements is promoted by incorporating *Pattern-driven MAS Design*.

Design System Dynamics deals with the behaviour of the agents, their interactions, and agent organisations. Capabilities of the agents are identified and their behaviour is specified. The interactions between the agents are designed and interaction patterns and protocols are applied if possible. A suitable system organisation is selected and a self-organisation algorithm is specified if necessary. *Develop Solution Increment* can be performed after these design activities have been completed. Tests are carried out in *Test Solution* and if all tests pass, the code is integrated and a build is created. *Ongoing Tasks* deals with the submission and integration of change requests.

The elaboration phase ends with the *Life Cycle Architecture Milestone* that signifies that the most important aspects of the system, agent, and organisational architecture are completed. The most risky requirements have been tackled and appropriate solutions have been incorporated into the design.

The **construction phase** marks a shift from design and requirements elicitation towards implementation and preparation for an eventual release. While the overall structure of an iteration in this phase is similar to prior ones, the overall design has become stable and most design activities are no longer performed. Release and documentation activities are newly introduced.The phase ends with the *Initial Operational Capability Milestone*, an extended prototype that is usable as a standalone product. Testing is mostly finished and a preliminary product documentation as well as plans for deployment are available.

The final iterations of the process are part of the **transition phase** in which development is wrapped up and a final release is created and deployed. Change requests no longer result in new requirements or changes in the design but have to be realised on the code level. Product documentation and training documents are finished and product training starts. Release preparations are completed and the final release is deployed. The transition phase ends with the *Product Release Milestone* including the accepted final product, complete training and documentation, as well as successful deployment.

5   Evaluation and Comparison to Other AOSE Processes

The validation of a software engineering process is difficult from a methodical point of view. Ideally, the process is tested in a productive environment for the creation of a software product with an experienced team of software engineers and developers who can compare the effort to previous experiences with other methodologies. Such an approach, however, is not feasible in the scope in which AOSE methodologies are created at the moment. Instead, we rely on qualitative evaluation and validation criteria. Tran et al. [8,11] have introduced a catalogue of criteria that are used in Table 2 to show the characteristics of PosoMAS and to compare it to other approaches. It is important to note that the table only captures if a process has explicit supporting content for a certain criterion. It is, e.g., possible to build proactive systems with PosoMAS even though the process does not include specific support for them. The process website contains a detailed description of the criteria and comparisons under different aspects and for additional methodologies at `http://posomas.isse.de`.

The basis for these evaluations are simulated development efforts for two case studies: a self-organising emergency response system and a power management system. The former system is highly connected and includes sensors, information retrieval and distribution, as well as a pronounced human component. The power management case study on the other hand puts the focus on self-organisation and self-optimisation in a fully autonomous system. It is available as an example run at `http://posomas.isse.de` along with a detailed description and a selection of artefacts. This diversity allows us to demonstrate that PosoMAS is applicable to a wide range of open multi-agent systems if tailored appropriately.

The development of PosoMAS and the accompanying validation provided a number of lessons that have been integrated in the process and its documentation. First and foremost, the distinction of *architecture areas* is vital for the

Table 2. Characteristics of PosoMAS, O-MasE, Prometheus, and ASPECS based on [8–11, 16, 19]. More details on criteria and values on http://posomas.isse.de.

Criteria	PosoMAS	O-MasE	Prometheus	ASPECS
Process-Related Criteria				
Development lifecycle	Iterative-incremental risk-value life cycle	Depends on base process	Iterative across all phases	Iterative-incremental life cycle
Coverage of the lifecycle	Conceptualisation, Analysis, Design, (Test, Deployment, Management)	Analysis, Design	Analysis, Design	Analysis, Design, Test, Deployment
Development perspectives	Hybrid	Top-Down	Bottom-Up	Top-Down
Application Domain	Any	Any	Any	Any
Size of MAS	Not Specified	Not Specified	Not Specified	Not Specified
Agent paradigm	Heterogeneous	Heterogeneous	BDI	Holonic
Model Validation	Yes	Consistency	Consistency and completeness	No
Refinability	Yes	Yes	Yes	Yes
Approach towards MAS development	Object-Oriented, Non-Role-Based	Object-Oriented, Role-Based, Goal-Oriented	Object-Oriented, Non-Role-Based	Role-Based, Knowledge Engineering
Meta-model based	No	Yes	No	Yes
Model-Related Criteria				
Syntax and Semantics	Medium	High	High	High
Model transformations	Yes	Yes	Yes	Yes
Consistency	Yes	Yes	Yes	Yes
Modularity	Yes	Yes	Yes	Yes
Abstraction	Yes	Yes	Yes	Yes
Autonomy	Yes	Yes	Yes	Yes
Adaptability	No	Yes	No	Yes
Cooperation	Yes	Yes	Yes	Yes
Inferential capability	No	Yes	Yes	No
Communication	Yes	Yes	Yes	Yes
Reactivity	Yes	Yes	Yes	Yes
Proactivity	No	Yes	Yes	Yes
Concurrency	No	Yes	No	No
Model Reuse	Yes	Yes	Yes	Yes
Supportive Feature Criteria				
Software and methodological support	Yes	Yes	Yes	Yes
Open systems and scalability	Yes	No	No	Yes
Dynamic structure	Yes	Yes	No	Yes
Performance and robustness	Yes	No	Yes	Yes
Support for conventional objects	Yes	No	Yes	Yes
Support for self-interested agents	Yes	No	No	Yes
Support for ontologies	No	No	No	Yes

creation of a modular, flexible design. Many of the problems with the initial system design in early iterations were caused by a misunderstandings about which parts of the design were on the agent level, which on the system level and in the environment, and which are part of the organisation design. These areas have thus been discriminated more thoroughly and according tasks and guidance has been disentangled. Second, the concept of *scope* and thus of the system boundaries has been overhauled and extended from the guidance provided by the OpenUP or existing AOSE processes. Essentially, everything outside the scope the system has to interact with, can not simply be ignored but assumptions must be captured and the environment has to be modelled accordingly. Finally, a specialised UML profile containing stereotypes for agents, methods that are part of an agents interface, and external components was introduced to mark specific concepts in the agent and system models.

6   Discussion and Future Work

This paper introduced PosoMAS, a novel agent-oriented software engineering process for the class of large-scale open self-organising systems. It is based on a risk-value lifecycle and incorporates practices both for agile development and for the principled design and implementation of self-organising systems. It has been validated in two case studies and compared with a number of other agent-oriented processes.

The level of abstraction differs tremendously between different processes. While the OpenUP is very abstract, without domain- or problem-specific guidance, Prometheus, ASPECS and other AOSE-processes are very concrete and prescribe solution approaches, techniques, and models in great detail. The latter approach excels when a system fits the assumptions made by giving much more hands-on support. However, it is rare that a product fits the assumptions perfectly. PosoMAS tries to find a middle ground between these extremes by providing guidance without forcing adherence to a special paradigm and by formulating method content in a way that lends itself to process customisation and tailoring. The comparisons in Table 1 and Table 2 can provide indications of the strength and weaknesses of the different processes.

Most processes impose a certain way of thinking about the system under construction. Prometheus enforces the use of BDI-agents, O-MaSE puts the focus on organisations, and ASPECS forces developers to think in terms of ontologies and holarchies. PosoMAS has been designed to be independent of most of these factors but still contains elements that favour certain solutions, e.g., using the Observer/Controller architectural pattern as the basis for adaptation. When choosing a process, the development team has to make sure that the perspective taken by the process is compatible with the product.

Future work includes the creation and integration of additional method content, especially w.r.t. deployment and testing of self-organising systems. Furthermore, the method content will be combined with the principles of the Scrum methodology to yield a truly agile process. These efforts will be accompanied by evaluations and refinement of the method content. Our hope, however, is that by making PosoMAS and all method content available as a repository at http://posomas.isse.de both in browsable form and as EPF source code, other researchers and practitioners will start using the practices and the framework they provide to adapt the process, create new methodologies, and enrich the content with their own ideas and concepts[3].

Acknowledgements. This research is partly sponsored by the research unit *OC-Trust* (FOR 1085) of the German Research Foundation. The authors thank Julian Kienberger for his input on the comparison of existing AOSE approaches.

References

1. Steghöfer, J.P., Anders, G., Siefert, F., Reif, W.: A system of systems approach to the evolutionary transformation of power management systems. In: Proc. of INFORMATIK 2013 – Workshop on Smart Grids. LNI, vol. P-220. Bonner Köllen Verlag (2013)
2. Bernard, Y., Klejnowski, L., Müller-Schloer, C., Pitt, J., Schaumeier, J.: Enduring institutions and self-organising trust-adaptive systems for an open grid computing infrastructure. In: Proc. of the 2012 Sixth IEEE Int. Conf. on Self-Adaptive and Self-Organizing Systems Workshop (SASOW), pp. 47–52. IEEE (2012)
3. Sudeikat, J., Steghöfer, J.P., Seebach, H., Reif, W., Renz, W., Preisler, T., Salchow, P.: On the combination of top-down and bottom-up methodologies for the design of coordination mechanisms in self-organising systems. Information and Software Technology 54(6), 593–607 (2012)
4. Eberhardinger, B., Steghöfer, J.P., Nafz, F., Reif, W.: Model-driven Synthesis of Monitoring Infrastructure for Reliable Adaptive Multi-Agent Systems. In: Proc. of the 24th IEEE Int. Symposium on Software Reliability Engineering (ISSRE 2013). IEEE Computer Society, Washington, D.C (2013)
5. Steghöfer, J.P., Behrmann, P., Anders, G., Siefert, F., Reif, W.: HiSPADA: Self-Organising Hierarchies for Large-Scale Multi-Agent Systems. In: 9th Int. Conf. on Autonomic and Autonomous Systems, ICAS 2013, Lisbon, Portugal, pp. 71–76. IARIA (March 2013)
6. Kroll, P., Kruchten, P.: The Rational Unified Process Made Easy—A Practitioner's Guide to the RUP. Addison-Wesley Professional (2003)
7. Henderson-Sellers, B., Gonzalez-Perez, C., Ralyte, J.: Comparison of method chunks and method fragments for situational method engineering. In: 19th Australian Conf. on Software Engineering, ASWEC 2008, pp. 479–488 (2008)
8. Tran, Q.N.N., Low, G.C.: Comparison of ten agent-oriented methodologies. In: Agent-oriented Methodologies, pp. 341–367. Idea Group, Hershey (2005)
9. Cossentino, M., Hilaire, V., Molesini, A., Seidita, V.: Handbook on Agent-Oriented Design Processes. Springer, Heidelberg (2014)
10. Padgham, L., Winikoff, M.: Developing Intelligent Agent Systems. John Wiley & Sons, Ltd. (2005)

---

11. Tran, Q.-N.N., Low, G., Williams, M.-A.: A preliminary comparative feature analysis of multi-agent systems development methodologies. In: Bresciani, P., Giorgini, P., Henderson-Sellers, B., Low, G., Winikoff, M. (eds.) AOIS 2004. LNCS (LNAI), vol. 3508, pp. 157–168. Springer, Heidelberg (2005)
12. Al-Hashel, E., Balachandran, B.M., Sharma, D.: A Comparison of Three Agent-Oriented Software Development Methodologies: ROADMAP, Prometheus, and MaSE. In: Apolloni, B., Howlett, R.J., Jain, L. (eds.) KES 2007, Part III. LNCS (LNAI), vol. 4694, pp. 909–916. Springer, Heidelberg (2007)
13. Dam, K.H., Winikoff, M.: Comparing agent-oriented methodologies. In: Giorgini, P., Henderson-Sellers, B., Winikoff, M. (eds.) AOIS 2003. LNCS (LNAI), vol. 3030, pp. 78–93. Springer, Heidelberg (2004)
14. Bernon, C., Gleizes, M.-P., Peyruqueou, S., Picard, G.: ADELFE: A methodology for adaptive multi-agent systems engineering. In: Petta, P., Tolksdorf, R., Zambonelli, F. (eds.) ESAW 2002. LNCS (LNAI), vol. 2577, pp. 156–169. Springer, Heidelberg (2003)
15. Bauer, B., Müller, J.P., Odell, J.: Agent UML: A formalism for specifying multi-agent software systems. In: Ciancarini, P., Wooldridge, M.J. (eds.) AOSE 2000. LNCS, vol. 1957, pp. 91–103. Springer, Heidelberg (2001)
16. Cossentino, M., Gaud, N., Hilaire, V., Galland, S., Koukam, A.: ASPECS: an agent-oriented software process for engineering complex systems. Autonomous Agents and Multi-Agent Systems 20(2), 260–304 (2010)
17. DeLoach, S.A., Wood, M.F., Sparkman, C.H.: Multiagent Systems Engineering. IJSEKE 11(3), 231–258 (2001)
18. Abdelaziz, T., Elammari, M., Unland, R.: A Framework for the Evaluation of Agent-Oriented Methodologies. In: 4th Int. Conf. on Innovations in Information Technology, IIT 2007, pp. 491–495 (November 2007)
19. DeLoach, S.A., Garcia-Ojeda, J.C.: O-MaSE – a customisable approach to designing and building complex, adaptive multi-agent systems. IJAOSE 4(3), 244–280 (2010)
20. Pavón, J., Gómez-Sanz, J.: Agent oriented software engineering with INGENIAS. In: Mařík, V., Müller, J.P., Pěchouček, M. (eds.) CEEMAS 2003. LNCS (LNAI), vol. 2691, pp. 394–403. Springer, Heidelberg (2003)
21. Caire, G., Coulier, W., Garijo, F., Gomez, J., Pavon, J., Leal, F., Chainho, P., Kearney, P., Stark, J., Evans, R., Massonet, P.: Agent oriented analysis using message/UML. In: Wooldridge, M.J., Weiß, G., Ciancarini, P. (eds.) AOSE 2001. LNCS, vol. 2222, pp. 119–135. Springer, Heidelberg (2002)
22. Eberhardinger, B., Seebach, H., Knapp, A., Reif, W.: Towards testing self-organizing, adaptive systems. In: Merayo, M.G., de Oca, E.M. (eds.) ICTSS 2014. LNCS, vol. 8763, pp. 180–185. Springer, Heidelberg (2014)
23. van Lamsweerde, A., Letier, E.: From object orientation to goal orientation: A paradigm shift for requirements engineering. In: Wirsing, M., Knapp, A., Balsamo, S. (eds.) RISSEF 2002. LNCS, vol. 2941, pp. 325–340. Springer, Heidelberg (2004)
24. Cheng, B., Sawyer, P., Bencomo, N., Whittle, J.: A goal-based modeling approach to develop requirements of an adaptive system with environmental uncertainty. In: Schürr, A., Selic, B. (eds.) MODELS 2009. LNCS, vol. 5795, pp. 468–483. Springer, Heidelberg (2009)
25. Ramirez, A.J., Cheng, B.H.C.: Design patterns for developing dynamically adaptive systems. In: Proc. of the Workshop on Software Engineering for Adaptive and Self-Managing Systems, SEAMS 2010, pp. 49–58. ACM, New York (2010)
26. Horling, B., Lesser, V.: A survey of multi-agent organizational paradigms. The Knowledge Engineering Review 19(04), 281–316 (2004)

27. Richter, U., Mnif, M., Branke, J., Müller-Schloer, C., Schmeck, H.: Towards a generic observer/controller architecture for Organic Computing. In: 36. Jahrestagung der GI. LNI, vol. 93, pp. 112–119. GI (2006)
28. Pinyol, I., Sabater-Mir, J.: Computational trust and reputation models for open multi-agent systems: a review. Artificial Intelligence Review 40(1), 1–25 (2013)
29. Seidita, V., Cossentino, M., Gaglio, S.: A repository of fragments for agent systems design. In: Proc. of the Workshop on Objects and Agents (WOA 2006), Catania, Italy, pp. 130–137 (September 2006)
30. Cossentino, M., Gleizes, M.-P., Molesini, A., Omicini, A.: Processes engineering and AOSE. In: Gleizes, M.-P., Gomez-Sanz, J.J. (eds.) AOSE 2009. LNCS, vol. 6038, pp. 191–212. Springer, Heidelberg (2011)
31. Eclipse Foundation: Openup (2013), http://epf.eclipse.org/wikis/openup/ (accessed September 2, 2013)
32. Gustafsson, B.: Openup – the best of two worlds. Methods & Tools (2008)

Experiments with Social Capital in Multi-agent Systems

Patricio E. Petruzzi, Dídac Busquets, and Jeremy Pitt

Department of Electrical and Electronic Engineering
Imperial College London, Exhibition Road, London, SW7 2BT, UK
{p.petruzzi12,didac.busquets,j.pitt}@imperial.ac.uk

Abstract. Social scientist define social capital as a feature or attribute of an organisation or an individual that facilitates cooperation to achieve mutual benefit and enhances their ability to solve collective action problems. In this paper we present a set of experiments on an electronic version of social capital in two different scenarios of repeated pairwise interactions amongst agents. The results show that (i) social capital can be represented in a computational form, and (ii) that the use of social capital does indeed support effective collective action. These results offer a convincing demonstration that being able to represent and reason about (electronic) social capital provides a compelling alternative solution to cooperation dilemmas in multi-agent systems.

Keywords: Social capital, self-organising systems, electronic institutions.

1 Introduction

Social capital has been defined by Ostrom and Ahn [10] as "an attribute of individuals that enhances their ability to solve collective action problems". They observed that social capital has multiple forms, especially the form of institutions, defined as collections of conventional rules by which people mutually agree to regulate their behaviour. They also suggested that trust was the 'glue' that enabled these various forms of social capital to be leveraged for solving collective action problems, for example, the sustainability of a common-pool resource.

However, we would argue that there are certain social processes, in particular the commodification of social concepts such as friendship, loyalty and privacy, that act as a kind of 'social acetate' for trust, thereby diminishing the value of social capital in helping people to resolve collective action problems [12] .

In other work, (e.g.[13]), it has been examined how formal models of social processes, in particular Elinor Ostrom's institutional design principles [9] and Nicholas Rescher's theory of distributive justice [15] , can be used in self-organising electronic institutions to achieve a fair and sustainable allocation of resource in 'technical' systems, such as ad hoc and sensor networks.

In this paper we report on a set of experiments based on two player games that enables us to pursue further work on n-player games and evaluate social capital

H.K. Dam et al. (Eds.): PRIMA 2014, LNAI 8861, pp. 18–33, 2014.

for successful collective action. Moreover, we have observed that through social capital, agents are able to self-organise, deciding with whom to interact as well as to what institutions to join. These aspects are key when trying to assess to what extent can electronic institutions be 'injected' into socio-technical systems, and computational intelligence (embodied in the form of software agents) be used to help people in the process of fair allocation of physical resources, such as energy and water.

2   Social Capital

Capital in its most basic sense can be understood as a set of assets capable of generating future benefits for at least some individuals [4]. Social Capital theory gained importance through the integration of classical sociological theory with the description of an intangible form of capital. Through the social capital concept researchers have tried to propose a synthesis between the value contained in the communitarian approaches and individualism professed by the *rational choice theory*.

Social capital has been defined by Putnam as "the features of social organization, such as networks, norms and trust, that facilitate coordination and cooperation for mutual benefit" [14], by Bourdieu and Wacquant as "the aggregate of the actual or potential resources which are linked to possession of a durable network of more or less institutionalized relationships of mutual acquaintance and recognition..." [1] and by Ostrom and Ahn as "an attribute of individuals that enhances their ability to solve collective action problems" [10].

Ostrom and Ahn observed that social capital has multiple forms, of which they identified three:

- *'trustworthiness'*, as distinct from trust, and related to reputation, being a shared understanding of someone's willingness to honour agreements and commitments;
- *social networks*, including strong and weak ties, identifying both channels through which people communicate or other social realtions; and
- *institutions*, identified as sets of conventional rules by which people voluntarily and mutually agree to regulate their behaviour.

They also suggested that *trust* itself was the 'glue' that enabled these various forms of social capital to be leveraged for solving collective action problems (see Figure 1), for example, the sustainability of a common-pool resource. Social capital generates 'reliance' trust and, where reliance trust can be seen as a complexity-reducing decision-making short-cut which helps resolve collective action problems.

Inspired by an analysis of trust as comprising a belief component and an expectation component [3], we model the trust decision (i.e. a mapping between a game and social capital inputs to a cooperate (or not) output) as reasoning about three components:

- the belief that there is a rule;

– the expectation that someone else's behaviour will conform to that rule; and
– the expectation that a third party will punish behaviour that does not conform to the rule.

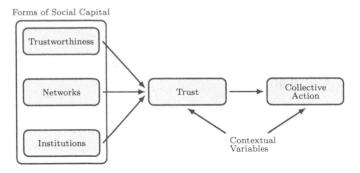

Fig. 1. Ostrom and Ahn's social capital model

[12] identify several examples of computer systems which represent and reason with social capital in computational form, including forgiveness in e-commerce, legitimate claims for fair resource allocation in open networks, and demand-side self-organisation in SmartGrids.

For example, one feature of open systems is the expectation of error, but there are many dimensions of 'error', including a distinction between intentional and unintentional violations, gradations of seriousness, and so on. Human society has evolved a standard mechanism for recovering from error in general: *forgiveness*. From the psychological literature, four positive motivations for forgiveness can be identified, comprising twelve constituent signals. This has been formalised in a computational model of forgiveness [17], which uses fuzzy logic to compute a forgiveness decision from given weights associated with each of the twelve signals. The critical aspect of this forgiveness model is that some of the constituent signals, for example 'prior beneficial relationship' are an indication of some form of social capital.

Similarly, a theory of distributive justice based on legitimate claims [15] was used in a computational model for self-organised, 'fair' resource allocation [13]. In this model the representation of some of the claims – notably the claims according to efforts and sacrifices, and according to socially-useful services – provide a ranking based on quantitative representation of a form of social capital.

In the next two sections we present two different models for representing and reasoning with an electronic version of social capital and the experiments we have carried out. The first model is based on a single form of social capital, while the second one comprises the three forms identified by Ostrom and Ahn, making it more appropriate for a wider set of scenarios.

3   Cooperative Situation: Favours as Social Capital

As a first approach to represent social capital, we base our model on the *trustworthiness* form. In particular, we have focused on representing and reasoning about direct interactions between agents in pairwise situations. In such pairwise interactions, each agent is confronted with the decision of whether to choose an action that will favour the other agent or not. The agents keep track of the favours received from (and done to) each other agent, which will be then used to decide whether to do a favour to a given agent. The rationale of the model is that the more favours an agent does, the more social capital it is associated with, and the more likely other agents will be willing to give back favours.

3.1 Scenario: Electricity Exchange Arena

In this particular scenario, each day is divided in twenty-four time slots of one hour. Consumers demand amounts of electricity for each time slot based on their needs. Using a predefined allocation method, consumers receive an allotment which may or not be in their demands (only the time slots can vary, the amount of electricity is always assigned as requested). After the initial distribution, consumers can start exchanging their allocations. To measure and compare the allocation results, the consumers' satisfaction is the proportion of electricity received in their preferred time slots. We consider better average consumer satisfaction as effective collective action.

To facilitate the pairwise exchange of the slot assignments, consumers publish the slot times they are willing to interchange in a "classified advertising board". Using this board, consumers can locate slots they are interested in and send offers to the owners. Only two consumers participate in an exchange and they swap time slots for the same amount of electricity; there are no payments involved. Consumers accept or deny offers based in their electricity needs.

3.2 Experiments

We have implemented the Electricity Exchange Arena using PreSage2 [5], a Java platform for developing discrete time driven animation and simulations of collective adaptive systems. The simulation was populated with ninety-six consumers who demand four time slots of electricity for each day. The request was fixed with one kilowatt-hour at each slot. Initially, the slot were assigned using Random and Optimum allocation methods. The first assigns the demands randomly to the available slots and the second performs the allocations maximising the average consumer satisfaction. Both methods consider the consumption average for each day and assign the slots up to that limit, i.e. sixteen kilowatt-hour for each slot.

Two type of consumers were added to the system. *Selfish Consumers* that only accept exchanges where the offered allocation is in their interest, i.e. a time slot that is in its preferences, but was not received at the initial allocation. And, *Social Consumers* that keep the count of favours done and received by checking at every exchange if the allocation received is in their interest. They accept an offer when is beneficial, as the Selfish consumers, but also if they owe a favour to who sends the offer. By doing so, they will not decrease their satisfaction, since the consumer is not interested in any of the two allocations involved in the exchange, but it will improve their Social Capital.

A simulation day consists of: consumers demand electricity slots, the allocation method assigns these slots, and at last, the consumers to perform pairwise exchanges between them. The simulations were run for fifty sequential days and the results were averaged over fifty runs.

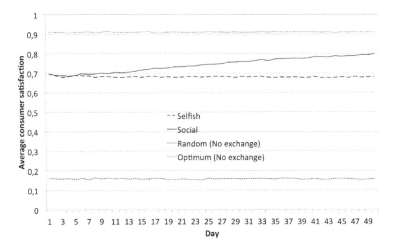

Fig. 2. Average consumer satisfaction at the end of each day

In Figure 2 we show the average consumer satisfaction at the end round for each day. The lowest consumer satisfaction is achieved by the random method, without any exchange. Once they start performing exchanges, the Selfish Consumers improve their results, but their satisfaction does not increase over time. Using Social Capital, Social Consumers start performing as the Selfish Consumers. As a result of previous exchanges perceived as favours, Social Consumers start giving back these favours exchanging slots their a not interested in, helping others to get the allocations they need. This helps the Social Consumers to increase their satisfaction over the Selfish Consumers. And at last, the Optimum allocator achieved the highest consumer satisfaction average, and since there is no better allocation distribution, no exchanges were performed.

Although using a centralised allocation method (Optimum) shows better results, using Social Capital lightly under-performs and relives the systems from the scalability issues. Including more consumer flexibility into the Optimum Allocation method will require a more complex algorithm. But then, with exchanges, the more flexible a consumer is, the more Social Capital it will be able to generate. In the end, consumers can also add more constraints or more flexibility to their demands without altering the operation of the whole system, which is not possible in a centralised allocation.

Figure 3 shows the average satisfaction during the exchange period for the first, the twenty-fifth and the fiftieth day for Selfish and Social Consumers.

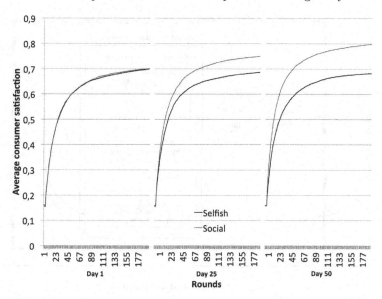

Fig. 3. Average consumer satisfaction during the first, twenty-fifth and fiftieth day

At the end of the first day both perform evenly since very few favours take place. After twenty-five days, Social Consumers have got a high satisfaction average, because they pay back favours received from previous days. At last, on day fifty, the consumers' satisfaction is higher because more exchanges occurred.

These results show that the use of social capital does improve performance at an individual level (i.e. agents being more satisfied), and also, and more importantly, at a collective level (i.e. achieving a more efficient use of the electricity while reducing consumption peaks). Moreover, we can observe that the effect of social capital increases in the long-term, thus making it suitable for scenarios where the interaction between agents is repeated over time.

However, one limitation of this cooperative situation is that it relies purely on direct interactions of each of the agents individually (i.e. an agent only knows about the favours done to and by itself), and therefore does not take advantage of the experiences of other agents, which could be shared and used to gain more knowledge about other agents (including those with which an agent has never interacted with). To overcome this limitation, we present a competitive situation to represent social capital using not only the individual experience, but also the other two forms of social capital identified by Ostrom and Ahn, namely *networks* and *institutions*.

4 Competitive Situation: Multiple Forms of Social Capital

While, as shown in the previous section, relying on past experiences is an important part of decision making when interacting with another agent, it has some limitations. One of them is that it only takes into account the view of the own

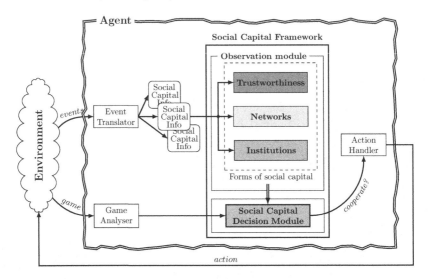

Fig. 4. Social Capital Framework

agent, thus omitting experiences of other agents. Although this could not be a problem in scenarios where the frequency of interacting with the same agent is high, thus allowing to have a rather good model of the other agents, it can become an important issue in scenarios where interactions are sparse. In such situations, an agent might have very few past experiences, or even none at all, with which it should reason and make a decision of how to behave in a pairwise interaction with a given agent. This kind of scenario is quite common in domains such as electronic marketplaces, grid computing, and other large-scale systems with many agents and a low frequency of interaction with the same agents.

Thus, it makes sense to use information coming from other sources to better model the social capital of each agent. These other sources include information about past experiences of other agents, as well as information regarding the social networks agents belong to, and also including information about institutions, such as their rules and their members. The combination of all this information then allows to build a much better model of the social capital for each agent. To this end, we present a formal framework that captures information related to the three forms of social capital. Moreover, the framework has been designed to be domain-independent, being applicable to any particular scenario.

4.1 Social Capital Framework

We propose a formal framework to represent and reason about (an electronic version of) social capital. The framework comprises an observation model in which actions enhance or diminish the different forms of social capital, and a decision-making model which uses the information from the forms of social capital to decide to cooperate or not with another agent.

Figure 4 shows a schematic view of the framework. Agents sense from the environment different events that they translate into Social Capital Information.

This information is the input of the Social Capital Framework and includes information about when an agent cooperates or not; what messages are sent or received and all the institutional actions such as joining, leaving, sanctioning, etc. The three forms of social capital (Trustworthiness, Networks and Institutions) will store the information received and aggregate it. When the agent needs information about another agent or an institution, it will query the Social Capital Decision Module which will combine all the information from the forms of social capital into a value from zero to one, where zero is *no cooperation* and one is *full cooperation*.

4.2   Scenario: Cooperation Game

To evaluate the Social Capital Framework we defined a theoretical scenario called Cooperation Game. The Cooperation Game is a strategic game were a population of agents is repeatedly randomly paired to play a game against each other. At every round, each player has a randomly designated opponent and a two-player strategic game to play. Table 1 shows the four pairwise games selected and their payoff matrix. Once paired, players must choose either to *Cooperate, Defect* or *Refuse to play*. Then, the payoff matrixes are applied and they receive or lose points depending on what they have played. If one of the players refuses to play, the game is cancelled and agents do not receive or lose any points. A global count of points is kept for all the players and it is used to evaluate their performance over the time.

Table 1. Payoff matrix of all four pairwise games

	C	D			C	D			C	D			C	D
C	2,2	-2,3		C	1,1	-1,-1		C	1,1	-1,-1		C	1,1	-1,-1
D	3,-2	1,1		D	-1,-1	1,1		D	-1,-1	-2,-2		D	-1,2	-2,-2
	Prisoner's dilemma				Coordination				Full convergence				Partial Convergence

Another feature of the cooperation game are institutions. They define how agents should play in a certain game and apply sanctions to its members when misbehaving, i.e. an institution rule could be that agents playing prisoner's dilemma against other members of the institution should cooperate. And, if an agent defects, the institution will sanction it losing a stipulated amount of points. Players can create, join and leave institutions while playing the game. They can also invite others to join the ones they are members of.

Algorithm 1 shows a step-by-step procedure of the cooperation game. At the beginning of each round, random pairs of agents are generated and a specific pairwise game is selected for each of the pairs. We called this a Match. Then, players select the action they want to play in that scenario (lines 9-11). At the end of the round the players actions are grouped with their matches and the outcome is calculated (line 13). Here players will gain or lose points based on their actions and the game's payoff matrix (line 14). Institutions apply their

Algorithm 1. Cooperation Game

1: $A \leftarrow$ set of n agents
2: $G \leftarrow$ set of m games
3: $t \leftarrow 0$
4: **repeat**
5:    $p \leftarrow generate\_random\_pairs(A, G)$
6:    **for** each pair $(i, j, g) \in p$ **do**
7:       create match $m_{ij}(g)$
8:    **end for**
9:    **for** each agent $i \in A$ **do**
10:       play $action_i$
11:    **end for**
12:    **for** each pair $(i, j, g) \in p$ **do**
13:       $mr_{ij} \leftarrow match\_result(g, action_i, action_j)$
14:       $update\_points(mr_{ij})$
15:       $institutional\_sanctions(mr_{ij})$
16:    **end for**
17:    create new institutions
18:    update institution membership
19:    $t \leftarrow t + 1$
20: **until** $t == T_{lim}$

---

sanctions based on the match results (line 15), agents that violate the rules of the institutions they are member of get sanctioned. At last, new institutions are created and the members of the institutions are updated, all based on agent's requests during that round. This process is repeated for every round till the end of the simulation.

We have implemented different agents types. In this section we will focus on the Social Players which are the ones we are interested on, the other agents will be explained in the next section.

Social Players are agents who participate in the cooperation game and have some form social capital included in their decision-making. Algorithm 2 describes their behaviour in a round of the simulation. When a round starts, players receive a random and limited amount of the results of other players matches (i.e. each agent will receive a different set of results). We use it to model agents observation, communication with other agents or any form of publishing results that will deficiently spread the match results to other agents. Social agents update their social capital with this information (lines 5-7). Subsequently, they again update their social capital with all the information received by the institutions they are member of (lines 8-10). All institutions send information about who joined, left, was sanctioned, was rewarded or was expelled. Also if an institution called a vote to accept a new member, the vote is sent at this point. Next, the player has a probability q of creating an institution (line 11). The configuration of the institution are generated randomly based on the five customisable aspects explained before, two institutions with the same characteristics are not allowed. With a probability r and with a probability s social players will join or leave a

---

Algorithm 2. Social Agent

1: E ← set of n institutional events
2: R ← set of m other match results
3: I ← set of o institutions joined by the agent
4: J ← set of p invitations to join institutions
5: **for** each match result $mr \in R$ **do**
6:     create social interaction si_{mr} {Updates the SC Observation Module}
7: **end for**
8: **for** each event $e \in E$ **do**
9:     create social interaction si_e {Updates the SC Observation Module}
10: **end for**
11: create new institution, with probability q
12: join random institution, with probability r
13: leave random institution, with probability s
14: **for** each invitation $j \in J$ **do**
15:     **if** $accept(j)$ **then**
16:         join j
17:     **end if**
18: **end for**
19: **for** each institution $i \in I$ **do**
20:     **if** not $cooperate(i)$ **then** {Queries the Institutions form of SC}
21:         leave i
22:     **end if**
23: **end for**
24: opp_t ← $current\_match\_opponent$
25: **if** $cooperate(opp_t)$ **then** {Queries the SC Decision Module}
26:     play cooperate
27: **else**
28:     play refuse_to_play
29: **end if**
30: **if** opp_{t-1} played cooperate **then**
31:     send invitation to my institution
32:     create social interaction si_{coop} {Updates the SC Observation Module}
33: **end if**
34: **if** opp_{t-1} played not_cooperate **then**
35:     create social interaction si_{not_coop} {Updates the SC Observation Module}
36: **end if**

---

random institution respectively (lines 12-13). In this cases, a Boltzmann distribution of the institutions based on their social capital value is used to choose one (when choosing which one to leave the value is inverted using $1 - value_{sc}$). The next step is to process the invitations to join institutions. In order to decide whether to accept it or not, players check the social capital for the institution and for the player who sends the invitation. If this values are greater than a certain threshold, the invitation is accepted (lines 14-18). Following, the agent checks the social capital of each institution it is member of. If the value is lower than a threshold, the agent will leave the institution (lines 19-23). After, the current opponent is retrieved and the action to play is chosen according to this opponent's social capital. If the opponent's social capital value is lower that a threshold, social players refuse to play against this opponent (lines 25-29). At last, they receive the information about last match result and they update their social capital accordingly (lines 30-36).

4.3   Experiments

In order to evaluate our social capital framework, we use the cooperation game defined above with different type of agents. In particular, we have used the following agents: *Social*, *Probabilistic*, *Random* and *Dominant Strategy* players. As explained in the previous section, social players are agents that implement any form of social capital. In our set up, we used all the possible combinations of agents using one, two and the three forms of social capital. Probabilistic players also use social capital but, even if the social capital advices them to cooperate, they play defect in a pre-defined percentage of rounds. The social capital decision module used in *Social* and *Probabilistic* agents is the average of each active form of social capital of the agent.

Table 2. Simulation players

Player name	Forms of social capital	% of Defects
SocialPlayer-TNI	Trustworthiness, Networks, Institutions	0
SocialPlayer-NI	Networks, Institutions	0
SocialPlayer-TI	Trustworthiness, Institutions	0
SocialPlayer-TN	Trustworthiness, Networks	0
SocialPlayer-T	Trustworthiness	0
SocialPlayer-N	Networks	0
SocialPlayer-I	Institutions	0
Probabilistic-TNI-0.1	Trustworthiness, Networks, Institutions	10
Probabilistic-T-0.25	Trustworthiness	25
Probabilistic-N-0.25	Networks	25
Probabilistic-I-0.25	Institutions	25
Probabilistic-TNI-0.25	Trustworthiness, Networks, Institutions	25
Probabilistic-TNI-0.5	Trustworthiness, Networks, Institutions	50
Probabilistic-TNI-0.75	Trustworthiness, Networks, Institutions	75
RandomPlayer	NA	50
DominantPlayer	NA	NA

Random players arbitrary choose their action. Dominant Strategy agents play the Nash equilibrium action in each game: defect in prisoner's dilemma and coordination games, and cooperate in full and partial convergence. Dominant Strategy and Random players do not participate in any institution and do not implement any form of social capital. Table 2 shows the characteristics of each of the players.

The simulation has been populated with ten agents of each type, for a total of 160 agents. The average values of ten simulations have been used for the results in this section.

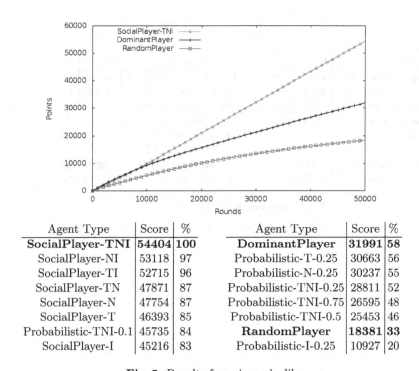

Agent Type	Score	%	Agent Type	Score	%
SocialPlayer-TNI	**54404**	**100**	**DominantPlayer**	**31991**	**58**
SocialPlayer-NI	53118	97	Probabilistic-T-0.25	30663	56
SocialPlayer-TI	52715	96	Probabilistic-N-0.25	30237	55
SocialPlayer-TN	47871	87	Probabilistic-TNI-0.25	28811	52
SocialPlayer-N	47754	87	Probabilistic-TNI-0.75	26595	48
SocialPlayer-T	46393	85	Probabilistic-TNI-0.5	25453	46
Probabilistic-TNI-0.1	45735	84	**RandomPlayer**	**18381**	**33**
SocialPlayer-I	45216	83	Probabilistic-I-0.25	10927	20

Fig. 5. Results for prisoner's dilemma

With this setup, our first experiment was run the simulation playing always prisoner's dilemma. The results are shown in Figure 5. The plot shows the evolution of the average points achieved by the different type of agents (for the sake of clarity we only show the type obtaining the most points, and the *Dominant* and *Random* agents). On the right hand side of the figure we show the average of the final score for each type of agent in the last round of the simulations, as well as the percentage of points w.r.t the best score. We can see how at the beginning *Dominant Strategy* players outperform the rest. Due to the lack of interaction between the agents, the forms of social capital do not have any information, and *Social* and *Probabilistic* players get defected by *Dominant Strategy* players.

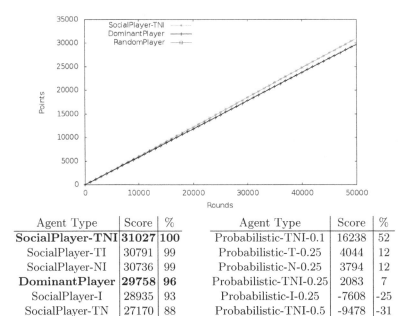

Agent Type	Score	%	Agent Type	Score	%
SocialPlayer-TNI	**31027**	**100**	Probabilistic-TNI-0.1	16238	52
SocialPlayer-TI	30791	99	Probabilistic-T-0.25	4044	12
SocialPlayer-NI	30736	99	Probabilistic-N-0.25	3794	12
DominantPlayer	**29758**	**96**	Probabilistic-TNI-0.25	2083	7
SocialPlayer-I	28935	93	Probabilistic-I-0.25	-7608	-25
SocialPlayer-TN	27170	88	Probabilistic-TNI-0.5	-9478	-31
SocialPlayer-N	27109	87	**RandomPlayer**	**-10913**	**-35**
SocialPlayer-T	26366	85	Probabilistic-TNI-0.75	-17849	-38

Fig. 6. Results for full convergence

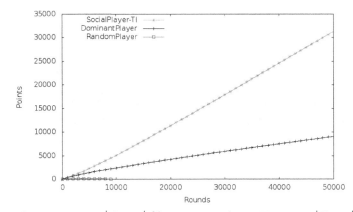

Agent Type	Score	%	Agent Type	Score	%
SocialPlayer-TI	**31318**	**100**	**DominantPlayer**	**9080**	**29**
SocialPlayer-TNI	30242	97	Probabilistic-T-0.25	7097	23
SocialPlayer-NI	29866	95	Probabilistic-N-0.25	6719	21
SocialPlayer-TN	28571	91	Probabilistic-TNI-0.25	5579	18
SocialPlayer-N	28485	91	Probabilistic-TNI-0.5	1160	4
SocialPlayer-T	27350	87	Probabilistic-I-0.25	-285	-1
SocialPlayer-I	24042	77	Probabilistic-TNI-0.75	-589	-2
Probabilistic-TNI-0.1	20826	66	**RandomPlayer**	**-2506**	**-8**

Fig. 7. Results for all four games

As the game evolves, each form of social capital starts collecting information and feeding their decision modules. Then, players with any form of social capital start refusing to play against the *Dominant Strategy* players. At around round 8000, the *Social* player with Trustworthiness, Networks and Institutions forms of social capital outperforms the *Dominant Strategy* player. *Random* players under performs all, but one, other players. A huge difference can be seen between *Social* players using any form of social capital, and the rest of the players.

Figure 6 shows the results when playing full convergence game at every round. *Social* and *Dominant Strategy* players equally play cooperate in this scenario and their scores are similar. The difference between them is that social capital prevents *Social* players of being defected by the *Probabilistic* ones. When refusing to play against some *Probabilistic* agents, *Social* players are minimising the amount of lost points. The damage control policy enforced by social capital helps agents to obtain better results. *Random* players get negative results and are not shown in the figure.

In the last scenario, shown in Figure 7, the same type of agents as the previous experiments now play all four pairwise games. At each round, when the opponent is randomly selected, one of the four games is also randomly chosen. When playing multiple games, actions in one game can affect the future interactions in other games. In this scenario, *Dominant Strategy* players defecting in prisoner's dilemma and coordination games affect their ability to play in full and partial convergence. Because *Social* and *Probabilistic* players were defected by the *Dominant Strategy* players they refuse to play against them in future interactions, no matter what game they are playing. When the other refuse to play against *Dominant Strategy* players, these lose the opportunity of wining more points at those games. As with the Prisoner's dilemma, in this case the use of social capital by *Social* players allows them to achieve the best results.

5   Related Work

Action-selection for repeated games has been addressed using different approaches, from multi-agent learning [2], to using the concept of trust [7]. The latter is the closest to our approach, since trustworthy is actually one of the forms of social capital we have presented. Trust (see [11] for a review of trust and reputation models for open multi-agent systems) is built by the agents through repeated interactions with the other agents, and it is used to decide actions such as with what agent to interact, or whether to cooperate with a given agent. This idea has also been incorporated in some game theoretical models for repeated games [6]. The first model we have presented, based on favours, could be seen as a form of trust, using only direct experiences (i.e. not taking into account indirect trust nor reputation) to build a model of the social capital of other agents.

While trust is indeed quite an appropriate metric to predict some agent's behaviour, it is based only on the interactions of agents (either experienced first hand or communicated through reputation values). To include other sources of information relevant to social capital, we have presented a competitive situation, using the social capital framework. Our framework enhances the individual view of each agent by treating trustworthy as one of the forms of social capital, and complementing it with information regarding the social network of the agent as well as the information coming from institutions.

Cooperative behaviour can also be achieved through repeated interactions and the desire of the agents to avoid retaliation threats in case of non-cooperative behaviour [8]. In this case, though, cooperation does not arise from a willingness to do so, but rather from the objective of reducing the probability of being punished.

Norms can also lead to cooperative behaviour. Norms can be learned from repeated social interactions using, e.g., reinforcement learning [16] or through aggregation techniques (ensemble methods) [18]. After a sequence of interactions, agents might learn that cooperation is beneficial. This can then be explicitly stated as a norm, or implicitly internalised by the agents as a social convention. In the case of explicit norms, the compliance to them could be incorporated in the update of the social capital related to institutions.

6   Conclusions and Future Work

In this paper we have presented two models for representing social capital and reported the experiments we have performed with them. We started with a cooperative situation, which takes into account past experiences of the agents, in form of 'favours', to compute the social capital accrued by each agent. While we obtained successful results with this first approach, we identified the need of extending the model to cope with more realistic scenarios, such as large-scale socio-technical systems, where relying only on direct interactions would not be feasible. We then presented the social capital framework, which includes the three forms of social capital and takes advantage of a richer set of information to compute and reason with social capital.

The results with both models show that the use of social capital clearly benefits the agents individually, as well as the system as a whole. One of the main effects of using social capital is the facilitation to achieve win-win situations, where the two agents involved in a pairwise interaction benefit from behaving cooperatively.

We have also observed that social capital acts as a catalyst for self-organisation: agents decide with whom to interact with according to their social capital, and they also use the social capital information to join or leave institutions. Thus, we believe that social capital will play a key role in socio-technical systems where long-term collective goals will only be achievable through cooperation of the participants.

We plan to perform further tests with the presented models by providing agents the ability to adapt or learn, so that they can change their behaviour 'on-the-fly'. This would allow us, for instance, to assess whether a critical mass of 'social agents' would be enough to pervade a cooperative behaviour amongst all participants of the system.

We propose to extend the current two-payer games to n-player games scenario to support our claim that the use of Social Capital does indeed support effective collective action.

References

1. Bourdieu, P., Wacquant, L.: An invitation to reflexive sociology. Chicago University Press (1992)
2. Bowling, M., Veloso, M.: Multiagent learning using a variable learning rate. Artificial Intelligence 136(2), 215–250 (2002)
3. Jones, A.J.: On the concept of trust. Decision Support Systems 33(3), 225–232 (2002)
4. Lachmann, L.: Capital and its structure. Sheed, Andrews and McMeel (1978)
5. Macbeth, S., Pitt, J., Schaumeier, J., Busquets, D.: Animation of self-organising resource allocation using presage2. In: 6th IEEE Conference on Self-Adapting and Self-Organising Systems (SASO), pp. 225–226 (2012)
6. Mailath, G.J., Samuelson, L.: Repeated Games and Reputations: Long-Run Relationships. Oxford University Press (2006)
7. Mayer, R.C., Davis, J.H., Schoorman, F.D.: An Integrative Model of Organizational Trust. The Academy of Management Review 20(3), 709–734 (1995)
8. Myerson, R.B.: Game theory - Analysis of Conflict. Harvard University Press (1997)
9. Ostrom, E.: Governing the Commons. Cambridge University Press (1990)
10. Ostrom, E., Ahn, T.: Foundations of Social Capital. Edward Elgar Publishing (2003)
11. Pinyol, I., Sabater-Mir, J.: Computational trust and reputation models for open multi-agent systems: a review. Artificial Intelligence Review 40(1), 1–25 (2013)
12. Pitt, J., Nowak, A.: The reinvention of social capital for socio-technical systems. IEEE Technology and Society Magazine 33(1), 27–80 (2014)
13. Pitt, J., Busquets, D., Macbeth, S.: Distributive justice for self-organised common-pool resource management. ACM Transactions on Autonomous and Adaptive Systems (to appear, 2014)
14. Putnam, R.D.: The prosperous community: Social capital and public life. The American Prospect, 35–42 (1993)
15. Rescher, N.: Distributive Justice. Bobbs-Merrill (1966)
16. Sugawara, T.: Emergence and stability of social conventions in conflict situations. In: 22nd International Joint Conference on Artificial Intelligence (IJCAI), pp. 371–378 (2011)
17. Vasalou, A., Pitt, J.: Reinventing forgiveness: A formal investigation of moral facilitation. In: Herrmann, P., Issarny, V., Shiu, S.C.K. (eds.) iTrust 2005. LNCS, vol. 3477, pp. 146–160. Springer, Heidelberg (2005)
18. Yu, C., Zhang, M., Ren, F., Luo, X.: Emergence of social norms through collective learning in networked agent societies. In: 12th International Conference on Autonomous Agents and Multi-Agent Systems (AAMAS), pp. 475–482 (2013)

Intermediary-Based Self-organizing Mechanism in Multi-agent Systems

Mengzhu Zhang, Yifeng Zhou, and Yichuan Jiang[*]

School of Computer Science and Engineering, Southeast University, Nanjing, China
zmzseu@126.com, yfzhouseu@hotmail.com, yjiang@seu.edu.cn

Abstract. Self-organizing mechanism in multi-agent systems can improve the system performance by adapting the structure among agents. However, in most previous work, each agent can only adapt the relations by itself. This may induce a problem that the overloaded agents have to consume a fraction of precious load on adaptation. Here, we propose a novel self-organizing mechanism which enables some underloaded agents to act as the intermediary to perform the relation adaptation for the overloaded agents. Through experiments, our self-organizing mechanism has validated the effectiveness.

Keywords: self-organization, intermediary agent, execution agent.

1 Introduction

The scale expansion of computing systems requires autonomy of each component to adapt to dynamic environment without manual intervention [1]. Self-organization incarnating characteristics of autonomic computing system, was defined by [2]. Agent-based modeling [3, 4] is a natural way to model systems [5] and often allocates agents in a problem solving environment, e.g., task allocation environment. Adaptation of the system network structure is one typical form of self-organization, because tasks should be accomplished among multiple networked agents.

The centralized mechanisms are widely studied in the issue of self-organization. Bou et al. [6] presented a centralized adaptation approach to allow autonomic institutions to adapt dynamic circumstances. Miralles et al. [7] divided the system into meta-level and domain-level, where agents in meta-level could monitor and reorganize the structure. However, if central control agents predefined are unavailable due to some failure, it will cause the collapse of the entire system.

To solve the shortcomings of centralized methods, Glinton et al. [8] designed a token-based algorithm in team formation domain. However, their mechanism was based on probability which resulted in some non-ideal consequences. Kota et al. [9] proposed a decentralized self-organizing mechanism based on historical interaction. However, in these decentralized mechanisms, each agent adapts relations by itself in each time step, which may increase redundant adaptation costs.

---

[*] Corresponding author.

H.K. Dam et al. (Eds.): PRIMA 2014, LNAI 8861, pp. 34–41, 2014.

In this paper, we propose a novel decentralized self-organizing mechanism in which two roles of agents are introduced: the *execution role* and the *intermediary role*. Agents which act these two roles are denoted by *execution agent* and *intermediary agent*. Execution agents aim at executing tasks while intermediary agents help execution agents to adapt relations. Some underloaded agents can act as intermediary agents to take up the responsibility for relation adaptation. However, once an intermediary agent perceives that it is no longer fit for acting the current role, it can switch current role to execution agent. The core idea of our mechanism is the division of labor and results from the heterogeneity of each agent. Through a series of experiments, the performance of our self-organizing mechanism has been validated by comparing with some benchmark models, e.g., K-Adapt [9] and TBM [8].

The remainder of this paper is organized as follows: In Section 2, the task allocation environment is introduced. In Section 3, the intermediary-based self-organizing mechanism is presented. Section 4 shows the results and analyses of the experiments. Finally, some conclusions are discussed in Section 5.

2   Task Allocation Environment

In this section, we will introduce our organization model in detail. Our environmental configuration is based on the organization model proposed by Kota et al. [9].

A task T_j is composed of a set of patterns and T_j can be represented as $T_j = \{P_{set}^j, Comp_{set}^j, R_j\}$. P_{set}^j represents a set of patterns and a pattern P_z is presented as $P_z = \{SI_{set}^z, Dep_{set}^z\}$. SI_{set}^z is a set of service instances(denoted as SI) in demand and Dep_{set} reveals the execution sequence of SIs. Each task T_j can be described as an out-tree and each node of the tree represents a subtask ST_j, requiring one particular SI and the computation load of executing one ST_j which is denoted by $Comp_j$. The entire computation load in demand of one task composes $Comp_{set}$. Meanwhile, a reward R_j is endowed to T_j initially and decreases with execution time. If T_j cannot be finished in time, R_j is negative and T_j should be aborted. Dep_{set} defines execution sequence representing which subtask should be executed preferentially.

In [9], Kota et al. defined three relations: acquaintance, peer-to-peer and superior-subordinate relation. For the sake of simplicity, only the acquaintance relation and the peer-to-peer relation are retained in our model. An agent can be denoted as $a_x = \{Cap_x, Load_x, EAC_x, EPP_x\}$. Cap_x represents the SIs that a_x can provide and $Load_x$ indicates the capacity of a_x. EAC_x and EPP_x represent the acquaintance relation set and the peer-to-peer relation set of a_x respectively.

The load of a_x in time step t consists of five parts in our system:

- The acquaintance relation load: the load of maintaining acquaintance relations. An acquaintance relation costs K_1 load.
- The peer-to-peer relation load [9]: the load of maintaining peer-to-peer relations. Each peer-to-peer relation costs K_2 load.
- The management load [9]: the load of considering peer-to-peer agents while transferring a task. The factor K_3 denotes the coefficient of management load.
- The adaptation load [9]: the load of proposing relation adaptation. The factor K_4 represents the coefficient of adaptation load.

- The task execution load [9]: the sum of task computation load executed. The computation load expended by a_x for executing a task is denoted as $Comp_i(t)$.

Therefore, a_x's current load in one time step t can be calculated as:

$$load_x(t) = K_1 \cdot |EAC_x| + K_2 \cdot |EPP_x| + K_3 \cdot M_{man}(t) + K_4 \cdot A_{meas}(t) + \sum_{i}^{i \in Task_x} Comp_i(t). \qquad (1)$$

In Equation (1), $|EAC_x|$ and $|EPP_x|$ represent the size of EAC_x and EPP_x. The factor $M_{man}(t)$ is the total number of relations considered while allocating tasks in time step t and $A_{meas}(t)$ is the number of times considered by a_x to adapt relations.

The profit of the system $Profit_{sys}$ [9] is presented by Equation (2).

$$\begin{aligned} Profit_{sys} &= Reward_{sys} - Comm_{sys} - Adap_{sys} \\ &= \sum_{j}^{j \in Task_{set}} (R_j - exe\_time_j) - \sum_{x}^{x \in Agent_{set}} C_{comm} \cdot C_x - \sum_{x}^{x \in Agent_{set}} (C_{meas} \cdot a^x_{meas} + C_{adjs} \cdot a^x_{adjs}) \end{aligned} \qquad (2)$$

- $Reward_{sys}$: the pure rewards of the system, derived from the accomplishment of tasks. R_j represents the reward of task T_j and exe_time_j is the execution time steps of T_j. $Task_{set}$ is the set of tasks which have been accomplished successfully.
- $Comm_{sys}$: the communication cost of executing tasks. C_{comm} is the coefficient of communication cost and C_x is the number of the times of delivering tasks to a_x's peer-to-peer neighbors. $Agent_{set}$ represents the set of all the agents in the system.
- $Adap_{sys}$: the cost of reorganization. $Adap_{sys}$ is composed of the measure cost and the adjustment cost. The measure cost, referring to the cost of proposing an adaptation requirement. C_{meas} represents the coefficient of considering one adaptation and a^x_{meas} represents the total amount of considering adaptations of a_x. The adjustment cost indicates that a cost should be paid if a pair of agents really decides to change a peer-to-peer relation. C_{adjs} is the coefficient of changing one peer-to-peer relation and a^x_{adjs} is the total amount of change of a_x.

3   Intermediary-Based Self-organizing Mechanism

$Load_x$ is like the limited processing ability. Then, if a_x spends a large amount of load on adapting relations, the load for executing tasks will not be enough. In our model, agents can be divided into two kinds according to the role they play: the *execution agent* (EA) and the *intermediary agent* (IA). In this section, the responsibilities of different agents and the role switch mechanism will be represented.

3.1   The Social Contact Process

When the system starts to work, all the agents only know their peer-to-peer neighbors. However, as the system begins to execute tasks, agents should select appropriate agents from EAC_x to adapt relations. We suppose that in one time step, an EA can only decide to execute tasks or make acquaintance relation with other agents. Only idle agents which have no tasks to execute can perform social contact process. Similarly, if an IA receives no adaptation requests from EAs, it can also perform social contact process. The detailed process is that an idle agent a_x chooses an agent a_y from EPP_x or EAC_x randomly and adds all unacquainted agents from EPP_y and EAC_y to EAC_x.

3.2   The Execution Agents

During the execution process, each agent may be allocated a set of tasks. If an EA has no ability to execute a subtask, it will seek a least busy peer-to-peer agent who has the ability. Each EA a_x computes the busy degree (BDE) by Equation (3):

$$BDE_x = \frac{NIT_x}{WT_x}. \tag{3}$$

In Equation (3), WT_x represents the number of time steps a_x acting current role and NIT_x is the number of time steps a_x possessing tasks. Obviously, larger BDE_x means a_x is busy with executing tasks. Meanwhile, a_x keeps a record of the utilization condition of all kinds of service instances using Equation (4):

$$res_{x \to i}(t) = \omega \cdot res_{x \to i}(t-1) + \sum_{z=0}^{m} 1 / ne_z \,(\omega < 1). \tag{4}$$

In Equation (4), $res_{x \to i}(t)$ is the a_x's demand of SI_i. And ω is a decay factor implying that past record turns insignificant. $\sum 1 / ne_z$ represents m unfinished subtasks requiring SI_i and ne_z represents the number of peer-to-peer agents which can provide SI_i. In one time step, the average value of total agents' $res_{x \to i}(t)$ is represented by N_i. If $res_{x \to i}(t) > \alpha \cdot N_i$, a_x needs SI_i urgently and α is an adjustment factor. Agent a_x records all the $res_{x \to i}(t)$ exceeding the threshold. Then, if a_x has an IA acquaintance, a_x submits the requirement to the IA and the IA will handle with the candidate selection problem. The agent a_x needs to wait for the reply from IA and then connects another EA according to the recommendation. In contrast, if there are no IA acquaintances, EA should reorganize the structure by itself.

Destroying a peer-to-peer relation is also significant as keeping a useless relation induces cost for both sides. Thus, a_x evaluates all the peer-to-peer relations (Equation (5)). If conditions in Equation (6) are met, a peer-to-peer relation can be destroyed.

$$score\_pp_{x \to l}(t) = \sum_{k \in Cap_l} res_{x \to k}(t). \tag{5}$$

$$
\begin{aligned}
&\frac{BDE_x}{BDE_x + BDE_l} \cdot score\_pp_{x \to l}(t) + \frac{BDE_l}{BDE_x + BDE_l} \cdot score\_pp_{l \to x}(t) < \beta \cdot avg\_score_{x \leftrightarrow l}, \\
&avg\_score_{x \leftrightarrow l} = \frac{BDE_x}{BDE_x + BDE_l} \cdot avg\_score_{x \to ne}(t) + \frac{BDE_l}{BDE_x + BDE_l} \cdot avg\_score_{l \to ne}(t), \\
&avg\_score_{x \to ne}(t) = \frac{\sum_{d \in EPP_x} score\_pp_{x \to d}(t)}{\left| EPP_x \right|}
\end{aligned} \tag{6}
$$

The factor β is also an adjustment factor and $avg\_score_{x \to ne}(t)$ represents the average evaluation of a_x's peer-to-peer neighborhood. Therefore, $avg\_score_{x \leftrightarrow l}$ is the average evaluation of both a_x and a_l's peer-to-peer neighborhood. Equation (6) means that the relation can be destroyed if one relation's contribution is less than that of both agents' neighborhood multiplied by β.

3.3   The Intermediary Agents

The main responsibility of intermediary agents is satisfying their clients' requests to recommend appropriate candidate agents. Therefore, a significant issue is that who will be recommended by IAs to clients. IAs rate acquaintances by Equation (7).

$$score\_acq_{x \to q}(t) = \frac{\sum_{k \in Cap_{set}^q} res_{p \to k}(t) \cdot F(k)}{BDE_q}, F(k) = \begin{cases} 1, & res_{p \to k} > \alpha \cdot N_k \\ 0, & otherwise \end{cases}. \tag{7}$$

An IA a_x scores its acquaintance agents via Equation (7). Firstly, IA a_x selects a client a_p with highest BDE_p as the prior client. If a_p needs SI_k and agent a_q which is scored can provide SI_k, $F(k)$ equals to 1. $\sum_{k \in Cap_{set}^q} res_{p \to k}(t) \cdot F(k)$ represents the degree that agent a_q can satisfy a_p. According to Equation (7), a_x sorts its acquaintances in descending order and the one with highest score is the most appropriate candidate for client agent. Then, IA a_x removes the part of demand which have been satisfied and continues this circulation until all requirements are satisfied. After finishing this circulation, all the requirements of a_p become 0 and IA a_x can dispose the next client.

3.4   Role Switching Mechanism

In this section, the mechanism of role switching between EA and IA will be described. After a pre-defined inspection time steps IT of executing tasks, EAs and IAs will calculate the fitness for the current role in every time step by Equation (8):

$$FE_x = BDE_x \cdot \frac{N}{|EAC_x| + |EPP_x|}, \quad FI_x = \frac{NoR_x}{clock_x} \cdot \frac{|EAC_x|}{N}. \tag{8}$$

FE_x represents the fitness of EA_x. If EA_x has no tasks to execute and gets acquaintance with many other agents, it may be fit for acting as an IA. In addition, an IA needs to keep acquaintance relations with at least over half of the whole agents because an excellent intermediary should have a mass of interpersonal relations.

FI_x represents the fitness of IA_x, where NoR_x represents total number of adaptation requirements and $clock_x$ is the time steps of a_x's existent time of the current role. If a_x perceives its fitness of the current role is lower than a threshold value (defined as one fifth of the average value of overall fitness of EAs or IAs), it will change its role. If a_x determines to act as an IA, all of its acquaintances can release their acquaintance relations load because this new IA will adapt the relations for them.

4   Experimental Validation

To demonstrate the effectiveness of our mechanism, named *Intermediary-Adapt*, other three mechanisms will be compared with Intermediary-Adapt: Central [9], K-Adapt [9], and Token-Based mechanism (TBM) [8].

- Central [9]: This is a centralized mechanism meaning after executing a subtask, a_x will deliver the next subtask to another agent which has largest spare capacity and the capability to accomplish it. Central mechanism is impractical and unrealistic but can be regarded as an upper bound of the performance evaluation.
- K-Adapt [9]: Agents take advantage of meta-reasoning approach to decide when and how to adapt relations.
- Token-Based mechanism (TBM) [8]: Every agent sends a token to a neighbor then the neighbor decides to forward or accept the token with a probability. Once a token is accepted, the sender and the receiver will establish a relation.

In our experiments, the original network is a random network and the average degree is set as 6. Initially, each agent is endowed with some kinds of SIs based on a Resource Probability (*RP*). In each task allocation run, 1000 tasks are randomly created. In one time step, certain tasks are randomly assigned to certain agents and are in proportion to the number of agents *N*. Each trial is performed with 500 replications.

We list some parameters in Table 1 to clarify the setting of our experiments and these parameters are set similar to [9].

Table 1. Parameters setting

Parameters	Values	Explanations
RP	0.3	Resource Probability
Load	10~30 randomly	The load of an agent
NoP	4,6,8,10,12	The number of total patterns
NSI	10	The number of SIs
IT	30	The inspection time of a new role
α	10,15	The adjustment factor of SIs
β	0.02	The adjustment factor of peer-to-peer agent
ω	0.7	The decay factor
K_1	0.03	The coefficient of an acquaintance relation load
K_2	0.1	The coefficient of a peer-to-peer relation load
K_3	0.1	The coefficient of allocation load
K_4	0.1	The coefficient of adaptation load
C_{comm}	0.1	The cost of one communication
C_{meas}	0.01	The cost of one adaptation requesting
C_{adis}	0.1	The cost of one real adaptation

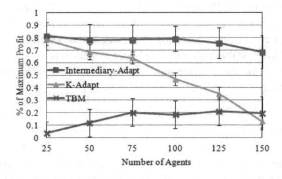

Fig. 1. The percentage of maximum profit of *Intermediary-Adapt*, *K-Adapt* and *TBM* respectively with an increase of *N*. $\alpha=10$, $K_1=0.03$

Fig.1 demonstrates the results of the percentage of the maximum profit (Central), derived from Intermediary-Adapt, K-Adapt and TBM with an increase of N. It is clearly exhibited that Intermediary-Adapt outperforms the other mechanisms obviously with the increase of N. When N increases, the load of maintaining relations gradually becomes heavy and the performance of K-adapt rapidly decreases. Because TBM adapts relations on the basis of probability, it performs worst. However, in our system, IAs undertake the load of maintaining acquaintance relations and relation adaptation for EAs and EAs can fully utilize their load to execute tasks. Therefore, Intermediary-Adapt reveals higher efficiency than other mechanisms. However, the standard deviations show that K-Adapt is the most stable. The reason for this is that in our system, agents change their roles although the IT can avoid them to change roles too frequently. The stability of Intermediary-Adapt will be our future work.

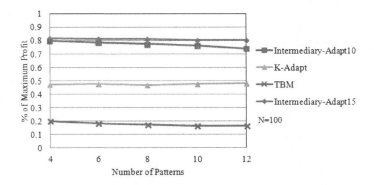

Fig. 2. The system profit with the increase of *NoP*. The square line indicates that $\alpha=10$ and the rhombus line represents that $\alpha=15$.

The influence of number of patterns (*NoP*) on the final performance of the system is also discussed in Fig.2. As shown in Fig.2, when tasks become dissimilar (*NoP* increases), Intermediary-Adapt outperforms the other mechanisms. It can be clearly found in Fig.2 that when $\alpha=15$, it performs better and remains more stable, nearly 80% of the maximum profit. However, when the adjustment factor α is 10, there is a slight decline of Intermediary-Adapt. The probable reason is that with the increase of *NoP*, the utilization condition of all kinds of service instances changes greatly, and a high α contributes to the stabilization of EAs' peer-to-peer sets.

In conclusion, Intermediary-Adapt shows its high efficiency and performs well in different environments.

5   Conclusion

This paper introduced a novel self-organizing mechanism in multi-agent system aiming at improving the performance in a task allocation environment. All agents in the system can switch between the two roles: *execution role* and *intermediary role*. Agents which act these two roles are denoted by *execution agent* (*EA*) and *intermediary agent* (*IA*). Some underloaded agents act as IAs spontaneously. By undertaking the relation adaptation work for overloaded EAs, IAs help overloaded EAs to save the load of relation adaptation. Hence, EAs can fully utilize the load to execute tasks. To validate the effectiveness of our mechanism named *Intermediary-Adapt*, a series of experiments have been conducted. Compared with the Central, K-Adapt and TBM mechanisms, Intermediary-Adapt performs better than K-Adapt and TBM, and can achieve nearly 80% performance of the Central mechanism.

Acknowledgements. This work was supported by the National Natural Science Foundation of China (No.61170164, No.61472079), the Program for Distinguished Talents of Six Domains in Jiangsu Province (No.2011-DZ023), and the Funds for Distinguished Young Scholars of Jiangsu Province (BK2012020).

References

1. Kephart, J.O., Chess, D.M.: The Vision of Autonomic Computing. Computer 36, 41–50 (2003)
2. Serugendo, G.D.M., Gleizes, M.P., Karageorgos, A.: Self-Organization in Multi-Agent Systems. The Knowledge Engineering Review 20(02), 165–189 (2005)
3. Jiang, Y., Jiang, J.C.: Understanding Social Networks from a Multiagent Perspective. IEEE Transactions on Parallel and Distributed Systems 25(10), 2743–2759 (2014)
4. Jiang, Y., Jiang, J.C.: Diffusion in Social Networks: A Multiagent Perspective. IEEE Transactions on Systems, Man, and Cybernetics: Systems (in press, 2014)
5. De Wolf, T., Holvoet, T.: Towards Autonomic Computing: Agent-based modelling, dynamical systems analysis, and decentralised control. In: 1st IEEE International Conference on Industrial Informatics, Banff, Alberta, Canada, pp. 470–479. IEEE Press, New York (2003)
6. Bou, E., López-Sánchez, M., Rodriguez-Aguilar, J.A.: Self-Configuration in Autonomic Electronic Institutions. In: Coordination, Organization, Institutions and Norms in Agent Systems Workshop at ECAI, Riva Del Garda, Italy, pp. 1–9. IOS Press, Amsterdam (2006)
7. Miralles, J.C., López-Sánchez, M., Esteva, M.: Multi-Agent System Adaptation in a Peer-to-Peer Scenario. In: ACM Symposium on Applied Computing, Honolulu, Hawaii, USA, pp. 735–739. ACM Press, New York (2009)
8. Glinton, R., Sycara, K., Scerri, P.: Agent Organized Networks Redux. In: 23rd Association for the Advancement of Artificial Intelligence, Chicago, Illinois, USA, pp. 83–88. AAAI Press, California (2008)
9. Kota, R., Gibbins, N., Jennings, N.R.: Decentralized Approaches for Self-Adaptation in Agent Organizations. ACM Transactions on Autonomous and Adaptive Systems 7(1), 1 (2012)

Estimating the Degrees of Neighboring Nodes in Online Social Networks

Jooyoung Lee[1] and Jae C. Oh[2]

[1] Innopolis University, Kazan, Russia
j.lee@innopolis.ru
[2] Department of Electrical Engineering and Computer Science
Syracuse University, Syracuse, NY, USA
jcoh@ecs.syr.edu

Abstract. We propose an agent centric algorithm that each agent (i.e., node) in a social network can use to estimate each of its neighbor's degree. The knowledge about the degrees of neighboring nodes is useful for many existing algorithms in social networks studies. For example, algorithms to estimate the diffusion rate of information spread need such information. In many studies, either such degree information is assumed to be available or an overall probabilistic distribution of degrees of nodes is presumed. Furthermore, most of these existing algorithms facilitate a macro-level analysis assuming the entire network is available to the researcher although sampling may be required due to the size of the network. In this paper, we consider the case that the network topology is unknown to individual nodes and therefore each node must estimate the degrees of its neighbors. In estimating the degrees, the algorithm correlates observable activities of neighbors to Bernoulli trials and utilize a power-law distribution to infer unobservable activities. Our algorithm was able to estimate the neighbors' degrees in 92% accuracy for the 60867 number of nodes. We evaluate the mean squared error of accuracy for the proposed algorithm on a real and a synthetic networks.

Keywords: Online social networks, degree estimations, distributed computation.

1 Introduction

As online social networks gained significant popularity, understanding the characteristics of social networks became an essential task for many application areas. Many existing studies in social networks uses a macro-level approach to a variety of problems including diffusion of influence, malicious node detection, and efficiency of communication networks [1]. Recent research interest has been shifting to a micro-level or a node-level reasoning. These studies focus on designing algorithms for an individual node within a social network to reason about the characteristics of the social network it belongs. Due to privacy protection in social networks and their dynamic characteristics and extremely large sizes, such node-level reasoning is extremely challenging.

Among many properties of social networks, researchers accept the *degree distribution* of a network as the most essential property in understanding the structure of the network. The degree distribution $P(k)$ of a network is the fraction of nodes in the network with degree k. Therefore, many have realized the importance of reasoning about

H.K. Dam et al. (Eds.): PRIMA 2014, LNAI 8861, pp. 42–56, 2014.

degree distributions in social networks and studied it in-depth [2]. However, as alluded by the definition, the knowledge of degree distribution does not provide information on the degree of any arbitrarily chosen node; it merely gives a probability value for each possible degree. The degree of a node represents the importance, or influential power, of the node because a higher-level of connections implies a higher level of diffusion may the node facilitate. If a node knows the degree of a neighbor, it may infer to the popularity of the neighbor [3]. Attempts to estimate degree distributions of networks have been made by, but not limited to, [1], [4], and [5].

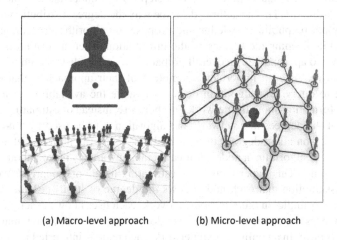

(a) Macro-level approach   (b) Micro-level approach

Fig. 1. The difference between macro and micro level approaches to social network analysis. In general, a macro-level analysis is conducted offline using a collected data set, while a micro-level is an online analysis that can continuously update the belief about the world.

However, most researchers have employed a macro-level approach, such as graph sampling, to estimate degrees of nodes in social networks. In a distributed reputation management knowledge of the second degrees–i.e., the sum of degrees of neighbors– is important [6]. Figure 1 presents the difference between macro and micro-level approaches. In a macro-level approach, shown in Figure 1 (a), also referred to as a global method, there is an entity outside of a given network that can observe everything about the network such as the number of users, degrees, etc. Therefore, the goals of a macro-level approach is often to analyze structure of the network and learn interesting properties of the network, from an objective view with offline data sets collected. On the other hand, in a micro-level approach, shown in Figure 1 (b), also referred to as a distributed method, the observing entity is a member of the network and therefore it can only access private information, such as its own degree. Usually, a micro-level approach can be used for an online algorithm capable of updating its knowledge over time. For example, on a sensor network, where each node itself is a tiny computer, it is infeasible for each node to have global view of the entire system at any time [7]. Therefore, in distributed systems like sensor networks, tasks are solved completely locally by each node running distributed (node-centric) algorithms. One the other hand, a macro-level approach generally requires an offline data set that is sampled for a given period of time. In this paper, we introduce a node-centric, i.e., micro-level, algorithm to estimate degrees of neighboring nodes.

2   Background and Motivation

Estimating the degree distribution is the first step toward understanding the nature of networks according to [1]. The authors describe why the degree distribution of a social network may not be public knowledge and proposes an algorithm to estimate it from a database while keeping the privacy of the information. Their algorithm is a macro-level algorithm to approximate an overall probabilistic degree distribution of a network as defined above. Also an important assumption of their approach is that databases are available to query. Our algorithm does not assume the availability of a database containing information about the network. Furthermore, instead of estimating an overall distribution of the degrees in a network, our algorithm is to be used by a node within a network to reason about degrees of its neighbors. Using the preferential attachment model [8] and our algorithm, a node within a social network can reason about the entire network it belongs. This paper focuses on estimating neighbors' degrees. We make a reasonable assumption that each node knows the degree of itself, i.e., the number of neighbors. For example, in the *Facebook* network, each user knows exactly how many *friends* (neighbors) he or she has but the user does not always know how many *friends* his/her *friends* have. In an online social network, each node is interested in knowing the degrees of its neighbors for various reasons such as to find the most influential neighbor to spread information in the network and to select a neighbor who is most likely to share quality information. Another practical example is on sensor networks. A node in a sensor network can choose a neighbor that may have the highest degree among its neighbors to transfer/spread information it gathered to the entire network as fast as it can. From the best of our knowledge, no attempt has been made to estimate degrees of neighboring nodes in a distributed manner.

In [9], authors attempt to estimate the degree distributions of a network using different sampling algorithms including random walks; this is again a macro-level approach. [10] introduces three estimators, namely, maximum likelihood estimator, mark and recapture, and random walker, to estimate the size of a social network. The second degree of a node is the sum of all degrees of the node's neighbors as defined in [3]. They also suggest that the distribution of second degrees is of interest since it is a good approximation of PageRank [11]. They prove that the distribution of second degrees follow a power law in Buckley–Osthus model which is a generalization of the Barabási–Albert model.

Most of the existing researches focus on the topology of given networks and studies the degree (or second degree) distributions based only on the topological information. However, to be able to deal with real world networks, in which nodes and edges are dynamically changing, one cannot assume that the topology of networks are known in advance and, therefore, the presented methods above are not suitable for distributed and dynamic environment.

3 An Algorithm for Estimating Each Neighbor's Degree

In this section, we discuss our algorithm and explain how each node within a social network can use the algorithm to estimate the degrees of its neighbors. We first present an overview of the algorithm then present several important definitions to help the readers to understand the algorithm in detail. Then we present an important proposition with a proof to show that our algorithm indeed can compute accurate degree values if the numbers of observations about its neighbors follow a certain proportionality condition (Definition 10). We also show that straightforwardly counting the number of observations does not yield good estimations because there are unobservable activities. We use a beta distribution and a power-law distribution models to extrapolate the observed activities to estimating the degrees of neighbors. This idea turned out to be quite effective in discovering hidden neighbors of neighboring nodes as we show in the experiments section.

3.1 An Overview of the Algorithm

We assume that the observer node can perceive some activities of its neighbors and we call the observed activities as *observations* (Definition 5). In reality, a user cannot collect every *observation* of their neighbors. Furthermore, there are nodes that are connected to a node that do not make any observable activities. For example, users of a Facebook wall (a node) may be just reading the posting. In this case, the reading activities are not observable; nevertheless these nodes are still connected to the node and important from the information diffusion or the connectivity concerns. We also assume that, without loss of generality, the differences among the numbers of observations made on neighbors are relative to the degrees of neighbors. If a user can see its neighbor interacting a lot with others, the user can infer the neighbor has a lot of friends (neighbors) compared to another neighbor that has less interactions.

The overall idea of our algorithm is the following. Each node estimates neighbors' degrees based on *observations* made about each neighbor that are proportionally bounded by the current estimation of the total activities – captured by N_v below – between its neighbors and the second neighbors. We consider each *observation* as Bernoulli trial, the number of seen *observations* so far as the number of successes and the number of unseen (expected) *observations* as the number of failures. As a new *observation* is introduced, the success probability is updated by the beta distribution. The numbers of *observations* made about each neighbor are statistically proportional to each other. Therefore, estimating the neighbors' degrees directly from the number of *observations* without applying to the Bernoulli trials will not capture the statistical properties of the degree distribution of the neighbors. Then, each node adjusts the distribution of second degrees according to a power-law distribution, because previous studies including [12] have shown that degree distributions of social networks follow Power-law distribution. Finally, we apply the principle of maximum likelihood to estimate the degree of each neighbor.

3.2 Useful Definitions

We define some useful terms in this Section. Figure 2 shows a node v's second neighbors where one of its neighbors is i. We assume that the degree information of a node is only known to itself.

Definition 1. *Let $deg(i)$ be the true degree of a node i. Then, use $deg_v(i)$ as v's estimation of i's degree. See Figure 2.*

Definition 2. *Let N_v be v's estimated second degree. Then, $N_v = \sum_{i \in Ne_v} deg_v(i)$. See Figure 2.*

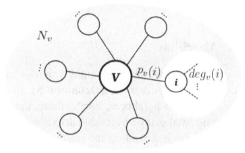

Fig. 2. The second neighborhood of a node v and one of its neighbors, i

Definition 3. *Consider a network $G =< V, E >$ where V is a set of nodes and E is a set of connections. For a given node, $v \in V$, we denote the neighbors of v as Ne_v.*

Definition 4. *Given a node v and a neighbor i, let $p_v(i)$ be v's estimated probability that i is connected to a node in each trial according to a binomial distribution.*

We employ *Erdős-Rényi model* [13] to define distribution of degrees of v's neighbors. Under the model, the probability that the degree of i is k given $p_v(i)$ follows a binomial distribution.

According to *Erdős-Rényi model* [13], v's estimated probability that i's degree is k given $p_v(i)$ is defined as follows.

$$Pr_v(deg(i) = k | p_v(i), N_v) = \binom{N_v - 2}{k-1} \cdot p_v(i)^{k-1} \cdot (1 - p_v(i))^{n-k-1} \quad (1)$$

However, $p_v(i)$ and N_v are not known to v and we explain a method to estimate $p_v(i)$ and N_v using Beta distribution in Definition 7. Once $p_v(i)$ and N_v are estimated, $p_v(i)$ for each neighbor i is adjusted according to a power-law distribution. Finally, v estimates $deg_v(i)$ using the maximum likelihood principle. A step by step procedure is given in Algorithm 1.

3.3 Defining Observations

Generally, in a social network, a node in the network can observe interactions between its neighbors and others. For example, on *Facebook*, a user can observe its *friends'* interactions with others through *wall* postings and *likes*. Intuitively, the degree of a neighbor is correlated to the number of observed and unobserved interactions. We define observed activities as *observations*. An example of an unobserved interaction on *Facebook* includes reading a posting without making any comments.

Definition 5 (Observation). *Given a node v, an observed interaction between v's neighbor i and i's neighbors is defined as an observation, $o_v(i, t)$, where t is the time of the interaction. Also, a time-ordered list of v's observations on i is defined as $O_v(i)$ and O_v is a time-ordered list of $\bigcup_{i \in Ne_v} O_v(i)$.*

We use the beta-binomial distribution to update $p_v(i)$ when an *observation* occurs. Since the belief about neighbors' degrees follows a binomial distribution according to [14], we can compute the probability of a neighbor i having a degree k using Equation (1). Also, as the beta distribution captures the prior and posterior beliefs of a binomial distribution, each node can update the belief about the degree of each neighbor with the beta distribution considering each *observation* as a binomial trial.

Now we are ready to discuss a method to compute $p_v(i)$ which is needed in Equation 1. If the posterior distributions are in the same family as the prior probability distribution, the prior and posterior are then called conjugate distributions, and the prior is called a conjugate prior for the likelihood [15]. In Definition 6, conjugate prior and posterior distribution are defined when the likelihood function is binomial.

Definition 6 (Conjugate distributions). *If a prior distribution of $p_v(i)$, v's estimation of the probability that i is connected to an additional node, follows $Beta(a, b)$ and if the likelihood has a binomial distribution, i.e., $f(x|p_v(i)) = \binom{n}{x}(p_v(i))^x(1 - p_v(i))^{n-x}$, the posterior distribution of $p_v(i)$ given x is $Beta(a + x, n + b - x)$.*

Next, we extend the idea from Definition 6 to compute $p_v(i)$ in Definition 4, given a node v and its neighbor i.

Definition 7. *Given a node v, $p_v(i)$ follows $Beta(deg(v), deg(v) + 1)$. Then the estimated posterior distribution of $p_v(i)$ is $Beta(deg(v) + |O_v(i)|, N_v + deg(v) + 1 - |O_v(i)|)$.*

Definition 7 proposes a method to estimate $p_v(i)$. This process is repeated for each *observation*, $o_v(i, t)$ as described in Algorithm 1. The two parameters for the beta distribution represent the estimated degree of i and the estimated second degree of v, respectively. Since v is only aware of its own neighbors before any *observation* has been made, v's initial estimation of the second degree is $deg(v) + 1$ (the number of v's neighbors plus itself), as in line 6 of Algorithm 1. Also without any information about neighbors' degrees, initially v assumes for all the neighbors have the same degrees with itself [14], as in line 5 of Algorithm 1. Then, upon each *observation*, v updates $p_v(i)$ with the expected value of the posterior beta distribution and update $deg_v(i)$ with k that gives the maximum likelihood, $Pr_v(\cdot)$ as defined in Equation (1), as in line 8-16 in Algorithm 1.

Algorithm 1. An Algorithm for Estimating Neighbors' Degrees

1: **Input:** $O_v = \{o_v(i,t) | i \in Ne_v\}$
2: **Output:** $\{p_v(i), deg_v(i) | i \in Ne_v\}, N_v$
3: **for all** $i \in Ne_v$ **do**
4:   $p_v(i) \leftarrow \frac{deg(v)}{2*deg(v)+1}$
5:   $deg_v(i) \leftarrow deg(v)$
6:   $N_v \leftarrow deg(v) + 1$
7: **end for**
8: **for each** $o_v(i,t) \in O_v$ **do**
9:   $vel(o_v(i,t)) \leftarrow \frac{1}{t-t'}$
10:   **if** $\int_0^t vel(o_v(i,t))\mathrm{d}t \geq 0$ **then**
11:     $p_v(i) \leftarrow \frac{deg(v)+|O_v(i)|}{2*deg(v)+N_v+1}$
12:     $p_v(i) \leftarrow \frac{p_v(i)}{\sum_{l \in Ne_v} p_v(l)}$
13:     $N_v \leftarrow \sum_{j \in Ne_v} deg_v(j)$
14:     $deg_v(i) \leftarrow \arg\max_k\{Pr_v(deg(i) = k | p_v(i), N_v)\}$
15:   **end if**
16: **end for**

Definition 7 is implemented in Algorithm 1 to estimate the degree of each neighbor and the second degree of a node. Each node executes Algorithm 1 locally to estimate degrees of its neighbors without help of global knowledge about the network. From line 4-6 in Algorithm 1, the node initializes the variables as explained in Definition 7. From line 11-14, v updates estimations of $deg_v(i)$ upon each *observation*. In line 14, in particular, the binomial distribution from Equation (1) is used to find the degree which gives the maximum probability of $Pr_v(deg(i) = k | p_v(i), N_v)$, where k is tested from 1 to N_v. In line 12, *Barabási-Albert* algorithm [8] is applied after each estimation to redistribute $p_v(i)$ since many social networks are known to follow a power-law degree distribution [16]. The time complexity of the algorithm for each *observation* is the second degree of a node due to the maximum likelihood estimation of degrees.

3.4 Stopping Criterion for the Algorithm

Observations can be unlimited for real social networks. Therefore, without using a stopping criterion, a node could run Algorithm 1 forever. We use the velocity of *observations* as a soft stopping criterion. Notice that our algorithm is an online algorithm that can stop and restart depending on the velocity value defined in Definition 8. It is a soft stopping criterion because the value of velocity changes positively or negatively over time.

Definition 8 (Velocity). *Consider a node v and its* $O_v(i)$. *Given any two consecutive observations from* $O_v(i)$, *say* $o_v(i, t')$ *and* $o_v(i, t)$ *where* $t' < t$, *the velocity associated with* $o_v(i, t)$ *at time t, i.e.,* $vel(o_v(i, t))$, *is* $\frac{1}{t-t'}$. *If the observation* $o_v(i, t)$ *is the first observation in* $O_v(i)$ *then* $vel(o_v(i, t))$ *is zero. Notice that time of occurrence, say t, is relative time.*

Upon each *observation*, an observer node (in our algorithm, node v) not only updates its belief about the degree of the *observee* node (in our algorithm, node i), but also compute the velocity associated with each *observation*.

Definition 9 explains how velocities of observations are used to stop and resume the degree estimation process.

Definition 9 (Stopping criterion). *Given a node v and a neighbor i, for each observation* $o_v(i, t)$, *v can compute the sum of the velocities from 0 to t using* $\int_0^t vel(o_v(i, t))dt$. *Algorithm 1 stops the degree estimation of i if* $\int_0^t vel(o_v(i, t))dt < 0$ *and begins the estimation process again when the integral becomes positive,* $\int_0^t vel(o_v(i, t))dt \geq 0$.

Notice that the stopping criteria only applies to the neighbors of v that satisfy the conditions described. At any given time, a node v can refer to the current estimated degrees of neighbors.

3.5 Proportionality

Proportionality is a ratio of *observations* to the degree of each neighbor. We formally define *proportionality constant* in Definition 10. The *proportionality constant* is used only for analysis purposes since true degrees of neighbors are not known to each node.

Definition 10 (Proportionality constant). *We define the proportionality constant,* $c_v(i)$, *as* $\frac{|O_v(i)|}{deg(i)}$ *for all* $i \in Ne_v$.

Note that $c_v(i)$ equals 1 only when the number of v's observed interactions of i, $|O_v(i)|$, is the same as i's degree, $deg(i)$. Since it is impractical that v observes the exact same number of interactions of i as i's degree, i.e., $c_v(i) = 1$ for all $i \in Ne_v$, merely counting the number of *observations* to estimate neighbors' degrees is not enough.

4   Experiments

We present two experiments to evaluate our algorithm. First, we apply the algorithm on a scale-free network created by *Barabási-Albert* Model [8]. Then we apply the algorithm to a real world social network data from *Facebook*.

4.1   Degree Estimations on Neighboring Nodes in *Barabási-Albert* Network

We generated a scale-free network based on *Barabási-Albert* model using *Cytoscape* [17]. We consider each edge as an interaction between the two nodes connected; this is the same as the base case when the edge belonging to these two nodes represents the only interaction made by the two nodes. Recall that an *observation* is defined as $o_v(i, t)$ where v is the observing node, i is the observed node, and t is the time of the interaction. Then, we generate the time stamps t using random assignments. For example, consider a node v that has two neighbors, i and j, with degrees 1 and 3 respectively. Then, v's observation set includes 4 *observations*, i.e., $O_v = \{o_v(i, t_1), o_v(j, t_2), o_v(j, t_3), o_v(j, t_4)\}$ where $\{t_1, t_2, t_3, t_4\}$ is a randomly generated ordered time sequence.

The generated scale-free network has 300 nodes and 2561 edges. To study an average behavior, we conducted multiple experiments with different time sequences. The error is measured as the estimated degree divided by the true degree for each neighbor subtracted from 1, i.e., $(1 - \frac{deg_v(i)}{deg(i)})$ for all $i \in Ne_v$ for a node v, where the perfect accuracy is 1. Then we compute the mean squared errors of the accuracies for each node. We define the mean squared error (MSE) for each node, v, as $\frac{1}{deg(v)} \sum_{i \in Ne_v} (1 - \frac{deg_v(i)}{deg(i)})^2$.

Figure 3 shows changes of estimated degrees over each *observation*. We picked a node with a typical behavior, which has 21 neighbors and we show the degree

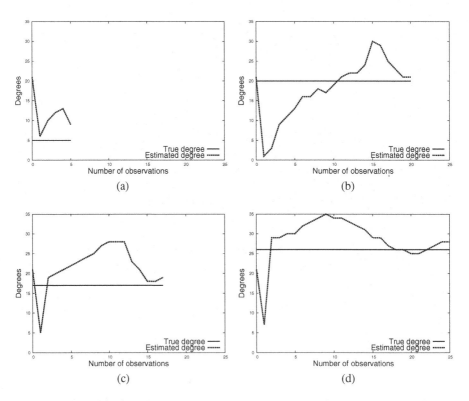

Fig. 3. Estimated neighbors' degrees over each *observation*

estimations on four of the neighbors. Typical behavior of degree estimations starts from the degree of the observer node, 21 in this case, and as soon as the first *observation* is made, the estimated degree decreases due to the changes in shape parameters of Beta distribution according to Definition 7. Then, the estimated degree increases and converges to the true degree of the observed node. The straight lines in each subfigure represent the true degrees of the observed nodes $(5, 20, 17$ and 26 respectively). The initial estimation of neighbors' degrees is the degree of the observer node, which is 21 in this case. x-axis shows the number of *observations* so far and y-axis shows the estimated degrees of the observed nodes over the *observations* made so far. For example, in Figure 3a, the observer node had 5 *observations* on the *observee* node and the estimated the degree of the *observee* is 9 at the end of *observations*. In Figure 3b and 3c, the estimations are reasonably accurate (20 to 21 and 17 to 19 respectively). On the other hand, in Figure 3a the estimation is 9 but the true degree is 5. This is because the true degree value is quite small. Our algorithm seems to have a lower bound for the true degree values for a reasonable performance. We show this result in Table 1 by comparing mean squared errors for the nodes with degrees above 5.

Table 1. Mean squared errors with increasing noise

Noise probability	0	0.2	0.4	0.6	0.8
MSE	0.6111	0.6132	0.6921	0.6831	0.7092
MSE $_{(deg > 5)}$	0.2037	0.2151	0.2265	0.2297	0.2394

We show MSEs with different noise probabilities in Table 1. We also show the results of nodes with degree values above 5 only. When the noise probability is 0, we use degrees of nodes as number of *observations*, i.e., $c_v(i) = 1$ for all $v \in V$ and $i \in Ne_v$. Then, we add or remove an *observation* from each node with the probability of $0.2, 0.4, 0.6$ and 0.8, respectively for each experiment. As the table shows MSE values do not increase much over increased noise probabilities.

We also computed MSEs for nodes that have degrees greater than 5 only since nodes with very small degrees have relatively high value of MSE. Since each observer node's initial estimations for neighbors' degrees are the degree of itself, it takes a number of *observations* to converge to true degrees of neighbors. However, when the number of *observations* is too small, i.e., small degrees, in this case, the resulting estimation is likely to produce more errors. For example, if a node with degree 1 was estimated to have degree 3, than the MSE is 4 which hurts the average MSE. We observe that the algorithm is resilient to noises since MSE values do not increase much as more noise is added.

We test the performance of the algorithm with different proportionality constants, i.e., $\frac{|O_v(i)|}{deg(i)} = c$ for all $v \in V$ and $i \in Ne_v$, where $c = 1, 2, 3, 4, 5$ (Note that we only multiply the number of *observations* since degrees of nodes are fixed). This is to test if the algorithm can tolerate numerous number of *observations* as it often happens in real world applications. Table 2 shows MSEs with different proportionality constants defined in Definition 10. We use the proportionality constants as estimators to compute

Table 2. Mean squared errors with different proportionality constants

Proportionality constant (c)	1	2	3	4	5
MSE	0.6111	0.8104	0.8120	0.8047	0.8096
MSE $_{(deg > 5)}$	0.2037	0.2128	0.2001	0.2205	0.2097

the MSEs in each experiment. We observe that both MSE and $MSE(deg > 5)$ stays about the same as c increases, which implies that the algorithm can estimate degrees of neighbors with accurate proportionality.

4.2 Degree Estimations on Neighboring Nodes in *Facebook* User Network

In real applications of social networks, the number of *observations* rarely agrees with (if not at all) the degrees of observed nodes (*observees*). In *Facebook* user network, some *Facebook* users may not have any activities at all even when they have many *friends* and other users may have more activities than the number of *friends*. Such "activities" include postings on the *walls* (observable) and reading the postings from the *walls* (not observable). If the *observee*'s *page* is actively engaged with other users, the observer can observe more *observations* of the *observee* than its number of *friends*. Also, if the *observee* is not engaged, the observer may not encounter any *observation* on the *observee*. We examine our algorithm with real *Facebook* user network data to evaluate how the algorithm performs when not all interactions are observed.

Facebook is one of the most popular and widely used online social network all around the world. By the end of March 2014, *Facebook* had 1.28 billion monthly active users worldwide and 802 million users log on to Facebook daily, according to *Facebook* newsroom. We used data sets from [18] which contains links between users and communications (collected from September 14, 2004 to January 22, 2009) among users via wall feature. The resulting network from user links consisted of $60,867$ nodes and $1,048,576$ edges. Some statistics of the network are given in Table 3.

Table 3. Statistics of the *Facebook* user network data

Statistics	Value
♯ Nodes	60867
♯ Edges	1048576
Average degree	17.22
Network diameter	15
Average Path Length	4.39
Modularity	0.602
♯ Communities	219

The smallest degree in the network is 1 and the largest degree is $1,903$ where the average degree is approximately 17, which tells us there are only a few users with very large degrees. Also, the maximum distance between two users (network diameter) is

15 and the average distance between any two users is 4.39 which are comparable with other social networks presented in [19]. Finally, the modularity of 0.602 is considered relatively high as [20] presented that the value usually falls between 0.3 and 0.7.

One of the important and innovative assumptions that our algorithm makes is that the degree distribution of the social network follows a power-law distribution. In Figure 4 (a), we show that the degree distribution of *Facebook* users from the data obeys power-law. In Figure 4 (b), we show the cumulative distribution function (CDF) of x, $P(x)$, where x is a degree of a node. We highlighted the graph presented in Figure 4 (b) to clearly see the power-law distribution (x ranges from 1 to 200). To verify if the degrees of *Facebook* users truly follow a power-law distribution, we use a goodness-of-fit test via a bootstrapping procedure, suggested by [21]. The hypothesis, that the data set actually follows a power-law, is tested by estimating the model parameters and then calculating the goodness-of-fit between the data and the power-law. We used *poweRlaw* package by [22] to perform the test. According to [21], the hypothesis, that the given data points follow a power-law, is valid if the resulting value is greater than 0.1. *Facebook* user data set produced a value of 0.98 which proves that the degree distribution of *Facebook* users follows a power-law.

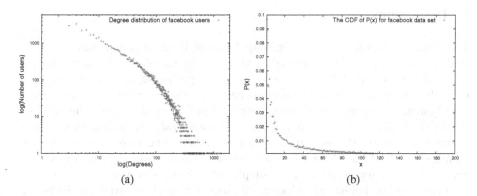

(a)   (b)

Fig. 4. Degree distribution of *Facebook* users follows power-law

The *Facebook wall* communication data shows the source (the user who writes to a wall), the target (the user whose wall has received a message from the source), and the time of the interaction (when the message was written to the wall). Notice that reading activities are not included in the data. Any user in *Facebook* can run our algorithm to find out how many *friends* each of its *friend* has.

Table 4. Statistics of estimation results on *Facebook* user network

	MSE	MSE(>50)	Observed	Estimation Ratio
Average	1.3906	0.7345	26.90%	0.9214

To test the performance of our algorithm, we run this algorithm for each user, for each *observation* (wall communication) from its neighbors. Table 4 shows the results of how the algorithm performs given *Facebook wall* activities. We compute the deviations from the perfect proportionality (Estimation ratio) assuming the proportionality constant is 1, i.e., $1 - \frac{|O_v(i)|}{deg(i)}$. In the table, *Observed* column shows the average percentage of *observations* each user could make. For example, if the degree of a user a is 10 and its neighbor b could observe 10 wall communications of a, than it is 100% *observed*. In this dataset, only 26.9% is observed which is challenging for the algorithm. It is comparable with the case when the proportionality constant (c) is 4 in Table 2 (since 25% observed is approximately when $c = \frac{1}{4}$). As *MSE* and *MSE(>50)* columns in Table 4 shows, the results are not as good, compared with the synthetic scale-free network used in Section 4.1. However, *MSE(>50)* of the estimation is 0.7345 which is close to the results from the generated network. Also, the average *Estimation Ratio* (estimated degree divided by true degree) is 0.9214 (1 being the perfect estimation) which is high.

If we purely count the number of *observations* to estimate degrees of neighbors, the *Estimation ratio* would be only 0.2690 compared to 0.9214. By applying our algorithm to estimate degree of neighbors, we achieved 0.9214 accuracy ratio which is more than three times better result.

5   Discussions

Traditional research focused on estimating degree distributions using macro-level algorithms. Because the size of network is huge, usually sampling is made to estimate degree distributions [14]. Our focus is to compute a precise degree of each neighboring node from an observer node within the network (therefore, micro-level approach). Our algorithm accommodates dynamic natures of online social networks, introducing the notion of *observations* which are obtained from interactions (or communications) among nodes (users). However, if we merely count the number of *observations* for the estimated degree of a neighbor, only active neighbors are discovered. In other words, in *Facebook* wall communications, if we simply count the number of *observations* to be estimated degrees of observed nodes, only the users who explicitly write on *observee*'s walls are counted. In reality, there are more readers (who silently read communications of others) than writers (who writes on walls). Although readers are currently inactive, they are potential writers and they should be also considered when estimating degrees of neighbors. The proposed algorithm combines the concept of Bernoulli trials and a power-law distribution to reason about hidden neighbors' of neighbors (readers).

In our experiments, we tested the algorithm on a synthetic scale-free network and *Facebook* user network. For the scale-free network experiment, we presented the mean squared errors of the accuracies. We added noise *observations* to show that the algorithm can estimate degrees of neighbors with incomplete information. In *Facebook* user network experiments, we tested the algorithm with wall communications among users as *observations*. Due to incomplete *observations*, average proportionality constant is as low as 0.2690, the results are not better than that of the scale-free network experiment.

6   Conclusions and Future Work

The proposed algorithm is based on the assumption that the number of activities of nodes is positively related to the degrees of nodes. In real life, the assumption is reasonable because people who have more connections have more social activities compared to people who do not.

However, there are certain relationships that are unique to online social networks. For example, many celebrities are neighbors with fans on online social networks. In this case, it becomes difficult to estimate the degrees of the celebrities from their neighbors point of view because they only interact with very few of their online neighbors. Note that, if degrees are estimated based only on the number of interactions (*observations*), hidden neighbors (connected but never interact with) may not be discovered. Our algorithm can capture hidden but potentially active neighbors because it can infer about unseen activities through the mechanisms of Bernoulli trials and power-law distributions.

Our algorithm can be further improved by utilizing additional information. In some applications, types of activities matter and certain types of *observations* are more valuable in estimating degrees of neighbors. By selectively using *observations* instead of all the *observations*, we can improve quality of the estimations. For example, on *Twitter* network, activities such as *follow* should be weighted more compared to the activities such as *tweet* and *retweet*. We can also extend our work by applying our algorithm recursively to enable users to capture the global view of the network, e.g. degree distributions of the entire network it belongs.

References

1. Hay, M., Li, C., Miklau, G., Jensen, D.: Accurate estimation of the degree distribution of private networks. In: Proceedings of the 2009 Ninth IEEE International Conference on Data Mining, ICDM 2009, pp. 169–178. IEEE Computer Society, Washington, DC (2009)
2. Snijders, T.A.B.: Accounting for degree distributions in empirical analysis of network dynamics. Proceedings of the National Academy of Sciences, 109–114 (2003)
3. Kupavskii, A., Ostroumova, L., Shabanov, D.A., Tetali, P.: The distribution of second degrees in the buckley-osthus random graph model. Internet Mathematics 9(4), 297–335 (2013)
4. Wang, T., Chen, Y., Zhang, Z., Xu, T., Jin, L., Hui, P., Deng, B., Li, X.: Understanding graph sampling algorithms for social network analysis. In: ICDCS Workshops, pp. 123–128. IEEE Computer Society (2011)
5. Ribeiro, B.F., Towsley, D.: On the estimation accuracy of degree distributions from graph sampling. In: CDC, pp. 5240–5247 (2012)
6. Lee, J.Y., Oh, J.C.: A model for recursive propagations of reputations in social networks. In: Proceedings of the 2013 IEEE/ACM International Conference on Advances in Social Networks Analysis and Mining, ASONAM 2013, pp. 666–670. ACM, New York (2013)
7. Lenzen, C., Wattenhofer, R.: Distributed Algorithms for Sensor Networks. Philosophical Transactions of the Royal Society A 370(1958) (January 2012)
8. Albert, R., Barabási, A.L.: Statistical mechanics of complex networks. Rev. Mod. Phys. 74(1), 47–97 (2002)
9. Ribeiro, B.F., Towsley, D.: On the estimation accuracy of degree distributions from graph sampling. In: CDC, pp. 5240–5247 (2012)

10. Ye, S., Wu, S.F.: Estimating the size of online social networks. In: Elmagarmid, A.K., Agrawal, D. (eds.) SocialCom/PASSAT, pp. 169–176. IEEE Computer Society (2010)
11. Page, L., Brin, S., Motwani, R., Winograd, T.: The pagerank citation ranking: Bringing order to the web. Technical Report 1999-66, Stanford InfoLab (November 1999)
12. Mislove, A., Marcon, M., Gummadi, K.P., Druschel, P., Bhattacharjee, B.: Measurement and analysis of online social networks. In: Proceedings of the 7th ACM SIGCOMM Conference on Internet Measurement, IMC 2007, pp. 29–42. ACM, New York (2007)
13. Erdös, P., Rényi, A.: On random graphs, I. Publicationes Mathematicae (Debrecen) 6, 290–297 (1959)
14. Galeotti, A., Goyal, S., Jackson, M.O., Vega-Redondo, F., Yariv, L.: Network games. Review of Economic Studies 77(1), 218–244 (2010)
15. Casella, G., Berger, R.: Statistical Inference. Duxbury Resource Center (June 2001)
16. Csanyi, G., Szendroi, B.: Structure of a large social network. Physical Review E 69(3) (March 2004); 036131 PT: J; PN: Part 2; PG: 5
17. Shannon, P., Markiel, A., Ozier, O., Baliga, N.S., Wang, J.T., Ramage, D., Amin, N., Schwikowski, B., Ideker, T.: Cytoscape: a software environment for integrated models of biomolecular interaction networks. Genome Research 13(11), 2498–2504 (2003)
18. Viswanath, B., Mislove, A., Cha, M., Gummadi, K.P.: On the evolution of user interaction in facebook. In: Proceedings of the 2nd ACM SIGCOMM Workshop on Social Networks (WOSN 2009) (August 2009)
19. Mislove, A., Marcon, M., Gummadi, K.P., Druschel, P., Bhattacharjee, B.: Measurement and analysis of online social networks. In: Proceedings of the 5th ACM/USENIX Internet Measurement Conference (IMC 2007) (2007)
20. Newman, M.E.J., Girvan, M.: Finding and evaluating community structure in networks. Phys. Rev. E 69(2), 026113 (2004)
21. Clauset, A., Shalizi, C.R., Newman, M.E.J.: Power-law distributions in empirical data. SIAM Rev. 51(4), 661–703 (2009)
22. Gillespie, C.S.: Fitting heavy tailed distributions: the poweRlaw package (2014), R package version 0.20.5

Towards Convention Propagation
in Multi-layer Social Networks

Smitha Keertipati, Bastin Tony Roy Savarimuthu, and Maryam A. Purvis

University of Otago, Dunedin, New Zealand
keesm110@student.otago.ac.nz,
{tonyr,tehrany}@infoscience.otago.ac.nz

Abstract. Most work on convention propagation have focused on single-layer networks. This work a) highlights the need for studying convention propagation in multi-layer networks, b) presents results comparing the speed of convention propagation in single-layer vs. multi-layer networks and c) demonstrates the role of influencer agents in convention propagation in multi-layer networks.

1 Introduction

The impact of different configurations of networks on the spread of information, rumours, norms, diseases etc. is being studied in many disciplines including sociology and epidemiology. Several other domains such as traffic management and marketing have benefited from the use of network propagation principles to their advantage. For example, the knowledge of network principles have been used in re-routing passengers arriving in a central hub that provides different modes of transport [5]. Marketing personnel could identify paths in networks that can expedite the faster uptake of a particular product [1, 2]. In this paper, we are interested in the spread of conventions as studied in the field of normative multi-agent systems (NorMAS) using simulations [10].

A simple view of networks categorizes networks into single-layer and multi-layer networks. A multi-layer network consists of many layers where a node (or nodes) in one of the layers might also be present in the other layers. There have been a wide-range of studies on the characteristics of different types of single-layer networks such as random, small-world and scale-free networks (see [7] for an overview). Researchers in NorMAS have investigated how conventions propagate in single-layer networks [3, 11]. However, the characteristics of information diffusion in multi-layer networks has attracted researchers' attention only recently [4, 8] in various domains. In MAS, the interest in exploring the applicability of multi-layer networks has been very recent [6] and this paper investigates the spread of conventions on top of multi-layer networks.

2 Single vs. Multi-layer Networks

This section aims to present an overview of single vs. multi-layer networks to highlight the need for studying convention propagation in multi-layer networks.

A single-layer network normally refers to individuals connected in a particular context such as work and hobby. Nowadays, it is estimated that an average individual is a

H.K. Dam et al. (Eds.): PRIMA 2014, LNAI 8861, pp. 57–64, 2014.

member of more than one social network. For example, an individual may be a part of LinkedIn, Facebook and Google+ networks. Each network can be considered as a layer. So, an individual who has an account in all the three networks is a part of a three layer network. However, the nodes an individual is connected to in a particular layer will be different. An individual in a multi-layer network can spread the information from one network to other networks.

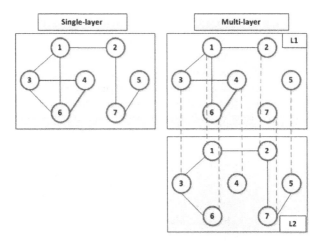

Fig. 1. An example of single and multi-layer networks

Figure 1 shows an example of single- and multi-layer networks. The single-layer network on the left shows the structure of a community where individuals are modelled as nodes and their relationships are shown as links (or edges). The multi-layer network on the right shows the different layers of relationships between individuals in a community. The first layer L1 could correspond to a social network between members on Facebook and the second layer L2 could be the Word of Mouth (WoM) network in the community. The dotted lines indicate that the nodes in L1 and L2 are the same individuals. It can be observed that not all nodes are connected to others in the same layer. For example nodes 5 and 7 are connected in L2, but not in L1. It can be observed that L1 and L2 can be superimposed to create the single-layer network on the left. Superimposition here implies the graph sum[1] of L1 and L2. If L2 is superimposed on top of L1, we get the same nodes (all seven) and the eight links (all links in L1 and L2 with the elimination of duplicates). The superimposition of L1 on top of L2 will yield the same result. So, the order of superimposition does not matter.

Most work that consider network topologies have restricted themselves to a single-layer network where the differences in influences of nodes that are spread across different layers have not been investigated. For example, nodes 3 and 4 are only connected

---

[1] A brief description of graph sum can be found at
http://mathworld.wolfram.com/GraphSum.html

in L1 and not in L2. These two nodes represent individuals that are further apart (physically) but are connected through an online social network. Such differences are often
ignored in single-layer networks that aggregate different layers into one through superimposition of layers, since the aim of these networks is to provide a simplified view
of relationships in a community. However, differentiating different layers of networks
is important because people are connected to each other through a range of networks
and the *layered* structure has a significant impact on the dynamics of information propagation in a community of agents such as the speed of convention propagation and the
extent of spread in a network.

In what follows, we compare the speed of information propagation of single and
multi-layer networks. The speed of information propagation between two nodes is referred to as cascade time (CT) in a network and is measured in hop lengths. Using the
simple example shown in Figure 1, we compare the CTs in the two types of networks.
Table 1 shows the CTs between two nodes in five different network settings. Assuming
that the time taken for information propagation between two adjacent nodes that are
connected is one, the CT for the path from nodes 4 to 5 in single-layer network (SL)
is 5. The information propagation from nodes 4 to 5 is unachievable in L1 or L2 alone
because there is no path between the two.

Each layer in a multi-layer network has certain properties. *Medium delay* (D_m) represents the time taken for a piece of information to flow between two adjacent nodes in
a given layer. For example, the D_m in WoM networks is generally greater than online
networks such as Facebook or Twitter. When information propagates across layers from
the same node, there would be a delay because of *medium switch* (D_s). For example,
D_s captures the time to transfer a message from Twitter to Facebook or from a WoM
network to Twitter. The CT between nodes a and b is given by:

$$CT_{ab} = \sum_{i=1}^{x} D_{m(L1)} + \sum_{j=1}^{y} D_{m(L2)} + \sum_{k=1}^{z} D_s \tag{1}$$

where x represents the number of links in layer 1 through which information propagates,
y represents the number of links in layer 2, and z represents the node switches between
the two layers.

Using the formula presented above, we compute the CT along the path from node 4
to 5 in the multi-layer network shown in Figure 1 under three varying circumstances.

Case 1. ML_0 represents a multi-layer network where $D_m=1$ between two adjacent
nodes in both layers (L1 and L2) and there is no medium switch delay ($D_s=0$). Let us
assume that the information originates in node 4 in L1. In order for this information to
be spread to node 5, this information needs to cross layers (i.e. L2 to L1 at node 2). The
path followed in L1 would be 4-3-1-2. So, the sum of D_m along the path from 4 to 2 in
L1 is 3. The information needs to cross layers since a path exists in L2 between nodes 2
and 5. The path followed in L2 is 2-7-5. So, the sum of D_m along the path from nodes
2 to 5 in L2 is 2. The sums of D_m for the path from nodes 4 to 5 is 5. Since D_s is zero,
CT_{45} is 5.

Case 2. ML_1 represents a multi-layer network where $D_m=1$ between two adjacent
nodes in both layers L1 and L2 and the medium switch delay is one ($D_s=1$). In this

Table 1. Cascade times along two different paths in five different network configurations

Cascade time	SL	L1	L2	ML_0	ML_1	ML_2
CT_{45}	5	-	-	5	6	8
CT_{67}	3	-	4	3	4	5

case CT between nodes 4 and 5 becomes 6. CT for ML_1 is one unit higher than ML_0 because of the network switch at node 2.

Case 3. ML_2 represents a multi-layer network where D_m=1 in L1 and D_m=2 in L2 and medium switch cost (D_s=1). This models a case where medium delays are different in different layers (e.g. the medium delay cost in Twitter might be 1 and for WoM might be 2). In this case, the CT between 4 to 5 rises to 8. The D_m along the path between 4 to 2 in L1 is 3. The D_m along the path between nodes 2 and 5 in L2 is 4. The medium switch delay at node 2 is 1. So, CT_{45} in this case is 8.

The same type of calculations for information propagation between nodes 6 and 7 (where origin is node 6 of L2) are presented in the second row of the table. The three cases presented above demonstrate that multi-layer networks are at best equal to single-layer networks (case 1) and most often are slower than single-layer networks (cases 2 and 3). Multi-layer networks are often slow in information propagation because the spread is influenced by the nature of the underlying medium and/or the network switch delays across layers.

3 Experimental Model

In this section, we discuss how to construct different types of network topologies and also model how conventions propagate on top of these networks.

We employ a simple contagion spreading model for the study of convention propagation. Similar to the spreading of a contagion such as a virus, a convention propagates from one node to another if one of them has the convention and there is an edge connecting the two. For example, if node A is connected to five other nodes, then, upon adopting a convention, node A spreads the convention to other agents. In the next time step, all the five nodes adopt the convention. This simple model has been used so as to focus on the dynamics of convention propagation in different types of networks. A similar contagion-based model has been used to study convention spreading [9].

While there have been multitude of models for generating single-layer networks (see [7]), there are relatively few approaches used in the literature to model multi-layer networks. Two approaches used are the merging and the splitting approaches where a multi-layer network is built by either merging two simple networks or splitting a simple network into multiple networks [6]. We employed the splitting approach in this work.

A Splitting Approach for the Generation of Multi-layer Networks - We created an initial single-layer network consisting of certain number of agents (e.g. 100). Three types of networks were considered - Erdos-Renyi (ER) random network, Watts-Strogatz

(WS) small-world network and Barabasi-Albert (BA) scale-free network. Once a single-layer network is generated, in order to create the multi-layer network consisting of two-layers, we duplicated all the nodes in the single layer in both layers of the multi-layer network. Then using the two splitting mechanisms (type 1 and 2) discussed below we assign the links to the two-layers.

Type 1 - For type 1, edges from the single-layer network are split between the two layers of the multi-layer network using a pair of probability values. For example, let us consider values 0.1 and 0.9. For each edge in the single-layer network a random number between 0 and 1 is generated. If the random number (r) is less than 0.1, a new edge is created in layer 1. Else if r is between 0.1 and 0.9 a new edge is created in layer 2. Else, the edge goes in layer 1 or layer 2 based on generating a new probability value between 0 and 1 (i.e. if the new value is less than 0.5 the link goes to layer 1 or else it goes to layer 2). Using this approach, an edge is assigned only to one of the two layers. This splitting mechanism generates interdependent networks. Nodes in these type of multi-layer networks remain in a single layer but send information back and forth to other layers.

Type 2 - These multi-layer networks differ from type 1 in that they allow duplication of edges between the two layers (i.e., the same link between any two nodes of the single-layer network can exist in different layers). The else part of the condition in Type 1 is modified. If the random number r is greater than or equal to 0.9, then the edge is added to both layers. So, there is a 10% chance that each edge is present in both the layers. Type 2 models modern social networks where the same individual in a community can belong to two different networks and can be connected to the same member(s) of the community in both of these networks.

To study the spread of conventions, we choose a certain number of individuals who are the originators of conventions (or norm entrepreneurs). In the experiments we conducted, we measured the time taken for a convention to spread from this originator to the entire network.

4   Experiments

In this section we describe the experiments conducted to compare the speed of convention propagation in two different networks and the role of influencer agents on convention propagation.

4.1   Convention Propagation Speeds in Single- vs. Multi-layer Networks

Section 2 shows that the cascade times along certain paths are slower in multi-layer networks than single-layer networks. In this experiment we empirically investigate the average cascade times for convention convergence in the whole network. For the single-layer network, we randomly chose an agent as the norm entrepreneur which starts propagating the convention. We first generated a particular type of network (e.g. Erdos-Renyi (ER) network) with 100 nodes. Then for each network, we conducted 10 experiments. In each experiment a randomly selected node becomes the norm entrepreneur. We conducted experiments on 100 networks of the same type (i.e. ER network). In total

1000 experiments were conducted. Also, we conducted similar experiments for small-world and scale-free networks. We measured the average time taken to reach a 100% convergence.

Multi-layer networks were also initialized using a similar approach. Convergence times were measured for multi-layer networks that were generated using Type 1 and Type 2 mechanisms. We investigated Types 1 and 2 using three different pairs of probability values for edge assignment. These were a) 0.1 and 0.9, b) 0.3 and 0.7 and c) 0.5 and 0.5. The experiments for multi-layer networks for different probability value pairs are named Types 1a, 1b, 1c, 2a, 2b and 2c (6 experiments).

The experimental results for a Watts-Strogatz (WS) small-world network is shown in Figure 2. Two observations can be made from the figure. First, convention propagation in SL is always faster than ML network. This is because of the delay in network switches which are absent in SL network. Second, the convention propagation in type 2 is faster than type 1 setting. This is because of the duplicate links in type 2 which increase the speed of convention propagation in type 2 multi-layer network. However, the smaller proportion of these duplicate links in the multi-layer type 2 network isn't sufficient to match the speed of convergence to that of the SL network. These were also noted in ER and BA networks. These fairly intuitive results confirm that multi-layer networks indeed slow down convention spreading in realistic settings.

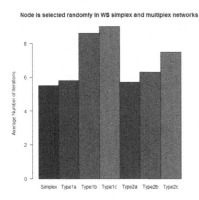

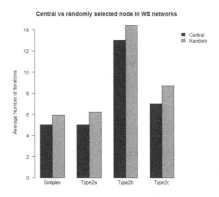

Fig. 2. Convention propagation in WS networks when node is selected at random

Fig. 3. Comparison of convention propagation using central node vs random node in single-layer and multi-layer networks

4.2   Role of Centrality-Based Influencer Agents

To investigate the role of influencer agents, we conducted experiments that compare the speed of convention propagation in both of these networks by starting convention propagation by selecting a different agent to start convention propagation. In the first approach, a norm entrepreneur agent was chosen randomly. In the other approach, based on degree centrality, a hub node is chosen. This hub node has an account in both layers. We conducted 100 experiments (each experiment with a different network of a certain type such as ER network).

The result of this experiment is shown in Figure 3. It can be observed that starting convention propagation using a node selected based on degree centrality is faster than using a node selected at random. This is consistent with the definition of centrality that the centrality of a node measures a node's relative importance within a network. The more central the node, the more influential it is, in the network.

4.3 Role of Multiple Influencer Agents

As opposed to the use of single influencer agent as discussed above, we conducted experiments using multiple influencer agents. The influencer agents in a network are measured by ranking nodes in descending order of degree centrality. The impact of using multiple influencer agents in an ER single-layer network is shown in Figure 4. It can be observed that, even though the hub node is the most connected in any given network, using this node in isolation is slower than using multiple agents to start convention propagation. It can also be observed that as the number of influencer agents increases, the number of iterations taken to fully converge decreases. This is because propagation is started from multiple sources that are located in different areas of the network. This allows the information to be spread over a longer distance much faster than if only one influencer agent is used. Figure 5 shows the impact of using multiple influencer agents in an ER multi-layer network. It can be observed that as the number of influencer agents increases, the speed of propagation also increases. This is consistent with the results for the ER single-layer network. We note that the role of influencer agents in single-layer networks have been studied by other researchers [3, 11]. Our study shows that the results hold for multi-layer networks also.

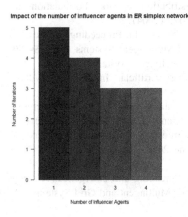

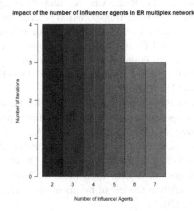

Fig. 4. Convention propagation using multiple influencer agents in an ER single-layer network

Fig. 5. Convention propagation using multiple influencer agents in an ER multi-layer network

4.4   Discussion

Our work is different from other researchers in the area of NorMAS (e.g. [3, 11]) as they are limited to single layer networks. The work of Li et al. [6] considers multi-layer networks, but assumes that the same nodes are present in the all the layers of the network. In our work, we relax this assumption and allow for nodes to be absent from one of the layers of the multi-layer network.

This work in progress paper makes three contributions to the study of convention propagation in multi-layer networks. First, we have shown that the spread of information is faster in single-layer networks in most realistic situations than multi-layer networks. Second, we have shown through our experimental results how the spread of convention propagation can be improved in single-layer and multi-layer networks through the use of seeded influencer agents. We are currently extending our model by considering the weights of edges since some individuals are more influential over others. In the future, we will investigate a threshold based model where an individual adopts a convention if certain proportion of its neighbours adopt it. Also, the agent will have the ability to decide whether to adopt a convention and whether to propagate a convention to its neighbours.

References

1. Achrol, R.S., Kotler, P.: Marketing in the network economy. The Journal of Marketing, 146–163 (1999)
2. Choi, H., Kim, S.-H., Lee, J.: Role of network structure and network effects in diffusion of innovations. Industrial Marketing Management 39(1), 170–177 (2010)
3. Franks, H., Griffiths, N., Jhumka, A.: Manipulating convention emergence using influencer agents. Autonomous Agents and Multi-agent Systems 26(3), 315–353 (2013)
4. Gomez, S., Diaz-Guilera, A., Gomez-Gardeñes, J., Perez-Vicente, C.J., Moreno, Y., Arenas, A.: Diffusion dynamics on multiplex networks. Physical Review Letters 110(2), 028701 (2013)
5. Lapierre, S.D., Ruiz, A.B., Soriano, P.: Designing distribution networks: Formulations and solution heuristic. Transportation Science 38(2), 174–187 (2004)
6. Li, Z., Jiang, Y.: Cross-layers cascade in multiplex networks. In: Proceedings of the 2014 International Conference on Autonomous Agents and Multi-agent Systems, pp. 269–276. International Foundation for Autonomous Agents and Multiagent Systems (2014)
7. Mitchell, M.: Complex systems: Network thinking. Artificial Intelligence 170(18), 1194–1212 (2006)
8. Mucha, P.J., Richardson, T., Macon, K., Porter, M.A., Onnela, J.-P.: Community structure in time-dependent, multiscale, and multiplex networks. Science 328(5980), 876–878 (2010)
9. Salazar, N., Rodríguez-Aguilar, J.A., Arcos, J.L.: Infection-based norm emergence in multi-agent complex networks. In: Proceeding of the 2008 Conference on ECAI 2008, pp. 891–892. IOS Press, Amsterdam (2008)
10. Savarimuthu, B.T.R., Cranefield, S.: Norm creation, spreading and emergence: A survey of simulation models of norms in multi-agent systems. Multiagent and Grid Systems 7(1), 21–54 (2011)
11. Sen, S., Airiau, S.: Emergence of norms through social learning. In: Proceedings of the Twentieth International Joint Conference on Artificial Intelligence (IJCAI), pp. 1507–1512. AAAI Press (2007)

Efficient Task Decomposition in Crowdsourcing

Huan Jiang and Shigeo Matsubara

Department of Social Informatics, Kyoto University, Kyoto 606-8501, Japan
jiang@ai.soc.i.kyoto-u.ac.jp, matsubara@i.kyoto-u.ac.jp

Abstract. In order to facilitate crowdsourcing-based task solving, complex tasks are decomposed into smaller subtasks that can be executed either sequentially or in parallel by workers. These two task decompositions attract a plenty of empirical explorations in crowdsourcing. However the absence of formal study makes difficulty in providing task requesters with explicit guidelines on task decomposition. In this paper, we formally present and analyze those two task decompositions as vertical and horizontal task decomposition models. Our focus is on addressing the efficiency (i.e., the quality of the task's solution) of task decomposition when the self-interested workers are paid in two different ways — equally paid and paid based on their contributions. By combining the theoretical analyses on worker's behavior and simulation-based exploration on the efficiency of task decomposition, our study 1) shows the superiority of vertical task decomposition over horizontal task decomposition in improving the quality of the task's solution; 2) gives explicit instructions on strategies for optimal vertical task decomposition under both revenue sharing schemes to maximize the quality of the task's solution.

Keywords: Task decomposition, task dependence, task difficulty, solution quality, efficient crowdsourcing.

1   Introduction

Crowdsourcing is admired as one of the most lucrative paradigm of leveraging collective intelligence to carry out a wide variety of tasks with various complexity. This very success is dependent on the potential for *decomposing* the complex tasks into smaller pieces of subtasks, such that each subtasks becomes low in complexity, requires little cognitive effort to be completed by an individual.

After decomposing a complex task into multiple small subtasks, a collective of crowds (or workers) execute the subtasks either *independently* or *dependently*. When the subtasks are structured independently, multiple workers are recruited to collaborate *in parallel*, and subtask's quality depends only upon the effort of the worker who performs it. By contrast, when there are dependencies among the subtasks, workers are organized to collaborate *sequentially*, and subtask's quality depends on efforts of multiple workers who jointly produce output. In the sequential process, subtask dependence mainly characterized in the striking feature that one worker's output is used as the starting point for the following worker, which makes the assumption that following worker can do better based

H.K. Dam et al. (Eds.): PRIMA 2014, LNAI 8861, pp. 65–73, 2014.

on quality solution provided by previous worker hold (see [4]). CrowdForge [1] and Soylent [2] delineate case studies on article writing and word processing respectively with sequential process, and they both come up with high quality final outcomes. It is worth noting that, TurKit [3] presents iterative workflow for complex tasks solving. However, such iterative workflows without task decomposition are beyond the scope of this paper.

We define two task decompositions as *horizontal task decomposition* for independent subtasks, and *vertical task decomposition* for dependent subtasks. To illustrate the concepts, we refer to the following crowdsourcing-based *proofreading* task as example, wherein an article containing three paragraphs requires spelling, style and grammar error correction. In this context, the article could be horizontally decomposed into three pieces of subtasks that each has one paragraph and be performed by one worker independently. Meanwhile, the original article could also be vertically decomposed into three sequential subtasks, as "Find-Fix-Verify" proposed by Bernstein et al. [2].

Our research focuses on the complex tasks decomposition in crowdsourcing, wherein the complex tasks can be decomposed and executed in both independent and dependent way. Of particular interest are the work that aim at analyzing workers' strategic behaviors, comparing the *efficiency* of two task decompositions, in terms of *final quality*, and finally generating explicit instructions on strategies for optimal task decomposition. Different from the works that provide efficient solutions for applications with independent subtasks (e.g., [6]), Long et al. [5] first investigates the interdependent subtask allocation in crowdsourcing systems, which has the most relevant background to our research.

We summarize our main contribution in the following. In Section 2, we formally construct the models for both vertical and horizontal task decompositions. The dependence among subtasks is formalized as the degree to which a subtask's difficulty depends on the qualities of the other subtasks. In Section 3, we rigorously analyze the strategic behaviors of the workers, and find that contribution-based sharing scheme provides more incentives for workers to exert higher efforts on difficult subtasks. In Section 4, we conduct simulations to analyze and compare the efficiency of two task decomposition. We conclude that in general, vertical task decomposition strategy outperforms the horizontal one in improving the quality of the final solution, and give explicit instructions the *optimal strategy* (i.e., arrangement of subtasks with different difficulties for final quality maximization) under vertical task decomposition situation from the task requester's point of view.

2   The Model

In this section we consider the complex task, e.g., proofreading, that can be both vertically and horizontally decomposed into N ($N > 1$) subtasks. In both situations, N workers contribute their efforts, such as time and resources, to N subtasks respectively. The amount of effort exerted by worker i to subtask i is characterized by e_i, which is normalized to scale $[0, 1]$.

2.1 Vertical Task Decomposition

Find-Fix-Verify: The output of Find stage is the *patches* that may have spelling and grammar errors and need corrections or edits. The quality of patches could be evaluated by how well they cover the true positions [5]. The output of Fix stage is the corrections of the errors in those patches. The quality of fix task could be evaluated by the number and the average validity of the proposed corrections. Last, in Verify stage, workers accept or reject the corrections and edit to improves the proofreading result. The quality of the final solution can be viewed as the *cumulative qualities* obtained from all subtasks.

Definition 1 (Final quality). *The quality of the final solution (Q) to the complex task is the cumulative qualities of all the N decomposed subtasks, i.e.,*

$$Q(\mathbf{e}) = \sum_{i=1}^{N} q_{vertical}^i \tag{1}$$

where $\mathbf{e} = (e_1, \cdots, e_N)$, *and* $q_{vertical}^i$ *is the quality function of subtask i.*

Since each subtask takes the output from the previous subtask as input, the quality of each subtask is also positively related to the quality of the previous subtask. Formally, the subtask quality function is governed by the following form.

Assumption 1. *The quality of subtask i's solution depends not only on the effort exerted by worker i, but also on the quality of previous subtask's solution, i.e.,*

$$q_{vertical}^i = f^i(q_{vertical}^{i-1}, e_i) \tag{2}$$

where f^i *increases with* e_i *at a decreasing rate, i.e.,*

$$\partial f^i / \partial e_i > 0 \quad and \quad \partial^2 f^i / \partial e_i \partial e_i < 0 \tag{3}$$

Remark 1. The recursive definition of f^i directly implies that the quality of subtask i's solution depends also on the efforts from all the prior workers. Hence, we can rewrite Eq. (2) equivalently as $q_{vertical}^i = f^i(e_1, \cdots, e_i)$, and any increase in the efforts from the previous workers also leads to an improvement on the quality of subtask i, i.e., $\forall k \in \{1, \cdots, i\}$, $\partial f^i / \partial e_k > 0$. Last, note that, for the first subtask ($i = 1$), the quality function is simplified as $q_{vertical}^1 = f^1(e_1)$.

Before we illustrate how does $q_{vertical}^i$ depend on $q_{vertical}^{i-1}$, we first introduce the concept of *subtask difficulty*. Take Find stage for example, articles that consist more frequent in long and compound sentences, indicate more grammatical errors, and thus require considerable effort for locating the true positions. Thus, low difficulty indicates high marginal contribution based on the same level of effort, which is formalized as follows.

Definition 2 (Subtask difficulty). *We endow subtask i with weight* $\omega_i \in (0, 1)$ *as its difficulty. Subtask i is said to be more difficult than subtask j (i.e., $\omega_i > \omega_j$), iff for any effort level l*

$$f_{e_i}^i(e_i, e_{-i} = \mathbf{e}_{N-1}) \mid_{e_i = l} < f_{e_j}^j(e_j, e_{-j} = \mathbf{e}_{N-1}) \mid_{e_j = l} \tag{4}$$

where $\mathbf{e}_{N-1}$ *is the effort levels of all other* $N-1$ *workers. Furthermore,* $\sum_{i=1}^{N} \omega_i = 1$.

Now, we continue with the Find-Fix-Verify example to illustrate how does $q_{vertical}^{i-1}$ affect $q_{vertical}^i$ by altering the difficulty of subtask i. As Find stage, Fix stage also has its own intrinsic difficulty. Nevertheless, its difficulty can be altered by the quality of the Find task. For example, high quality of Find task due to phrase-level error location reduces the difficulty of Fix task, however, low quality due to the noisy patches can make Fix task more difficult.

Assumption 2 (Quality dependency). *The difficulty of subtask i decreases as the efforts on previous subtasks increase, i.e., $\forall k \leq i - 1$, if $e_k < e_k'$, then*

$$f_{e_i}^i(e_{-k}, e_k) < f_{e_i}^i(e_{-k}, e_k') \tag{5}$$

Remark 2. It is worth noting that an increase in the effort previous subtasks not only increases the quality of subtask i in quantity (Eq. (3)), but also, according to Eq. (5), enables greater marginal increase on subtask i's quality.

2.2 Horizontal Task Decomposition

In horizontal task decomposition, the complex task is decomposed into N subtasks with no interdependencies, which implies $\partial^2 f^i / \partial e_j \partial e_i = 0$ $(i \neq j)$. N workers devote efforts independently to their own subtasks for individual utility maximization. The quality function of the final solution is defined as Eq. (1), i.e., $Q(\mathbf{e}) = \sum_{i=1}^N q_{horizontal}^i$, where $q_{horizontal}^i$ is the quality function of subtask i.

In contrast to vertical task decomposition, where each worker concentrates on a single stage of the workflow (take proofreading for example, Find, Fix or Verify), in horizontal task decomposition, each worker gives considerations to all stages. This makes the worker have to divide his effort among all stages. We assume that the effort e_i, exerted by worker i to subtask i, can be viewed as being distributed among N stages as in the vertical task decomposition situation, proportionally to the difficulties of the stages. This assumption simplifies the results without sacrificing much in terms of generality.

Assumption 3 (Horizontal subtask quality function). *The quality of the solution to subtask i only depends on the effort exerted by worker i, which is distributed among N stages proportionally to their difficulties. Hence, $q_{horizontal}^i = \sum_{k=1}^N f^k(\omega_1 e_i, \cdots, \omega_k e_i)$.*

2.3 Revenue Sharing Schemes

Definition 3 (Group-based revenue sharing). *Under the group-based revenue sharing scheme, each worker receives an equal share of the total revenue given by the task requester, i.e., $R_i = Q(e_i)/N$. Therefore, worker i's utility is $\pi(e_i) = Q(\mathbf{e})/N - c(e_i)$.*

Definition 4 (Contribution-Based revenue sharing). *Under the contribution-based revenue sharing scheme, each worker receives reward determined by his/her marginal contribution to the final task solution, i.e., $R_i(e_i) = Q_{e_i}(e_i) \cdot e_i$. Thus, worker i's utility is $\pi(e_i) = Q_{e_i}(e_i) \cdot e_i - c(e_i)$.*

Assumption 4 (Cost function). *In order to execute subtask i, worker i exerts an effort level e_i with a cost $c(e_i)$. The cost increases with the effort, and it increases at an increasing rate, i.e., $c_{e_i} = \frac{dc}{de_i} > 0$ and $c_{e_i e_i} = \frac{d^2 c}{de_i^2} > 0$.*

3   Strategic Behaviors

Proposition 1. *Under both vertical and horizontal task decomposition strategies, for individual utility maximization, 1) when group-based sharing scheme is applied, workers devote higher efforts to easy subtasks than difficult subtasks. On the contrary, 2) under contribution-based sharing scheme, workers devote efforts to easy subtasks no less than difficult subtasks.*

According to Proposition 1, although contribution-based revenue sharing may provide workers with more incentives to perform difficult subtasks than group-based revenue sharing, they both indicate the fact that workers are more inclined to perform easy subtasks. This is consistent with findings in worker behavior studies in crowdsourcing, and highlights the need for task decomposition design.

4   Task Decomposition Strategy Analysis and Comparison

We construct simulation aiming at explicitly evaluating and comparing the efficiencies, in terms of the final quality (Eq. (1)), of two task decomposition strategies. It is worth noting that, besides the 2-subtask and 3-subtask situation presented in the following, we also explored the situations for $N = 4, \cdots, 9$, which not shown here due to limited space but generate the similar results. It is worth noting that by considering the existing applications such as Soylent, N=9 for the vertical decomposition seems not small.

Subtask Quality Functions. We simulate the task solving process under the assumption of subtask quality functions in the *Cobb-Douglas form*. We assume there are N workers for N subtasks, and for subtask i, the quality functions under vertical and horizontal task decompositions are respectively defined as

$$q_{vertical}^i(e_1, \cdots, e_i) = \prod_{k=1}^{i} e_k^{\omega_k} \quad \text{and} \quad q_{horizontal}^i(e_i) = \sum_{k=1}^{N} \prod_{r=1}^{k} (\omega_r e_i)^{\frac{\omega_r}{N}}$$

where $\omega_i \in (0, 1)$ is the difficulty of subtask i, and $\sum_{i=1}^{N} \omega_i = 1$.

Cost Functions. We specify the cost function for worker i as $c(e_i) = e_i^2$.

4.1   Efficiency Comparison of Two Task Decompositions

Two-subtask situation is depicted in Fig. 1 to illustrate the efficiency difference between vertical and horizontal task decomposition strategies. We endow each of two subtasks with a weight ($\omega_1, \omega_2 \in (0, 1)$), which is restricted to one decimal

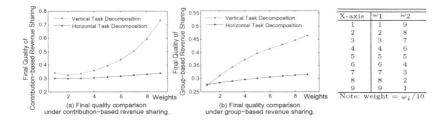

Fig. 1. Comparison of vertical and horizontal task decompositions. Generally, vertical decomposition outperforms horizontal decomposition in terms of final quality.

place. Then, we exhaustively examine the final quality under all the combinations of two weights, as given in the table in Fig. 1. As can be seen in Fig. 1 (a) and (b), vertical task decomposition strategy is superior to the horizontal one, under both group-based and contribution-based revenue sharing schemes.

4.2 Vertical Task Decomposition Strategy

As the qualities of the prior subtasks improve, the positive support they provide become strong, which makes the subsequent subtasks more dependent on the prior ones. Further, in the extreme situation where all subtasks have the highest qualities with all workers exert their highest efforts ($e=1$), the dependence among subtasks become strongest, which can be viewed as the intrinsic dependence among the sequential subtasks.

Definition 5. *Given a succession of N subtasks, the sequential dependence between subtasks $i-1$ and i is defined as*

$$\partial^2 q^i / \partial e_{i-1} \partial e_i |_{e_1 = \cdots = e_{i-1} = e_i = 1} = \omega_{i-1}\omega_i, \tag{6}$$

and the total dependence among all subtask is $\sum_{i=2}^{N} d(e_{i-1}, e_i)$.

As we do for the two-subtask situation, we respectively endow 3 subtasks with weights ω_1, ω_2, ω_3, which are restricted to one decimal place as well, and then exhaustively examine all combinations of the weights, i.e., a permutation of $\{0.1, 0.2, \cdots, 0.9\}$ with a restriction that the sum of three weights equals 1. As shown in Table 1, for 3-subtask situation, there are a total of 36 combinations, and they are sorted in a *lexicographic manner*, i.e., $(\omega_1, \omega_2, \omega_3)$ occurs before $(\omega_1', \omega_2', \omega_3')$ iff $\omega_1 < \omega_1'$, or $\omega_1 = \omega_1'$ and $\omega_2 < \omega_2'$, or $\omega_1 = \omega_1'$ and $\omega_2 = \omega_2'$ and $\omega_3 < \omega_3'$.

Lessons Learned on Group-Based Revenue Sharing Scheme. In Fig. 2, we explore 3-subtask situation under group-based revenue sharing scheme.

Table 1. Weight combinations for 3-subtask situation

	(a)												(b)												
X-axis	1	2	$\cdots$	8	9	10	$\cdots$	15	16	$\cdots$	21	22	23	1	$\cdots$	3	4	5	6	7	8	$\cdots$	10	11	12	13
ω_1	1	1	$\cdots$	1	2	2	$\cdots$	2	3	$\cdots$	3	4	4	4	$\cdots$	4	5	5	5	5	6	$\cdots$	6	7	7	8
ω_2	1	2	$\cdots$	8	1	2	$\cdots$	7	1	$\cdots$	6	1	5	2	$\cdots$	4	1	2	3	4	1	$\cdots$	3	1	2	1
ω_3	8	7	$\cdots$	1	7	6	$\cdots$	1	6	$\cdots$	1	5	1	4	$\cdots$	2	4	3	2	1	3	$\cdots$	1	2	1	1

Note: weight $= \omega_i/10$

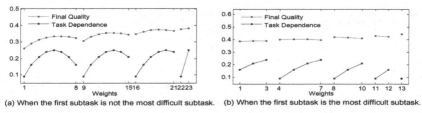

(a) When the first subtask is not the most difficult subtask.   (b) When the first subtask is the most difficult subtask.

Fig. 2. Efficiency estimation of vertical task decomposition strategy under group-based revenue sharing scheme. In general, series of subtasks begin with high difficulties generate high efficiency with respect to the final quality.

Lesson 1. *The highest final quality brought by the series of subtasks begin with high difficulty is superior to that brought by the series of subtasks begin with low difficulty under group-based revenue sharing scheme. (See Fig. 2 (a).)*

Lesson 2. *When the first subtask is the most difficult subtask, for the series of subtasks begin with the same difficulty, the highest task dependence given by the convex weights (i.e., $\omega_1 \geq \omega_2$ and $\omega_2 \leq \omega_3$) leads to the highest final quality.*

As can be observed in Fig. 2 (b), in four series of subtasks begin with weight 0.5, there are two with convex weights (4.(0.5,0.1,0.4) and 5.(0.5,0.2,0.3), with task dependence 0.09 and 0.16), and the higher task dependence (x-axis value 5), gives us the highest final quality among these four series of subtasks.

Example 2. Suppose the task requester has to choose among three very similar task decompositions, as (0.3,0.4,0,3), (0.4,0.3,0.3) and (0.4,0.4,0.2). According to Lesson 1, he would prefer the series of subtasks start with a more difficult subtask and eliminate option (0.3,0.4,0,3). Furthermore, according to Lesson 2, convex weights (0.4,0.3,0.3) is the decomposition, among all series of subtasks starts with difficulty 0.4, that leads to the highest final quality. So the task requester can construct his preference as $(0.4,0.3,0.3) \succ (0.4,0.4,0.2) \succ (0.3,0.4,0,3)$.

Lessons Learned on Contribution-Based Revenue Sharing Scheme. We explore the 3-subtask situation under contribution-based sharing scheme in Fig. 3.

Lesson 3. *When the first subtask is not the most difficult subtask, given a segment of weights on the first k ($k < N$) subtasks, the highest weight of all the possible weights on the $(k+1)-th$ subtask leads to the highest final quality.*

As in Fig. 3 (a), given the weight on the first subtask equaling 0.1 (X axis scale is 1 to 8), all possible weights on the second subtask are 0.2, 0.3, $\cdots$ 0.8, then the highest weight on the second subtask which equals 0.8 gives us the highest final quality among all the series of subtasks begin with weight 0.1.

Lesson 4. *When the first subtask is the most difficult subtask, 1) the more difficult the first subtask is, the more efficient is the contribution-based revenue sharing scheme; 2) for the series of subtasks begin with the same difficulty, highest task dependence leads to the highest final quality. (See Fig. 3 (b).)*

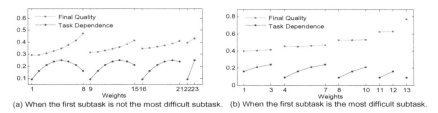

(a) When the first subtask is not the most difficult subtask.   (b) When the first subtask is the most difficult subtask.

Fig. 3. Efficiency estimation of vertical task decomposition strategy under contribution-based revenue sharing scheme

From the incentive viewpoint, it is true that decomposing a task into subtasks is worse than assigning the whole task to one worker. However, the latter makes difficult to find a worker who is willing to choose this task due to its limited resources. If we incorporate worker availability into discussions, Lesson 4 1) does not necessarily reduce the demand of crowdsourcing.

Example 3. Suppose the task requester is restricted to start with the subtask of a given difficulty. When the first subtask is not the most difficult subtask, (e.g., with difficulty 0.3), according to Lesson 3, the optimal decomposition is the one whose second subtask's difficulty is the highest among all possible difficulties (in this case, $0.1, \cdots, 0.6$), so the optimal decomposition is (0.3,0.6,0.1). When the first subtask is the most difficult subtask, (e.g., with difficulty 0.5), according to Lesson 4, the optimal decomposition is (0.5,0.4,0.1) with the highest dependence 0.24 among all series of subtasks start with difficulty 0.5.

5   Conclusion

In this paper we have formally presented and analyzed vertical and horizontal task decomposition models which respectively specify the relationship between subtask quality and the worker's effort level in the presence of positive and none dependence among subtasks. We conclude that in general, vertical task decomposition strategy outperforms the horizontal one in improving the quality of the final solution, and furthermore give explicit instructions the optimal strategy under vertical task decomposition from the task requester's point of view.

Acknowledgments. The work is partially supported by a Grant-in-Aid for Scientific Research (S) (24220002, 2012-2016) from Japan Society for the Promotion of Science (JSPS).

References

1. Kittur, A., Smus, B., Khamkar, S., Kraut, R.E.: Crowdforge: crowdsourcing complex work. In: Proceedings of the 24th Annual ACM Symposium on User Interface Software and Technology, pp. 16–19 (2011)
2. Bernstein, M.S., Little, G., Miller, R.C., Hartmann, B., Ackerman, M.S., Karger, D.R., Crowell, D., Panovich, K.: Soylent: a word processor with a crowd inside. In: Proceedings of the 23nd Annual ACM Symposium on User Interface Software and Technology, pp. 313–322 (2010)
3. Little, G., Chilton, L.B., Goldman, M., Miller, R.C.: Exploring iterative and parallel human computation processes. In: Proceedings of the ACM SIGKDD Workshop on Human Computation, p. 25 (2010)
4. Kulkarni, A., Can, M., Hartmann, B.: Collaboratively crowdsourcing workflows with turkomatic. In: Proceedings of the ACM 2012 Conference on Computer Supported Cooperative Work, pp. 1003–1012 (2012)
5. Tran-Thanh, L., Huynh, T.D., Rosenfeld, A., Ramchurn, S.D., Jennings, N.R.: Budgetfix: budget limited crowdsourcing for interdependent task allocation with quality guarantees. In: AAMAS, pp. 477–484 (2014)
6. Tran-Thanh, L., Venanzi, M., Rogers, A., Jennings, N.R.: Efficient budget allocation with accuracy guarantees for crowdsourcing classification tasks. In: AAMAS, pp. 901–908 (2013)

On the Equivalence of Defeasible Deontic Logic and Temporal Defeasible Logic*

Marc Allaire and Guido Governatori

NICTA Queensland, Brisbane, Australia

Abstract. In this paper we formally prove that compliance results derived from temporal defeasible logic are equivalent to the ones obtained in the standard defeasible deontic logic. In order to do so we first introduce an operator allowing us to translate rules from the standard to the temporal framework. Then we consider the sets of obligations used in the compliance checking algorithm from [19] and prove that they are isomorphic to the previously defined operator. Being able to add time to standard deontic logic will allow for a better and more elegant representation of obligations and improvement in computational efficiency.

1 Introduction

An important aspect of Normative Multi-Agent Systems (NorMAS) is to study whether the behaviour of an agent complies with the regulations governing the environment in which the agents is situated.

According to standard agent architectures (for example, the seminal BDI architecture) an agent is equipped with a plan library, and after the deliberation phase (i.e., the phase in the life-cycle of an agent when the agent identifies what goals the agent commits to), the agent select which plan has to be executed to reach the goals. An agent plan has to be understood as in classical AI, where a plan is just a sequence of actions or tasks, where every task can be associate to its pre-conditions and post-conditions of effects [14].

The notion of compliance has been investigated in the field of business processes [22,39]. A business process model is a self-contained, temporal and logical order in which a set of activities are executed to achieve a business goal. Typically a process model describes what needs to be done and when (control flow), who is going to do what (resources), and on what it is working on (data). The combination of tasks and connectors defines the possible ways in which a process can be executed. Where a possible execution, called *process trace* or simply *trace*, is a sequence of tasks respecting the order given by the connectors. In this perspective a trace is isomorphic to a plan, thus a business process can be understood as a set of traces/plan, or in other words a business process is the plan library an organisation has to achieve a particular business objective.

Governatori and Rotolo [19] propose to use PCL (Process Compliance Logic), an extension of defeasible logic with deontic operators including an operator to handle the

---

* NICTA is funded by the Australian Government through the Department of Communications and the Australian Research Council through the ICT Centre of Excellence Program.

H.K. Dam et al. (Eds.): PRIMA 2014, LNAI 8861, pp. 74–90, 2014.

combination of violations and compensations [18] for the modelling of norms in a business process compliance point of view. The deontic operators offer a rich conceptual model of obligations able to capture all type of obligations when one consider their validity and compliance aspects over a sequence of tasks or a timelime. Furthermore, they propose a linear time algorithm to check whether a process trace complies with a regulation (modelled in PCL). The proposed model has been implemented and successfully validated with industry scale case studies [23]. The obligation types captured by the deontic operators have an essential temporal nature, thus [21] presented a temporalised version of the logic. An important features of the resulting logic is that it can check whether a given theory is compliant using only the proof theory of the logic itself without any external algorithm.

The aim of this paper is to study the relationships between the notions of compliance proposed in [19] and [21]. We are going to show that the temporal model of [21] is able to simulate that of [19].

The structure of the paper is as follows: in the next section we outline the basics of defeasible logic and deontic defeasible logic (PCL). In Section 3 we outline the idea of business process compliance, and in Section 4 we recall the linear time algorithm presented in [19] to check if a trace is compliant with a set of norms. In the next section we outline the temporal defeasible deontic logic of [21]. Section 6is dedicated to establish the relationships between the two logic. In Section 7 we summarise the results and shortly discuss related work.

2   Defeasible Deontic Logic

Defeasible reasoning as presented in [31] is a non-monotonic type of reasoning where one cannot reach a full, undoubted conclusion because any conclusion can always be defeated if further evidence of the contrary is demonstrated. Both computer scientists and philosophers have shown an interest in this field. The philosophical interest can be traced back to ancient Greece and Aristotle. Although the scientific reasoning is built on deductive logic, for everyday life we rely mainly on defeasible reasoning. We try to make general statements out of personal experience, for example we could say that all birds fly. This proposition would be true until we experience a bird that cannot fly such as a penguin. This would defeat the first rule.

Computer science interest in defeasible logic has grown during the last 40 years especially in the field of artificial intelligence. An intelligent program needs a formal representation of the world, a formal language to represent knowledge, causality and ability in order to achieve its given goal. This requirement was first described in [35].

Defeasible Logic was first introduced by Donal Nute in [37] as a formalism to represent defeasible reasoning in a logical way. As stated in [4] defeasible logic is a flexible non-monotonic formalism able to represent a large set of non-monotonic reasoning intuitions. Several powerful implementations have been proposed with good complexity properties allowing a feasible computational time. This has been made possible by the design of defeasible logic that makes implementation easy yet efficient.

Let us introduce the basics of Defeasible Logic as given in [3]. A defeasible theory gives us five different ways of representing knowledge *facts*, *strict rules*, *defeasible rules*, *defeaters* and a *superiority relation*.

Facts are indisputable statements for example Tux is a penguin which could be written formally as *penguin(Tux)*

Strict Rules are rules as in classical logic. It is the kind of rule we find in scientific reasoning. The conclusion is irrefutable if the premises also are. These are formally represented as:

$$penguin(X) \rightarrow bird(X)$$

Defeasible Rules are rules that can be defeated by evidence of the contrary. To draw a parallel with everyday reasoning one could generalize from experience that "Birds fly" a statement that would be true until the opposite is derived. These rules are formally represented as:

$$bird(X) \Rightarrow flies(X)$$

Defeaters are weaker rules that cannot be used to draw any conclusion but can prevent one. They are used to defeat other rules (hence the name) because they produce evidence of the contrary.

$$heavy(X) \rightsquigarrow \neg flies(X)$$

From this defeater we cannot conclude that because someone or something is heavy it cannot fly, it is only here to prevent the conclusion of *flies(X)*.

Superiority relation is used to create an order in a rule set. It is important to note that this relation does not have the properties of a proper order relation, it is not transitive. When we have two different rules which derive something and its negation we cannot draw a conclusion since defeasible logic is sceptical. The superiority relation allows us to come to a conclusion. For example:

$$r: \quad\quad bird(X) \Rightarrow flies(X)$$
$$r': \quad brokenWing(X) \Rightarrow \neg flies(X)$$
$$r' > r$$

In this case we cannot reach a conclusion since r and r' reach opposite conclusions. By introducing the superiority relation we say that r' is strictly stronger than r and therefore we can conclude that the bird cannot fly.

Now that we are more familiar with the concepts of defeasible logic we can show how we can reach a defeasible conclusion using its proof theory. Four proof types for a conclusion have been defined. Given a Defeasible Theory D

$+\Delta q$ means that the literal q is definitely provable in D;
$-\Delta q$ means that the literal q is definitely refuted in D;
$+\partial q$ means that the literal q is defeasibly provable in D
$-\partial q$ means that the literal q is defeasibly refuted in D.

In [3] provability is defined using the concept of *derivation* of a conclusion from a Defeasible Theory D. Where, formally a Defeasible Theory D is a triple $(F, R, >)$ of set of facts F, set of rules R and superiority relation $>$. A derivation P can be seen as several steps in a demonstration. At step $P(i)$ of the proof we have a given set $(F, R, >)$ from this we can prove $P(i+1)$ either definitely or defeasibly. In what follows we restrict our attention to the propositional variant of the logic built on a set of atomic propositions (the examples given so far can be consider as schema corresponding to the set of all their ground instances). A literal is either an atomic proposition or its negation. Given a literal l, we use $\sim l$ to denote its complement, that is $\neg p$ if $l = p$, where p is an atomic proposition, and p if $l = \neg p$. A rule is an expression

$$r: A(r) \hookrightarrow C(r)$$

where r is the label of the rule; $A(r)$, the antecedent of the rule, is a (possibly empty) t set of literals; $C(r)$, the conclusion of the rule, is a literal; and $\hookrightarrow \in \{\rightarrow, \Rightarrow, \leadsto\}$. Given a set of rules R we use $R[q]$ to denote the set of rules whose head is q, i.e., $C(r) = q$, R_s is the set of the strict rules in R, and R_{sd} is the subset of strict and defeasible rules in R.

To reach a definitive conclusion $+\Delta q$ we need to have a strict rule that deduces q or have q as a fact. We will not get into details about how to definitely prove a literal since the focus of this article is more on defeasible proofs. We refer the reader to [3] for the full details.

The following definition exposes how to defeasibly conclude a literal q at $P(i+1)$.

Definition 1. *If $P(i+1) = +\partial q$ then either*

1. $+\Delta q \in P(1..i)$ *or*
2. (a) $\exists r \in R_{sd}[q], \forall a \in A(r) : +\partial a \in P(1..i)$ *and,*
   (b) $-\Delta \sim q \in P(1..i)$ *and,*
   (c) $\forall s \in R[\sim q]$ *either*
      i. $\exists a \in A(s) : -\partial a \in P(1..i)$ *or*
      ii. $\exists t \in R[q]$ *such that* $\forall a \in A(t) : +\partial a \in P(1..i)$ *and* $t > s$

In less mathematical terms this definition means that in order to defeasibly prove q we can follow two paths. Either prove that q is definitely provable or work the defeasible part. For the defeasible path, three conditions apply:

1. there is a rule r that concludes q for a set of literals $A(r)$ such as every $a \in A(r)$ has been defeasibly proven in a previous step $P(1..i)$ and,
2. $\sim q$ has not been definitively proven in a previous step $P(1..i)$ and,
3. for every rule s that conclude $\neg q$ for a literal a either
   (a) a has been defeasibly refuted in a previous step $P(1..i)$ or
   (b) there is an applicable rule t that concludes q such as $t > s$

2.1 Using Defeasible Deontic Logic to Represent Legal Norms and Regulations

Regulations and legal norms are an important concern for government and businesses. They are complex and hard to study especially when multiple regulations written separately are applied to a given situation. In a world where compliance to regulation is becoming both harder and more important because of their growing number and the sanctions applied for non compliance, a normative logical framework is needed to be able to reason about regulations.

Deontic logic is the branch of symbolic logic concerned with the logic of obligations and permissions. Therefore it is exactly the kind of logical framework we want to be able to express regulations. Unfortunatel, y standard deontic logic is unable to represent simple notions of normative reasoning such as prima-facie obligations or contrary-to-duty obligations [36]. This lack of expressibility has driven away the very people that would have used deontic logic the most [38].

Let us take a closer look at prima-facie obligation for example and see how we can express these in the light of defeasible logic. Prima-facie means "at first sight" hence a prima-facie obligation is an obligation that stands at first sight, one that can be defeated if new facts can prove otherwise. We can see that this type of obligation can easily be expressed using defeasible logic, it is defeasible by definition. Furthermore regulations contain exceptions that are easily represented using defeasible logic.

There are many benefits to use a logical framework to represent regulations, some of those are presented in [2]. They are subdivided into two main area of application:

- **The Understanding and Application of Regulations** for agents not familiar with legal writing and do not want to study a regulation yet being under the obligation to comply.

    Decision support: If an agent take a decision, is the agent compliant? The agent can run its process against a set of regulations and see if it complies. A formal framework for expressing processes and norms is needed too in this case.

    Explanation: The agent can examine the complete reasoning chain that lead to the given answer. It is therefore easier for the agent to understand what cause this answer for their request or what caused non-compliance.

- **The Creation of Regulation** for assisting legal professional in their work.

    Anomaly detection Having a formal logical framework backing the drafting of regulation allows for an easy detection of anomalies such as inconsistencies or loops.

    Hypothetical reasoning It is possible, like for decision support, to inspect the effects of a regulation on the entire system.

    Debugging When a regulation is not yielding the expected answer to a given query it is possible to debug it.

Now that we explained the need for a logical framework for legal reasoning and how good deontic defeasible logic is we can introduce the different types of obligations. Indeed to accurately represent the complexity of norms and regulations it is necessary to have a range of different types of obligations to be able to translate legal text into an equivalent logical representation as explained in [19]. There are three main types of obligations [16]:

- **Achievement Obligation:** There is an obligation to meet once before the deadline. For example *You must change your tires before they are worn out*
- **Maintenance Obligation:** There is an obligation to meet at all instant before the deadline. For example *You must provide for your children until they are 18*
- **Punctual Obligation:** There is an obligation to meet at one instant. They must be fulfilled at the same moment they were triggered.

We will use the modal operators O^a, O^m and O^p for, respectively, achievement, maintenance and punctual obligations.

Now that we described the broad range of obligations giving us the necessary vocabulary to translate regulations into our logical framework, we are still missing one critical point of regulations: reparation chains. If an obligation is violated, you are not complying with the regulation unless there is a reparation chain that kicks in and leaves you in an unoptimal but still compliant situation.

For example let us consider the following rules:

$$r: \quad invoice \Rightarrow O^p pay$$
$$r': \quad \neg pay \Rightarrow O^a payFine$$

They can be reduced and be expressed as a $\otimes$-expression such as these two obligation cannot be seen any more as independent.

$$r: invoice \Rightarrow O^p pay \otimes O^a payFine$$

We can now create chains of obligations started by a given set of literal and giving the actor a chance to stay compliant even if an obligation was violated [20].

3   Business Process Compliance

Business Process Compliance [22,39] is the research area studying techniques to ensure that the business processes of an organisation do not violate the regulations and the law governing the business. To formalise business process compliance two components are needed. The first is a formalism to represent the norms. In Section 2 we proposed Deontic Defeasible Logic for this task. The second component is the representation of the business processes. This has been extensively studied in the field of business process modelling, see [9]. A business process model is defined as a self-contained, temporal and logical order in which a set of activities are executed to achieve a business goal. Typically a process model describes what needs to be done and when (control flow), who is going to do what (resources), and on what it is working on (data). Many different formalisms (Petri-Nets, Process algebras, ...) and notations (BPMN, YAWL, EPC, ...) have been proposed to represent business process models. Besides the difference in notation, purposes, and expressive power, business process languages typically contain *tasks* and *connectors*, where a task corresponds to a (complex) business activity, and connectors (e.g., sequence, and-join, and-split, (x)or-join, (x)or-split) define the relationships among tasks to be executed. The combination of tasks and connectors defines the possible ways in which a process can be executed. Where a possible execution, called *process trace* or simply *trace*, is a sequence of tasks respecting the order given by the connectors.

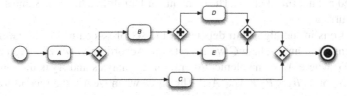

Fig. 1. Example of a business process model in standard BPMN notation

Consider the process in Figure 1, in standard BPMN notation, where we have a task A followed by an xor split. In the xor split in one of the branches we have task B followed by the and-split of a branch with task D, and a brach consisting of only task E. The second branch of the xor-split has only one task: C. The traces corresponding to the process are $\langle A, C \rangle$, $\langle A, B, D, E \rangle$ and $\langle A, B, E, D \rangle$.

Compliance is not only about the tasks that an organisation has to perform to achieve its business goals, but it is concerned also on their effects (i.e., how the activities in the tasks change the environment in which they operate), and the artefacts produced by the tasks (for example, the data resulting from executing a task or modified by the task) [27]. To capture this aspect [40] proposed to enrich process models with semantic annotations. Each task in a process model can have attached to it a set of semantic annotations. An annotation is just a set of formulas giving a (partial) description of the environment in which a process operates. Then, it is possible to associate to each task in a trace a set of formulas corresponding to the state of the environment after the task has been executed in the particular trace.

4   An Algorithm for Business Process Compliance

In the previous sections we described the framework used to express laws and regulations in a proper logical way, and we paired it with business process modelling. In the following we will present the business process compliance algorithm proposed in [19].

For a given business process the algorithm starts by computing all the possible traces, all possible executions of the business process. The reachability graph is computed first using the method described in [34]. From this all possible executions of the process are drawn. Now that we have all possible traces we will focus on one. For each task in the trace several actions are performed. The first step is to compute the state corresponding to the task. We cumulate the effects or semantic annotations attached to task using an update semantics, that is, in case of a conflict, the literal in the current task prevails over the the literal form the previous task. Then, a call is made to the rule engine with the informations about the task. It will return the new obligations generated by these antecedents. These new rules are added to the Current set which contains all rules in-force at a given task. The elements in Current are triples $[T, R, C]$, where T is a task identifier, R is a rule label and C is an $\otimes$-expression. T is the task where rule R triggers the chain of obligations C. The sets Violated and Compensated, as their names suggest, are used to keep track of which obligations in force have been violated and which violations have been compensated for. In both cases the structure of their elements is $[T, R, C, V]$, where T, R and C are as before and V is a literal indicating which obligation in the chain C has been violated. The Unfulfilled set contains all achievement and maintenance rules that were triggered but not fulfilled yet. The elements of Unfulfilled have the same structure as those of Current.

The operations in the algorithm depend on the set of $\otimes$-chains of obligations and on which element of an $\otimes$-chain C we operate on. Accordingly, we will explode C as either $A_1 \otimes A_2$, where A_1 is the element/literal under analysis and A_2 is the remainder of the $\otimes$-chain, or as $B_1 \otimes B_2 \otimes A_1 \otimes A_2$.[1] The cases when we use the second format is

---

[1] Any $\otimes$-chain C can be reduced to one of the two expression given the equivalence $A \equiv A \otimes \bot$.

when the "current" $\otimes$-chain C is the compensation of a previous violation. The use of B_2 is used to signify that that compensation can be used to compensate the violation of an obligation that itself is a compensation; similarly for A_2. Finally, the "add" and "remove" functions add or remove an element from a given set.

The Terminated set contains rules that were terminated according to the following definition from [19]. A chain C is terminated by a task n if C was active at task n and that another rule r triggered at task n derives the opposite of C. The rule r must not be weaker than the rule that originally yielded C.

for all $C \in$ Current **do**
   if $A_1 = O^p B$ **then**
      if $B \in S$ **then**
         remove($[T, R, A_1 \otimes A_2]$, Current)
         if $[T, R, B_1 \otimes B_2 \otimes A_1 \otimes A_2, B_2] \in$ Violated **then**
            add($[T, R, B_1 \otimes B_2 \otimes A_1 \otimes A_2, B_2]$, Compensated)
         end if
      else
         remove($[T, R, A_1 \otimes A_2]$, Current)
         add($[T, R, A_1 \otimes A_2, B]$, Violated)
         add($[T, R, A_2]$, Current)
      end if
   end if
   if $A_1 = O^a B$ **then**
      if $B \in S$ **then**
         remove($[T, R, A_1 \otimes A_2]$, Current)
         remove($[T, R, A_1 \otimes A_2]$, Unfulfilled)
         if $[T, R, B_1 \otimes B_2 \otimes A_1 \otimes A_2, B_2] \in$ Violated **then**
            add($[T, R, B_1 \otimes B_2 \otimes A_1 \otimes A_2, B_2]$, Compensated)
         end if
      else
         add($[T, R, A_1 \otimes A_2]$, Unfulfilled)
      end if
   end if
   if $A_1 = O^m B$ **then**
      if $b \notin S$ or $\neg B \in S$ **then**
         add($[T, R, A_1 \otimes A_2, B]$, Violated)
         add($[T, R, A_2]$, Current)
      end if
   end if
end for

for all $C \in$ Terminated **do**
   if $C \in$ Unfulfilled **then**
      add($[T, R, A_1 \otimes A_2, A_1]$, Violated)
      add($[T, R, A_2]$, Current)
   end if
   if $A_1 = O^a$ **then**
      remove($[T, R, A_1 \otimes A_2]$, Current)
   end if
end for

Given a trace/plan we extract the effects of each task in it, and for each task, we first compute the defeasible extension of the logic to determine what are the obligation in force, i.e., the obligations to be included in Current. Then we apply the algorithm above for each task.

At the end of the trace/plan we determine if the trace/plan is compliant. A trace/plan is compliant if

1. Current is empty (meaning that all pending obligation have been fulfilled); and
2. All obligations in Violated are also in Compensated.

For a stronger notion of compliance, the second condition can be replaced by that the set Violation is empty. In the former case, the meaning is that there were some violations, but they were compensated for. The stronger notion, on the other hand, requires that there are no violations at all.

5   Temporal Defeasible Deontic Logic

Adding time in defeasible deontic logic is a much anticipated feature because it implements at the source the essence of deadline allowing us, as we will see later on, to represent obligation types elegantly. In [24] extensions to include time in the logic are proposed and we will use these semantics and notations.

The presentation in this section is based on [21] which introduces new notations, semantics and concepts to deal with time in defeasible deontic logic. They represent time as a discrete linear order of instants $\mathscr{T} = (t_1, t_2, \ldots, t_n)$.

The following list sums up the notations introduced in [21] and their semantics:

- If l is a literal then l^t is a temporal literal. We will refer to the set of temporal literal as *TLit*. We also introduce $\top$ and $\bot$ which are also temporal literals, they are propositions that are respectively always complied with and impossible to comply with.
- If l^t is a temporal literal then Ol^t and its negation are deontic literals meaning that the obligation to do l holds at time t. We will refer to the set of deontic literals as *DLit*.
- If a^{t_a} and b^{t_b} are temporal literals, $t \in \mathscr{T}$ and $x \in \{a, m, p\}$ (for achievement, maintenance, and punctual) then $a^{t_a} \otimes_t^x b^{t_b}$ is an $\otimes$-chain used to express chain of reparation in laws. If $x = p$, then we impose that $t = t_a$; otherwise that $t > t_a$.
- If α is an $\otimes$-chain, t and $t_a \in \mathscr{T}$ and a^{t_a} is a temporal literal then $\alpha \otimes_t^x a^{t_a}$ is an $\otimes$-chain. A deontic expression is an $\otimes$-chain composed of temporal literals or sub-$\otimes$-chain and finishing with $\bot$.

An $\otimes$-chain like $\alpha \otimes_t^a a^{t_a} \otimes_{t'}^y b^{t_b} \otimes \bot$ means that the violation of α who holds until time t triggers an achievement obligation a from t_a to t'.

Temporal defeasible logic also defines new defeasible proof conditions. Definition 2 shows when a rule is applicable at index i, meaning that the obligation at index i in the $\otimes$-chain is in force.

Definition 2. *A rule r is applicable at index i in a proof P at line $P(n+1)$ iff*

1. $\forall a \in A(r)$
   (a) if $a \in TLit$, then $a \in F$ and
   (b) i. if $a = Ol^t$ then $+\partial l^t \in P(1..n)$
       ii. if $a = \neg Ol^t$ then $-\partial l^t \in P(1..n)$ and
2. $\forall c_j \in C(r),\ 1 \leq j \leq i$
   (a) if $mode(c_j) = punctual$, then $c_j \notin F$ or $\sim c_j \in F$
   (b) if $mode(c_j) = achievement$, then $\forall t,\ start(c_j) \leq t \leq end(c_j),\ c_j^t \notin F$ or $\sim c_j^t \in F$
   (c) if $mode(c_j) = maintenance$, then $\exists t,\ start(c_j) \leq t \leq end(c_j),\ c_j^t \notin F$ or $\sim c_j^t \in F$

In [21] different proof conditions are defined for each obligation type. In Definition 3 we present them in a condensed form. x is used to represent the mode of the obligation, it can be replace by one of a, m, p.

Definition 3. If $P(n+1) = +\partial p^t$ then

1. $\exists r \in R_{\Rightarrow}^x [p^t, i]$, r is applicable at index i and,
2. $\forall s \in R[\sim p^t, j]$ either
   (a) s is discarded at index j
   (b) $\exists w \in R_{\Rightarrow}^x [p^t, k]$, w is applicable at index k and $w \succ s$
3. $\exists x \in R_{\Rightarrow}^{a,m} \left[p^{t'}, i' \right]$, $t' < t$, $end(t') \geq t$
   (a) x is applicable at index i', and
   (b) $\forall y \in R \left[\sim p^{t''}, j' \right]$, $t' \leq t'' < t$ either
       i. y is discarded at index j' or
       ii. $\exists z \in R \left[\sim p^{t''}, k' \right]$, z is applicable at k' and $z \succ y$; and for $+\partial^a$
   (c) $\forall t''',\ t'' < t''' \leq t,\ p^{t'''} \notin F$.

Conditions 1. and 2. are enough to defeasibly prove a punctual obligation. Condition 3. only applies for maintenance and achievement obligations. The final line 3.c only applies to achievement obligations for which fulfilment terminates the obligation.

The last step is to give the conditions under which a theory is compliant. Checking compliance simply amount to show that $-\partial \bot$, and, conversely non-compliance is signalled by $+\partial \bot$.

6 From Defeasible Deontic Logic to Temporal Defeasible Deontic Logic

In this section we present constructions that allow us to encode the norms regulating a business process and the semantic annotations of the process in Temporal Defeasible Logic and to check compliance directly in that logic. In addition the computation is equivalent to the same compliance results as the combination of Defeasible Deontic Logic and the compliance algorithm presented in Section 4.

A defeasible theory is defined by the tuple $(F, R, >)$ where F is a finite set of literals, R a finite set of rules and $>$ a superiority relation on R. In the context of business process compliance we consider $S_1, \ldots, S_n$ sets of literals representing the literals attached to every task. Therefore for each task we have a different theory. At task n we have

$F = \bigcup\limits_{i=1}^{n} S_i \setminus \{\sim l : l \in S_i\}$, we also refer to F at task n as State(n). The set of rules stays the same although the obligations in force can change from one task to another.

A temporal defeasible theory is not so different from its classical counterpart. It is defined by the tuple $(F^t, R^t, \succ)$ where F^t is a finite set of temporal literals, R^t is a finite set of temporal rules and $\succ$ is a superiority relation on R^t. The Facts and Rule sets are dependent of the current task in a given trace. We highlight this dependence in the following.

We are defining the $\mathscr{T}$ operator which takes a defeasible theory and a point in time and returns the temporal equivalent, formally defined as:

$$\mathscr{T} : \mathbb{N} \times (F, R, >) \to (F^t, R^t, \succ) \tag{1}$$

Every literal in F is temporally annotated with the task number it is attached to. We know that at a given task F is the union of the previous S_i therefore at a given task t we have.

$$F^t = \{q^t \mid \forall q \in S_t\} \tag{2}$$

Every rule in R is basically translated by annotating temporally with the current task number all its antecedent and consequent. Hence the temporal rule arising from a classical rule depends on the task number in a given trace. For each task in every possible trace we define a set of temporal rules corresponding to the body of "classic" rules. All of the antecedents and effects of the rules are annotated with the task number which will play the role of time as the set of task numbers is isomorphic to $\mathbb{N}$ which is a perfect candidate for time. Since defeasible deontic logic does not include deadlines we transform achievement and maintenance obligations to permanent ones defining a parametric deadline using the *viol* operator.

Let us introduce the mode function that returns the mode of a given obligation:

$$mode(O) = \begin{cases} a & \text{if } O \text{ is an achievement obligation} \\ p & \text{if } O \text{ is a punctual obligation} \\ m & \text{if } O \text{ is a maintenance obligation} \end{cases} \tag{3}$$

Here we will show how the set of temporal rules R^t is derived from the set of classical rules R. First in (4) we define a general form for classical rules we will use to define how we translate to temporal rules.

$$\forall r \in R, \quad r : a_1, \dots, a_n \Rightarrow p_1 \otimes \cdots \otimes p_m \tag{4}$$

In (5) we introduce one of the tools we will need for this demonstration: the *naf* operator [5]. It stands for negation as failure which means that we failed to prove an element. It is defined as:

$$
\begin{aligned}
r_1 : & \quad \Rightarrow naf\ p \\
r_2 : & \quad \neg p \Rightarrow naf\ p \\
r_3 : & \quad p \Rightarrow \neg naf\ p \\
& \quad r_3 > r_2 > r_1
\end{aligned}
\tag{5}
$$

In other words we have *naf p* either when p has not been concluded or $\neg p$ has been concluded. If p is concluded then this rule is stronger than the other two and we conclude $\neg naf\ p$

For demonstration purposes we introduce in 6 the *viol* function which takes an obligation and returns the index of the task where it was violated. If the obligation is never violated it returns the index of the last task. This will allow us to express chain of reparation from the classical framework where no deadlines are defined into the temporal one where we need deadlines. This *viol* operator will create artificial parametrized deadlines for chain of obligations as it will be presented next.

$$viol(X): Obligations \rightarrow \mathbb{N} \tag{6}$$

– For a maintenance obligation $O^m p$, *viol* will return the index of the first task where the obligation is applicable and we can conclude *naf p*.

$$\text{At task } i \text{ if we have: } O^m p, naf\ p \in F$$
$$\text{then: } viol(O^m p) = i \tag{7}$$

– For an achievement obligation $O^a p$, *viol* will return the index of the first task where the obligation is applicable, we can conclude *naf p*, and the obligation is lifted at the next task (this can be done with defeaters).

$$\text{At task } i \text{ if we have: } O^a p, naf\ p, \neg O^a p \in F$$
$$\text{then: } viol(O^a p) = i \tag{8}$$

– It is not necessary to define *viol* for punctual obligations since they are always violated or fulfilled at the task after they were triggered. For example $O^p p$ is triggered at task i then it is either complied with or *viol* will return $i+1$.

Now we will show how we translate temporally each of these rules, given a classical rule r in the form defined in 4 at a given task t the set of temporal rules is composed of rules.

$$r_i: a_1, \dots, a_n \Rightarrow p_1 \otimes \cdots \otimes p_m \tag{9}$$

$$r_i(task): a_1^{task}, \dots, a_n^{task} \Rightarrow^{mode(p_1)}$$
$$p_1^{task} \otimes_{viol(p_1)}^{mode(p_2)} p_2^{viol(p_1)} \cdots \otimes_{viol(p_{m-1})}^{mode(p_m)} p_m^{viol(p_{m-1})} \otimes \bot \tag{10}$$

Now we are considering the sets of obligations we find in the algorithm for business process compliance checking. In this we find at each task three main sets of obligations and literals: Current, Violated and State. They contain respectively obligations in force at the given task, obligations that were violated in previous tasks and deontic literals attached to the current or previous tasks. We aim to prove that the transformation of these sets from classical formalism to temporal is isomorphic and our transformation bijective. All these set are depending on the current task we consider, they will be referred as: Set(n).

First let us prove that

$$\text{if } p \in \text{State}(n) \text{ then } +\partial p^n$$

this is trivially proven by definition of our translation where every literal associated with a task is annotated temporally with the task number in the trace. Therefore if p is in the State(n) it has been proven at a step $(1..n)$.

Now what about

$$\text{if } q \in \text{Current}(n) \text{ then } +\partial O q^n$$

If an obligation is in force at a task n in the classical formalism is it also in the temporal one, in other word is the rule applicable at the index where it triggers q. If q is in the set of current obligation it means that there is a rule r that yields q at task k and that this rule was fired meaning all of the antecedents have been proven. In other words:

$$\forall a \in A(r), \ a \in \text{State}(k)$$

so if a is a literal then $a \in \text{Facts}$

or if a is an obligation Ol then $+\partial l^{1..k}$

Or, the conditions on the Antecedents for a rule to be applicable are:

- if the antecedent is a litteral then it must be in the Facts (attached to a previous task)
- if the antecendent is an obligation then it must have been defeasibly proven before-hand.

Both conditions are met so the rule would also trigger in temporal defeasible logic. Now we have to see if it would trigger at the right index in the $\otimes$-chain.

If $q = Ol$ is part of an $\otimes$-chain like $A_1 \otimes \cdots \otimes A_n \otimes q \otimes B_1 \otimes \cdots \otimes B_n$ and if q is in current that means that for all obligation A_i, $-\partial A_i$ has been proven for a previous task $(1..k-1)$. Let m be the task where the rule was triggered first. Which translates into:

- for punctual obligations this means we either have $\neg l$ at task k when the obligation was triggered or that l was not in the State set at task k.
- for achievement obligations this means that we have $\neg l$ at a task between m and $k-1$
- for maintenance obligations this means that we either have $\neg l$ at a task between m and $k-1$ or that l was not in the State set at a given task between m and k

Whatever the obligation this means that at some point we were able to conclude $-\partial A_i$ for all the obligations before q which means that the rule r is also applicable at the index where it triggers q implying that q is also in the set of Current obligations in the temporal formalism.

We can easily translate this reflection to the Violated set. If a obligation Ol is in the violated set this means that at some task between $1..n$ we have one of the three conditions aforementioned for each type of obligation. Which trivially translates into being able to prove $-\partial l$ at some task $(1..n)$ implying that the obligation is also in the Violated set in the temporal formalism.

The use of Temporal Defeasible Deontic Logic allows us to use the same logic to model norms, semantic annotations and to check whether a process is compliant. This can be done by simply computing the extension of the theory encoding all such information. This means that this logic offers an holistic and more conceptually sound approach to the problem of business process compliance. In addition the temporal framework is expected to improve the computational efficiency of the system. For now we check compliance at each task of the business process collecting the new rules and forwarding them to the next task. With time we could do all of this at once. With temporal rules we would only need to create traces which would yield a set of temporal literals and check this set against the set of temporal rules. Let us consider again the example in Figure 1. In this case we have first to compute all the possible traces; as we have seen we have three traces, namely $\langle A,C \rangle$, $\langle A,B,D,E \rangle$ and $\langle A,B,E,D \rangle$. Each trace corresponds to a serialisation of the process. After the serialisation we go though each task, accumulate effects, derive rules in force, check for compliance and then forward effects and obligations to the next task. For a trace of size n we have to do each operation n times. The result of [8] shows that the problem of checking whether a business process is compliant with a set of norms is an NP-complete problem, however, the temporal approach could eliminate some of the overheads of the other method. In particular if we add time though, we only need to do the computation of the extension only once for each trace instead of repeating it for each task in the trace. In the worst case the total number of temporal literals given as facts is equal to the sum of literals used as semantic annotations in the single traces. Similarly, the number of rules in the temporal version does not exceed the number of rules in the non-temporal version times the number of the tasks in a trace. On the other hand the computation of what obligations have been fulfilled, violated and compensated is part of the computation of the extension, and not of what obligation chains are in force, and then calling the compliance checking algorithm. However, a proper experimental evaluation is required to determine whether the temporal approach speeds up the computation.

7   Summary and Related Work

This paper first presents defeasible deontic logic as presented in [18] and later extensions by [21] with time. This new framework is better suited to represent obligations as these often feature temporal deadlines. However, to the best of our knowledge no work in the field has so far attempted to formally prove that the results from the compliance checking algorithm introduced in [19] yields the same compliance results when porting a theory from the classical to the temporal framework. This proof introduces a new operator to translate a set of rules and then shows that sets of obligations from the compliance algorithm are isomorphic to it. Or in other words that this operator defines a bijection from the classical to the temporal formalism. This result paves the way for future work in adapting the compliance checking algorithm to the temporal framework.

The literature on norm compliance is NorMAS is large (see, e.g., [11,1,13,25,7,29,12,30]). However, to the best of our knowledge no work in the field has so far attempted to model a *legal* compliance pertaining to realistic systems where complex norm-enforcement mechanisms such as $\otimes$-chains are combined with a rich ontology of obligations as the one described here.

The literature on business process compliance is equally vast (see, e.g., [15,33,10,32,6]). But it suffers form the same problems as that in NorMAS. Most of these approaches fails to address the proper modelling of norms and normative reasonings. See [26] for a detailed evaluation and comparison of various business process compliance frameworks. Most of such approaches are based on first oder logic or temporal logic and limited to check the structural compliance of a processes (e.g., correct order of the tasks and presence or absence of tasks). In addition [28] shows that first order logic is not appropriate for the modelling of legal reasoning. Similarly there are some concerns that temporal logics, and in particular LTL, might not be able to model compliance requirements [17].

References

1. Alberti, M., Gavanelli, M., Lamma, E., Chesani, F., Mello, P., Torroni, P.: Compliance verification of agent interaction: a logic-based software tool. Applied Artificial Intelligence 20(2-4), 133–157 (2006)
2. Antoniou, G., Billington, D., Governatori, G., Maher, M.J.: On the modeling and analysis of regulations. In: ACIS 1999, pp. 20–29 (1999)
3. Antoniou, G., Billington, D., Governatori, G., Maher, M.J.: Representation results for defeasible logic. ACM Transactions on Computational Logic 2(2), 255–287 (2001)
4. Antoniou, G., Billington, D., Governatori, G., Maher, M.J., Rock, A.: A family of defeasible reasoning logics and its implementation. In: ECAI 2000, pp. 459–463. IOS Press (2000)
5. Antoniou, G., Maher, M.J., Billington, D.: Defeasible logic versus logic programming without negation as failure. J. Log. Program. 42(1), 47–57 (2000)
6. Awad, A., Weidlich, M., Weske, M.: Visually Specifying Compliance Rules and Explaining their Violations for Business Processes. Journal of Visual Languages & Computing 22(1), 30–55 (2011)
7. Boella, G., Broersen, J., van der Torre, L.: Reasoning about constitutive norms, counts-as conditionals, institutions, deadlines and violations. In: Bui, T.D., Ho, T.V., Ha, Q.T. (eds.) PRIMA 2008. LNCS (LNAI), vol. 5357, pp. 86–97. Springer, Heidelberg (2008)
8. Colombo Tosatto, S., Governatori, G., Kelsen, P.: Business process regulatory compliance is hard. IEEE Transactions on Services Computing (2014)
9. Dumas, M., La Rosa, M., Mendling, J., Reijers, H.A.: Fundamentals of Business Process Management. Springer (2013)
10. Elgammal, A., Türetken, O., van den Heuvel, W.J.: Using patterns for the analysis and resolution of compliance violations. Int. J. Cooperative Inf. Syst. 21(1), 31–54 (2012)
11. Pasquier, P., Flores, R., Chaib-draa, B.: Modelling flexible social commitments and their enforcement. In: Gleizes, M.-P., Omicini, A., Zambonelli, F. (eds.) ESAW 2004. LNCS (LNAI), vol. 3451, pp. 139–151. Springer, Heidelberg (2005)
12. Gabaldon, A.: Making golog norm compliant. In: Leite, J., Torroni, P., Ågotnes, T., Boella, G., van der Torre, L. (eds.) CLIMA XII 2011. LNCS, vol. 6814, pp. 275–292. Springer, Heidelberg (2011)
13. García-Camino, A., Rodríguez-Aguilar, J.-A., Vasconcelos, W.W.: A Distributed Architecture for Norm Management in Multi-Agent Systems. In: Sichman, J.S., Padget, J., Ossowski, S., Noriega, P. (eds.) COIN 2007. LNCS (LNAI), vol. 4870, pp. 275–286. Springer, Heidelberg (2008)
14. Ghallab, M., Nau, D., Traverso, P.: Automated planning – theory and practice. Elsevier (2004)
15. Goedertier, S., Vanthienen, J.: Designing Compliant Business Processes with Obligations and Permissions. In: Eder, J., Dustdar, S. (eds.) BPM Workshops 2006. LNCS, vol. 4103, pp. 5–14. Springer, Heidelberg (2006)
16. Governatori, G.: Business Process Compliance: An Abstract Normative Framework. IT-Information Technology 55, 231–238 (2013)

17. Governatori, G.: Thou shalt is not you will. Tech. Rep. 8026, NICTA (2014)
18. Governatori, G., Rotolo, A.: Logic of violations: A Gentzen system for reasoning with contrary-to-duty obligations. Australasian Journal of Logic 4, 193–215 (2006)
19. Governatori, G., Rotolo, A.: A conceptually rich model of business process compliance. In: APCCM 2010, pp. 3–12. ACS (2010)
20. Governatori, G., Rotolo, A.: Norm compliance in business process modeling. In: Dean, M., Hall, J., Rotolo, A., Tabet, S. (eds.) RuleML 2010. LNCS, vol. 6403, pp. 194–209. Springer, Heidelberg (2010)
21. Governatori, G., Rotolo, A.: Justice delayed is justice denied: Logics for a temporal account of reparations and legal compliance. In: Leite, J., Torroni, P., Ågotnes, T., Boella, G., van der Torre, L. (eds.) CLIMA XII 2011. LNCS, vol. 6814, pp. 364–382. Springer, Heidelberg (2011)
22. Governatori, G., Sadiq, S.: The journey to business process compliance. In: Cardoso, J., van der Aalst, W. (eds.) Handbook of Research on BPM, pp. 426–454. IGI Global (2009)
23. Governatori, G., Shek, S.: Regorous: a business process compliance checker. In: ICAIL 2013, pp. 245–246. ACM (2013)
24. Governatori, G., Terenziani, P.: Temporal extensions to defeasible logic. In: Orgun, M.A., Thornton, J. (eds.) AI 2007. LNCS (LNAI), vol. 4830, pp. 476–485. Springer, Heidelberg (2007)
25. Grossi, D., Aldewereld, H., Dignum, F.P.M.: *Ubi lex, ibi poena*: Designing norm enforcement in E-institutions. In: Noriega, P., Vázquez-Salceda, J., Boella, G., Boissier, O., Dignum, V., Fornara, N., Matson, E. (eds.) COIN 2006. LNCS (LNAI), vol. 4386, pp. 101–114. Springer, Heidelberg (2007)
26. Hashmi, M., Governatori, G.: A methodological evaluation of business process compliance management frameworks. In: Song, M., Wynn, M.T., Liu, J. (eds.) AP-BPM 2013. LNBIP, vol. 159, pp. 106–115. Springer, Heidelberg (2013)
27. Hashmi, M., Governatori, G., Wynn, M.T.: Business process data compliance. In: Bikakis, A., Giurca, A. (eds.) RuleML 2012. LNCS, vol. 7438, pp. 32–46. Springer, Heidelberg (2012)
28. Herrestad, H.: Norms and formalization. In: ICAIL 1991, pp. 175–184. ACM (1991)
29. Hübner, J.F., Boissier, O., Bordini, R.: From organisation specification to normative programming in multi-agent organisations. In: Dix, J., Leite, J., Governatori, G., Jamroga, W. (eds.) CLIMA XI. LNCS, vol. 6245, pp. 117–134. Springer, Heidelberg (2010)
30. Knorr, M., Gabaldon, A., Gonçalves, R., Leite, J., Slota, M.: Time is up! – norms with deadlines in action languages. In: Leite, J., Son, T.C., Torroni, P., van der Torre, L., Woltran, S. (eds.) CLIMA XIV 2013. LNCS, vol. 8143, pp. 223–238. Springer, Heidelberg (2013)
31. Koons, R.: Defeasible reasoning. In: Zalta, E.N. (ed.) The Stanford Encyclopedia of Philosophy (Spring 2014) http://plato.stanford.edu/archives/spr2014/entries/reasoning-defeasible/
32. Ly, L.T., Rinderle-Ma, S., Göser, K., Dadam, P.: On enabling integrated process compliance with semantic constraints in process management systems - requirements, challenges, solutions. Information Systems Frontiers 14(2), 195–219 (2012)
33. Maggi, F., Montali, M., Westergaard, M., van der Aalst, W.: Monitoring Business Constraints with Linear Temporal Logic: An Approach Based on Colored Automata. In: Rinderle-Ma, S., Toumani, F., Wolf, K. (eds.) BPM 2011. LNCS, vol. 6896, pp. 132–147. Springer, Heidelberg (2011)
34. Mailund, T., Westergaard, M.: Obtaining memory-efficient reachability graph representations using the sweep-line method. In: Jensen, K., Podelski, A. (eds.) TACAS 2004. LNCS, vol. 2988, pp. 177–191. Springer, Heidelberg (2004)
35. McCarthy, J., Hayes, P.: Some philosophical problems from the standpoint of artificial intelligence. Stanford University, USA (1968)

36. McNamara, P.: Deontic logic. In: Zalta, E.N. (ed.) The Stanford Encyclopedia of Philosophy (Spring 2014), http://plato.stanford.edu/archives/spr2014/entries/logic-deontic/

37. Nute, D.: Defeasible logic. In: Handbook of Logic in Artificial Intelligence and Logic Programming, vol. 3, pp. 353–395. Oxford University Press (1994)

38. Nute, D. (ed.): Defeasible deontic logic. Springer (1997)

39. Sadiq, S., Governatori, G.: Managing regulatory compliance in business processes. In: vom Brocke, J., Rosemann, M. (eds.) Handbook on Business Process Management 2, pp. 265–288. Springer, Heidelberg (2015)

40. Sadiq, W., Governatori, G., Namiri, K.: Modeling control objectives for business process compliance. In: Alonso, G., Dadam, P., Rosemann, M. (eds.) BPM 2007. LNCS, vol. 4714, pp. 149–164. Springer, Heidelberg (2007)

Multi-agency Is Coordination
and (Limited) Communication

Piotr Kaźmierczak[1,2], Thomas Ågotnes[2], and Wojciech Jamroga[3,4]

[1] Department of Computing, Mathematics and Physics, Bergen University College,
Bergen, Norway
[2] Department of Information Science and Media Studies, University of Bergen,
Bergen, Norway
[3] Computer Science and Communication, and Interdisciplinary Centre for Security,
Reliability and Trust, University of Luxembourg, Luxembourg
[4] Institute of Computer Science, Polish Academy of Sciences, Warsaw, Poland
phk@hib.no, thomas.agotnes@infomedia.uib.no, w.jamroga@ipipan.waw.pl

Abstract. Systems within the agent-oriented paradigm range from ones
where a single agent is coupled with an environment to ones inhabited
by a large number of autonomous entities. In this paper, we look at what
distinguishes single-agent systems from multi-agent systems. We claim
that *multi*-agency implies limited coordination, in terms of action and/or
information. If a team is characterized by full coordination both on the
level of action choice and the available information, then we may as well
see the team as a single agent in disguise. To back the claim formally,
we consider a variant of Alternating-time Temporal Logic ATL where
each coalition operates with a single indistinguishability relation. For
this variant, we propose a truth-preserving translation of formulas and
models in the syntactic fragment of ATL where only singleton coalitions
are allowed. In consequence, we show that assuming unified view of the
world on part of each coalition reduces the full language of ATL to its
single-agent fragment when a model is given.

1 Introduction

Agent-based models become a suitable foundation for IT environments nowadays. More and more systems involve social as much as technological aspects, and
even those that focus on technology are often based on distributed components
exhibiting self-interested, goal-directed behavior. Moreover, the components act
in environments characterized by incomplete information and uncertainty. The
field of *multi-agent systems* [28] studies the whole spectrum of phenomena ranging from agent architectures to communication and coordination in agent groups
to agent-oriented software engineering. The theoretical foundations are mainly
based on game theory and formal logic.

Systems within the agent-oriented paradigm display various degrees of mul-
tiplicity, from systems where a single agent is coupled with an environment
(often used e.g. in agent-oriented programming), to massively populous ones

H.K. Dam et al. (Eds.): PRIMA 2014, LNAI 8861, pp. 91–106, 2014.

used e.g. for agent-based simulation. What distinguishes a single-agent system from a *multi*-agent system is an interesting question in itself. In particular, is it enough that a system consists of multiple *modules* to call it multi-agent? What about semi-autonomous entities that act according to "orders" dispatched from a central unit? Or entities that act autonomously but they pursue a common goal, and act according to a joint plan? All these cases clearly display different degrees of autonomy and agency.

In this paper, we claim that multi-agency implies limited coordination, in terms of action and/or information. That is, different agents may collaborate, but they are inherently separated: each agent is individually responsible for executing his/her actions, and does that based on his/her individual view of the situation. Putting it in another way, if a team is characterized by full coordination both on the level of action/strategy choice and the available information, then we may as well see the team as a single (though composite) agent.

To back the claim formally, we use Alternating-time Temporal Logic ATL [4,5] that combines elements of game theory, temporal logic, and epistemic logic in a neat formal framework. Coordination of coalitional strategies is implicitly given "for free" in the semantics of ATL, but the logic has many semantic variants for reasoning about coalitional play under different patterns of uncertainty. We consider a variant of ATL where each coalition operates by definition with a single indistinguishability relation (e.g., the distributed knowledge relation). For this variant, we propose a truth-preserving translation of formulas and models in the syntactic fragment of ATL where only singleton coalitions are allowed. In consequence, we show that assuming unified view of the world on part of each coalition reduces the full language of ATL to its single-agent fragment, at least when a model is given.

The main purpose of this study is philosophical. We want to understand the different degrees of autonomy and agency that arise in complex systems. Still, the reduction that we propose can be potentially used to implement model checking for some interesting semantic variants of ATL.

We begin by introducing the relevant syntactic and semantic variants of ATL in Sections 2 and 3. Then, we present our main result in Section 4. We conclude with some final remarks in Section 5.

Related Work. ATL has been studied extensively in the last 15 years. The research can be roughly divided into the computational and conceptual strands. The conceptual strand focuses on looking for the "right" semantics of ability, especially in the presence of imperfect or incomplete information. ATL has been combined with epistemic logic [24,25,1,16], and several semantic variants were defined that match various possible interpretations of strategic ability [22,18,16]. Multiple extensions have been considered, e.g., with explicit reasoning about strategies, rationality assumptions and solution concepts [26,23,27,9], agents with bounded resources [3,8], coalition formation and negotiation [7], opponent modeling and action in stochastic environments [15,21] and reasoning about irrevocable plans and interplay between strategies of different agents [2,6]. Besides providing a palette of different formal interpretations for the concept of strategic ability, the research brought benefits in analysis of related verification problems, such as module checking [17].

In this paper, we are especially interested in works that redefine the "uniformity" conditions for coalitional play, based on a *single* epistemic relation for the whole coalition [13,11,14,10]. Philosophically, this amounts to assuming members of the coalition to share their knowledge (or, conversely, propagate their uncertainty) at each step while executing a joint strategy. We show that – at least in the context of model checking – such a coalition can be seen as a single agent executing compound actions *in unison*.

2 Reasoning about Abilities of Agents and Coalitions

Alternating-time Temporal Logic ATL [4,5] is a non-normal modal logic that allows for expressing properties of multi-agent systems. Specification in ATL is usually based on formulae of type $\langle\!\langle A \rangle\!\rangle \varphi$, expressing that the group of agents A has a strategy to enforce the temporal property φ no matter what the other agents do. Formulae of ATL are interpreted in *concurrent game structures* that assume synchronous execution of actions from all the agents in the system. We begin by defining the models formally. Then, we present the syntax and the semantic clauses for relevant variants of the logic.

2.1 Models: Concurrent Game Structures

In the most general case, formulas of ATL are interpreted over *imperfect information concurrent game structures* (ICGS), defined as follows:

Definition 1 (Imperfect Information Concurrent Game Structures [22]).
An ICGS is an 8-tuple $M = \langle \Sigma, \Pi, Q, C, d, \delta, \sim, \pi \rangle$, where:

- *Σ is a finite set of agents;*
- *Π is a finite set of propositional letters;*
- *Q is a finite set of states;*
- *C is a finite set of choices/actions;*
- *$d : Q \times \Sigma \to \wp(C)$ is a guard function that specifies which actions are enabled for whom and where. It is assumed that in any state at least one choice must be enabled for each agent. We will usually write $d_a(q)$ instead of $d(q, a)$;*
- *$\delta : Q \times C^\Sigma \to Q$ is a deterministic transition function;*
- *$\sim: \Sigma \to \wp(Q \times Q)$ is a family of equivalence relations (one per agent) indicating states that are indistinguishable from agents' perspectives, and*
- *$\pi : Q \to \wp(\Pi)$ is a valuation of atomic propositions.*

Additionally, it is usually assumed that the ICGS assigns the same sets of choices to indistinguishable states; formally: if $q \sim_a q'$ then $d_a(q) = d_a(q')$.

We illustrate how ICGS are used to model multi-agent systems on the following example.

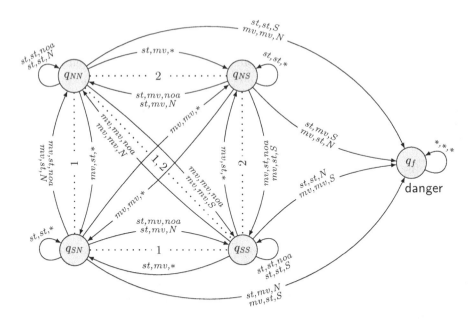

Fig. 1. A simple model of coordinated defense (M_1). The wildcard ($*$) matches any action of the appropriate player.

Example 1 (Coordinated Defense). Two guards (agents 1 and 2) are supposed to protect a sensitive area from attack. They conduct surveillance of the area in parallel, from two separate locations. These can be different floors in a building, or different hills giving view to a military zone, etc. At any moment, each guard is in a position that allows him to protect either the North or the South entry to the area, but not both at the same time. Moreover, a guard can stay in the same place (action st) or move to the other side of the surveillance area (action mv). However, the landscape is confusing and the guards are no experts in reading landscape signs; in consequence, both entries and surveillance points look the same to each guard. On the other hand, guard 1 can recognize when he is in the North position and guard 2 is in the South position, because only then he can see the light from the other guard's torch. Likewise, guard 2 can only distinguish the situation when he is in the North and the other guard is in the South.

The attack – executed by the third agent a, the "attacker" – can be conducted either from the North (action N) or from the South (action S). The attacker can also refrain from attacking (action noa). The attack is only successful if it targets a position which, in the very next moment, will not be protected by any of the guards. In such case, the system proceeds to the "failure" state q_f, labeled by the atomic proposition danger.

A simple model of the scenario is depicted in Figure 1. The set of players is $\Sigma = \{1, 2, a\}$. States, transitions (represented by solid arrows), indistinguishability relations (represented by dotted lines), and valuation of atomic propositions can be easily read off the picture.

2.2   Syntax: ATL and Single-Agent ATL

The language of alternating-time temporal logic, formally referred to as $\mathcal{L}_{\text{ATL}}$, is defined by the following grammar:

$$\varphi ::= \top \mid p \mid \neg\varphi \mid \varphi \wedge \varphi \mid \langle\!\langle A \rangle\!\rangle \bigcirc \varphi \mid \langle\!\langle A \rangle\!\rangle \square \varphi \mid \langle\!\langle A \rangle\!\rangle \varphi \, \mathcal{U} \, \varphi$$

where p is a propositional symbol and A is a subset of agents (called sometimes a *coalition*). We will write $\langle\!\langle a_1, a_2, \dots \rangle\!\rangle$ instead of $\langle\!\langle \{a_1, a_2, \dots \} \rangle\!\rangle$. The temporal operator $\bigcirc$ stands for "in the next moment", $\square$ for "always from now on", and $\mathcal{U}$ for "strong until". We use the usual abbreviations of Boolean operators, plus the standard abbreviation for "sometime in the future": $\lozenge\varphi \equiv \top \, \mathcal{U} \varphi$.

We also define a syntactic fragment of ATL called the *single-agent* ATL , that allows only singleton coalitions in the formulae. The fragment, to which we will refer as $\mathcal{L}_{1\text{ATL}}$, is formally defined as follows:

$$\varphi ::= \top \mid p \mid \neg\varphi \mid \varphi \wedge \varphi \mid \langle\!\langle a \rangle\!\rangle \bigcirc \varphi \mid \langle\!\langle a \rangle\!\rangle \square \varphi \mid \langle\!\langle a \rangle\!\rangle \varphi \, \mathcal{U} \, \varphi$$

where p is a propositional symbol and a is an agent.

Example 2. The following formulae specify possible requirements on the Coordinated Defense scenario: $\langle\!\langle 1, 2 \rangle\!\rangle \square \neg\mathsf{danger}$ (the guards can effectively protect the system from attacks forever), $\neg\langle\!\langle 1, 2 \rangle\!\rangle \lozenge \langle\!\langle 1, a \rangle\!\rangle \bigcirc \mathsf{danger}$ (the guards cannot compromise the system in such a way that, at some future moment, guard 1 can collude with the attacker for a successful attack).

2.3   Semantic Variants of ATL

Semantic variants of ATL are usually derived from different assumptions about agents' capabilities. Can the agents "see" the current state of the system, or only a part of it? Can they memorize the whole history of observations in the game? Different answers to these questions induce different semantics of strategic ability. In this section, we recall the "canonical" variants as proposed in [22]. There, a taxonomy of four strategy types was introduced and labeled as follows: I (resp. i) stands for *perfect* (resp. *imperfect*) *information*, and R (resp. r) refers to *perfect recall* (resp. *no recall*). In essence, the semantics of ATL in [22] is parameterized with the strategy type – yielding four different semantic variants of the logic, labeled accordingly (ATL$_{\text{IR}}$, ATL$_{\text{Ir}}$, ATL$_{\text{iR}}$, and ATL$_{\text{ir}}$).

The following types of strategies are used in the respective semantic variants:

- Ir: $f_a : St \to Act$ such that $f_a(q) \in d(a, q)$ for all q;
- IR: $f_a : St^+ \to Act$ such that $f_a(h) \in d(a, q_n)$ for all $h = q_0, \dots, q_n$;

– ir: like Ir, with the additional constraint that $q \sim_a q'$ implies $f_a(q) = f_a(q')$;
– iR: like IR, with the additional constraint that $h \approx_a h'$ implies $f_a(h) = f_a(h')$, where $h \approx_a h'$ iff $h[i] \sim_a h'[i]$ for all i.

That is, strategy f_a is a conditional plan that specifies agent a's actions in each state of the system (for memoryless agents) or for every possible history of the system evolution (for agents with perfect recall). Moreover, imperfect information strategies specify the same choices for indistinguishable states (resp. histories). Finally, a collective xy-strategy F_A for a group of agents $A \subseteq \Sigma$ is a tuple of xy-strategies $(f_a)_{a \in A}$, one for each agent.

A *computation* is an infinite sequence of states $\lambda = q_0, q_1, \ldots$, and we say it is an *outcome* of strategy F_A from state q if $q_0 = q$ and for each $i > 0$, there are $c_a \in C$ choices for $a \in \Sigma \setminus A$, such that $q_{i+1} = \delta(q_i, \mathbf{c})$ where $\mathbf{c}_a = f_a([q_i]_a)$ if $a \in A$, and $\mathbf{c}_a = c_a$ for the opponents. Outcomes are therefore computations that start from the given state and follow the strategy. The set of all the outcome paths of strategy F_A from state q on is denoted by $out(q, F_A)$.

Given an ICGS M, state q and formula φ, we interpret the formula as follows:

– $M, q \models_{xy} \langle\!\langle A \rangle\!\rangle \bigcirc \varphi$ iff there exists an xy-strategy F_A for A such that, for every q' with $q \sim_A q'$, and every $\lambda \in out(q', F_A)$, we have $\lambda[1] \models_{xy} \varphi$.
– $M, q \models_{xy} \langle\!\langle A \rangle\!\rangle \Box \varphi$ iff there exists an xy-strategy F_A for A such that, for every q' with $q \sim_A q'$, and every $\lambda \in out(q', F_A)$, we have $\lambda[i] \models_{xy} \varphi$ for every position $i \geq 0$.
– $M, q \models_{xy} \langle\!\langle A \rangle\!\rangle \varphi_1 \mathcal{U} \varphi_2$ iff there exists an xy-strategy F_A such that, for every q' with $q \sim_A q'$, and every $\lambda \in out(q', F_A)$, there is a position $i \geq 0$ such that $\lambda[i] \models_{xy} \varphi_2$, and for all positions $0 \leq j < i$ we have $\lambda[j] \models_{xy} \varphi_1$.

In the above clauses, one element is not properly defined yet – namely, the coalitional indistinguishability relation $\sim_A$. Epistemic logic suggests several "canonical" ways in which collective indistinguishability can be constructed. The epistemic relation for *"everybody knows"* is defined as the union of individual relations: $\sim_A^E = \bigcup_{a \in A} \sim_a$. The relation for *common knowledge* ($\sim_A^C$) is the transitive closure of $\sim_A^E$. Furthermore, the epistemic relation for *distributed knowledge* is defined as the intersection of individual relations: $\sim_A^D = \bigcap_{a \in A} \sim_a$. Since we focus on coalitions that can freely communicate and exchange information, we assume that $\sim_A = \sim_A^D$. Notice that the distinction is not relevant for the main result in this paper, which proceeds by embedding coalition-uniform abilities in 1ATL. This is because, for individual agents, $\sim_{\{a\}}^D = \sim_{\{a\}}^E = \sim_{\{a\}}^C = \sim_a$.

We illustrate how the semantics works on the Coordinated Defense example.

Example 3. For model M_1 from Example 1 and formulae from Example 2 we have the following. $M_1, q_{SN} \models_{ir} \langle\!\langle 1, 2 \rangle\!\rangle \Box \neg \mathsf{danger}$ because (i) the coalition $\{1, 2\}$ has distributed knowledge that the initial state is precisely q_{SN} and (ii) from q_{SN}, the memoryless strategy where each guard does st in every state avoids q_f no matter what the attacker does. On the other hand, $M_1, q_{NN} \not\models_{ir} \langle\!\langle 1, 2 \rangle\!\rangle \Box \neg \mathsf{danger}$ because the only way to avoid a successful attack right after the game begins is that one guard stays, and one moves to the other position. Since they use memoryless strategies, the staying guard must execute st forever. Moreover, the moving guard will not see that he has changed his position (as $q_{NN} \sim_1 q_{SN}$ and $q_{NN} \sim_2 q_{NS}$). Since they can only use uniform strategies, the moving guard must execute mv forever – but that means that the area can be successfully attacked in two steps from the start. Finally, memory matters: $M_1, q_{NN} \models_{iR} \langle\langle 1, 2 \rangle\rangle \square \neg$danger. To see this, consider any strategy where one guard always stays, and the other one moves in the first moment, and stays from then on. We leave it up to the reader to check that the strategy succeeds from $\{q_{NN}, q_{SS}\}$, i.e., both states that the guards jointly consider possible at the beginning.

As a *logic*, we will understand the language together with the chosen semantic interpretation. For the logics used in this paper, we will use the notation $L_{xy} = (\mathcal{L}_L, \models_{xy})$. For example, 1ATL$_{ir}$ denotes the logic with the syntax defined by $\mathcal{L}_{1ATL}$ and the semantics by $\models_{ir}$.

3   A Different Concept of Coalitional Uniformity

The uniformity conditions presented in Section 2.3 are based on the assumption that each member of the coalition executes its part of the joint plan on its own. Thus, the execution of every next step is based on the agent's individual view of the situation. A number of papers redefine uniformity of coalitional strategies, using instead a *single* epistemic relation for the whole coalition [13,11,14,10]. This amounts to assuming members of the coalition to establish their *joint view of the situation* at each step while executing the joint strategy. Thus, at each step they either fully share their individual knowledge, or aggregate their uncertainty. [13,11,14] take the first approach by defining coalitional uniformity on top of the distributed knowledge relation. In [10], the opposite stance is adopted, by assuming that members of a coalition must choose same actions in states that are connected by the common knowledge relation. The main motivation for the semantic variations was quest for a variant of ATL with imperfect information, perfect recall, and decidable model checking.[1] However, the research was conceptually interesting in its own right.

We formalize the intuitions from [13,11,14,10] by changing the set of available strategies as follows.

Definition 2 (Coalition-uniform strategies). *A collective memoryless strategy f_A is coalition-uniform iff $q \sim_A q'$ implies $f_a(q) = f_a(q')$ for every $q, q' \in St$ and $a \in A$. Likewise, a collective perfect recall strategy f_A is coalition-uniform iff $h \approx_A h'$ implies $f_a(h) = f_a(h')$ for every $h, h' \in St^+$ and $a \in A$.*

Note that uniformity constraints are relevant only for the imperfect information case. Depending on the type of recall, we will denote the new variant of ATL

---

[1] It is well known that "standard" ATL with imperfect information and perfect recall makes verification undecidable even for very simple formulae and regular models [12].

by ATL^c_{ir} or ATL^c_{iR}, with "c" standing for *imperfect information with coalition-uniform strategies*. Let $y \in \{r, R\}$. The interpretation of strategic modalities in ATL^c_{iy} is defined below:

- $M, q \models^c_{\text{iy}} \langle\!\langle A \rangle\!\rangle \bigcirc \varphi$ iff there exists a set of coalition-uniform y-strategies F_A, such that for all q' with $q \sim_A q'$ and all computations $\lambda \in out(q', F_A)$ we have $\lambda[1] \models^c_{\text{iy}} \varphi$.
- $M, q \models^c_{\text{iy}} \langle\!\langle A \rangle\!\rangle \Box \varphi$ iff there exists a set of coalition-uniform y-strategies F_A, such that for all q' with $q \sim_A q'$ and all computations $\lambda \in out(q', F_A)$ we have $\lambda[i] \models^c_{\text{iy}} \varphi$ for all i.
- $M, q \models^c_{\text{iy}} \langle\!\langle A \rangle\!\rangle \varphi_1 \mathcal{U} \varphi_2$ iff there exists a set of coalition-uniform y-strategies F_A such that $\forall q' \sim_A q$ and $\forall \lambda \in out(q', F_A)$, there exists a position $i \geq 0$ such that $\lambda[i] \models^c_{\text{iy}} \varphi_2$, and for all positions $0 \leq j < i$, we have $\lambda[j] \models^c_{\text{iy}} \varphi_1$.

In line with [13,11,14], we assume $\sim_A = \sim^D_A$ and $\approx_A = \approx^D_A$. That is, members of a coalition are able to freely communicate while executing the strategy. We believe, however, that our results carry over to the other notions of collective indistinguishability.

Example 4. Now, we have that $M_1, q_{NN} \models^c_{\text{ir}} \langle\!\langle 1, 2 \rangle\!\rangle \Box \neg \mathsf{danger}$. A successful strategy makes one guard do st in every state, and the other guard move in $\{q_{NN}, q_{SS}\}$ and stay elsewhere.

4 Translating Coalition-Uniform ATL to Single-Agent ATL

In this section we present a truth-preserving translation from ATL^c_{iy} to 1ATL_{iy}.

4.1 Reconstruction of Models

We first propose a reconstruction of ICGS's that replaces relevant coalitions by single agents. The idea is as follows: for every coalition A occurring in a given formula φ, we remove the agents in A from Σ, and instead add a new agent a_A. The actions of a_A are combinations of actions from agents in A. Thus, the new set of agents will consist of new agents representing coalitions from φ, plus those agents that did not appear in any coalition. Now, it can be the case that some "old" agents have become part of several different "coalitional" agents a_A. If their choices agree across the new coalitional actions then the transition specified in the original model is executed. Otherwise, the system proceeds to a new "conflict" state $q_\perp$ labeled with a new atomic proposition null.

Definition 3 (Model Translation). *We define a function T which given an ICGS $M = \langle \Sigma, \Pi, Q, C, d, \delta, \sim, \pi \rangle$ and an ATL^c_{iy} formula φ with coalitions $A_1, \ldots, A_n$ of (where $A_1, \ldots, A_n \subseteq \Sigma$), translates them into a concurrent game structure $T(M, \varphi) = M' = \langle \Sigma', \Pi', Q', C', d', \delta', \sim', \pi' \rangle$.*
$\Sigma' = \{a_{A_1}, \ldots, a_{A_n}\} \cup \{\Sigma \setminus \bigcup_n A_n\} \cup \{a_d\}$ is the new set of agents, which has new agents $\{a_{A_1}, \ldots, a_{A_n}\}$ that correspond to coalitions occurring in φ, and all

the old agents except for those that belonged to coalitions in φ. There is also an extra agent in Σ' which we denote as 'a_d' ("dummy"). For the sake of brevity we will refer to 'old' agents (those that do not belong to coalitions occurring in φ) as $\{a_1, \ldots, a_m\}$. Also, in order to be able to refer to former members of coalitions $A_1, \ldots, A_n$, we adopt the following notation:

$$A_1 = (a_1^1, a_2^1, \ldots, a_{l_1}^1)$$
$$A_2 = (a_1^2, a_2^2, \ldots, a_{l_2}^2)$$
$$\vdots$$
$$A_n = (a_1^n, a_2^n, \ldots, a_{l_n}^n)$$

And we also say that there are k agents in the original structure M.

We introduce one new propositional symbol 'null' and one new state $q_\perp$:

$$\Pi' = \Pi \cup \{null\}$$
$$Q' = Q \cup \{q_\perp\}$$

We now define the set of choices C' and a function of enabled choices d' simultaneously. We say that:

$$d'_a(q') = \begin{cases} d_a(q) & \text{if } a \in \{a_1, \ldots, a_m\} \text{ and } q' \neq q_\perp, \\ \prod_{b \in A_j} d_b(q) & \text{if } a = a_{A_j} \text{and } q' \neq q_\perp, \\ \{empty\} & \text{if } a = a_d \text{ or if } q' = q_\perp, \end{cases}$$

where $q' \in Q'$, $q \in Q$ and $a \in \Sigma'$. We say the set C' is simply an image of the function d', and we refer to members of C' as c'.

The new transition function, δ', handles non-empty intersections of coalitions that lead to (potentially) conflicting choices. Whenever two (or more) singleton coalitions have enabled choices that would lead to different states, it produces transitions to a special conflict state $q_\perp$:

$$\delta'(q', (c'_{a_1^1}, \ldots, c'_{a_{l_1}^1}), \ldots, (c'_{a_1^n}, \ldots, c'_{a_{l_n}^n}),$$

$$c'_d, c'_1, \ldots, c'_m) = \begin{cases} \delta(q, x_1, \ldots, x_k) & \text{when } A_1 \cap \ldots \cap A_n = \emptyset \text{ or} \\ & \forall_{i,j \in \{1,\ldots,n\}} \forall_{r \in \{1,\ldots,l_i\}} \forall_{s \in \{1,\ldots,l_j\}} \\ & a_r^i = a_s^j \Rightarrow c'_{a_r^i} = c'_{a_s^j} \\ q_\perp & \text{otherwise.} \end{cases}$$

where $x_i = c'_j$ if $a_i = a_j \in \{a_1, \ldots, a_m\}$ and $c'_{a_o^j}$ if $a_i = a_o^j \in A_j$.

The indistinguishability relation remains the same for old agents, and for new agents it becomes the intersection of relations for members of old coalitions:

$$\sim'_a = \begin{cases} \sim_a \cup \{q_\perp, q_\perp\} & \text{if } a \in \{a_1, \ldots, a_n\} \\ \bigcap_{b \in A_j} \sim_b & \text{if } a = a_{A_j} \\ \{q_\perp, q_\perp\} & \text{if } a = a_d \end{cases}$$

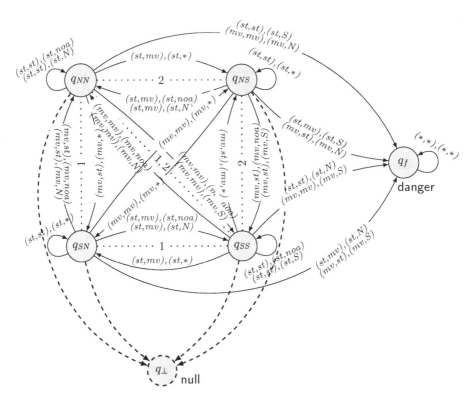

Fig. 2. Translation of model M_1 for formula $\langle\langle 1,2\rangle\rangle\Diamond\langle\langle 1,a\rangle\rangle\bigcirc$ danger. Dashed arrows depict transitions to the "conflict" state $q_\perp$.

Finally, we label the special state $q_\perp$ with a new propositional symbol null: $\pi'(q) = \{null\}$ for $q = q_\perp$ and $\pi(q)$ otherwise.

Example 5. The translation of the coordinated defense model M_1 for formula $\langle\langle 1,2\rangle\rangle\Diamond\langle\langle 1,a\rangle\rangle\bigcirc$ danger is presented in Figure 2.

4.2   Translation of Formulas

The formula translation is straightforward. We substitute each coalition A with agent a_A, and insert the proposition null so that the opponents can only lose by enforcing a conflict.

Definition 4 (Formula Translation). *We define the function* $t : \mathcal{L}_{\text{ATL}} \to \mathcal{L}_{1\text{ATL}}$ *which translates an* ATL *formula over* Σ *to a single-agent* ATL *formula over* Σ' *inductively in the following way:*

$$t(p) = p$$
$$t(\neg\varphi) = \neg t(\varphi)$$
$$t(\varphi \wedge \psi) = t(\varphi) \wedge t(\psi)$$
$$t(\langle\!\langle\emptyset\rangle\!\rangle \bigcirc \varphi) = \langle\!\langle a_d\rangle\!\rangle \bigcirc (null \vee t(\varphi))$$
$$t(\langle\!\langle\emptyset\rangle\!\rangle\Box\varphi) = \langle\!\langle a_d\rangle\!\rangle\Box(null \vee t(\varphi))$$
$$t(\langle\!\langle\emptyset\rangle\!\rangle\varphi\,\mathcal{U}\psi) = \langle\!\langle a_d\rangle\!\rangle(null \vee t(\varphi))\,\mathcal{U}(null \vee t(\psi))$$
$$t(\langle\!\langle A\rangle\!\rangle \bigcirc \varphi) = \langle\!\langle a_A\rangle\!\rangle \bigcirc (null \vee t(\varphi))$$
$$t(\langle\!\langle A\rangle\!\rangle\Box\varphi) = \langle\!\langle a_A\rangle\!\rangle\Box(null \vee t(\varphi))$$
$$t(\langle\!\langle A\rangle\!\rangle\varphi\,\mathcal{U}\psi) = \langle\!\langle a_A\rangle\!\rangle(null \vee t(\varphi))\,\mathcal{U}(null \vee t(\psi))$$

where $p \in \Pi$, $null \in \Pi'$, $A \subseteq \Sigma$, *and* $a_A, a_d \in \Sigma'$.

Example 6. According to the translation, our formula $\langle\!\langle 1,2\rangle\!\rangle\Diamond\langle\!\langle 1,a\rangle\!\rangle\bigcirc\mathsf{danger}$ becomes now $\langle\!\langle a_{\{1,2\}}\rangle\!\rangle\Diamond(null \vee \langle\!\langle a_{\{1,a\}}\rangle\!\rangle\bigcirc(null \vee \mathsf{danger}))$.

4.3   Main Result: The Embedding Is Truth-Preserving

In order to prove correctness of our translation we need some additional definitions and lemmas:

Definition 5 (Complexity of formulas). *The complexity* $c : \mathcal{L}_{\text{ATL}^c_{xy}} \to \mathbb{N}$ *is defined inductively as follows:*

$$c(p) = 1$$
$$c(\neg\varphi) = 1 + c(\varphi)$$
$$c(\varphi \wedge \psi) = 1 + \max(c(\varphi), c(\psi))$$
$$c(\langle\!\langle A\rangle\!\rangle \bigcirc \varphi) = c(\langle\!\langle\emptyset\rangle\!\rangle \bigcirc \varphi) = 1 + c(\varphi)$$
$$c(\langle\!\langle A\rangle\!\rangle\Box\varphi) = c(\langle\!\langle\emptyset\rangle\!\rangle\Box\varphi) = 1 + c(\varphi)$$
$$c(\langle\!\langle A\rangle\!\rangle\varphi\,\mathcal{U}\psi) = c(\langle\!\langle\emptyset\rangle\!\rangle\varphi\,\mathcal{U}\psi) = 1 + c(\varphi) + c(\psi)$$

Lemma 1. $T(M, \neg\varphi)$ *is equivalent to* $T(M, \varphi)$.

Proof. T takes a structure and a formula as its arguments, but the only part of the formula taken into consideration is the coalition predicate. Since negation does not affect it, we say that the above expressions are equivalent.   □

We can now state the main result in this paper.

Theorem 1. *Given an* ICGS M, *a state* $q \in M$ *and an* ATL^c_{iy} *formula* φ, *the following equivalence holds:*

$$M, q \models \varphi \iff T(M, \varphi), q \models t(\varphi)$$

Proof. Let φ be a formula. The proof is by induction on $c(\psi')$ for all subformulas ψ' of φ.

Base Case. If $M, q \models p$ then $T(M, \varphi), q \models t(p)$, because $t(p)$ is p, and for every $q \in Q$, $\pi'(q) = \pi(q)$. The same argument applies in the other direction, so if $T(M, \varphi), q \models t(p)$ then $M, q \models p$.

Induction Hypothesis. For all subformulas ψ of φ such that $c(\psi) < c(\psi')$, and all $q \in Q$: $M, q \models \psi \iff T(M, \varphi), q \models t(\psi)$.

Case for $\psi' = \neg\psi$. Follows directly from the induction hypothesis and Lemma 1.

Case for $\psi' = \psi_1 \wedge \psi_2$. If ψ' is a conjunction, it is trivially true that whenever $M, q \models \psi_1 \wedge \psi_2$, then $T(M, \varphi), q \models t(\psi_1 \wedge \psi_2)$. The other direction follows as well, since $t(\psi_1 \wedge \psi_2)$ translates into $t(\psi_1) \wedge t(\psi_2)$.

Case for $\psi' = \langle\!\langle A \rangle\!\rangle \bigcirc \psi$.

($\Rightarrow$) We want to show that:

$$M, q \models \langle\!\langle A \rangle\!\rangle \bigcirc \psi \Rightarrow T(M, \varphi), q \models \langle\!\langle a_A \rangle\!\rangle \bigcirc (null \vee t(\psi))$$

Assume that $\exists F_A \forall_{q_1 \sim_A q} \forall \lambda \in out(q_1, F_A), M, \lambda[1] \models \psi$, where $F_A = \{f_a : a \in A\}$ is a coalition-uniform set of strategies. We must show that $\exists f_{a_A} \forall_{q'_1 \sim'_{a_A} q} \forall \lambda' \in out(q'_1, f_{a_A}), T(M, \varphi), \lambda'[1] \models (null \vee t(\psi))$. We define the strategy f_{a_A} for agent a_A in $T(M, \varphi)$ as follows: $f_{a_A}(q') = \prod_{a \in A} f_a(q')$ when $q' \in Q$, and $f_{a_A}(q') = empty$ when $q' = q_\perp$. Let $q'_1 \sim_{a_A} q$ and $\lambda' \in out(q'_1, f_{a_A})$. We must show that $T(M, \varphi), \lambda'[1] \models (null \vee t(\psi))$. From Definitions 2 and 3 we have that $q'_1 \sim_{a_A} q$ implies that $q'_1 \sim_A q$. That $\lambda' \in out(q'_1, f_{a_A})$ means that there is a choice $c'_a \in d'_a(q'_1)$ for each agent $a \in \Sigma'$ such that $c'_{a_A} = f_{a_A}(q'_1)$. We now define some notation: for any $h \in \{1, \dots, n\}$, we have that $c'_{a_{A_h}} = (c^h_1, \dots, c^h_{l_h}) \in d'_{a_{A_h}}(q'_1) = \prod_{a \in A_h} d_a(q'_1)$, so for every agent $a \in \Sigma$ such that $a \in A_h = \{a^h_1, \dots, a^h_{l_h}\}$, let $i^h_a \in \{1, \dots, l_h\}$ be such that $a = a^h_{i^h_a}$ (a is agent number i^h_a in the enumeration of A_h). We thus have that $c^h_{i^h_a} \in d(q'_1)$ is the choice of agent a in the choice $c'_{a_{A_h}}$ of the coalition A_h. We now consider two cases.

The first case is that there exist A_h and A_l such that $A_h \cap A_l \neq \emptyset$ but $c^h_{i^h_a} \neq c^l_{i^l_a}$ (the choice made by a in the two coalitions differ). In this case $\delta'(q'_1, \mathbf{c}) = q_\perp$, and thus $T(M, \varphi), \lambda'[1] \models null$ and we are done.

Assume, then, the second case, that whenever there are one or more coalitions with a as a member, they all agree on the choice for agent a, i.e., $c^h_{i^h_a} = c^l_{i^l_a}$ whenever $a \in A_h \cap A_l$. We now define a choice $c_a \in d_a(q'_1)$ for each agent $a \in \Sigma$ in the original model M, as follows. When $a \notin A_h$, for all h, let $c_a = c'_a$; $c_a \in d_a(q'_1)$ because $d'_a(q'_1) = d_a(q'_1)$. When $a \in A_h$ for some h, let $c_a = c^h_{i^h_a}$ for some h such that $a \in A_h$ (this is well-defined by the assumption that all coalitions with a as a member agree on the choice of a). Let h be such that $A = A_h$ (since ψ' is a subformula of φ, A is one of the coalitions occurring in φ). Let $a \in A$. We have that $c'_{a_A} = f_{a_A}(q'_1) = \prod_{a \in A} c_a$ and $c_a = c^h_{i^h_a}$ by the definitions above, and thus $c_a = c^h_{i^h_a} = f_a(q'_1)$. Since $c_a = f_a(q'_1)$ for any $a \in A$, there is a $\lambda \in out(q'_1, F_A)$

such that $\lambda[1] = \delta(q_1', \mathbf{c})$, and we thus have that $M, \delta(q_1', \mathbf{c}) \models \psi$.[2] By the induction hypothesis, $T(M, \varphi), \delta(q_1', \mathbf{c}) \models t(\psi)$. By Definition 3 we have that $\delta'(q_1', \mathbf{c}') = \delta(q_1', \mathbf{c})$, and thus that $T(M, \varphi), \delta(q_1', \mathbf{c}) \models t(\psi)$. By definition of $\mathbf{c}'$, $\delta'(q_1', \mathbf{c}') = \lambda'[1]$. Thus, $T(M, \varphi), \lambda'[1] \models t(\psi)$, and we are done.

($\Leftarrow$) We want to show that:

$$T(M, \varphi), q \models \langle\!\langle a_A \rangle\!\rangle \bigcirc (null \vee t(\psi)) \Rightarrow M, q \models \langle\!\langle A \rangle\!\rangle \bigcirc \psi$$

Assume that $\exists f_{a_A} \forall_{q_1 \sim'_{a_A} q} \forall \lambda' \in out(q_1, f_{a_A}), T(M, \varphi), \lambda'[1] \models (null \vee t(\psi))$. We must show that $\exists F_A \forall_{q_1 \sim_A q} \forall \lambda \in out(q_1, F_A), M, \lambda[1] \models \psi$.
We define a coalition-uniform set of strategies $F_A = \{f_a : a \in A\}$ for coalition $A = \{a_1, \ldots, a_r\}$ as follows: for every $a = a_j \in A$ and any $q' \in Q$, $f_a(q') = c_j$, where $(c_1, \ldots, c_r) = f_{a_A}(q)$. For $q' = q_\perp$ and $a \in A$, $f_a(q') = empty$. From Definition 3 it is easy to see that F_A is a (collective) strategy in M (i.e., $f_a(q') \in d_a(q')$ for each $a \in A$) and from uniformity of f_{a_A} and Definition 3 it follows that F_A is coalition-uniform ($q' \sim_A q'' \Rightarrow f_a(q') = f_a(q'')$ for each $a \in A$).
Let $q_1 \sim_A q$. We know that $q \neq q_\perp$, because $q_\perp \notin Q$ and we also know that $q_1 \neq q_\perp$, because $q_\perp$ is indistinguishable only from itself. Hence, from Definitions 2 and 3 we get that $q_1 \sim_A q$ implies $q_1 \sim'_{a_A} q$.
Let $\lambda \in out(q_1, F_A)$. It is easy to see that also $\lambda \in out(q_1, f_{a_A})$: $T(M, \varphi)$ includes all the states of M; all the strategies F_A and f_{a_A} "do the same thing" in those states; the other agents have the same actions available in those states. Thus, $T(M, \varphi), \lambda[1] \models null \vee t(\psi)$. But it cannot be that $T(M, \varphi), \lambda[1] \models null$, because $null$ is only satisfied in $q_\perp$ and $q_\perp$ is not a state in λ (since λ is a computation in M). So, $T(M, \varphi), \lambda[1] \models t(\psi)$, and by the induction hypothesis, $M, \lambda[1] \models \psi$. Thus, $M, q \models \langle\!\langle A \rangle\!\rangle \bigcirc \psi$.

Case for $\psi' = \langle\!\langle A \rangle\!\rangle \psi_1 \mathcal{U} \psi_2$.

($\Rightarrow$) The proof of this case proceeds in a similar way to the previous case. We want to show that:

$$M, q \models \langle\!\langle A \rangle\!\rangle \psi_1 \mathcal{U} \psi_2 \Rightarrow T(M, \varphi), q \models \langle\!\langle a_A \rangle\!\rangle (null \vee t(\psi_1)) \mathcal{U} (null \vee t(\psi_2))$$

Assume that $\exists F_A$ such that $\forall_{q_1 \sim_A q} \forall \lambda \in out(q_1, F_A)$, there is a position $i > 0$ in λ, such that $M, \lambda[i] \models \psi_2$ and for all positions $0 \leq j < i$, $M, \lambda[j] \models \psi_1$, where $F_A = \{f_a : a \in A\}$ is a coalition-uniform set of strategies. We must show that $\exists f_{a_A} \forall_{q_1 \sim'_{a_A} q} \forall \lambda' \in out(q_1', f_{a_A})$, there is a position $i' > 0$ in λ', such that $T(M, \varphi), \lambda'[i'] \models (null \vee t(\psi_2))$ and for all positions $0 \leq j' < i'$, $T(M, \varphi), \lambda'[j'] \models (null \vee t(\psi_1))$. We define the strategy f_{a_A} for agent a_A in $T(M, \varphi)$ like before: $f_{a_A}(q') = \prod_{a \in A} f_a(q')$ when $q' \in Q$, and $f_{a_A}(q') = empty$ when $q' = q_\perp$. Let $q_1 \sim'_{a_A} q$ and $\lambda' \in out(q_1, f_{a_A})$.
It is now easy to see, in the same way as in the $\bigcirc$-case, that there exists an M-computation $\lambda \in out(q_1, F_A)$ such that either (i) $\lambda[j] = \lambda'[j]$ for all

---

[2] Throughout the rest of the proof we use the following notation: $\mathbf{c}$ is the action profile where the choice of agent $a \in \Sigma$ is c_a and $\mathbf{c}'$ is the action profile where the choice of agent $a \in \Sigma'$ is c_a'.

$j \geq 0$, or (ii) there exists a $k \geq 0$ such that $\lambda[j] = \lambda'[j]$ for all $0 \leq j < k$ and $\lambda'[j] = q_\perp$ for all $j \geq k$. In case (i) we are done by the induction hypothesis. We argue that we are also done in case (ii). If $k > i$ where i is such that $M, \lambda[i] \models \psi_2$, we are done by the induction hypothesis like in case (i). If $k \leq i$ we are also done: we have that $M, \lambda[j] \models \psi_1$ for all $j \leq k$; by the induction hypothesis $T(M, \varphi), \lambda[j] \models t(\psi_1)$ for all $j \leq k$ and thus $T(M, \varphi), \lambda'[j] \models t(\psi_1)$ for all $j \leq k$; and $T(M, \varphi), \lambda'[k] \models null$.

($\Leftarrow$) The proof in this direction is exactly like the proof in the same direction for the $\bigcirc$-case.

Case for $\psi' = \langle\!\langle A \rangle\!\rangle \Box \psi$. analogous to the $\mathcal{U}$-case. $\Box$

5   Conclusions

In this paper, we look closer at the issue of executable strategies for coalitions acting under imperfect or incomplete information. Based on ideas from existing literature, we propose the "coalition-uniform" semantics for Alternating-time Temporal Logic where uniformity of coalitional strategies is based on the *distributed knowledge* relation for the coalition. We also show that ATL with the new semantics can be embedded in the syntactic restriction of the logic that talks only about abilities of individual agents. This is done through a translation of models and formulae that preserves the truth of formulae in the context of a given model. We take it as a formal counterpart of our argument that coalitions whose members can fully coordinate their actions and share their knowledge should be seen as *de facto* single compound agents. We also note that the translation can be used to implement model checking of coalition-uniform ATL with verification tools for more standard variants of the logics, such as MCMAS [19] and SMC [20].

Acknowledgements. Piotr Kaźmierczak's research was supported by the Research Council of Norway project 194521 (FORMGRID). Wojciech Jamroga acknowledges the support of the National Research Fund (FNR) Luxembourg under the project GALOT (INTER/DFG/12/06), as well as the support of the 7th Framework Programme of the European Union under the Marie Curie IEF project ReVINK (PIEF-GA-2012-626398).

References

1. Ågotnes, T.: Action and knowledge in alternating-time temporal logic. Synthese 149(2), 377–409 (2006); Section on Knowledge, Rationality and Action
2. Ågotnes, T., Goranko, V., Jamroga, W.: Alternating-time temporal logics with irrevocable strategies. In: Samet, D. (ed.) Proceedings of TARK XI, pp. 15–24 (2007)
3. Alechina, N., Logan, B., Nguyen, H.N., Rakib, A.: Resource-bounded alternating-time temporal logic. In: Proceedings of AAMAS, pp. 481–488 (2010)

4. Alur, R., Henzinger, T.A., Kupferman, O.: Alternating-time Temporal Logic. In: Proceedings of the 38th Annual Symposium on Foundations of Computer Science (FOCS), pp. 100–109. IEEE Computer Society Press (1997)
5. Alur, R., Henzinger, T.A., Kupferman, O.: Alternating-time Temporal Logic. Journal of the ACM 49, 672–713 (2002)
6. Brihaye, T., Da Costa, A., Laroussinie, F., Markey, N.: ATL with strategy contexts and bounded memory. In: Artemov, S., Nerode, A. (eds.) LFCS 2009. LNCS, vol. 5407, pp. 92–106. Springer, Heidelberg (2008)
7. Bulling, N., Dix, J.: Modelling and verifying coalitions using argumentation and ATL. Inteligencia Artificial, Revista Iberoamericana de Inteligencia Artificial 14(46), 45–73 (2010)
8. Bulling, N., Farwer, B.: On the (un-)decidability of model checking resource-bounded agents. In: Proceedings of ECAI. Frontiers in Artificial Intelligence and Applications, vol. 215, pp. 567–572. IOS Press (2010)
9. Chatterjee, K., Henzinger, T.A., Piterman, N.: Strategy logic. In: Caires, L., Vasconcelos, V.T. (eds.) CONCUR 2007. LNCS, vol. 4703, pp. 59–73. Springer, Heidelberg (2007)
10. Diaconu, R., Dima, C.: Model-checking alternating-time temporal logic with strategies based on common knowledge is undecidable. Applied Artificial Intelligence 26(4), 331–348 (2012)
11. Dima, C., Enea, C., Guelev, D.: Model-checking an alternating-time temporal logic with knowledge, imperfect information, perfect recall and communicating coalitions. In: Proceedings of GANDALF, pp. 103–117 (2010)
12. Dima, C., Tiplea, F.: Model-checking atl under imperfect information and perfect recall semantics is undecidable. CoRR, abs/1102.4225 (2011)
13. Guelev, D.P., Dima, C.: Model-checking strategic ability and knowledge of the past of communicating coalitions. In: Baldoni, M., Son, T.C., van Riemsdijk, M.B., Winikoff, M. (eds.) DALT 2008. LNCS (LNAI), vol. 5397, pp. 75–90. Springer, Heidelberg (2009)
14. Guelev, D., Dima, C., Enea, C.: An alternating-time temporal logic with knowledge, perfect recall and past: axiomatisation and model-checking. Journal of Applied Non-Classical Logics 21(1), 93–131 (2011)
15. Jamroga, W.: A temporal logic for stochastic multi-agent systems. In: Bui, T.D., Ho, T.V., Ha, Q.T. (eds.) PRIMA 2008. LNCS (LNAI), vol. 5357, pp. 239–250. Springer, Heidelberg (2008)
16. Jamroga, W., Ågotnes, T.: Constructive knowledge: What agents can achieve under incomplete information. Journal of Applied Non-Classical Logics 17(4), 423–475 (2007)
17. Jamroga, W., Murano, A.: On module checking and strategies. In: Proceedings of the 13th International Conference on Autonomous Agents and Multiagent Systems AAMAS 2014, pp. 701–708 (2014)
18. Jamroga, W., van der Hoek, W.: Agents that know how to play. Fundamenta Informaticae 63(2-3), 185–219 (2004)
19. Lomuscio, A., Qu, H., Raimondi, F.: MCMAS: A model checker for the verification of multi-agent systems. In: Bouajjani, A., Maler, O. (eds.) CAV 2009. LNCS, vol. 5643, pp. 682–688. Springer, Heidelberg (2009)
20. Pilecki, J., Bednarczyk, M., Jamroga, W.: Synthesis and verification of uniform strategies for multi-agent systems. In: Bulling, N., van der Torre, L., Villata, S., Jamroga, W., Vasconcelos, W. (eds.) CLIMA 2014. LNCS, vol. 8624, pp. 166–182. Springer, Heidelberg (2014)

21. Schnoor, H.: Strategic planning for probabilistic games with incomplete informa-
    tion. In: Proceedings of AAMAS 2010, pp. 1057–1064 (2010)
22. Schobbens, P.Y.: Alternating-time logic with imperfect recall. Electronic Notes in
    Theoretical Computer Science 85(2), 82–93 (2004)
23. van der Hoek, W., Jamroga, W., Wooldridge, M.: A logic for strategic reasoning.
    In: Proceedings of AAMAS 2005, pp. 157–164 (2005)
24. van der Hoek, W., Wooldridge, M.: Cooperation, knowledge and time: Alternating-
    time Temporal Epistemic Logic and its applications. Studia Logica 75(1), 125–157
    (2003)
25. van Otterloo, S., Jonker, G.: On Epistemic Temporal Strategic Logic. Electronic
    Notes in Theoretical Computer Science 126, 77–92 (2004); Proceedings of LCMAS
    2004
26. van Otterloo, S., van der Hoek, W., Wooldridge, M.: Preferences in game logics.
    In: Proceedings of AAMAS 2004, pp. 152–159 (2004)
27. Walther, D., van der Hoek, W., Wooldridge, M.: Alternating-time temporal logic
    with explicit strategies. In: Samet, D. (ed.) Proceedings TARK XI, pp. 269–278.
    Presses Universitaires de Louvain (2007)
28. Wooldridge, M.: An Introduction to Multi Agent Systems. John Wiley & Sons
    (2002)

Bounded Model Checking for Weighted Interpreted Systems and for Flat Weighted Epistemic Computation Tree Logic*

Bożena Woźna-Szcześniak[1], Ireneusz Szcześniak[2],
Agnieszka M. Zbrzezny[1], and Andrzej Zbrzezny[1]

[1] IMCS, Jan Długosz University
Al. Armii Krajowej 13/15, 42-200 Częstochowa, Poland
{b.wozna,a.zbrzezny,agnieszka.zbrzezny}@ajd.czest.pl
[2] Department of Telecommunications, AGH University of Science and Technology
al. Mickiewicza 30, 30-059 Kraków, Poland
iszczesniak@kt.agh.edu.pl

Abstract. The paper deals with the SAT- and ROBDD-based bounded model checking (BMC) methods for the existential fragment of a flat weighted epistemic computation tree logic (FWECTLK) interpreted over weighted interpreted systems. We implemented the both BMC algorithms, and compared them with each other on several benchmarks for multi-agent systems.

1 Introduction

Interpreted systems (ISs) [4] are the most widely studied models of multi-agent systems (MASs) [14], which are designed for reasoning about the agents' epistemic and temporal properties. An important restriction in these models is that there are no costs associated with agents' actions. The models become more expressive when this restriction is dropped. For example, the formalism of the *weighted interpreted systems* (WISs) [16] extends ISs to make the reasoning possible about not only temporal and epistemic properties, but also about agents' quantitative properties. In the paper we use this weighted formalism as the model of MASs.

The past ten years in the area of MASs have witnessed considerable research in verification techniques aimed at assessing automatically whether a MAS meets its intended specifications. One of the leading techniques in this area is the *symbolic model checking* [3]. Unfortunately, due to the agents' complex nature, the practical applicability of model checking is strongly restricted by the so-called "state-space explosion problem", i.e., an exponential growth of the system state space with the number of agents. To alleviate this problem, a number of techniques, including the SAT- and ROBDD-based bounded model checking

---

* Partly supported by National Science Centre under the grant No. 2011/01/B/ST6/05317.

H.K. Dam et al. (Eds.): PRIMA 2014, LNAI 8861, pp. 107–115, 2014.

(BMC) [12,7,11], have been put forward. These have been successful in allowing users to tackle larger MASs, but it is still difficult to verify MASs with many agents and cost constraints on agents' actions. The aim of this paper is to contribute to overcome this shortcoming.

To model check the requirements of MASs, various extensions of temporal logics [3] with epistemic [4], beliefs [14], and deontic (representing the distinction between ideal/correct behaviour and actual – possibly incorrect – behaviour of the agents) [9] modalities have been proposed. In this paper we aim at completing the picture of applying the ROBDD-based BMC techniques to MASs by looking at the existential fragment of a flat weighted CTLK [12] (FWECTLK) interpreted over WISs. Note that the first ROBDD-based BMC method for MAS has been proposed in [7], and it deals with ECTLK and with ISs. Then, in [10] and [11] ROBDD-based BMC methods for RTECTLK over IISs and for ELTLK over ISs, respectively, have been defined and compared to the corresponding SAT-based BMC method.

The original contributions of the paper are the following. First of all, we define and implement a ROBDD-based BMC technique for FWECTLK and for WISs. Secondly, we implement the BMC techniques for FWECTLK and for WISs that has been introduced in [15], but not implemented and experimentally evaluated. Finally, we evaluate these two BMC methods experimentally by means of the *weighted generic pipeline paradigm* [16] and the *weighted bits transmission problem* [16]. We do not compare our results with other model checkers for MASs, e.g. MCMAS [8] or MCK [5], simply because they do not support FWECTLK and WIS. Some comparison of our BMC algorithms on the LTLK subset of FWECTLK can be found in [11].

The structure of the paper is as follows. In Section 2 we recall the formalism of WISs which we will use throughout the paper. Next, we define FWECTLK, and interpret it over WISs. Finally, we introduce the fixed point characterisation of FWECTLK which we use in the ROBDD-based BMC algorithms. In Section 3 we define the ROBDD-based BMC for FWECTLK and for WIS. In Section 4 we discuss our experimental results, and finally in Section 5 we conclude the paper.

2   Preliminaries

WISs. Let $Ag = \{1, \ldots, n\}$ be a non-empty and finite set of agents, $\mathcal{E}$ a special agent that is used to model the environment in which the agents operate, and $\mathcal{PV}$ a set of propositional variables. The *weighted interpreted system* (WIS) is a tuple $(\{L_{\mathbf{c}}, \iota_{\mathbf{c}}, Act_{\mathbf{c}}, P_{\mathbf{c}}, t_{\mathbf{c}}, \mathcal{V}_{\mathbf{c}}, d_{\mathbf{c}}\}_{\mathbf{c} \in Ag \cup \{\mathcal{E}\}})$, where $L_{\mathbf{c}}$ is a non-empty set of *local states*, $\iota_{\mathbf{c}} \subseteq L_{\mathbf{c}}$ is a non-empty set of *initial states*, $Act_{\mathbf{c}}$ is a non-empty set of *possible actions*, $P_{\mathbf{c}} : L_{\mathbf{c}} \to 2^{Act_{\mathbf{c}}}$ is a *protocol function* which defines rules according to which actions may be performed in each local state, $t_{\mathbf{c}} : L_{\mathbf{c}} \times Act \to L_{\mathbf{c}}$ with $Act = \prod_{\mathbf{c} \in Ag \cup \mathcal{E}} Act_{\mathbf{c}}$ (each element of Act is called a *joint action*) is a (partial) *evolution function*, $\mathcal{V}_{\mathbf{c}} : L_{\mathbf{c}} \to 2^{\mathcal{PV}}$ is a *valuation function* which assigns to each local state a set of propositional variables that are assumed to be true at that state, and $d_{\mathbf{c}} : Act_{\mathbf{c}} \to \mathbb{N}$ is a *weight function*.

For a given WIS we define a *model* as a tuple $M = (Act, S, \iota, T, \mathcal{V}, d)$, where $Act = \prod_{\mathbf{c} \in Ag \cup \mathcal{E}} Act_{\mathbf{c}}$ is a set of joint actions, $S = \prod_{\mathbf{c} \in Ag \cup \mathcal{E}} L_{\mathbf{c}}$ is a set of all *possible global states* (let $s = (\ell_1, \dots, \ell_n, \ell_{\mathcal{E}})$ be a global state, then $l_{\mathbf{c}}(s)$ denotes the local component of agent $\mathbf{c} \in Ag \cup \{\mathcal{E}\}$ in s), $\iota = \prod_{\mathbf{c} \in Ag \cup \mathcal{E}} \iota_{\mathbf{c}}$ is the set of all possible initial global states, $\mathcal{V} : S \to 2^{\mathcal{PV}}$ is the valuation function defined as $\mathcal{V}(s) = \bigcup_{\mathbf{c} \in Ag \cup \{\mathcal{E}\}} \mathcal{V}_{\mathbf{c}}(l_{\mathbf{c}}(s))$, $d : Act \to \mathbb{N}$ is a "joint" weight function defined as follows: $d((a_1, \dots, a_n, a_{\mathcal{E}})) = \sum_{\mathbf{c} \in Ag \cup \{\mathcal{E}\}} d_{\mathbf{c}}(a_{\mathbf{c}})$, $T \subseteq S \times Act \times S$ is a transition relation defined as follows: $(s, a, s') \in T$ (or $s \xrightarrow{a} s'$) iff $t_{\mathbf{c}}(l_{\mathbf{c}}(s), a) = l_{\mathbf{c}}(s')$ for all $\mathbf{c} \in Ag \cup \{\mathcal{E}\}$; we assume that the relation T is total, i.e. for any $s \in S$ there exists $s' \in S$ and a non-empty joint action $a \in Act$ such that $s \xrightarrow{a} s'$.

Given a WIS one can define the indistinguishability relation $\sim_{\mathbf{c}} \subseteq S \times S$ for agent $\mathbf{c}$ as follows: $s \sim_{\mathbf{c}} s'$ iff $l_{\mathbf{c}}(s') = l_{\mathbf{c}}(s)$. Moreover, a *path* in M is an infinite sequence $\pi = s_0 \xrightarrow{a_1} s_1 \xrightarrow{a_2} s_2 \xrightarrow{a_3} \dots$ of transitions. For such a path and $m \in \mathbb{N}$, by $\pi(m)$ we denote the m-th state s_m. Next, by $\pi[j..m]$ we denote the finite sequence $s_j \xrightarrow{a_{j+1}} s_{j+1} \xrightarrow{a_{j+2}} \dots s_m$ with $m - j$ transitions and $m - j + 1$ states, and by $D\pi[j..m]$ we denote the (cumulative) weight of $\pi[j..m]$ that is defined as $d(a_{j+1}) + \dots + d(a_m)$ (hence 0 when $j = m$). By $\Pi(s)$ we denote the set of all the paths starting at $s \in S$, and $\Pi = \bigcup_{s^0 \in \iota} \Pi(s^0)$.

FWECTLK. Our specification language is the existential fragment of a flat weighted CTLK (FWECTLK) which extends ECTLK [12] with cost constraints on *non-nested* temporal modalities. FWECTLK is a subset of WECTLK [15] (i.e., the weighted ECTLK with cost constraints on *all* temporal modalities) for which the SAT-based BMC has been defined. In the syntax of FWECTLK we assume the following: $p \in \mathcal{PV}$ is an atomic proposition, $\mathbf{c} \in Ag$, $\Gamma \subseteq Ag$, I is an interval in $\mathbb{N} = \{0, 1, 2, \dots\}$ of the form: $[a, \infty)$ and $[a, b)$, for $a, b \in \mathbb{N}$ and $a \neq b$. The FWECTLK formulae are defined by the following grammar:

$$\varphi ::= \mathbf{true} \mid \mathbf{false} \mid p \mid \neg p \mid \varphi \wedge \varphi \mid \varphi \vee \varphi \mid EX\varphi \mid E(\varphi U \varphi) \mid EG\varphi \mid \overline{K}_{\mathbf{c}}\varphi \mid \overline{E}_{\Gamma}\varphi \mid \overline{D}_{\Gamma}\varphi \mid \overline{C}_{\Gamma}\varphi$$
$$\psi ::= \varphi \mid EX_I\varphi \mid E(\varphi U_I\varphi) \mid EG_I\varphi \mid \overline{K}_{\mathbf{c}}\psi \mid \overline{E}_{\Gamma}\psi \mid \overline{D}_{\Gamma}\psi \mid \overline{C}_{\Gamma}\psi$$

E (for some path) is the path quantifier. X (neXt time), U (until), and G (always) are the standard temporal modalities. X_I (weighted neXt time), U_I (weighted until), and G_I (weighted always) are the weighted temporal modalities. The modality $\overline{K}_{\mathbf{c}}$ is dual to $K_{\mathbf{c}}$ (agent $\mathbf{c}$ knows), so $\overline{K}_{\mathbf{c}}$ is read as "agent $\mathbf{c}$ does not know whether or not". The modalities $\overline{D}_{\Gamma}$, $\overline{E}_{\Gamma}$, and $\overline{C}_{\Gamma}$ are the dualities to the standard group epistemic modalities representing distributed knowledge in the group Γ, everyone in Γ knows, and common knowledge among agents in Γ.

In the semantics we assume the following definitions of epistemic relations: $\sim_{\Gamma}^{E} \overset{def}{=} \bigcup_{\mathbf{c} \in \Gamma} \sim_{\mathbf{c}}$, $\sim_{\Gamma}^{C} \overset{def}{=} (\sim_{\Gamma}^{E})^{+}$ (the transitive closure of $\sim_{\Gamma}^{E}$), $\sim_{\Gamma}^{D} \overset{def}{=} \bigcap_{\mathbf{c} \in \Gamma} \sim_{\mathbf{c}}$, where $\Gamma \subseteq Ag$. A FWECTLK formula φ is *true* in the model M (in symbols $M \models \varphi$) iff $M, s^0 \models \varphi$ for some $s^0 \in \iota$ (i.e. φ is true at some initial states of the model M). For every $s \in S$, the relation $\models$ is defined inductively with the classical rules for the ECTL fragment of FWECTLK, and with the following rules for epistemic and weighted temporal modalities:

$M, s \models \mathrm{EX}_I \alpha$ iff $(\exists \pi \in \Pi(s))(D\pi[0..1] \in I$ and $M, \pi(1) \models \alpha)$,

$M, s \models \mathrm{EG}_I \alpha$ iff $(\exists \pi \in \Pi(s))(\forall i \geq 0)(D\pi[0..i] \in I$ implies $M, \pi(i) \models \alpha)$,

$M, s \models \mathrm{E}(\alpha \mathrm{U}_I \beta)$ iff $(\exists \pi \in \Pi(s))(\exists i \geq 0)(D\pi[0..i] \in I$ and $M, \pi(i) \models \beta$

                   and $(\forall j < i)M, \pi(j) \models \alpha)$,

$M, s \models \overline{\mathrm{K}}_{\mathbf{c}} \alpha$ iff $(\exists \pi \in \Pi)\ (\exists i \geq 0)(s \sim_{\mathbf{c}} \pi(i)$ and $M, \pi(i) \models \alpha)$,

$M, s \models \overline{\mathrm{Y}} \alpha$ iff $(\exists \pi \in \Pi)(\exists i \geq 0)(s \sim \pi(i)$ and $M, \pi(i) \models \alpha)$,

              where $\overline{\mathrm{Y}} \in \{\overline{\mathrm{D}}_\Gamma, \overline{\mathrm{E}}_\Gamma, \overline{\mathrm{C}}_\Gamma\}$ and $\sim \in \{\sim_\Gamma^D, \sim_\Gamma^E, \sim_\Gamma^C\}$.

The *model checking problem* asks whether $M \models \varphi$.

Note that the formulae for the "eventually", and "weighted eventually" are defined as standard: $\mathrm{EF}\varphi \overset{df}{=} \mathrm{E}(\mathbf{true}\mathrm{U}\varphi)$, and $\mathrm{EF}_I\varphi \overset{df}{=} \mathrm{E}(\mathbf{true}\mathrm{U}_I\varphi)$.

Fixed Point Characterisation of FWECTLK. Let W be a finite set and $\tau : 2^W \to 2^W$ a *monotone* function, i.e. $X \subseteq Y$ implies $\tau(X) \subseteq \tau(Y)$ for all $X, Y \subseteq W$. The set $X \subseteq W$ is a *fixed point* of τ if $\tau(X) = X$. One can prove that if τ is monotone, then there exist the least fixed point of τ (denoted by $\mu X.\tau(X)$) and the greatest fixed point of τ (denoted by $\nu X.\tau(X)$).

Let $[\![M, \varphi]\!]$ (or $[\![\varphi]\!]$, if M is implicitly understood) be the set of all the reachable states of the model M at which φ holds, $S_R \subseteq S$ denote the set of all the reachable states of M, $pre_\exists(X)$ be a set of all the reachable states from which a transition to some state in a finite set $X \subseteq S_R$ is possible, and $pre_\sim(\mathbf{c}, X)$ be a set of all the reachable states that are epistemically equivalent with respect to agent $\mathbf{c}$ to some state in a finite set $X \subseteq S_R$, and $In(I)$ be a set of all the reachable states with the value of the cumulative weight that belongs to the interval I. Furthermore, let $\alpha,\ \beta$ be some FWECTLK formulae. We define the following sets: $[\![\mathbf{true}]\!] \overset{df}{=} S_R$, $[\![\mathbf{false}]\!] \overset{df}{=} \emptyset$, $[\![p]\!] \overset{df}{=} \{s \in S_R \mid p \in \mathcal{V}(s)\}$, $[\![\neg p]\!] \overset{df}{=} S_R \setminus [\![p]\!]$, $[\![\alpha \wedge \beta]\!] \overset{df}{=} [\![\alpha]\!] \cap [\![\beta]\!]$, $[\![\alpha \vee \beta]\!] \overset{df}{=} [\![\alpha]\!] \cup [\![\beta]\!]$, $[\![\mathrm{EX}\alpha]\!] \overset{df}{=} pre_\exists([\![\alpha]\!])$, $[\![\mathrm{EX}_I\alpha]\!] \overset{df}{=} pre_\exists([\![\alpha]\!]) \cap In(I)$, $[\![\mathrm{EG}\alpha]\!] \overset{df}{=} \nu X.[\![\alpha]\!] \cap pre_\exists(X)$, $[\![\mathrm{EG}_I\alpha]\!] \overset{df}{=} \nu X.(S_R \setminus In(I) \cup [\![\alpha]\!]) \cap pre_\exists(X)$, $[\![\mathrm{E}(\alpha\mathrm{U}\beta)]\!] \overset{df}{=} \mu X.[\![\beta]\!] \cup ([\![\alpha]\!] \cap pre_\exists(X))$, $[\![\mathrm{E}(\alpha\mathrm{U}_I\beta)]\!] \overset{df}{=} \mu X.(In(I) \cap [\![\beta]\!]) \cup ([\![\alpha]\!] \cap pre_\exists(X))$, $[\![\overline{\mathrm{K}}_{\mathbf{c}}\alpha]\!] \overset{df}{=} pre_\sim(\mathbf{c}, [\![\alpha]\!])$, $[\![\overline{\mathrm{E}}_\Gamma\alpha]\!] \overset{df}{=} \bigcup_{\mathbf{c} \in \Gamma} pre_\sim(\mathbf{c}, [\![\alpha]\!])$, $[\![\overline{\mathrm{D}}_\Gamma\alpha]\!] \overset{df}{=} \bigcap_{\mathbf{c} \in \Gamma} pre_\sim(\mathbf{c}, [\![\alpha]\!])$, $[\![\overline{\mathrm{C}}_\Gamma\alpha]\!] \overset{df}{=} \nu X.[\![\overline{\mathrm{E}}_\Gamma(\alpha \wedge X)]\!]$. How to compute the above sets by means of ROBDDs we will show in the next section.

3   ROBDD-Based Bounded Model Checking

Algorithm 1 of [7] defines the ROBDD-based BMC for a temporal property. It stops either if some witness for the verified FWECTLK formula is discovered, or a fixed point in the construction of the state space is detected. The set R denotes the set of reachable states, and initially it is equal to the set ι. The set R_p is an auxiliary set of reachable states, and initially it is empty. The algorithm operates on submodels of the model M. For $R \subseteq S$ such that $\iota \subseteq R$ the submodel M_R is a tuple $(Act, R, \iota, T_R, \mathcal{V}_R, d)$ with $T_R = T \cap R^2$, and $\mathcal{V}_R : R \to 2^{\mathcal{PV}}$ defined by $\mathcal{V}_R(s) = \mathcal{V}(s)$ for all $s \in R$. Furthermore, $R_\rightsquigarrow$ defines the set of successors of all the states in $R \subseteq S_R$. The complete set of reachable states S_R is obtained by computing the least fixed point $\mu R.\iota \cup R \cup R_\leadsto$. Thus, in each iteration (except the last one) the set R is extended with $R_\leadsto$.

Sets of the reachable states satisfying FWECTLK formulae are computed by Algorithm 2 that takes a FWECTLK formula φ as input. It has access to all the relevant parts of the model M, and it returns the set of states satisfying the formula φ. For this it calls Algorithms 3, 4, 5, respectively, if EG, EG_I, EU, EU_I, or $\overline{C}_\Gamma$ is the root of the input's parse tree. The correctness of Algorithm 2 for the ECTLK part follows from the results for CTL described, e.g. in [6] and from the results for CTLK described in [13]. The correctness of $[\![ ]\!]_{EG_I}$ and $[\![ ]\!]_{EU_I}$ can be proven in a similar way as Theorems 3.19 and 3.20 of [6].

Algorithm 1. BMC(φ: FWECTLK formula, $M = (Act, S, \iota, T, \mathcal{V}, d)$: model)

1. $R := \iota$; $R_p := \emptyset$;
2. **while** $R \neq R_p$ **do**
3.   **if** $\iota \subseteq [\![M_R, \varphi]\!]$ **then**
4.   **return true**; {Witness to WECTLK formula found}
5.   **end if**
6. $R_p := R$; $R := R \cup R_\leadsto$;
7. **end while**
8. **return false**; {Fixed point reached}

Algorithm 2. The algorithm $[\![ ]\!]$

case

φ is **true**: return R; φ is **false**: return $\emptyset$;

$\varphi \in \mathcal{PV}$: return $\mathcal{V}|_R(\varphi)$; φ is $\neg p$ and $p \in \mathcal{PV}$: return $S|_R \setminus [\![M_R, \alpha]\!]$;

φ is $\alpha \vee \beta$: return $[\![M_R, \alpha]\!] \cup [\![M_R, \beta]\!]$; φ is $\alpha \wedge \beta$: return $[\![M_R, \alpha]\!] \cap [\![M_R, \beta]\!]$;

φ is $\mathrm{EX}\alpha$: return $pre_\exists([\![M_R, \alpha]\!])$; φ is $\mathrm{EX}_I\alpha$: return $pre_\exists([\![M_R, \alpha]\!]) \cap In(I)$;

φ is $\mathrm{EG}\alpha$: return $[\![M_R, \mathrm{EG}\alpha]\!]_{EG}$; φ is $\mathrm{EG}_I\alpha$: return $[\![M_R, \mathrm{EG}_I\alpha]\!]_{EG_I}$;

φ is $\mathrm{E}(\alpha\mathrm{U}\beta)$: return $[\![M_R, \mathrm{E}(\alpha\mathrm{U}\beta)]\!]_{EU}$; φ is $\mathrm{E}(\alpha\mathrm{U}_I\beta)$: return $[\![M_R, \mathrm{E}(\alpha\mathrm{U}_I\beta)]\!]_{EU_I}$;

φ is $\overline{K}_c\alpha$: return $pre_\sim(\mathbf{c}, [\![M_R, \alpha]\!])$; φ is $\overline{E}_\Gamma\alpha$: return $\bigcup_{c \in \Gamma} pre_\sim(\mathbf{c}, [\![M_R, \alpha]\!])$;

φ is $\overline{D}_\Gamma\alpha$: return $\bigcap_{c \in \Gamma} pre_\sim(\mathbf{c}, [\![M_R, \alpha]\!])$; φ is $\overline{C}_\Gamma\alpha$: return $[\![M_R, \overline{C}_\Gamma\alpha]\!]_{\overline{C}}$;

end case

Algorithm 3. Computing $[\![M_R, \mathrm{EG}\alpha]\!]_{EG}$ and $[\![M_R, \mathrm{EG}_I\alpha]\!]_{EG_I}$

1. $Y := [\![M_R, \alpha]\!]$; $X := \emptyset$;	1. $Y := R \setminus In(I) \cup [\![M_R, \alpha]\!]$; $X := \emptyset$;
2. **while** $X \neq Y$ **do**	2. **while** $X \neq Y$ **do**
3. $X := Y$; $Y := Y \cap pre_\exists(Y)$;	3. $X := Y$; $Y := Y \cap pre_\exists(Y)$;
4. **end while**	4. **end while**
5. **return** Y	5. **return** Y

Algorithm 4. Computing $[\![M_R, \mathrm{E}(\alpha\mathrm{U}\beta)]\!]_{EU}$ and $[\![M_R, \mathrm{E}(\alpha\mathrm{U}_I\beta)]\!]_{EU_I}$

1. $W := [\![M_R, \alpha]\!]$; $X := \emptyset$;	1. $W := [\![M_R, \alpha]\!]$; $X := \emptyset$;
2. $Y := [\![M_R, \beta]\!]$;	2. $Y := [\![M_R, \beta]\!] \cap In(I)$;
3. **while** $X \neq Y$ **do**	3. **while** $X \neq Y$ **do**
4. $X := Y$; $Y := Y \cup (W \cap$	4. $X := Y$; $Y := Y \cup (W \cap$
$pre_\exists(Y))$;	$pre_\exists(Y))$;
5. **end while**	5. **end while**
6. **return** Y	6. **return** Y

Algorithm 5. Computing $[\![M_R, \overline{C}_\Gamma \alpha]\!]_{\overline{C}}$.

1. $Y := [\![M_R, \alpha]\!]$; $X := \emptyset$;
2. **while** $X \neq Y$ **do**
3. $X := Y$; $Y := \bigcup_{\mathbf{c} \in \Gamma} pre_\sim(\mathbf{c}, X)$;
4. **end while**
5. **return** Y

4   Experimental Results

We consider two scalable scenarios, which we use to evaluate the performance of our ROBDD-based BMC algorithm and SAT-based BMC [15] for the verification of several properties expressed in WECTLK and FWECTLK, respectively.

The first benchmark is the *weighted generic pipeline paradigm* (WGPP) WIS model [16]. Let Min denote the minimum cost incurred by Consumer to receive the data produced by Producer, and p denote the cost of producing data by Producer. We have tested WGPP with the local weight functions as in [16] and when they were multiplied by 10^3 and 10^6 on the following specifications:

$\varphi_1 = \overline{\mathrm{K}}_P\mathrm{EF}_{[Min,Min+1)}CReady$ - it expresses that it is not true that Producer knows that always the cost incurred by Consumer to receive data is Min.

$\varphi_2 = \overline{\mathrm{K}}_P\mathrm{EF}(PSend \wedge \overline{\mathrm{K}}_C\overline{\mathrm{K}}_P\mathrm{EG}_{[0,Min-p)}CReady)$ - it states that it is not true that Producer knows that always if it produces data, then Consumer knows that Producer knows that Consumer has received data and the cost is less than $Min - p$. Let us note that this formula belongs to the WECTLK language, but not to the FWECTLK language.

The number of the considered k-paths is equal to 2 for φ_1 and 4 for φ_2, respectively. The length of the counterexample for φ_1 and for both BMC methods ranges from $k = 4$ for one node to $k = 23$ for 125 nodes, while for φ_2 ranges from $k = 3$ for one node to $k = 10$ for 25 nodes.

The second benchmark of our interest is the *weighted bits transmission problem* (WBTP) WIS model [16]. This system is scaled according to the number of bits the $\mathcal{S}$ wants to communicate to $\mathcal{R}$. We have tested the WBTP on the following specifications. Let $a \in \mathbb{N}$ and $b \in \mathbb{N}$ be the costs of sending, respectively, bits by Sender and an acknowledgement by Receiver. Then,

$\phi_1 = \mathrm{EF}_{[a+b,a+b+1)}(\mathbf{recack} \wedge \overline{\mathrm{K}}_\mathcal{S}(\overline{\mathrm{K}}_\mathcal{R}(\bigwedge_{i=0}^{2^n-2}(\neg \mathbf{i}))))$, i.e. it is not true that if an ack is received by $\mathcal{S}$, then $\mathcal{S}$ knows that $\mathcal{R}$ knows at least one value of the n-bit numbers except the maximal value, and the cost is $a + b$.

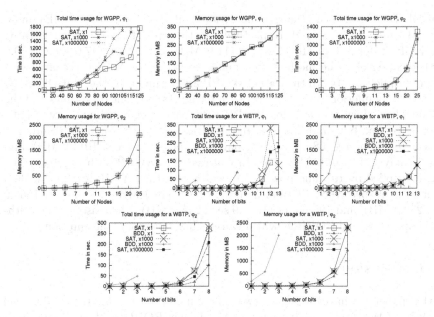

Fig. 1. SAT-based BMC: WGPP with n nodes. SAT- and ROBDD-based BMC: WBTP with n bits integer value.

$\phi_2 = \mathrm{EF}_{[a+b,a+b+1)}(\overline{\mathrm{K}}_{\mathcal{S}}(\bigwedge_{i=0}^{2^n-1}(\overline{\mathrm{K}}_{\mathcal{R}}(\neg \mathbf{i}))))$, i.e. it is not true that $\mathcal{S}$ knows that $\mathcal{R}$ knows the value of the n-bit number and the cost is $a + b$.

The number of the considered k-paths is equal to 3 for ϕ_1 and $2^n + 2$ for ϕ_2, respectively. The length of the counterexamples for both formulae and both methods is equal to 2 for any $n > 0$.

Performance Evaluation. For the tests we have used a computer with I7-3770 processor, 32 GB of RAM, and running Arch Linux with the kernel 3.15.5. We set the CPU time limit to 1800 seconds. Moreover, we used PicoSAT [1] in version 959 to test the satisfiability of the propositional formulae generated by our SAT-based BMC (SAT-BMC) encoding, and we used the CUDD library in version 2.5.0 (http://vlsi.colorado.edu/~fabio/CUDD/) for the manipulation of ROBDDs.

In the case of SAT-BMC, the experimental results show that when we scale up the weights for both benchmarks and for all properties, the computation time and the memory usage grows linearly, regardless of the considered number of nodes or n-bit integer value (see Fig. 1). The sensitivity to growing weights follows from the encoding of the cumulative weight. Namely, the number of bits that is required to encode the cumulative weight depends on the number of agents, on the bound k, and the maximal weight appearing in the system.

As one can see from the line charts in Fig. 1, for the ROBDD-based BMC (ROBDD-BMC) method the impact of the growing weights on the performance of the method is even more marked. Namely, in the time limit set and for the WBTP scenario with basic weights (b.w.) and with b.w. multiplied by 10^3, our

ROBDD-BMC can verify the formula ϕ_1 for 8 bits (86.4 sec.; 1395.1 MB) and 3 bits (43.0 sec.; 20008.5 MB), respectively. In the case of ϕ_2 our ROBDD-BMC can verify it for 8 bits (100.0 sec.; 1411.9 MB) and 3 bits (47.6 sec.; 2009.0 MB), respectively. The method was unable to verify the WBTP scenario with b.w. multiplied by 10^6. In the case of WGPP and formula φ_1, the ROBDD-BMC is remarkably inferior to the SAT-BMC in terms of the verification times and the consumed memory. Namely, for WGPP with basic weights (b.w.), b.w. multiplied by 10, and b.w. multiplied by 100, ROBDD-BMC can calculate results for, respectively, 4 nodes (68.2 sec.; 2746.6MB), 2 nodes (23.9sec.; 1011.9 MB), and 1 node only (44.0sec.;1384.9 MB). In contrast, for WGPP with basic weights, b.w. multiplied by 10^3, and b.w. multiplied by 10^6, the SAT-BMC can calculate results for, respectively, 125 nodes (1768.8 sec.; 344.4 MB), 115 nodes (1656.0 sec.; 284.5 MB), and 105 nodes (1699.9 sec.; 245.0 MB). The reason is the arithmetic operations on ROBBDs which cause a huge memory consumption.

5   Conclusions

In this paper we have presented two different approaches for bounded model checking of WISs: via a reduction to SAT and via ROBDDs. The two methods have been tested and compared with each other on two scalable benchmarks. The experimental results revealed that for the WIS the SAT-based BMC significantly outperforms the ROBDD-based BMC. Therefore, in our future work we are going to define the SMT-based BMC encoding for WISs and for WECTLK, and compare this encoding with the SAT-based encoding.

References

1. Biere, A.: PicoSAT essentials. Journal on Satisfiability, Boolean Modeling and Computation 4, 75–97 (2008)
2. Bryant, R.: Graph-based algorithms for boolean function manipulation. IEEE Transaction on Computers 35(8), 677–691 (1986)
3. Clarke, E.M., Grumberg, O., Peled, D.A.: Model Checking. The MIT Press (1999)
4. Fagin, R., Halpern, J.Y., Moses, Y., Vardi, M.Y.: Reasoning about Knowledge. MIT Press (1995)
5. Gammie, P., van der Meyden, R.: MCK: Model checking the logic of knowledge. In: Alur, R., Peled, D.A. (eds.) CAV 2004. LNCS, vol. 3114, pp. 479–483. Springer, Heidelberg (2004)
6. Huth, M.R.A., Ryan, M.D.: Logic in Computer Science: Modelling and Reasoning about Systems. Cambridge University Press (2000)
7. Jones, A.V., Lomuscio, A.: Distributed BDD-based BMC for the verification of multi-agent systems. In: Proc. of AAMAS 2010, pp. 675–682. IFAAMAS (2010)
8. Lomuscio, A., Qu, H., Raimondi, F.: MCMAS: A model checker for the verification of multi-agent systems. In: Bouajjani, A., Maler, O. (eds.) CAV 2009. LNCS, vol. 5643, pp. 682–688. Springer, Heidelberg (2009)
9. Lomuscio, A., Sergot, M.: Deontic interpreted systems. Studia Logica 75(1), 63–92 (2003)

10. Męski, A., Woźna-Szcześniak, B., Zbrzezny, A.M., Zbrzezny, A.: Two approaches to bounded model checking for a soft real-time epistemic computation tree logic. In: Omatu, S., Neves, J., Rodriguez, J.M.C., Paz Santana, J.F., Gonzalez, S.R. (eds.) Distrib. Computing & Artificial Intelligence. AISC, vol. 217, pp. 483–491. Springer, Heidelberg (2013)
11. Męski, A., Penczek, W., Szreter, M., Woźna-Szcześniak, B., Zbrzezny, A.: BDD-versus SAT-based bounded model checking for the existential fragment of linear temporal logic with knowledge: algorithms and their performance. Autonomous Agents and Multi-Agent Systems 28(4), 558–604 (2014)
12. Penczek, W., Lomuscio, A.: Verifying epistemic properties of multi-agent systems via bounded model checking. Fundamenta Informaticae 55(2), 167–185 (2003)
13. Raimondi, F.: Model Checking Multi-Agent Systems. PhD thesis, UCL (2006)
14. Wooldridge, M.: An introduction to multi-agent systems, 2nd edn. John Wiley & Sons (2009)
15. Woźna-Szcześniak, B.: SAT-based bounded model checking for weighted deontic interpreted systems. In: Correia, L., Reis, L.P., Cascalho, J. (eds.) EPIA 2013. LNCS, vol. 8154, pp. 444–455. Springer, Heidelberg (2013)
16. Woźna-Szcześniak, B., Zbrzezny, A.M., Zbrzezny, A.: SAT-based bounded model checking for weighted interpreted systems and weighted linear temporal logic. In: Boella, G., Elkind, E., Savarimuthu, B.T.R., Dignum, F., Purvis, M.K. (eds.) PRIMA 2013. LNCS, vol. 8291, pp. 355–371. Springer, Heidelberg (2013)

Assumption-Based Argumentation Equipped with Preferences

Toshiko Wakaki

Shibaura Institute of Technology
307 Fukasaku, Minuma-ku, Saitama-city, Saitama, 337–8570 Japan
twakaki@sic.shibaura-it.ac.jp

Abstract. The existing approaches which map the given explicit preferences into standard assumption-based argumentation frameworks (ABAs) reveal some difficulties such as generating a huge number of rules and so on. To overcome them, we present an assumption-based argumentation framework equipped with preferences (p_ABA). It increases the expressive power of ABA by incorporating preferences between sentences into the framework. The semantics of p_ABAs is given by $\mathcal{P}$ extensions selected from extensions of ABAs based on the given sentence ordering. The advantages of our approach are that not only it enables us to express different kinds of preferences such as preferences over rules, over goals, over decisions by means of sentence orderings in p_ABAs but we also successfully obtain solutions from $\mathcal{P}$ extensions of the p_ABAs expressing the respective knowledge for various applications such as epistemic reasoning, practical reasoning, decision-making with preferences and so on in a uniform way without suffering from difficulties of existing ones.

1 Introduction

Assumption-Based Argumentation (ABA) [6,12] as well as Abstract Argumentation (AA) [11] are general-purpose argumentation frameworks. One of the essential differences between them is that arguments of ABAs are structured, while those of AA are not structured but abstract. Besides, as for preferences which are often required to resolve conflicts between arguments, neither of these two approaches have the mechanism to deal with explicit preferences.

Hence in order to enable Dung's AAs to deal with explicit preferences, several approaches such as Amgoud *et al.*'s preference-based argumentation framework (PAF) [1,2], Bench-Capon's value-based argumentation framework (VAF) [3] and Modgil's extended argumentation framework (EAF) [16] have been proposed to incorporate preferences into AA. In PAF (resp. VAF), for example, preferences are expressed by the ordering of arguments (resp. values).

On the other hand, in regards to ABAs, a considerable number of studies [27,17,26] to treat preferences have been done for applications such as epistemic and practical reasoning with preferences, decision-making with preferences and so on. In [26], for example, for reasoning beliefs, goals, decisions with preferences, the epistemic (resp. practical, decision) frameworks with preferences are defined, and then such pre-defined frameworks are mapped into the respective ABAs from

H.K. Dam et al. (Eds.): PRIMA 2014, LNAI 8861, pp. 116–132, 2014.

which solutions are obtained. That is, the given explicit preferences are treated in those mappings from such frameworks to the respective ABAs. However there exist difficulties in such mapping approaches. For example, a huge number of rules and assumptions are generated in the the most-preferred ABA mapped from a tiny decision-making framework with preferences (*edf*) [17]. Moreover as to practical reasoning, Toni *et al.* showed nothing about how to solve the famous *punishment example with preferences* [4] based on ABA and left it as future work though they [18,27] represented the knowledge of the problem excluding preferences over goals in the framework of ABA as far as we know.

Thus the motivation and aim of this study is to overcome such difficulties of the existing approaches. As stated in [28], they adopted such mappings to standard ABAs for the given explicit preferences since ABAs have a mechanism to deal with implicit preferences. Indeed, in the field of nonmonotonic reasoning and logic programming, it is well-known that preference knowledge can be implicitly encoded in default rules of Reiter's default theory as well as logic programs based on answer set semantics [20]. However, for example, the logic programming languages provide a rather weak mechanism for specifying priorities in a program (see [24]), and hence in the literature [10], numerous approaches for logic programs with explicit preferences have been proposed so far. Thus our basic idea to overcome difficulties addressed above is to extend ABA to incorporate explicit preferences in the framework. Thereby we propose an assumption-based argumentation framework equipped with preferences (p_ABA, for short), which contains explicit preferences over sentences. We provide a method to lift preferences over sentences to preferences over arguments. Accordingly we can freely give any semantics to the proposed p_ABA based on either the argument ordering or the sentence ordering. In this paper, as an approach to achieve our aim, the semantics of p_ABAs is given by $\mathcal{P}$-argument extensions along with $\mathcal{P}$-assumption extensions, which are selected from extensions of the associated argumentation frameworks by making use of such preferences.

The advantages of our approach are that first, it successfully overcomes difficulties of the existing approaches [17,18,27]. That is, compared with them, "good" decisions are easily obtained from $\mathcal{P}$ extensions of the p_ABA which has far less rules, contraries and assumptions than theirs by expressing the knowledge of the *edf* faithfully. In addition, for the well-known punishment example [4] as to practical reasoning, our approach provides a solution based on the p_ABA expressing the problem with preferences faithfully. Second, by expressing different kinds of preferences such as preferences over rules, over goals, or over decisions by means of sentence orderings in p_ABAs, we can obtain solutions from $\mathcal{P}$ extensions for various applications such as epistemic and practical reasoning with preferences, decision-making with preferences in a uniform and domain-independent way. Third, though in [31,30], the underlying languages are restricted to PLPs [24] to build the non-abstract PAFs, p_ABAs along with ABAs do not have such a restriction for the languages. Nonetheless fourth, p_ABAs instantiated with PLPs capture the semantics of the PLPs under the stable semantics, denoting the generalization of Dung's result [11, Theorem 49].

This paper is organized as follows. Section 2 gives preliminaries. Section 3 presents an ABA framework equipped with preferences, its applications to decision-making, practical reasoning and epistemic reasoning with preferences along with some complexity results. Section 4 discusses related work, while Section 5 concludes this paper.

2   Background: Assumption-Based Argumentation, Prioritized Logic Programming

Definition 1 ([12,17]). *An ABA framework is a tuple $\langle \mathcal{L}, \mathcal{R}, \mathcal{A}, \mathcal{C} \rangle$ where*

- $(\mathcal{L}, \mathcal{R})$ *is a deductive system, with $\mathcal{L}$ a* language *consisting of countably many sentences and $\mathcal{R}$ a set of inference rules of the form $b_0 \leftarrow b_1, \ldots, b_m (m \geq 0)$.*
- $\mathcal{A} \subseteq \mathcal{L}$, *is a (non-empty) set, referred to as* assumptions.
- $\mathcal{C}$ *is a total mapping from $\mathcal{A}$ into $2^{\mathcal{L}}$, where $\mathcal{C}(\alpha)$ is referred to as the* contrary *of $\alpha \in \mathcal{A}$.*

When presenting an ABA framework, we often omit presenting $\mathcal{L}$ explicitly as we assume $\mathcal{L}$ contains all sentences appearing in $\mathcal{R}$, $\mathcal{A}$ and $\mathcal{C}$. Given a rule r of the form: $b_0 \leftarrow b_1, \ldots, b_m$, we use the following notation: $head(r) = b_0$ and $body(r) = \{b_1, \ldots, b_m\}$. We often write $b_0 \leftarrow body(r)$ instead of $b_0 \leftarrow b_1, \ldots, b_m$. As in [12], we enforce that ABA frameworks are *flat*, namely assumptions do not occur in the head of rules.

In ABA, *arguments* are deduction of claims using rules and supported by assumptions, and *attacks* are directed at assumptions as follows:

Definition 2 ([12]). *Given an ABA framework $\langle \mathcal{L}, \mathcal{R}, \mathcal{A}, \mathcal{C} \rangle$,*

- *an argument for (the claim) $c \in \mathcal{L}$ supported by $K \subseteq \mathcal{A}$ ($K \vdash c$ in short) is a (finite) tree with nodes labelled by sentences in $\mathcal{L}$ or by τ standing for the empty body of rules, the root labelled by c, leaves either τ or assumptions in K, and non-leaves b with, as children, the elements of the body of some rule with head b. Note that this definition of argument allows for one-node arguments. These arguments consist solely of a single assumption, say $\alpha \in \mathcal{A}$, and they are denoted by $\{\alpha\} \vdash \alpha$.*
- *an argument $K_1 \vdash c_1$ attacks an argument $K_2 \vdash c_2$ iff $c_1 \in \mathcal{C}(\alpha)$ for $\alpha \in K_2$.*

Definition 3 ([12]). *Let $\mathcal{F} = \langle \mathcal{L}, \mathcal{R}, \mathcal{A}, \mathcal{C} \rangle$ be an ABA framework. Then, the abstract argumentation framework $AF_{\mathcal{F}}$ corresponding to $\mathcal{F}$ is $AF_{\mathcal{F}} = (AR, attacks)$ such that*

- *each argument $A \in AR$ has the form: $K \vdash c$ as defined in Definition 2.*
- $(A, B) \in attacks$ *if and only if an argument A attacks an argument B.*

The various abstract argumentation semantics are defined in the context of an ABA framework [12,9]. We focus on the admissibility semantics. For a set $\mathcal{A}rgs$ of arguments, let $\mathcal{A}rgs^+$ be $\{A \mid$ there exists an argument in $\mathcal{A}rgs$ that attacks $A\}$. Then $\mathcal{A}rgs$ is *conflict-free* iff $\mathcal{A}rgs \cap \mathcal{A}rgs^+ = \emptyset$. $\mathcal{A}rgs$ *defends* an argument A iff each argument that attacks A is attacked by an argument in $\mathcal{A}rgs$ [9].

Definition 4 ([11,12,9]). Let $\langle \mathcal{L}, \mathcal{R}, \mathcal{A}, \mathcal{C} \rangle$ be an ABA framework, and AR be the associated set of arguments. Then $\mathcal{A}rgs \subseteq AR$ is:

- a complete argument extension iff $\mathcal{A}rgs$ is conflict-free and $\mathcal{A}rgs = \{A \in AR \mid \mathcal{A}rgs \text{ defends } A\}$.
- a preferred (resp. grounded) argument extension iff it is a (subset) maximal (resp. minimal) complete argument extension.
- a stable argument extension iff it is conflict-free and attacks any argument in $AR \setminus \mathcal{A}rgs$.

Originally the various ABA semantics [12] are described in terms of sets of assumptions. A set $\mathcal{A}sms$ of assumptions is said to attack an assumption α iff $\mathcal{A}sms$ enables the construction of an argument for the claim belonging to $\mathcal{C}(\alpha)$. Then assumption extensions are similarly defined like argument extensions [11,9]. Caminada *et al.* [9] showed that there is a one-to-one correspondence between assumption extensions and argument extensions under many of admissibility-based semantics as follows.

Theorem 1. ([9, Theorem 6]). [1] *Let* $\langle \mathcal{L}, \mathcal{R}, \mathcal{A}, \mathcal{C} \rangle$ *be an ABA framework, AR be the set of all arguments that can be constructed using this ABA framework and $Sname \in \{complete, preferred, grounded, stable\}$. Then*

- *if $\mathcal{A}sms \subseteq \mathcal{A}$ is a Sname assumption extension, then* `Asms2Args`$(\mathcal{A}sms)$ *is a Sname argument extension, and*
- *if $\mathcal{A}rgs \subseteq AR$ is a Sname argument extension, then* `Args2Asms`$(\mathcal{A}rgs)$ *is a Sname assumption extension,*

where `Asms2Args`$: 2^{\mathcal{A}} \to 2^{AR}$ *and* `Args2Asms`$: 2^{AR} \to 2^{\mathcal{A}}$ *are functions such that*
`Asms2Args`$(\mathcal{A}sms) = \{K \vdash c \in AR \mid K \subseteq \mathcal{A}sms\}$
`Args2Asms`$(\mathcal{A}rgs) = \{\alpha \in \mathcal{A} \mid \alpha \in K \text{ for some } K \vdash c \in \mathcal{A}rgs\}$.

For notational convenience, let $claim(Ag)$ stand for the claim c of an argument Ag such that $K \vdash c$. For a set E of arguments, $claims(E)$ is defined as follows:
$$claims(E) = \{c \mid K \vdash c \in E\}.$$

Definition 5 ([20,19]). An extended logic program (ELP) is a set of rules of the form: $L \leftarrow L_1, \ldots, L_m, not\ L_{m+1}, \ldots, not\ L_n,$

where L and L_i are classical literals, i.e. either atoms or atoms preceded by the classical negation symbol $\neg$ and $n \geq m \geq 0$. The symbol "*not*" denotes negation as failure. We call a literal preceded by "*not*" an NAF-literal. An ELP is called a *normal logic program* (NLP) if every literal in the program is an atom. Hereafter let Lit_P be the set of all ground literals in the language of an ELP P and HB_P be the Herbrand base of an NLP P.

The semantics of an ELP P is given by either *answer sets* [20,19] or *paraconsistent stable models* [23]. Both are defined as subsets of Lit_P. (See details in [31].)

---

[1] In [9, Theorem 6], the theorem is proved for ABA=$\langle \mathcal{L}, \mathcal{R}, \mathcal{A}, ^- \rangle$, where $^-$ is a total mapping from $\mathcal{A}$ into $\mathcal{L}$. Similarly using $\mathcal{C}$ instead of $^-$, it can be also proved for the extended ABA=$\langle \mathcal{L}, \mathcal{R}, \mathcal{A}, \mathcal{C} \rangle$.

Answer sets (resp. paraconsistent stable models) of an NLP P may be called *stable models* [19].

Prioritized logic programs used in this paper is shown as follows.

Definition 6 (Prioritized Logic Programs, PLPs [24]). Given an ELP P, let $\mathcal{L}_P = Lit_P \cup \{not\ p|\ p \in Lit_P\}$ and $\preceq$ be a preorder relation on $\mathcal{L}_P$. For $e_1, e_2 \in \mathcal{L}_P$, $e_1 \preceq e_2$ is called a *priority* standing for " e_2 *has a higher or equal priority than* e_1". As usual, $e_1 \prec e_2$ iff $e_1 \preceq e_2$ and $e_2 \not\preceq e_1$.

A *prioritized logic program* (PLP) is defined as a pair (P, Φ), where P is an ELP and Φ is a binary relation on $\mathcal{L}_P$ consisting of priorities.

The declarative semantics of a PLP (P, Φ) is given by *preferred answer sets* [24] (resp. *preferred paraconsistent stable models* [31]). In what follows, let Φ^* be the reflexive and transitive closure of Φ, that is, a preorder.

Definition 7 (Preference relation: $\sqsubseteq_{as}$ [24,31]). Given a PLP (P, Φ), the preference relation $\sqsubseteq_{as}$ over the set of answer sets (resp. paraconsistent stable models) of P is defined as follows: For any answer sets (resp. paraconsistent stable models) S_1, S_2 and S_3 of P,

1. $S_1 \sqsubseteq_{as} S_1$,
2. $S_1 \sqsubseteq_{as} S_2$ if for some literal $e_2 \in S_2 \setminus S_1$,
    (i) there is a literal $e_1 \in S_1 \setminus S_2$ such that $e_1 \preceq e_2 \in \Phi^*$, and
    (ii) there is no literal $e_3 \in S_1 \setminus S_2$ such that $e_2 \prec e_3 \in \Phi^*$,
3. if $S_1 \sqsubseteq_{as} S_2$ and $S_2 \sqsubseteq_{as} S_3$, then $S_1 \sqsubseteq_{as} S_3$.

Obviously $\sqsubseteq_{as}$ is a preorder. We write $S_1 \sqsubset_{as} S_2$ if $S_1 \sqsubseteq_{as} S_2$ and $S_2 \not\sqsubseteq_{as} S_1$.

Definition 8 (Preferred answer sets / Preferred paraconsistent stable models [24,31]). Let (P, Φ) be a PLP. Then, an answer set (resp. a paraconsistent stable model) S of P is called a *preferred answer set* (resp. a *preferred paraconsistent stable model*) of (P, Φ) if $S \sqsubseteq_{as} S'$ implies $S' \sqsubseteq_{as} S$ (with respect to Φ) for any answer set (resp. paraconsistent stable model) S' of P.

3   ABA Frameworks Equipped with Preferences

3.1   ABA Frameworks with Preferences

We propose ABA frameworks equipped with preferences (p_ABAs, for short), which incorporate explicit priorities between sentences into ABAs. The semantics of p_ABAs is given $\mathcal{P}$ extensions. Not only do p_ABAs overcome difficulties of the existing approaches but p_ABAs instantiated with PLPs [24] capture the semantics of the PLPs. Hereafter let $Sname \in \{complete, preferred, stable, grounded\}$.

Definition 9. Given an ABA $\langle \mathcal{L}, \mathcal{R}, \mathcal{A}, \mathcal{C} \rangle$, let $\preceq$ be a binary relation over $\mathcal{L}$, which is a preorder, that is, reflexive and transitive. As usual, $c' \prec c$ iff $c' \preceq c$ and $c \not\preceq c'$. For any sentences c, c', $c' \preceq c$ (resp. $c' \prec c$) means that c is at least as preferred as c' (resp. c is strictly preferred to c').

Definition 10 . An *ABA framework equipped with preferences* (a *p_ABA framework*, or *p_ABA* for short) is defined as a tuple:

$$\langle \mathcal{L}, \mathcal{R}, \mathcal{A}, \mathcal{C}, \preceq \rangle$$

where $\langle \mathcal{L}, \mathcal{R}, \mathcal{A}, \mathcal{C} \rangle$ is the ABA framework and $\preceq$ is a preorder relation over $\mathcal{L}$.

The semantics of a p_ABA framework is defined as the minimal *Sname* extensions w.r.t. the preference relation $\sqsubseteq_{ex}$. First of all, we show how the given sentence ordering $\preceq$ is lifted to the argument ordering $\leq$ as follows.

Definition 11 (Argument Orderings $\leq$). Given a p_ABA $\langle \mathcal{L}, \mathcal{R}, \mathcal{A}, \mathcal{C}, \preceq \rangle$, let $AF_{\mathcal{F}} = (AR, attacks)$ be the argumentation framework constructed from the associated ABA, $\mathcal{F} = \langle \mathcal{L}, \mathcal{R}, \mathcal{A}, \mathcal{C} \rangle$. Then $\leq$ (resp. $<$) is defined as the binary relation over AR derived from $\preceq$ as follows.
For any arguments $Ag_1, Ag_2 \in AR$ such that $K_1 \vdash c_1$ and $K_2 \vdash c_2$,

$$Ag_1 \leq Ag_2 \quad \text{if} \quad c_1 \preceq c_2$$
$$Ag_1 \nleq Ag_2 \quad \text{if} \quad c_1 \npreceq c_2$$

where $c_i = claim(Ag_i)$ $(i = 1, 2)$, and $Ag_1 < Ag_2$ iff $Ag_1 \leq Ag_2$ and $Ag_2 \nleq Ag_1$.

Proposition 1 . $\leq$ *is a preorder.*

Proof: *This is proved in a similar way to Proposition 4.2 in [31].*

The preference relation $\sqsubseteq_{ex}$ denoting the extension ordering is defined based on either the sentence ordering $\preceq$ or the argument ordering $\leq$ as follows.

Definition 12 (Preference relations $\sqsubseteq_{ex}$). Given a p_ABA $\langle \mathcal{L}, \mathcal{R}, \mathcal{A}, \mathcal{C}, \preceq \rangle$, let $\mathcal{E}$ be the set of *Sname* argument extensions of the argumentation framework $AF_{\mathcal{F}} = (AR, attacks)$ corresponding to the ABA framework $\mathcal{F} = \langle \mathcal{L}, \mathcal{R}, \mathcal{A}, \mathcal{C} \rangle$ under *Sname* semantics and $f : 2^{AR} \times 2^{AR} \rightarrow 2^{AR}$ be the function as follows:

$$f(U, V) = \{X | \; claim(X) = claim(Y) \text{ for } X \in U, \; Y \in V\}.$$

Then the preference relation $\sqsubseteq_{ex}$ over $\mathcal{E}$ (i.e. $\sqsubseteq_{ex} \subseteq \mathcal{E} \times \mathcal{E}$) is defined as follows. For any *Sname* argument extensions, E_1, E_2 and E_3 from $\mathcal{E}$,

1. $E_1 \sqsubseteq_{ex} E_1$,
2. $E_1 \sqsubseteq_{ex} E_2$ if for some argument $Ag_2 \in E_2 \setminus \Delta_2$ [2],
   (i) there is an argument $Ag_1 \in E_1 \setminus \Delta_1$ s.t. $claim(Ag_1) \preceq claim(Ag_2)$ and,
   (ii) there is no argument $Ag_3 \in E_1 \setminus \Delta_1$ s.t. $claim(Ag_2) \prec claim(Ag_3)$,
   where $\Delta_1 = f(E_1, E_2)$ and $\Delta_2 = f(E_2, E_1)$,
3. if $E_1 \sqsubseteq_{ex} E_2$ and $E_2 \sqsubseteq_{ex} E_3$, then $E_1 \sqsubseteq_{ex} E_3$;

$\sqsubseteq_{ex}$ is a preorder due to the items no.1 and no.3. We say that E_2 is *preferable* to E_1 with respect to $\preceq$ if $E_1 \sqsubseteq_{ex} E_2$ holds. We write $E_1 \sqsubset_{ex} E_2$ if $E_1 \sqsubseteq_{ex} E_2$ and $E_2 \not\sqsubseteq_{ex} E_1$. $E_1 \sqsubseteq_{ex} E_2$ is called "a *preference between extensions*".

---

[2] In [30, Definitions 23]), the weaker conditions such as $E_2 \setminus E_1$ and $E_1 \setminus E_2$ are used. They should be corrected by replacing them with $E_2 \setminus \Delta_2$ and $E_1 \setminus \Delta_1$.

Proposition 2. *Let $\sqsubseteq'_{ex}$ be a preference relation (i.e. $\sqsubseteq'_{ex} \subseteq \mathcal{E} \times \mathcal{E}$) which is defined by replacing $claim(Ag_1) \preceq claim(Ag_2)$ and $claim(Ag_2) \prec claim(Ag_3)$ with $Ag_1 \leq Ag_2$ and $Ag_2 < Ag_3$ in the item no. 2 of Definition 12. Then $\sqsubseteq'_{ex}$ coincides with $\sqsubseteq_{ex}$.*

Now the semantics of a p_ABA framework is given by *Sname* $\mathcal{P}$ extensions which are selected as the minimal *Sname* extensions w.r.t. $\sqsubseteq_{ex}$ as follows.

Definition 13 ($\mathcal{P}$-extensions). Given a p_ABA framework $\langle \mathcal{L}, \mathcal{R}, \mathcal{A}, \mathcal{C}, \preceq \rangle$, let $\mathcal{E}$ be the set of *Sname* argument extensions of $AF_{\mathcal{F}} = (AR, attacks)$ corresponding to the ABA framework $\langle \mathcal{L}, \mathcal{R}, \mathcal{A}, \mathcal{C} \rangle$ under *Sname* semantics. Then a *Sname* argument extension $E \in \mathcal{E}$ is called a *Sname* $\mathcal{P}$-argument extension of the p_ABA framework if $E \sqsubseteq_{ex} E'$ implies $E' \sqsubseteq_{ex} E$ (with respect to $\preceq$) for any $E' \in \mathcal{E}$. In other words, E is a *Sname* $\mathcal{P}$-argument extension of the p_ABA framework iff $E \not\sqsubseteq_{ex} E'$ for any $E' \in \mathcal{E}$.

For a *Sname* $\mathcal{P}$-argument extension E, $\texttt{Args2Asms}(E)$ is called a *Sname* $\mathcal{P}$-assumption extension. Both a *Sname* $\mathcal{P}$-argument extension and a $\mathcal{P}$-assumption extension may be called a *Sname* $\mathcal{P}$ extension for short.

When preferences are not available, *Sname* $\mathcal{P}$ extensions of p_ABAs coincide with *Sname* extensions of ABAs as follows.

Proposition 3 (Generalization). *Let $\langle \mathcal{L}, \mathcal{R}, \mathcal{A}, \mathcal{C}, \preceq \rangle$ be a p_ABA, where $\preceq = \emptyset$. Then E is a Sname $\mathcal{P}$ extension of p_ABA $\langle \mathcal{L}, \mathcal{R}, \mathcal{A}, \mathcal{C}, \emptyset \rangle$ iff E is a Sname extension of the ABA $\langle \mathcal{L}, \mathcal{R}, \mathcal{A}, \mathcal{C} \rangle$.*

The sceptical (resp. credulous) query-answering problem is defined as follows:

Definition 14 (Sceptical / Credulous Query-Answering). Given a p_ABA $\langle \mathcal{L}, \mathcal{R}, \mathcal{A}, \mathcal{C}, \preceq \rangle$, let $AF_{\mathcal{F}} = (AR, attacks)$ be the argumentation framework constructed from $\mathcal{F} = \langle \mathcal{L}, \mathcal{R}, \mathcal{A}, \mathcal{C} \rangle$, and $E_1, \ldots, E_x$ be *Sname* $\mathcal{P}$-argument extensions of the p_ABA. Then for an argument $Ag \in AR$,
- Ag is sceptically *justified* under *Sname* semantics iff $Ag \in E_i$ for $\forall E_i$;
- Ag is credulously *justified* under *Sname* semantics iff $Ag \in E_i$ for $\exists E_i$.

Next we show that under the stable semantics, p_ABAs instantiated with PLPs [24] can capture the semantics of the PLPs as the generalization of Dung's theorem [11, Theorem 49], which is described in the context of ABAs as follows.

Lemma 1. *([11, Theorem 49]). Let $\mathcal{F}(P) = \langle \mathcal{L}_P, P, HB_{not}, \mathcal{C} \rangle$ be the ABA framework instantiated with an NLP P, where $HB_{not} = \{not\ p \mid p \in HB_P\}$, $\mathcal{L}_P = HB_P \cup HB_{not}$, $\mathcal{C}(not\ p) = \{p\}$ for $not\ p \in HB_{not}$. Then the argumentation framework corresponding to the ABA framework $\mathcal{F}(P)$ is $AF_{\mathcal{F}}(P) = (AR_P, attacks)$ defined as follows:*

$$AR_P = \{K \vdash k \mid K \subseteq HB_{not} \text{ is a support for } k \in HB_P \text{ w.r.t. } P\}$$
$$\cup \{\{not\ k\} \vdash not\ k \mid k \in HB_P\},$$
$$K \vdash h \text{ attacks } K' \vdash h' \quad iff \quad \exists h^* \in K' \text{ such that } h \in \mathcal{C}(h^*).$$

Then a Herbrand interpretation M is a stable model of P iff there is a stable extension E of $AF_{\mathcal{F}}(P)$ such that $M \cup \neg.CM = claims(E)$, where $\neg.CM = \{not\ a \mid a \in HB_P \setminus M\}$.

For the p_ABA instantiated with a PLP (P, Φ), *claims* is the order-preserving mapping (i.e. *order-isomorphism* [31]) w.r.t. $\sqsubseteq_{ex}$ and $\sqsubseteq_{as}$ as shown as follows.

Theorem 2. (Order-embeddings). *Given a PLP (P, Φ) for an NLP P and $\Phi \subseteq \mathcal{L}_P \times \mathcal{L}_P$, let $\mathcal{F}(P, \Phi) = \langle \mathcal{L}_P, P, HB_{not}, \mathcal{C}, \Phi^* \rangle$ be the p_ABA framework instantiated with the PLP, where $\mathcal{F}(P) = \langle \mathcal{L}_P, P, HB_{not}, \mathcal{C} \rangle$ is the ABA framework instantiated with P. Then it holds that, for stable extensions E_1, E_2 of the argumentation framework $AF_{\mathcal{F}}(P)$ corresponding to $\mathcal{F}(P)$ and stable models (i.e. answer sets) M_1, M_2 of P,*

$$E_1 \sqsubseteq_{ex} E_2 \quad iff \quad M_1 \sqsubseteq_{as} M_2 \quad for\ M_i \cup \neg.CM_i = claims(E_i) \quad (i = 1, 2).$$

Proof: See appendix. $\qquad\qquad\qquad\qquad\qquad\qquad\qquad\qquad\qquad\qquad$ $\square$

As the generalization of Dung's Theorem [11], the following theorem holds for the p_ABA instantiated with (P, Φ) based on Theorem 2.

Theorem 3. *Let $\langle \mathcal{L}_P, P, HB_{not}, \mathcal{C}, \Phi^* \rangle$ be the p_ABA framework instantiated with a PLP (P, Φ), where P is an NLP, $\mathcal{L}_P = HB_P \cup HB_{not}$ and $\Phi \subseteq \mathcal{L}_P^2$. Then M is a preferred stable model (i.e. a preferred answer set) of a PLP (P, Φ) iff there is a stable $\mathcal{P}$-extension E of $\langle \mathcal{L}_P, P, HB_{not}, \mathcal{C}, \Phi^* \rangle$ instantiated with the PLP such that $M \cup \neg.CM = claims(E)$.*

Proof: *See appendix.* $\qquad\qquad\qquad\qquad\qquad\qquad\qquad\qquad\qquad\qquad$ $\square$

As the generalization of Theorem 3, the following corollary holds for the p_ABA instantiated with a PLP (P, Φ) where P is an ELP, denoting that there is a one-to-one correspondence between the preferred paraconsistent stable models of a PLP and stable $\mathcal{P}$-extensions of the p_ABA instantiated with the PLP.

Corollary 1. *Let $\langle \mathcal{L}_P, P, Lit_{not}, \mathcal{C}, \Phi^* \rangle$ be the p_ABA framework instantiated with a PLP (P, Φ), where P is an ELP, $Lit_{not} = \{not\ L \mid L \in Lit_P\}$, $\mathcal{L}_P = Lit_P \cup Lit_{not}$, $\mathcal{C}(not\ L) = \{L\}$ for not $L \in Lit_{not}$ and $\Phi \subseteq \mathcal{L}_P^2$. Then M is a preferred paraconsistent stable model of a PLP (P, Φ) iff there is a stable $\mathcal{P}$-extension E of $\langle \mathcal{L}_P, P, Lit_{not}, \mathcal{C}, \Phi^* \rangle$ instantiated with the PLP such that $M \cup \neg.CM = claims(E)$, where $\neg.CM = \{not\ L \mid L \in Lit_P \setminus M\}$.*

Proof: *(Sketch) By regarding each $\neg L \in Lit_P$ as a newly introduced atom [23], this is proved in a similar way to Theorem 3 based on Theorem 2.*

3.2   Application to Decision-Making with Preferences

In [17], decision-making problems with preferences are solved based on the notion of *extended decision functions* (*edfs*). In our approach, 'good' decisions are easily obtained from preferred $\mathcal{P}$-extensions of the p_ABA faithfully expressing a given *edf* without suffering from difficulties occurred in the existing approach [17].

Definition 15 ([17])**.** An extended decision framework $\langle \mathtt{D}, \mathtt{A}, \mathtt{G}, \mathtt{DA}, \mathtt{GA}, \mathtt{P} \rangle$, has:

- a set of decisions $\mathtt{D} = \{d_1, \ldots, d_n\}, n > 0$;

- a set of attributes $\mathsf{A} = \{a_1, \ldots, a_m\}, m > 0$;
- a set of goals $\mathsf{G} = \{g_1, \ldots, g_\ell\}, \ell > 0$;
- a partial order over goals P (i.e. $\mathsf{P} \subseteq \mathsf{G} \times \mathsf{G}$), representing the preference ranking of goals;
- two tables: $\mathsf{DA}_{i,j}$, of size$(n \times m)$, and $\mathsf{GA}_{i,j}$, of size$(\ell \times m)$, such that
  - for every $\mathsf{DA}_{i,j}, 1 \le i \le n, 1 \le j \le m$, $\mathsf{DA}_{i,j}$ is either 1, representing that decision d_i has attribute a_j, or 0, otherwise;
  - for every $\mathsf{GA}_{i,j}, 1 \le i \le \ell, 1 \le j \le m$, $\mathsf{GA}_{i,j}$ is either 1, representing that goal g_i is satisfied by attribute a_j, or 0, otherwise.

Our solution for such a decision-making problem is given in the following definition, where the p_ABA expressing a given *edf* has the greatly simplified framework compared with *the most preferred ABA* defined in [17, Definition 5].

Definition 16. Given an extended decision framework $edf = \langle \mathsf{D}, \mathsf{A}, \mathsf{G}, \mathsf{DA}, \mathsf{GA}, \mathsf{P} \rangle$, let $\mathcal{PF}_{edf} = \langle \mathcal{L}, \mathcal{R}, \mathcal{A}, \mathcal{C}, \preceq \rangle$ be the p_ABA framework corresponding to *edf*, where

- $\mathcal{R}$ is such that: for all k, i, j such that $1 \le k \le n, 1 \le i \le m$ and $1 \le j \le \ell$:
  - if $\mathsf{DA}_{k,i} = 1$, then $a_i \leftarrow d_k \in \mathcal{R}$;
  - if $\mathsf{GA}_{j,i} = 1$, then $g_j \leftarrow a_i \in \mathcal{R}$;
- $\mathcal{A}$ is D;   and $\mathcal{C}$ is such that $\mathcal{C}(d_k) = \mathsf{D} \setminus \{d_k\}$ for $d_k \in \mathsf{D}$;
- $\preceq$ is the reflexive and transitive closure of $\mathsf{P} \subseteq \mathsf{G} \times \mathsf{G}$.

Let E be a preferred $\mathcal{P}$-argument extension of $\mathcal{PF}_{edf}$. Then $d \in \mathsf{D}$ is called a selected decision if the argument $\{d\} \vdash d$ is in E. In other words, d is a selected decision if $d \in \mathtt{Args2Asms}(E) \cap \mathsf{D}$ for a preferred $\mathcal{P}$-assumption extension $\mathtt{Args2Asms}(E)$ of $\mathcal{PF}_{edf}$.

Example 1. ([17, Example 1]). An agent is to choose accommodation in London. Decisions (D) are: hotel (jh) and Imperial College Halls (ic). Attributes (A) are: £50, £70, in South Kensington (inSK), and in a backstreet (backSt). Goals (G) are: *cheep, near* and *quiet*. The preference P is: *near > cheap > quiet*. DA and GA are shown in Figure 1 ([17, Table.1]). Then the p_ABA framework corresponding to this *edf* is $\mathcal{PF}_{edf} = \langle \mathcal{L}, \mathcal{R}, \mathcal{A}, \mathcal{C}, \preceq \rangle$, where

- $\mathcal{R}$: $£70 \leftarrow jh$, $inSK \leftarrow jh$, $backSt \leftarrow jh$, $£50 \leftarrow ic$,
  $inSK \leftarrow ic$, $cheap \leftarrow £50$, $near \leftarrow inSK$, $quiet \leftarrow backSt$;
- $\mathcal{A} = \mathsf{D} = \{jh, ic\}$; $\mathcal{C}(jh) = \{ic\}$, $\mathcal{C}(ic) = \{jh\}$;
- $\preceq = \{(cheep, near), (quiet, cheep), (quiet, near)\}$
     $\cup \{(X, X) | X \in \mathsf{G} = \{near, cheep, quiet\}\}$

	£50	£70	inSK	backSK
jh	0	1	1	1
ic	1	0	1	0

	£50	£70	inSK	backSK
near	0	0	1	0
cheap	1	0	0	0
quiet	0	0	0	1

Fig. 1. DA(left) and GA(right)

Arguments are constructed from the ABA $\mathcal{F}_{edf}=\langle\mathcal{L},\mathcal{R},\mathcal{A},\mathcal{C}\rangle$ as follows:

- $A_1 : \{jh\} \vdash £70$ • $A_2 : \{jh\} \vdash inSK$ • $A_3 : \{jh\} \vdash near$
- $A_4 : \{jh\} \vdash backSt$ • $A_5 : \{jh\} \vdash quiet$ • $B_1 : \{ic\} \vdash £50$ • $B_2 : \{ic\} \vdash inSK$
- $B_3 : \{ic\} \vdash near$ • $B_4 : \{ic\} \vdash cheap$ • $\alpha : \{jh\} \vdash jh$ • $\beta : \{ic\} \vdash ic$

Then $AF_{edf} = (AR, attacks)$ is also constructed from ABA $\mathcal{F}_{edf}$, where $attacks = \{(\alpha,\beta),(\beta,\alpha)\}\cup\{(\beta,A_i)|1 \le i \le 5\}\cup\{(\alpha,B_j)|1 \le j \le 4\}$.

In this case, AF_{edf} has two preferred extensions E_1, E_2 as follows:
$$E_1 = \{\alpha, A_1, A_2, A_3, A_4, A_5\}, \qquad E_2 = \{\beta, B_1, B_2, B_3, B_4\},$$
with $\texttt{Args2Asms}(E_1)=\{jh\}$ and $\texttt{Args2Asms}(E_2)=\{ic\}$.

W.r.t. E_1 and E_2, $E_1 \sqsubseteq E_2$ is derived since $quiet \preceq cheap$ for $claim(A_5) = quiet$ and $claim(B_4) = cheap$, where $E_1 \setminus \Delta_1 = \{\alpha, A_1, A_4.A_5\}$ and $E_2 \setminus \Delta_2 = \{\beta, B_1, B_4\}$. Hence E_2 (resp. $\{ic\}$) is the preferred $\mathcal{P}$-argument (resp. $\mathcal{P}$-assumption) extension of p_ABA $\mathcal{PF}_{edf}$. Thus we can obtain the expected result "ic" as the selected decision.

Remark. It should be noticed that in [17, Example 4], the most preferred ABA: $\langle\mathcal{L},\mathcal{R},\mathcal{A},\mathcal{C}\rangle$ for this small edf is derived, where 53 rules in $\mathcal{R}$, 14 assumptions in $\mathcal{A}$ and 14 $contraries$ for $\mathcal{C}$ are generated.

3.3 Application to Practical Reasoning with Preferences

Our approach provides a solution for the famous punishment example [4] owing to preferences over goals expressed in the p_ABA, whereas how to treat those preferences based on ABAs was not shown in Toni *et al.*'s approach [18,27].

Example 2. (The punishment example [4]). A judge needs to decide how best to punish a criminal found guilty, while deterring the general public, rehabilitating the offender, and protecting society from further crime. The judge can choose among three forms of punishment: (i) imprisonment, (ii) a fine, or (iii) community service, as possible decisions (D). The judge believes that: (i) promotes deterrence and protection to society, but it demotes rehabilitation; (ii) promotes deterrence but has no effect on rehabilitation and protection of society; (iii) promotes rehabilitation but demotes deterrence. Then the problem is to find the best way (i.e. decisions) to meet goals (G) in some order, where G=$\{punish, deter, rehabilitate, protect\}$. In [18], the problem without preferences is represented as the ABA framework $\mathcal{F}= \langle\mathcal{L},\mathcal{R},\mathcal{A},\mathcal{C}\rangle$, where

- $\mathcal{A}=\{prison, fine, service, \alpha, \beta, \gamma, \delta\}$, where D$=\{prison, fine, service\} \subseteq \mathcal{A}$,
- $\mathcal{C}(prison)=\{fine, service\}$, $\mathcal{C}(fine)=\{prison, service\}$
  $\mathcal{C}(service)=\{prison, fine\}$, $\mathcal{C}(\alpha)=\{\neg deter\}$, $\mathcal{C}(\beta)=\{deter\}$,
  $\mathcal{C}(\gamma)=\{\neg rehabilitate\}$, $\mathcal{C}(\delta)=\{rehabilitate\}$,
- $\mathcal{R}$ consists of nine rules:

  $punish \leftarrow prison$ $deter \leftarrow prison, \alpha$ $rehabilitate \leftarrow service, \gamma$
  $punish \leftarrow fine$ $deter \leftarrow fine, \alpha$ $\neg rehabilitate \leftarrow prison, \delta$
  $punish \leftarrow service$ $\neg deter \leftarrow service, \beta$ $protect \leftarrow prison.$

Arguments are constructed from $\mathcal{F}$ as follows:

- $A_1 : \{prison\} \vdash prison$ • $A_2 : \{fine\} \vdash fine$ • $A_3 : \{service\} \vdash service$
- $A_4 : \{\alpha\} \vdash \alpha$ • $A_5 : \{\beta\} \vdash \beta$ • $A_6 : \{\gamma\} \vdash \gamma$ • $A_7 : \{\delta\} \vdash \delta$

- $B_1 : \{prison\} \vdash punish$ • $B_2 : \{fine\} \vdash punish$ • $B_3 : \{service\} \vdash punish$
- $C_1 : \{prison, \alpha\} \vdash deter$ • $C_2 : \{fine, \alpha\} \vdash deter$
- $C_3 : \{service, \beta\} \vdash \neg deter$ • $D_1 : \{service, \gamma\} \vdash rehabilitate$
- $D_2 : \{prison, \delta\} \vdash \neg rehabilitate$ • $H : \{prison\} \vdash protect$.

Then, the argumentation framework $AF_{\mathcal{F}} = (AR, attacks)$ corresponding to ABA $\mathcal{F}$ has three preferred argument extensions E_1, E_2, E_3 as follows:

- $E_1 = \{A_3, A_5, A_6, B_3, C_3, D_1\}$,   with Args2Asms$(E_1)=\{service, \beta, \gamma\}$,
- $E_2 = \{A_2, A_4, A_6, A_7, B_2, C_2\}$,   with Args2Asms$(E_2)=\{fine, \alpha, \gamma, \delta\}$,
- $E_3 = \{A_1, A_4, A_7, B_1, C_1, D_2, H\}$,   with Args2Asms$(E_3)=\{prison, \alpha, \delta\}$,

where $claims(E_1) = \{service, \beta, \gamma, punish, \neg deter, rehabilitate\}$,
$claims(E_2) = \{fine, \alpha, \gamma, \delta, punish, deter\}$,
$claims(E_3) = \{prison, \alpha, \delta, punish, deter, \neg rehabilitate, protect\}$.

Here since there is no extension satisfying all goals contained in G, preferences over goals (P $\subseteq$ G $\times$ G) such that $deter \preceq rehabilitate \preceq punish$ are taken into account in [4]. However Toni *et al.* [18,27] left this for future research. In contrast, our approach enables us to represent such preferences in p_ABA$=\langle \mathcal{L}, \mathcal{R}, \mathcal{A}, \mathcal{C}, \preceq \rangle$, where $\preceq= \{(deter, rehabilitate), (rehabilitate, punish), (deter, punish)\}$
$\cup \{(x, x)|x \in \{punish, deter, rehabilitate, protect\}\}$.
Then $E_2 \sqsubseteq E_1$ is derived since $\Delta_1 = f(E_1, E_2) = \{A_6, B_3\}$, $\Delta_2 = f(E_2, E_1) = \{A_6, B_2\}$ and $deter \preceq rehabilitate$ for $claim(C_2) = deter$ and $claim(D_1) = rehabilitate$. Similarly $E_3 \sqsubseteq E_1$ is derived. Since E_1 is obtained as the unique preferred $\mathcal{P}$-extension of the p_ABA, *community service* is decided as judge's punishment since $A_3 \in E_1$ or Args2Asms$(E_1) \cap$ D$=\{service\}$ as suggested in [4].

3.4   Application to Epistemic Reasoning with Preferences

Toni addressed in [28] that if a rule of ABA has one or more assumptions in the body, then it is *defeasible*, otherwise it is *strict*. In fact, in [25, Definition 15], the ABA corresponding to a defeasible framework $\langle D, S \rangle$ wrt $\mathcal{L}_d$ is shown as $\delta=\langle \mathcal{L}_d \cup \mathcal{A}_\delta, \mathcal{R}_\delta, \mathcal{A}_\delta, \mathcal{C}_\delta \rangle$, where $\mathcal{R}_\delta$ is defined as $\{X \leftarrow Y, \alpha(Y \rightarrow X) \mid Y \rightarrow X \in D\} \cup S$ by using a bijective function $\alpha : D \rightarrow \mathcal{A}_\delta$. Besides in [26], for the additional preferences over defeasible rules, she defined frameworks for reasoning about beliefs (referred to as *epistemic frameworks*) based on defeasible rules and preferences over them, and provided a mapping from them to standard ABAs.

In our approach, the additional preferences over defeasible rules are faithfully expressed in p_ABAs without providing the extra mapping to ABAs as follows.

Definition 17. Given a p_ABA $\langle \mathcal{L}, \mathcal{R}, \mathcal{A}, \mathcal{C}, \preceq \rangle$, let $\mathcal{R}$ be divided into two disjoint sets R_{df} and R_{st}, where R_{df} (resp. R_{st}) be a set of defeasible (resp. strict) rules in a sense of ABA [28], and $\mathcal{N}$ be a partial function from R_{df} to $\mathcal{L}$ denoting that a sentence $\mathcal{N}(r) \in \mathcal{L}$ expresses the name for the rule $r \in R_{df}$. Suppose that a preference relation $\preceq_{\mathcal{R}}$ on R_{df} is additionally given for the p_ ABA, where $r \preceq_{\mathcal{R}} r'$ stands for "r' is preferred to r" for defeasible rules $r, r' \in R_{df}$. Then the situation is expressed by p_ABA$=\langle \mathcal{L}, \mathcal{R}', \mathcal{A}, \mathcal{C}, \preceq' \rangle$, where $\mathcal{R}'= \mathcal{R} \cup \{n \leftarrow body(r), n' \leftarrow body(r')| \ r \preceq_{\mathcal{R}} r' \text{ for } n = \mathcal{N}(r) \text{ and } n' = \mathcal{N}(r')\}$ and $\preceq'= \preceq \cup \{(n, n')| \ r \preceq_{\mathcal{R}} r' \text{ for } n = \mathcal{N}(r) \text{ and } n' = \mathcal{N}(r')\}$.

Example 3. In Example 1 of [26], the ABA framework corresponding to the epistemic framework ϵ is shown as $\langle \mathcal{L}_\epsilon, \mathcal{R}_\epsilon, \mathcal{A}_\epsilon, \mathcal{C}_\epsilon \rangle$, where $\mathcal{R}_\epsilon = \{q \leftarrow a_1; \ p \leftarrow q, a_2; \ r \leftarrow a_3; \ \neg p \leftarrow r, a_4\}$, $\mathcal{A}_\epsilon = \{a_1, a_2, a_3, a_4\}$, $\mathcal{C}_\epsilon(a_1) = \{\neg q\}$, $\mathcal{C}_\epsilon(a_2) = \{\neg p\}$, $\mathcal{C}_\epsilon(a_3) = \{\neg r\}$, and $\mathcal{C}_\epsilon(a_4) = \{p\}$. In this case, $\mathcal{R}_\epsilon = R_{df}$ and $R_{st} = \emptyset$. Now suppose that the second rule whose name is $n_2 = \mathcal{N}(p \leftarrow q, a_2)$ is preferred to the last rule whose name is $n_4 = \mathcal{N}(\neg p \leftarrow r, a_4)$, the situation is expressed by p_ABA$=\langle \mathcal{L}, \mathcal{R}, \mathcal{A}, \mathcal{C}, \preceq \rangle$, where $\mathcal{L}=\mathcal{L}_\epsilon \cup \{n_1, n_2, n_3, n_4\}$, $\mathcal{R}=\mathcal{R}_\epsilon \cup \{n_2 \leftarrow q, a_2; n_4 \leftarrow r, a_4\}$, $\mathcal{A}=\mathcal{A}_\epsilon$, $\mathcal{C}=\mathcal{C}_\epsilon$ and $n_4 \preceq n_2$, that is, $\preceq = \{(n_4, n_2)\}$. Hence the p_ABA has the unique preferred $\mathcal{P}$-assumption extension Args2Asms$(E)=\{a_1, a_2, a_3\}$ for its unique preferred $\mathcal{P}$-argument extension E.

3.5 Some Complexity Results

We next address some complexity results of our approach.

Lemma 2. *([14]). Let (AR, attacks) be an argumentation framework. Then deciding the existence of a stable extension of (AR, attacks) is NP-complete.*

Lemma 3. *For a p_ABA $\langle \mathcal{L}, \mathcal{R}, \mathcal{A}, \mathcal{C}, \preceq \rangle$, let S be a set of arguments of the ABA $\langle \mathcal{L}, \mathcal{R}, \mathcal{A}, \mathcal{C} \rangle$. Then deciding whether S is a stable $\mathcal{P}$-extension of $\langle \mathcal{L}, \mathcal{R}, \mathcal{A}, \mathcal{C}, \preceq \rangle$ is in* coNP.

Proof. The argumentation framework $AF_{\mathcal{F}}=(AR,\ attacks)$ corresponding to the ABA $\mathcal{F} = \langle \mathcal{L}, \mathcal{R}, \mathcal{A}, \mathcal{C} \rangle$ is constructible from the ABA in polynomial time. Besides whether $S \subseteq AR$ is a stable extension of $AF_{\mathcal{F}}$ is decided in polynomial time. For a stable extension S, it is not a stable $\mathcal{P}$-extension iff there exists another stable extension S' such that $S \sqsubset_{ex} S'$, while checking whether $S \sqsubset_{ex} S'$ holds for another stable extension S' is done in polynomial time. A guess for a stable extension S' is verifiable in polynomial time, thus deciding whether S is not a stable $\mathcal{P}$-extension is in NP, and the result follows. $\square$

Theorem 4. *Let $\langle \mathcal{L}, \mathcal{R}, \mathcal{A}, \mathcal{C}, \preceq \rangle$ be a p_ABA. Then*

(i) *Deciding the existence of a stable $\mathcal{P}$-extension of $\langle \mathcal{L}, \mathcal{R}, \mathcal{A}, \mathcal{C}, \preceq \rangle$ is NP-complete.*

(ii) *Deciding whether an argument is contained in some stable $\mathcal{P}$-extension of $\langle \mathcal{L}, \mathcal{R}, \mathcal{A}, \mathcal{C}, \preceq \rangle$ is in Σ_2^P.*

Proof.

(i) $\langle \mathcal{L}, \mathcal{R}, \mathcal{A}, \mathcal{C}, \preceq \rangle$ has a stable $\mathcal{P}$-extension iff the argumentation framework $(AR,\ attacks)$ which is constructed from the ABA $\langle \mathcal{L}, \mathcal{R}, \mathcal{A}, \mathcal{C} \rangle$ in polynomial time has a stable extension. Hence the result holds by Lemma 2.

(ii) To see the membership in Σ_2^P, first guess a set $S \subseteq AR$ containing an argument. Then, whether such S is a stable $\mathcal{P}$-extension can be verified in polynomial time with a call to an NP-oracle [15] due to Lemma 3. Hence the decision problem is in $\text{NP}^{\text{NP}}=\Sigma_2^P$. $\square$

4   Related Work

Toni stated in [28] that the philosophy behind ABA is to translate preferences and defeasible rules into ABA rules plus ABA assumptions. Hence their approaches [17,18,27] need to provide the domain-dependent mapping functions from pre-defined frameworks to standard ABAs to deal with explicit preferences, which eventually reveals difficulties shown in Examples 1 and 2. In addition, though a huge number of rules [17] are generated in the ABA mapped from the tiny *edf* in Example 1, they showed no computational complexities of their mapping approach. Our approach overcomes such drawbacks of their approaches.

Bondarenko *et al.* [5] proposed an *assumption-based frameworks with preferences* which includes preferences between formulae. However, we cannot obtain solutions of the problems given in Examples 1 and 2 based on their approach since the given preferences do not affect *attacks* between sets of assumptions.

$ASPIC^+$ [21] is a general-purpose argumentation framework with structured arguments, and has a mechanism to deal with explicit preferences. Prakken [21] showed that ABA is a special case of $ASPIC^+$ with only strict inference rules ($\mathcal{R}_s$), only assumption-type premises ($\mathcal{K}_a$) (respectively corresponding to rules $\mathcal{R}$ and the assumptions $\mathcal{A}$ in ABA) and no preferences, while sets of defeasible rules, the ordinary premises and axioms (i.e. $\mathcal{R}_d$, $\mathcal{K}_p$, $\mathcal{K}_n$) of $ASPIC^+$ are empty, where $\mathcal{K} = \mathcal{K}_n \cup \mathcal{K}_p \cup \mathcal{K}_a \subseteq \mathcal{L}$ [22]. *attacks* of ABA corresponds to (*contrary-undermining*) *attacks* of $ASPIC^+$. W.r.t. preferences, the framework of $ASPIC^+$ is equipped with priority orderings $\leq$ on $\mathcal{R}_d$ [3] and $\leq'$ on $\mathcal{K}_p$ [22], whereas p_ABA contains the ordering $\preceq$ on $\mathcal{L}$. As to the semantics of $ASPIC^+$, priority ordering on arguments is derived from both $\leq$ and $\leq'$ based on the last-link and weakest-link principles, and then by taking account of such argument ordering, the altered argumentation framework with a modified successful *attacks* (i.e. *defeat*) is constructed, to which Dung's argument-based semantics is applied. Then when applying $ASPIC^+$ to problems shown in Examples 1 and 2, $\mathcal{A}$ and $\mathcal{R}$ of each ABA become $\mathcal{K}_a$ and $\mathcal{R}_s$ of the reconstructed $ASPIC^+$, while $\mathcal{K}_p$ is empty. Thus it is impossible to express the given preferences P over goals $\mathsf{G} \subseteq \mathcal{L} \setminus \mathcal{K}$ as $\leq'$ in the framework of $ASPIC^+$ since $\leq' \subseteq \mathcal{K}_p \times \mathcal{K}_p$. Moreover even if the argument ordering generated from the sentence ordering $\preceq$ shown in Examples 1 and 2 based on Definition 11 are used in $ASPIC^+$, they do not affect *attacks*, denoting that *defeat* coincides with *attacks*, and hence problems of these examples cannot be solved based on the theory of $ASPIC^+$.

W.r.t. Caminada and Amgoud's rationality postulates [8], Prakken [21] showed the conditions under which an argumentation theory of $ASPIC^+$ with preferences satisfies those postulates. On the other hand, p_ABA can also satisfies rationality postulates as far as the embedded ABA satisfies them under the conditions shown in [13,21]. To the best of our knowledge, there have been shown no correspondence between the semantics of an underlying language with preferences of $ASPIC^+$ and the semantics of $ASPIC^+$, whereas we show that p_ABAs instantiated with Sakama and Inoue's PLPs [24] can capture the

---

[3] When each defeasible rule in $\mathcal{R}_d$ is expressed by the ABA rule [25,28] belonging to $R_{df} \subseteq \mathcal{R}$, the ordering $\leq$ on $\mathcal{R}_d$ is mapped to $\preceq_\mathcal{R}$ on R_{df} defined in section 3.4.

semantics of the PLPs under the stable semantics as shown in Theorem 3 and Corollary 1.

The non-abstract PAF [31,30] built from (P, Φ) for an ELP P and $\Phi \subseteq Lit_P^2$ captures the semantics of the PLP under the stable semantics, while the p_ABA instantiated with (P, Φ) for an ELP P and $\Phi \subseteq \mathcal{L}_P^2$ s.t. $\mathcal{L}_P = Lit_P \cup Lit_{not}$ captures the semantics of the PLP according to Corollary 1. Thus the class of PLPs to build such non-abstract PAFs is a subset of the class of PLPs used to instantiate p_ABAs since priorities between NAF-literals are not allowed in the former but allowed in the latter. In addition, a language of p_ABA is not restricted to a PLP [24] but is generally defined as a logical language.

Brewka *et al.* [7] proposed prioritized abstract dialectical frameworks (PADFs). When we apply their approach to Examples 1 and 2, each p_ABA is translated into the respective PADF $(AR, \emptyset, attacks, <)$ whose semantics coincides with that of Amgoud *et al.*'s PAF=$(AR, attacks, <)$ [1] due to [7, Proposition 11]. Then since the strict argument ordering $<$ derived from $\preceq$ does not affect *attacks* in both examples, we cannot obtain solutions of these examples based on PADFs.

5   Conclusion

We presented an assumption-based argumentation framework equipped with preferences (p_ABA). It maintains all the features of ABA based on Proposition 3. As a main contribution, our approach based on p_ABAs overcomes difficulties of the existing approaches [17,18,27] as shown in section 3.2 and 3.3.

As for computation, though Toni *et al.*'s approach [17] can make use of proof procedures [12,28] to compute admissible sets of assumptions of the mapped ABAs, the generation of the most-preferred ABA from the tiny *edf* in Example 1 was found to be expensive as addressed in [17]. Nonetheless they showed no complexity of their approach. In contrast, $\mathcal{P}$-argument extensions of our approach can be computed by slightly modifying the ASP encodings [32,29] which were developed to compute $\mathcal{P}$ extensions of PAFs [31,30] based on answer set programming [20]. $\mathcal{P}$-assumption extensions are computed from $\mathcal{P}$-argument extensions by using `Args2Asms` in polynomial time. As to complexity, querying tasks for p_ABAs shown in Definition 14 lie at the second level complexity classes of the polynomial hierarchy even under the stable semantics due to Theorem 4.

Our future work is to explore whether proposed p_ABA framework can capture the semantics of the other type of logic programs with preferences [10] excluding Sakama and Inoue's PLPs [24] by giving it the other type of semantics.

References

1. Amgoud, L., Cayrol, C.: On the acceptability of arguments in preference-based argumentation. In: Proceedings of UAI 1998, pp. 1–7 (1998)
2. Amgoud, L., Vesic, S.: Repairing preference-based argumentation frameworks. In: Proceedings of IJCAI 2009, pp. 665–670 (2009)
3. Bench-Capon, T.J.M.: Persuasion in practical argument using value-based argumentation frameworks. J. Logic Comput. 13(3), 429–448 (2003)

4. Bench-Capon, T.J.M., Prakken, H.: Justifying actions by accruing arguments. In: Proceedings of COMMA 2006, pp. 247–258 (2006)
5. Bondarenko, A., Toni, F., Kowalski, R.A.: Assumption-Based framework for non-monotonic reasoning. In: Proceedings of LPNMR 1993, pp. 171–189 (1993)
6. Bondarenko, A., Dung, P.M., Kowalski, R.A., Toni, F.: An abstract, argumentation-theoretic approach to default reasoning. Artificial Intelligence 93, 63–101 (1997)
7. Brewka, G., Ellmauthaler, S., Strass, H., Wallner, J.P., Woltran, S.: Abstract Dialectical Frameworks Revisited. In: Proceedings of IJCAI 2013, pp. 803–809 (2013)
8. Caminada, M., Amgoud, L.: On the evaluation of argumentation formalisms. Artificial Intelligence 171(5-6), 286–310 (2007)
9. Caminada, M., Sa, S., Alcantara, J., Dvorak, W.: On the difference between assumption-based argumentation and abstract argumentation. In: Proceedings of BNAIC 2013, pp. 25–32 (2013)
10. Delgrande, J.P., Schaub, T., Tompits, H., Wang, K.: A Classification and survey of preference handling approaches in nonmonotonic reasoning. Computational Intelligence 20(2), 308–334 (2004)
11. Dung, P.M.: On the acceptability of arguments and its fundamental role in non-monotonic reasoning, logic programming, and n-person games. Artificial Intelligence 77, 321–357 (1995)
12. Dung, P.M., Kowalski, R.A., Toni, F.: Assumption-based argumentation. In: Rahwan, I., Simari, G.R. (eds.) Argumentation in Artificial Intelligence, pp. 199–218. Springer (2009)
13. Dung, P.M., Thang, P.M.: Closure and consistency rationalities in logic-based argumentation. In: Balduccini, M., Son, T.C. (eds.) Logic Programming, Knowledge Representation, and Nonmonotonic Reasoning. LNCS, vol. 6565, pp. 33–43. Springer, Heidelberg (2011)
14. Dunne, P.E., Bench-Capon, T.J.M.: Coherence in finite argument systems. Artificial Intelligence 141, 187–203 (2002)
15. Eiter, T., Gottlob, G.: Complexity results for disjunctive logic programming and application to nonmonotonic logics. In: Proceedings of ILPS 1993, pp. 266–278 (1993)
16. Modgil, S.: Reasoning about preferences in argumentation frameworks. Artificial Intelligence 173, 901–934 (2009)
17. Fan, X., Craven, R., Singer, R., Toni, F., Williams, M.: Assumption-based argumentation for Decision-Making with preferences: A Medical Case Study. In: Leite, J., Son, T.C., Torroni, P., van der Torre, L., Woltran, S. (eds.) CLIMA XIV 2013. LNCS, vol. 8143, pp. 374–390. Springer, Heidelberg (2013)
18. Gaertner, D., Toni, F.: CaSAPI: a system for credulous and sceptical argumentation. In: Proceedings of ArgNMR (2007)
19. Gelfond, M., Lifschitz, V.: The stable model semantics for logic programming. In: Proceedings of ICLP/SLP 1998, pp. 1070–1080. MIT Press (1988)
20. Gelfond, M., Lifschitz, V.: Classical negation in logic programs and disjunctive databases. New Generation Computing 9, 365–385 (1991)
21. Prakken, H.: An abstract framework for argumentation with structured arguments. Argumentation and Computation 1, 93–124 (2010)
22. Prakken, H.: Some Reflections on Two Current Trends in Formal Argumentation. In: Artikis, A., Craven, R., Kesim Çiçekli, N., Sadighi, B., Stathis, K. (eds.) Sergot Festschrift 2012. LNCS, vol. 7360, pp. 249–272. Springer, Heidelberg (2012)

23. Sakama, C., Inoue, K.: Paraconsistent stable semantics for extended disjunctive programs. J. Log. Comput. 5(3), 265–285 (1995)
24. Sakama, C., Inoue, K.: Prioritized logic programming and its application to commonsense reasoning. Artificial Intelligence 123, 185–222 (2000)
25. Toni, F.: Assumption-based argumentation for closed and consistent defeasible reasoning. In: Satoh, K., Inokuchi, A., Nagao, K., Kawamura, T. (eds.) JSAI 2007. LNCS (LNAI), vol. 4914, pp. 390–402. Springer, Heidelberg (2008)
26. Toni, F.: Assumption-based argumentation for selection and composition of services. In: Sadri, F., Satoh, K. (eds.) CLIMA VIII 2007. LNCS (LNAI), vol. 5056, pp. 231–247. Springer, Heidelberg (2008)
27. Toni, F.: Assumption-based argumentation for epistemic and practical reasoning. In: Casanovas, P., Sartor, G., Casellas, N., Rubino, R. (eds.) Computable Models of the Law. LNCS (LNAI), vol. 4884, pp. 185–202. Springer, Heidelberg (2008)
28. Toni, F.: A tutorial on assumption-based argumentation. Argument and Computation 5(1), 89–117 (2014)
29. Wakaki, T., Nitta, K.: Computing argumentation semantics in answer set programming. In: Proceedings of JURISIN 2008, pp. 32–41 (2008), the revised version is in Hattori, H., Kawamura, T., Idé, T., Yokoo, M., Murakami, Y. (eds.) JSAI 2008. LNCS, vol. 5447, pp. 254–269. Springer, Heidelberg (2009)
30. Wakaki, T.: Preference-based argumentation capturing prioritized logic programming. In: McBurney, P., Rahwan, I., Parsons, S. (eds.) ArgMAS 2010. LNCS, vol. 6614, pp. 306–325. Springer, Heidelberg (2011)
31. Wakaki, T.: Preference-based argumentation built from prioritized logic programming. Journal of Logic and Computation (2013), doi:10.1093/logcom/exs066
32. Wakaki, T., Tatsuzawa, M.: Computing preference-based argumentation in answer set programming. In: Proceedings of JURISIN 2013 (2013)

Appendix: Proofs of Theorems

Proof of Theorem 2. According to Lemma 1, there exist a stable model M of a NLP P and a stable extension E of the argumentation framework $AF_{\mathcal{F}}(P)$ corresponding to the ABA framework $\mathcal{F}(P) = \langle \mathcal{L}_P, P, HB_{not}, \mathcal{C} \rangle$ such that $M \cup \neg.CM = claims(E)$ where $\mathcal{L}_P = HB_P \cup HB_{not}$. Note that for any sets $S \subseteq HB_P$, $T \subseteq HB_P$ and any ground atom $L \in HB_P$, $L \in S \setminus T$ means $L \in S$ and $L \notin T$, while $not\ L \in S \setminus T$ means $L \notin S$ and $L \in T$. Then for stable models M_1, M_2, it holds that for a ground atom $L \in HB_P$,

- $L \in M_1 \setminus M_2$ iff $L \in M_1$ and $L \notin M_2$ iff $L \in (M_1 \cup \neg.CM_1)$ and $L \notin (M_2 \cup \neg.CM_2)$ iff $L \in (M_1 \cup \neg.CM_1) \setminus (M_2 \cup \neg.CM_2)$;
- $not\ L \in M_1 \setminus M_2$ iff $L \notin M_1$ and $L \in M_2$ iff $not\ L \in \neg.CM_1$ and $not\ L \notin \neg.CM_2$ iff $not\ L \in (M_1 \cup \neg.CM_1)$ and $not\ L \notin (M_2 \cup \neg.CM_2)$ iff $not\ L \in (M_1 \cup \neg.CM_1) \setminus (M_2 \cup \neg.CM_2)$.

Then w.r.t. stable models M_1, M_2 of P and stable extensions E_1, E_2 of $AF_{\mathcal{F}}(P)$ such that $M_i \cup \neg.CM_i = claims(E_i)$ $(i = 1, 2)$, it holds that, for $e_1 \in \mathcal{L}_P$,

$e_1 \in M_1 \setminus M_2$,

iff $e_1 \in ((M_1 \cup \neg.CM_1) \setminus (M_2 \cup \neg.CM_2))$

iff $e_1 \in (claims(E_1) \setminus claims(E_2))$

iff there is an argument $Ag_1 \in E_1$ with $claim(Ag_1) = e_1$ such that $K \vdash e_1$

and no argument $Ag_2 \in E_2$ with $claim(Ag_2) = e_1$ such that $K' \vdash e_1$,

iff $Ag_1 \in E_1 \setminus \Delta_1$ with $e_1 = claim(Ag_1)$,

$\quad$ where $\Delta_1 = \{A \in E_1 \mid claim(A) = claim(B) \; for \; A \in E_1, \; B \in E_2\}$. $\qquad$ (1)

Similarly for $e_2 \in \mathcal{L}_P$, it holds that,

$\quad e_2 \in M_2 \setminus M_1$ iff $Ag_2 \in E_2 \setminus \Delta_2$ with $e_2 = claim(Ag_2)$,

$\quad$ where $\Delta_2 = \{B \in E_2 \mid claim(A) = claim(B) \; for \; A \in E_1, \; B \in E_2\}$. $\quad$ (2)

Thus due to (1), (2), it holds that,

$\quad \exists e_2 \in M_2 \setminus M_1$ and $\exists e_1 \in M_1 \setminus M_2$ such that $e_1 \preceq e_2 \in \Phi^*$

iff $\exists Ag_2 \in E_2 \setminus \Delta_2$ with $e_2 = claim(Ag_2)$ and

$\quad \exists Ag_1 \in E_1 \setminus \Delta_1$ with $e_1 = claim(Ag_1)$ such that $e_1 \preceq e_2 \in \Phi^*$. $\qquad$ (3)

Therefore, it is obviously derived that,

$\quad \exists Ag_2 \in E_2 \setminus \Delta_2[\; \exists Ag_1 \in E_1 \setminus \Delta_1$ such that $e_1 \preceq e_2 \in \Phi^*$

$\qquad \wedge \neg \exists Ag_3 \in E_1 \setminus \Delta_1$ s.t. $e_2 \prec e_3 \in \Phi^*]$ for $e_j = claim(Ag_j)$ $(1 \leq i \leq 3)$

iff $\exists e_2 \in M_2 \setminus M_1[\exists e_1 \in M_1 \setminus M_2$ such that $e_1 \preceq e_2 \in \Phi^*$

$\qquad \wedge \neg \exists e_3 \in M_1 \setminus M_2$ such that $e_2 \prec e_3 \in \Phi^*]$. $\qquad$ (4)

(4) means that $E_1 \sqsubseteq_{ex} E_2$ iff $M_1 \sqsubseteq_{as} M_2$ for $M_i \cup \neg.CM_i = claims(E_i)$ $(i = 1, 2)$ w.r.t. the item no.2 of Definition 12 and that of Definition 7. Since both $\sqsubseteq_{ex}$ and $\sqsubseteq_{as}$ are reflexive and transitive, obviously it also holds that, $E_1 \sqsubseteq_{ex} E_2$ iff $M_1 \sqsubseteq_{as} M_2$ w.r.t. items no.1 and no.3 of these definitions. $\qquad \square$

Proof of Theorem 3. For a PLP(P, Φ), let AS be the set of all stable models of an NLP P and $\mathcal{E}$ be the set of all stable extensions of the argumentation framework $AF_{\mathcal{F}}(P)$ corresponding to the ABA framework $\mathcal{F}(P) = \langle \mathcal{L}_P, P, HB_{not}, \mathcal{C} \rangle$. Then, it follows that,

$\quad M \in AS$ is a preferred stable model of a PLP (P, Φ)

iff $M \sqsubseteq_{as} M'$ implies $M' \sqsubseteq_{as} M$ (with respect to Φ) for any $M' \in AS$

iff w.r.t. $E \in \mathcal{E}$ such that $M \cup \neg.CM = claims(E)$, $E \sqsubseteq_{ex} E'$ implies $E' \sqsubseteq_{ex} E$

$\quad$ for any $E' \in \mathcal{E}$ s.t. $M' \cup \neg.CM' = claims(E')$ (due to Theorem 2)

iff $E \in \mathcal{E}$ is a stable $\mathcal{P}$-extensions of the p_ABA $\langle \mathcal{L}_P, P, HB_{not}, \mathcal{C}, \Phi^* \rangle$. $\qquad \square$

Approximating Constraint-Based Utility Spaces Using Generalized Gaussian Mixture Models

Rafik Hadfi and Takayuki Ito

Department of Computer Science and Engineering, Nagoya Institute of Technology
Gokiso, Showa-ku, Nagoya 466-8555, Japan
rafik@itolab.nitech.ac.jp, ito.takayuki@nitech.ac.jp

Abstract. Complex negotiations are characterized by a particular type of utility spaces that is usually non-linear and non-monotonic. An example of such utility spaces are constraint-based utility spaces. The multitude of constraints' shapes that could potentially be used by the negotiating agents makes any opponent modeling attempt more challenging. The same problem persists even when the agent is exploring her own utility space as to find her optimal contracts. Seeking a unified form for constraint-based utility representation might shed some light on how to tackle these problems.

In this paper, we propose to find an approximation for constraint-based preferences, used mainly in complex negotiation with non-linear utility spaces. The proposed approximation yields a compact form that unifies a whole family of constraints (Cubic, Bell, Conic, etc.). Results show that the new canonical form can in fact be an alternative representation for all known constraint-based utility functions. Additionally, it leads us to a potential parametric model that could be used for opponent modeling in complex non-linear negotiations.

1 Introduction

Preferences are fundamental for the analysis of human choice behavior, and for autonomous agents to make decisions in a desirable and rational way. Consequently, they are becoming of increasing importance in many areas of artificial intelligence such as multi-agent systems [2], game theory [16], decision making [10], social choice [9], constraint satisfaction [5] and so forth.

Since an autonomous agent is capable of experiencing the consequences of her acts, she must have the means of evaluating and of comparing those effects. For instance, representing her preferences as a utility function allows her to choose among a number of competing alternatives [11]. Choosing the right utility function is therefore crucial, as it affects directly the well-being and the welfare of the agent. When choosing a utility function, several aspects have to be addressed, such as the domain being considered, the risk, the uncertainty, the rationality of the opponent(s), etc. For example, in real-world negotiations, constraint-based utility functions offer a practical way to reason about the preferences' of the agents. These preferences are non-linear, non-monotonic, and usually defined over multiple and interdependent issues. This situation is challenging for the negotiating agents in the sense that it yields complex utility spaces, and therefore makes traditional negotiation mechanisms impractical. In such encounters, agents usually do not share their preferences as to avoid exploitation. It is therefore common that

H.K. Dam et al. (Eds.): PRIMA 2014, LNAI 8861, pp. 133–140, 2014.

an agent tries to model the opponent's behavior in order to predict her future offers. This could allow both agents to find a mutually satisfactory outcome, measured in terms of utility gain. In the case where we are certain that the utility space of the opponent is constraint-based, it would be interesting to find the parametrization that governs the opponent's utility model, despite the multitude of constraints' representations.

In this work, we provide a canonical and compact form for constraint-based utility functions that unifies a number of well known constraint-based utility functions, that is, cubic, bell and conic constraints. This leads us to new insights on how to model the preferences of opponents with constraint-based utilities. Several utility representations are being used in automated negotiation, whether for the internal representation of the agent preferences, or whenever the agent is reasoning about her opponent's preferences. Generally, and consistently with the economics literature, the most widely used utility representation exhibits constant relative risk aversion (CRRA) known as the power family or logarithmic utility function [17]. Some use the utility function that exhibits constant absolute risk aversion (CARA) known as the exponential utility function. However, the most commonly used form is based on a general form of utility functions that includes discounting or risk aversion as parametrization [12]. Another alternative for preferences modeling relies on the assumption that the agent's preferences are generated by a random utility model (RUM), which makes the agent utility function composed of a deterministic component and a stochastic unobserved error component [1]. Similar approaches inspired from Machine Learning were largely used for Opponent Modeling. For instance, [18] develops a concession strategy based on Gaussian processes as to predict the opponent's future concessions given her offers. Our adopted representation is instead based on constraints, defined in terms of geometric regions of the utility spaces. They could in fact be defined in terms of shapes like cubes, bell curves, planes or cones, as they were studied in [8,15,13,6,7]. One problem with this representation is that each constraint is to be defined separately, which can be impractical especially with the fact that we are dealing with highly complex domains. To this end, we propose a parametric representation that can fit any possible shape and that is defined as a Mixture of Generalized Gaussians. The new approximation is compact, unified and could reduce the complexity of the optimal contracts search as well as the generation of negotiation scenarios. Additionally, having a parametric form for this type of utility functions could help in modeling the topology of the opponent's utility space by defining prior distributions on the unknown opponent's model, and then use Machine Learning techniques to predict her moves [4]. This of course comes with the assumption that the agents' utility spaces are constraint-based, which is at least true for the non-linear negotiation domains of the ANAC competition [12] in its fifth year.

The paper is structured as following. Next, we provide the general form the constraint-based utility spaces we are interested in. In section 3, we provide our canonical parametric form. In section 4, we provide the approximation. In section 5, we provide an experimental analysis. Finally, we conclude and highlight the future directions.

2   Preliminaries

We start from the general setting of non-linear multi-issue negotiation of [8]. That is, N agents are negotiating over n issues $i_{k \in [1,n]} \in \mathbb{I}$, with $\mathbb{I} = \{i_k\}_{k=1}^n$, forming an

$n-$dimensional utility space. The issue k, namely i_k, takes its values from a set $\mathbb{I}_k$ where $\mathbb{I}_k \subset \mathbb{Z}$. A contract $\boldsymbol{x}$ is a vector of issue values $\boldsymbol{x} \in \mathcal{I}$ with $\mathcal{I} = \times_{k=1}^{n} \mathbb{I}_k$. An agent's utility function is defined in terms of constraints, making the utility space a constraint-based utility space. That is, a constraint $c_{j \in [1,m]}$ is a region of the total $n-$dimensional utility space. We say that the constraint c_j has value $w(c_j, \boldsymbol{x})$ for contract $\boldsymbol{x}$ if c_j is satisfied by $\boldsymbol{x}$. That is, when the contract point $\boldsymbol{x}$ falls within the hyper-volume defined by c_j, namely $hyp(c_j)$. The utility of an agent for a contract $\boldsymbol{x}$ is thus defined as in (1).

$$u(\boldsymbol{x}) = \sum_{c_{j \in [1,m]}, \ \boldsymbol{x} \in hyp(c_j)} w(c_j, \boldsymbol{x}) \tag{1}$$

In the following, we distinguish three types of constraints: Cubic constraints, Bell constraints and Conic constraints, shown in Figure 1. More details about constraint-based utility spaces and their usage could be found in [14,13,15].

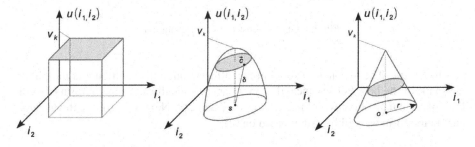

Fig. 1. Cubic, Bell and Conic Constraints

3 Canonical Utility Representation

We start from the intuition that the Generalized Gaussian Distribution (2) could in fact represent a multitude of geometric shapes that could approximate the constraints' shapes we are dealing with. Precisely, the exponent ρ in (2) controls the asymptotic behavior of the function branches (right and left, in the one dimensional case). For the moment, we only focus on the one dimensional case before generalizing.

$$g(x; \rho, \mu, \beta) = \frac{\rho}{2\beta\Gamma(\frac{1}{\rho})} e^{-(\frac{|x-\mu|}{\beta})^\rho} \tag{2}$$

Γ being the gamma function. As it is shown in Figure 2, choosing $\rho = 2$ gives the classical bell curve, or Gaussian distribution. If $\rho \to +\infty$ with $2|\rho$, the previously Gaussian-shaped curve will morph into square wave. Similarly, if $\rho \in [1, 2]$, we get a single-peaked function [3] that could approximate a conic-shaped constraint in its one dimensional case. Thus, depending on the exponent ρ, it is possible to reproduce the three different structures (Cube, Cone, Bell). Particularly, let us take the angle φ defining the slope of the left branch (conversely $-\varphi$ for the right branch) of a 2$-$dimensional

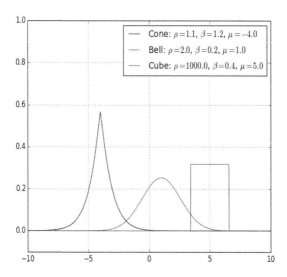

Fig. 2. GGD for constraints representation

bell-like curve. The exponent ρ could in fact affect φ and thus contribute in morphing the shape of the bell. For instance, if ρ grows asymptotically, the general form (2) will look like a square curve with $\lim_{\rho \to +\infty} \varphi = \frac{\pi}{2}$ and $2|\rho$. Next, we propose the general parametric form we will be using, based on (2).

Canonical Form. From (2), we construct a parametrization that corresponds to the partial weight term $w(c_j, \boldsymbol{x})$ in (1). By exchanging the parametrization (ρ, β, μ) in (2) with $(\gamma_j, \beta_j, \zeta_j)$, we re-scale the width, length, height for the n dimensions of the constraint, yielding (3). For example, if the contract point $\boldsymbol{x}$ is located in the hypervolume (or concavity) defined by the n-dimensional function f_j, we get $f_j(\boldsymbol{x}; \pi_j) > 0$.

$$f_j(\boldsymbol{x}; \pi_j) = \gamma_j + \beta_j e^{-\sum_{i=1}^{n} |\zeta_{j,i} x_i - \mu_{j,i}|^{\rho_j}} \tag{3a}$$

$$\pi_j = \rho_j, \beta_j, \gamma_j, \delta_j, \mu_j, \zeta_j \tag{3b}$$

$$\boldsymbol{x} = (x_1, \ldots, x_i, \ldots, x_n) \tag{3c}$$

Accounting for all the m constraints gives the total utility, defined as mixture of Generalized Gaussians (4), which is compatible with its constraint-based counterpart (1).

$$u(\boldsymbol{x}) = \sum_{j=1}^{m} f_j(\boldsymbol{x}; \pi_j) \tag{4}$$

4   Constraints Approximation

It is important to find the right correspondence between the constraint and its fitting function f from the geometric characteristics of the constraint.

4.1 Two Dimensional Case

We start from the general form (5).

$$f(x; \rho, \beta, \gamma, \delta, \mu, \zeta) = \gamma + \beta e^{\delta - |\zeta x - \mu|^\rho} \qquad (5)$$

Next, we show how we approximate the three types of constraints. Depending on the constraint shape, we mainly rely on ρ to firstly define the general shape, as in (6), and then we need to adjust few parameters in f in order to map the correct constraint's dimensions. Next, we take these cases one by one.

$$f(x; \rho, \beta, \gamma, \delta, \mu, \zeta) \begin{cases} 1 \leq \rho \leq 2 & \text{if Conic} \\ \rho = 2 & \text{if Bell} \\ 100 \leq \rho, \ 2|\rho & \text{if Cubic} \end{cases} \qquad (6)$$

Cubic. We take the example of a 2–dimensional cube, *i.e.*, a square. From (5) we compute the two bounds (7) delimiting the square according to the x axis. These specific points are the inflection points provided from the derivative(s) of f. They need to be determined in order to fit the length l and height β of the square, with $l = |\frac{2}{\zeta}(\frac{\rho-1}{\rho})^{1/\rho}|$.

$$x_1 = \frac{1}{\zeta}(\frac{\rho - 1}{\rho})^{1/\rho} - \frac{\mu}{\zeta} \qquad (7a)$$

$$x_2 = -\frac{1}{\zeta}(\frac{\rho - 1}{\rho})^{1/\rho} - \frac{\mu}{\zeta} \qquad (7b)$$

As example, let us take a square delimited by four points $[a, b, c, d]$. Given the square length $l = 19.38$, height $h = 4.19$, we get the parameterization: $\rho = 10^2$, $\beta = 1.5$, $\gamma = -2$, $\delta = 0$, $\mu = 0.432$ and $\zeta = 0.103$. In order to compare the accuracy of the fit we measure the areas (8a) of the constraint ($[a, b, c, d]$) and its approximation in (8b).

$$\mathcal{A}_{square} = h \times l = da \times ab \qquad (8a)$$

$$\mathcal{A}_f = \int_{\frac{-\mu}{\zeta} - \frac{L}{2}}^{\frac{-\mu}{\zeta} + \frac{L}{2}} f(x) - \gamma \, dx \qquad (8b)$$

Thus, $\mathcal{A}_f = 203.328$ and $\mathcal{A}_{l \times h} = 203.49$, which leads to $\lim_{\rho \to \infty} \mathcal{A}_f = \mathcal{A}_{square}$.

Bell. The bell shape is preserved by taking $\rho = 2$ and by defining the width, radius and height based on (β, ζ, μ).

Cone. The branches are straight segments, therefore (5) needs to be linear for those branches. Since the exponential component of (5) is of the form $e^{g(x)}$, $g(x)$ should be logarithmic to yield a linear representation. However, since we are restricted to the general form of (5) we ought to represent the logarithmic function as Taylor series. We start from the simple case of $log(x) = -\sum_{\rho=1}^{\infty} \rho^{-1}(1 - x)^\rho$. Rewriting (3) according to a Taylor aproximation gives (9).

$$f(x; \beta, \gamma, \delta, \mu, \zeta) = \gamma + \beta e^{\delta - \sum_{\rho=1}^{\infty} \rho^{-1}|\zeta x - \mu|^\rho} \qquad (9)$$

It is possible to linearize the branches and lower the two bottom inflection points by removing the ρ^{-1} term under the summation in (9) and preserve the general form (3). After fitting the mean μ/ζ of the cone, the approximation of a two dimensional cone of height β, an apex angle proportional to ζ, and a center μ/ζ is given in (10).

$$f(x; \beta, \gamma, \delta, \mu, \zeta) = \gamma + \beta e^{\delta - \sum_{\rho=1}^{\infty} |\zeta x - \mu|^\rho} \tag{10}$$

4.2   General Case

In the following, we take the general case of a $n-$dimensional utility space with a contract point (3c). Most of the constraints are symmetrical with respect to the dimensions, which is due to the absolute value in (3a). Hence, we assume that $\delta = 0 \; \forall x_i, \; i \in [1, n]$. Similarly, we assume that ζ is invariant for all dimensions, although it could be defined in a specific way for each dimension and therefore yield a parallelepiped instead of a cube. Let us now take the constraints one by one. For an $n-$dimensional utility space, a cube-constraint utility function is represented as in (11). It relies only on the exponent ρ as it should be large ($\rho \simeq 10^3$) and even. In this case, ρ could control the precision of the fit by flexibly adjusting φ to any right angle of the cube.

$$f(\boldsymbol{x}; \rho, \beta, \gamma, \delta, \mu, \zeta) = \gamma + \beta e^{- \sum_{i=1}^{n} |\zeta x_i - \mu_i|^\rho} \tag{11}$$

We note that for cubes, β acts like the height of the cube and is equivalent to the utility that will be assigned to any contract contained in the cube. For a bell, we need to choose an exponent $\rho = 2$ as to fit an $n-$dimensional Gaussian distribution. It is important that the result in (12) is adequately fitted to the real dimensions of the bell to be approximated. This could be done by finding the right relationship between the width, radius, center of the bell and the parameters ζ and μ. For instance, by assuming that the width of the bell is equal to $2\sigma \sqrt{log(2)}$, σ being the standard deviation of (12).

$$f(\boldsymbol{x}; \beta, \gamma, \delta, \mu, \zeta) = \gamma + \beta e^{- \sum_{i=1}^{n} |\zeta x_i - \mu_i|^2} \tag{12}$$

Finally, for an $n-$dimensional utility space, a cone-constraint utility function is represented as in (13).

$$f(\boldsymbol{x}; \beta, \gamma, \delta, \mu, \zeta) = \gamma + \beta e^{- \sum_{\rho=1}^{\infty} \sum_{i=1}^{n} |\zeta x_i - \mu_i|^\rho} \tag{13}$$

We can clearly see the Taylor expansion in the exponent, necessary for the linearization of the exponential form.

5   Experimental Analysis

We propose few examples of $3-$dimensional cubic and conic constraints, and see how they could be approximate based on the general form (3).

Herein, we evaluate the alignment, or the fitting, between the constraints and their functional approximations. The bell constraint is unchanged, whether it is defined using our functional parametric form, or as a Bell, Gaussian or Normal distribution in the large sense. To this end, we use two approaches: one is by random sampling from the constraint and then counting the contracts that fall within the concavity of f by getting $f(x) > 0$. The second approach computes the volume of the constraint and compares it to the integral of the approximated function. If the approximation is adequate, bother measures should coincide. We start by randomly selecting n contracts from the cube constraint. One contract $x = (x_1, x_2, x_3)$ is selected by picking each x_i, $i \in [1, 2, 3]$, within the bounds defined by the width, length and height of the cube. Let us take the example where we want to approximate a cube with a function f. One way of evaluating how good is this approximation, is to generate random contract points within the cube, and check if the same contracts fall within the concavity of f. It is possible to have 100% of the contracts fall in both the cube and the concavity of the function f. As another evaluation, we can to compute the volume of f as $V_f = \int_{x=-\theta+\mu_1}^{\theta+\mu_1} \int_{y=-\theta+\mu_2}^{\theta+\mu_2} f(x; \rho, \beta, \gamma, \delta, \mu, \zeta) \, dy \, dx$, with $\theta = \frac{1}{\zeta}(\frac{\rho-1}{\rho})^{1/\rho}$. In our example, we found that both volumes coincide by yielding $V_f = 635.797$ and $V_{cube} = 636.0$. We also note that in this case, ρ affects largely the precision of the approximation ($\lim_{\rho \to \infty} V_f = V_{cube}$).

As another example, we selected n contracts from a randomly generated cone constraint. In our evaluation, for $n = 100$ contracts, we got 93% contracts, with $V_{cone} = 50.26$ and $V_f = 31.62$ being the integration of of f. It i possible to enhance this precision by adjusting the ζ of the function until it covers the relatively important parts of the cone.

6   Conclusion

We have provided a practical way to approximate a family of constraint-based utility function based on one unified parametric form. The new representation reduces the complexity inherent to the definition of the constraints and adds more flexibility when hard constraints are present.

As a future direction to be investigated, we are thinking about using the current parametric form for Opponent Modeling. In fact, we have shown how the constraints' descriptions could collapse to fewer parameters (3b) that could potentially be defined using prior distributions and the underlying hyper-parameters. Particularly, these parameters could be estimated using well known Machine Learning techniques, for instance as a Generalized Gaussian Process [18].

References

1. Azari Soufiani, H., Diao, H., Lai, Z., Parkes, D.C.: Generalized random utility models with multiple types. In: Burges, C., Bottou, L., Welling, M., Ghahramani, Z., Weinberger, K. (eds.) Advances in Neural Information Processing Systems 26, pp. 73–81. Curran Associates, Inc. (2013)

2. Aziz, H.: In: Shoham, Y., Leyton-Brown, K. (eds.) Multiagent Systems: Algorithmic, Game-theoretic, and Logical Foundations. Cambridge University Press (2008); SIGACT News 41(1), 34–37 (2010)
3. Coombs, C., Avrunin, G.: Single-peaked Functions and the Theory of Preference: A Generalization of S-R Theory. Michigan mathematical psychology program, University of Michigan, Department of psychology (1976)
4. Do, C.B., Batzoglou, S.: What is the expectation maximization algorithm? Nature Biotechnology 26(8), 897–900 (2008)
5. Farinelli, A., Rogers, A., Jennings, N.R.: Agent-based decentralised coordination for sensor networks using the max-sum algorithm. Journal of Autonomous Agents and Multi-Agent Systems 28(3), 337–380 (2014), http://eprints.soton.ac.uk/350670/
6. Fujita, K., Ito, T., Klein, M.: A secure and fair negotiation protocol in highly complex utility space based on cone-constraints. In: Proceedings of the 2009 International Joint Conference on Intelligent Agent Technology (IAT 2009) (2009)
7. Hadfi, R., Ito, T.: Addressing complexity in multi-issue negotiation via utility hypergraphs. In: AAAI (2014)
8. Ito, T., Hattori, H., Klein, M.: Multi-issue negotiation protocol for agents: Exploring non-linear utility spaces. In: Proceedings of the 20th International Joint Conference on Artificial Intelligence (IJCAI 2007), pp. 1347–1352 (2007)
9. Johnson, P.E.: Social Choice: Theory and Research. Quantitative Applications in the Social Sciences, vol. 123. SAGE Publications (1998)
10. Keeney, R.L., Raiffa, H.: Decisions with multiple objectives. Cambridge University Press (1993)
11. Keeney, R., Raiffa, H.: Decisions with multiple objectives preferences and value tradeoffs. Behavioral Science 39(2), 169–170 (1994)
12. Lin, R., Kraus, S., Baarslag, T., Tykhonov, D., Hindriks, K., Jonker, C.M.: Genius: An integrated environment for supporting the design of generic automated negotiators. Computational Intelligence 30(1), 48–70 (2014)
13. Lopez-Carmona, M.A., Marsa-Maestre, I., De La Hoz, E., Velasco, J.R.: A region-based multi-issue negotiation protocol for nonmonotonic utility spaces. Computational Intelligence 27(2), 166–217 (2011)
14. Marsa-Maestre, I., Lopez-Carmona, M.A., Velasco, J.R., de la Hoz, E.: Effective bidding and deal identification for negotiations in highly nonlinear scenarios. In: Proceedings of The 8th International Conference on Autonomous Agents and Multiagent Systems, AAMAS 2009, vol. 2, pp. 1057–1064. International Foundation for Autonomous Agents and Multiagent Systems, Richland (2009)
15. Marsa-Maestre, I., Lopez-Carmona, M., Carral, J., Ibanez, G.: A recursive protocol for negotiating contracts under non-monotonic preference structures. Group Decision and Negotiation 22(1), 1–43 (2013)
16. von Neumann, J., Morgenstern, O.: Theory of games and economic behavior, 2nd edn. Princeton University Press, Princeton (1947)
17. Wakker, P.P.: Explaining the characteristics of the power (crra) utility family. Health Economics 17(12), 1329–1344 (2008)
18. Williams, C.R., Robu, V., Gerding, E.H., Jennings, N.R.: Using gaussian processes to optimise concession in complex negotiations against unknown opponents. In: Proceedings of the 22nd International Joint Conference on Artificial Intelligence. AAAI Press (2011)

Deliberative Argumentation for Smart Environments

Juan Carlos Nieves, Esteban Guerrero, Jayalakshmi Baskar, and Helena Lindgren

Department of Computing Science
Umeå University
901 87, Umeå, Sweden
{jcnieves,esteban,jaya,helena}@cs.umu.se

Abstract. In this paper, an *argumentation-based deliberative approach* for fusing contextual information obtained from heterogeneous sources using *a multi-agent system* is introduced. The system is characterized by three different agents: *an Environment Agent, an Activity Agent* and *a Coach Agent*. These agents consider data from heterogenous sources of data. As a method for aggregating data and supporting decision-making, so-called *agreement rules* are instrumental in the argumentation-based deliberative method. The aggregation rules will be associated to specific beliefs related to the services of each agent.

1 Introduction

As a result of the daily activities of humans, there can be a vast and increasing volume of a variety of data that is collected from different sources, *e.g.,* sensors from smart environments. The data is typically represented using a variety of formats, *e.g., relational databases, rule-based knowledge bases, etc.* Moreover, these data sources are consulted by using different query engines, in order to serve the human with useful information. Consequently, providing services, such as support for decision-making by synthesizing the relevant sources of data, represents a fundamental challenge in information management.

In this paper, an *argumentation-based deliberative approach* for fusing contextual information from heterogeneous sources using *a multi-agent system* is introduced. *Deliberation dialogues* aim at reasoning for deciding upon what action to make (also called *practical reasoning* in literature) and have been explored by several authors in the argumentation literature [1,2,3,8]. The argumentation-based deliberative approach introduced in this paper, is motivated by the design and construction of *As-A-Pal*, a smart home environment functioning as a part of the As-A-Pal architecture initially presented in [9]. The As-A-Pal project aims at developing an agent-based assessment and intervention infrastructure, where *personalized interventions* are provided, which can be viewed as services. Therefore, our multi-agent system is described in terms of the services supported by As-A-Pal.

The paper presents the following two major contributions: 1) a multi-agent approach designed to fuse contextual information from heterogeneous sources; and 2) an argumentation-based deliberative method based on argument inquiry dialogues [3], Well-Founded Semantics (WFS) [4] and *agreement rules*. The materialization of the

H.K. Dam et al. (Eds.): PRIMA 2014, LNAI 8861, pp. 141–149, 2014.

multi-agent approach is based on three software agents: *an Environment Agent*, *an Activity Agent* and *a Coach Agent*. These three agents have different goals and different capabilities; however, they are collaborative in order to provide services to a user in smart environments. The design of these agents follows the conceptual models of Activity Theory [7]. The inquiry dialogues support both data aggregation and decision making from heterogenous sources of data. The deliberative method is based on both knowledge bases expressed in terms of logic programs with negation as failure and WFS [4]. We show that our approach is sound *w.r.t.* the inference of WFS. Moreover, we show that deciding whether an agreement rule is committed is decidable in polynomial time.

The article is organized as follows: Section 2 introduces our suggested multi-agent approach. Section 3 introduces our argumentation-based deliberative method. In the last section, our conclusions and future work are presented.

2   A Multi-agent Systems for Providing Intelligent Services

In this section, we present the first contribution of this paper, which is a multi-agent approach designed to deliver personalized services in a smart environment.

Since human activity performance is complex, we apply *activity-theoretical models* for capturing motives, goals, composite actions, the role of tools, and the levels of complexity of actions [7]. The use of activity-theoretical models is justified by the following three reasons. Firstly, *Activity Theory* emphasizes that human activity is affected by the environment, and dependent on the availability and the characteristics of *tools*, which enable and mediate activity. Consequently, the physical environment is taken into consideration, when a human actor is moving around, finding tools to use in activities. Secondly, activity is composed of actions in an hierarchy of complexity, which is dynamic, and puts challenges on technology aimed at recognizing and evaluating activity in an ambient assisted living environment [7]. For instance, the human can conduct her breakfast routine in different ways, even cook her porridge in different ways. The selection of procedure depends on several factors, some which the human is aware of, and some selections are done automatically, without thinking. For a support system to know and decide if, or at which point, the system should interfere for giving support is a non-trivial task. Thirdly, Activity Theory emphasizes the *changing nature of activity* and human ability to perform activity, driven by motives, goals, challenges and focus shifts, which in turn drives development [7]. The concept *zone of proximal development* (ZPD) is applied, where a human Actor is expected to be able to perform an activity with the assistance of a more skillful peer, until the autonomy is reached. In our scenario, the intervention in the form of the As-A-Pal system functions as the more skillful peer, for the purpose to improve activity performance. These three activity-theoretical perspectives are captured by the so called *Environment Agent*, *Activity Agent* and *Coach Agent*, see Figure 1.

The agents have been partially implemented in the As-A-Pal smart environment. They supplement the *Domain Agent*, previously introduced [9], which has the role of a domain expert in our multi-agent systems. However, in this work, we focus on the other three agents. The three agents are human-centered, i.e. they take the human Actor as the starting point while providing the personalized services. As-A-Pal is a smart environment where the acronym As-A-Pal refers to *Agent-Supported Assessment for*

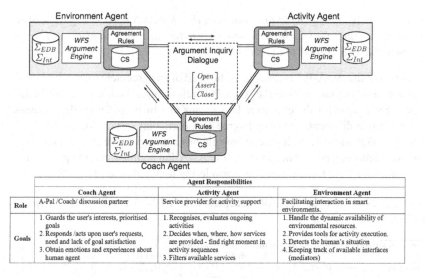

Fig. 1. Interaction between agents and their goals

Agent Responsibilities		
Coach Agent	**Activity Agent**	**Environment Agent**
Role A-Pal /Coach/ discussion partner	Service provider for activity support	Facilitating interaction in smart environments.
Goals 1. Guards the user's interests, prioritised goals 2. Responds /acts upon user's requests, need and lack of goal satisfaction 3. Obtain emotions and experiences about human agent	1. Recognises, evaluates ongoing activities 2. Decides when, where, how services are provided - find right moment in activity sequences 3. Filters available services	1. Handle the dynamic availability of environmental resources. 2. Provides tools for activity execution. 3. Detects the human's situation 4. Keeping track of available interfaces (mediators)

Adaptive and Personalized Ambient Assisted Living. As-A-Pal also refers to "like a friend", an artificial companion that knows the immediate needs of the human actor, her preferences, priorities and abilities, so that adaptive and personalized services tailored to the current context can be provided.

3   A Deliberative Argumentation Approach

In Section 2, a multi-agent architecture was introduced. One of the main issues to deal with in this architecture, is to reach agreements between its agent in order to select the best service to offer to an end-user. In this section, an argumentation approach is presented, which manages agreements between the As-A-Pal architecture's agents. This argumentation approach will be basically an operational implementation of *an deliberation dialogue*. A deliberation dialogue is characterized as a dialogue occurring when two or more parties aim to agree on an action in some situation. To implement deliberation dialogues between the As-A-Pal's agents, we provide each agent with a set of so-called *agreement rules*. An agreement rule is basically *a consensus* in which the different participant of a deliberation dialogue agree. Agreement rules will be associated to specific *goals* related to *the services* of the As-A-Pal architecture. Hence, an agreement rule will be defined as follows.

Let us start presenting the following notation: given a logic-based theory T, $\mathcal{L}_T$ denotes the set of atoms which appears in T.

Definition 1. *An agreement rule is of the form:*

$$\alpha : a_0 \leftarrow a_1, \ldots, a_n$$

in which $\alpha \in \mathbb{N}$, $a_i (0 \le i \le n)$ is an atom such that for each $a_i (1 \le i \le n)$ either exists an agent Ag such that its logic-based knowledge base is Σ and $a_i \in \mathcal{L}_\Sigma$ or $a_i \in \mathcal{L}_{AR}$ such that AR is a set of agreement rules, and $a_0 \ne a_i (1 \le i \le n)$.

In the context of the As-A-Pal architecture, the head of an agreement rule, *a.i.* a_o, will be associated to a particular belief of the As-A-Pal architecture. For instance, this belief can be a service suitable for the end user. This means that by considering the trueness of an agreement rule different agents will agree on a particular service for a user.

According to Definition 1, each agreement rule has a natural number attached. This natural number denotes a preference level. In the As-A-Pal architecture, the preference levels are managed by the *Coach Agent* by considering user-satisfiability.

Example 1. Let us consider a couple of agreement rules of the As-A-Pal smart environment as illustration:

AR1	$\alpha_1 : service(reminder, Z, M) \leftarrow optimal\_mediator(Z, M), \neg past\_activity(Z,$ $takenpills), requested\_service(Z, reminders).$
AR2	$\alpha_2 : optimal\_mediator(Z, M) \leftarrow mediator(M), is\_near(M, Z), current\_activity(Z, X),$ $acivity\_object(M, X).$

In these agreement rules, we are assuming that predicates such as $mediator(M)$ and $is\_near(M, Z)$ belong to the knowledge base of the environment agent. Moreover, the predicates $current\_activity(Z, X)$ belongs to the knowledge base of the activity agent. Therefore, the agents have to interact in order to decide if a given agreement rule holds true in a given state of the As-A-Pal system.

The general idea of our approach is to consider an *argument inquiry dialogue* in order to validate the trueness of a given agreement rule. If an agreement rule holds true in an given state of the As-A-Pal architecture, then the head of the given agreement rule holds the trueness of a particular believe in the whole As-A-Pal system.

Inspired by [3], our argument inquiry dialogues are based on three basic moves: *open*: $\langle x, open, \ dialogue(ai, \gamma) \rangle$, *assert*: $\langle x, assert, \langle S, a \rangle \rangle$ and *close*: $\langle x, close, dialogue(ai, \gamma) \rangle$ in which x denotes an agent, $\langle S, a \rangle$ is an argument, γ denotes *an agreement rule* and ai means "argument inquiry dialogue". It should be noted that the format of these moves are not exactly the same as the ones introduced by [3]. Our moves are applied to only the *argument inquiry dialogue type*, which can be opened only by applying an agreement rule as a topic. This means that the nested process between argument inquiry dialogues is only induced by agreement rules. Moreover, the arguments suggested by assert-moves will be constructed based on the deductive arguments introduced in [6]. We have implemented an argumentation engine, which constructs these arguments from a logic program [6][1]. Given a logic program Σ, $\mathcal{A}_\Sigma$ denotes the set of arguments built from Σ.

From hereon, we apply the definition of dialogue introduced in [3]. D_r^t denotes a dialogue which is a sequence of moves $[m_r, \dots, m_t]$ involving a set of participants $\mathcal{I}$, where $r, t \in \mathbb{N}$. As in [3], we apply the restriction that a dialogue *terminates* whenever all the participants of a dialogue have made a close move in a consecutive form.

---

[1] This argumentation engine can be downloaded from:
   http://esteban-guerrero.tumblr.com/argengine

In addition, it is allowed to open another dialogue without terminating the ongoing dialogue, which allows us to manage multi-nested dialogues.

In the following we present the protocol of an argument inquiry dialogue as a sequence of general steps. Let $\mathcal{I}$ be the finite set of participants of a dialogue. We identify each agent from $\mathcal{I}$ by a natural number this means that $\mathcal{I} = 1, \ldots, n$ such that $i = \langle \Sigma^i, AR^i, CS^i \rangle$ in which Σ^i denotes the knowledge base of agent i, AR^i denotes a set of agrement rules which belongs to agent i and CS^i denotes a commitment store of agent i. Σ^i and CS^i are basically extended normal logic programs. As it is done in [3], a dialogue is attached by a query store. Hence, an argument inquiry dialogue works as follows:

Step Argument Inquiry Dialogue

---

1 One of the participant agents starts the argumentation inquiry dialogue with the move $\langle x, open, dialogue(ai, \gamma) \rangle$.

2 The query store QS is updated.

3 Each participant agent i performs one of the following moves:

  1. $\langle i, assert, \langle S, a \rangle \rangle$ if $\langle S, a \rangle \in \mathcal{A}_\Sigma$, $a \in QS$ in which $\Sigma = \Sigma^i \cup \bigcup_{j \in \mathcal{I} \text{ and } i \neq j} CS^j$ and none of the participants have asserted the argument $\langle S, a \rangle$ in the dialogue before. The commitment store of the agent i is updated.

  2. $\langle i, open, dialogue(ai, a_0 \leftarrow a_1, \ldots, a_n) \rangle$ if $a_0 \in QS$, $\alpha : a_0 \leftarrow a_1, \ldots, a_n \in AR^i$ and there is no previous open move in the dialogue with $a_0 \leftarrow a_1, \ldots, a_n$ as its topic. The dialogue go to Step 1 in a recursive way.

  3. $\langle i, close, dialogue(ai, \gamma) \rangle$ if the agent i is unable to perform one of the previous steps.

There are formal conditions *w.r.t. well-formed argument inquiry dialogues*, which basically argue that all the moves *extend* an initial dialogue and all the participants of the dialogue have the opportunity to perform a move (see [3] for the formal definitions).

Given an argument inquiry dialogue, its outcome is defined as follows:

Definition 2. *Let D_r^t be a well-formed argument inquiry dialogue. The outcome of D_r^t is: $Outcome_{ai}(D_r^t) = \mathcal{A}_\Sigma$ such that $\Sigma = \bigcup_{i \in \mathcal{I}} CS^i$.*

As we can see in Definition 2, the outcome of an argument inquiry dialogue is basically the set of arguments, which we can build from the commitment stores of all the participating agents.

In order to define when an agreement rule γ is *committed* by a set of agents $\mathcal{I}$, let us introduce the concept of *an agrement atom*. Let $i = \langle \Sigma, AR, CS \rangle$ be an agent. $a \in \mathcal{L}_{AR}$ is called *an agrement atom* iff $a \notin \mathcal{L}_\Sigma$ and it does not exist an agent $j = \langle \Sigma^j, AR^j, CS^j \rangle$ such that $a \in \mathcal{L}_{\Sigma^j}$. This means that agreement atoms only appears in agreement rules.

We will say that an agreement rule γ is *committed* by a set of agents $\mathcal{I}$ as follows:

Definition 3. *Let D_r^t be a well-formed argument inquiry dialogue involving a set of participant $\mathcal{I}$ and $m_r = \langle x, open, dialogue(ai, \gamma) \rangle$ such that $x \in \mathcal{I}$ and $\gamma = a_0 \leftarrow a_1, \ldots, a_n$ is an agreement rule. γ is a committed agreement rule by $\mathcal{I}$ w.r.t. D_r^t if for each $a_i (1 \leq i \leq n)$ one of the following conditions hold:*

1. *if a_i is not an agreement atom, then $\langle S, a_i \rangle \in Outcome_{ai}(D_r^t)$.*
2. *if a_i is an agreement atom, then there exist a sub-well-formed argument inquiry dialogue D_q^j such that $m_q = \langle agent, open, dialogue(ai, a_i \leftarrow a_1, \ldots, a_k) \rangle$ and $a_i \leftarrow a_1, \ldots, a_k$ is a committed agreement rule by $\mathcal{I}$ w.r.t. D_q^j.*

An important property of a committed agreement rule is that this rule holds true by the well-founded model of the resulting program of the join of all the commitment stores and agreement rules of the participating agents.

Theorem 1. *Let D_r^t be a well-formed argument inquiry dialogue involving a set of participant $\mathcal{I}$ and $m_r = \langle x, open, dialogue(ai, \gamma) \rangle$ such that $x \in \mathcal{I}$, $\gamma = a_0 \leftarrow a_1, \ldots, a_n$ is an agreement rule. If γ is a committed agreement rule by $\mathcal{I}$ w.r.t. D_r^t iff $a_i \in T(1 \leq i \leq n)$ such that $\Sigma = \bigcup_{i \in \mathcal{I}} CS^i \cup AR^i$ and $WFS(\Sigma) = \langle T, F \rangle$.[2]*

Another relevant property of a committed agreement rule is that deciding whether an agreement rule is committed is decidable in polynomial time.

Proposition 1. *Let γ be an agreement rule, $\mathcal{I}$ be a set of agents and D_r^t be an argument inquiry dialogue. Deciding whether γ is a committed agreement rule by $\mathcal{I}$ w.r.t. D_r^t is decidable in polynomial time .*

Since more than one agreement rule could hold committed in a given moment, we will consider the preference level of each agreement rule for selecting the best service, which the As-A-Pal architecture can provide to an end-user.

Definition 4. *Let $\gamma_a = \alpha_a : a_0 \leftarrow a_1, \ldots, a_n$ and $\gamma_b = \alpha_b := b_0 \leftarrow b_1, \ldots, b_n$ be committed agreement rule. γ_a is preferred than γ_b if $\alpha_a < \alpha_b$.*

Whenever an agent has to take a decision about which service to provide, it will take the service supported by a preferred committed agreement rule. If there are two committed agreement rules with the same preference level, the agent will take one of the these committed agreement rules in a random way. We could think that taking a committed agreement rule in a random way could be a drawback of our approach. However, the preference level of each agreement rule will be updated according to the user satisfaction with the choice. In this setting, an agreement rule, which supports a service with a poor user satisfiability will decrease its preference level. The update of preference levels will be managed by the coach agent.

---

[2] $WFS(\Sigma) = \langle T, F \rangle$ denotes the 3-valued model of the logic program Σ. Informally speaking, T denotes the set of atoms which are inferred true and F denotes the set of atoms which are inferred false. See [4] for the formal definition of the well-founded model.

Example 2. Let us introduce a simple example of a well-formed argument inquiry dialogue. To reduce space in the presentation, we will associate some abbreviations to the grounded predicates of the knowledge bases of the agents:

Predicate	Acronym	Predicate	Acronym
$service(reminder, rut, walker\_tablet)$	s1	$optimal\_mediator(rut, walker\_tablet)$	om
$past\_activity(rut, takenpills)$	pa	$requested\_service(rut, reminders))$	rs
$mediator(walker\_tablet)$	mwt	$is\_near(walker\_tablet, rut)$	nwt
$current\_activity(rut, walking)$	cw	$activity\_object(walker\_tablet, walking)$	awt
$current\_activity(rut, takenpills)$	ctp		

In this example, we consider the agreement rules introduced in Example 1. Let us suppose that the agreement rule AR1 belongs to Coach Agent. AR1 aims to provide a reminder to the user about her medication. Before considering this reminder, Coach Agent needs to know whether the user has taken her medication. If not, Coach Agent needs to know if there is an optimal mediator, *e.g.*, a digital interface, near the user for delivering the reminder. To find an optimal mediator is a goal of Environment Agent. Hence, we assume that AR2 belongs to Environment Agent. To record activities performed by the user is a goal of Activity Agent. Given this scenario, Coach agent opens an argument inquiry dialogue: $\langle 1, open, dialogue(ai, s1 \leftarrow om, \neg pa, rs \rangle$. Table 1 illustrates the moves of the dialogue.

Table 1. An example of an argument inquiry dialogue. m_t denotes the moves conducted by the agents. They are denoted as follows: Coach Agent (1), Environment Agent (2) or Activity Agent (3).

t	CS_1^t	CS_2^t	CS_3^t	m_t	QS_t
1				$\langle 1, open, dialogue(ai, s1 \leftarrow om, \neg pa, rs)\rangle$	$QS_1 = \{om, \neg pa, rs\}$
2				$\langle 2, open, dialogue(ai, om \leftarrow mwt, nwt, cw, awt)\rangle$	$QS_2 = \{ mwt, nwt, cw, awt\}$
3			$cw \leftarrow \top$	$\langle 3, assert, \langle\{cw \leftarrow \top\}, cw\rangle\rangle$	
4				$\langle 1, close, dialogue(ai, om \leftarrow mwt, nwt, cw, awt)\rangle$	
5		$mwt \leftarrow \top$		$\langle 2, assert, \langle\{mwt \leftarrow \top\}, mwt\rangle\rangle$	
6			$awt \leftarrow \top$	$\langle 3, assert, \langle\{awt \leftarrow \top\}, awt\rangle\rangle$	
7				$\langle 1, close, dialogue(ai, om \leftarrow mwt, nwt, cw, awt)\rangle$	
8		$nwt \leftarrow \top$		$\langle 2, assert, \langle\{nwt \leftarrow \top\}, nwt\rangle\rangle$	
9				$\langle 3, close, dialogue(ai, om \leftarrow mwt, nwt, cw, awt)\rangle$	
10				$\langle 1, close, dialogue(ai, om \leftarrow mwt, nwt, cw, awt)\rangle$	
11				$\langle 2, close, dialogue(ai, om \leftarrow mwt, nwt, cw, awt)\rangle$	
12			$\neg pa \leftarrow not\ pa, not\ ctp$	$\langle 3, assert, \langle\{\neg pa \leftarrow not\ pa, not\ ctp\}, \neg pa\rangle\rangle$	
13	$rs \leftarrow \top$			$\langle 1, assert, \langle\{rs \leftarrow \top\}, rs\rangle\rangle$	
14				$\langle 2, close, dialogue(ai, s1 \leftarrow om, \neg pa, rs)\rangle$	
15				$\langle 3, close, dialogue(ai, s1 \leftarrow om, \neg pa, rs)\rangle$	
16				$\langle 1, close, dialogue(ai, s1 \leftarrow om, \neg pa, rs)\rangle$	

As can be observed in Table 1, $AR1$ is a committed agreement rule by all agents *w.r.t.* D_1^{16}. Moreover, D_1^{16} is a well-formed argument inquiry dialogue. Let us observe that D_1^{16} has the sub-dialogue D_2^{11} which is also well-formed. Given that the atom $service(reminder, rut, walker\_tablet)$ is an agreement atom which suggests to deliver a reminder to the user Rut, Coach Agent can deliver a reminder to Rut in order to remind her to take her medication.

4   Conclusions and Future Work

In this paper, a multi-agent approach designed to fuse contextual information from heterogeneous sources in an ambient assisted living environment is presented. In particular, three agents have been introduced: the *Environment Agent*, the *Activity Agent* and the *Coach Agent*. The design of these agents follows conceptual models of Activity Theory, in order to capture the ambiguous and changing nature of human activity, and human preferences, needs, ability and motives. By introducing the concept of *agreement rules*, an argumentation-based deliberative method based on *argument inquiry dialogues* was also introduced. We show that our approach is sound *w.r.t.* the inference of the Well-Founded Semantics (WFS) (Theorem 1). Moreover, we show that deciding whether an agreement rule is committed is decidable in polynomial time (Proposition 1).

Our model of a deliberative process in smart environments was inspired by Black and Hunter's inquiry dialogue systems [3]. However, unlike Black and Hunter's inquiry dialogue system [3], which is based on *Defeasible Logic Programming* for capturing knowledge and reasoning, we apply and implement logic programs with negation as failure and the WFS [4] for capturing knowledge and reasoning.

Our approach is conceptually close to the HERA project [10], which is an AAL system that provides specialized assisted living services for elderly people. From the knowledge representation point of view, our approach is similar to the one suggested by [11] in which the underlying mechanism for capturing the knowledge base relies on Extended Disjunctive Programs under the Answer Set Semantics [5].

In future work, we will focus on two main issues: 1) A combination of our argument inquiry dialogues with warrant inquiry dialogues in order to allow the agents to disagree with assert moves; 2) a complete implementation of our approach, using message-oriented middleware (MOMs) such as Data Distribution Service (DDS) for implementing argument inquiry dialogues.

Acknowledgements. This research is partly funded by VINNOVA (Sweden's innovation agency) and the Swedish Brain Power.

References

1. Amgoud, L., Prade, H.: Reaching agreement through argumentation: A possibilistic approach. In: Principles of Knowledge Representation and Reasoning: Proceedings of the Ninth International Conference (KR 2004), Whistler, Canada, June 2-5, pp. 175–182. AAAI Press (2004)

2. Atkinson, K., Bench-Capon, T., Walton, D.: Distinctive features of persuasion and deliberation dialogues. Argument and Computation 4(2), 105–127 (2012)

3. Black, E., Hunter, A.: An inquiry dialogue system. Autonomous Agents and Multi-Agent Systems 19(2), 173–209 (2009)

4. Gelder, A.V., Ross, K.A., Schlipf, J.S.: The well-founded semantics for general logic programs. Journal of the ACM 38(3), 620–650 (1991)

5. Gelfond, M., Lifschitz, V.: Classical negation in logic programs and disjunctive databases. New Generation Computing 9(3-4), 365–385 (1991)

6. Guerrero, E., Nieves, J.C., Lindgren, H.: Arguing through the Well-founded Semantics: an Argumentation Engine. Submitted to a Journal (2014)
7. Kaptelinin, V.: Activity theory: Implications for human-computer interaction. In: Nardi, B. (ed.) Context and Consciousness. Activity Theory and Human Computer Interaction, pp. 103–116. MIT Press (1996)
8. Kraus, S., Sycara, K.P., Evenchik, A.: Reaching agreements through argumentation: A logical model and implementation. Artif. Intell. 104(1-2), 1–69 (1998)
9. Lindgren, H., Surie, D., Nilsson, I.: Agent-supported assessment for adaptive and personalized ambient assisted living. In: Corchado, J.M., Pérez, J.B., Hallenborg, K., Golinska, P., Corchuelo, R. (eds.) Trends in Practical Applications of Agents and Multiagent Systems. AISC, vol. 90, pp. 25–32. Springer, Heidelberg (2011)
10. Marcais, J., Spanoudakis, N., Moraitis, P.: Using argumentation for ambient assisted living. In: Iliadis, L., Maglogiannis, I., Papadopoulos, H. (eds.) EANN/AIAI 2011, Part II. IFIP AICT, vol. 364, pp. 410–419. Springer, Heidelberg (2011)
11. Sá, S., Alcântara, J.: Cooperative dialogues with conditional arguments. In: Proceedings of the 11th International Conference on Autonomous Agents and Multiagent Systems, vol. 1, pp. 501–508. International Foundation for Autonomous Agents and Multiagent Systems (2012)

Development of Traffic Simulator Based on Stochastic Cell Transmission Model for Urban Network

Sho Tokuda[1], Ryo Kanamori[2], and Takayuki Ito[3]

[1] Department of Computer Science and Engineering,
Graduate School of Engineering Nagoya Institute of Technology,
Gokiso-cho, Showa-ku, Nagoya, Aichi 466-8555, Japan
`tokuda.sho@itolab.nitech.ac.jp`
[2] Institute of Innovation for Future Society, Nagoya University,
Furo-cho, Chikusa-ku, Nagoya, Aichi 464-8601, Japan
`kanamori.ryo@nagoya-u.jp`
[3] School of Techno-Business Administration,
Graduate School of Engineering Nagoya Institute of Technology,
Gokiso-cho, Showa-ku, Nagoya, Aichi 466-8555, Japan
`ito.takayuki@nitech.ac.jp`

Abstract. This study proposes the modified stochastic cell transmission model (M-SCTM), which can be used to apply the conventional SCTM to urban networks. Although SCTM can represent an uncertainty of traffic state and changing travel demand or supply conditions, it has been applied to a freeway or a simple network that has only one origin-destination pair. In M-SCTM, we introduce vehicle agents and their route choice behavior on an urban network for application to more complex urban networks. From the results of an empirical study, we confirm the reproducibility of traffic volume and travel time that are calculated by M-SCTM.

Keywords: Traffic simulation, stochastic cell transmission model, urban network, route search.

1 Introduction

Traffic simulators are currently used to evaluate transportation policies for smoothing traffic flow. A traffic simulator can predict temporal and spatial traffic jams, and the uncertainty of traffic state. To evaluate traffic control measures, a high-accuracy traffic simulator is required.

The stochastic cell transmission model (SCTM) [1], [2] has been proposed as a macro traffic simulation model of high accuracy. SCTM can represent an uncertainty of traffic state and changing travel demand or supply conditions. So far, SCTM has only been applied to freeways and simple networks that are one-to-one origin-destination networks.

In this study, we propose a modified stochastic cell transmission model (M-SCTM) for applying SCTM to urban networks. As general roads are large-scale

H.K. Dam et al. (Eds.): PRIMA 2014, LNAI 8861, pp. 150–165, 2014.

and complicated networks, there are some problems when SCTM is applied directly. First, setting a turning ratio at diverging points in urban networks is difficult. A turning ratio represents the ratio of flow from a diverging point to each branch destination. In SCTM, a turning ratio is set beforehand in networks, and vehicles choose a route depending on the turning ratio. However, calculation of a turning ratio requires detailed data, including the amount of flow from a diverging point to each branch destination. Furthermore, a turning ratio is used inaccurately to represent a driver's route choice behavior at diverging points. Therefore, we create a vehicle agent, calculate each vehicle agent's shortest path under traffic conditions at the starting time period, and adjust the flow at each diverging and merging point according to the number of vehicle agents at each diverging and merging point. Since the traffic flows are modeled as vehicle agents, we assume M-SCTM to be a mesoscopic model, and regard our simulation as a multi-agent simulation. Second, SCTM cannot represent network structure around adjacent intersections. To represent adjacent intersections, we propose a method to represent subsystems. As an empirical study, due to comparing M-SCTM with SCTM in dynamic process of density in subsystems, we conduct a simulation with the same settings and confirm the accuracy of M-SCTM. Also, we use famous road network data of Kichijoji and Mitaka City in Tokyo, Japan. From the results of utilizing M-SCTM with this network data, we confirm the reproducibility of each vehicle's travel time.

The multi-agent simulation has been extensively studied, since the characteristics of an agent, which is autonomous, collaborative, and reactive, is required in traffic and transportation management [3]. Agents can operate without centralized control, and this feature helps to implement automated traffic control management systems. Furthermore, multi-agent systems can connect to distributed subsystems, and can be extended to large-scale multi-agent simulations.

The outline of this paper is as follows: Section II gives some background and touches on an issue with SCTM. Section III presents a solution to the issue and introduces M-SCTM. Section IV provides the empirical study on a segment of Kichijoji and Mitaka City in Tokyo. Lastly, Section V highlights conclusions and future research issues.

2 Stochastic Cell Transmission Model

2.1 Descriptions

The stochastic cell transmission model (SCTM) was developed by A. Sumalee et al. [1], [2]. SCTM represents a road segment using multiple cells and makes one subsystem consisting of two cells. The overall network is composed by each subsystem interconnecting with other subsystems. SCTM can simulate the traffic dynamics of a road with stochastic demands and supplies. In general, the demand and supply are uncertain, and the prediction of the traffic state becomes inaccurate due to the changing traffic state. In SCTM, the uncertainty of demand is represented by adding a noise sequence to each outflow to subsystems.

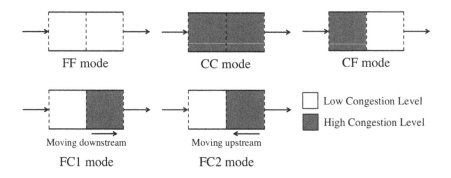

Fig. 1. Five modes of subsystem [1]

On the contrary, the uncertainty of supply is represented by adding a noise sequence to each subsystem parameter. All the noise sequences are assumed to follow Gaussian processes. Due to noise addition, the inflow and each parameter are assumed to be random variables.

SCTM utilizes the concept of mode, which is based on the switching-mode model [4], [5]. The five modes represent the congestion levels of two cells in each subsystem. The five modes are FF (Free flow-Free flow) mode, CC (Congestion-Congestion) mode, CF (Congestion-Free flow) mode, FC1 (Free flow-Congestion1) mode, and FC2 (Free flow-Congestion2) mode as depicted in Fig. 1. In Fig. 1, a white cell represents the traffic state as free flow, and a red cell represents the traffic flow as congestion. FF mode represents that the first cell and second cell are free flow. CC mode represents that the first cell and second cell are congestion. CF mode represents that the first cell is congestion and the second cell is free flow. FC mode represents that the first cell is free flow and the second cell is congestion. FC mode can be divided into two additional modes. FC1 mode represents that the wavefront is moving to the second cell. FC2 mode represents that the wavefront is moving to the first cell.

The mode in a subsystem is defined by the parameters of the two cells in the subsystem. However, the mode is non-unique because the parameters are random variables. Thus, an occurrence probability of each mode in a subsystem can be defined as in (1). In FF mode, the occurrence probability can be represented as in (1a):

$$P_{FF}(k) = Pr(\rho_u(k) < \rho_{c,1}(k) \cap \rho_d(k) < \rho_{c,2}(k)), \qquad (1a)$$

where $P_{FF}(k)$ is the occurrence probability of FF mode at time k, $\rho_u(k)$ and $\rho_d(k)$ are the densities of the first and second cells at time k, respectively, $\rho_{c,1}(k)$ and $\rho_{c,2}(k)$ are the critical densities that mean the threshold of congestion of the first and second cells at time k, respectively. In CC mode, the occurrence probability can be represented as in (1b):

$$P_{CC}(k) = Pr(\rho_u(k) \geq \rho_{c,1}(k) \cap \rho_d(k) \geq \rho_{c,2}(k)), \qquad (1b)$$

where $P_{CC}(k)$ is the occurrence probability of CC mode at time k. In CF mode, the occurrence probability can be represented as in (1c):

$$P_{CF}(k) = Pr(\rho_u(k) \geq \rho_{c,1}(k) \cap \rho_d(k) < \rho_{c,2}(k)), \qquad (1c)$$

where $P_{CF}(k)$ is the occurrence probability of CF mode at time k. In FC mode, the occurrence probability can be represented as in (1d):

$$P_{FC}(k) = 1 - (P_{FF}(k) + P_{CC}(k) + P_{CF}(k)), \qquad (1d)$$

where $P_{FC}(k)$ is the occurrence probability of FC mode at time k. The calculation of the occurrence probabilities of FC1 mode and FC2 mode is different from the others. In FC1 mode, the occurrence probability can be represented as in (1e):

$$P_{FC1}(k) = P_{FC}(k)Pr(v_{f,1}(k)\rho_u(k) \leq w_{c,2}(k)(\rho_{J,2}(k) - \rho_d(k))), \qquad (1e)$$

where $P_{FC1}(k)$ is the occurrence probability of FC1 mode at time k, $v_{f,1}(k)$ is the free-flow speed of the first cell at time k, $w_{f,2}(k)$ is the backward wave speed of the second cell at time k, $\rho_{J,2}(k)$ is the jam density of the second cell at time k. In FC2 mode, the occurrence probability can be represented as in (1f):

$$P_{FC2}(k) = P_{FC}(k)Pr(v_{f,1}(k)\rho_u(k) > w_{c,2}(k)(\rho_{J,2}(k) - \rho_d(k))), \qquad (1f)$$

where $P_{FC2}(k)$ is the occurrence probability of FC2 mode at time k.

In SCTM, the dynamics of a subsystem's density is defined by the following formulation as in (2):

$$\rho(k+1) = (A_0 + \sum_{i=1}^{p} A_i\omega_i(k))\rho(k) + (B_0 + \sum_{i=1}^{p} B_i\omega_i(k))\lambda(k) + Bu(k), \qquad (2)$$

where $\rho(k)$ is the vector of a subsystem's density at time k, $\omega(k)$ and $\lambda(k)$ are random vectors to be dependent on a subsystem's mode, $u(k) = (q_u(k), q_d(k))$ is the vector comprised of inflow $q_u(k)$ and outflow $q_d(k)$ at time index k, A_i, B_i, $i = 0, 1, 2$, and B are constant matrices to be dependent on a subsystem's mode. A_i, B_i, B, $\omega(k)$, and $\lambda(k)$ are represented under each mode as follows:

FF mode:

$$A_1 = \begin{bmatrix} -\frac{T_s}{l_1} & 0 \\ \frac{T_s}{l_2} & 0 \end{bmatrix}, A_2 = \begin{bmatrix} 0 & 0 \\ 0 & -\frac{T_s}{l_2} \end{bmatrix}, B = \begin{bmatrix} \frac{T_s}{l_1} & 0 \\ 0 & 0 \end{bmatrix},$$

$$B_0 = 0_{2\times2}, \qquad B_1 = 0_{2\times2}, \qquad B_2 = 0_{2\times2},$$

$$\omega(k) = \begin{bmatrix} v_{f,1}(k) & v_{f,2}(k) \end{bmatrix}^T, \lambda(k) = \begin{bmatrix} 0 & 0 \end{bmatrix}^T,$$

CC mode:

$$A_1 = \begin{bmatrix} -\frac{T_s}{l_1} & 0 \\ 0 & 0 \end{bmatrix}, A_2 = \begin{bmatrix} 0 & \frac{T_s}{l_1} \\ 0 & -\frac{T_s}{l_2} \end{bmatrix}, B = \begin{bmatrix} 0 & 0 \\ 0 & -\frac{T_s}{l_2} \end{bmatrix},$$

$$B_0 = 0_{2\times2}, \qquad B_1 = -A_1, \qquad B_2 = -A_2,$$

$$\omega(k) = \begin{bmatrix} w_{c,1}(k) \; w_{c,2}(k) \end{bmatrix}^T, \; \lambda(k) = \begin{bmatrix} \rho_{J,1}(k) \; \rho_{J,2}(k) \end{bmatrix}^T,$$

CF mode:

$$A_1 = \begin{bmatrix} -\frac{T_s}{l_1} & 0 \\ 0 & 0 \end{bmatrix}, \; A_2 = \begin{bmatrix} 0 & 0 \\ 0 & -\frac{T_s}{l_2} \end{bmatrix}, \; B = 0_{2\times2},$$

$$B_0 = \begin{bmatrix} 0 & -\frac{T_s}{l_1} \\ 0 & \frac{T_s}{l_2} \end{bmatrix}, \; B_1 = -A_1, \qquad B_2 = 0_{2\times2},$$

$$\omega(k) = \begin{bmatrix} w_{c,1}(k) \; v_{f,2}(k) \end{bmatrix}^T, \; \lambda(k) = \begin{bmatrix} \rho_{J,1}(k) \; Q_M(k) \end{bmatrix}^T,$$

FC1 mode:

$$A_1 = \begin{bmatrix} -\frac{T_s}{l_1} & 0 \\ \frac{T_s}{l_2} & 0 \end{bmatrix}, \; A_2 = 0_{2\times2}, \; B = \begin{bmatrix} \frac{T_s}{l_1} & 0 \\ 0 & -\frac{T_s}{l_2} \end{bmatrix},$$

$$B_0 = 0_{2\times2}, \qquad B_1 = 0_{2\times2}, \; B_2 = 0_{2\times2},$$

$$\omega(k) = \begin{bmatrix} v_{f,1}(k) \; 0 \end{bmatrix}^T, \; \lambda(k) = \begin{bmatrix} 0 \; 0 \end{bmatrix}^T,$$

FC2 mode:

$$A_1 = 0_{2\times2}, \; A_2 = \begin{bmatrix} 0 & \frac{T_s}{l_1} \\ 0 & -\frac{T_s}{l_2} \end{bmatrix}, \; B = \begin{bmatrix} \frac{T_s}{l_1} & 0 \\ 0 & -\frac{T_s}{l_2} \end{bmatrix},$$

$$B_0 = 0_{2\times2}, \; B_1 = 0_{2\times2}, \qquad B_2 = \begin{bmatrix} 0 & -\frac{T_s}{l_1} \\ 0 & \frac{T_s}{l_2} \end{bmatrix},$$

$$\omega(k) = \begin{bmatrix} 0 \; w_{c,2}(k) \end{bmatrix}^T, \; \lambda(k) = \begin{bmatrix} 0 \; \rho_{J,2}(k) \end{bmatrix}^T,$$

where T_s is the sampling duration, l_1 and l_2 are the lengths of the first and second cells, $v_{f,1}(k)$ and $v_{f,2}(k)$ are the free-flow speeds of the first and second cells at time k, $w_{c,1}(k)$ and $w_{c,2}(k)$ are the backward wave speeds of the first and second cells at time k, $\rho_{J,1}(k)$ and $\rho_{J,2}(k)$ are the jam densities of the first and second cells at time k, $Q_M(k)$ is the maximum flow of a cell at time k. Finally, the overall effect of the five modes needs to be estimated, namely joint traffic density. The probability distribution of the joint traffic density is defined by merger among all probability distributions of the density in each mode. The mean of the joint traffic density is represented by the following formulation as in (3):

$$E(\bar{\rho}(k)|\theta(k)) = \sum_s P_s E(\bar{\rho}(k)|\theta_s(k)) = \sum_s P_s(k)E(\rho_s(k)), \qquad (3)$$

where $\bar{\rho}(k)$ is the joint traffic density at time k, $P_s(k)$ is the occurrence probability of the mode $s \in \{FF, CC, CF, FC1, FC2\}$ at time k, $\rho_s(k)$ is the traffic density in the mode s at time k, the parameter set is defined as $\sum_s P_s(k) = 1$, $\{\theta(k)\} = \{\theta_s(k)\}$, $\theta_s(k) = (P_s, \rho_s(k))$.

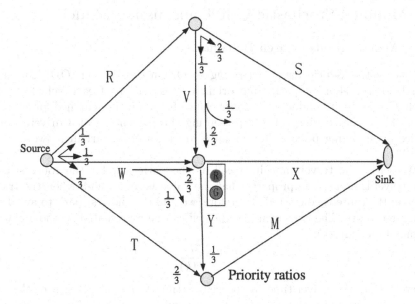

Fig. 2. Simple network in Zhong et al. [6]

2.2 Problems for Application to Urban Network

When it comes to applying SCTM to general roads, there are some problems. Zhong et al. [6] apply SCTM to a simple network as depicted in Fig. 2. The simple network sets the turning ratio at diverging points and includes only one origin and one destination of drivers. The turning ratio is the value that represents in which direction vehicles move and how vehicles move at diverging points. The calculation of a turning ratio requires detailed data, including the amount of flow from the diverging point to each branch destination. Moreover, as there are multiple pairs of origins and destinations of drivers in an urban network, it is difficult to set the turning ratio to urban networks. Thus, applying SCTM to urban networks is difficult.

Moreover, SCTM can't represent adjacent intersections. The network utilized in Zhong's study is represented as one intersection. Therefore, with Zhong's expression method of networks, although one intersection can be represented, one adjacent intersection can't be represented in urban networks. If Zhong's expression method represents an adjacent intersection, the duplication of cells is generated. The duplication of cells suggests the situation where one cell is assigned by two subsystems. If there is duplication of a cell, the movement of vehicles does not proceed well. Thus, the expression method needs to be changed when SCTM represents a general road.

3   Modified Stochastic Cell Transmission Model

3.1   Agent's Route Search Behavior

We create the vehicle agent according to Origin-Destination (OD) flow, and search for the shortest path from origin to destination of each vehicle agent. Each vehicle agent conducts the route choice based on the searched for shortest path. Thus, the turning ratio, representing the percentage of a driver's route choice at diverging points, doesn't have to be set to an urban network as in SCTM.

We select the travel time in a cell as the path cost for the route search. The travel time has the property that the value becomes high when the traffic state in the route is congested. Therefore, we find the shortest path to avoid the congested route. The travel time in the cell can be represented by the following formulation as in (4):

$$t(k) = \frac{l}{v(k)}, \tag{4}$$

where $t(k)$ is the travel time in the cell at time k, l is the length of the cell, $v(k)$ is the speed of traffic flow at time k. v can be represented by Greenshields model [7]. Greenshields model can be represented by the following formulation as in (5):

$$v(k) = v_f(k) \left(1 - \frac{\rho(k)}{\rho_j(k)}\right), \tag{5}$$

where v_f is the free-flow speed at time k, ρ is the traffic density at time k, ρ_j is the jam density at time k. v_f suggests the traffic speed when the traffic density is zero. ρ_j suggests the traffic density when the traffic speed is zero. (4) and (5) can represent the flow-density relation, the travel time is long when the traffic density of a cell is high, and the travel time is short when traffic density in the cell is low.

The route search is conducted before vehicle agents are created, and each vehicle agent with the result of the route search is put on its origin in the network. Then, the vehicle agent moves from its origin to its destination according to its own route. We assume that drivers with a destination choose the shortest path and avoid a congested route when one is encountered. In our study, Dijkstra's algorithm [8] is utilized to search for the shortest path.

We now describe the flow of the simulation. First, the travel time in a cell is set as the path cost. Next, a vehicle agent's shortest path from its origin to its destination is searched for, and the vehicle agent has its own shortest path. The vehicle agent chooses a route according to its shortest path and aims at its destination.

3.2   Dynamic State Inside Subsystem

The representation of dynamic state of the traffic flow needs to determine how many vehicle agents can move to the next cell. To sum up, we need to define the amount of flow from the upstream cell to the downstream cell in a subsystem. As in (3), we define the probability distribution of flow inside the subsystem in each mode, and estimate the overall effect of the five modes, namely joint flow inside the subsystem. The probability distribution of flow inside the subsystem in each mode is represented by the following formulation as in (6):

$$q_{FF}(k) = v_{f,1}(k)\rho_1(k), \tag{6a}$$

$$q_{CC}(k) = w_{c,2}(k)(\rho_{J,2}(k) - \rho_2(k)), \tag{6b}$$

$$q_{CF}(k) = Q_m(k), \tag{6c}$$

$$q_{FC1}(k) = v_{f,1}(k)\rho_1(k), \tag{6d}$$

$$q_{FC2}(k) = w_{c,2}(k)(\rho_{J,2}(k) - \rho_2(k)), \tag{6e}$$

where $q_{FF}(k)$, $q_{CC}(k)$, $q_{CF}(k)$, $q_{FC1}(k)$, and $q_{FC2}(k)$ are the traffic flow inside the subsystem in FF mode, CC mode, CF mode, FC1 mode, and FC2 mode at time k. The overall effect of the five modes is defined by merger among all probability distributions of flow inside the subsystem in each mode. The mean of the joint flow inside a subsystem is represented by the following formulation as in (7):

$$E(q(k)) = \sum_s P_s(k)E(q_s(k)), \tag{7}$$

where $q(k)$ is the joint flow inside a subsystem at time k, $P_s(k)$ is the probability of occurrence in mode $s \in \{FF, CC, CF, FC1, FC2\}$ at time k, $q_s(k)$ is the flow inside a subsystem in mode s at time k. Eventually, we assume the amount of flow from the upstream cell to the downstream cell in a subsystem as in (7).

The density of the two cells of the subsystem can be defined by the number of vehicle agents and the lengths of the cells. The densities of the upstream cell and downstream cell can be defined by the following formulation as in (8):

$$\rho_1(k+1) = \frac{n_1(k)}{l_1}, \tag{8a}$$

$$\rho_2(k+1) = \frac{n_2(k)}{l_2}, \tag{8b}$$

where $\rho_1(k)$ and $\rho_2(k)$ are the densities of the upstream cell and downstream cell in a subsystem at time k, $n_1(k)$ and $n_2(k)$ are the numbers of vehicle agents in a cell at time k, $l_1(k)$ and $l_2(k)$ are the lengths of the upstream cell and downstream cell. We must perform some traces of the place where each vehicle agent exists because the vehicle agents move according to the result of the route search. Therefore, we can confirm the number of vehicle agents in each cell.

3.3 Dynamic State among Multiple Adjacent Subsystems

Next, we need to represent the dynamic state of traffic flow among adjacent subsystems. Thus, we must define the amount of flow among multiple adjacent subsystems. In an urban network, there are multiple diverging flows from diverging points and merging flows to merging points. Although the calculation of flow between two neighboring subsystems can be conducted in the same way as SCTM, dynamic state of flow at diverging and merging points in an urban network need to be taken into account.

First, we describe the dynamic state of the traffic flow between two adjacent subsystems in SCTM. To define the flow between two adjacent subsystems, the sending flow from each upstream subsystem needs to be defined under different congestion levels. To determine the sending flow from the upstream subsystem $S(k)$ at time k, the probability of the mode in the upstream subsystem is defined as in (1). The two events to determine $S(k)$ exist under different modes in the upstream subsystem. If the mode of an upstream subsystem is FF mode or CF mode, $S(k)$ equals $v_{f,1}(k)\rho_1(k)$, and if it is CC mode or FC mode, $S(k)$ equals $Q_1(k)$. $v_{f,1}(k)$ is the free-flow speed in the second cell of an upstream subsystem at time k, $\rho_1(k)$ is the traffic density of the second cell of an upstream subsystem at time k, and $Q_1(k)$ is the maximum flow of the second cell of an upstream subsystem at time k. Then, the receiving flow to downstream subsystems is determined according to the probability of the mode of downstream subsystems. Subject to the congestion conditions of downstream subsystems and $S(k)$, the receiving flow can be classified by the following four events:

1. If the mode of downstream subsystems is FF mode or FC mode and $S(k)$ is less than or equal to $Q_2(k)$, then $R_{j,1}(k)$ equals $S(k)$;
2. If the mode of downstream subsystems is FF mode or FC mode and $S(k)$ is more than $Q_2(k)$, then $R_{j,2}(k)$ equals $Q_2(k)$;
3. If the mode of downstream subsystems is CC mode or CF mode and $S(k)$ is less than or equal to $w_{c,2}(k)(\rho_{J,2}(k) - \rho_2(k))$, then $R_{j,3}(k)$ equals $S(k)$;
4. If the mode of downstream subsystems is CC mode or CF mode and $S(k)$ is less than $w_{c,2}(k)(\rho_{J,2}(k)-\rho_2(k))$, then $R_{j,4}(k)$ equals $w_{c,2}(k)(\rho_{J,2}(k)-\rho_2(k))$;

where $Q_2(k)$ is the maximum flow of the first cell of a downstream subsystem at time k, $w_{c,2}(k)$ is the backward wave speed of the first cell of a downstream subsystem at time k, $\rho_{J,2}(k)$ is the jam density of the first cell of a downstream subsystem at time k, $\rho_2(k)$ is the traffic density of the first cell of a downstream subsystem at time k. $R_{j,1}(k)$, $R_{j,2}(k)$, $R_{j,3}(k)$, and $R_{j,4}(k)$ are the receiving flows in subsystem j in each event at time k. The probabilities of each event can be represented by the following formulation as in (9):

$$P_1(k) = (P_{FF}(k) + P_{FC}(k))Pr(S(k) \leq Q_2(k)), \tag{9a}$$
$$P_2(k) = (P_{FF}(k) + P_{FC}(k))Pr(S(k) > Q_2(k)), \tag{9b}$$
$$P_3(k) = (P_{CC}(k) + P_{CF}(k))Pr(S(k) \leq w_{c,2}(k)(\rho_{J,2}(k) - \rho_2(k))), \tag{9c}$$
$$P_4(k) = (P_{CC}(k) + P_{CF}(k))Pr(S(k) > w_{c,2}(k)(\rho_{J,2}(k) - \rho_2(k))), \tag{9d}$$

where $P_1(k)$, $P_2(k)$, $P_3(k)$, and $P_4(k)$ are the probabilities of each event at time k. Eventually, the overall effect of the four events, the joint receiving flow, needs to be estimated. The overall effect of the four events is defined by merger among all probability distributions of receiving flow in each event such as in (3). Then, the mean of the joint receiving flow is represented by the following formulation

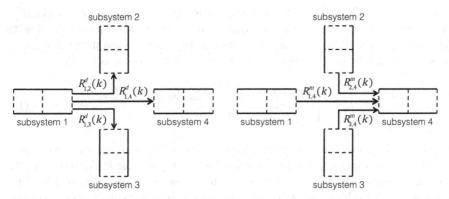

(a) Diverging flow at diverging point   (b) Merging flow at merging point

Fig. 3. Adjustment of flow at diverging and merging points

as in (10)

$$E(R_j(k)|\chi(k)) = \sum_y P_y(k)E(R_j(k)|\chi_y(k))$$

$$= \sum_y P_y(k)E(R_{j,y}(k)), \tag{10}$$

where $R_j(k)$ is the joint receiving flow in subsystem j at time k, $P_y(k)$ is the occurrence probability of the event $y \in \{1, 2, 3, 4\}$ at time k, $R_{j,y}(k)$ is the receiving flow in subsystem j in the event y at time k, the parameter set is defined as $\sum_y P_y(k) = 1$, $\{\chi(k)\} = \{\chi_y(k)\}$, $\chi_y(k) = (P_y(k), R_y(k))$.

Second, we describe the dynamic state of traffic flow at diverging and merging points. Although the traffic flow in one-to-one adjacent subsystems $R_j(k)$ can be represented as in (10), the dynamic state of traffic flow at diverging and merging points can't be defined in the same way. Since traffic flow at diverging and merging points is in one-to-many, many-to-one, or many-to-many neighboring subsystems as in Fig. 3, $R_j(k)$ needs to be adjusted. We adjust the flow at diverging points according to the ratio of the number of vehicle agents to be aimed at each branch destination. The adjustment of the flow from the diverging subsystem to some other subsystem can be represented by the following formulation as in (11):

$$R_{i,j}^d(k) = \frac{n_{2,j}^i(k)}{\sum_j n_{2,j}^i(k)} R_j(k), \tag{11}$$

where $R_{i,j}^d(k)$ is the flow from the diverging subsystem i to subsystem j at time k, $n_{2,j}^i(k)$ is the number of vehicle agents to be aimed at subsystem j at the second cell of diverging subsystem i at time k. For example, the flows from subsystem 1 to each subsystem are represented as in Fig. 3(a). Because a merging point's capacity may fall into overflow, we also need to adjust the flow at merging points as in Fig. 3(b). Therefore, if the capacity of a merging point is more than $R^d_{i,j}$, then the flow at merging points is adjusted according to the ratio of the flow to the merging point. The adjustment of the flow from some subsystems to merging subsystems can be represented by the following formulation as in (12):

$$R^m_{i,j}(k) = \begin{cases} R^d_{i,j}(k) & (\sum_i R^d_{i,j}(k) \le C_{1,j}(k)) \\ \frac{R^d_{i,j}(k)}{\sum_i R^d_{i,j}(k)} C_{1,j}(k) & (otherwise) \end{cases} \tag{12}$$

where $R^m_{i,j}(k)$ is the flow from subsystem i to the merging subsystem j at time k, $C_{1,j}(k)$ is the capacity of the first cell in subsystem j at time k. For example, the flows from each subsystem to each subsystem 4 are represented as in Fig. 3(b). Eventually, the vehicle agents move between neighboring subsystems according to the amount of flow to be adjusted by (11), (12).

3.4 Assignment Method of Subsystem

In Zhong's study, four subsystems are utilized to represent an intersection. One link represents one cell, and cells facing each other across an intersection are assigned to the same subsystem in Zhong's study. However, if Zhong's assignment method is applied to an adjacent intersection as depicted in Fig. 4, the duplication of cells occurs. Both assignment methods of SCTM and M-SCTM are depicted in Fig. 5. In Fig. 5, the color of each cell represents which subsystem cells are assigned, then same-color cells are assigned by the same subsystem. The duplication of cells suggests the situation where one cell is assigned by two subsystems as depicted in Fig. 5(a). The blue cell and the brown cell, the yellow cell and the purple cell are overlapping in Fig. 5(a). When the traffic simulation is conducted, there should not be duplication of cells. If one cell is assigned to multiple subsystems, a problem with the movement of vehicles occurs. The flow between two adjacent subsystems becomes incorrect, and vehicles cannot move from an arbitrary cell to their destination cells. If there is a problem with

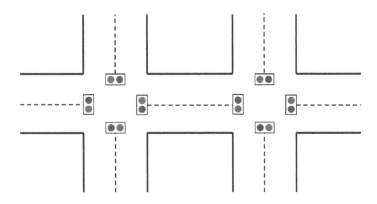

Fig. 4. Adjacent intersections

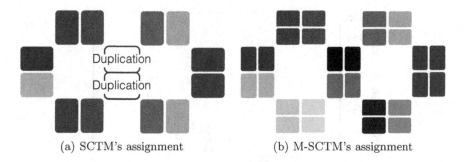

(a) SCTM's assignment	(b) M-SCTM's assignment

Fig. 5. Different kind of assignment method in each model

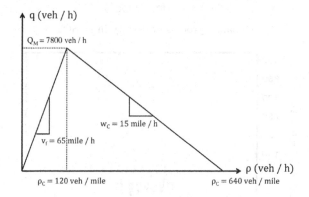

Fig. 6. Fundamental flow-density diagram of parameters[6]

the movement of vehicles, the simulation cannot be implemented. Because general roads include multiple intersections, the assignment method of subsystems should be more detailed.

Therefore, in M-SCTM, one link is represented as two cells; thus two cells are assigned by one subsystem. M-SCTM can represent adjacent intersections without the duplication of cells. An adjacent intersection is assigned a subsystem as depicted in Fig. 5(b). In Fig. 5(b), there is no duplication of cells in an adjacent intersection.

4   Empirical Study

4.1   Accuracy Verification of M-SCTM

To confirm the accuracy of M-SCTM, we compare it with the result of Zhong's study [6]. We conduct a simulation with the same settings as Zhong's study, and compare M-SCTM and SCTM in terms of the dynamic process of density of cells. In Zhong's study, a simple network as in Fig. 2 is utilized. In Fig. 2, the length of all links is 1 mile. The simulation time increment is 5 seconds and the

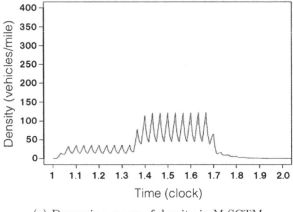

(a) Dynamic process of density in M-SCTM

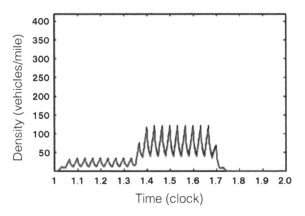

(b) Dynamic process of density in Zhong's study

Fig. 7. Result of dynamic process of density in each model

signal has a cycle time of 2 minutes. The fundamental flow-density diagram of the parameters is depicted in Fig. 6. The means of the parameter uncertainties are assumed to be 0, and the standard deviations of parameter uncertainties are assumed to be 5%. The inflow at time k $q_u(k)$ is given as follows:

$$q_u(k) = \begin{cases} 6,000\,vehicles/hour & (0 \leq k \leq 20\,minutes) \\ 21,000\,vehicles/hour & (20 \leq k \leq 40\,minutes) \\ 0\,vehicles/hour & (40 \leq k \leq 60\,minutes) \end{cases}$$

We plot the output of the simulation based on M-SCTM of the dynamic process of density of link R as depicted in Fig. 7(a), and show the result of the dynamic process of density of link R in Zhong's study in Fig. 7(b). In 7(a) and 7(b), the horizontal axis is the density of link R, and the vertical axis is the

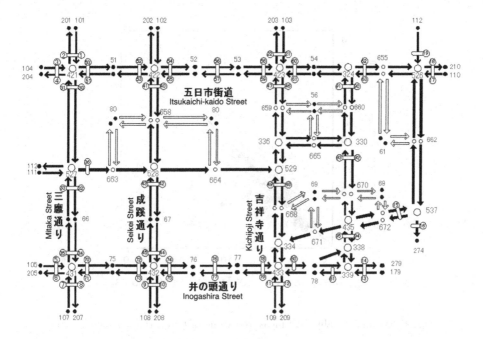

Fig. 8. Urban network of Kichijoji and Mitaka City

simulation time. Compared with Fig. 7(b), Fig. 7(a) is similar with respect to the dynamic process of density. From the results of dynamic process of density, we also find that M-SCTM has the same accuracy as SCTM.

4.2   Reproducibility Verification of M-SCTM

Next, to verify the reproducibility of the traffic simulation based on M-SCTM in an urban network, we conduct an empirical study using the observation data from the surveillance of number plates in the benchmark data set of Kichijoji and Mitaka City [9]. Kichijoji and Mitaka City are in Tokyo, Japan as depicted in Fig. 8. To search for each driver's route, the path cost in a cell is set at the travel time. We choose 130 minutes as the whole simulation time, and throw approximately 18,000 vehicles into the network. The standard deviations of the parameter uncertainties are assumed to be 10%. As the output of the simulation, the travel time that it takes the vehicle to move from its origin to its destination is obtained. In terms of the travel time, we compare the output from the simulation based on M-SCTM and the observation data.

We plot the output of the simulation based on M-SCTM of the travel time of each vehicle as depicted in Fig. 9. In Fig. 9, the horizontal axis is the estimated value, the vertical axis is the measured value, red points are output data in M-SCTM, and the black line is a straight line of 45 degrees. The black line denotes that the error between the estimated value and the measured value is

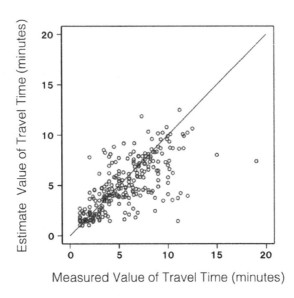

Fig. 9. Estimated value and measured value of travel time of each vehicle

smaller when red points are closer to the line. As shown in Fig. 9, the red dots are clustered around the black line. We calculate the correlation coefficient of the estimate value with the measured value, and the resulting value is approximately 0.7. Moreover, we calculate the regression coefficient in the case where the intercept of the regression line is zero. The resulting value is approximately 0.8. From the results, we find high validity of the traffic simulation based on M-SCTM. Also, the error between the estimated value and the measured value is small, and the reproducibility of the simulation based on M-SCTM is appropriate.

5   Conclusion

In this paper, a modified stochastic cell transmission model (M-SCTM) was proposed for applying SCTM to urban networks. M-SCTM can be utilized to apply traffic simulations to networks in which the turning ratio is not set by introducing a route search algorithm. Moreover, M-SCTM can be utilized to estimate the traffic state of the large-scale networks. To verify the accuracy of the simulation based on M-SCTM, we compared the output of our simulator with the result of Zhong's study in terms of dynamic process of density of the arbitrary cell. The result revealed that M-SCTM can conduct a simulation with as much accuracy as SCTM. Moreover, to verify the reproducibility of the simulation based on M-SCTM, we compared the estimated value and the measured value in terms of the travel time of each vehicle. We found the reproducibility of the traffic simulation based on M-SCTM to be appropriate.

A future research issue is the parameter estimation of each cell. Although we set constant values as the parameters for each cell, the parameters should be estimated from a measured value on each road as in [10]. Furthermore, although we utilized Dijkstra's algorithm and found the shortest path, we need to select an alternative method to represent a driver's route choice, such as Dial's algorithm [11].

References

1. Sumalee, A., Zhong, R., Pan, T., Szeto, W.Y.: Stochastic cell transmission model (SCTM): A stochastic dynamic traffic model for traffic state surveillance and assignment. Transportation Research Part B 45, 507–533 (2011)
2. Sumalee, A., Pan, T., Zhong, R., Uno, N., Indra-Payoong, N.: Dynamic stochastic journey time estimation and reliability analysis using stochastic cell transmission model: Algorithm and case studies. Transportation Research Part C: Emerging Technologies 35, 63–285 (2013)
3. Chen, B., Cheng, H.H.: A review of the applications of agent technology in traffic and transportation systems. IEEE Transactions on Intelligent Transportation Systems, 485–497 (2010)
4. Muñoz, L., Sun, X., Horowitz, R., Alvarez, L.: Traffic Density Estimation with the cell transmission model. In: Proceedings of the American Control Conference, Denver, Colorado, USA, pp. 3750–3755 (2003)
5. Sun, X., Muñoz, L., Horowitz, R.: Highway Traffic State Estimation Using Improved Mixture Kalman Filters for Effective Ramp Metering Control. In: 42th IEEE Conference on Decision and Control, vol. 6, pp. 6333–6338 (2003)
6. Zhong, R., Sumalee, A., Pan, T., Lam, W.: Stochastic cell transmission model for traffic network with demand and supply uncertainties. In: Transportmetrica A: Transport Science, P567–P602 (2013)
7. Greenshields, B.D.: A study of traffic capacity. Highway Research Board 14, 448–477 (1935)
8. Dijkstra, E.W.: A note on two problems in connexion with graphs. Numerische Mathematik 1, 269–271 (1959)
9. Traffic Simulation Clearinghouse.: Public Website for Verification Data in Traffic Simulation Clearinghouse,
   `http://www.i-transportlab.jp/bmdata/KichijojiBM/ave-dataset/`
   `ave-index.html`
10. Fransson, M., Sandin, M.: Framework for Calibration of a Traffic State Space Model. In: Master of Science in Communication and Transport Engineering, P42–P48 (2012)
11. Dial, R.B.: A probabilistic multi-path traffic assignment model which obviates path enumeration. Transportation Research 5, 83111 (1971)

A Scalable Workbench for Large Urban Area Simulations, Comprised of Resources for Behavioural Models, Interactions and Dynamic Environments

Leonel Enrique Aguilar Melgar[1], Maddegedara Lalith[2], Muneo Hori[2],
Tsuyoshi Ichimura[2], and Seizo Tanaka[2]

[1] Department of Civil Engineering, University of Tokyo, Bunkyo,
Tokyo 113-8656, Japan
[2] Earthquake Research Institute, University of Tokyo, Bunkyo,
Tokyo 113-0032, Japan
{leaguilar,lalith,hori,ichimura,stanaka}@eri.u-tokyo.ac.jp

Abstract. A multi-agent based large urban area evacuation simulator
is developed with the aim of addressing the limitations of the present
large area simulators. Environment model of sub-meter details and agents
which can visually perceive it are implemented, so that complex evacuees
behaviours can be included, making it possible to study scenarios beyond
those covered by the existing simple models. A mathematical framework
is extended to include sufficient expressiveness and an overview of the
developed software is presented in the context of this framework. Further
details of the agent system and available agents' functions are presented.
In order to increase the results' reliability, a parallel tool for automatic
calibration of the agent interactions according to observed human behaviours is included. Finally, demonstrative applications of the software
highlighting the need of detailed modelling are presented.

1 Introduction

Extensive studies of a wide range of possible evacuation scenarios and preparations are necessary to prevent large loss of lives from the anticipated
mega-tsunamis. Current software for large area evacuation simulations use highly
simplified models, in which environment and evacuees are modelled as 1D networks and queues. Although these simplified models give useful insights for some
scenarios, there are many important scenarios demanding detailed model of environment and complex agents, e.g. night time evacuation during a festival with
many visitors. Moreover, software capable of taking details into account are
restricted to smaller domains as they don't scale beyond a few CPUs[1]. Therefore, there is a great need for developing a scalable large urban area simulator
supporting detailed models of environment and complex agents.

In order to address the above need, a multi agent based evacuation simulation software, including sub-meter level details of large urban area, supporting

H.K. Dam et al. (Eds.): PRIMA 2014, LNAI 8861, pp. 166–181, 2014.
© Springer International Publishing Switzerland 2014

the modelling of evacuees' behaviours in details, is developed. This tool can be used by expert teams as an experimental playground to quantitatively evaluate the effects of different scenarios and mitigation measures in an exploratory manner. Basic agents' interaction which have a significant effects on the evacuation time have been included, e.g. collision avoidance[2], vision[2], navigation[2] and communication. Other features are incorporating agents' past experiences in their decision making, inclusion of dynamic changes of environment like tsunami inundation, visual identification of road blockages, etc. Additionally, an HPC enhanced tool to automatically calibrate the model to the target population, application scenario, etc., is developed. In order to provide reliability to the software, implemented interactions are calibrated and validated by comparing them to observation data[2]. Furthermore, a scalable parallel computing extension is developed[5], and Monte Carlo simulation capability is implemented to account for the uncertainties and introduce robustness.

Section 2 introduces an extended mathematical framework, and the design of the agent based system. Section 3 presents tools created to support the design of behavioural and environmental scenarios. Section 4 elaborates on the need to calibrate the models with observation results and introduces an HPC enhanced automatic calibration tool. Section 5 presents demonstrative applications of the evacuation simulation software to highlight the need of detailed modelling and simulation.

2   Model

2.1   Mathematical Framework

The agent based system is time step driven and architectural wise the agents would fall in the category of cognitive agents. The implementation of cognition and behavioural models is not part of the software itself, but considered as exploratory scenarios. This section presents the mathematical framework of the system, based upon the dynamical system framework by Laubenbacher et. al. [3].

Let $A = \{a_1, a_2, ..., a_n\}$ represent the set of all the n agents in the simulation. Considering i^{th} agent's state composed of internal (personal or inaccessible to other agents) and external (observable or deducible by other agents) states, $s_i = \{s_i^{int}, s_i^{ext}\}$; defining its neighbourhood as $N_i = \{N_i^{env}, N_i^{agent}\}$, consisting of environment and agent neighbourhoods, which are defined as the region of the environment and the agents it can interact with, respectively; and denoting $x_i = \{s_i, N_i\}$ as the agent's local system state in the local system space, $x_i \in X_i^*$; the agent execution can be conceptualized as:

$$f_i : X_i^* \to X_i^*, \tag{2.1}$$

where the time evolution of the agent's local system is given by $x_i^{t+\Delta t} = f_i(x_i^t)$. The system's active environment is then described by $Env^* = \bigcup_{i=1}^n N_i^{env}$. Although formally the active environment is a subset of the whole environment,

$Env^* \subseteq Env$, for practical purposes they will be referred indistinctively. The evolution of dynamical environment is defined by a set of update functions

$$\lambda_j : Env \to Env. \qquad (2.2)$$

The state space of the whole system is the assembly of all local system state spaces, $X^n = \bigcup_{i=1}^{n} X_i^*$. By defining the evolution function of the system state as the assembly of all local and environment update functions, the following discrete dynamical system is built.

$$\phi = (f_1, f_2, ..., f_n, \lambda_1, \lambda_2, ..., \lambda_m) : X^n \to X^n \qquad (2.3)$$

Agents' dependency graph, G_{dep}, is formed by considering agents as vertices and forming links between any pair of interacting agents based on proximity, visibility, communication, etc.

$$G_{dep} = (V, E) \qquad (2.4)$$

where,

$$V = \{a | a \in A\}$$

$$E = \{(a, b) | (a \neq b) \wedge (a, b \in A)$$
$$\wedge ((N_a^{env} \cap N_b^{env} \neq \emptyset) \vee ((a \in N_b^{agent}) \vee (b \in N_a^{agent})))\}$$

If interfering concurrent interactions take place, the specification on the assembly of the global state has to be given. In this context, an agent has been formalized as $a = \{f, s\}$, the agent's local system as $syst_{local} = \{f, x\}$, and the multi agent system $syst = \{\phi, x^n\}$ where $x^n \in X^n$.

2.2   In the Context of Tsunami Evacuation Simulation

As exposed in [3], every permutation in the order of application of f_i defines a different dynamical system. In many cases, such as tsunami evacuation simulation, the order dependence in the application of f_i would signify the inclusion of unacceptable unfairness in the simulation. Hence, the system is formulated as a parallel discrete dynamical system.

Heterogeneity in crowds is introduced by varying each agent's state, s, and/or the local update functions, f. As it would be impractical to specialize every f_i and s_i non intersecting subsets, $F^\tau \subseteq F$, $S^\tau \subseteq S$ are created, where $F = \{f_1, .., f_n\}$ and $S = \{s_1, ..., s_n\}$. τ stands for the agent type label. From now on $a^\tau = \{f^\tau, s^\tau\}$ will refer to a representative member of the specialized subgroup with label τ. f^τ is specialized based on the role of an agent and the information it posses, while s^τ is specialized based on agent's physical capabilities and role.

The dynamical system is then composed by a base scenario and its complementing parameters. A base scenario consists of the essential elements to be explored such as environment damage models, mitigation measures, essential initial conditions, and the set of local update functions encompassing different behavioural models. In this formalism, the evacuation simulation system can be abstracted as a configuration reachability problem, in which, given a scenario, it is analysed if undesired states (bottle necks, high percentage of casualties, etc.) or desired states (high percentage of agents evacuated, feasible retrofitting costs, etc.) have been reached.

The exploration of the complete phase space is impossible as there are an uncountable number of initial conditions and possible states. Therefore, the analysis is constrained to the most probable trajectories inside this dynamical system. Monte Carlo simulations are performed, leaving the basic parameters of the scenario unchanged in order analyse the stability of these trajectories and thereby produce robust results.

2.3   The General Agent's State - s

Each agent possess a unique state s which is composed of an internal state s^{int} and an external state s^{ext}. s^{int} encompasses their desired moving direction, desired speed, past experiences such a blocked roads, recognized neighbours, what lies in their visual range, etc. s^{int} is inaccessible to other agents. The external state s^{ext} is the information other agents can observe, such as position, physical extension, current moving direction and other features that are deducible by the neighbours such as speed. The physical occupancy of pedestrians are modelled as circles.

2.4   The General Local Update Function - f

The power of the implemented agent based model stems from the local system update functions f. The agent's local system update function encompass its behaviour, actions and interactions models, categorized in *See*, *Think* and *Act*. f is constituted by a basic set of functions g, grouped in objects, $f = g^1 \circ g^2 \circ \ldots \circ g^m$. Implemented constitutive functions are briefly explained below. Further explanation of some of these functions, g, can be found in section 3.

g^{eyes}: Scans N^{env} and creates a visual boundary in s^{int} based on agent's sight distance, which is 50m or longer.

$g^{identify\_env}$: Scans visual boundary and extracts features such as open paths.

$g^{navigate}$: Chooses which path to take out of those identified in $g^{identify\_env}$, based on an agent's destination.

$g^{identify\_inter}$: Recognizes agents to interact with, based on visibility, interaction radius, etc.

g^{coll_av}: Finds a collision free velocity to reach the path chosen in $g^{navigate}$, evading collision with neighbours identified in agents $g^{identify\_inter}$.

$g^{path\_planning}$: Finds paths with different characteristics, see section 3.

$g^{is\_path\_blocked}$: Visually identifies whether the desired path is blocked, see section 3.

$g^{find\_and\_follow}$: Finds a suitable agent and follows it, see section 3.

$g^{deliver\_message}$: Delivers a message to another agent
$g^{execute\_actions}$: Executes desired actions such as move
g^{update}: Updates an agent's state

See consists of g^{eyes}. *Think* encompasses the exploratory behavioural scenarios providing a basic workbench for an agent designer to focus on the cognition and behavioural models of the agents by applying any of the predefined g functions or adding their own. The basic constituents of *Think* are $g^{identify\_env}$, $g^{navigate}$, $g^{identify\_inter}$ and g^{coll_av}. *Act* is composed of $g^{execute\_actions}$ and g^{update}. By specializing *Think*, from now on referred as behavioural model, a different agent type τ is introduced. An example is presented in Figure 1.

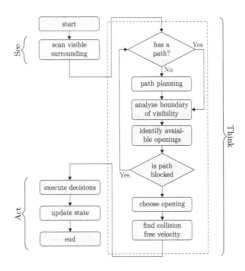

Fig. 1. Local system update function f, and a behavioural specialization example f^τ

2.5   Specialization of Agents - a^τ

Currently, three types of agents with simple behavioural models have been implemented to demonstrate the versatility of the framework and the use of the supporting tools provided; the agents' behavioural models are simple compared to those of their real human counterpart, but complex compared to those of existing large area simulators. Even highly idealized scenarios can expose flaws in evacuations plans. For example, ideal agents with perfect knowledge the environment, capable of finding the best path to destinations, and not getting tired after a long walk may end up drowning in the tsunami or not reaching a shelter. Thus, highlighting the need of the inclusion of mitigation measures such as additional vertical shelters, reinforcement of bridges or roads in critical paths, etc. Results of these idealized scenarios provide an upper bound, and should be improved to bring them as close to real life as possible. The software presented in this work provides a workbench to explore different behavioural models, which would ideally be supported with observation data or expert's consensus. A brief description of the three types of implemented agents are presented below.

Resident - $a^{resident}$: Represents a local resident of the analysed area. $s^{resident}$ possess a mental map of the environment, and uses $g^{path\_planning}$ to find paths according to its desired constrains and past experiences. These agents are able to store, in $s^{resident}$, experiences such as blocked roads. Additionally they know the location of possible evacuation areas.

Visitor - $a^{visitor}$: Represent non-resident people in the interest area. They don't possess any additional information of the environment aside from what they can visually perceive. Their main evacuation mechanism is to seek a visible high ground or to follow other evacuees using $g^{find\_and\_follow}$.

Officials - $a^{official}$: This type of agents represents figures of authority, such as law enforcement, event staff, etc. Their main task is to facilitate fast and smooth evacuation by independently or collectively planning the areas to be covered by each with $g^{path\_planning}$, and commanding or delivering information to other agents with $g^{deliver\_message}$. $s^{officials}$ also possess a mental map of the environment which can be updated through communication.

2.6 Environment - *Env*

A detailed model of the environment is included to facilitate sophisticated sensing and behavioural models of agents, thereby overcoming the limitations of the currently used simplified models. The developed software can accommodate environments with the physical extent of 100's of km^2, in sub-meter details. The environment is modelled as a hybrid of vector and raster, consisting of grids and graphs (see Figure 2) so that advantages of each of the schemes can be exploited. Model-wise the environment can be conceptualized as how an agent perceives its visible surroundings and what they know about it. The grid represent the current state of the dynamically changing environment, including tsunami inundation and earthquake induced damages. The grid can be visually perceived by the agents, providing a base for sophisticated sensing and behaviours, and full use of traversable spaces. In contrast, the graph represents an abstraction of this detailed environment suitable for agents' geographical knowledge representation. Agents discover mismatches between their knowledge and the reality, and stores those experiences with reference to this graph. The graph provides support for thought processes such as path planning and identification of known regions, otherwise computationally intensive with a grid environment. The graph enables compilation of statistical summaries of simulation results, which are convenient for analysis by evacuation planners.

In order to model earthquake induced damages, $\lambda^{earthquake}$ is implemented by coupling with a physics based structural seismic response simulator called IES[4]. $\lambda^{tsunami}$ is introduced to include given tsunami inundation data.

2.7 A Brief on Parallel Scalability

In order to handle the high computational cost emanating from complex agents, a scalable parallel computing extension based on balanced task decomposition is implemented [5]. Preliminary scalability analysis, using 2 million agents in a

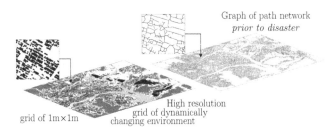

Graph of path network
prior to disaster

High resolution
grid of dynamically
changing environment

grid of 1m×1m

Fig. 2. Hybrid model of grid and graph environments. Grid is dynamically updated, reflecting changes in the environment. The graph is static and represents the path network before the disaster.

$18km^2$ urban environment, is performed attaining 94.8% strong scalability up to 2048 cores, see table 1. Strong scalability defined as $\frac{\left(\frac{T_m}{T_n}\right)}{\left(\frac{n}{m}\right)}$ with T_k being the runtime with k number of CPU cores and $n \geq 2m$. Making use of the presence of disconnected sub-graphs in G_{dep} to implement embarrassing parallelization is not possible due to two several reasons; the number of disconnected sub-graphs is usually much lesser than the required number of CPUs and the links in G_{dep} can rapidly change.

Table 1. Parallel scalability

number of cores	runtime (s)	strong scalability (%)
512	1873.456	
1024	916.2538	102.2
2048	483.2215	94.8

3   Constitutive Functions Examples - *g*

Visitor Agent Evacuation Mechanism - $g^{find\_and\_follow}$. Starts by visually recognizing someone to follow, from now on referred as a target. If a visitor doesn't have a target or the target is out of vision it tries to find a new target to follow. If no target can be seen it will continue walking in the direction of the last seen target. If the target wasn't moving in the previous time step it stops following it. Only the agents moving away are considered as candidate targets and the one with the smallest speed difference is chosen as the target. In order to avoid possible overcrowding, visitors extrapolate the target agent's movement and sets the extrapolated point as their temporary desired destination. Depending on the distance to the targets, visitors adjust speed to keep up with the target.

Interaction with the Dynamically Changing Environment - $g^{is\_path\_blocked}$. Earthquake induced damages in the environment are unknown to evacuees unless they witness or encountered those while evacuating or receive information from other agent's who have experienced them. To mimic this, the grid environment is dynamically updated, according to the earthquake induced damages $\lambda^{earthquake}$ and/or inundation data $\lambda^{tsunami}$. Agents visually discover incongruences by comparing the available paths in their mental map and what they perceive with their vision, and update their mental map based on these experiences. Figure 3 shows the initially planned path of a resident agent and the re-planned path after visually detecting that the previous path is blocked.

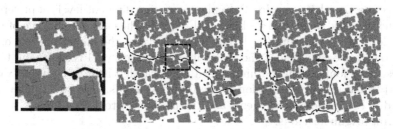

Fig. 3. Blue arrow, observed agent. Left, blocked road zoom in. Center, initial path plan as the agent doesn't know the road is blocked. Right, as the agent gets close enough and visually identifies that the road is blocked, it re-plans its path.

3.1   Path Planning Algorithms - $g^{path\_planning}$

In order support complex behavioural models several standard path planning algorithms are included: shortest path, closest destination and path to that, shortest path with way-points, k mutually independent paths, etc. These are insufficient for the target applications, where people tend to choose safer paths according to time availability and perceived level of danger. Especially, in the case of earthquakes people tend to take paths with longer stretches of wider roads to lower the probability of encountering blocked roads, depending on the intensity of ground shaking they experienced.

Width/Number of Agents Preference. Standard Dijkstra algorithm allows the use of strong constrains such as minimum road width. But for the above mentioned purpose weaker constrains reflecting the preference for wider roads are needed.

Algorithm 5 shows the modified Dijkstra algorithm to find the destination which has the longest stretch of the path with preferred width and reachable within the given time/length constraints. The required inputs are: a known node in the topological graph nearest to the agents current location, minimum preferred width, preferred width and level of preference. The bias is introduced in the way the graph edges lengths are perceived. Roads narrower than their minimum preference are unaffected, while roads wider than its preference will be perceived as reduced in length. The reduction factor is interpolated for the roads in between (see algorithm 5 lines 9-11). While exploring nodes of the graph, we keep track of actual distances, and a node is explored only if the actual distance is less than the maximum allowable for the agent (see algorithm 5 line 14).

This maximum allowed distance is an agent's personal goal, currently calculated using the tsunami arrival time and the agent's average speed, which is an ideal case.

In the case of volunteers, the same algorithm using the number of agents as the bias parameter, instead of the width, is used to make them find paths giving priority to roads with more evacuees.

Preference Level Example. Path planning using different levels of preference with the modified algorithm is shown in Figure 4. The considered range of preference level factors is from $(0, 1]$. The lower the value the higher interest of the agent to traverse wide roads. The path with preference level 1 is equivalent to the shortest path found with the unmodified Dijkstra algorithm. The use of values above 1 would introduce aversion to the use wider roads. This could potentially be used to command official agents and rescue services to search for lost visitors in narrow neighbourhoods.

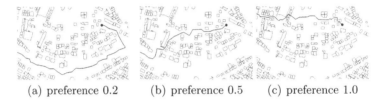

(a) preference 0.2   (b) preference 0.5   (c) preference 1.0

Fig. 4. Effect of different levels of preference, evacuation area assumed to be on the left edge of the domain

4   An Automated Parallel Calibration/Optimization Tool

Given that evacuations during tsunamis involve a large number of lives, it is of primary concern to improve the reliability of the simulation results. Human behaviours change according to the situation, time of the day, area, country, etc. It is impossible to have a model with a unique set of parameters reproduce all the possible situations. The best solution is to provide a versatile tool for calibrating the evacuation simulator to the target population, using field observations. For this purpose an automatic calibration tool is developed. The evacuation simulation software is then used as a mapping from the parameter space to the observation space. The search ranges in the parameter space have to be properly restricted with reasonable upper and lower bounds for each parameter, excluding infeasible regions. These bounds are usually based on physical restrictions, e.g. speed should be between zero and running speed. Then a measure of the disagreement between the evacuation simulator results and observations can be casted to a suitable error norm, and the problem of optimum calibration can be reduced to an error minimization problem. As an example, given a regression on the observed data or a fundamental diagram, $r(x)$, and n simulation data points (y_i, x_i) in the observation space, the optimal calibration can be found by

---

Algorithm 1: Modified Dijkstra algorithm

---

input : Starting node s, preference factor pF, boolean
        functor `IsADestination()`, interpolation function
        `In()`, maximum allowed distance l_{max}, Positive
        weighted graph $G = (V, E, l, \boldsymbol{w})$ (l-length,$\boldsymbol{w}$-width,
        of the edges), $\boldsymbol{w_{min}}$, $\boldsymbol{w_{pref}}$
output: *path* to destination and its *length*

1 **for** $\forall u \in V$ **do** pd$(u)= \infty$; parent$(u)= -1$;
  /* d-distance,pd-perceived distance, nd-new
  distance, npd-new perceived distance   */
2 pd$(s)= 0$; d$(u)= 0$;
3 *priority_queue*.add$(s$,pd$(s))$;
4 **while not** *priority_queue*.empty$()$ **do**
5     $u = priority\_queue$.top$()$;
6   **if** `IsADestination`(u) **then break**$()$;
7   *priority_queue*.pop$()$;
8   **for** $\forall (u, v) \in E$ **do**
9   **if** $w(u,v)< w_{min}$ **then** $pl(u, v) = l(u, v)$;
10   **else if** $w(u,v)> w_{pref}$ **then** $pl(u, v) = pF * l(u, v)$;
11   **else** $pl(u, v) =$In$(pF, w_{min}, w_{pref}) * l(u, v)$;
12   npd$(v)=$pd$(u)+pl(u, v)$;
13   nd$(v)=$d$(u)+l(u, v)$;
14   **if** pd$(v) >$ npd(v) **and** npd$(v) < l_{max}$ **then**
15   d$(v)=$nd(v);
16   pd$(v)=$npd(v);
17   parent$(v)=u$;
18   *priority_queue*.add$(v$,pd$(v))$;
19 **if** `IsADestination`(u) **then** // Extracts the path
20   *length* $=$ d(u);*path*.pushBack(u);
21   **while** $u \neq s$ **do** $u =$ parent(u); *path*.pushBack(u);
22 **return** *path* , *length*

Fig. 5. Preference based Dijkstra algorithm

minimizing the L^1-norm defined as $\sum_{i=1}^{n} |r(x_i) - y_i|$. Another useful measure is L^∞-norm which concentrates on the reduction outliers.

4.1   Search Strategies and Parallelization

This search for an optimal calibration is a combinatorial optimization problem, for which a parallel meta-heuristic trajectory based approach is considered. Different approaches can be adapted to explore the search space. Currently, two approaches are implemented in the automated calibration tool. The first is a progressive search which introduces small random perturbations to the parameters at a small neighbourhood of a given parent point, and move to the parameter set that has the lowest error. If no neighbouring point with a lower error is found after a predefined maximum number of random perturbations, more aggressive perturbations are applied and the search is restarted at a new point. The second approach is based on simulated annealing, which inverts the former process by starting with more aggressive perturbations and reducing the level of aggressiveness as the search progresses.

This process is computationally intensive as for every trial parameter set a complete simulation has to be performed. Furthermore, in order to assure that the simulation is not being fitted to an outlier/special case scenario Monte Carlo simulations are performed. Monte Carlo simulation and the presence of many independent search fronts increase the parallel vocation of the problem. The automated tool utilizes the Message Passing Interface (MPI) to communicate and spawn the processes. Figure 6 shows the search with 2 levels of paralellization.

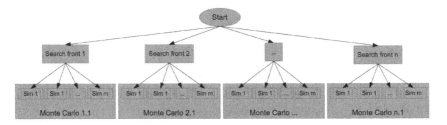

Fig. 6. Two layers of parallelism (search and Monte Carlo parallelism)

4.2   An Application: Calibrating Collision Avoidance Algorithm

The automated tool is applied to calibrate collision avoidance algorithm according to the observations by Wiederman et. al.[2]. Figure 7 shows the results obtained by the randomized search algorithm in a parametric space of 8 dimensions. The L^1 norm criteria with 10 search fronts and 100 Monte Carlo simulations per search are used.

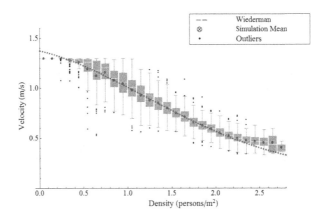

Fig. 7. Calibration results for the collision avoidance validation problem

4.3   Other Applications

The parallel calibration tool is designed to attach to any client application, with minimal requirements and changes for the client application. The client application, such as the presented evacuation simulator, would ideally use the Message Passing Interface to communicate back with the calibration/optimization tool.

This tool could prove useful in order to assess the versatility of the different agent based tools. Answering questions such as if the current model is enough to reproduce the observed behaviour or if further improvements are needed in order to capture the essence of the phenomena and ultimately discovering features or lack of them in the models.

5 Demonstrative Applications of the Evacuation Simulation Framework

As a demonstrative application of the developed system, several hypothetical scenarios are presented, grouped in three scenario sets. These scenarios demand a detailed model of environment, the use of all available traversable area and complex agent functions, rendering the simulators with simplified models insufficient. Further, these scenarios showcase the developed software ability to perform quantitative evaluation of mitigation measures and the use of some of the presented behavioural models.

5.1 Problem Setting

The domain considered is a Japanese coastal urban area (see Figure9(a)), which has experienced several historical tsunamis. The extent of the domain considered is 9.6×5.4 km^2, modelled with a grid of 1m^2 resolution. All the areas which are not occupied by buildings or water bodies are considered traversable. The agents have a complete aversion to the use of paths of less than 3m width. All the regions with an elevation greater than 30m, shown in green in Figure 9(a), are considered as evacuation areas.

The earthquake induced damages are estimated based on the physics based seismic response analysis of all the buildings in the selected domain, due to the strong ground motion data of Kobe earthquake in 1995. The seismic response analysis is performed using IES[4]. The threshold drift angle of 0.005 [7,8] is used to determine the damage state of buildings, and the width of the occupied area is increased by 40% of the building height if the building is deemed damaged. The grid is updated using tsunami inundation data, by Takashi et. al. [6], every 5 minutes.

The composition of the agent population is set according to the city's population. 57,000 evacuees are considered, and their properties are given in Table 2.

Table 2. Properties of the agents

Age	<50 years	>50 years
Speed /(m/s)	55	45
Percentage	1.43±0.11	1.39±0.19
Pre-evacuation time /(s)	1000±600	
Sight distance /(m)	50m	

Number of Cases for Monte-Carlo Simulation Due to the presence of random variables like the properties and the distribution of evacuees, the considered scenarios are stochastic in nature, thus Monte-Carlo simulations are performed to improve the reliability of the results. To decide a sufficient number of samples required for the Monte Carlo simulation, 1000 simulations are performed initially and the convergence of the standard deviation, with respect to the number of simulations, is analysed. The minimum number of simulations per scenario is decided to be 400 simulations according to the results shown in Figure 8.

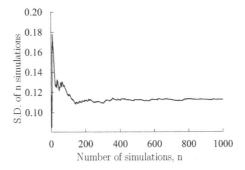

Fig. 8. Standard deviation of cumulative agents evacuated at the end of 40 minutes for 1000 simulations

5.2   The Effect of Tsunami Inundation and Earthquake Damages on Evacuation Time

To evaluate the effects of earthquake induced damages and tsunami inundation on the evacuation process, four scenarios are considered: undamaged environment, only with earthquake damages, only with tsunami inundation, and the combined effect of earthquake damages and inundation. These four scenarios constitute the scenario set 1. For these only resident agents are considered, which are initially located within a 20m distance from the buildings.

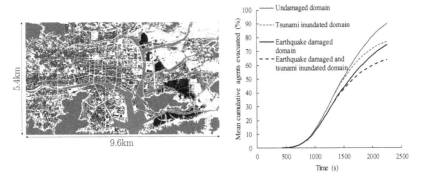

Fig. 9. Effect of earthquake induced damages and tsunami inundation. The simulated area (left). Blue, green and black indicate water bodies, above 30m elevations and buildings, respectively. Results of the 4 considered scenarios (right).

Figure 9(b) shows the cumulative number of agents evacuated for each case. Through detailed analysis of results, it is found that the inundation of key bridges is the deterrent of the smooth evacuation of the agents.

In order to assess the importance of these key bridges shown in Figure 10(a), simulations are performed blocking them, grouped in scenario set 2. Comparison of the results with that of the above tsunami inundation case indicates that inundation of these key brides is the main deterrent of fast evacuation. Further, it is found that the introduction of tsunami shelters near this bridges rectify this problem, proving to be a very effective mitigation measure.

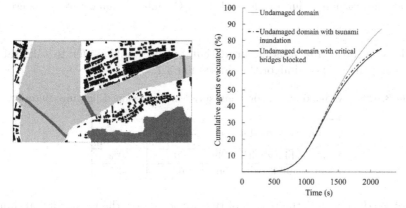

Fig. 10. Effect of critical buildings. Critical bridges (left). Results tsunami inundation and bridge blocking (right).

5.3   The Effect of Lighting in Night Time Evacuation

The final set of scenarios requiring detailed model of environment and complex agents are in the context of a night time evacuation during a hypothetical summer festival. It is assumed to be a full moon night; an earthquake has damaged the environment and caused power failure; and the evacuation is triggered by a tsunami arriving in 15 minutes. Further, visitors are assumed to have no knowledge of the environment. The visibility, which requires both detailed model of environment and complex agents, is crucial for the survival of visitors since following others is their only mean of reaching an evacuation area.

18,000 visitors and 18,000 residents are assumed to be participating in the festival, which take place in a $14km^2$ area, see Figure 11(a). Festival attendees are distributed across the streets and open spaces, while additional 39,000 residents are distributed over the whole domain. With full moon, 0.2lux of lighting[11] and 15m sight distance [11,10] are assumed. In order to explore the mitigation measures of installing emergency lighting of 15lux [12] at 30m spacing which is equal to common street lighting[12], another scenario with 30m visibility is considered. Maximum speed of agents under these lighting conditions are shown

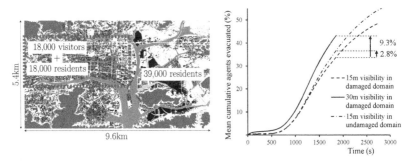

Fig. 11. Simulation of a special event evacuation. Domain and the distributions of agents for the evacuation during a festival (left). Cumulative number of agents evacuated (right).

in table 3. Additionally it is assumed that people would prefer to take safer paths, using the proposed algorithm in section 3.1.

Table 3. Effective maximum pedestrian speed under assumed lighting conditions

Lighting conditions	Age	
	<50 years	>50 years
15m visibility with 0.2lux	70%	50%
30m visibility with 15lux	90.6%	83%

Figure 11(b) presents the results of the two scenarios; the means of 400 simulations, using 12,800 CPU cores of the K-computer, with different agent distributions. As seen, the low lighting conditions have significantly reduced the number of agents evacuated, in comparison to an ordinary day. Further, it is observed that providing lighting of 15lux enhances the ability of the visitor agents to identify and follow other evacuees, increasing the number of visitors evacuated by 5%. To further explore the importance of lighting condition, the scenario with moon lighting is simulated excluding the effect of earthquake damages. As shown in Figure 11(b), for this specific setting, lighting conditions have a higher impact than the strengthening of buildings against earthquake induced damages.

6   Concluding Remarks

A large urban area simulator with sub-meter resolution environment and agents with complex functionality is presented. A mathematical framework is extended to add sufficient expressiveness to present details of the simulator and a brief overview of the model is given in this context. The software is designed to be used by experts as an experimental workbench to quantitatively evaluate different scenarios and mitigations measures in an exploratory manner. An automatic calibration tool is included with the evacuation simulator so that agents' interactions and behaviours can be easily calibrated according to the available observations of evacuees behaviours. Finally, demonstrative applications of the evacuation simulation framework and its exploratory capability are presented. The presented demonstrations highlight the need of detailed agent based models for exploring scenarios which can't be simulated with typical large area evacuation simulators.

Acknowledgments. This work was supported by JSPS KAKENHI Grant Number 24760359. Part of the results is obtained using K computer at the RIKEN Advanced Institute for Computational Science.

References

1. Cosenza, B., Cordasco, G., De Chiara, R., Scarano, V.: Distributed Load Balancing for Parallel Agent-Based Simulations. In: 19th International Euromicro Conference on Parallel, Distributed and Network-based Processing, pp. 62–69 (2011)
2. Melgar, L.E.A., Lakshman, W.M.L., Hori, M., Ichimura, T., Tanaka, S.: On the Development of an MAS Based Evacuation Simulation System: Autonomous Navigation and Collision Avoidance. In: Boella, G., Elkind, E., Savarimuthu, B.T.R., Dignum, F., Purvis, M.K. (eds.) PRIMA 2013. LNCS, vol. 8291, pp. 388–395. Springer, Heidelberg (2013)
3. Laubenbacher, R., Jarrah, A.S., Mortveit, H.S., Ravi, S.S.: Agent Based Modeling, Mathematical Formalism for, Computational Complexity, pp. 88–14. Springer New York (2012)
4. Hori, M., Ichimura, T.: Current state of integrated earthquake simulation for earthquake hazard and disaster. J. of Seismology, 307–321 (2007)
5. Wijerathne, M.L., Melgar, L.A., Hori, M., Ichimura, T., Tanaka, S.: HPC enhanced large urban area evacuation simulations with vision based autonomously navigating multiagents. Procedia Computer Science, 1515–1524 (2013)
6. Takahashi, N., Kaneda, Y., Inazawa, Y., Baba, T., Kikkojin, M.: Tsunami inundation modelling of the 2011 tohoku earthquake using three-dimensional building data for Sendai, Miyagi prefecture, Japan. Tsunami Events and Lessons Learned, Advances in Natural and Technological Hazard Research (35), 89–98 (2014)
7. Xue, M., Ryuzo, O.: Examination of vulnerability of various residential areas in china for earthquake disaster mititgation. In: The 9th International Conference on Urban Earthquake Engineering/4th Asia Conference on Earthquake Engineering, Tokyo, pp. 1931–1936 (2012)
8. Galambos, T.V., Ellingwood, B.: Serviceability Limit States: Deflection. Journal of Structural Engineering, ASCE, 67–84 (1986)
9. Bohannon, R.W.: Comfortable walking speed of adults aged 20-79 years: reference values and determinants. Age and Ageing 26, 15–19 (1997)
10. Nichols, T.F., Powers, T.R.: Moonlight and night visibility. U.S. Army Training Center Human Research Unit, Presidio of Monterey, California, (January 11, 1964), Use-ip ltd. Lux light level chart. Pdf
11. Honeywell (February 2014), Emergency lighting design guide. Pdf
12. Ouellette, M.J., Rea, M.S.: Illuminance Requirements for Emergency Lighting. Journal of the Illuminating Engineering Society, 37–42 (1989), Arizona transportation department, City of Glendale. Street lighting manual. Pdf, 2006 14

Synthetic Population Initialization and Evolution-Agent-Based Modelling of Population Aging and Household Transitions

Mohammad-Reza Namazi-Rad, Nam Huynh, Johan Barthelemy, and Pascal Perez

SMART Infrastructure Facility, University of Wollongong, NSW 2522, Australia
{mrad,nhuynh,johan,pascal}@uow.edu.au

Abstract. A synthetic population (SP) aims at faithfully reproducing actual social entities, individuals and households, and their characteristics as described in a population census. Depending on the quality and completeness of the input data sets, as well as the number of variables of interest and hierarchical levels (usually, individual and household), a reliable SP should be able to reflect the actual physical social entities, with their characteristics and specific behavioural patterns. This paper presents a methodology to construct a reliable dynamic synthetic population for the Illawarra Region-Australia. The two main components in the population synthesizer presented in this paper are *initialization* and *evolution*. Iterative proportional fitting procedure (IPFP) is presented to help with the initialization of the population using 2011 Australian census. Then, population aging and evolution is projected using an agent-based modeling (ABM) technique over ten years.

Keywords: Agent-Based Modelling, Household Transitions, Iterative Proportional Fitting Procedure, Population Dynamics, Synthetic Reconstruction.

1 Introduction

Complex social systems are formed by a composition of multiple intelligent agents interacting with each other within an environment, and can be modelled as a collection of entities called agents (that are, individuals and/or collective entities such as households or institutions). Amongst other innovative tools, dynamic micro-simulation and agent-based modelling (ABM) techniques can be used to simulate the actions and interactions of autonomous agents with a view to assessing their effects on the network as a whole. It is the role of activity-based models (such as ABM) to provide each agent with specific goals and associated means. Such models need the population of agents with their demographic characteristics to be generated. Then, the agent's behaviours are to be simulated. The importance of simulating reliable area-specific synthetic populations for activity-based modeling has received more attention recently [1-3]. A reliable area-specific synthetic population (SP) should be able to give a believable picture on how population entities or agents have to perform certain

H.K. Dam et al. (Eds.): PRIMA 2014, LNAI 8861, pp. 182–189, 2014.

tasks or display behavioural patterns which consequences are of interest to researchers and practitioners.

The main objective in this study is to generate a representative area-specific SP and to simulate the SP dynamics using an ABM technique. The purpose of generating a dynamic SP is to create a valid representation of the population spatially distributed while addressing the daily population transitions. In the current study, the key components in simulating a dynamic SP are *initialization* and *evolution*. Initialization involves simulating the baseline area-specific population of individuals and households in a way that the simulated population meets aggregate-level information from the census. In this paper, the synthetic reconstruction (SR) approach is presented to help with initialization of the population using 2011 Australian census. Once the initial population is generated, in order to evolve the population, the dynamics within the population should be modelled. An ABM of population aging and household transitions is presented in this paper to simulate the population dynamics over a ten years period. A case study is also presented that uses the algorithm to initialize a synthetic population for the Illawarra Region in 2011 and evolves this population over ten years.

2   Population Synthesis

In order to generate a reliable SP, tabulating multi-dimensional tables of agents' socio-demographics is needed. This can come from an area-specific fully informative database which use both census and survey data. However, such a database may not exist in practice. Even if a rich database is available, accessing the required data form this database is generally very costly or/and problematic due to privacy and confidentiality issues. Therefore, most official statistical agencies and researchers try to estimate cross-classified small area population counts that are of acceptable quality using marginal counts. Here, we present standard approaches to overcome this challenge.

2.1   Generating Multi-way Tables

The iterative proportional fitting procedure (IPFP) has been used for adjusting a table of data in a way that table cells add up to totals in all required dimensions [4-5]. Here, the reason for developing IPFP is to estimate small area population counts for two or more cross-classified variables of interest within the SP to be generated. For instance, given a three-way $A \times B \times C$ contingency tables where the marginal probabilities are known, it is desired to estimate the cell probabilities, denoted by π_{abc} for all a, b, and c ($a \in \{1,...,A\}; b \in \{1,...,B\}; c \in \{1,...,C\}$). Having the population total, (denoted by N,) together with the cell probabilities estimated using the IPFP, cell frequencies are to be calculated. Here, each cell frequency is denoted by N_{abc}, where each subscript refers to one variable (or dimension). When performing a summation over one variable (or dimension), the marginal totals are $N_{ab.}$, $N_{.bc}$, and $N_{a.c}$ where a dot is replaced with the subscript referring to the omitted demotion. When performing a summation over two variables (or dimensions) the marginal totals are $N_{a..}$, $N_{.b.}$, and $N_{..c}$. The probability associated with each cell frequency is presented by π with the same subscripts.

IPFP was originally proposed by [4] as an algorithm leading to a minimizer of the Pearson χ^2 statistic. A classical IPFP to be used for population reconstruction uses a representative sample data. This data is basically used to generate the initial values for the cell probabilities. Then, using IPFP, the cell probabilities in a multi-way cross-table are adjusted in a way that the table cells add up to totals in all required dimensions. When the marginal counts are available for each variable, one iteration (in 3 dimensions) is done by executing the following equations in turn.

$$\pi_{abc}^{(1)} = \frac{\pi_{abc}^{(0)}}{\sum\limits_{a=1}^{A} \pi_{abc}^{(0)}} \times \frac{N_{.bc}^{(0)}}{N} \ ; \ \ \pi_{abc}^{(2)} = \frac{\pi_{abc}^{(1)}}{\sum\limits_{b=1}^{B} \pi_{abc}^{(1)}} \times \frac{N_{a.c}^{(1)}}{N} \ ; \ \ \pi_{abc}^{(3)} = \frac{\pi_{abc}^{(2)}}{\sum\limits_{c=1}^{C} \pi_{abc}^{(2)}} \times \frac{N_{ab.}^{(2)}}{N} \ .$$

This three-step cycle will be repeated until convergence to a desired accuracy is attained. This technique can be used for tabulating multi-dimensional tables.

2.2   Synthetic Reconstruction of Individuals and Households Population

The SR approach has been traditionally used by researchers [3][6] for generating the initial SP using both disaggregated- and aggregated-level data. This method first uses available disaggregated-level data while assuming that it is a fully representative sample of the target population. This is generally referred to as the *seed data*. Then, population units (with the required socio-demographics) are randomly drawn from the representative disaggregated-level data and populated within the target area using a weighting technique so that the marginal distribution follows the aggregated-level information coming from one source covering the complete population (e.g. census data). One way to do this is to use the deterministic re-weighting algorithm to allocate a certain weight to each unit record within the disaggregated-level data and consider the weights as a distribution of probabilities derived from the available aggregated-level data. The multi-way tabulation of agents' socio-demographics obtained from the IPFP algorithm is basically used to calculate such weights [3-5].

2.3   An Agent-Based Model for Population Dynamics

Once the initial synthetic population is generated, an ABM algorithm can be used to generate the population dynamics. Such algorithm includes individuals and households that perform several activities (e.g. having a newborn, getting married or divorced, changing household type etc.) with bounded rationality. ABM combines elements of game theory, complex systems, emergence, computational sociology, and evolutionary programming to offer a versatile and spatially explicit approach to social simulation and to simulate the actions and interactions of autonomous agents. An ABM is a computer-assisted simulation that tries to mimic the micro-level behaviours within a real system in order to study possible macro-level effects and outcomes [7]. In order to do so, an ABM needs to simulate the simultaneous operations and interactions of multiple agents, in an attempt to represent individual agents, their behaviours, natural decision making and interactions [8-9].

A certain number of characteristics are considered in this study to define any specific individual within the synthetic population. The individuals within the synthetic population will then form single-member and multimember households with certain demographics. The individuals considered in this study are: *i*) 'U15Child': an dependent individual aged under 15, *ii*) 'O15Child': an dependent individual aged over 15, *iii*) 'Student': an individual who is a university student, *iv*) 'Married': an aged over 15 in a married/de facto relationship, *v*) 'LoneParent': an aged over 15 not in a married/de facto relationship and have a dependent children, & *vi*)'Other': none of the case mentioned before. Eight types of household relationship used in the algorithm are: **(1)**'*Couple*': households having 2 'Married' individuals; no 'U15Child', 'Student', 'O15Child' individuals; with or without individuals of other types, **(2)**'*CoupleU15*': households having 2 'Married' individuals; at least 1 'U15Child' individual; no 'Student', 'O15Child' individuals; with or without individuals of other types, **(3)**'*CoupleU15O15*': households having 2 'Married' individuals; at least 1 'U15Child' individual; at least 1 'Student' individual or 1 'O15Child' individual; with or without individuals of other types, **(4)** '*CoupleO15*': households having 2 'Married' individuals; no 'U15Child' individuals; at least 1 'Student' individual or 1 'O15Child' individual; with or without individuals of other types, **(5)**'*LoneParentU15*': households having 1 'LoneParent' individual; at least 1 'U15Child' individual; no 'Student', 'O15Child' individuals; with or without individuals of other types, **(6)**'*CoupleU15O15*': households having 1 'LoneParent' individual; at least 1 'U15Child' individual; at least 1 'Student' individual or 1 'O15Child' individual; with or without individuals of other types, **(7)**'*CoupleO15*': households having 1 'LoneParent' individual; no 'U15Child' individuals; at least 1 'Student' individual or 1 'O15Child' individual; with or without individuals of other types, **(8)**'*Other*': households having no 'Married', 'LoneParent', 'U15Child', 'Student', 'O15Child' individuals; with 1 or more individuals of other types.

In the current study, the newborns are given to females with higher probabilities of having a newborn baby calculated based on age-specific fertility rates. Each newborn is given a new ID and specific attributes (i.e. sex, age and household type). These new agents are added into the individual pool as well as the respective household members list. The algorithm then re-calculates the attributes of the household the new individual belongs to. At each time step, the algorithm also determines the probability of dying based on individuals' sex and age. In case of death, the algorithm removes the deceased individual from his/her household and from the pool of individuals. Then, the algorithm re-calculates the household's attributes and the attributes of the members of this household. Some special cases need ad hoc procedures. For example, if only children aged less than 15 remain in a household, they are removed from the individual and household pools. Likewise, if a household becomes empty, it is to be removed from the pool of household.

Divorcing algorithm applies only to households with 2 'Married' individuals. These individuals are considered divorced if at least one of them satisfies the probability of divorcing. In the current algorithm, the divorced males move out of the family and construct new households of type 'Other'. Their relationships are also changed to 'Other'.

The divorced females remain in their current households with other individuals. Marrying algorithm applies to individuals having different genders. Individuals available for marrying are determined based on their age and gender and are stored in a list. The selection of any two individuals out of this list for marriage is random, with priority given to individuals from two different households. For married individuals, a new household is constructed to accommodate them. If any of the marrying individuals is of type 'LonePa-rent', any children of his/hers will follow him/her to the new household. A diagram is presented in Figure 1 to show all the aforementioned steps in generating the synthetic population dynamics.

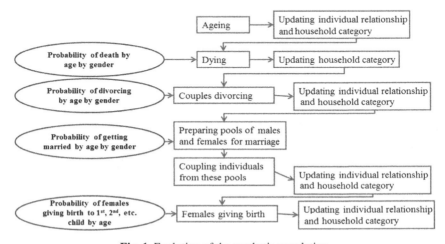

Fig. 1. Evolution of the synthetic population

The main advantage of this ABM algorithm over similar algorithms used for simulating the synthetic population dynamics (e.g. [2][10]) is the fact that this algorithm re-evaluates the type of each household at the end of each evolution step based on the new status/attributes of its residents. This ensures the consistency and integrity between the household type and its compositional residents.

3   Dynamic Synthetic Population of the Illawarra

The study area in this paper is the Illawarra region in NSW Australia with the total population of 365388 individuals in 2011. Illawarra is the coastal region situated immediately south of Sydney and north of the Shoalhaven or South Coast region (see Figure 2). The smallest geographic area defined in the Australian Statistical Geography Standard (ASGS) is Statistical Level 1 (SA1) for which the required data is available to our study. The algorithm presented in section 2.1 & 2.2 is used to initialize the SA1-specific SP based on the 2011 census data provided by Australian Bureau of Statistics (ABS). The sets of ABS tables used for this purpose include individual-related tables (e.g. distribution of age by gender, & relationship in household by age by gender) as well as household related tables (e.g. age by sex tables; family composition tables; and family composition by gender and age). A 1% Basic Census Sample File (CSF) is available to this study through the Confidentialised Unit Record File (CURF) microdata system. This data is used for calculating the initial cell values in the multi-dimensional table of socio-characteristics (e.g. age, sex and household type) required in our synthetic population. Then, the IPFP algorithm is used for adjusting a table of data in a way that table cells add up to SA1-specific marginal totals. We then need to assign individuals to households in such a way that we maintain the distributions as close as possible to both the individual demographics per SA1and the household demographics of that area.

Once the SA1-specific initial synthetic population is simulated, the ABM algorithm presented in section 2.3 is used to generate the population dynamics over ten years. It will be noted that, the net

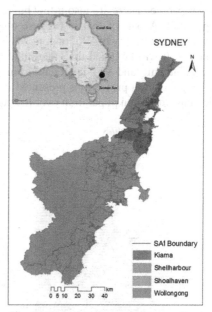

Fig. 2. Map of study area (Illawarra Region)

migration is considered in the algorithm while the migrated population are assumed to have similar characteristics to the current residents. The distribution of household types in the Illawarra simulated SP for 2011-2021 is demonstrated in Figure 3. As can be seen, proportion of lone individuals and parents without children are expected to increase within the region while the proportion of families with children is expected to decrease, gradually.

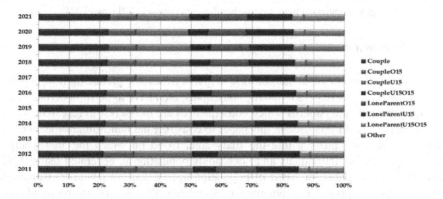

Fig. 3. Household type structure of the Illawarra population 2011-2021

The population pyramid presented in Figure 4 shows at a glance the age distribution of the simulated SP of Illawarra in 2011 and 2021. This pyramid narrows toward the top. This is because the death rate is higher among older people than among younger people. There are also a few bulges and narrower parts in the middle part of the pyramid. A part of that is because of young students who come to the area to study at the University of Wollongong. This area is also targeted by older people after retirement. It will be noted that, the initial SP (for the target area) is simulated based on available unit- and SA1-level data from Australian Census 2011. The two-sex age-specific population projections presented in Figure 4 follow the rules used by ABS in projecting Australian population over the next century [11].

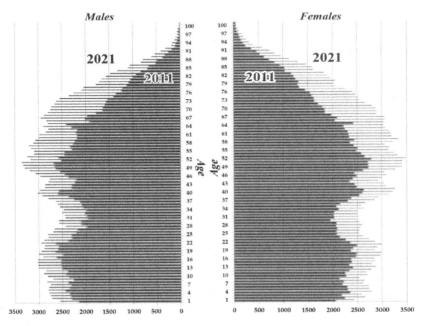

Fig. 4. Population pyramid for the Illawarra region in 2011 and 2021

4   Discussion

A reliable area-specific SP should be able to give a believable picture on how population entities or agents (e.g. individuals, households, etc.) have to perform certain tasks or display behavioural patterns which consequences are of interest to researchers and practitioners. The IPFP is used in this paper to construct the multi-dimensional cross-tables for the small areas within the study area, based on which the area-specific initial population of individuals and households population is generated using 2011 Australian census data. An ABM of population ageing and household transitions is then presented to project the dynamics of simulated SP. Several micro-simulation techniques are presented in the literature for such a purpose [3]. However, dynamic micro-simulation techniques have their own limitations and cannot reflect the agent-specific autonomy and behaviours in a complex network.

This paper presents an agent-based algorithm to generate the dynamic synthetic population which specifies the individual and household characteristics at each time period at the smallest geographical level for which the required data is available. The main purpose in this paper is to generate a reliable dynamic synthetic population of the study area based on available data. Evolution discussed in this paper involves the ageing of each individual and drawing of age-dependent life-event probabilities (e.g. birth, death, marriage, and divorce). Unfortunately, these vital rates are not available to this study for the target areas at SA1 level and the rates available for the larger areas are used. The occurrence of the life events influences both individual and household entities. Evolution uses a discrete event simulation model with a time-dependent feedback loop triggering either probabilistic or incremental changes to individual states. At any point in time, each individual is characterized by a significant number of state variables. These state variables describe personal attributes such as sex and age, relationship and family type. This means that the current model does not take into account other element is evolution of population such as residential mobility and job allocations to the individuals. This study also does not consider different scenarios of changing in area-specific vital rates over time. These are the subjects for future research studies.

References

1. Harland, K., Heppenstall, A., Smith, D., Birkin, M.: Creating Realistic Synthetic Populations at Varying Spatial Scales: A Comparative Critique of Population Synthesis Techniques. Journal of Artificial Societies and Social Simulation 15, 1–24 (2012)
2. Geard, N., McCaw, J.M., Dorin, A., Korb, K.B., McVernon, J.: Synthetic Population Dynamics: A Model of Household Demography. Journal of Artificial Societies and Social Simulation 16(1), 8 (2013)
3. Namazi-Rad, M., Mokhtarian, P., Perez, P.: Generating a dynamic synthetic population - Using an age-structured two-sex model for household dynamics. PLoS ONE 9 (4), e94761 (2014)
4. Deming, W.E., Stephan, F.F.: On a Least Squares Adjustment of a Sampled Frequency Table When the Expected Marginal Totals are Known. Annals of Mathematical Statistics 11(4), 367–484 (1940)
5. Bishop, Y.M.M., Fienberg, S.E., Holland, P.W.: Discrete Multivariable Analysis: Theory and Practice. MIT Press, Cambridge (1975)
6. Farooq, B., Bierlaire, M., Hurtubia, R., Flötteröd, G.: Simulation Based Population Synthesis. Transportation Research Part B: Methodological 58, 243–263 (2013)
7. Wooldridge, M., Jennings, N.: Intelligent agents: Theory and practice. Knowledge Engineering Review 10(2), 115–152 (1995)
8. Grimm, V., Revilla, E., Berger, U., Jeltsch, F., Mooij, W.M., Railsback, S.F., Thulke, H., Weiner, J., Wiegand, T., DeAngelis, D.L.: Pattern-Oriented Modeling of Agent-Based Complex Systems: Lessons from Ecology. Science 310, 987–991 (2005)
9. Barreteau, O., Bots, P., Daniell, K., Etienne, M., Perez, P., Barnaud, C., Bazile, D., Becu, N., Castella, J.C., Dare, W., Trebuil, G.L.: Participatory Approaches. In: Edmonds, B., Meyer, R. (eds.) Simulating Social Complexity: A Handbook, ch. 10. Springer (2013)
10. Billari, F.C., Prskawetz, A., Diaz, B.A., Fent, T.: The "Wedding-Ring": An Agent-Based Marriage Model Based on Social Interaction. Demographic Research 17, 59–82 (2007)
11. Australian Bureau of Statistics: Population Projections, Australia, 2012 (base) to 2101. (cat. no. 3235.0) (2012)

Intelligent Collision Avoidance between Autonomous Agents Using Adaptive Local Views

Fan Liu and Ajit Narayanan

Auckland University of Technology
School of Computing and Mathematical Sciences, New Zealand
{rliu,ajnaraya}@aut.ac.nz
http://www.aut.ac.nz

Abstract. We propose a nature-inspired, intelligent collision management approach for use by multiple autonomous agents. This approach is calculated by each agent involved in possible collision through its own local view and without communication with other agents or central control. The approach uses both the current position and the velocity of other local agents to compute a future trajectory in order to both predict collision and avoid it. Our approach is capable of dealing with static obstacles and is developed in conjunction with a common kinematics metric 'Minimal Predicted Distance (MPD)' ensuring all agents remain free of collision while attempting to follow their goal direction, thus making the procedure well-suited for real-time applications. We build on prior work related to rectangular roundabout ('rectabout') and introduce the concept of hybrid rectabout for collision avoidance that takes into account heterogeneous agents, i.e. variable speed and variable size. Each agent has its own speed (and local view), and senses its surroundings and acts independently without central coordination or communication with other agents. We apply our hybrid rectabout maneuver to WowWee Rovio mobile robots and provide both analytic and empirical results to show that our fully decentralized, non-communicative and distributed approach generates collision-free motions.

Keywords: Hybrid Rectangular Roundabout, Decentralized Collision Avoidance, Minimum Enclosing Rectangle.

1 Introduction

Collision avoidance is an important issue in multi-agent systems that involve planning, searching or coordination. Many decentralized approaches [1–3] have been presented recently. However, such techniques require a global-view or communication between agents. If we look at humans going by foot in crowded areas or driving by car in urban traffic, however, we observe very little collision and no obvious communication between these agents. The challenge is to achieve the same flexibility with autonomous agents involved in traversing a common

H.K. Dam et al. (Eds.): PRIMA 2014, LNAI 8861, pp. 190–205, 2014.

and shared space for the purposes of reaching a goal without colliding with one another.

In this paper, the main contribution focuses on two aspects. First, we present a hybrid rectabout procedure for navigation of multiple mobile robots or agents that explicitly considers heterogeneity (i.e. variable speed and variable size of agents). Second, we present both practical demonstrations and experimental simulations to demonstrate scalability and efficiency, taking into account Minimal Predicted Distance (MPD, more details below) between all the autonomous agents and the velocity of each agent. The approach is 'nature inspired' because of its use of theories taken from human pedestrian collision avoidance. The approach is 'intelligent' because of its use of traffic regulations and conventions. It is also fully decentralized, with each agent taking responsibility independently for detecting and avoiding collisions through local views / maps and local decision-making.

The hybrid rectabout is an extension of the Minimum Enclosing Rectangle-based (MER-based) rectabout [4, 5] that was introduced to address similar issues in multiagent simulation. However, the rectabout formulation had some limitations. All agents were required to be homogeneous (same size and speed). This meant that all agents had the same local view. To extend the applicability of MER-based rectabout to heterogeneous agents, the procedure needs to take into account variable speed of agents as well as variable size of agents. Both require adaptive local views since variable speed of agents means not just that agents are moving at different speeds from each other but also that an agent can vary its own speed while moving. Size of agent is, however, constant. The aim of this paper is to extend the MER-based rectabout procedure to deal with heterogeneous agents (variable speed of agents and various sizes of agent), hence the term 'hybrid'. To deal with this hybrid nature of agents the adaptive MER-based rectabout procedure to be described below is also hybrid in that the size and location of the rectabout will vary to reflect the properties of the agent. Consequently, MPD is adaptive to change while the agent speed is variable. In addition, our approach takes into account both the kinematic constraints of an agent and sensor uncertainty, which makes it specifically suitable for navigation of autonomous agents.

Informally, the hybrid rectabout procedure to be described below builds on the implicit assumption that other agents make similar collision avoidance reasoning via MER. That is, knowledge of MER is built into each agent. It consists of two components: Minimal Predicted Distance (MPD) detection and hybrid rectabout collision avoidance algorithm. The MPD is a metric inspired by real human pedestrian collision avoidance behaviour (for a review, see [6–8] and more details below). As far as we are aware, this was the first time that MPD had been used for addressing collision problems in fully decentralized and distributed multi-agent systems. The hybrid MER-based rectabout collision avoidance algorithm is a pairwise approach which computes and navigates agents' moving direction by following a 'keep right' rule at the rectabout. This rule can be changed if necessary to 'keep left'.

We have implemented and applied our new approach for heterogeneous agents to a set of WowWee Rovio mobile robots moving in an indoor environment using independent sensing and WiFi-based wireless remote control. Our experiments show that our approach achieves direct, collision-free and oscillation-free navigation in an environment containing multiple mobile robots and dynamic obstacles, even with some uncertainty in position and velocity. We also demonstrate the ability to handle static obstacles and the low computational requirements and scalability and efficiency of the hybrid rectabout in simulations of multiple virtual agents.

2   Problem Definition

2.1   Collision Issues

The problem we discuss in this paper is formally defined as follows. Let there be a set of n agents sharing an environment. For simplicity we assume the agents move in the plane $\mathbb{R}^2$. Each agent A has a current position p_A, a current velocity v_A. An agent's position can be obtained through sensors on the agent and the information can be broadcast through a WiFi-based remote control if necessary. In other words, all we need to demonstrate our new approach is that an agent can observe another agent when it 'comes into view' and that every agent knows what its position is in relation to the configuration space. These parameters are part of the agent's external state. Furthermore, each agent can have a different speed while moving from start location to goal location, for instance, starting slow and speeding up.

The task is for each agent A to independently and simultaneously calculate a new velocity v_A^{new} for itself such that, at an emergent level, all agents are guaranteed to be conflict-free for at least a certain amount of time (one time step in our experiments) when they would continue to move at their new velocity. As a secondary objective, each agent should calculate its new velocity as close as possible towards its goal orientation so that, at an emergent level, all agents reach their goal. The agents are not allowed to negotiate with each other, and can only use observations of the other agent's current position and velocity. However, each of the agents may assume that the other agents use the same strategy as itself to select a new velocity.

2.2   Minimal Predicted Distance

Inspiration from nature comes from Olivier et al. [7, 8], who proposed a new minimal predicted distance metric to investigate how pedestrians effortlessly and without communication avoid each other repeatedly and in a variety of different circumstances while still reaching their goals with minimum disruption to their paths. Given two persons with positions p_i and p_j, for $i, j = 1, 2, i \neq j$, each person is considered as a moving obstacle for the other. At each instant t, $MPD(t)$ represents the distance at which a person would meet the other if they did not perform motion adaptation after instant t. According to the model of MPD [7], the future trajectory for each person is modeled as follows:

$$p'(t, u) = p(t) + (u - t)\boldsymbol{v(t)}, \tag{1}$$

where u is a future time instant with $u, t > 0$ and $u > t$, $p(t)$ and $\boldsymbol{v(t)}$ are the position and velocity at time instant t, respectively. Their experimental studies showed that MPD is constant and that walkers adapt their motion only when MPD is small. Therefore, we can predict potential collisions by computing the absolute distance between p_i and p_j at each time instant t:

$$MPD(t) = \min_{u} \left\| p'_i(t, u) - p'_j(t, u) \right\|. \tag{2}$$

MPD is a strategy adopted by each agent for predicting potential collision risk. It is also a strategy that attempts to explain how individual humans implicitly adapt their motion and proposes implicit rules that humans naturally and intuitively follow for this adaptation. We further develop this strategy to devise a computational, geometric approach to compute a conflict-free solution for each agent separately and autonomously.

The further effects on MPD for two pedestrians walking at different speeds are revealed in [6], where computing the MPD with respect to motion adaptation shows the extent to which how much MPD is adapted when the speed s or orientation θ of two walkers varies. We formalize this as:

$$MPD_{ij}(t) = f(p_i(t, u), p_j(t, u), \theta_i, s_i, \theta_j, s_j), \tag{3}$$

Physical agents will typically calculate paths that suit their own needs. The moves of two or more agents will need to be separated by a minimal safety distance, Ω, to ensure no collisions. If two moves along planned paths never take agents within Ω of one another, we say they are conflict-free. That is, paths can intersect but moves along these paths cannot. Put differently, paths can be time-independent but moves along these paths cannot. Formally, moves along paths are conflict-free if and only if

$$\forall t, \forall p_i, p_j, i \neq j, MPD_{ij}(t) > \Omega, \tag{4}$$

where $MPD_{ij}(t)$ is the Euclidean distance between two positions at each time step, and Ω is the grid size dynamically adapted to the configuration space to compute the minimal safety distance.

2.3   Collision and Conflict Definition

The agents considered here are modeled as point masses. However, physical agents have actual size constraints and we need to take physical size into account in the theoretical model. Liu et al. [9] investigated all possible collision types between two moving agents in a configuration grid space, where the collision avoidance condition is to not occupy the same position during the same time-step when following paths, but rather to keep moving within a minimal safety distance at all times. This minimal safety distance has been studied in [6–8] and is considered a useful metric for minimal predicted distance. Collision can be defined as follows:

Definition 1 (Collision State)
A collision occurs between agents A_i and A_j when

$$\mathcal{C}_{ij} \Leftrightarrow \|p_i - p_j\| < \Omega(A_i, A_j), \tag{5}$$

where $\mathcal{C}_{ij}$ represents the collision between two agents A_i and A_j, Ω is a distance threshold for the minimal safety distance, which in turn is the absolute distance between the agents' geometric centers. Thus, we have the non-collision state description as follow:

Definition 2 (Non-Collision State)

$$\mathcal{S}_{ij} \Leftrightarrow \|p_i - p_j\| \geq \Omega(A_i, A_j), \tag{6}$$

where $\mathcal{S}_{ij}$ represents the non-collision state of the two agents corresponding to $\mathcal{C}_{ij}$ condition.

Definition 3 (Conflict State)
Another situation that must be accounted for is when collision would occur if two agents do not perform motion adaptation at a future time instant t. According to Equation 2, a conflict occurs between agents A_i and A_j if the agents are not currently in a collision situation but will enter a collision situation at time u if they do not perform motion adaptation. Equation 7 gives the definition of this conflict:

$$\mathcal{H}_{ij}(t) \Leftrightarrow \mathcal{S}_{ij}(t) \wedge MPD(u) < \Omega(A_i, A_j), \tag{7}$$

where $\mathcal{H}_{ij}(t)$ represents conflict between two agents A_i and A_j at time instant t taking into account the future time u (Equation 2). '$\wedge$' is the conjunction operator.

3   Collision Avoidance

In this section, we describe how agents avoid collisions with each other. We briefly review the idea of MER [10] and MER-based rectabout [4, 5], and then introduce our formulation of hybrid MER-based rectabout that we use for heterogeneous multi-agent navigation.

3.1   Local View Definition

We define a local view LV in front of the current position of an agent and only take into account the agents and any other obstacles inside this local view. The local view has to be of a minimum size to ensure satisfactory conflict detection. If the configuration space is considered as consisting of a grid of squares or rectangles, the size of which is equal to the size of the agent, each agent has 8 moving directions at each time step, as shown in Figure 1(a) and a wait action, plus front local view, as shown in Figure 1(b) and (c). Our approach requires each agent to consider its moves within its front local view at each time step, so each agent potentially has 9 legal actions. Each of these legal actions is a solution to the constraint satisfaction problem in which each agent must determine a move from $\{E,S,W,N,NE,SE,SW,NW,wait\}$, as shown in Figure 1(a), provided that the chosen move does not lead to collision with another agent.

The front local view will be restricted to the region that the agent can actually see, given the direction of motion of the agent, its view angle, and the position of any static obstacles (and perhaps other agents). The LV needs to be updated once the new velocity v is computed. Fixed and dynamic obstacles will be presented in the LV of each agent, not in a global data structure to be shared by all agents. The size of the individual squares in the LV will vary according to the size of the agent.

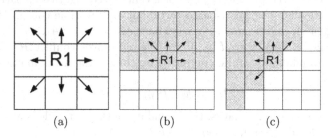

(a)   (b)   (c)

Fig. 1. (a) 8 possible moving directions. (b) and (c) The front local view (LV) of the agent.

3.2 MER Representation

According to Das et al. [10], given a set of points $P = \{p_1, p_2, ..., p_k\}$ with $p_k \in \Re^2$, the minimum enclosing square (or rectangle) of P is the smallest square (or rectangle) that contains all points of P. For the purposes of this paper, the smallest square or rectangle is defined to be the smallest rectangle that contains a given number k such that $\frac{n}{2} < k \leq n$ of x-consecutive points in a set of n points in the plane. The problem of computing k-square and k-rectangle has been investigated since 1991 (for a review, see [10–14]). MER has been applied in various areas, such as pattern recognition [15], facility location [16], similarity search [17, 18] and collision detection [5]. In order to classify the k-square with respect to the number of points η present on its boundary, Das et al. [10] investigated all different possibilities of k-squares. As a result, no k-square is possible with $\eta = 0$ or 1. The only possibility with $\eta = 2$ is that the two points appear at the two diagonally opposite corners of the corresponding k-squares. In this study, $k = \eta = 2$ is the MER or MES that the agents are searching for, as shown in Figure 2.

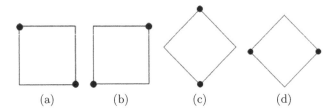

(a)   (b)   (c)   (d)

Fig. 2. MER of $\eta = 2$, with dots representing the position of the two agents. The orientation of the rectabout can differ according to the local view.

3.3   MER-Based Rectabout

The MER-based rectabout [4, 5] addresses the problem of collision caused by autonomous agents through moving independently and having only a limited capability to detect the potential risk of collision. The description below is a formal overview of the procedure and not a centralized algorithm. Each agent is assumed to calculate the MER-based rectabout and possible collision for itself. Given an agent A_i and n number of neighbour agents $A = \{A_1, A_2, ..., A_n\}$ with $1 \leq j \leq n$ in its local view LV, if two agents' moves conflict $\mathcal{H}_{ij}$, a virtual rectangular roundabout can be computed by calculating a minimum enclosing rectangle,

$$R^{ij} = MER(p_i, p_j), \tag{8}$$

where $p_i, p_j \in R^{ij}, \eta \equiv 2$. That is, the boundary of the rectangle is also included in the rectangle. Then, a new velocity is calculated over R^{ij}.

To calculate the new velocity $\boldsymbol{v}$ over R^{ij} for deconfliction between A_i and A_j, we calculate the other two diagonal opposite corner points p_i' and p_j', and we have

$$\mathrm{p}' = \begin{cases} q_1 & \min\{x_i, x_j\} \ and \ \min\{y_i, y_j\}, \\ q_2 & \min\{x_i, x_j\} \ and \ \max\{y_i, y_j\}, \\ q_3 & \max\{x_i, x_j\} \ and \ \min\{y_i, y_j\}, \\ q_4 & \max\{x_i, x_j\} \ and \ \max\{y_i, y_j\}. \end{cases} \tag{9}$$

Here, p_i, p_j correspond to two distinct elements of p'. Then we have another two points p_i' and p_j'

$$\{p_i', p_j'\} = \mathrm{p}' \cap \neg \{p_i, p_j\}. \tag{10}$$

The new velocity $\boldsymbol{v}_i'$ can be calculated as

$$p_i' - p_i = (x_i' - x_i) \wedge (y_i' - y_i). \tag{11}$$

For $x < 0$,

$$v_i' = \begin{cases} (-1, -1) & \text{if } y < 0, \\ (-1, 0) & \text{if } y = 0, \\ (-1, 1) & \text{if } y > 0. \end{cases}$$

For $x = 0$,

$$v_i' = \begin{cases} (0, -1) & \text{if } y < 0, \\ (0, 1) & \text{if } y > 0. \end{cases}$$

For $x > 0$,

$$v_i' = \begin{cases} (1, -1) & \text{if } y < 0, \\ (1, 0) & \text{if } y = 0, \\ (1, 1) & \text{if } y > 0. \end{cases}$$

3.4   Hybrid MER-Based Rectabout

In our experiments below, all agents are allowed to move at various speeds. Different speeds require different local views to take into account any other agents in their path, given their speed. The size of agents' LVs and of the squares making up their LVs will determine the size of the roundabout for that agent. This will allow agents independently to calculate a possible collision and place a virtual roundabout on their paths in case they need to use it to avoid collisions. If one agent is moving at a very high speed (e.g. motorway or highway), the agent will need a larger view to react to any hazard and keep a minimum safety distance from other agents. Therefore, LVs and minimal safety distances are scaled by velocity. The larger the LV, the further ahead the agents can plan. If one agent's speed is one grid (agent size $\Phi(A)$ is also one grid) at one move, then setting that agent's LV to grid size two can be guaranteed collision-free. According to Definition 1 and 2, different agents may have various physical sizes and the handling of agents with different size is taken into account. Thus, we can write the relationship between minimum local view LV, speed and physical sizes for agents as

$$LV_{min} = \begin{cases} \pi(\|v\| + \Phi(A)) & \text{if } \|v\| > 0, \\ 0 & \text{if } \|v\| = 0. \end{cases} \tag{12}$$

Equation 4 is not applicable to multiple agent systems with various speed. According to Equation 12, an agent's speed affects that agent's LV and a larger LV affects roundabout location. In hybrid-speed multi-agent systems, we can have a simple formula to calculate the minimal safety distance:

$$\Omega(t) = \|v\|, \|v\| > 0 \tag{13}$$

and therefore Equation 4 can be rewritten for agent A_i calculation as

$$\forall t, \forall p_i, p_j, i \neq j, MPD_{ij}(t) > \|v_i\|, \tag{14}$$

which can be applicable to hybrid speed multiple agent systems.

3.5   Static Obstacles

We have discussed how agents avoid collisions with each other, but typical multi-agent environments also contain static obstacles. We can follow the same approach as above, with a key difference being that fixed obstacles do not move, so they can be treated as object $\|v\| = 0$. We can generally assume that obstacles are modeled as the same size of grid unit due to our simulations being based on a grid environment. Let **O** be a one grid unit static obstacle, and let A be an agent positioned at p_A. Then the virtual rectabout induced by obstacle **O** is defined as (see Figure 3(a) and (b)):

$$R^{AO} = MER(p_A, p_O) \tag{15}$$

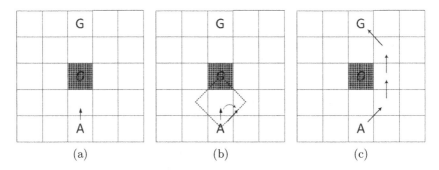

(a)   (b)   (c)

Fig. 3. A and G represent agent A and agent's goal, respectively. (a) A configuration of an agent A and a static obstacle **O**. (b) Geometric illustration of how a rectabout is located to resolve collision between the agent and static obstacle using hybrid rectabout. (c) Here the path for the agent is tracked for avoiding the static obstacle using keep right traffic rule.

In case of obstacles, the agent employs the hybrid rectabout to calculate a new velocity to move around such obstacles. This guarantees that there always exists a valid velocity for the agent that avoids collisions with the fixed obstacle. The direction of motion around obstacles towards the agent's goal can be obtained by the agent using standard path planning techniques, e.g. the A* algorithm [19]. Figure 3(c) shows the tracked path of how the agent avoids the static obstacle to reach its goal.

4   Experimentation

4.1   Implementation Details

We implemented our approach for a set of WowWee Rovio mobile robots using independent sensing and WiFi-based wireless remote control. The WowWee Rovio is a differential-drive mobile robot. It has three individual omni-directional wheels. There are ten various drive and turn speeds in both forward and reverse directions and its shape is a rectangular car-like robot.

All calculations were performed on a 3.2GHz Intel Core i5 system with 4GB of memory running Microsoft Windows XP. However, to ensure that our approach applies when each agent uses its own on-board sensing and mobile laptop for computing, only the WiFi signal sending was carried out centrally. The calculations for each agent were performed in separate and independent processes that did not communicate with each other.

4.2   Experimental Results

Using the WowWee Rovio mobile robots, we tested our approach in the following two scenarios.

1. Two robots are deployed on two sides of the field and have to move to their goal positions on the other side using the hybrid rectabout avoiding collision. The video link is `http://youtu.be/nitsNOSxs9Q`.

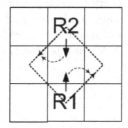

Fig. 4. Solid arrow line is the intended trajectory. Dotted arrow line is the deconfliction trajectory. The central dotted rectangle is a virtual rectabout enclosing two robots R1 and R2.

2. Four robots are distributed evenly on a square, and their goal is to navigate to the antipodal position on the circle. In doing so, the robots will form a dense crowd in the middle. The video link is `http://youtu.be/1YQY3TZJzwM`.

In addition, we tested the heterogeneity and scalability of our approach in the following two simulated scenarios.

1. **Heterogeneity:** The simulation demonstrates a heterogeneous group of five virtual agents navigating from one side to the other, negotiating around each other in the center. For the path computation, each agent employs the A* algorithm [19] to navigate from the initial position to the goal position with a minimum local view. Each agent is able to detect conflict with any other agent and computes a virtual rectabout based on MER ($MER(p_1, p_2)$). A new velocity is planned along the path of MER and the agents follow a shared 'keep right' traffic rule to resolve the conflict independently. The virtual

Fig. 5. Illustration shows the start positions of four robots

rectabout is removed after one time-step, after which each agent needs to independently operate the process again, since the information around the agent always changes with every time step. However, agents always attempt to use A* planning path towards their own goal position at every time-step. Figure 6 shows snapshots of collision avoidance for six agents while adhering to their chosen paths. The video link is `http://youtu.be/1XHEiOLScXY`.

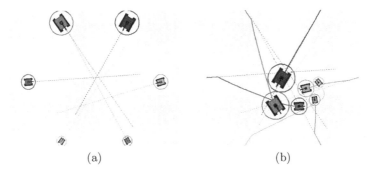

(a)   (b)

Fig. 6. Six hybrid agents (variable size and speed) avoiding collision with each other. (a) soon after starting. (b) after avoiding collisions.

2. **Scalability:** In order to test the performance of our method we varied the number of agents in different configuration space (200x200 grid, 300x300 grid and 400x400 grid) to see how our approach scales when the number of agents increases. We performed our experiments on an Intel Core(TM) i5 processor 3.20 GHz with 4GByte of memory. Each scenario was repeated 10 times and results were averaged. All start and goal positions were generated randomly. All agents have various speed (1 to 3 grid per move step) and these were randomly assigned for each agent at the initial position.

The agents with higher speed require larger local views, leading to increasing computation time in comparison to homogeneous settings. Figure 7 shows the total running time for various numbers of agents with various speed. We note that the total running time of our method scales nearly linearly with the number of heterogeneous agents. Furthermore, the computation time increases as the density of agents increases, as would be expected given that deadlock is more frequent with high density. An agent enters a 'wait' state for one or more moves if it is in deadlock. As long as one agent in a deadlock situation can move, such deadlock is temporary [4].

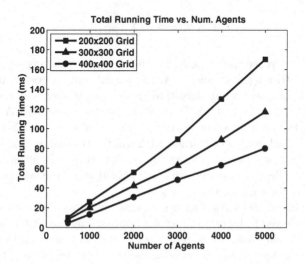

Fig. 7. The total running can be seen to scale almost linearly with the number of heterogeneous agents

4.3 Comparison

We conducted a number of simulations for comparison against two other decentralized approaches for which we could produce code based on the published algorithms: Satisficing Game Theory (SGT) algorithm by Hill et al. ([20]) and Distributed Reactive Collision Avoidance (DRCA) algorithm by Lalish and Morgansen ([1]): (1) Computation Time: how long the algorithm needs to compute deconfliction between agents in path conflict; and (2) Solution Efficiency: how efficient the solution is for collision avoidance. The scenario is referred to as a choke point because, without deconfliction, all the agents would meet at the center. In order to fairly compare these three algorithms, the hybrid rectabout algorithm has been set up for this simulation such that each agent has a constant speed (1 grid / move). The agent's size is the same as the grid size, so each agent has information only within the two grid front local view of itself, which is the same as in Hill et al. and Lalish.

Computation Time: A simulation of the hybrid rectabout algorithm for deconflicting 32 agents, the densest choke pattern demonstrated by Hill et al. [20]. Our hybrid rectabout algorithm consumed 0.1953 milliseconds for the mean running time for deconfliction, compared to 0.1180 seconds in DRCA and 127.3804 seconds in SGT. The reason for the increased time in SGT is that their approach requires communication and priority for deconfliction, unlike our approach.

Solution Efficiency: The efficiency of the maneuver is defined as the average of the percentage of moving cost (or time delay) in arrival from start position to goal position:

$$Efficiency = \frac{1}{n} \sum_{i=1}^{n} \frac{C_r^i}{C^i}, \tag{16}$$

where C_r^i is the reference moving cost for the ith agent (moving straight without considering other agents), and C^i is the actual moving cost taken for the ith agent. The hybrid rectabout algorithm attained an efficiency of 88.9%, compared to 87.6% in DRCA and 85.7% in SGT. However, the DRCA algorithm breaks some of the guarantees of safety for this simulation, in other words, it does not always work for this situation with safety. Meanwhile, the SGT algorithm has collisions occurring in its experiments (recorded 19 out of 32 agents). Importantly, no collisions occurred with our hybrid rectabout algorithm which guaranteed safety for each agent.

We also conducted 100 virtual agents moving simultaneously across a circle, the scenario is referred to by [21]. All agents approaching the center of the circle and the agents moving toward the perimeter of the circle have to pass through the center. The timings of this scenario for the hybrid rectabout and three other variations of velocity obstacles (Velocity Obstacle [22], Optimal Reciprocal Collision Avoidance (ORCA) [23], Hybrid Reciprocal Velocity Obstacle [21]) are shown in Table 1.

Table 1. Timing of simulations of 100 virtual agents moving simultaneously across a circle using Hybrid Rectabout and three variations of velocity obstacles algorithms

Algorithm	Computation Time (ms)
Hybrid Rectabout	**0.77**
Velocity Obstacle	0.81
Optimal Reciprocal Collision Avoidance	0.83
Hybrid Reciprocal Velocity Obstacle	1.24

Figure 8 shows the comparison of the timings for this scenario with an increasing number of virtual agents moving across a circle. The timing of the hybrid rectabout requires less time to complete (significant $p \leqslant 0.1$, lower CI -0.68, upper CI 0.02).

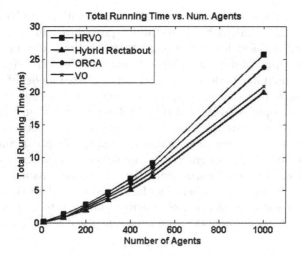

Fig. 8. Comparison of the timing of simulations of increasing numbers of virtual agents moving simultaneously across a circle of increasing circumference between hybrid rectabout and other 3 algorithms

5 Conclusions

Collision avoidance has a long history in both agent-based and robotics research, and there exist many approaches, only some of which have been mentioned here. Nearly all previous approaches assume some degree of communication, access to a global map, priority allocation or central coordination. In this paper, we have introduced a novel and intelligent hybrid rectabout procedure for navigation of multiple robots or autonomous agents using nature-inspired techniques. We take into account the obstacles in the environment as well as uncertainty in position and velocity. We also consider the dynamics and kinematics of the agents, thereby allowing us to implement our approach on WowWee Rovio mobile robots. The kinematic research on minimal predicted distance between two human walkers is applied for the first time to deal with agent collision problems in conjunction with a hybrid rectabout maneuver. We use MPD to detect the possible collisions in agent trajectories. The agents involved in conflict will compute a rectabout and re-plan a new velocity when MPD is below the threshold. This process is repeated until all agents achieve their goals, but each of the agents acts completely independently without central coordination and does not communicate with other agents.

The hybrid rectabout for mutual avoidance provides a powerful method for a multiple heterogeneous agent avoidance maneuver. At present, most agent search-based algorithms assume all agents have the same physical size (e.g. particles in PSO), travel at the same speed (e.g. ants in ACO) or have the same kinematic constraints (e.g. autonomous robots). Simulations involving such autonomous agents rarely take into account the need to avoid collision, which makes the application of these algorithms to real-world situations problematic. Our findings indicate that a MER-based rectabout procedure can be appended to the search algorithm used by agents (e.g. A*) with little additional cost, resulting in greater applicability to real-world navigation and therefore increased plausibility. We would like to develop a more sophisticated model of uncertainty that takes into account uncertainty in position and velocity as given by sensors of the agent, and apply it to the hybrid rectabout formulation. The other future direction is to apply our approach for avoiding collisions between swarms or groups of agents with no communication or central coordination. Such collision avoidance is often overlooked or ignored in mobile multi-agent and swarm-based approaches and simulations. Swarm simulations frequently assume that swarm members can fly through each other. The lack of collision detection and avoidance severely limits the application of swarm technology to real-life problems (e.g. fleets of autonomous cars taking humans safely and reliably to their destinations).

References

1. Lalish, E., Morgansen, K.A.: Distributed reactive collision avoidance. Autonomous Robots 32(3), 207–226 (2012)
2. Platzer, A., Clarke, E.M.: Formal verification of curved flight collision avoidance maneuvers: A case study. In: Cavalcanti, A., Dams, D.R. (eds.) FM 2009. LNCS, vol. 5850, pp. 547–562. Springer, Heidelberg (2009)
3. Škrjanc, I., Klančar, G.: Optimal cooperative collision avoidance between multiple robots based on bernstein-bézier curves. Robotics and Autonomous Systems 58(1), 1–9 (2010)
4. Liu, F., Narayanan, A.: A human-inspired collision avoidance method for multi-robot and mobile autonomous robots. In: Boella, G., Elkind, E., Savarimuthu, B.T.R., Dignum, F., Purvis, M.K. (eds.) PRIMA 2013. LNCS, vol. 8291, pp. 181–196. Springer, Heidelberg (2013)
5. Liu, F., Narayanan, A.: Roundabout collision avoidance for multiple robots based on minimum enclosing rectangle (demonstration). In: Proceedings of the Twelfth International Joint Conference on Autonomous Agents and Multiagent Systems (AAMAS 2013), Saint Paul, Minnesota, USA, pp. 1375–1376. IFAAMAS (May 2013)
6. Olivier, A.H., Marin, A., Grétual, A., Berthoz, A., Pettré, J.: Collision avoidance between two walkers: Role-dependent strategies. Gait & Posture 38(4), 751–756 (2013)
7. Olivier, A.H., Marin, A., Grétual, A., Pettré, J.: Minimal predicted distance: A common metric for collision avoidance during pairwise interactions between walkers. Gait & Posture 36(3), 399–404 (2012)
8. Olivier, A.-H., Marin, A., Grétual, A., Pettré, J.: Minimal predicted distance: A kinematic cue to investigate collision avoidance between walkers. Computer Methods in Biomechanics and Biomedical Engineering 15(1), 240–242 (2012)
9. Liu, F., Narayanan, A., Bai, Q.: Effective methods for generating collision free paths for multiple robots based on collision type (demonstration). In: Proceedings of the Eleventh International Joint Conference on Autonomous Agents and Multiagent Systems (AAMAS 2012), Valencia, Spain, pp. 1459–1460. IFAAMAS (June 2012)

10. Das, S., Goswami, P.P., Nandy, S.C.: Smallest k-point enclosing rectangle and square of arbitrary orientation. Information Processing Letters 94(6), 259–266 (2005)
11. Aggarwal, A., Imai, H., Katoh, N., Suri, S.: Finding k points with minimum diameter and related problems. Journal of Algorithms 12(1), 38–56 (1991)
12. Eppstein, D., Erickson, J.: Iterated nearest neighbors and finding minimal polytopes. Discrete & Computational Geometry 11(1), 321–350 (1994)
13. Mahapatra, P.R.S., Karmakar, A., Das, S., Goswami, P.P.: k-enclosing axis-parallel square. In: Murgante, B., Gervasi, O., Iglesias, A., Taniar, D., Apduhan, B.O. (eds.) ICCSA 2011, Part III. LNCS, vol. 6784, pp. 84–93. Springer, Heidelberg (2011)
14. Segal, M., Kedem, K.: Enclosing k points in the smallest axis parallel rectangle. Information Processing Letters 65(2), 95–99 (1998)
15. Pang, S., Liu, F., Kadobayashi, Y., Ban, T., Inoue, D.: Training minimum enclosing balls for cross tasks knowledge transfer. In: Huang, T., Zeng, Z., Li, C., Leung, C.S. (eds.) ICONIP 2012, Part I. LNCS, vol. 7663, pp. 375–382. Springer, Heidelberg (2012)
16. Drezner, Z., Hamacher, H.W.: Facility Location: Applications and Theory. Springer, Berlin (2002)
17. De, M., Maheshwari, A., Nandy, S.C., Smid, M.H.M.: An in-place min-max priority search tree. Computational Geometry 46(3), 310–327 (2013)
18. Nandy, S.C., Bhattacharya, B.B.: A unified algorithm for finding maximum and minimum object enclosing rectangles and cuboids. Computers & Mathematics with Applications 29(8), 45–61 (1995)
19. Nilsson, N.J.: Principles of Artificial Intelligence. Springer, Berlin (1982)
20. Hill, J., Archibald, J., Stirling, W., Frost, R.: A multi-agent system architecture for distributed air traffic control. In: Proceedings of AIAA Guidance, San Francisco, California, USA, pp. 1936–1946. American Institute of Aeronautics and Astronautics (AIAA) (August 2005)
21. Snape, J., van den Berg, J., Guy, S.J., Manocha, D.: The hybrid reciprocal velocity obstacle. IEEE Transactions on Robotics 27(4), 696–706 (2011)
22. Fiorini, P., Shiller, Z.: Motion planning in dynamic environments using velocity obstacles. International Journal of Robotic Research 17(7), 760–772 (1998)
23. van den Berg, J., Guy, S.J., Lin, M.C., Manocha, D.: Reciprocal n-body collision avoidance. In: Proceedings of The 14th International Symposium of Robotics Research (ISRR 2009), Lucerne, Switzerland, pp. 3–19. Springer (August 2009)

Locating Malicious Agents
in Mobile Wireless Sensor Networks

Yuichi Sei and Akihiko Ohsuga

Graduate School of Information Systems
The University of Electro-Communications, Tokyo, Japan
{sei,ohsuga}@is.uec.ac.jp

Abstract. A compromised node in wireless sensor networks can be used
to create false messages by generating them on their own or by fabricat-
ing legitimate messages received from other nodes. Our goal is to locate
the compromised nodes that create false messages. Existing studies can
only be used in situations where sensor nodes do not move. However, it
is possible that nodes move because of wind or other factors in real situations. We improve existing studies for detecting compromised nodes in
mobile wireless sensor networks. In the proposed method, an agent exists
on each node and it appends its ID and a k-bit code to an event message
and the sink detects a compromised node by a statistical method. Our
method can be used in static and dynamic environments. Simulations we
conducted prove the effectiveness of our method.

Keywords: Wireless sensor networks, Security, Malicious agent detection.

1 Introduction

Wireless sensor networks (WSNs) can detect events such as forest fires and in-
truders. An agent exists on each sensor node in a WSN, and the agent creates an
event message and delivers it to the *sink* over multi-hop paths. Because WSNs
are unattended, an adversary could capture and compromise some of the sensor nodes. In so doing, the adversary can extract all information such as the
secret keys stored in the nodes, and the adversary can insert malicious agents
into the nodes. Then, these nodes can then be used to create false messages,
i.e., generate false messages on their own and/or fabricate legitimate messages
they have received from other nodes. They can waste a significant amount of
network resources. Moreover, they can also generate network congestion by creating many false event messages to prevent a legitimate event message from
being transmitted to the sink.

Although there are many works on detecting such false messages
[29,32,16,1,34], they cannot detect malicious agents that creating false messages.

Studies on traceback in wireless sensor networks include ones [30,33] on detecting malicious agents that create false messages. However, these methods can
only be used in situations where there is only one malicious agent and the routing

H.K. Dam et al. (Eds.): PRIMA 2014, LNAI 8861, pp. 206–221, 2014.

path from it to the sink is static. Although Authenticated K-sized Probabilistic Packet Marking (AK-PPM) [26] can be used in environments where the routing paths are changeable, it cannot identify malicious agents that fabricate messages. Light-weight Packet Marking (LPM) [20] can be used in situations where there are many malicious agents. However, LPM can only detect a *suspicious node group*, which contains a suspicious node n, nodes that had sent messages to node n, and nodes that had received messages from node n. If nodes can move, the number of nodes in a suspicious node group can be very large. Therefore, the effectiveness of LPM goes away in this case.

We use the packet marking method to detect nodes that created false messages, that is, the source nodes that generate false messages and the nodes that fabricated messages. In our method, each forwarding node appends its ID and a k-bit message authentication code (MAC) [13] to the message. If the length of the bits of a MAC is normal, such as 128 bits [5], there is a lot of communication traffic for forwarding a message. In our method, we can set k to be small, e.g., only 1 bit. Of course, malicious agents can generate a correct MAC with high probability if k is small. Even so, we can detect malicious agents by using a statistical procedure when some false messages reach the sink.

The rest of this paper is organized as follows. Section 2 presents the models of false messages and sensor networks. Section 3 discusses the related methods and their problems. Section 4 presents the design of our algorithm. Section 5 presents the results of our simulations. Section 6 discusses several design issues in our method. Section 7 summarizes this paper.

2   System Model

In this section, we define our assumed sensor network model in this paper and the model of false message attacks.

2.1   Model of WSNs

We assume a WSN composed of many small sensor nodes. Each sensor node has extremely limited computational power and storage. We assume that sensor nodes are not equipped with tamper-resistant hardware.

The nodes can detect an event of interest. Each of the detecting nodes reports the signal it senses to the sink. In our model, we assume that the destination of messages is the sink. We assume that the sink has sufficient computational power and storage.

An agent exists on each node and the agent has a role of controlling the node. Agent-based wireless sensor networks are widely studied such as [2,19]. We use "node" and "agent" interchangeably.

These assumptions are fairly general in studies of wireless sensor networks.

We also assume that sensor nodes can move because of wind or reasons of applications. Many studies, such as [15,25] target mobile wireless sensor networks.

2.2   Attack Model

Adversaries could compromise multiple sensor nodes in a WSN. They can extract all information such as secret keys from the compromised nodes. The compromised node can be used to create false messages, i.e., generate false messages by itself and/or fabricate messages it has received from other nodes. They can waste a significant amount of network resources. Therefore, we want to eliminate these malicious nodes as quickly as possible. Moreover, they can also generate network congestion by creating many false event messages to prevent a legitimate event message from being transmitted to the sink.

Malicious agents can mount other attacks such as sinkhole attacks [9] and wormhole attacks [12,11]. These attacks are beyond the scope of this paper. We can use existing studies such as [24,31,18] for these attacks.

3   Related Work

3.1   Overview

In this section, we describe related works on detecting malicious agents and their problems.

There are currently three ways of detecting malicious agents: verifying the integrity of the code running on a node, monitoring conducted by the nodes themselves, and traceback from the sink. Verifying the integrity of the code mechanism [21,28,8] can check whether or not the suspicious node is compromised. Because this mechanism requires a high cost, this mechanism is usually used only after detecting a suspicious node using other mechanisms.

In our proposal, the sink can detect a malicious agent at a high probability, i.e., it can detect a suspicious node. Therefore, verifying the integrity of the code running on a node, and the use of our proposal can coexist. The monitoring done by nodes mechanisms [17,23,3] is vulnerable to collusion attacks because the monitor nodes may be compromised as well. We would need to use these kinds of mechanisms if we wanted to send and receive messages within only the sensor nodes without a sink. However, we take into account a situation where the destination of the messages from the nodes is the sink. Therefore, we can assign the task of detecting malicious agents to the sink, not to the nodes.

Related works of traceback from the sink are given below. Probabilistic Nested Marking (PNM) [30] modified a packet marking algorithm [4,22] used on the Internet into one for wireless sensor networks. In PNM, each forwarding node appends its message authentication code (MAC) as well as its ID with some probability. Because several nodes append their MACs, PNM can detect fabricated messages. The sink constructs an attack graph from false messages in the same way as a probabilistic packet marking algorithm on the Internet.

However, the sink can only construct the attack graph in situations where there is only one source node of messages and the routing path is static. Moreover, it must also receive a lot of false messages before they can construct an attack graph and locate a malicious agent.

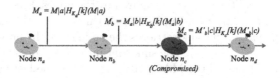

Fig. 1. Base algorithm of LPM and PM4M

The mechanism in [33] can detect the source node that generated the false messages from fewer false messages than PNM. However, it cannot detect the node that fabricated a message. It also cannot be used in environments where the routing paths are changeable.

Authenticated K-sized Probabilistic Packet Marking (AK-PPM) scheme was proposed for packet traceback in mobile ad hoc networks [26]. This method can be used in environments where the routing paths are changeable. Although AK-PPM can identify the source node that creates a message, it cannot identify malicious agents that fabricate messages.

Light-weight Packet Marking (LPM) [20] can detect the source node that generated false messages and also can detect the malicious agents that fabricate messages. However, LPM assumes that the positions of nodes are static. Therefore, we cannot use these methods or other related work in situations where sensor nodes can move because of wind or other factors.

3.2   LPM

The algorithm of LPM consists of two parts; marking at nodes and verification at the sink. The algorithm of marking at nodes is the same as our proposed Probabilistic Marking for Mobile WSNs (PM4M) in this paper.

In LPM, *every* forwarding node appends its ID and a *k-bit* MAC to messages. The basic scheme is shown in Fig. 1. We express a stream concatenation as |.

Marking at the Nodes. We assume that each sensor node n_u has a unique ID u and shares a unique secret key K_u with the sink. H represents a secure hash function, and it is shared among all the nodes and the sink. $H_{K_u}[k](m)$ means the k-bit MAC of message m calculated from a shared hash function H and node n_u's secret key K_u. The initial message M may contain the event type detected at node n_a, the detected time, and the location among other things. After creating an initial message M, node n_a calculates the MAC of $M|a$ by using its key K_a and creates the message $M_a = M|a|H_{K_a}[k](M|a)$. The next node n_b receives message M_a. Node n_b calculates the MAC of $M_a|b$ by using its key K_b and creates message M_b.

Verification at the Sink. When the sink receives the final message $M_{n_r} = M_{n_{r-1}}|n_r|H_{K_r}(M_{n_{r-1}}|n_r)$, it starts a verification process. The sink has the shared hash function H and all the secret keys shared by the nodes. First, the sink calculates the MAC of $M_{n_{r-1}}|n_r$ by using key K_r. If this value is the same as the one included in message M_{n_r}, the sink retrieves the node ID of the previous hop $r-1$ and verifies $H_{K_{r-1}}(M_{n_{r-2}}|n_{r-1})$. The sink continues this process until it finds an incorrect MAC or verifies all the MACs. The node with the last verified MAC is called the **Last Verified Node (LVN)**. A malicious agent (the node that created false messages and/or the forwarding node that fabricated legitimate messages) is located within a one-hop neighborhood of the LVN if k is sufficiently large.

However, the malicious agent and its one-hop neighbor node do not become always an LVN if k is small. Consider the situation shown in Fig. 1. When node n_c fabricates a message, the LVN is node n_c if k is sufficiently large. Otherwise, the candidates of an LVN are all the nodes between the source node and the malicious agent, i.e., nodes n_a, n_b, n_c in this example.

Problem of LPM. A malicious agent can choose to append a legitimate MAC or a false MAC to a false message after it has created the false message. In the example of Fig. 1, node n_c changes message M_b into a false message M_b', then it appends to string $M_b'|c$ a legitimate MAC $H_{K_c}[k](M_b'|c)$. We call this attack a **legitimate MAC attack**. On the other hand, node n_c can append a false MAC to a fabricated message M_b' after it changes message M_b to M_b'. We call this attack a **false MAC attack**. In this case, the LVN is always node n_d. In LPM, it is assumed that malicious agents always append a legitimate MAC. Even if this assumption is incorrect, we can detect malicious agents within a one-hop neighbor node in situations where the positions of nodes are static. However, if the number of neighbor nodes of a malicious agent is large, the successful detection rate also decreases.

For example, assume that the number of neighbor nodes of a malicious agent is 10. In this case, the number of nodes of a suspicious node group that LPM can detect is 11. If we capture each node physically and check the physical memory one by one to determine whether or not the node is actually compromised, the successful detection rate is $(\sum_i^{11} 1/i)/11 = 0.27$ on average. Moreover, the condition goes from bad to worse when we assume that nodes can move. In this case, the suspicious node group contains all nodes that had been neighbor of the malicious agent. If the number of nodes of the suspicious node group is 50, the successful detection rate is $(\sum_i^{50} 1/i)/50 = 0.09$.

4   PM4M: Probabilistic Marking for Mobile WSNs

4.1   Notations

Logical Node. Let the routing path of a false message be $p_i = \langle\{a, b, ...\}\rangle$ (here, $a, b...$ represents the node IDs). A set of all the routing paths of the false messages the sink has received is represented by $P = \{p_1, ..., p_d\}$. The value d is the number of times the sink received false messages.

We call a node which is located downstream of n_u (that is, situated nearer the sink in relation to n_u) and is i-hop away from node n_u a **logical node** $n_{u[i]}$

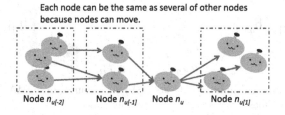

Each node can be the same as several of other nodes because nodes can move.

Node $n_{u[-2]}$ Node $n_{u[-1]}$ Node n_u Node $n_{u[1]}$

Fig. 2. Logical nodes

($i > 0$). Examples are shown in Fig. 2. We call a node which is located upstream of n_u and is i-hop away from node n_u a logical node $n_{u[-i]}$ ($i > 0$).

The node ID of an LVN in routing path p_i is represented by $L[p_i]$. The order of node n_u appearing in path p_i is represented by $M_u[p_i]$ (the order of the source node is 1.) The order of the LVN appearing in path p_i is represented by $M_L[p_i] = M_{L[p_i]}[p_i]$.

We define

$$b_{u[i]} = |\{j | p_j \in P \land u \in p_j \land M_L[p_j] - M_u[p_j] = i\}|. \tag{1}$$

$b_{u[i]}$ represents the number of times that the number of hops from node n_u to the LVN is i. Furthermore, let us define

$$b_u = b_{u[0]}. \tag{2}$$

That is, b_u represents the number of times node n_u became an LVN.

Let us introduce the notation $b_{u[i]}\langle S \rangle$ to represent the number of times logical node $n_{u[i]}$ became an LVN as a result of legitimate MAC attacks on logical nodes $\{n_{u[s]} | s \in S\}$. Of course, the sink cannot know this value. For example, imagine a situation where logical node $n_{u[5]}$ of node n_u mounted legitimate MAC attacks several times and logical node $n_{u[1]}$ became an LVN twice. In this case, $b_{u[1]}\langle\{5\}\rangle = 2$. Suppose further that logical node $n_{u[6]}$ mounted legitimate MAC attacks several times and logical node $n_{u[1]}$ became an LVN three times. In this case, $b_{u[1]}\langle\{6\}\rangle = 3$ and $b_{u[1]}\langle\{5, 6\}\rangle = 5$.

Let us introduce another notation $b_{u[i]}(j, v)$ to represent the number of times logical node $n_{u[i]}$ became an LVN of a message passed at n_v which is j hops away from n_u. That is,

$$b_{u[i]}(j, v) = |\{s | p_s \in P \land u \in p_s \land M_L[p_s] - M_u[p_s] = i$$
$$\land v \in p_s \land M_v[p_s] - M_u[p_s] = j\}| \tag{3}$$

Previous Nodes of a Node that Became an LVN. The sink manages a **previous node set** PN_u for each node n_u. PN_u includes IDs of nodes that transmitted a message to n_u and n_u became an LVN of the message. That is,

$$PN_u = \{v | b_u(-1, v) \geq 1\}. \tag{4}$$

We also define the function $PN_u.\text{get}(v)$. This function returns $b_u(-1, v)$.

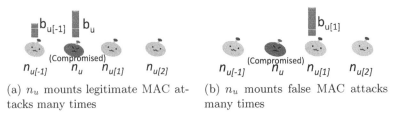

(a) n_u mounts legitimate MAC attacks many times

(b) n_u mounts false MAC attacks many times

Fig. 3. Observational results when n_u mounts legitimate/false MAC attacks many times

Next Nodes of a Node that Became an LVN. The sink manages a **next node set** NN_u for each node n_u. NN_u includes IDs of nodes that received a message from n_u and n_u became an LVN of the message. That is,

$$NN_u = \{v|b_u(1,v) \geq 1\}. \tag{5}$$

We also define the function $NN_u.get(v)$. This function returns $b_u(1,v)$.

4.2   Concept of Determining Malicious Agents in PM4M

In Fig. 1, node n_c mounts a legitimate MAC attack. In this case, one of the nodes that transmitted the message to node n_c, that is node n_a, n_b, or n_c, becomes an LVN. The probability that node n_c becomes an LVN is $1 - 2^{-k}$. The probability that $n_{c[-i]}$ becomes an LVN is $2^{-k \cdot i} \cdot (1 - 2^{-k})$. Therefore, node n_c is most likely to become an LVN.

On the other hand, if node n_c mounted a false MAC attack, $n_{c[1]}$, that is node n_d in this example, always becomes an LVN.

Therefore,

- When n_u mounts legitimate MAC attacks many times,
  1. The result $b_u \gg b_{u[1]}$ will be observed (Fig. 3(a)).
- When n_u mounts false MAC attacks many times,
  2. The result $b_{u[1]} \gg b_{u[2]}$ and
  3. $b_{u[1]} \gg b_u$ will be observed (Fig. 3(b)).

Then, we consider the reasons for the observed results just mentioned above.

Situation 1 : The reasons why $b_u \gg b_{u[1]}$ are,
  - a. n_u mounted legitimate MAC attacks,
  - b. PN_u mounted false MAC attacks, or
  - c. $n_{u[i]}(i \geq 1)$ mounted legitimate MAC attacks and it just happened that way.

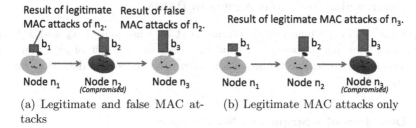

(a) Legitimate and false MAC attacks

(b) Legitimate MAC attacks only

Fig. 4. Indistinguishable situations from observed effects

Situation 2 : The reasons why $b_{u[1]} \gg b_{u[2]}$ are,

    a. n_u mounted false MAC attacks,

    b. NN_u mounted legitimate MAC attacks, or

    c. $n_{u[i]} (i \geq 2)$ mounted legitimate MAC attacks and it just happened that way.

Situation 3 : The reason why $b_{u[1]} \gg b_u$ is,

    a. n_u mounted false MAC attacks, or

    b. $n_{u[i]} (i \geq 1)$ mounted legitimate MAC attacks and it just happened that way.

If we can eliminate the possibility of c. in Situation 1, we can cut the list of candidates of suspicious nodes to n_u and nodes of PN_u. In the same way, we can cut the list of candidates of suspicious nodes to n_u and nodes of NN_u if we can eliminate the possibility of c. in Situation 2. We can cut the list of candidates of suspicious nodes to only n_u if we can eliminate the possibility of b. in Situation 3.

To do this, we propose the detection method PM4M for legitimate/false MAC attacks. PM4M can identify a suspicious node, but its identification is not always correct because it is a probabilistic method. To confirm whether a node is actually compromised or not requires another more costly method described in Section 3.1. The use of PM4M enables us to restrict this more costly determination to the set of identified suspicious nodes.

We cannot distinguish between the two situations in Fig. 4 from observed effects. In this case, we determine **suspicious node group**. In Fig. 4, the suspicious node group includes nodes n_2 and n_3. We randomly choose one node from the group (here, assume that we choose n_2) and determine that n_2 is a suspicious node. Then the sink confirms whether n_2 is actually compromised or not by another more costly method. If n_2 is a malicious agent, we eliminate the other node n_3 from the suspicious node group. Otherwise, the sink determines that n_3 is a suspicious node and confirms whether n_3 is actually compromised or not by the costly method. Therefore, the theoretical maximum **successful detection rate** is 2/3.

4.3   Determining Malicious Agents in PM4M

We propose PM4M which can determine that at least one of n_u and PN_u is suspicious. Then we propose a method that can cut the list of candidates of suspicious nodes to realize the situation where the successful detection rate is higher than th.

4.4   Detection of a Suspicious Node Group

Let $B_{u[i]}$ be the random variable of the number of times logical node $n_{u[i]}$ became an LVN, and let $W_{u[i]}$ be the random variable of the number of times logical node $n_{u[i]}$ mounted a legitimate MAC attack. The conditional probability of n_u becoming LVNs $b_u - i$ times as a result of legitimate MAC attacks of $n_{u[j]}$ $(j \geq 1)$ given that $n_{u[i]}$ became LVNs $b_{u[i]}$ times is calculated by

$$
\begin{aligned}
\xi_1(u, i) &= P(B_{u[0]}\langle 1, \ldots\rangle = b_u - i | B_{u[1]}\langle 1, \ldots\rangle = b_{u[1]}) \\
&= P(B_{u[0]}\langle 1\rangle = b_u - i | B_{u[1]}\langle 1\rangle = b_{u[1]})
\end{aligned}
\tag{6}
$$

From Lemma 1 described in Appendix A,

$$
= 2^{k+b_{u[1]}k} \cdot (1 + 2^k)^{-1-b_{u[1]}-b_u+i} \cdot {}_{b_{u[1]}+b_u-i}C_{b_{u[1]}}
$$

Let $\Xi_1(u, \alpha)$ be the conditional probability of at least one of nodes of PN_u and n_u mounting attacks α times given that n_u became LVNs b_u times. We get from Equation 6

$$
\Xi_1(u, \alpha) = \sum_{i=\alpha}^{b_u} \xi_1(u, i).
\tag{7}
$$

We consider that the set of nodes of PN_u and n_u is a suspicious node group. The number of nodes of the suspicious node group could be large. In the following subsection, we describe how to reduce the number of the suspicious nodes.

4.5   Determination of Which Nodes of Node n_u and Nodes PN_u Are Suspicious Node

The sink can determine that at least one of n_u and nodes PN_u is suspicious node by using the method described above. We propose methods that can cut the list of candidates of suspicious nodes.

Method 1. $\Xi_1(v, 1)$ where $v \in PN_u$ is the probability that n_u and n_v mounted attacks one or more times. When this value is larger than th, the probability that node n_u mounted a legitimate MAC attack or n_v mounted a false MAC attack is higher than th, therefore, the sink determines that n_u and n_v are the suspicious node group.

Method 2.   We assume that n_u is legitimate. We calculate $\omega = b_u - \max_v(PN_u.get(v))$ and $\Xi_1(u, \omega+1)$. For example in Fig. 5, $\max_v(PN_u.get(v)) = 5$. When $\Xi_1(u, \omega + 1)$ is larger than th, the probability that node n_u mounted

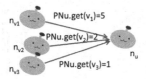

Fig. 5. n_{v_1} forwarded messages to n_u and n_u became LVNs five times as a result of these messages, n_{v_2} forwarded messages to n_u and n_u became LVNs twice as a result of these messages, and n_{v_3} forwarded messages to n_u and n_u became an LVN once of these messages.

legitimate MAC attack or nodes of PN_u mounted false MAC attacks $\omega + 1$ times is higher than th. Even if all nodes of PN_u except for $n_{\mathrm{argmax}_v(PN_u.get(v))}$ are malicious agents, they could mount false MAC attacks only ω times. That is, the probability that one of nodes n_u and $n_{\mathrm{argmax}_v(PN_u.get(v))}$ is compromised is higher than th. Therefore, the sink determines that n_u and $n_{\mathrm{argmax}_v(PN_u.get(v))}$ are the suspicious node group. For example in Fig. 5, if the probability that nodes of PN_u mounted attacks more than three times, we can determine that n_{v_1} and/or n_u mounted attacks at least once.

Method 3. Assume that the probability that many nodes of PN_u are malicious agents is high. In this case, if the sink determines that all nodes of PN_u are suspicious nodes, the successful detection rate can be higher than th.

Here, the expected value of successful detection rate when n_u is confirmed to be legitimate and the sink determines that all nodes of PN_u are suspicious nodes is calculated by

$$\varXi_3(u) = \sum_{i=1}^{b_u} \xi_1(u, b_u - i) \cdot \varPsi(i), \tag{8}$$

where

$$\varPsi(i) = \min_V(|\{v|V \subseteq PN_u \wedge \sum_{v \in V} PN_u.get(v) \geq i\}|)/(1 + |PN_u|).$$

For example, see Fig. 5. In this case, $\varPsi(i) = 1, 1, 1, 1, 1, 2, 2, 3$ $(i = 1, ..., 8)$. Specifically,

1. The sink confirms that $\varXi_1(u, 1) \geq th$ and $\varXi_3(u) \geq th$.
2. The sink determines that n_u and $n_{\mathrm{argmax}_v(PN_u.get(v))}$ are the suspicious node group and confirms whether each node is compromised or not.
3. If both of the two nodes are legitimate, the sink determines that all nodes of $PN_u - \{\mathrm{argmax}_v(PN_u.get(v))\}$ are suspicious nodes.

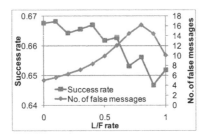

Fig. 6. Results of legitimate and false MAC attacks

5 Evaluation

5.1 Evaluation Index

Existing studies and our proposed method detects a *suspicious node* which is thought to mount attacks of creating false messages with high probability. Our proposed method is a statistical one, that is, we cannot detect malicious agents without misdetection. It is a costly task to determine whether or not the suspicious node is *actually* compromised because we need to capture the suspicious node physically and check the physical memory of it. Therefore, we want to reduce the number of occurrences of misdetection.

On the other hand, we want to detect malicious agents as soon as possible because they can waste a significant amount of network resources by creating false messages.

Therefore, we use a *successful detection rate* and the *number of false messages* to measure our proposed method and existing studies. Let S_s be the set of nodes that a sink determines as suspicious nodes and let S_c be the set of nodes that are actually malicious agents within S_s. The successful detection rate is calculated by $|S_c|/|S_s|$. The number of false messages represents the number of false messages created by malicious agents until the sink detect all malicious agents.

5.2 Evaluation Results

We conducted simulations to verify our analysis. The simulator has the basic routing algorithm [10]. We set the length of the bits of the node ID to 10 by default and the bit length of a MAC to 64 in PNM.

In the first experiment, we set $th = 0.66$. Then, we varied the ratio of legitimate MAC attacks and false MAC attacks (L/F). L/F represents the ratio of false MAC attacks. The result is shown in Fig. 6. The figure shows that the successful detection rate is around th. When we set the ratio to 0.8, the number of false messages had a largest value.

Next, we compared our proposed PM4M with existing studies PNM and LPM. We set the number of forwarding nodes on a path to 30 and the routing path

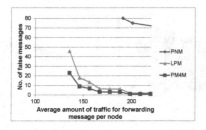

Fig. 7. Maximum number of false messages as much as possible without detection

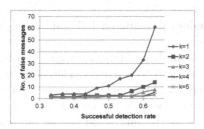

Fig. 8. Maximum number of false messages as much as possible without detection with varying the length of MAC k

was fixed. The first node was the source node of a message and the 15th node was set as a malicious agent. The last node forwarded the messages it received to the sink. The 15th node always fabricated the messages it received. The node mounted false MAC attacks in combination with legitimate MAC attacks as much as possible without detection. The source node repeatedly generated a message until the sink determined which node was the malicious agent. We counted the number of false messages sent from the malicious nodes. This process was repeated 10,000 times. Figure 7 shows the results. We know from the figure that PM4M could detect malicious agents earlier than PNM and LPM. Because LPM assume that malicious agents do not mount false MAC attacks, LPM needs more number of false messages until the sink detects the malicious agents.

We analyzed the number of false messages a malicious agent can mount false MAC attacks and legitimate MAC attacks as much as possible without detection with varying k. The results are shown in Fig. 8. If we want the successful detection rate to be around 2/3, the sink needs relatively many false messages to detect a malicious agent, e.g., 60 when $k = 1$. However, this value is still less than that of PNM and LPN.

Finally, we conducted an experiment to verify whether our method is resilient to changes in routing paths. The number of sensor nodes was set to 1,000. One of them repeatedly generated a message. We set the number of malicious agents from 10 to 100. When a malicious agent received a message, the node fabricated

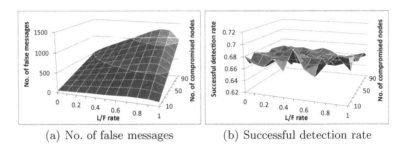

(a) No. of false messages   (b) Successful detection rate

Fig. 9. Results of mobile wireless sensor networks

the message with a random probability. L/F rate of each node is at random. Figure 9 shows the results.

Figure 9(a) shows the number of false messages needed all malicious agents until the sink detected all malicious agents. They indicate that the number of false messages needed per malicious agent until the sink detected all malicious agents is relatively stationary even if the number of malicious agents increases.

Figure 9(b) indicates that the sink could determine malicious agents around 66% of the time.

6   Discussion

In this section, we discuss cost overhead of our method.

Many works in WSNs set the default packet size to about 40 bytes [7], [6]. When the average number of neighbor nodes is 5 and the average number of hops from the source node to the sink is 20, the average overhead is $(\sum_{i}^{20}(1+3)\cdot i)/20 = 42$ bits $= 6$ bytes if we set k to 1. Therefore, the overhead rate is 15%.

This value is much less than that of existing works for packet traceback as shown in Section 5. Moreover, we may reduce the average overhead by combining methods for detecting false messages. Although existing works of detecting false messages [29,32,34,27,14] cannot identify the nodes that create false messages, they can notify the sink of the existence of false messages. Only when the sink recognizes the necessity to identify the malicious agent that creates false messages, it floods a message to the network to start using the PM4M protocol. When the sink identifies and removes the malicious agent, it floods a message to stop using the PM4M protocol.

Moreover, if we want to avoid physically checking for determining whether or not the node is actually compromised because of cost, we can remove malicious nodes "logically". For example, the sink can let all nodes ignore malicious nodes by message flooding when it detects them.

7   Conclusion

We described a method to detect a malicious agent that created a false message and report it to the sink. Existing works can only be used in situations where sensor nodes have fixed positions. The method described above uses a k-bit MAC algorithm and a logical node to deal with changes in positions of nodes. Mathematical analysis and simulations show that compared with related methods, it needs fewer false messages to detect a malicious agent.

Acknowledgements. This work was supported by JSPS KAKENHI Grant Numbers 24300005, 26330081, 26870201.

References

1. Cao, Z., Deng, H., Guan, Z., Chen, Z.: Information-theoretic modeling of false data filtering schemes in wireless sensor networks. ACM Trans. Sensor Networks 8(2), 1–19 (2012)
2. Chen, M., Kwon, T., Yuan, Y., Leung, V.C.: Mobile agent based wireless sensor networks. Journal of Computers 1(1), 14–21 (2006)
3. Dini, G., Lo Duca, A.: Towards a reputation-based routing protocol to contrast blackholes in a delay tolerant network. Ad Hoc Networks 10(7), 1167–1178 (2012)
4. Dong, Q., Banerjee, S., Adler, M., Hirata, K.: Efficient probabilistic packet marking. In: Proc. IEEE ICNP, pp. 368–377 (2005)
5. Ganesan, P., Venugopalan, R., Peddabachagari, P., Dean, A., Mueller, F., Sichitiu, M.: Analyzing and modeling encryption overhead for sensor network nodes. In: Proc. ACM WSNA, pp. 151–159 (2003)
6. Gezer, C., Niccolini, M., Buratti, C.: An IEEE 802.15.4/ZigBee based wireless sensor network for Energy Efficient Buildings. In: Proc. IEEE WiMob., pp. 486–491. IEEE (2010)
7. Hansen, M.T.: Asynchronous group key distribution on top of the cc2420 security mechanisms for sensor networks. In: Proc. ACM WiSec, pp. 13–20 (2009)
8. Jin, X., Putthapipat, P., Pan, D., Pissinou, N., Makki, S.K.: Unpredictable Software-based Attestation Solution for node compromise detection in mobile WSN. In: 2010 IEEE Globecom Workshops, pp. 2059–2064 (2010)
9. Karlof, C., Wagner, D.: Secure routing in wireless sensor networks: Attacks and countermeasures. In: IEEE SNPA, pp. 113–127 (2003)
10. Karp, B., Kung, H.T.: GPSR: Greedy perimeter stateless routing for wireless networks. In: Proc. ACM MOBICOM, pp. 243–254 (2000)
11. Khalil, I., Bagchi, S., Nina-Rotaru, C.: Dicas: Detection, diagnosis and isolation of control attacks in sensor networks. In: SecureComm, pp. 89–100 (2005)
12. Khalil, I., Bagchi, S., Shroff, N.B.: Liteworp: Detection and isolation of the wormhole attack in static multihop wireless networks. Comput. Netw. 51(13), 3750–3772 (2007)
13. Krawczyk, H., Bellare, M., Canetti, R.: HMAC: Keyed-hashing for message authentication. In: iETF - Network Working Group (February 1997), RFC2104
14. Li, F., Wu, J.: A probabilistic voting-based filtering scheme in wireless sensor networks. In: ACM IWCMC, pp. 27–32 (2006)
15. Liu, B., Dousse, O., Nain, P., Towsley, D.: Dynamic Coverage of Mobile Sensor Networks. IEEE Trans. Parallel and Distributed Systems 24(2), 301–311 (2013)
16. Lu, R., Member, S., Lin, X., Zhu, H.: BECAN: A Bandwidth-Efficient Cooperative Authentication Scheme for Filtering Injected False Data in Wireless Sensor Networks. IEEE Trans. Parallel Distrib. Syst. 23(1), 32–43 (2012)

17. Marti, S., Giuli, T.J., Lai, K., Baker, M.: Mitigating routing misbehavior in mobile ad hoc networks. In: Proc. ACM MOBICOM, pp. 255–265 (2000)
18. Platon, E., Sei, Y.: Security software engineering in wireless sensor networks. Progress in Informatics 5(1), 49–64 (2008)
19. Ramadan, R.A.: Agent Based Multipath Routing in wireless sensor networks. In: IEEE Symposium on Intelligent Agents, pp. 63–69 (2009)
20. Sei, Y., Ohsuga, A.: Need Only One Bit: Light-weight Packet Marking for Detecting Compromised Nodes in WSNs. In: Proc. 7th SECURWARE, pp. 134–143 (2013)
21. Seshadri, A., Perrig, A., van Doorn, L., Khosla, P.: SWATT: Software-based attestation for embedded devices. In: Proc. IEEE S&P, pp. 272–282 (2004)
22. Song, D.X., Perrig, A.: Advanced and authenticated marking schemes for IP traceback. In: IEEE INFOCOM, pp. 878–886 (2001)
23. Wang, G., Zhang, W., Cao, G., Porta, T.: On supporting distributed collaboration in sensor networks. In: Proc. IEEE MILCOM, pp. 752–757 (2003)
24. Wood, A.D., Stankovic, J.A.: Denial of service in sensor networks. Trans. IEEE Computer 35(10), 54–62 (2002)
25. Xu, E., Ding, Z., Dasgupta, S.: Target Tracking and Mobile Sensor Navigation in Wireless Sensor Networks. IEEE Trans. Mobile Computing 12(1), 177–186 (2013)
26. Xu, Z., Hsu, H., Chen, X., Zhu, S., Hurson, A.R.: AK-PPM: An authenticated packet attribution scheme for mobile ad hoc networks. In: Balzarotti, D., Stolfo, S.J., Cova, M. (eds.) RAID 2012. LNCS, vol. 7462, pp. 147–168. Springer, Heidelberg (2012)
27. Yang, H., Ye, F., Yuan, Y., Lu, S., Arbaugh, W.: Toward resilient security in wireless sensor networks. In: ACM MOBIHOC, pp. 34–45 (2005)
28. Yang, Y., Wang, X., Zhu, S., Cao, G.: Distributed software-based attestation for node compromise detection in sensor networks. In: Proc. IEEE SRDS, pp. 219–230 (2007)
29. Ye, F., Luo, H., Lu, S., Zhang, L.: Statistical en-route filtering of injected false data in sensor networks. IEEE Journal on Selected Areas in Communications 23(4), 839–850 (2005)
30. Ye, F., Yang, H., Liu, Z.: Catching "Moles" in Sensor Networks. In: Proc. IEEE ICDCS, p. 69 (2007)
31. Ye, F., Zhong, G., Lu, S., Zhang, L.: Gradient broadcast: a robust data delivery protocol for large scale sensor networks. Wirel. Netw. 11(3), 285–298 (2005)
32. Yu, Z., Guan, Y.: A dynamic en-route scheme for filtering false data injection in wirelesssensor networks. In: Proc. IEEE INFOCOM, pp. 1–12 (2006)
33. Zhang, Q., Zhou, X., Yang, F., Li, X.: Contact-based traceback in wireless sensor networks. In: Proc. IEEE WiCom, pp. 2487–2490 (2007)
34. Zhu, S., Setia, S., Jajodia, S., Ning, P.: An interleaved hop-by-hop authentication scheme for filtering of injected false data in sensor networks. In: IEEE S&P, pp. 259–271 (2004)

A   Definition and Proof of Lemma1

Lemma 1

$$P(B_{u[0]}\langle 1 \rangle = j | B_{u[1]}\langle 1 \rangle = b_{u[1]}) = 2^{k+b_{u[1]}k} \cdot (1+2^k)^{-1-b_{u[1]}-j} \cdot {}_{b_{u[1]}+j}C_{b_{u[1]}}. \quad (9)$$

Proof. From Bayes' theorem and total probability theorem, we get

$$P(B_{u[0]}\langle 1 \rangle = j | B_{u[1]}\langle 1 \rangle = b_{u[1]})$$

$$= \sum_{w=0}^{\infty} \left[P(W_{u[1]} = w | B_{u[1]}\langle 1 \rangle = b_{u[1]}) \cdot \frac{P(B_{u[0]}\langle 1 \rangle = j \wedge B_{u[1]}\langle 1 \rangle = b_{u[1]} | W_{u[1]} = w)}{P(B_{u[1]}\langle 1 \rangle = b_{u[1]} | W_{u[1]} = w)} \right]. \tag{10}$$

From Bayes' theorem, the conditional probability of $n_{u[1]}$ creating a false message w times given that it became an LVN $b_{u[1]}$ times by itself, is

$$P(W_{u[1]} = w | B_{u[1]}\langle 1 \rangle = b_{u[1]})$$

$$= \frac{P(W_{u[1]} = w) \cdot P(B_{u[1]}\langle 1 \rangle = b_{u[1]} | W_{u[1]} = w)}{\sum_{w'=0}^{\infty} P(W_{u[1]} = w') \cdot P(B_{u[1]}\langle 1 \rangle = b_{u[1]} | W_{u[1]} = w')}, \tag{11}$$

where $P(B_{u[1]}\langle 1 \rangle = b_{u[1]} | W_{u[1]} = w)$ represents the conditional probability of node $n_{u[1]}$ becoming an LVN $b_{u[1]}$ times by itself given that $n_{u[1]}$ created false messages w times.

Assume that node $n_{u[1]}$ mounted a legitimate MAC attack and the sink detects that the message is a false one. If the verification of the next node to $n_{u[1]}$ fails, $n_{u[1]}$ becomes an LVN. This probability is $1 - 2^{-k}$. If the verification of the node next to $n_{u[1]}$ succeeds, $n_{u[1]}$ does not become an LVN. This probability is 2^{-k}. Therefore,

$$P(B_{u[1]}\langle 1 \rangle = b_{u[1]} | W_{u[1]} = w) = {}_wC_{b_{u[1]}}(1 - 2^{-k})^{b_{u[1]}}(2^{-k})^{w-b_{u[1]}}. \tag{12}$$

In a similar way, we get

$$P(B_{u[0]}\langle 1 \rangle = j \wedge B_{u[1]}\langle 1 \rangle = b_{u[1]} | W_{u[1]} = w)$$

$$= {}_wC_{b_{u[1]}} \cdot {}_{w-b_{u[1]}}C_j \cdot (1 - 2^{-k})^{b_{u[1]}} \left\{ 2^{-k}(1 - 2^{-k}) \right\}^j \tag{13}$$

$$\cdot \left\{ 1 - (1 - 2^{-k}) - 2^{-k}(1 - 2^{-k}) \right\}^{w-b_{u[1]}-j}$$

$P(W_{u[1]} = w')$ in Eq. 11 represents the probability that $n_{u[1]}$ created false messages w times. Since the number of times that $n_{u[1]}$ became an LVN by itself is $b_{u[1]}$, the number of times that $n_{u[1]}$ created w' should be greater than or equal to $b_{u[1]}$. Therefore, when $w' < b_{u[1]}$, $P(W_{u[1]} = w') = 0$. When $j \geq b_{u[1]}$, we can assume that every $P(W_{u[1]} = w')$ has the same value, because a malicious agent can create false messages an arbitrary number of times. Therefore, we get from Equations 11 and 12

$$P(W_{u[1]} = w | B_{u[1]}\langle 1 \rangle = b_{u[1]}) = \frac{P(B_{u[1]}\langle 1 \rangle = b_{u[1]} | W_{u[1]} = w)}{\sum_{j=b_{u[1]}}^{\infty} P(B_{u[1]}\langle 1 \rangle = b_{u[1]} | W_{u[1]} = w')} \tag{14}$$

$$= (2^{-k})^{1-b_{u[1]}+w}(1 - 2^{-k})^{b_{u[1]}}(2^k - 1){}_wC_{b_{u[1]}}.$$

From these equations, we get

$$P(B_{u[0]}\langle 1 \rangle = j | B_{u[1]}\langle 1 \rangle = b_{u[1]}) = 2^{k+b_{u[1]}k} \cdot (1 + 2^k)^{-1-b_{u[1]}-j} \cdot {}_{b_{u[1]}+j}C_{b_{u[1]}}. \tag{15}$$

Improving Simulation of Continuous Emotional Facial Expressions by Analyzing Videos of Human Facial Activities

Thi Duyen Ngo, Thi Hong Nhan Vu, Viet Ha Nguyen, and The Duy Bui

University of Engineering and Technology,
Vietnam National University, Hanoi, Vietnam
{duyennt,nhanvth,hanv,duybt}@vnu.edu.vn

Abstract. Conversational agents are receiving significant attention from multi-agent and human computer interaction research societies. In order to make conversational agents more believable and friendly, giving them the ability to express emotions is one of research fields which have drawn a lot of attention lately. In this paper, we propose a work on analysis of how emotional facial activities happen temporally. Our goal is to find the temporal patterns of facial activity of six basic emotions in order to improve the simulation of continuous emotional facial expressions on a 3D face of an embodied agent. Using facial expression recognition techniques, we first analyze a spontaneous video database in order to consider how facial activities are related to six basic emotions temporally. From there, we bring out the general temporal patterns for facial expressions of the six basic emotions. Then, based on the temporal patterns, we propose a scheme for displaying continuous emotional states of a conversational agent on a 3D face.

Keywords: Human Computer Interaction, 3D Conversational Agents, Emotional Facial Expressions, Continuous Emotional State, Temporal Pattern, FACS.

1 Introduction

Conversational agents become more and more common in multimedia world of films, educative applications, e-business, computer games and so on. Many techniques have been developed to enable these agents to behave in a human-like manner. In order to do so, they are simulated with similar communicative channels as humans, such as voice, head and eyes movement, manipulator and facial expression (3; 11; 25; 6). Moreover, they are also simulated with emotion and personality (8; 18; 38; 45). Emotions have been studied for a long time and results show that they play an important role in human cognitive functions. Picard has summarized this in her "Affective Computing" (35). In fact, emotions play an extremely important role during the communication between people. People usually assesses others' emotional states, probably because of their good indication of how the person feels, what the person could do next, and how he is about to act. For this assessment, the human face is the most communicative part of the body for expressing emotions (14). It is recognized that a link exists between facial activity

H.K. Dam et al. (Eds.): PRIMA 2014, LNAI 8861, pp. 222–237, 2014.
© Springer International Publishing Switzerland 2014

and emotional states. This is asserted in Darwin's pioneer publication "The expression of the emotions in man and animals" (10). It is undoubted that conversational agents need emotional states and a way to facially express emotions in a real way in order to improve their communication with humans. Therefore, the accurate selection as well as timing of facial expressions according to emotional sates would improve the realism of conversational agents. To provide conversational agents with the ability to express emotions, firstly, we need to have knowledge about the relationship between emotion and facial activity. Up to now, many researches on this relationship have been done(e.g., (15; 20; 16; 12; 43; 32)). However, most of them focus on analyzing the relationship without taking time factors into account. In other words, they analyzed the relationship but did not examine it in the time domain. Also, techniques for creating facial expression from emotions have been developed (e.g. (34; 21; 41; 7)). These works concentrate on producing static facial expressions from emotions, e.g. (7). For expressing continuous emotional states of an agent, not much attention has been paid except the study in (5). In this work, Bui et al. brought out a scheme for generating facial expressions from continuous emotional states. In each small interval of time, emotional state is mapped directly to facial expressions which are then displayed on a 3D face. This one to one mapping, however, is not realistic in case there is a high activated state that lasts for a long time. In that situation, a facial expression might stay on the face for quite a long time. This may reduce remarkably the realism of conversational agents.

In this paper, we focus on an analysis of how emotional facial activities vary over time. Our goal is to find the temporal patterns of facial activities of six basic emotions in order to improve the simulation of continuous emotional facial expressions on a 3D face of an embodied agent. To perform this task, we first analyze a spontaneous video database automatically using facial expression recognition techniques. Our hypothesis is that the facial expressions happen in series with decreasing intensity when a corresponding emotion is triggered. For example, when an event happens, which triggers the happiness of a person, he/she would not smile in full intensity during the time the happiness lasts. Instead, he/she would express a series of smiles in decreasing intensity. In order to verify our hypothesis, movements of features on the face are detected and matched automatically with predefined patterns. Based on the temporal patterns, we propose a scheme for displaying continuous emotional states of a conversational agent on a 3D face. Experiments are conducted to verify the improvement of the new facial expression simulation approach. Experimental results show that produced emotional facial expressions are more natural and believable.

The rest of the paper is organized as follows. Section 2 presents a summary on related work. After that, in Section 3, we describe our facial expression analysis process. We then propose our mechanism to convert continuous emotional states of an agent to facial expressions in Section 4. We then test our model in an emotional conversational agent and show result in Section 5.

2 Related Work

Most of researches on the relationship between emotion and facial activity follow one of three main views: the basic emotions view, the cognitive view and the dimensions view. The basic emotions view (e.g., (44; 14; 13; 23) is the most popular one which assumes that there is a small set of emotions that can be distinguished discretely from one another by facial expressions. The cognitive view assumes that emotions are triggered by a cognitive evaluation/appraisal process of an individual's situation (4; 40). The dimensions view was proposed by researchers who believe that emotional states are fundamentally differentiated on a small number of dimensions, and that facial activity is linked to these dimensions (e.g., (39)). The psychological studies from these views have a significant effect on our understanding of the link between emotion state and facial activity. These studies also play a very important role in the task of simulating and recognizing emotional facial expressions on computers. According to Kappas (24), the basic emotions view is most useful in the context of diagnosing emotions from facial actions. Compared to research within the two other views, research within the basic emotions view provides more empirical evidence on the relationship between emotion and facial activity. Moreover, the predictions of the basic emotions view are usually so clear to confirm or reject. In our opinion, the results from research within the basic emotions view are most useful in simulating the relationship between emotion and facial activity.

In order to objectively capture the richness and complexity of facial expressions, behavioral scientists found it necessary to develop objective coding standards. The Facial Action Coding System (FACS) (15) is one of the most widely used expression coding system in the behavioral sciences. FACS was developed by Ekman and Friesen to identify all possible visually distinguishable facial movements. It involves identifying the various facial muscles that individually or in groups cause changes in facial behaviors. These changes in the face and the underlying muscles that caused these changes are called Action Units (AU). The FACS is made up of several such action units. Related to the relationship between emotions and facial activity, each AU codes the fundamental actions of individual or groups of muscles typically seen while producing facial expressions of emotion. FACS provides an objective and comprehensive language for describing facial expressions and relating them back to what is known about their meaning from the behavioral science literature.

Up to now, there have been quite many proposed researches followed the basic emotion view to simulate the relationship between emotion and facial activity. Extensive research in (15) showed that certain combinations of action units are linked to the six "universal" facial patterns of the emotions. EMFACS (20) was proposed by Friesen and Ekman, which is similar to FACS but considers only emotion-related facial actions. Ekman and Hager (16) also presented a database called facial action coding system affect interpretation database (FACSAID), which allows to translate emotion related FACS scores into affective meanings. In (12), all images in a database which consisted of pictures in neutral, six basic, and fifteen compound emotions were FACS coded in order to analysis the relationship between emotions and facial activity. Tian et al. have developed the Automatic Face Analysis (AFA) system which can automatically recognize six upper face AUs and ten lower face AUs (43). Most of the proposed works attempt at dealing with basic emotions and some attempts at dealing with non-basic emotions. However there have been very few attempts at considering the temporal dynamics of the face. Temporal dynamics refers to the timing and duration of facial activities.

The important terms that are used in connection with temporal dynamics are: onset, apex and offset (17). Onset is the instance when the facial expression starts to show up, apex is the point when the expression is at its peak and offset is when the expression fades away. Similarly, onset-duration is defined as the time taken from start to the peak, apex-duration is defined as the total time at the peak and offset-duration is defined as the total time from peak to the stop. Pantic and Patras have reported successful recognition of facial AUs and their temporal segments (32). By doing so, they have been able to recognize a much larger range of expressions. However, this research only analyzing single AUs, it did not mention to facial expression "pattern" for emotions in the time domain.

In the research field of conversational agents, one interesting research question which has received much attention is expressing emotions on faces of conversational agents. Until now, there are several proposed methods. These methods can be classified into two categories: static emotion representation methods and dynamic emotion representation methods. In the first category, several researchers including Kurlander (27), Latta (28), Raouzaiou (37), Albrecht (2) used the emotional wheel described by Plutchik (36) to develop facial animation systems. This emotional wheel model enables researchers to create mechanisms to map emotional state to universally recognized facial expressions. However, this model is only static emotion representation. It does not provide any consistent mechanism for creating emotional facial expressions. So any facial expression can be displayed at any time, independently from the previous emotional facial expression. This is a considerable weakness. Another drawback of the static representation is that emotions vary relatively slowly, so a change of expression from an emotion to the opposite emotion takes remarkable time, which is not very appropriate. The second method type, dynamic emotion representations, including the systems of Reilly (38),Velásquez (45), Kshirsagar and Magnenat-Thalmann (26), Paiva (31), Bui (7), and Tanguy (42), selects which emotional facial expressions should be displayed from emotions dynamically. Dynamic emotion representations keep track over time of changes in emotion intensities, represent emotional momentums, and therefore provide a consistent mechanism for creating emotional facial expressions and eliminate the limitation of static emotion representation methods. It can be seen that dynamic emotion representation is better than static emotion representations. However, existing dynamic representation systems only deal with expressing emotions without real time conditions. In fact, human emotions are very complicated and we usually can not know in advance how one's emotion will occur. In case there is an emotion that lasts for a long time, mapping one to one from given emotions to facial expression will reduce the realism of conversational agents. In fact this is almost always true because emotions tend to decay slower than facial expressions do. Our solution in this paper will eliminate this limitation.

3 Emotional Facial Expression Analysis

3.1 Database

In our work, we use a spontaneous facial expression database which consist of video sequence selected from three databases namely MMI (1; 33), FEEDTUM (47), DISFA (29).

MMI Facial Expression Database (1; 33) contains posed and spontaneous expressions but only spontaneous ones being used in our research. These expressions belong to part IV and part V of the MMI database. These two parts consist of video sequences that express six basic emotions. These video sequences were collected through experiments in which researchers showed the participants images, videos, short clips of cartoons and comedy shows, or sound of the stimuli to induce emotions. The FEEDTUM database (47) consists of elicited spontaneous emotions of 18 subjects. Beside the neutral state, the content of the database covers the emotions such as anger, disgust, fear, happiness, sadness and surprise for each subject, which have been recorded three times. To elicit the emotions as natural as possible it was decided to play several carefully selected stimuli videos and record the participants reactions. In the DISFA database (29), twenty-seven young adults were video recorded by a stereo camera while they viewed video clips intended to elicit spontaneous emotion expression. To form the database used in our work, from the three databases above, video sequences in which the human face begins with a neutral expression, proceeds to a peak expression which is fully FACS coded, and then gets back to the neutral state were selected. Because our goal is to find the temporal "pattern" of facial activity of emotion, such selected video sequences will be suitable to be used in the analyzing process. Finally, there are 215 selected video sequences: 67 video for happy emotion, 25 video for sad emotion, 25 video for angry emotion, 33 video for disgust emotion, 30 video for fear emotion, and 35 video for surprise emotion. These videos are arranged into six categories according to the six emotions they belong to.

3.2   Facial Activity Analysis Process

Our emotional facial activity analysis process is illustrated in Figure 1. The input of the system is a video sequence which is processed by the system frame by frame. For each frame, the Face Detector detects the face and returns its location. Then the ASM Fitting perform fitting task and returns ASM shape of the face. From this shape, Face Normalization module carries out the normalizing task in order to change the shape to the common size. Finally, the AUs Intensity Extractor module extract AUs intensity related to each of six basic emotions using feature points obtained from ASM Fitting and then Face Normalization modules. The construction and detail operation of the four modules are presented in the following.

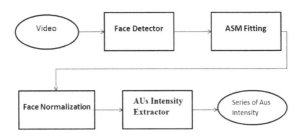

Fig. 1. Block diagram of the emotional facial activity analyzing system

A. Face Detector: We start by detecting the face inside the scene. For each frame of the input video, the Face Detector module check whether or not is there a human face, and provide the approximate location and size of the detected face. In this work, we have selected Viola Jones algorithm (46) for face detection because it is known to work robustly for large inter-subject variations and illumination changes. The result of face detection algorithm is illustrated in Figure 2(a).

B. ASM Fitting: This module extracts feature points from the detected face using ASM fitting algorithm. Within the face region passed from the Face Detector, we search the exact location of facial landmarks using Active Shape Model (9). Among the various types of deformable face models, we use Active Shape Model (ASM) for several reasons. ASM is arguably the simplest and fastest method among deformable models, which fit our need to track a large number of frames in multiple videos. Furthermore, ASM is also known to generalize well to new subjects due to its simplicity. We trained ASM with manually collected 68 landmark locations from a set of still images. The ASM method detects facial landmarks through a local-based search constrained by a global shape model which statistically learned from training data. The output of ASM Fitting module is location of 68 feature points (facial landmark)(we call this as ASM shape) as illustrated in Figure 2(b).

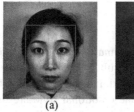 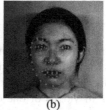

(a)   (b)

Fig. 2. (a)Face Detection; (b) Facial landmarks

C. Face Normalization: Due to variations in head pose and/or camera positions, the face size in frames of the same video sequence maybe not same. Since then the ASM shapes of these frame are also not at the same size. This may lead to the less accuracy in analysis results. So it needs performing normalization task in order to set all the shapes into a common size. In our work, we use the distance between the centers of eyes for normalization. All the shapes will be normalized so that in their normalized reproductions the distance between the centers of eyes equal to that in the other ASM shapes.

D. AUs Intensity Extractor: This component extracts facial features related to each of six basic emotions using feature points (facial landmarks) obtained from ASM Fitting and then Face Normalization modules. It uses normalized landmark locations to calculate the intensity of Action Units (AUs) which are related to the emotion style of the input video. We follow the basic emotion view and base on research of Ekman (15), Shichuan (12) about the link between combinations of action units and the six universal

Table 1. Description of six basic emotions ((15; 12))

Emotion	Action Unit	Facial Feature	Emotion	Action Unit	Facial Feature
Happiness	AU12	Lip Corner Puller	Disgust	AU15	Lip Corner Depressor
	AU25	Lips Part		AU16	Lower Lip Depressor
Sadness	AU1	Inner Brow Raiser	Anger	AU4	Brow Lowerer
	AU4	Brow Lowerer		AU5	Upper Lid Raiser
	AU15	Lip Corner Depressor		AU7	Lid Tightener
				AU17	Chin Raiser
Fear	AU1	Inner Brow Raiser	Surprise	AU1	Inner Brow Raiser
	AU2	Outer Brow Raiser		AU2	Outer Brow Raiser
	AU4	Brow Lowerer		AU5	Upper Lid Raiser
	AU5	Upper Lid Raiser		AU25	Lips Part
	AU20	Lip Stretcher		AU26	Jaw Drop
	AU25	Lips Part			
	AU26	Jaw Drop			

facial patterns of the emotions anger, disgust, fear, sadness, surprise, and happiness. For each emotion, there is a set of related AUs to classify it from the others, as showed in Table 1.

3.3   Results of Analysis

For a video of each emotion, from the landmark locations, the intensity of each related AU is calculated frame by frame. As a result, we have a temporal series of intensity values for each AU. This series is extracted and graphing. Finally, series and graphic results of all AUs from all videos of one emotional style are used to generalize the temporal pattern for facial expressions of that emotion. By observing these graphics, we bring out a hypothesis that the facial expressions happen in series with decreasing intensity when a corresponding emotion is triggered. Thence, we proposed pre-defined temporal patterns for facial expressions of six basic emotions. The temporal pattern for facial expressions of the happiness and the sadness is depicted in Figure 3(a) and the temporal pattern for facial expressions of the disgust, angry, fear, and surprise emotions is depicted in Figure 3(b). In this pattern, we see that there are solid line part and dash line part. The difference between these two parts is that the solid line part is always present while the dash line part may be absent. This can be explained as follows. The internal emotional states are the cause of the appearance of external facial activities which occur in order to produce facial expressions expressing that emotion. When the internal emotional states with sufficient intensity take place in a duration, it will lead to emergence of the external facial activities and then facial expressions in this duration. If this duration is short, the facial expressions also appear in short time; then only the solid line part in the pattern appears. Conversely, if this duration is long, the facial expressions also appear in long time. Then in addition to the solid line part, the dash line part in the pattern also appears. As shown in the pattern, although the internal emotional state may have constant sufficient intensity in a long time, the corresponding facial expressions are not always at the same intensity in this long duration. On the other hand, the facial

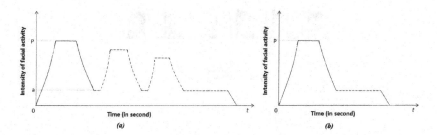

Fig. 3. (a): Temporal pattern for facial expressions of happiness and sadness. (b): Temporal pattern for facial expressions of fear, angry, disgust, and surprise emotions.

expressions appear with the intensity corresponding to the intensity of the emotion, then stay in this state for a while, and then fall near the initial state. We call this process is a cycle. With happiness and sadness, this cycle repeats several times with decreasing intensity, then the facial expressions are kept at a constant low intensity until the end of the long duration. With four remaining emotions, the facial expressions often occur in only one cycle and then the facial expressions are kept at a constant low intensity.

We define a cycle of facial expressions as:

$$E = (P, Ts, Te, Do, Dr)$$

where P defines the target intensity of the expressions; Ts and Te are the starting time and the ending time of the cycle; Do, Dr are onset duration and offset duration of the expressions, respectively. The process in which the expressions occur in a cycle is described as a function of time:

$$F_e(t) = \begin{cases} P.\phi_+(t-Ts, Do) & \text{if} \quad (Ts < t < Ts + Do) \\ P & \text{if } (Ts + Do \leq t \leq Te - Dr) \\ P.\phi_-(t-Te+Dr, Dr) & \text{if} \quad Te - Dr < t < Te \end{cases}$$

where ϕ_+ and ϕ_- are the functions that describe the onset and offset phase of expressions. We follow Essa's work (19) to use exponential curves to fit the onset and offset portions of expressions. A function of the form $(e^{bx} - 1)$ is suggested for the onset portion, while a function of the form $(e^{c-dx} - 1)$ is suggested for the offset portion. Basing on the suggested functions, we derive two functions for the onset and offset portions. For the onset portion, we want to choose b so that:

$$\phi_+(0, Do) = e^{b.0} - 1 = 0 \text{ and } \phi_+(Do, Do) = e^{b.Do} - 1 = 1$$

From the second equation, the derived function to describe the onset portion is defined as:

$$\phi_+(x, Do) = exp(\tfrac{ln2}{Do}x) - 1$$

For the offset portion, we want to choose c and d so that:

$$\phi_-(0, Dr) = e^{c-d.0} - 1 = 1 \text{ and } \phi_-(Dr, Dr) = e^{c-d.Dr} - 1 = \tfrac{a}{P}$$

From the two equation, the derived function to describe the offset portion of a parameter activity is defined as:

$$\phi_-(x, Dr) = exp(ln2 - \tfrac{ln2-ln(\tfrac{a}{P}+1)}{Dr}x) - 1$$

In order to verify the reasonableness of the pre-defined temporal patterns, we have performed the fitting task for all temporal AU profiles. Figure 4 shows an example of

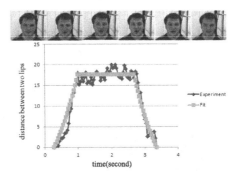

Fig. 4. Experiment and fitting temporal AU25 profiles of a subject in surprise emotion. TOP: Captured video frames at several time points from the whole video. BOTTOM: The temporal profiles show the distance between two lips which characterizes the intensity of AU25.

the temporal AU25 profiles of a representative subject in the surprise emotion. The subject displayed gradual increase of Lips Part (AU25) which is typical of a surprise expression. In the figure, the top part depicts captured video frames at several time points from the whole video. In the bottom part of the figure, the temporal profiles show the distance between two lips which characterizes the intensity of AU25. The darker points and darker line represent data obtained from experiment analysis. The paler points and paler line show fitting data using the pattern and function described above. If the distance between the centers of two eyes is normalized to 1, the sum of squares due to error (SSE) of the fit is 0.0207. Performing the fitting task for all temporal AU profiles, we found that the average of the sum of squares due to error (SSE) was 0.055 with the standard deviation was 0.078. These values show that the above temporal patterns and the fitting function are reasonable.

Our analysis results showed that in the happiness, the average duration of a cycle is about 3.5 seconds. It is usually not less than 1.5 seconds and not more than 6 seconds. In the sadness, the average duration of a cycle is about 5.3 seconds, and it is usually not less than 2 seconds and not more than 7 seconds. The analysis results also found that the average duration of a cycle for disgust emotion is about 3.6 seconds; the average duration of a cycle for angry and fear emotions is about 3 seconds; the average duration of a cycle for surprise emotion is about 2.7 seconds.

4   Our Mechanism for Simulating Continuous Emotional Facial Expressions

In this section, we propose our scheme to improve the conversion of continuous emotional states of an agent to facial expressions. We base on the temporal patterns in Section 3 to control the emotional facial expressions. The idea is that the facial expressions happen in series with decreasing intensity when a corresponding emotion is triggered. For example, when an event happens that triggered the happiness of a person, he/she would not smile in full intensity during the time the happiness lasts. Instead, he/she would express a series of smiles in decreasing intensity. Thus, emotional facial expressions appear only when there is a significant stimuli that changes the emotional states, otherwise, the expressions in the face is kept at low level displaying moods rather than emotions even when the intensities of emotions are high. The emotional expressions will not stay on the face for a long time while emotions decay slowly. However, the expressions of moods can last for much longer time on the face.

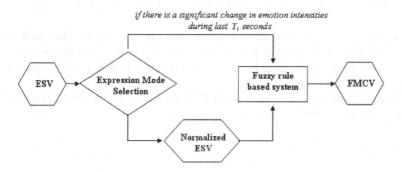

Fig. 5. The scheme to convert continuous emotional states of an agent to facial expressions (30)

We use the model in (30) to convert continuous emotional states of an agent to facial expressions. In order to perform our scheme with the idea above, we focus on improving the operation of Expression Mode Selection module. The model, as shown in Figure 5, consists of four components:

1. The input is a series of Emotion State Vector (ESV) over time. Each ESV is a vector of intensity of the six emotions at time t:
$$ESV^t = (e_1^t, e_2^t, \ldots, e_6^t) \text{ where } 0 \le e_i^t \le 1.$$

2. The output is a series of Facial Muscle Contraction Vector (FMCV) over time. Each FMCV is a vector of contraction level of 19 muscles in the right side of the 3D face model at time t:
$$FMCV^t = (m_1^t, m_2^t, \ldots, m_{19}^t) \text{ where } 0 \le m_i^t \le 1.$$

3. The Expression Mode Selection adjusts the series of ESV over time so that corresponding facial expressions happen temporally in the way similar to the temporal patterns found in Section 3. This module determines whether an emotional facial expression should be generated to express the current emotional state or the expressions in the 3D face kept at low level displaying moods rather than emotions. It firstly checks if there is a significant increase in the intensity of any emotion during last T_i seconds (the duration of an emotional expression cycle), that is if:
$$e_i^x - e_i^{x-1} > \theta$$
where $t - T_i \le x \le t$, t is the current time, and θ is the threshold to activate emotional facial expressions. (According to analytic results in Section 3, T_i has value of about 3.5 for happiness, 5.3 for sadness, 3.6 for disgust emotion, 3 for angry

and fear emotions, and 2.7 for surprise emotion). If there is a significant change, the ESV is converted directly to FMCV using the fuzzy rule based system proposed in (7); and the $cycle - tag_i$ is set to 1 for happy and sad emotions, is set to 3 for fear, angry, surprise, and disgust emotions. If not, the ESV is normalized as follows: t'_i is the time at which the most recent cycle ends, t is the current time,

- if $cycle - tag_i = 1$ and $t'_i + 3 \leq t \leq t'_i + 3 + T_i * 0.8$ then $e^t_i = e^t_i * 0.8$ and $cycle - tag_i = 2$
- if $cycle - tag_i = 2$ and $t'_i + 3 \leq t \leq t'_i + 3 + T_i * 0.6$ then $e^t_i = e^t_i * 0.6$ and $cycle - tag_i = 3$
- otherwise, e^t_i is normalized to lower intensity. In this way, the emotions are displayed as moods, the low-intensity and long-lasting state of emotions. After being normalized, the EVS is converted to FMCV using the same fuzzy rule based system.
4. The fuzzy rule based system converts from emotions (EVS) to facial muscle contraction levels (FMVS), which is proposed in (7).

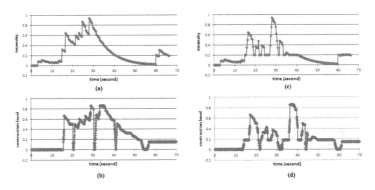

Fig. 6. (a): the intensity of emotion Happiness of Obie during the football match before applying our proposed model. (b): the contraction level of Zymgomatic Major - the smiling muscle to express Happiness before applying our proposed model. (c): the normalized intensity of emotion Happniness by our model to display on 3D face. (d): the contraction level of Zymgomatic Major after applying our proposed model.

5   Result and Evaluation

We use the emotional conversational agent presented in (5) to test our proposed mechanism in Section 4. This is the one we know so far that maps continuous emotional states to facial expressions; and we apply our proposed scheme on this agent to fix the unnaturalness. The agent is situated in the domain of a football supporter. Football is an emotional game. There are many events in the the game that trigger emotions of not only players but also of coaches, supporters, etc. Testing the football supporter's domain gives us the chance to test many emotions as well as the dynamics of emotions because the actions in a football match happen fast. The agent, named Obie, is a

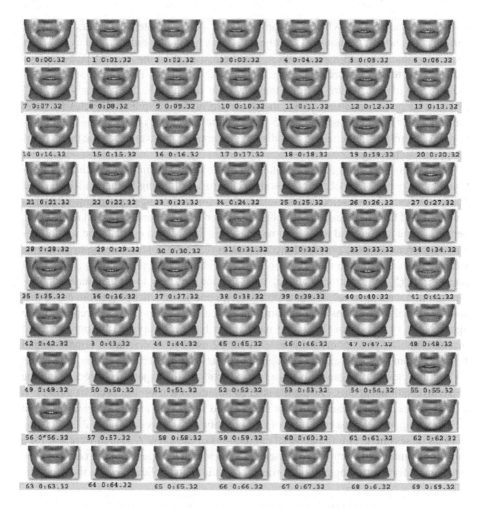

Fig. 7. Emotional facial expressions on the 3D face (frame by frame)

football (soccer) supporter agent. Obie is watching a football match in which a team, which he supports, is playing. Obie can experience different emotions by appraising events based on his goals, standards, and preferences. Obie can also show his emotions on a 3D talking head. Before applying our model, Obie sometimes displayed a visible facial expressions for a long duration when the emotions lasted for a long time. That gives the agent a mechanical look over time because an emotional facial expression with high intensity just stays on a human face for a few seconds. This can be easily seen in the intensity graph of emotion happiness and the contraction level graph of the smiling muscle Zymgomatic Major to express happiness in Figure 6(a) and (b). From the graph, we can see that the contraction level of Zymgomatic Major stays high for a long period, from second 15 to second 45. That means the 3D face "smiles" for about 30 seconds. After applying our model, Obie now displays his emotions in his 3D face in a much reasonable way. When the happy emotion with high intensity occurs for a long period, corresponding emotional facial expressions happen in only several cycles with decreasing intensity and time duration. For the rest of the time, the 3D face displays low level expressions expressing moods rather than emotions. This can be seen in Figure 6(c) and (d) and Figure 7. From these, we can see that, the 3D face only "smiles" twice, at second 16 and second 34; there are two or three expression cycles for each time, and the first cycle lasts about 3.5 seconds, the later cycles have diminishing duration. For the rest of the time, the face displays a happy mood even when the intensity of happy emotion is high.

We have also performed a user evaluation of the ability to simulate continuous emotional facial expressions of the proposed mechanism. Following Katherine Isbister and Patrick Doley (22), we selected user test method for evaluating experiments related to emotions and facial expressions. To obtain the user's assessment, we asked the users to perform some actions and answer some questions. In order to evaluate the advantages and effectiveness of our proposed mechanism in real-time conditions, the experiments were conducted with two conversational agents. The first agent (agent A) is the agent presented in (5). As mentioned above, this is the one we know so far that maps continuous emotional states to facial expressions; it uses one-to-one mapping (from emotional states to facial expressions) mechanism. The second agent (agent B) is a replica of the agent A but its one-to-one mapping mechanism has been replaced by our proposed mechanism. The two agents were tested with 12 users (6 males and 6 females) aged between 15 and 35 with an average age of 26 years. Each user test session took about 25 minutes. Sessions began with a brief introduction to the experiment process and the two conversational agents. During the next 10 minutes, the user watched two short clips of two agents. Finally, each user was interviewed separately about his/her assessment of the two agents. We asked a total of five questions as showed in Table 2. According to users' assessment, emotional facial expressions of the agent A, which were last for a quite long time, is less natural. And users also found that the agent B using our proposed mechanism for expressing emotions was more natural and believable than the agent A.

Table 2. Summary of interview results from the user test

Question	Negative	Middle	Positive
1. Could you understand emotions which the agent A expressed	0%	0%	100%
2. Could you understand emotions which the agent B expressed	0%	0%	100%
3. Naturalness of facial emotional expressions of the agent A	41.67%	41.67%	16.66%
4. Naturalness of facial emotional expressions of the agent B	0%	16.66%	83.34%
5. Is the agent B more natural and believable in expressing continuous emotional states than the agent A	0%	8.33%	91.67%

6   Conclusion

In this paper, we have presented a work on analysis of the relationship between emotions and facial activities in the time domain. Using facial expression recognition techniques to automatically analyze a spontaneous video database in order to consider how emotional facial activities happen temporally, we can extract the general temporal patterns for facial expressions of the six basic emotions. Then, based on the temporal patterns, we presented a scheme to convert continuous emotional states of a conversational agent to emotional facial expressions. The proposed idea is that the facial expressions happen in series with decreasing intensity when a corresponding emotion is triggered. The mechanism works well especially in case there is a high activated emotional state lasting for a long time. We have tested our mechanism on a football supporter agent and performed an user evaluation. The experiment results showed that produced emotional facial expressions were more natural and believable.

References

[1] http://mmifacedb.eu/

[2] Albrecht, I.: Faces and Hands- Modeling and animating anatomical and photorealistic models with regard to the communicative competence of virtual humans. PhD thesis, University at des Saarlandes (2005)

[3] Albrecht, I., Haber, J., Kähler, K., Schröder, M., Seidel, H.-P.: May i talk to you?:-) facial animation from text. In: Proceedings Pacific Graphics 2002, pp. 77–86 (2002)

[4] Arnold, M.B.: Emotion and personality. Psychological aspects. Columbia University Press, New York (1960)

[5] Bui, T.D., Heylen, D., Nijholt, A.: Building embodied agents that experience and express emotions: A football supporter as an example. In: Proc. CASA2004. Computer Graphics Society (2004)

[6] Bui, T.D., Heylen, D., Nijholt, A.: Combination of facial movements on a 3d talking head. In: Proc. CGI 2004. IEEE Computer Society (2004)

[7] Bui, T.D., Heylen, D., Poel, M., Nijholt, A.: Generation of facial expressions from emotion using a fuzzy rule based system. In: Stumptner, M., Corbett, D.R., Brooks, M. (eds.) Canadian AI 2001. LNCS (LNAI), vol. 2256, pp. 83–95. Springer, Heidelberg (2001)

[8] Bui, T.D., Heylen, D., Poel, M., Nijholt, A.: ParleE: An adaptive plan based event appraisal model of emotions. In: Jarke, M., Koehler, J., Lakemeyer, G. (eds.) KI 2002. LNCS (LNAI), vol. 2479, pp. 129–143. Springer, Heidelberg (2002)

[9] Cootes, T.F., Taylor, C.J., Cooper, D.H., Graham, J.: Active shape models-their training and application. Computer Vision and Image Understanding 61(1), 38–59 (1995)

[10] Darwin, C.: The expression of the emotions in man and animals. Univerity of Chicago Press, Chicago (1872/1965)

[11] DeCarlo, D.C., Revilla, M.S., Venditti, J.: Making discourse visible: Coding and animating conversational facial displays. In: Computer Animation (2002)

[12] Du, S., Tao, Y., Martinez, A.M.: Compound facial expressions of emotion. In: David, J. (ed.) Proceedings of the National Academy of Sciences. New York University, New York (2014)

[13] Ekman, P.: Emotion in the human face. Cambridge University Press, Cambridge (1982)

[14] Ekman, P., Friesen, W.V.: Unmasking the Face: A Guide To Recognizing Emotions From Facial Clues. Prentice-Hall, Englewood Cliffs (1975)

[15] Ekman, P., Friesen, W.V.: Facial Action Coding System. Consulting Psychologists Press, Palo Alto (1978)

[16] Ekman, P., Hager, J.: Facial action coding system affect interpretation database (facsaid), http://face-and-emotion.com/dataface/facsaid/description.jsp (retrieved)

[17] Ekman, P., Rosenberg, E.L.: What the face reveals: basic and applied studies of spontaneous expression using the facial action coding system (FACS), Illustrated Edition. Oxford
University Press (1997)

[18] El-Nasr, M.S., Yen, J., Ioerger, T.R.: FLAME-fuzzy logic adaptive model of emotions. Autonomous Agents and Multi-Agent Systems 3(3), 219–257 (2000)

[19] Essa, I.A., Pentland, A.: A vision system for observing and extracting facial action parameters. In: Proceedings of IEEE Computer Vision and Pattern Recognition Conference (1994)

[20] Friesen, W., Ekman, P.: EMFACS-7: Emotional Facial Action Coding System. University
of California, California (unpublished manual, 1983)

[21] Hayes-Roth, B., van Gent, R.: Story-making with improvisational puppets. In: Johnson,
W.L., Hayes-Roth, B. (eds.) Proceedings of the 1st International Conference on Autonomous Agents, pp. 1–7. ACM Press, New York (1997)

[22] Isbister, K., Doyle, P.: Design and evaluation of embodied conversational agents: a proposed taxonomy. In: Proceedings of AAMAS 2002 Workshop on Embodied Conversational
Agents? Let?s Specify and Evaluate Them!, Bologna, Italy (2002)

[23] Izard, C.E.: Emotions and facial expressions: A perspective from differential emotions theory. In: Russell, J.A., Fernandez-Dols, J.M. (eds.) The Psychology of Facial Expression.
Maison des Sciences de l'Homme and Cambridge University Press (1997)

[24] Kappas, A.: What facial activity can and cannot tell us about emotions. In: Katsikitis, M.
(ed.) The Human Face: Measurement and Meaning, pp. 215–234. Kluwer Academic Publishers, Dordrecht (2003)

[25] King, S.A., Parent, R.E., Olsafsky, B.: An anatomically-based 3d parametric lip model
to support facial animation and synchronized speech. In: Proceedings of Deform 2000,
pp. 7–19 (2000)

[26] Kshirsagar, S., Magnenat-Thalmann, N.: A multilayer personality model. In: Proceedings
of 2nd International Symposium on Smart Graphics, pp. 107–115. ACM Press (2002)

[27] Kurlander, D., Skelly, T., Salesin, D.: Comic chat. In: SIGGRAPH 1996: Proceedings of the
23rd Annual Conference on Computer Graphics and Interactive Techniques, pp. 225–236
(1996)

[28] Latta, C., Alvarado, N., Adams, S.S., Burbeck, S.: An expressive system for animating char-
acters or endowing robots with affective displays. In: Society for Artificial Intelligence and
Social Behavior (AISB), 2002 Annual Conference, Symposium on Animating Expressive
Characters for Social Interactions (2002)

[29] Mohammad Mavadati, S., Mahoor Mohammad, H., Bartlett, K., Trinh, P., Cohn, J.F.: Disfa:
A spontaneous facial action intensity database. IEEE Transactions on Affective Computing 4(2), 151–160 (2013)

[30] Ngo, T.D., Bui, T.D.: When and how to smile: Emotional expression for 3D conversational agents. In: Ghose, A., Governatori, G., Sadananda, R. (eds.) PRIMA 2007. LNCS,
vol. 5044, pp. 349–358. Springer, Heidelberg (2009)

[31] Paiva, A., Dias, J., Sobral, D., Aylett, R., Sobreperez, P., Woods, S., Zoll, C., Hall, L.:
Caring for agents and agents that care: Building empathic relations with synthetic agents.
In: Proceedings of the Third International Joint Conference on Autonomous Agents and
Multiagent Systems, pp. 194–201. IEEE Computer Society (1996)

[32] Pantic, M., Patras, I.: Detecting facial actions and their temporal segments in nearly frontal-
view face image sequences. In: Proc. IEEE Conf. Systems, Man and Cybernetics, vol. 4,
pp. 3358–3363 (2005)

[33] Pantic, M., Valstar, M.F., Rademaker, R., Maat, L.: Web-based database for facial expression analysis. In: Proc. 13th ACM Int'l Conf. Multimedia and Expo, pp. 317–321 (2005)

[34] Perlin, K., Goldberg, A.: Improv: A system for scripting interactive actors in virtual worlds.
Computer Graphics 30(Annual Conference Series), 205–216 (1996)

[35] Picard, R.: Affective Computing. MIT Press, Cambridge (1997)

[36] Plutchik, R.: Emotions: A general psychoevolutionary theory. In: Scherer, K.R., Ekman, P. (eds.) Approaches to Emotion. Lawrence Erlbaum, London (1984)

[37] Raouzaiou, A., Karpouzis, K., Kollias, S.D.: Online gaming and emotion representation. In: García, N., Salgado, L., Martínez, J.M. (eds.) VLBV 2003. LNCS, vol. 2849, pp. 298–305. Springer, Heidelberg (2003)

[38] Reilly, W.S.: Believable social and emotional agents. Technical Report Ph.D. Thesis. Technical Report CMU-CS-96-138, Carnegie Mellon University, Pittsburgh, PA, USA (1996)

[39] Russell, J.A.: Reading emotions from and into faces: Resurrecting a dimensional-contextual perspective. In: Russell, J.A., Fernndez-Dols, J.M. (eds.) The Psychology of Facial Expression. Cambridge University Press, New York (1997)

[40] Scherer, K.R.: What does facial expression express. In: Strongman, K. (ed.) International Review of Studies on Emotion, vol. 2. Wiley, Chichester (1992)

[41] Stern, A., Frank, A., Resner, B.: Virtual petz: A hybrid approach to creating autonomous, lifelike dogz and catz. In: Sycara, K.P., Wooldridge, M. (eds.) Proceedings of the 2nd International Conference on Autonomous Agents (Agents 1998), pp. 334–335. ACM Press, New York (1998)

[42] Tanguy, E.: Emotions: the Art of Communication Applied to Virtual Actors. PhD thesis, Universit of Bath (2006)

[43] Tian, Y., Kanade, T., Cohn, J.: Recognizing action units for facial expression analysis. IEEE Trans. Pattern Analysis and Machine Intelligence. 23(2), 97–115 (2001)

[44] Tomkins, S.S.: Affect, Imagery, Consciousness (Volume 1): The Positive Affects. Springer, New York (1962)

[45] Velásquez, J.D.: Modeling emotions and other motivations in synthetic agents. In: Proceedings of the 14th National Conference on Artificial Intelligence and 9th Innovative Applications of Artificial Intelligence Conference (AAAI-97/IAAI 1997), pp. 10–15. AAAI Press, Menlo Park (1997)

[46] Viola, P., Jones, M.: Robust real-time object detection, Tech. rep., Cambridge Research Laboratory Technical report series. (2) (2001)

[47] Wallhoff, F.: The facial expressions and emotions database homepage (feedtum), http://www.mmk.ei.tum.de/~waf/fgnet/feedtum.html

Adaptive User Interface Agent for Personalized Public Transportation Recommendation System: PATRASH

Hiroyuki Nakamura[1], Yuan Gao[1], He Gao[1], Hongliang Zhang[1],
Akifumi Kiyohiro[1], and Tsunenori Mine[2]

[1] Graduate School of ISEE, Kyushu University
744 Motooka, Nishi-ku, Fukuoka 8190395, Japan
[2] Faculty of ISEE, Kyushu University
744 Motooka, Nishi-ku, Fukuoka 8190395, Japan
`{nakamura,kiyohiro,mine}@ma.ait.kyushu-u.ac.jp`

Abstract. Public transportation guidance services, which are widely used nowadays, support our daily lives. However they have not fully been personalized yet. Regarding personalized services, an adaptive user interface plays a crucial role. This paper presents an Adaptive User Interface (AUI) agent of our personalized transportation recommendation system called PATRASH. To design and implement the agent, first, we collected and analyzed public transportation usage histories of 10 subjects so as to confirm the possibilities and effectiveness of the personalized route recommendation function. Then we propose a method to deal with user histories and evaluate the effectiveness of the proposed method based on click costs, comparing with two major transportation guidance systems in Japan. We also propose a decision-tree-based route recommendation method. The experimental results illustrate the effectiveness of the proposed method.

Keywords: Intelligent Transportation System, Personalized Recommendation, User Context, User History, Adaptive User Interface Agent.

1 Introduction

Our daily lives are supported by various Web-based services. One of those important services is a public transportation route and time table guidance service. The service is provided by many companies such as Yahoo, Jorudan, NAVITIME, goo, and Google. Their services are improved day by day, and provide us useful functions such as registration of routes or stations used frequently, notice of applicability of commuter pass, or existence of elevators. They also show us abnormal real traffic information such as delay or shut down routes when we search for routes. Although individuals have own different requirements, they unfortunately do not give us fully personalized services such as automatic registration of user routine routes, which are frequently used by users, prediction of departure and arrival stations to be used by the users, recommendation of

H.K. Dam et al. (Eds.): PRIMA 2014, LNAI 8861, pp. 238–245, 2014.

routes preferred by the users, and so on. We believe that prediction of user routine routes or arrival station is possible and then personalized functions would be indispensable for future transportation recommendation systems, at the thought of human mobility patterns[1]. To realize personalized services, an adaptive user interface (AUI) plays an important role; the AUI adapts to its user behaviors and provides information the user needs. Regarding public transportation recommendation systems, the AUI should be able to estimate the target place the user is heading for, considering the user contexts and usage histories. Since the AUI can learn its user behaviors to work for its user, the AUI can be regarded as an agent. We call the agent an AUI agent.

This paper presents an AUI agent of our personalized transportation recommendation system called PATRASH: Personalized Autonomous TRAnsportation recommendation System considering user context and History. The AUI agent estimates the user target place, recommends his/her suitable routes and timetable information considering his/her context and usage histories. Before designing the agent, we investigated if route recommendation functions of the agent could be effectively implemented. To this end, first, we collected, from 10 subjects, their public transportation usage histories for one month and analyzed them. The analyzed results promise us to distinguish individual routine routes from non-routine routes, and to recommend public transportation routes to them. Then, we investigated the effectiveness of the AUI of the PATRASH by comparing with two major transportation guidance systems in Japan from the point of view of click costs. We conducted comprehensive experiments with 3 subjects and 3 data sets. The experimental results illustrate the effectiveness of the AUI. In addition, we propose a decision-tree-based route recommendation method and show the validity of the proposed method through experimental results.

In what follows, Section 2 describes related work to show the position in this research; Section 3 describes the AUI of the PATRASH; Section 4 discusses effectiveness and possibilities of personalized recommendation functions based on user context and histories; Section 5 discusses two types of experimental results: (1) show the effectiveness of our AUI by comparing the three services. (2) show the effectiveness of our AUI agent; finally we conclude and describe our future work.

2   Related Work

An adaptive user interface (AUI) adapts user needs; the AUI shows information relevant to the users, by changing layout or elements according to user contexts, behaviors and their needs. There are a lot of researches conducted on the AUI to cover a variety of users and situations. [2] proposes a method for identifying user contexts, and devises the most significant factor to design AUI. [3] discussed problems of augmenting recommendation diversity by applying an organization interface design method to a commonly used list interface and compared an organization interface with a list interface. [4] examined the relative effects of predictability and accuracy on the usability of AUIs. [5] proposed culturally adaptive systems, which automatically generated personalized interfaces corresponding to cultural preferences.

This paper discusses an AUI agent that recommends a transportation route according to user context and histories.

3   AUI of PATRASH

The PATRASH records user public transportation usage histories consisting of a set of pairs of departure and arrival stations, with each pair of timetable information, and recommends route information suitable to a user via its AUI agent. Before discussing the recommendation function of the agent, we investigated how to reduce operations to search for the user route. We here consider the number of button clicks as the operations. We believe less button clicks make the user feel less stress. To this end, we first propose a container-based user interface of the PATRASH. The interface displays user routes and their time table information immediately when accessed. The interface provides a set of containers called **M**ore detailed route **I**nformation **C**ontainers: **MIC**s as its initial view. Each **MIC** indicates a route that was used by a user. The **MIC**s record the user route histories. We call the history **HoP**: **H**istory **o**f a set of **P**airs of departure and arrival stations. Clicking a **MIC** shows the user more detailed information of a route in the **MIC**.

To search for user routes, unlike most traditional guidance systems, the PATRASH gives the routes in **MIC**s immediately when accessed. Only if **MIC**s do not contain a route suitable for the user, the user issues a query to the PATRASH, where the query consists of a departure route station, a departure time, and a destination route station. The way of the PATRASH is, so to speak, "Show First, Search Next." To show routes appropriate to the user, routes in **MIC**s are dynamically varied according to the user contexts and histories.

4   Pre-liminal Investigation

To make confirmation of effectiveness and possibilities of personalized route recommendation considering user contexts and histories, we collected and analyzed public transportation usage histories of 10 subjects who were undergraduate students at K university. The investigation period was from the 1st to the 31st of August in 2013.

The average number of the **T**otal number of **B**us stops and **T**rain station: **TBT** used by the subjects is 81.2. The number of subjects whose TBT belongs to the range between 60 and 89 is 5, which is the half of all the subjects; the numbers of TBT in neighboring ranges between 30 and 59, and between 90 and 119 are 2, respectively. The exceptional subject is ID 1; she used the greatest number of TBT, 160. The average number of their **D**istinct **B**us stops or **T**rain stations: **DBT** is 11.2.

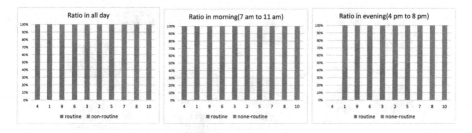

Fig. 1. Ratio between routine and non-routine routes: All day (Left), Morning (Middle), Evening (Right)

Route Station. We call a bus stop or a train station a **route station**; a route consists of a pair of route stations.

Routine or Non-Routine Route. We call r_{ij} a routine route of u_i if $freq(r_{ij}) \geq Ave(R_i) + Stdev(R_i)$, otherwise, a non-routine route of u_i.

where $freq(r)$ is a function that returns the number of times route r was used; r_{ij} is the jth route that user u_i used; R_i is a set of routes $r_{ij}(j = 1..m)$, m is the number of routes user u_i used; $Avg(R_i)$ and $Stdev(R_i)$ are the average frequency and the standard deviation of $freq(r_{ij}) \in R_i(j = 1..m)$, respectively.

According to the definitions above, the ratio between routine and non-routine routes for each subject is shown in Fig. 1 (Left). Subject with ID 4 only used his routine routes. On the other hand, three subjects with IDs 7, 8 and 10 didn't use their routine routes. It would be because the investigation period was in August when all the subjects were in summer vacation.

We further consider the routes of 7 subjects. Fig. 1 (Middle) shows the routine route ratio in the morning between 7 am and 11 am. The ratio of three subjects with IDs 1, 3, and 9 became 100%; the ratio of subjects with IDs 5 and 6 became decreased. The ratio of subject with ID 6 became increased in the evening between 4 pm and 8 pm shown in Fig. 1 (Right). Fig. 2 depicts a directed station diagram of subject with ID 1. Here a node and an edge denote a route station and a transition between route stations in the diagram, respectively. A number on the edge denotes a transition probability. From these investigations, we made sure that their destination would be determined by using a pair of a departure station and time. In addition, the ratio between routine and non-routine routes depends on users. Therefore personalized route recommendation would be possible and effective, in particular to the users who mainly use their routine routes.

5   Experiments

5.1   Evaluation of AUI

We compared the PATRASH with two major transportation guidance systems: Yahoo and Jorudan. Their applications individually record user departure and

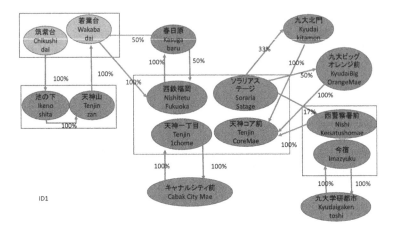

Fig. 2. State (Station, Stop) Transition Diagram

arrival route stations, but not by pairs. We call the history of their recorded stations, **History of Individual** departure and arrival route stations: **HoI**, in contrast with **HoP** of the PATRASH. To compare the three systems, we used **click cost** as a measure, where the click cost counts up all steps a user operated until the user got a suitable route.

Considering the ratio between routine and non-routine routes discussed in Section 4, we found that some subjects used less routine routes and others did more routine routes. Since the number of subjects were only 10, we chose three kinds of routine-route ratio: 30%, 50%, and 70%, which are corresponding to less, medium and more routine routes. We built a dataset to each ratio for each transportation guidance system, i.e. we totally built 9 datasets. Each dataset includes 100 pairs of route stations. The routes in the dataset were automatically generated so that the number of their occurrence times in the dataset followed a normal distribution. While, unlike the definition in Section 4, a routine route here means each pair of route stations that appears more than once, which is for the simplicity of generating the routes. We carried out experiments that each subject tried to search for route information in each dataset using the corresponding transportation guidance system. Each subject repeated this work 900 times: 3 datasets times 3 transportation guidance systems times 100 routes

We compared the click costs of the three systems. The average click costs for 30%, 50%, and 70% dataset by 3 subjects are shown in Table 1 (Left). The PATRASH took the lowest click costs and Yahoo did the highest. For 30% dataset, the PATRASH took 5.5 clicks per query, where a query consisted of a pair of route stations. Yahoo took 6.6 clicks per query. For 50% and 70% datasets, the PATRASH took the best performance. To make confirmation if there is any significant difference among the results, we conducted student's t-test. The results are shown in Table 1 (Middle and Right). Table 1 (Middle) shows that at 5% significance level, there are significant differences between the

Table 1. Average click cost (Left), p values of t-test: PATRASH vs Yahoo (Middle) and vs Jorudan (Right)

Guidance System	30%	50%	70%	PATRASH vs Yahoo			vs Jorudan		
				Subject	30%	50%	70%	30%	50%	70%
PATRASH	5.5	5.1	4.5	S1	9.7E-4	0.23	5.4E-3	0.020	0.96	6.1E-4
Yahoo	6.6	6.2	5.6	S2	2.2E-16	2.2E-16	1.9E-10	0.27	0.48	0.093
Jorudan	5.6	5.3	5.3	S3	1.1E-09	2.6E-07	5.8E-09	2.8E-4	1.3E-3	1.2E-08

PATRASH and Yahoo, except subject S1's 50% dataset. As shown in Table 1 (Right), except the results of subject S2 and 50% dataset of subject S1, at 5 % significance level, there are also significant differences. The results show the effectiveness of the **MIC**-based interface of the PATRASH.

5.2 Evaluation of Route Recommendation

When a user issues a query consisting of a departure route station, departure time, and the day of a week, the PATRASH AUI agent estimates his/her arrival route station considering his/her usage histories. Considering the user context, the agent can estimate his/her departure route station which would be near the current place and the departure time which would be just in a few minutes from the current time. These contexts can be obtained from GPS and clock time information of his/her mobile phone. In addition, user behavior such as picking out his/her mobile phone or the clock time approaching his/her planed time already had recorded in **HoP** become a trigger to tell the agent when the agent should recommend routes to the user.

We propose an decision-tree-based method as a route recommendation function of the agent. The method creates a prediction model which is incrementally learned from the user usage histories. If the model can recommend greater number of routes than the number specified by the user, the recommended routes candidates, except the top ranked route, are re-ranked based on the occurrence frequency of the routes and only the specific number of routes are selected. On the other hand, if the model can not recommend a sufficient number of routes specified by the user, insufficient numbers of routes are filled by the frequency-based method; the frequency-based method recommends a specific number of routes ranked in descending order of the number of routes occurred in the user usage histories. We used J4.8 of WEKA [6] to implement the method. To evaluate the effectiveness of the proposed method, using the usage histories of the 10 subjects described in Section 4, we compared with two methods: frequency-based and recency-based methods; the recency-based method recommends a specific number of routes ranked in the order of the latest used in the user histories. The two methods usually recommend routes without considering the departure route station for simplicity. As the evaluation measures, we employ precision and average precision defined by the following equations:

$$Precision = \frac{\Sigma_{i=1}^{n}\delta_i}{n} \qquad AveragePrecision = \frac{\Sigma_{i=1}^{n}\delta_i\frac{1}{r_i}}{n}$$

where δ_i returns 1 if the ith route used by a user is included in a list of routes recommended, 0 otherwise. r_i is the rank of the ith route in the list.

Table 2. Comparison on Recommendation Results

	# of routes	N5		N10		F5		F10		TF5		TF10	
		P	AP	P	AP	P	AP	P	AP	P	AP	P	AP
U1	80(16)	0.368	0.158	0.711	0.314	0.645	0.312	0.816	0.337	0.816	0.797	**0.829**	**0.799**
U2	35(16)	0.581	0.328	0.581	0.304	0.581	0.435	0.581	0.435	**0.710**	**0.677**	**0.710**	**0.677**
U3	40(12)	0.583	0.208	0.722	0.427	0.667	0.420	**0.778**	0.437	0.722	**0.688**	0.722	**0.688**
U4	32(4)	**1.000**	0.289	**1.000**	0.863	**1.000**	0.521	**1.000**	0.521	0.964	0.905	**1.000**	**0.910**
U5	24(12)	0.550	0.225	**0.600**	0.287	**0.600**	0.385	0.600	0.385	**0.600**	**0.560**	**0.600**	**0.560**
U6	51(13)	0.553	0.267	0.617	0.207	0.660	0.320	0.723	0.330	0.702	0.702	**0.745**	**0.708**
U7	33(25)	0.172	0.086	**0.241**	0.071	0.069	0.052	0.138	0.062	**0.241**	**0.241**	**0.241**	**0.241**
U8	32(12)	0.357	0.125	0.393	0.087	0.321	0.117	**0.679**	0.167	0.571	0.519	0.607	**0.534**
U9	52(17)	0.458	0.158	0.542	0.230	0.521	0.225	0.688	0.252	0.667	0.618	**0.708**	**0.622**
U10	27(14)	0.087	0.043	0.522	0.129	0.348	0.099	0.652	0.139	0.435	0.413	**0.696**	**0.473**
Ave.	40.6	0.471	0.189	0.593	0.292	0.541	0.289	0.665	0.307	0.643	0.612	**0.686**	**0.621**

Both the precision and the average precision consider if the route required by the user is recommended by the method. In addition, the average precision considers the rank of the route recommended by the method. The average precision is a measure commonly used by the Information Retrieval domain. Since the decision tree model requires at least 2 or 3 usage histories to learn the model, we excluded the first 3 usage histories from the evaluation. Experimental results are shown in Table 2. In table 2, the first row shows the method name, where first letter(s) of N, F, and TF denote a recency-based, frequency-based, and decision-tree-based methods, respectively; the latter number of 5 or 10 is the number of containers holding routes recommended. For example, N5 stands for the recency-based method with 5 containers. The next row shows the types of measurement: P and AP, which are precision and average precision, respectively. The first column is the ID of a subject and second one is the total number of routes the subject used, of which the number surrounded by parentheses is the distinct routes.

To confirm the significant difference at 5 % significance level, we conduct Wilcoxon signed rank test with continuity correction using R system[1]. On the precision, there was not a significant difference among three methods: TF5, TF10, and F10 since p values were over 0.3. On the average precision, TF5

---

[1] http://www.r-project.org/

and TF10 were clearly better than others. Then we compared TF5 with TF10 using Wilcoxon signed rank test with continuity correction as well. Since the p value was less than 0.05, there was a significant difference between TF5 and TF10 at 5 % significance level.

6   Conclusion and Future Work

This paper discussed the adaptive user interface agent of the PATRASH. The interface immediately provides a set of containers called **MICs** that keep user histories called HoPs. We conducted experiments to evaluate the effect of **MICs** by comparing the PATRASH with transportation guidance systems of Yahoo and Jorudan. The experimental results showed the click costs of the PATRASH were lowest among three systems. This shows the effect of **MICs**.

We also proposed a method for estimating an arrival route station according to a user query: a list of a departure route station, departure time, and the day of the week. The method learns user histories by decision tree J4.8 of WEKA. Experimental results showed that the proposed method took the best performance on the average precision.

We will start the service of the PATRASH in near future and investigate the effect of our AUI agent in real service.

Acknowledgment. This work was supported in part by NEDO under the METI of Japan, and JSPS KAKENHI Grant Number 26350357 and 26540183.

References

1. Gonzalez, M.C., Hidalgo, C.A., Barabasi, A.-L.: Understanding individual human mobility patterns. Nature 453(7196), 779–782 (2008)
2. Castillejo, E., Almeida, A., López-de-Ipiña, D.: User, context and device modeling for adaptive user interface systems. In: Urzaiz, G., Ochoa, S.F., Bravo, J., Chen, L.L., Oliveira, J. (eds.) UCAmI 2013. LNCS, vol. 8276, pp. 94–101. Springer, Heidelberg (2013)
3. Hu, R., Pu, P.: Enhancing recommendation diversity with organization interfaces. In: Proceedings of the 16th International Conference on Intelligent User Interfaces, pp. 347–350. ACM (2011)
4. Gajos, K.Z., Everitt, K., Tan, D.S., Czerwinski, M., Weld, D.S.: Predictability and accuracy in adaptive user interfaces. In: Proceedings of the SIGCHI Conference on Human Factors in Computing Systems, pp. 1271–1274. ACM (2008)
5. Reinecke, K., Bernstein, A.: Improving performance, perceived usability, and aesthetics with culturally adaptive user interfaces. ACM Transactions on Computer-Human Interaction (TOCHI) 18(2), 8 (2011)
6. Hall, M., Frank, E., Holmes, G., Pfahringer, B., Reutemann, P., Witten, I.H.: The weka data mining software: an update. ACM SIGKDD Explorations Newsletter 11(1), 10–18 (2009)

An Agent-Based Serious Game
for Decentralised Community Energy Systems

Aikaterini Bourazeri and Jeremy Pitt

Department of Electrical & Electronic Engineering
Imperial College London, Exhibition Road, London, SW7 2BT, UK

Abstract. Decentralised Community Energy Systems (dCES) are a type of SmartGrid in which a group of domestic residences form a common-pool resource for locally-generated and stored energy. In this paper, we argue that collective awareness is a pre-requisite for fair, sustainable and successful collective action in such systems, and that this awareness has to be shaped through affordances of the 'human-infrastructure interface'. Using a multi-agent simulator, we describe the development of a serious game for dCES which includes such affordances, and report on some preliminary results of an observational evaluation. This platform will be used in future work to test the hypothesis that collective awareness can improve the chances of successful collective action in dCES.

Keywords: collective action, collective awareness, serious games.

1 Introduction

Decentralised Community Energy Systems (dCES) are a type of SmartGrid in which a group of geographically co-located domestic residences form a common-pool resource for locally-generated and stored energy. These residences are installed with photovoltaic cells, small wind turbines or other renewable energy source and storage facilities; and each residence has a number of electrical devices the occupants wish to use. To do this, they have to provision to, and appropriate from, the common-pool energy resource.

In effect, this is a collective action situation, and the occupants need to work together to prioritise distribution, avoid blackouts, achieve a fair allocation, sustain the community over time, and so on. In this paper, we argue that collective awareness is a pre-requisite for fair, sustainable and successful collective action in such systems, and that this awareness has to be shaped through specific affordances of the 'human-infrastructure interface'.

Accordingly, this paper is structured as follows. Section 2 reviews other serious games for SmartGrids, and discusses dCES. Section 3 explains the concept of collective awareness in the context of dCES, and identifies five requirements for affordances of the interface. Section 4 describes the multi-agent system architecture and interface of the *Social Mpower* serious game, and reports on some preliminary results of an observational evaluation. Section 5 summarises and concludes with the prospect of further work to test the hypothesis that collective awareness can improve the chances of successful collective action in dCES.

H.K. Dam et al. (Eds.): PRIMA 2014, LNAI 8861, pp. 246–253, 2014.

2   Background and Motivation

Serious Games are used to build applications that simulate real-world events, and are intended to inform or train people in problem-solving skills. In this section, we review three Serious Games for energy systems; CityOne, PowerMatrix and Power House. However, none of these systems provides a platform for investigating the collective action problem-solving encountered in dCES.

2.1   Serious Games for Energy Systems

CityOne. IBM has designed the CityOne [3] game; a smarter planet game with main purpose to create an energy distribution network for a city to provide electricity in the most efficient way. Players take part in real-world problems and use new technologies to provide innovative solutions and make the water cleaner or banks more prosperous and user-centric. Through different missions, players learn how to prevent the over-utilisation of the grid or decrease the carbon emissions, while they investigate various environmental issues and better understand how a flexible and innovative IT infrastructure can revolutionise the energy and water industries.

PowerMatrix. In PowerMatrix [6] game provided by Siemens, players have the role of an energy manager and build power plants (combination of wind, solar and hydropower energy) to provide energy to their city. The main goal of this game is the city to grow and become wealthy and clean, and players have to develop a strategy for the optimum energy mix (power plants, wind farms, photovoltaic systems, biomass plants and so on). As the city starts to grow, population increases and more buildings are constructed, and so players have to balance the energy by tracking the energy resources, power consumption and generation. In case that more power is produced than the one needed, players should sell the energy surplus to avoid negative effects.

Power House. Stanford university designed the Power House [7] game to educate users on how to save energy and money. Different graphs and plots display the individual energy consumption, while users can track in real-time their progress and savings. Feedback is a very important feature as players get advices on how to reduce their energy use while maximising their profits.

2.2   Decentralised Community Energy Systems (dCES)

There are various problematic situations in power systems and distribution networks which need to be solved by an aggregated body, comprising a portfolio of smaller resources forming a kind of 'collective'. Virtual Power Plants (VPPs) are part of a partitioning/aggregation problem which include a central control body that collectively aggregates small generation units into a bigger power plant [8].

These aggregated or collective power plants can participate in the markets with higher quantities of energy or of related services, in order to have better prices. There are markets where small quantities are not accepted in todays IT support platforms. In addition, some small un-synchronised efforts may not bring at all a visible effect in the network, so small contributors may not participate at all if they think they are alone.

Usually, however, such aggregations are pre-arranged and usually are backed-up by legal contracts. When the focus is switched from the supply-side to the demand-side, it can be argued that there is a requirement for run-time self-organisation rather than pre-arrangement, and for social contracts rather than legal contracts.

In our conception of a decentralised Community Energy System, a group of geographically co-located residences is occupied by prosumers. The residences may have installed solar panels, small wind turbines or other renewable energy source; and the occupants have the usual requirements to operate their appliances. We also consider the issue of storage, and propose to consider the use of electric vehicles as a 'distributed battery'.

Therefore, in fact we have multiple co-dependent provision and appropriation systems, i.e. one for the energy distribution, one for storage, one for maintenance and investment, and so on. To investigate whether people can self-organise solutions to collective action problems in dCES, we propose to design and implement a Serious Game.

3   Collective Action and Awareness

In this section we give an example of how collective action and active participation of consumers could benefit the energy sector, whereas we identify collective awareness as a prerequisite for successful collective action. Moreover, we propose five requirements that could be used as the basis for designing a serious game to promote collective awareness in an energy system.

3.1   Collective Action in Energy Systems

In the energy sector there are many situations where problems need to be solved by involving either a big resource or an aggregated body containing a portfolio of smaller resources. However, even a large number of aggregated units may not bring about a visible effect on the network if their efforts are un-synchronised. Furthermore, such aggregations are pre-organised between 'large' organisations and usually are backed-up by legal contracts. We are concerned with synchro-nised action between individual users, which are dynamically self-organised and are brought about by social processes.

In a real-life scenario, a group of users are supplied from the same low volt-age (LV) network. In crowded distribution networks, there is the possibility of a power network overload due to excessive demand– which can cause temporary network congestion, bringing undesirable service interruptions. The bottleneck is at the transformer, which becomes overloaded during peak times. If its tem-perature increases a given limit, a switch trips the transformer and keeps it

disconnected for some time in order to cool down. After reduction of tempera-
ture, the switch reconnects the transformer.

Currently, people seem not know about the overload risk or to care much about
the issue. When the outage occurs, they just observe that the energy supply
has been interrupted and they ring the electric company's customer relations
department to complain.

If people are so readily reactive, one approach to solve this problem is to install
a smart meter in each domestic residence and alert customers to an incipient trip
event, in the hope they will reduce their consumption. However, the trip can only
be avoided with the participation of a 'critical mass' of customers. However,
one individual acting alone cannot be sure that others will also reduce their
consumption. If one individual does and everyone else does not, the individual
will not only lose from turning off his/her device, but also suffers the collective
loss from the subsequent power outage. Thus avoiding the trip event is critically
dependent on collective action.

3.2   Collective Awareness

Collective awareness is "an attribute of communities that helps them solve collective action problems", i.e. analogous to the way that social capital is defined
by Ostrom and Ahn [5] as "an attribute of individuals that helps them solve collective action problems. In communities in which collective awareness is barely
present, individuals are generally less willing to obey the norms or rules, or to
appreciate the consequences of their individual actions for the community. Individuals may take actions for common resources that are suboptimal from a
community-wide perspective, leading to depletion of those resources. They may
understand the situation they are in from a micro-level perspective (e.g. reducing
individual energy consumption) and might additionally recognise the macro-level
requirement (e.g. meeting national carbon dioxide emission pledges); however,
they might not be aware of interactions occurring at the meso-level which are
critical for mapping one to the other.

Therefore, collective awareness has a critical role in the formation of institutions, the regulation of behaviour within the context of an institution, and
the direction (or selection) of actions intended to achieve a common purpose.
We consider collective awareness as being different from mutual knowledge, and
we identify certain requirements for dCES as necessary conditions for achieving
collective awareness as a precursor to collective action. These requirements are:

- Interface cues for collective action: users participating in an action situation;
- Visualisation: appropriate presentation and representation of data, making
    what is conceptually significant perceptually prominent;
- Social networking: fast, convenient and cheap communication channels to
    support the propagation of data;
- Feedback: individuals need to know that their ('small', individual) action X
    contributed to some ('large', collective) action Y which achieved beneficial
    outcome Z;

- Incentives: typically in the form of social capital [5], itself identified as an attribute of individuals that helps them with solving collective action problems.

3.3   Requirements

We identify interface cues, visualisation, social networking, feedback and appropriate incentivation as sufficient requirements to design a serious game which promotes collective awareness for collective action.

Table 1. Serious Games for the Energy Sector

Game Elements	City One	PowerMatrix	Power House
Interface Cues	✓		
Visualisation	✓	✓	✓
Social Networking	✓	✓	
Feedback		✓	✓
Appropriate Incentivation		✓	

A critical appraisal of the above serious games for the energy sector concluded that some of the key requirements for successful collective action were omitted; therefore we developed the *Social Mpower* game, which satisfies all these requirements.

4   Platform, Interface and Observational Evaluation

In this section we give more details about the platform that used to build and manage a serious game for energy systems. The interface represents an energy community where players have to distribute resources in an economy of scarcity, whereas the observational evaluation tries to test our hypothesis that "collective awareness implies successful collective action".

4.1   Platform

A multi-agent simulator is used to provide an implementation route to gamification, whereas an application server and viewer are included to monitor and coordinate actions, providing at the same time data animation and visualisation.

Presage2 is a general purpose platform for developing and simulating collective adaptive systems [4]. For our research, we have extended Presage2 properties to use it as an experimental platform for computations (energy consumption), inter-agent communication and database integration. Agents written in Java represent avatars, electrical devices, solar panels and smart meter boards in a dCES. Energy consumption is calculated based on the operating time and the amount of electricity each of the electrical devices has assigned to use in a simulation period.

OpenSimulator is an open source multi-user 3D application server platform which supports virtual worlds and environments [2]. OpenSimulator has been customised and personalised to meet our preferences and requirements for a dCES. Our dCES is basically an energy community, where players can move their avatars all around, visit different houses, take part in individual or common activities and gather in a room called 'Deliberative Assembly', where the game rules are defined.

Imprudence is an open source viewer which supports OpenSimulator-based virtual worlds with main goal to provide a user interface that enhances the user experience [1]. We use Imprudence as the main interface for supporting and displaying our virtual energy community. Different communication channels are used for inter-communication between avatars and this can be done either on private or public mode.

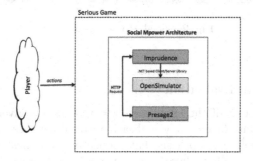

Fig. 1. Social Mpower Architecture

Figure 1 presents the 3-Layer architecture of *Social Mpower* game. The environment (player) interacts with the serious game through actions (clicking on objects, avatars, etc). The *Social Mpower* architecture includes three components; Imprudence viewer, OpenSimulator and Presage2. Imprudence communicates with Presage2 through HTTP requests. One action on the viewer brings an effect on the simulation platform. Imprudence is also connected to OpenSimulator through a web client/server library. Each viewer has a specific "Login URI" and through that is connected to the server. When the client viewer starts up, a name/password is required. Those details are sent to the OpenSimulator login service which sends back a specific IP address and port, enabling the viewer to connect to its region.

4.2 *Social Mpower* Interface

Social Mpower interface has been designed to simulate and represent an energy community. This community includes different houses equipped with electrical devices and smart meter boards which enable players (avatars) to consume and control energy. The energy of community is generated from "solar panels" installed on the roofs of those houses. *Social Mpower* provides different communication channels to promote social interaction and networking among players. Players use the provided electrical devices to do various tasks/jobs according to their preferences. The smart meter boards provide real-time information about the energy consumption either on individual or common basis (figure 2). The community has a maximum energy capacity fairly allocated among all players (avatars) and synchronisation/coordination is needed to solve potential energy problems.

Fig. 2. Social Mpower Game

4.3   Observational Evaluation

For the design and test of the experiments, emphasis was given on the different requirements – interface cues, visualisation, social networking, feedback and incentives – to prove our hypothesis that "collective awareness implies successful collective action". When these requirements were missing from the game, only 52% of the participants coordinated their behaviour and actions with their co-players to avoid a possible blackout in the system, whereas, when social networking and visualisation (energy consumption representation) were added to the game there was an increase up to 80% in coordinating action. Interface cues – players participate in an action situation – enabled and promoted participants to respond to occurred energy problems with 76% of them to treat energy as a common pool resource and avoid its depletion, but when there were missing only 19% of them tried to solve an occurred problem. Finally, provided feedback and rewards (in form of social capital) sustained players' interest with 85% of them to monitor regularly their energy consumption during the game and change their behaviour accordingly. When those two requirements were absent only 52% of players changed their energy behaviour.

5   Conclusion

In summary, we have reviewed Serious Games for energy systems, argued that collective awareness is a prerequisite for successful collective action in decentralised Community Energy Systems (dCES), identified the interface requirements and affordance or shaping collective awareness, and described a Serious

Game for dCES which manifests these features. We described some observational evaluations which informally indicate that these features do correlate with collective awareness.

In further work, we propose to conduct experiments with different subsets of these collective-awareness enhancing features enabled, and measure the impact on people's collective action problem-solving. In this way, we can investigate our primary experimental hypothesis, that increased collective awareness supports successful collective action. Other research directions include gamification of the system, so that appliances in the game are directly related to appliances in the (smart)house, and actions in the real world affect the state of the 'game'. In this context, the use of the SmartMeter for visualisation and synergising computational intelligence with human (social) intelligence could have a profound impact on collective action.

In conclusion, we would argue that this prosocial self-organising approach to demand-side energy management offers an opportunity to empower users in different roles in (or relations with) the infrastructure, e.g. prosumer, citizen, investor, etc.), and that this will lead to more responsible and sustainable energy use.

References

1. Champsas, I., Leftheris, I., Tsiatsos, T., Terzidou, T., Mavridis, A.: Opengames: A framework for implementing 3d collaborative educational games in opensim. In: 6th European Conference on Games Based Learning, p. 82. Academic Conferences Limited (2012)
2. Fishwick, P.A.: An introduction to opensimulator and virtual environment agent-based m&s applications. In: Proceedings of the 2009 Winter Simulation Conference (WSC), pp. 177–183. IEEE (2009)
3. IBM 2014: Cityone real world game, real world impact,
   http://www-01.ibm.com/software/solutions/soa/innov8/cityone/.
4. Macbeth, S., Pitt, J., Schaumeier, J., Busquets, D.: Animation of self-organising resource allocation using presage2. In: SASO, pp. 225–226 (2012)
5. Ostrom, E., Ahn, T.K.: Foundations of social capital (2003)
6. SIEMENS: Power matrix, a siemens initiative,
   http://www.powermatrixgame.com/en/index.html
7. STANFORD UNIVERSITY: Power house, game play to reduce energy use,
   http://powerhouse.stanford.edu/?q=welcome
8. Steghöfer, J.-P., Anders, G., Siefert, F., Reif, W.: A system of systems approach to the evolutionary transformation of power management systems. In: Proceedings of INFORMATIK 2013 – Workshop on Smart Grids. Lecture Notes in Informatics, vol. P-220, pp. 1–16. Bonner Köllen Verlag (2013)

Activity Recognition for an Agent-Oriented Personal Health System

Özgür Kafalı, Alfonso E. Romero, and Kostas Stathis

Department of Computer Science
Royal Holloway, University of London
Egham, TW20 0EX, UK
{ozgur.kafali,aeromero,kostas.stathis}@cs.rhul.ac.uk

Abstract. We present a knowledge representation framework that allows an agent situated in an environment to recognise complex activities, reason about their progress and take action to avoid or support their successful completion. Activities are understood as parameterised templates whose parameters consist of a unique name labelling the activity to be recognised, a set of participants co-involved in the carrying out of the activity and a goal revealing the desired outcome the participants seek to bring about. The novelty of the work is the identification of an activity lifecycle where activities are temporal fluents that can be started, interrupted, suspended, resumed, or completed over time. The framework also specifies activity goals and their associated lifecycle, as with activities, and shows how the state of such goals aids the recognition of significant transitions within and between activities. We implement the resulting recognition capability in the Event Calculus and we illustrate how an agent using this capability recognises activities in a personal health system monitoring diabetic patients.

1 Introduction

We study the problem of how to develop an activity recognition capability as part of a healthcare application with the aim of assisting a patient in the monitoring and management of his diabetes. This problem is important because the possibility of delegating parts of the monitoring and management of a diabetic's activity to a software application has the advantage of simplifying the patient's lifestyle. Amongst other things, a patient would not have to worry about where to systematically record regular measurements of his blood glucose, or how to distinguish trends that may determine his well-being and, in the ultimate analysis, his health. This is, however, a complex task because the application must be in position to recognise the patient's activities using sensor technology, relate these activities to medical guidelines that must be reasoned upon and interpreted in conjunction to medical expertise, as well as make suggestions that do not overwhelm the patient with notifications or requests for input information.

We argue that such a challenging application can be naturally developed as a multi-agent system for the following reasons. The problem of monitoring requires a continuous and dedicated software process that observes the condition of the patient. First, this process must also encapsulate its own state, to store information such as glucose measurements or patient profile information. In addition, the process must be both reactive, in order for example to alert the patient about significant events that are relevant

H.K. Dam et al. (Eds.): PRIMA 2014, LNAI 8861, pp. 254–269, 2014.

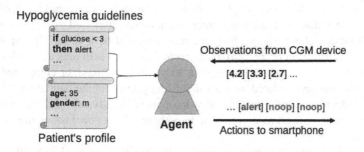

Fig. 1. Continuous Glucose Monitoring (CGM) Agent in COMMODITY$_{12}$ [12]

to his condition, but also proactive, to evaluate the significance of certain events, reason about their effects and choose appropriate action that will be to the benefit of the patient. Furthermore, the process must be also in a position to access and influence the environment via state-of-the-art sensor/actuation technologies, for instance, to measure glucose values or administer insulin respectively. Most importantly, the process should be able to interact and communicate with other similar processes representing the interests of doctors, hospitals, or family members of patients, to inform and alert of critical situations as they arise, and by using specific protocols, sometimes formal and strict, while other times informal and flexible.

From our involvement in the FP7 COMMODITY$_{12}$ project, we have been particularly preoccupied with developing a monitoring agent that is a specialised version of the KGP model [15]. Such an agent diagnoses [12], ontologically reasons about [14] and together with specialised agents predict [13] medical emergencies such as *hypoglycemia*. According to the International Classification of Diseases (ICD), hypoglycemia is defined as the patient's glucose level being below a certain threshold value. When it arises, it can produce a variety of symptoms and effects but the principal problems is an inadequate supply of glucose to the brain, resulting in impairment of function and, eventually, to permanent brain damage or death. According to the severity level of hypoglycemia, a series of actions may need to be taken immediately, including informing the doctor of the patient as soon as possible, to require advice, or to start an emergency protocol.

To address conditions such as hypoglycemia we have developed an agent prototype that monitors blood glucose levels of a diabetic patient as shown in Figure 1. The monitoring knowledge and guidelines required for conditions such as hypoglycemia, have been specified using a symbolic, computational logic approach combined with temporal reasoning of the kind supported by the Event Calculus [18]. This approach is particularly suitable for reasoning about observations according to medical guidelines and has been combined with diagnostic reasoning to provide the patient with suitable recommendations and explanation, even in the light of incomplete information. However, the current monitoring capability cannot cope with information that refers to lifestyle activities of the patient, which are key to diabetes management, especially activities about the patient's physical exercise and diet.

The contribution of this work is the specification of an activity recognition capability that is integrated within the logic-based agent architecture discussed in [12] to support reasoning about complex activities from the recognition of basic ones. The capability relies on the identification of an *activity lifecycle* that treats activities as special temporal fluents that can be started, interrupted, suspended, resumed, or completed over time. Such information is related with a similar lifecycle about the patient's goals and is amalgamated with a monitoring capability to improve the advice and explanation offered to the patient, as well as corroborate hypotheses about conclusions that require further action.

The rest of the paper is structured as follows. We motivate our work in Section 2, by presenting a specific scenario that will provide the rest of the paper a grounding for the ideas presented later. Section 3 reviews the relevant background on activity recognition and the type of approaches followed in a number of applications, not necessarily diabetes. In Section 4, we describe the components that make up our proposal. Section 5 presents the case study and reports performance results. Finally, we conclude the paper with Section 6, where we point out a discussion and possible extensions.

2   The Smart Street Scenario

Consider the following scenario.

> John, a *type 1 diabetic*, is returning home after having spent an evening to the movies with friends. The bus that he took to go home does not reach John's street directly, so John needs to walk back to his place. Once he alights from the bus, John's mobile phone app that monitors his diabetes recognised that he has started walking, so it asks John to confirm that he is going back home. After John's confirmation, the app estimates that the walk will be roughly 20-minutes. Halfway, however, John receives an alert informing him that the content of glucose in his blood is abnormally low (a hypoglycemia medical emergency). John did not have enough time to respond to this alert as he passed out and fell on the pavement. Immediately after John falling on the pavement, his doctor and family were informed, an ambulance was called and the nearest street light started flashing to attract attention of passers-by and help the ambulance locate John.

To support such a scenario we will assume that John's mobile app is developed as a software agent that monitors John's glucose with an insuline pump and recognises John's activities in relation to his diabetes. The insuline pump is a device that can measure blood glucose, holds an insulin cartridge and can deliver a continuous flow (basal rate) of insulin to the body in the press of button. In regular intervals, it can communicate with the mobile app about the patient's glucose measurements, so that the agent can detect abnormally high/low glucose readings.

The scenario above requires that when the glucose level was low the agent has taken a number of important steps. Immediately after sending the hypoglycemia alert, the agent also sent a message on the app's display asking whether John was feeling ok. As John did not respond to this message because he fainted. This was recognised by the agent because the person had fallen while he was suffering a hypoglycemia attack. As a result, the agent alerted first John's doctor, then John's family and an ambulance giving John's location. The scenario assuming further a neighbourhood e-infrastructure of the kind envisaged in Smart Cities [24]. Using such an e-infrastructure, the agent can observe the closest street light, also represented electronically as a software agent, requesting it to flash about John's medical emergency.

3 Activity Recognition

Activity recognition can be defined, in broad terms, as the task of automatically detecting different human behaviours from certain given input data. In the last years, many computational approaches have been proposed to solve this problem (see [25,4,1] and references therein). From the point of view of the type of input data received, an activity recognition usually belongs to one of these two main groups: video-based [1,25], where a computer is used to recognise a sequence of images with one or more persons performing a certain activity, and sensor-based activity recognition (often called "motion analysis"), which deals with data coming from sensors like accelerometers, gyroscopes and, in general, any readings which could be produced by a mobile or wearable device (mobile telephone, activity tracker, medical sensor, etc.) In this work we will mainly focus on the latter.

It can be noted that the definition of activity recognition given above is essentially too abstract and not many attempts to formalise this problem can be found. In this manner, the task of Activity Recognition is even treated as a "subproblem of computer vision" or of the field where it is applied, and it is not treated in itself. Apart of the lack of formal definitions of the task itself, activities are taken as primitive concepts, not dealing the majority of the available references with a proper definition of them, and just focusing on the computational solution of the problem. The definition of activity, in the general sense, remains an open question which we try to partially address in this work.

Despite this lack of formalisation, links with activity theory have been established mostly within the field of human computer interaction [16]. On the other hand, the contribution of Chen *et al.* [5] presents a formal framework of activities, which are modelled as concepts of an ontology, having specific relations among them, and which are later used to include semantic information into the model of activity recognition proposed.

From an operational perspective, most of the current approaches to activity recognition work follow a hierarchical scheme. This scheme is summarised in Figure 2: first, a stream of data coming from mobile sensors and other sources is available (in our previous example, Jonh's smartphone and the CGM). Second, this raw data is preprocessed in a standard manner to obtain usable features for the following stages. Then, using these features, computational models recognise a set of low-level *primitive events* (also known as *actions* in the literature [25]). These events for our example would correspond to simple physical actions such as *walk, stand, lie*. Finally, the primitive events together with the context (such as historical information and user conformations) are used to recognise (more complex) activities, represented in terms of the events which were captured in the previous level. For our concrete case, these are activities which are

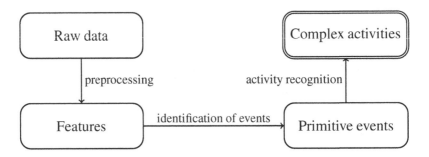

Fig. 2. General data flow for activity recognition

suitable for being monitored or treated by doctors (like for instance, the case that John has fainted). In this work we will mainly focus on the last step, represented in Figure 2 with a double box.

The methods for preprocessing raw data are highly dependent on the device type and its parameters, and we will not deal with them here. In order to detect basic events many alternatives techniques have been used: mainly supervised learning methods over tagged data (such as Hidden Markov Models, decision trees, neural networks). This subproblem has been successfully addressed by the previously mentioned techniques, resulting in very high values of accuracy (an exhaustive list is collected in [1] showing performances from 85% to 95%).

Next, we will review more carefully the methods for complex activity recognition, fundamentally those dealing with symbolic approaches. Apart from statistical models, two main solutions for this task has been proposed: syntactic methods and description-based methods. In syntactic methods, activities are defined as production rules of a grammar, reducing the problem of recognition to the one of parsing. In order to attain for uncertainty methods such as stochastic context grammars have often been used [20]. Joo and Chellappa propose a framework for recognition of events using attribute grammars [11]. They represent sequence of events as grammar rules as well as assigning attributes to each event. Primitive events are represented with terminal symbols. Using this representation, they look for patterns in video sequences that match corresponding rules. Each rule is associated with a probability telling how probable that sequence of events leads to the subject activity. They evaluate their approach with video data from two different domains: casing vehicles in a parking lot and departure of aircrafts. While their framework can successfully recognise such activities, it's not equipped to deal with the types of scenarios we have discussed in this paper, where the duration of an event and other contextual information are significant to recognition.

Ontologies are also utilised to represent and recognise events. In [8], the authors present an ontology based on the video event representation language (VERL). They use a logic-based markup language to represent composite events as sequences of primitive events as well using interval logic to capture temporal relations among events. They present a scenario where people are recognised while tailgating through a door. However, their rules are not as representative as ours and do not take into account contextual information. Nevatia *et al.* [21] define an ontology and a language to annotate video and describe complex activities as a function of simple activities. A very similar approach is taken in [26] where a symbolic approach to recognise temporal scenarios by specifying all its elements (e.g., characters, sub-scenarios, constraints) is presented.

Artikis *et al.* [3] study a variant of the Event Calculus for recognising composite events at run-rime using a stream of time-stamped simple derived events. In this system recognition of higher-level activities are treated as recognition of composite events but an activity (composite event) lifecycle as the one specified in section 4.2 is missing. So we can think of our framework as being more methodological for a specific class of applications where the goal achieved by an activity is an important requirement for the background knowledge of the recognition process. Knowing in advance the goals of participants in activities is an important consideration for applications such as the one we consider here, as they provide important contextual information in support of recognition. However, we do not recognise goals (or more generally the intentions of participants, as in [23]). Instead, we monitor an activity given the activity's goal and, where possible, we check that there are no activities or events that may interfere with the achievement of that goal.

There is also an important number of publications dealing with activity recognition and healthcare. For instance, a comparative of machine learning predictors for low-level activity recognition using body sensors is presented in [17]. In this study a lot of effort is made on the recognition of low-level events (which is done using different machine learning methods such as decision trees or Bayesian networks) and little is shown about the possible extension of recognising higher-level (complex) activities. Given the inherent risk of the application, most of the literature in this sub-field (and, in general, in sensor-based human activity recognition [19]) actually deals with recognition of low-level events, trying to find models achieving the minimum error.

For the specific case of diabetes not much work has been reported in the literature. One related work, where a system for monitoring diabetic patients (with an activity-recognition module) is presented in [10]. While there is an important description of the architecture of the system (e.g., the context of a smart home), there is not much discussion about the list of possible activities that could be recognised for this case of a diabetic patient, or about the different alternatives for activity recognition. The authors base their approach on Hidden Markov Models. Another interesting contribution is done by Han *et al.* [9], where the concept of "Disease Influenced Activity" is presented. Like many others, this contribution is also focused on monitoring uncommon patters (e.g., "frequent drinking" for diabetes) and presenting them to the doctor. In their approach they also make use of a Machine learning algorithm.

4   The Activity Recognition Framework

4.1   Architecture

Figure 3 shows how our agent framework, presented in the introduction, is extended with activity recognition to support the smart street scenario. We use dark font to represent the currently supported features of the monitoring agent within the personal health

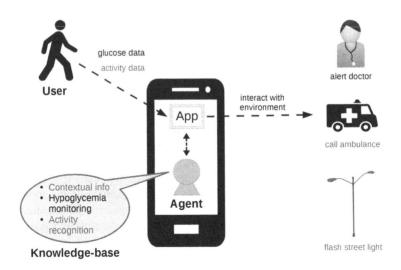

Fig. 3. Diabetes Monitoring and Management in our system. Components shown in red are the extended features for the Continuous Monitoring Agent.

system (as shown in Figure 1). We extend this original framework with a new set of features relevant to complex activity recognition. The agent is situated in the smart phone of the user and interacts with the application that receives input such as glucose and activity data from the sensors on the user. The agent's knowledge-base is also extended with logic rules regarding activity recognition to process activity data (see Sections 4.2 and 5) as well as contextual information about the user's environment (e.g., the user's current goal). The application also allows the agent to interact with the user's surroundings. In case of an emergency, the agent can call an ambulance and flash the street lights to attract attention as well as alerting the user's doctor.

4.2   Recognising Activities and Their Lifecycle Transitions in the Event Calculus

We are now ready to describe our activity recognition framework. In this framework an activity is understood as a parameterised template whose parameters consist of a label naming the activity, a set of participants co-involved in the carrying out of the activity and a goal revealing the desired outcome of the participants participating in it. The framework identifies an activity lifecycle that treats activities as temporal fluents that can be started, interrupted, suspended, resumed, or completed in time. The framework also proposes a template for activity goals and their associated lifecycle, similar to that of activities. Both lifecycles are presented in Fig.4.

We assume the notion of primitive events (e.g., walks, stands, lies), which are represented as input from the low level recognition system (see Fig.2). The framework differentiates between events, activities and activity transitions, caused by special events

Table 1. Domain-independent axioms of the Event Calculus

Predicate	Description
$happens\_at(E, T)$	Event E happens at time T
$initially(F = V)$	Fluent F has value V at time 0
$holds\_at(F = V, T)$	Fluent F has value V at time T
$holds\_for(F = V, [Ts, Te])$	Fluent F continuously has value V from time Ts to time Te
$broken\_during(F = V, [Ts, Te])$	Fluent F has changed value V from time Ts to time Te
$initiates\_at(E, F = V, T)$	Event E initiates value V for fluent F at time T
$terminates\_at(E, F = V, T)$	Event E terminates value V for fluent F at time T

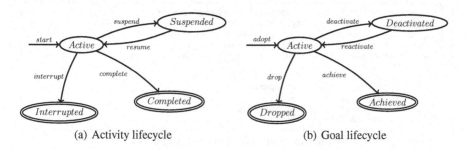

(a) Activity lifecycle   (b) Goal lifecycle

Fig. 4. Lifecycle of an activity and a goal. Double ellipses represent terminal states.

within an activity and according to the activity's lifecycle, or changes between activities. For example, the primitive event that a person stands provided as an input observation from a sensor, terminates the status of the activity of walking from active to suspended, and initiates standing.

To interpret and reason about events and activities we use the Event Calculus [18]. Table 1 summarises the domain-independent axioms used of the Event Calculus; these axioms assume multi-valued fluents as discussed in [2]. On top of the domain-independent axioms, our framework consists of the following additional components:

- an activity theory that regulates the activity lifecycle;
- a goal theory that regulates the goal lifecycle;
- a domain model that describes the recognition domain;
- an event narrative that contains the events that happened in the system.

We start with the generic components of the event recognition framework, i.e., the activity theory and the goal theory (see Section 5 for the domain model and the event narrative). Figure 4 describes the lifecycle of an activity (a) and a goal (b). The recognition of activities is driven by the goals of the user, which we represent as a modification of the goal lifecycle presented in [22] for our purposes. An activity is first activated due to a goal being adopted by the user and a low-level event happening to start the activity. While the activity is being performed, if the user's goal changes, then the activity is no longer required (e.g., the goal is *dropped*), then the activity is *interrupted*. If the goal remains, but another goal supersedes it temporarily (e.g., the goal is *deactivated*), then the activity is *suspended*. When the user reactivates the goal again, the activity is resumed. The activity completes successfully when the user achieves the goal, in which case the activity is *completed*.

Listing 1 presents the Event Calculus axioms specifying the domain independent activity theory. Lines (1-5) describe the events that happen when an activity is recognised to have been started (`started_at/2`), suspended (`suspended_at/2`), resumed (`resumed_at/2`), interrupted (`interrupted_at/2`), or eventually been completed (`completed_at/2`) at a specific time. Lines (7-11) describe how the recognised events initiate different values for the activity fluents; termination of these fluents are handled automatically by a generic `terminates_at/2` definition, see [2] (axiom 19).

```
1   happens_at(start(Activity), T):- started_at(Activity, T).
2   happens_at(suspend(Activity), T):- suspended_at(Activity, T).
3   happens_at(resume(Activity), T):- resumed_at(Activity, T).
4   happens_at(interrupt(Activity, T):- interrupted_at(Activity, T).
5   happens_at(complete(Activity), T):- completed_at(Activity, T).

7   initiates_at(start(A), A=active, T).
8   initiates_at(suspend(A), A=suspended, T).
9   initiates_at(resume(A), A=active, T).
10  initiates_at(interrupt(A), A=interrupted, T).
11  initiates_at(complete(A), A=completed, T).
```

Listing 1. Domain independent activity theory

Similar to the activity theory, Listing 2 presents the Event Calculus axioms for the goal theory. Lines (1-5) describe the events that happen when a goal is said to have been adopted (`adopted_at/2`), deactivated (`deactivated_at/2`), reactivated (`reactivated_at/2`), dropped (`dropped_at/2`), or eventually been achieved (`achieved_at/2`) at a specific time. Lines (7-11) describe now describe how the goal events initiate different values for the goal fluents.

```
1   happens_at(adopt(Goal), T):- adopted_at(Goal, T).
2   happens_at(deactivate(Goal), T):- deactivated_at(Goal, T).
3   happens_at(reactivate(Goal, T):- reactivated_at(Goal, T).
4   happens_at(drop(Goal, T):- dropped_at(Goal, T).
5   happens_at(achieve(Goal), T):- achieved_at(Goal, T).

7   initiates_at(adopt(G), G=active, T).
8   initiates_at(deactivate(G), G=deactivated, T).
9   initiates_at(reactivate(G), G=active, T).
10  initiates_at(drop(G), G=dropped, T).
11  initiates_at(achieve(G), G=achieved, T).
```

Listing 2. Domain independent goal theory

We show next how to develop the domain dependent part of our framework in order to support the activity recognition we envisage for our scenario. We represent an activity fluent as $activity(Name, Participants, Goal) = State$. The $Name$ is an atom (e.g., $walking$), the $Participants$ is either a list of atomic identifiers (e.g. $[john, peter]$ or a single such identifier (e.g. $john$), and $Goal$ is the name of a goal that specifies what the activity is seeking to achieve (e.g., at_home) with the possibility of a *null* value.

The *State* represents the current value of the fluent, drawn from the set of possible values *active, suspended, interrupted* and *completed*. We represent similarly a goal fluent as *goal(Name, Participants) = State*. The *Name* (e.g. *at_home*) and the *Participants* (e.g. *[john, peter]*) are defined like those of the activity fluent, what changes now is the current value of the *State*, drawn from the set of possible values *active, deactivated, dropped* and *achieved*.

```
1   started_at(activity(walking, P, G), T):-
2       holds_at(goal(G, P)=active, T),
3       happens_at(walks(P), T).

5   suspended_at(activity(walking, P, G)), T):-
6       happens_at(stands(P), T),
7       holds_at(activity(walking, P, G)=active, T).

9   resumed_at(activity(walking, P, G), T):-
10      holds_at(activity(walking, P, G)=suspended, T),
11      happens_at(walks(P), T).
12  ...

14  interrupted_at(activity(A, P, G)), T):- happens_at(drop(goal(G, P)), T).

16  completed_at(activity(A, P, G)), T):- happens_at(achieved(goal(G, P)), T).
```

Listing 3. An example of domain dependent activity theory

```
1   adopted_at(goal(G, P), T):- happens_at(adopt_goal_fromGUI(P, G), T).

3   deactivated_at(goal(G, P), T):- happens_at(deactivate_goal_fromGUI(P, G), T).

5   reactivated_at(goal(G, P), T):- happens_at(reactivate_goal_fromGUI(P, G), T).

7   dropped_at(goal(G, P), T):- happens_at(drop_goal_fromGUI(P, G), T).

9   achieved_at(goal(at_home, P), T):-
10      holds_at(location_of(P, L)=true, T),
11      holds_at(home_of(P, H)=true, T),
12      holds_at(location_of(H, L)=true, T).
```

Listing 4. An example of domain dependent goal theory

Listing 3 shows an extract of the domain dependent activity theory exemplified, in part, by the activity of *walking*. This is started once a low-level event *walks(P)* happens (stating that the participant *P* walks, see lines 1-3). We assume that the low-level activity recognition module will not send us more low-level *walk(P)* events, only when it recognises that walking has stopped and something else has happened. When a new (different) event is recognised by the low-level module, it will be communicated to the high-level one, which will in turn suspend the current activity. Lines (5-7) show how standing suspends walking. The *walking* activity is resumed (becomes *active* again) when a low-level *walks(P)* event happens (Lines 9-11). Any activity is interrupted when that activity's goal is dropped (Line 14), and, any activity is *completed* when that activity's goal has been achieved (Line 16).

Listing 4 shows an extract of a domain dependent goal theory exemplified, in part, by the goal of *at_home*. In this domain, we assume that the user manages directly the

Fig. 5. John's activities

goal from the graphical user interface (GUI) of the application. For any goal, actions of the user at the GUI are interpreted as internal events that cause the adoption of a new goal (Line 1) or the deactivation/reactivation/dropping of an existing goal (Lines 3, 5, and 7 respectively). Only the achievement of a goal is specified case by case; Line 9-12 shows an example of when the *at_home* goal is achieved.

5   Case Study

We now focus on the scenario described in Section 2. Let us first see the primitive events that lead to John falling on the street due to a hypoglycemia episode. Figure 5 shows the timeline of John's activities after he gets off the bus and heads home. We capture the temporal intervals of such activities using the predicate *holds_for/2*, implemented in our Event Calculus representation (see Table 1). It represents the validity period for activities that are in active or suspended state. This is shown in Listing 5.

```
happens_at(adopt_goal_fromGUI(john, at_home), 1).
happens_at(walks(john), 3).
happens_at(stands(john), 16).
happens_at(lies(john), 19).

holds_for(activity(walking, john, at_home)=active, [3,16]).
holds_for(activity(standing, john, null)=active, [16,19]).
holds_for(activity(lying, john, null)=active, [19,infPlus]).

holds_for(activity(walking, john, at_home)=suspended, [16,infPlus]).
holds_for(activity(standing, john, null)=suspended, [19,infPlus]).
```

Listing 5. Recognition of intervals for primitive activities

Using this knowledge only, we can recognise if someone is falling. Listing 6 describes the recognition of the composite event *falls*. The person must go from walking to standing, and then to lying in a short period of time in order to be recognised as a fall event. Note that this rule does not take into account the activity theory described in Section 4.2, and thus requires explicit temporal interval reasoning (i.e., the predicate *immediately_before/2*) to check the order of activities.

```
happens_at(falls(Person), T):-
    holds_for(activity(walking, Person, _)=active, [_,T1]),
    holds_for(activity(standing, Person, _)=active, [T2,T3]),
    holds_for(activity(lying, Person, _)=active, [T,_]),
    immediately_before(T1,T2),
    immediately_before(T3,T).

immediately_before(T1,T2):-
    T is T2-T1,
    T < 2.
```

Listing 6. Recognition of a fall event without the activity theory

Listing 7 improves the previous rule with the use of the activity theory. Here, since the states of the activities are handled by the activity theory, the rule does not need to check explicitly the validity periods of the activities as previously done with the $immediately\_before/2$ predicate shown in Listing 6.

```
happens_at(falls(Person), T):-
    holds_for(activity(lying, Person, _)=active, [T,_]),
    holds_for(activity(standing, Person, _)=suspended, [T,_]),
    holds_at(activity(walking, Person, _)=suspended, T).
```

Listing 7. Recognition of a fall event using the activity theory

In order to recognise that John has fainted, we must have additional knowledge about the environment as well as the intentions of John. Listing 8 describes this domain knowledge relevant to our scenario. John's goal is to walk home after watching the movie. As he starts walking home after he gets off the bus, he receives a hypoglycemia alert and stops to look at his smartphone. Unfortunately, he fell down soon after checking the alert. The agent running on his smartphone asks for John's status immediately after he fell.

```
happens_at(adopt_goal_fromGUI(john, at_home), 1).
happens_at(measurement(john, glucose, 2.8), 14).
happens_at(requests(john, confirm_status), 20).
```

Listing 8. Contextual information significant to recognising event interruption

Now we can combine this knowledge together with the formalisation of the fall event to conclude that John has fainted. Listing 9 describes these rules. We capture fainting as a special case of the fall event (e.g., the interruption of walking). In order to recognise that walking is interrupted (by an emergency) rather than just suspended for a period of time, we need additional contextual information as well as the fact that John has fallen. More specifically, the agent distinguishes fainting from falling if the following happens:

- John has the goal of walking and it has not been achieved yet;
- the agent has sent an alert to John following a hypoglycemia before he fell;
- the agent has asked John to confirm his status soon after he fell, and it has not received a response.

```
happens_at(faints(Person), T):-
    happens_at(raises_alert(Person, hypoglycemia), T1),
    happens_at(falls(Person), T2),
    happens_at(requests(Person, confirm_status), T),
    \+ happens_at(response(Person, status_ok), _),
    holds_at(goal(at_home, Person)=active, T),
    T1 < T2,
    T2 < T.
```

Listing 9. Recognition of a faint event

After the agent detects there is something wrong with John, it has to take appropriate action to make sure John is safe. Listing 10 describes the events that connects the agent with the environment. It can alert his doctor and call an ambulance as well as interacting with the street lights (provided a suitable infrastructure).

```
alert(doctor). %via the smartphone
alert(ambulance). %via the smartphone
alert(street_light). %via the smart city infrastructure
```

Listing 10. Ambient assisting during a faint event

Implementation and Supported Queries

We have implemented a prototype of the framework for the domain described in Section 5. We have used tuProlog for the implementation of the Event Calculus and Java to read the datasets generated for testing purposes.

```
Query 1
happens_at(falls(Person), T). --> yes.
Person / john   T / 19

Query 2
happens_at(falls(john), 15). --> no.

Query 3
happens_at(faints(john), T). --> yes.
T / 20

Query 4
happens_at(faints(Person), 20). --> yes.
Person / john
```

Listing 11. Supported queries

Listing 11 reports the different types of queries for *falls* and *faints* events. We have evaluated the framework with both grounded queries and queries involving variables. Our implementation of the Event Calculus allows fast query times and is able to answer queries with time given as a variable, e.g., *happens_at(faints(john), T)*.

6   Conclusions

We have presented an activity recognition capability that is integrated within a logic-based agent architecture to recognise complex activities related to diabetes monitoring.

The approach makes use of an *activity lifecycle*, in which activities are treated as temporal fluents that can change state according to events that occur through time. The framework also proposes a *goal lifecycle* for activity goals, similar to that of activities. The activity recognition capability then supports the monitoring agent to reason upon the link between the patient's activities and goals using their corresponding lifecycles, and provides advice and explanation to the patient, as well as detecting emergency situations.

We have motivated the work with a specific scenario illustrating how monitoring and recognising activities of a diabetic patient can be naturally conceived as a multi-agent systems problem. The approach we have developed is particularly suitable for symbolic reasoning agents that use monitoring observations according to medical guidelines, even in the light of incomplete information, and can take into account information that refers to the lifestyle of the patient.

The main emphasis of the work has been on motivating and conceptually organising the knowledge representation of the recognition in terms of activity and goal lifecycles. In this context, we have evaluated our proposed framework by outlining different ways to carry out the recognition of significant events for a case study with and without these lifecycles. We have also compared our work in the context of existing activity recognition frameworks and we have discussed how the key aspects of our framework extend the most relevant existing work.

As we have concentrated on the knowledge representation of complex activities we have decided not to carry out any performance evaluation of our Event Calculus implementation. The main reason for this choice is that Event Calculus performance is not an obstacle in the development of practical applications, since we could have used an *off-the-shelf* approach, for example see [3,6,7]. However, we believe that our version of the Event Calculus has merits, especially if combined with our recognition and agent monitoring framework, but this discussion is beyond the limited space of this paper. As part of future work, we plan to compare the performance of our implementation of the Event Calculus with similar approaches such as RTEC [3] and $\mathcal{REC}$ [6].

We have connected the lifecycle of an activity and a goal using one direction only, viz., our framework recognises activities first and then obtains knowledge of goals as part of the context provided by the patient (user). The other direction is also interesting, e.g., recognise goals from performed activities as described in [23]. This is particularly significant when agents are performing collaborative activities to achieve a common goal. Here, we have presented a simple goal structure. We will investigate how this can be extended and generalised with the integration of domain ontologies showing how our approach can be extended to other domains where run-time continuous monitoring is essential.

Acknowledgements. We thank the anonymous referees and Alexander Artikis for their helpful comments on a previous version of this paper. The work has been partially supported by the FP7 project COMMODITY$_{12}$ (www.commodity12.eu), funded by the European Union.

References

1. Aggarwal, J., Ryoo, M.: Human activity analysis: A review. ACM Comput. Surv. 43(3), 16:1–16:43 (2011)
2. Artikis, A., Sergot, M., Pitt, J.: Specifying norm-governed computational societies. ACM Trans. Comput. Logic 10(1), 1:1–1:42 (Jan 2009)
3. Artikis, A., Sergot, M., Paliouras, G.: Run-time composite event recognition. In: Proceedings of the 6th ACM International Conference on Distributed Event-Based Systems, DEBS 2012, pp. 69–80. ACM, New York (2012)
4. Avci, A., Bosch, S., Marin-Perianu, M., Marin-Perianu, R., Havinga, P.: Activity recognition using inertial sensing for healthcare, wellbeing and sports applications: A survey. In: 2010 23rd International Conference on Architecture of Computing Systems (ARCS), pp. 1–10. VDE (2010)
5. Chen, L., Nugent, C.D., Wang, H.: A knowledge-driven approach to activity recognition in smart homes. IEEE Transactions on Knowledge and Data Engineering 24(6), 961–974 (2012)
6. Chesani, F., Mello, P., Montali, M., Torroni, P.: A Logic-Based, Reactive Calculus of Events. In: Gavanelli, M., Riguzzi, F. (eds.) 24th Convegno Italiano di Logica Computazionale (CILC 2009) (2009)
7. Chittaro, L., Montanari, A.: Efficient temporal reasoning in the cached event calculus. Computational Intelligence 12(3), 359–382 (1996)
8. Francois, A.R.J., Nevatia, R., Hobbs, J.R., Bolles, R.C.: Verl: An ontology framework for representing and annotating video events. IEEE MultiMedia 12(4), 76–86 (2005)
9. Han, Y., Han, M., Lee, S., Sarkar, A.M., Lee, Y.-K.: A framework for supervising lifestyle diseases using long-term activity monitoring. Sensors 12(5), 5363–5379 (2012)
10. Helal, A., Cook, D.J., Schmalz, M.: Smart home-based health platform for behavioral monitoring and alteration of diabetes patients. Journal of Diabetes Science and Technology 3(1), 141–148 (2009)
11. Joo, S.W., Chellappa, R.: Recognition of multi-object events using attribute grammars. In: ICIP, pp. 2897–2900 (2006)
12. Kafalı, Ö., Bromuri, S., Sindlar, M., van der Weide, T., Aguilar-Pelaez, E., Schaechtle, U., Alves, B., Zufferey, D., Rodrguez-Villegas, E., Schumacher, M.I., Stathis, K.: COMMODITY12: A smart e-health environment for diabetes management. Journal of Ambient Intelligence and Smart Environments 5(5), 479–502 (2013)
13. Kafalı, Ö., Schaechtle, U., Stathis, K.: HYDRA: a HYbrid Diagnosis and monitoRing Architecture for diabetes. In: 16th International Conference on E-health Networking, Application & Services (HealthCom 2014), October 15-18. IEEE, Natal (2014)
14. Kafalı, Ö., Sindlar, M., van der Weide, T., Stathis, K.: $\mathcal{ORC}$: an $\mathcal{O}$ntology $\mathcal{R}$easoning $\mathcal{C}$omponent for diabetes. In: 2nd International Workshop on Artificial Intelligence and Netmedicine (NetMed 2013) (2013)
15. Kakas, A.C., Mancarella, P., Sadri, F., Stathis, K., Toni, F.: Computational logic foundations of KGP agents. J. Artif. Intell. Res (JAIR) 33, 285–348 (2008)
16. Kaptelinin, V.: Activity theory: Implications for human-computer interaction. In: Context and Consciousness: Activity Theory and Human-computer Interaction, pp. 103–116 (1996)
17. Kouris, I., Koutsouris, D.: A comparative study of pattern recognition classifiers to predict physical activities using smartphones and wearable body sensors. Technology and Health Care 20(4), 263–275 (2012)
18. Kowalski, R., Sergot, M.: A logic-based calculus of events. New Generation Computing 4(1), 67–95 (1986)
19. Lara, O.D., Labrador, M.A.: A survey on human activity recognition using wearable sensors. IEEE Communications Surveys & Tutorials 15(3), 1192–1209 (2013)

20. Minnen, D., Essa, I., Starner, T.: Expectation grammars: Leveraging high-level expectations for activity recognition. In: Proceedings of 2003 IEEE Computer Society Conference on Computer Vision and Pattern Recognition, vol. 2, pp. II–626. IEEE (2003)
21. Nevatia, R., Zhao, T., Hongeng, S.: Hierarchical language-based representation of events in video streams. In: Conference on Computer Vision and Pattern Recognition Workshop, CVPRW 2003, vol. 4, p. 39. IEEE (2003)
22. van Riemsdijk, M.B., Dastani, M., Winikoff, M.: Goals in agent systems: A unifying frame-work. In: Proceedings of the 7th International Joint Conference on Autonomous Agents and Multiagent Systems, AAMAS 2008, vol. 2, pp. 713–720 (2008)
23. Sadri, F.: Intention recognition in agents for ambient intelligence: Logic-based approaches. In: Bosse, T. (ed.) Agents and Ambient Intelligence, Ambient Intelligence and Smart Environments, vol. 12, pp. 197–236. IOS Press (2012)
24. Schaffers, H., Komninos, N., Pallot, M., Trousse, B., Nilsson, M., Oliveira, A.: Smart cities and the future internet: Towards cooperation frameworks for open innovation. In: Future Internet Assembly, pp. 431–446 (2011)
25. Turaga, P., Chellappa, R., Subrahmanian, V.S., Udrea, O.: Machine recognition of human activities: A survey. IEEE Transactions on Circuits and Systems for Video Technology 18(11), 1473–1488 (2008)
26. Vu, V.T., Bremond, F., Thonnat, M.: Automatic video interpretation: A novel algorithm for temporal scenario recognition. IJCAI 3, 1295–1300 (2003)

An Extended Agent Based Model for Service Delivery Optimization

Mohammadreza Mohagheghian[1], Renuka Sindhgatta[2], and Aditya Ghose[1]

[1] Decision Systems Laboratory
School of Computer Science and Software Engineering
University of Wollongong, NSW 2522 Australia
[2] IBM Research India
mm751@uowmail.edu.au
renuka.sr@in.ibm.com
aditya@uow.edu.au
http://www.dsl.uow.edu.au/

Abstract. Service delivery optimization has an important impact on organizational profitability, where changes in allocation of resources (e.g. humans, equipment and materials) to services increases profit. Simulation and optimization techniques generally suffer from three main drawbacks; firstly, the limited knowledge and skill of researchers in modeling social complexities. Secondly, having assumed that a fairly realistic model of the problem is simulated, finding optimal solutions requires an exhaustive search that is almost impossible in problems with a large search space. Thirdly, mathematical optimization techniques often require the acquisition of knowledge in a central unit, which is problematic e.g. for privacy reasons. This article introduces a new technique, which combines Agent Based Modeling (ABM) and Distribution Constraint Optimization (DCOP) to overcome these difficulties. Our empirical results present a successful model for finding optimized resourced allocation settings in comparison with two different ABM simulated models on a sample of a real-life service delivery problem

1 Introduction

The contributions of this paper are situated in the context of *service systems* as defined by Spohrer et al. [1] and specifically *service delivery systems* as defined by Ramaswamy et al. [2]. We address the problem of optimal resourcing (where the resources might be workers, IT resources or other equipment) in service delivery systems (we focus on allocating service workers to tasks, but this can be easily generalized). Optimal resourcing can have a major impact on cost-effectiveness. A number of studies have suggested that the resource allocation logic used in most service systems is often over-simplified, ad-hoc and significantly sub-optimal (see, for instance, [3]).

Simulation tools are often used for such problems, but do not, in general, generate optimal solutions. Using a simulation tool for optimization) requires

H.K. Dam et al. (Eds.): PRIMA 2014, LNAI 8861, pp. 270–285, 2014.
© Springer International Publishing Switzerland 2014

a trial-and-error approach that leverages the simulation to determine whether progressively more preferred solutions are indeed feasible (the role of the simulation in such settings is essentially as a feasibility checker). Using a simulation tool in this fashion is impractical if the space of potential solutions to explore is large [4]. Building accurate models of the social systems within which service delivery is situated is important, but difficult, and we are also obliged to replicate the potentially sub-optimal resource allocation logic of the actual system. We might also apply optimization tools, but modeling optimization problems is difficult. Indeed, it is widely recognized that a key impediment to the deployment of optimization solutions is the modeling bottleneck (good modeling requires the experience and expertise of good modelers, while good models can significantly contribute to the efficiency and effectiveness of the solving process). Existing work on combining simulation and optimization (see, for instance, [4] and [5]) does not help with our problem. Service systems are often complex multi-agent systems with a wide repertoire of agent types and inter-agent interactions for which it is difficult to devise mathematical (equational) models, as would be required by simulation or optimization tools.

In any organization, resource allocation systems are often embedded and distributed across a variety of processes, systems and decision making procedures. Changing the resource allocation logic is difficult, and sometimes meets resistance driven by organizational inertia. Making a *business case* for the deployment of improved resource allocation procedures can help, but we need to make reference to an "as-is" baseline, in order to demonstrate the extent to which an investment in optimization techniques might generate cost improvements. A simulation model helps answer this question by permitting us to explore, *in silico*, the implications of leaner resourcing (or heavier loading) on the existing systems.

It is generally known that building analytical (equational) models is difficult. This has motivated the development of agent-based modeling (ABM), which permits us to model complex systems by merely engaging in the much simpler exercise of modeling the behavior and interactions of the agents constituting the system. Our approach leverages ABM, but addresses the drawbacks of ABM - in particular, the difficulties associated with solving optimization problems discussed above - by devising a novel combination of ABM and distributed optimization, specifically distributed constraint optimization problem (DCOP) techniques. In the complex social settings involved in service delivery, much of the knolwedge relevant to the resource allocation problem remains local to specific agents and is also highly dynamic. This makes centralized optimization techniques impractical. Privacy concerns, or business-sensitive information can also prevent centralization (and hence centralized optimization). DCOP techniques do not require centralied handling of this knowledge.

Our novel combination of ABM and DCOP techniques in this paper has other benefits. Modeling all of the complex social interactions in a service delivery system can be difficult even in a DCOP model. We are able to model these interactions in a far easier fashion in an ABM model, while the DCOP model addresses only those that are directly relevant to the optimization problem. The combined ABM and DCOP model helps establish the baseline discussed earlier.

This paper extends the results of a previous study [19] which explores how a simple resource allocation policy (modeled in an ABM) could be improved by leveraging DCOP. In this study, we study two different ABM models: one identical to that considered in the previous study and a second (more sophistiacted) ABM model that allows agents to negotiate to find more optimal solutions. This study thus makes a more compelling case for the proposed approach, since it shows that even a more sophisticated resource allocation policy could be improved upon by using DCOP. This study also presents a more detailed empirical evaluation of the approach

In summary, our approach involves the following steps:

- The development of an ABM model for a service delivery system.
- Analysis of the ABM model to identify the best provisioning modes, while leaving the existing resource provisioning procedures and systems intact. This provides the baseline.
- The development of the second ABM model by exploiting the capacity of agents in inter-agents' collaboration in order to reach some degree of optimization.
- The modeling of the optimal resource allocation logic via a DCOP protocol based collection of interaction within the context of the ABM model, i.e., these interactions involve messaging between the agents modeled in the ABM model. This integrated model helps identify the cost saving accruing from optimal (or at least near-optimal) resource allocation.
- Resource allocation optimality comparisons between the baseline ABM model, enhanced ABM model, and the ABM combined with DCOP protocol model.

The rest of this paper addresses the deployment of this approach in a context closely based on the IT infrastructure management service offered by a large global service delivery business. The setting that we have modeled (involving service requests being dispatched by a central dispatcher to a pool of service workers) is on the simpler end of the spectrum of service delivery models, but an accurate reflection of the reality in this business. However, it is easy to extend the same approach to service delivery settings with a larger repertoire of actor/agent types and more complex interactions [6]. The results that we report suggest that significant efficiency gains are possible using our approach.

2   Background: Distributed Constraint Optimization Problem

DCOP techniques (sometimes referred to as DCOP *protocols*) help solve optimization problems where the relevant problem-solving knowledge (tyically represented in the form of constraints) is distributed across a collection of actors or agents (sometimes the optimization objectives are distributed as well - i.e., the objective functions are agent-specific) [7]. DCOP techniques are particularly useful in settings in which business-sensitive knowledge cannot be centralized or where privacy concerns prevent agents from sharing their knowledge with a central optimization solver. DCOP techniques build upon the class of Distributed Constraint Satisfaction Problem (DCSP) techniques by finding a complete assignment to the decision variables of interest that not only satisfies the problem constraints but also optimizes the relevant objective(s) [8]. Some of the better-known DCOP techniques include OptAPO [9], ADOPT [10] and its extensions [11][12], DPOP [13] and its extensions[14][15]. DCOP algorithms have been applied to a variety of problems (such as distributed scheduling[16], distributed sensor networks[17]).

3   Formal Problem Statement

In this section, we formalize the problem that we aim to address in this research. This formalization generalizes a number of service delivery settings, including generic customer care centers, government-to-citizen contact centers and technical support centers. The setting we use for the evaluation presented later in this paper is based on the IT infrastructure management service offered by a large organization.

The service systems of interest share a number of common characteristics. Services are delivered by Service Workers (SWs) who are typically profiled in terms of their qualifications and competencies. Clients of the service systems submit Service Requests; based on the metaphor of traditional service delivery centers where customers pick up a numbered ticket from a dispenser on arrival and go to service delivery counters when their numbers are called out, these Service Requests are often referred to as *problem tickets*, or simply *tickets*. SWs are often organized into groups based on specialist skillsets (e.g., database systems, operating system, servers etc. in the instance of an IT infrastructure management service). The model we present below does not address skill-based grouping, but can be easily extended to support settings where the nature of these groupings impacts the optimal allocation of service worker to ticket.

A ticket represents a request for a service initiated by a customer and sent to the service system. Tickets are characterized by their types such as operating system disk maintenance, user account access, patch management and so on (using, ideally, the same vocabulary used to describe SW skillsets). In this paper, we make the simplifying assumption that each ticket requires a single skill. This definition can be extended without much difficulty to deal with settings where a single ticket might require multiple skillsets to be deployed.

Formally, the problem is as follows. Given:

- A set $\mathcal{T} = \{T_1, \ldots, T_\tau\}$ of ticket types
- A set $\mathcal{S} = \{S_1, \ldots, S_\sigma\}$ of skills
- A set of N tickets, where each ticket is denoted by $Tkt_j^{T_t}$ with $j \in \{1, \ldots, N\}$ and $T_t \in \mathcal{T}$ (i.e., $Tkt_j^{T_t}$ is the j-th ticket, and is of type T_t) . Each ticket

is associated with either a deadline, or a priority indicator that effectively specifies a deadline (e.g., a priority-1 ticket must be processed in 30 minutes, a priority-2 ticket in 40 minutes and so on).

- A set of M SWs, where each service worker is denoted by SW_i^ς with $i \in \{1, \ldots, M\}$ and $\varsigma \subseteq S$ (i.e., SW_i^ς is the i-th service worker with ς representing the set of skill possessed by that worker).
- A function f_{ts} that determines the skill required to process a ticket of a certain type, where $f_{ts} : \mathcal{T} \to \mathcal{S}$.
- A vector p_s where $s \in \mathcal{S}$, providing, for each skill, the *standard* time taken by a service worker with that skill to process a ticket requiring that skill.
- A function f_{df} that determines the *real* time required for a service worker to complete a ticket with a particular skill required (for instance, $f_{df}(S_s, SW_i^\varsigma) = \bar{p}_s$). The real time is determined by the skill required for the ticket, the service worker performance factors such as experience, knowledge acquisition, and some other non-measurable or unknown modifiers. For example, a service worker can complete an account creation service in less time by practicing it over time.

Determine: An allocation of a service worker to each of the N tickets such that the objective function $max(\bar{C}_1, \ldots, \bar{C}_N)$ is *minimized*, where:

- C_{ij} denotes the completion time of the j-th ticket requiring skill S_s when processed by the i-th service worker. $C_{ij} = t_{ij} + \bar{p}_s$ where t_{ij} denotes the time when the service worker starts processing that particular ticket.
- $\bar{C}_j$ denotes the time at which the j-th ticket exits the system (completion time). (i.e. if j-th ticket is completed by i-th SW, then $\bar{C}_j = C_{ij}$)

We make the simplifying assumption that the standard time taken to process a ticket is uniquely determined by the skill that needs to be brought to bear to handle that ticket (not making this assumption adds to the complexity of the problem formulation, but the machinery presented later in this paper requires little modification). We assume that each SW has an "in-queue" of tickets allocated to that service worker. We also assume that there is no idle time between tickets in any of the queues. For example, if $SW_1^{\{S_1\}}$ is sequentially assigned to two tickets $Tkt_1^{T_1}$ and $Tkt_2^{T_1}$ with $f_{ts}(Tkt_1^{T_1}) = f_{ts}(Tkt_2^{T_1}) = S_1$, $C_{11} = 0 + \bar{p}_1$ and $\bar{C}_2 = C_{12} = C_{11} + \bar{p}_2$.

4   The ABM-Based Solutions

As discussed earlier, an agent-based simulation can help build a faithful representation of a complex social reality. In this section, we outline two ABM models that describe the current operations of the IT infrastructure management service discussed earlier.

4.1   The First ABM-Based Solution

The model firstly focuses on a simple model of dispatching service requests where for each service request received from the customer, the dispatcher first recognizes the skill required for the service request. Secondly, it identifies all SWs who have the skill for handling the request, and thirdly, the dispatcher randomly sends the service request in the form of a ticket to one of the competent SWs. In this service system, service tickets are allocated to service workers only by a *dispatcher*. In the model presented in [2], the dispatcher mediates the interaction between customers and service workers. Similarly, in our model, the dispatcher uses a simple resource allocation logic. The dispatcher uses the function f_{ts} to determine the skill required for the jobs. Tickets also have different priorities that indicate the urgency of the service request for completion. The dispatcher is responsible for sending each ticket to the input queue of a service worker, such that the SW's skill matches the skill required for the ticket. For example, if for ticket $Tkt_1^{T_2}$, $f_{ts}(Tkt_1^{T_2}) = S_1$, both $SW_1^{\{S_1\}}$ and $SW_2^{\{S_1,S_2\}}$ can be the nominee for this ticket.

Since, the dispatcher has the main role in determining which SW should take the coming ticket, the SWs have no influence on the scheduling of the tickets. Algorithm 1 represents the process of dispatching tickets.

Algorithm 1. ABM algorithm for dispatching tickets to SWs using a simple resource allocation logic

---

1: **while** receiving requests from customers **do**
2:    $Tkt_j^{T_t} \leftarrow$ the j th request with type T_t
3:    $S_s \leftarrow f_{ts}(Tkt_j^{T_t})$
4:    $SWlist \leftarrow$ a list of SWs initialized to empty
5:    **for** $i = 1$ to M **do**
6:       **if** $S_s \in \varsigma$ for SW_i^ς **then**
7:          add SW_i^ς to $SWlist$
8:       **end if**
9:    **end for**
10:    send $Tkt_j^{T_t}$ to a random SW from $SWlist$
11: **end while**

Running Example. Having described the simple resource allocation logic for dispatching service requests to suitable service workers, we illustrate the result via an example. In this example, we assume $\tau = 3, \sigma = 3, N = 4, M = 3$ which means a system of three SWs with three skills and a dispatcher that receives four tickets of three possible types.

Table 1. Tickets issued by the central dispatcher

Tickets	$Tkt_1^{T_1}$	$Tkt_2^{T_2}$	$Tkt_3^{T_3}$	$Tkt_4^{T_2}$
$f_{ts}(Ticekts)$	S_1	S_1	S_2	S_3

Table 1 indicates the sequence of four tickets issued to the dispatcher by the customers. The skill required for each ticket is identified by the function f_{ts} to help the dispatcher match the skills required with the SWs skills. Table 2 illustrates a matrix that indicates the processing time required for each pair of SWs' skills and tickets' skills. Processing time for the jth ticket on ith SW can be extracted from the following table.

Table 2. Processing time for different pairs of SWs' skills and tickets' skills

p	Ticket Skill (S_s)		
Service Workers	S_1	S_2	S_3
$SW_1^{\{S_1\}}$	20	∞	∞
$SW_2^{\{S_1,S_2\}}$	20	25	∞
$SW_3^{\{S_2,S_3\}}$	∞	25	30

Finally, with reference to Algorithm 1, the tickets are scheduled among the SWs. Table 3 represents the queues of tickets as well as the total times needed for completion of the services. Each SW is only given those services that match their skills. As a result, the makespan for this set of tickets is $max(\bar{C}_1, \ldots, \bar{C}_4) = 45$.

Table 3. Tickets Assigned based by matching skills

Service Workers	Ticket	Completion Time
$SW_1^{\{S_1\}}$	$Tkt_1^{T_1}$	20
$SW_2^{\{S_1,S_2\}}$	$Tkt_2^{T_2}, Tkt_3^{T_3}$	45
$SW_3^{\{S_2,S_3\}}$	$Tkt_4^{T_2}$	30
Makespan		45

4.2 The Second ABM-Based Solution

In the second ABM-based simulation, we used a function called f_{df} to assess the impact of SWs adaptation to their environment. In practice, there is a variety of reasons which cause SWs to complete the same types of tasks in different time duration. For instance, assume a particular SW receives different tickets with similar types in a row, such as installing different types of software on a client system. Based on the similarity of installing different software packages on the same client computer, the total time required for installing all of the software programs on the computer would be less than the summation of each of these tickets times completed in a different day. The repetition of similar types of tickets is one of the reasons resulting in the alteration of tickets processing times. The other reason for the change of processing time might be the location of tickets completed. An SW takes less processing time for completing several tickets in the same place compared to handling the same tickets in different locations. Hence, the SWs preferences for completing the tickets largely impacts on the problem objective (makespan). However, as indicated earlier, application of traditional mathematical tools suffers from two main issues; model complexities formulation and integration of information. The former pertains to the difficulties of understanding model components complexities, including their behaviors and decision making mechanisms, and the latter is impractical at least due to privacy concerns for integration of data. To overcome this dilemma, in this setting, we involve the SWs preferences factor, which enables them to have dialogue with other SWs over a decision for finding the best SW for handling the ticket (Fig. 1). To do so, when a i-th SW receives the j-th ticket with type T_t from the

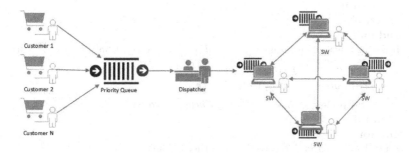

Fig. 1. The structure of a service system with four service workers including preferences

dispatcher, it estimates the time it requires for completing the ticket and stores in a value called $prefValue_i^{S_s}$. The preference value will then be shared with all other SWs within a message names *preference message*. Upon the arrival of the preference message, all SWs receive the message, estimate the time required for completing the type of ticket and inform the sender SW about that. Finally, in case any of the SWs offers less time for completing the j-ticket, the sender SW will transfer the ticket to the SW with the best offering time (Algorithm 2).

4.3   An Approach Combining ABM and DCOP

As mentioned earlier, there is no doubt about the necessity of combining ABM with some complementary tools that can reduce computational requirements by

---

Algorithm 2. The algorithm used under the second ABM model for reallocation of tickets between SWs

---

1: $SWQueue \leftarrow$ a list of tickets initialized to empty
2: **repeat**
3:     **for all** Tickets $Tkt_j^{T_t}$ received from the dispatcher **do**
4:         $S_s \leftarrow f_{ts}(Tkt_j^{T_t})$
5:         $SWQueue \leftarrow SWQueue \cup Tkt_j^{T_t}$
6:         $prefValue_i^{S_s} \leftarrow f_{df}(S_s, SW_i^c)$
7:         send preference message $(prefValue_i^{S_s})$ to all other SWs
8:         $prefValueList \leftarrow$ a list of received preference messages initialized to empty
9:         **repeat**
10:             **for all** preference messages $(prefValue_{i'\neq i}^{S_s})$ received from any $SW_{i'\neq i}^c$ **do**
11:                 $prefValueList \leftarrow prefValueList \cup prefValue_{i'\neq i}^{S_s}$
12:             **end for**
13:         **until** All preference messages received
14:         $prefValue_{i'\neq i}^{S_s} = min(prefValueList)$
15:         **if** $prefValue_{i'\neq i}^{S_s} < prefValue_i^{S_s}$ **then**
16:             **if** $Tkt_j^{T_t} \in SWQueue$ **then**
17:                 remove $Tkt_j^{T_t}$ from $SWQueue$
18:                 send $Tkt_j^{T_t}$ to $SW_{i'\neq i}^c$
19:             **end if**
20:         **end if**
21:     **end for**
22:     **for all** preference messages $(prefValue_{i'\neq i}^{S_{s'}})$ received from any $SW_{i'\neq i}^c$ **do**
23:         $prefValue_i^{S_{s'}} \leftarrow f_{df}(S_{s'}, SW_i^c)$
24:         **if** $prefValue_i^{S_{s'}} < prefValue_{i'\neq i}^{S_{s'}}$ **then**
25:             send preference message $(prefValue_i^{S_{s'}})$ to $SW_{i'\neq i}^c$
26:         **end if**
27:     **end for**
28:     **for all** tickets $Tkt_j^{T_t}$ received from other SWs **do**
29:         $SWQueue \leftarrow SWQueue \cup Tkt_j^{T_t}$
30:     **end for**
31:     implement the first ticket in $SWQueue$
32: **until** Exceeding Timeout

---

limiting the search space. In fact, not only this reduction should be considered, but also the new combination which can maintain the dynamic and distributed superiority of ABM. Moreover, the autonomy of the agents in ABM model is non-trivial. The contribution of this paper is associated with an application of DCOP's existing algorithms in an agent based modeling of a service delivery example with a simple resource allocation logic. In this paper, we applied ADOPT [10], which is a complete algorithm that can find the optimal or a solution in a user specified range of optimality. In ADOPT, each agent a_i has control over one variable x_i. The variable can take values from its domain D_i given. Constraints connect each pair of variables and limit the assignments they take. Between any pair of variables x_i and x_j, ADOPT uses valued constraints as a function $f_{ij} : D_i \times D_j \to \mathbb{N}$ that generates positive integers for the variables assignments. For a problem with a set of variables $\{x_1, x_2, \ldots, x_n\}$, set of domains $\{D_1, D_2, \ldots, D_n\}$, the objective is to find an assignment $\mathcal{A}$ that most minimizes the function $F(\mathcal{A}) = \sum_{x_i, x_j \in \{x_1, x_2, \ldots, x_n\}} f_{ij}(d_i, d_j)$. ADOPT allows agents to asynchronously change their variables' assignments, such that agents need not be inactive in order to receive a message from their neighbor agents. This important benefit improves the efficiency of the algorithm by manipulating the parallel computation among all agents, in comparison with its former DCOP algorithms that are mainly based on backtrack search, which require one agent to decide about the optimality of any final assignment. In order to facilitate the flow of messages, ADOPT takes advantage of a Depth First Search (DFS) tree, where agents are ordered in a tree based on their position in a constraint neighborhood graph. Although a DFS tree generation is an additional required step for ADOPT implementation, it is not considered a limitation for different problems, since any graph can be formed into a DFS tree.

Having described the basic elements of ADOPT, we formulate our problem using the ADOPT framework. In our model, each SW controls a set of variables that in fact indicate the decision of a SW to take or to not take some or all of the tickets. As such, using ADOPT we would be able to modify the assignments of tickets to service workers in a way that firstly, each SW is only taking the tickets that it has skills for, and secondly, the arrangement of tickets in each SW queue ensures that the optimized solution is achieved and makespan is minimized. To clarify, DCOP protocol facilitates an efficient distributed search through possible combinations of assignments of tickets to SWs leads the global optimized solution achievement. However, it is worthwhile to mention that agents only transfer the queued tickets between each other. Since any ticket is taken to be processed by any SW, that ticket would not be assigned a variable and therefore would not be counted in the DCOP algorithm.

Assuming N be the total number of tickets queued in each SW queue:

- Let $X = \{x_1, \ldots, x_N\}$ be the set of variables SW controls.
- Let $\Delta = \{\Delta_1, \ldots, \Delta_N\}$ be the set of domains where $\forall j \in \{1, \ldots, N\}, \Delta_j = \{0, 1\}$.

As mentioned earlier, ADOPT allows an agent to control only one variable. Thus, since in our settings we allocate each agent more than one variable, we define a new variable V with a new domain D that cross products of $\Delta_1 \times \ldots \times \Delta_N$ are elements of D. From now on, we use the notation $SW.\beta$ to address the element β of the SW. For instance, for a problem with $N = 2$, $SW.D = \{(0,0), (1,0), (0,1), (1,1)\}$ for $SW.V$. Given the new settings, we reformulate the service system problem as following;

- Let $\mathcal{V} = \{SW_1.V, \ldots, SW_M.V\}$ be the set of variables where M is the number of SWs.
- Let $\mathcal{D} = \{SW_1.D, \ldots, SW_M.D\}$ be the set of domains.
- For each pair of SWs (SW_a, SW_b) sharing a constraint between them (neighbors), cost function is defined as $f_{ab} : SW_a.D \times SW_b.D \to \mathbb{N}$.

– The problem objective is to find an assignment $\mathcal{A}^*$ such that $F(\mathcal{A}^*)$ is less than all other assignments

$$F(\mathcal{A}) = \min_{SW_i.V, SW_j.V \in \{SW_1.V, SW_2.V, \ldots, SW_M.V\}} f_{ij}(SW_i.D, SW_j.D)$$

For clarification of the above assumptions, we first need to define the concept of neighborhood. We define each pair of SWs neighbors if they are connected to each other by a constraint. We use soft constraints likewise in ADOPT in order to measure the value of each connected SWs assignments. This value is calculated by the cost function (f_{ab}). In our setting, every SW is connected to all other SWs which forms the problem as a complete graph. Likewise what we defined in section 3, f_{ab} is equivalent by makespan and is calculated by $max(\bar{C}_1, \ldots, \bar{C}_N)$ for a problem of N tickets. Considering the practical reality of the SWs completing the tasks in parallel, makespan would be the time required for a SW with the longest queue. As such, we try to minimize the longest queue by finding the best assignment $\mathcal{A}^*$. The final important issue is extending the constraints to n-ary constraints. So far, we demonstrated the binary constraints between any pair of SWs. In case we have more than two SWs, the algorithm requires to be compatible with constraints defined over more than two variables. In [10], the authors demonstrated the ability of ADOPT algorithm to be extended to n-ary constraints, although it can impact on the efficiency of the algorithm. Due to limitation of space, we did not mention the ADOPT pseudocode in this paper, however, we refer readers to cite [10] for this regard.

Example. In the following, we formulate a sample problem using the approach in section 4.3. As describing the algorithm for the above example requires a large number of steps and space, we have only described the problem metrics required for a small example with two SWs $SW_1^{\{S_1, S_2\}}$ and $SW_2^{\{S_1, S_2\}}$, for two tickets $Tkt_1^{T_1}$ and $Tkt_2^{T_1}$ with $f_{ts}(Tkt_1^{T_1}) = S_1$ and $f_{ts}(Tkt_2^{T_1}) = S_2$. For a problem of two tickets, each SW would require two variables $SW_1^{\{S_1, S_2\}}.x_1$, $SW_1^{\{S_1, S_2\}}.x_2$ and $SW_2^{\{S_1, S_2\}}.x_1$, $SW_2^{\{S_1, S_2\}}.x_2$.

The new variables for two service workers are defined by $SW_1^{\{S_1, S_2\}}.V$ and $SW_2^{\{S_1, S_2\}}.V$ with the identical domain $\{0, 1, 2, 3\}$ represents the cross products of original domains $\Delta_1 \times \Delta_2 = \{(0,0), (0,1), (1,0), (1,1)\}$.

5   Experimental Results

For our experiments, we have designed data that reflects real-life request arrivals. Throughout our experiments we examined the effect of each of three models on the defined system objectives; makespan, priority fulfillment, and tardiness. Makespan is defined as $max(\bar{C}_1, \ldots, \bar{C}_N)$ which is equivalent to the completion time of the last ticket to leave the system. Priority fulfillment reflects customer expectations for the completion of requests as in real-life problems where customers require some requests to be completed sooner than others. In our experiments we categorized tickets into four priority levels, $P1, P2, P3$ and $P4$. Tickets labeled as $P1$ are of the highest priority, whereas $P4$ tickets are recognized as the lowest priority ones. Since makespan and tardiness are measured by time, each SW perceives the priority of j-th ticket by its target completion time Ω_j. Henceforth, $P1, P2, P3, P4$ tickets are expected to be processed within $30, 40, 50, 60$ minutes from their time of arrival, respectively. Ticket arrival time follows a Poisson model pattern, distributed from minute 0 to minute 400. In total, there are 51 tickets generated in this time frame. Tardiness for j-th ticket (T_j) is measured by its completion time and target completion time by $T_j = max(C_j - \Omega_j, 0)$. Total tardiness is calculated by $\sum_{j=1}^{N} T_j$. In the end, we compare the effectiveness of three models in terms of the successful number of tickets that meet the priority levels.

In all three models, we applied three SWs $SW_1^{\{S_1,S_3\}}$ with skills S_1 and S_3, $SW_2^{\{S_1,S_2\}}$ with skills S_1 and S_2, and $SW_3^{\{S_2,S_3\}}$. The processing time required for tickets with skills S_1, S_2 and S_3 are 15, 20, and 25, respectively. For implementing the experiments, we used FRODO version 2.11 [18] freely accessible under GNU license.

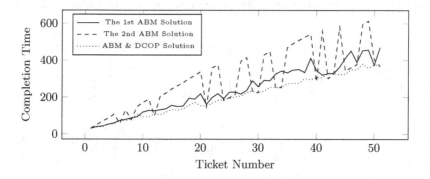

Fig. 2. Comparison between Completion Times

Fig. 2 compares the effectiveness of the three models in minimizing ticket completion times. This will eventually create better achievement in makespan. The first ABM model relies on the dispatcher decisions for assignment of tickets towards SWs. Although the dispatcher has the knowledge of distributing tickets to SWs with the right skill, the model lacks negotiations between SWs for finding the best solution that minimizes the makespan. This was included in the second ABM solution, with SWs negotiating over their preferences for taking a particular ticket (Algorithm 2). However, the improvements for minimizing tickets service time is only limited to few tickets such as the 6th, 8th, and 12th tickets. The reason for this occurrence is due to the limitation of the settings, considering that the size of the SWs tickets queue changes dependant on acceptance/rejection of tickets. In other words, an SW sends a ticket to an SW that can process a ticket in less time, yet it can cause accumulation of tickets in one SW queue and with adverse effects on makespan. Fig. 2 illustrates a remarkably consistent optimization in the reduction of tickets service time. This occurred by utilizing abilities of DCOP protocol for using SWs distributed knowledge to create an optimized solution. DCOP protocol facilitated the search process towards combinations of tickets assignments between SWs, merging to an optimized solution. Fig. 3 demonstrates the impact of three models in ticket tardiness. The third model presents the most successful minimization of tardiness, with the most number of tickets processed with zero tardiness. In all models, the number of tickets with positive tardiness happens more frequently as the number of tickets entering the system increases. Yet, when combining DCOP with ABM in the third model, the ability of the model to keep tardiness as low as possible is remarkable. Likewise in Fig. 2, the second model shows that only in a few occasions does it offer better results than the first model. Fig. 4 presents the significant impact of the three models on accumulated tardiness as the number of tickets entering the system increases over time. It can be concluded from both Fig. 3 and Fig. 4 that the first and second model end up with more poor results compared to the third model in case of customers requests for services increases. Having described the strong performance of combining ABM with DCOP in contrast to both simple and improved ABM models, it can be

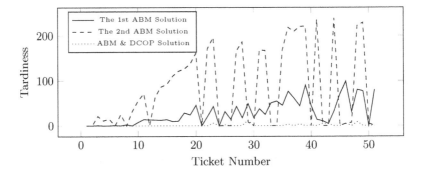

Fig. 3. Comparison between Tardiness

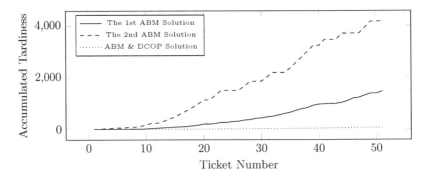

Fig. 4. Comparison between Accumulated Tardiness

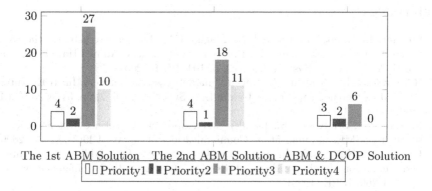

Fig. 5. Comparison between the number of Priorities Unfulfilled

expected that the increase of makespan and tardiness in the first and second models naturally cause failure to meet customers' priority requirements. Fig. 5 illustrates this effect by a comparison between models in exceeding the required time for processing tickets with different priorities.

6 Conclusion

Service delivery optimization is considered to be an important problem impacting on organizational profitability. However, service delivery optimization faces numerous difficulties, which hinder the suitable installation of resources for customer requests. A sub-optimum allocation of tasks to resources places the organization under the burden of unnecessary surplus costs. From this point of view, implementation of a system that can firstly, present a fair, detailed model of system current settings and secondly, provide optimized solutions, is necessary. This paper offers a novel solution which combines agent-based modeling (ABM) and distributed constraint optimization (DCOP) on a real-life sample of a service delivery problem. ABM is used to model the social context of service delivery, while the use of DCOP techniques enables us to bring dynamic knowledge (and insights) residing in service workers to bear on the optimal resource allocation problem. This eliminates the unrealistic requirement that all service workers continually communicate their local knowledge to a traditional (centralized) optimization solver. This paper completes and extends the previous model [19] similarly applied in service delivery problem. In our future work, we aim to develop the experiments to examine the efficiency of optimization using a variety of DCOP algorithms. We will also provide an extension of this problem to foster efficient group formations for solving those tasks requiring more than one service provider across multiple skills.

References

1. Spohrer, J., Vargo, S.L., Caswell, N., Maglio, P.P.: The service system is the basic abstraction of service science. In: Proceedings of the 41st Annual Hawaii International Conference on System Sciences, p. 104. IEEE (2008)
2. Ramaswamy, L., Banavar, G.: A formal model of service delivery. In: IEEE International Conference on, Services Computing, SCC 2008, vol. 2, pp. 517–520. IEEE (2008)
3. Maglio, P.P., Srinivasan, S., Kreulen, J.T., Spohrer, J.: Service systems, service scientists, SSME, and innovation. Communications of the ACM 49(7), 81–85 (2006)
4. Glover, F., Kelly, J.P., Laguna, M.: New advances for wedding optimization and simulation. In: Proceedings of 1999 Winter Simulation Conference, vol. 1, pp. 255–260. IEEE (1999)
5. Luo, Y., Lim, E.: Simulation-based optimization over discrete sets with noisy constraints. In: Proceedings of the 2011 Winter Simulation Conference (WSC), pp. 4008–4020. IEEE (2011)
6. Ghose, A.K., Koliadis, G.: Actor eco-systems: From high-level agent models to executable processes via semantic annotations (2007)
7. Yokoo, M., Ishida, T., Durfee, E.H., Kuwabara, K.: Distributed constraint satisfaction for formalizing distributed problem solving. In: Proceedings of the 12th International Conference on Distributed Computing Systems, pp. 614–621. IEEE (1992)
8. Yokoo, M., Hirayama, K.: Algorithms for distributed constraint satisfaction: A review. Autonomous Agents and Multi-Agent Systems 3(2), 185–207 (2000)
9. Mailler, R., Lesser, V.: Solving distributed constraint optimization problems using cooperative mediation. In: Proceedings of the Third International Joint Conference on Autonomous Agents and Multiagent Systems, vol. 1, pp. 438–445. IEEE Computer Society (2004)
10. Modi, P.J., Shen, W.-M., Tambe, M., Yokoo, M.: An asynchronous complete method for distributed constraint optimization. AAMAS 3, 161–168 (2003)
11. Yeoh, W., Felner, A., Koenig, S.: BnB-ADOPT: An asynchronous branch-and-bound DCOP algorithm. In: Proceedings of the 7th International Joint Conference on Autonomous Agents and Multiagent Systems, vol. 2, pp. 591–598. International Foundation for Autonomous Agents and Multiagent Systems (2008)
12. Yeoh, W., Felner, A., Koenig, S.: IDB-ADOPT: A depth-first search DCOP algorithm. In: Oddi, A., Fages, F., Rossi, F. (eds.) CSCLP 2008. LNCS, vol. 5655, pp. 132–146. Springer, Heidelberg (2009)
13. Petcu, A., Faltings, B.: A scalable method for multiagent constraint optimization. No. EPFL-REPORT-52705 (2005)
14. Petcu, A., Faltings, B., Parkes, D.C.: MDPOP: Faithful distributed implementation of efficient social choice problems. In: Proceedings of the Fifth International Joint Conference on Autonomous Agents and Multiagent Systems, pp. 1397–1404. ACM (2006)
15. Petcu, A., Faltings, B.: ODPOP: an algorithm for open/distributed constraint optimization. Proceedings of the National Conference on Artificial Intelligence 21(1), 703 (1999, 2006)
16. Liu, J.-S., Sycara, K.P.: Exploiting Problem Structure for Distributed Constraint Optimization. In: ICMAS, vol. 95, pp. 246–254 (1995)
17. Modi, P.J., Jung, H., Tambe, M., Shen, W.-M., Kulkarni, S.: A dynamic distributed constraint satisfaction approach to resource allocation. In: Walsh, T. (ed.) CP 2001. LNCS, vol. 2239, pp. 685–700. Springer, Heidelberg (2001)

18. Leaute, T., Ottens, B., Szymanek, R.: FRODO: a FRamework for Open/ Distributed Optimization Version 2.6. 2 User Manual (2010)
19. Mohagheghian, M., Sindhgatta, R., Ghose, A.: Combining Agent Based Modeling with Distributed Constraint Optimization for Service Delivery Optimization. In: Proceedings of the EDOC-2014 Workshop on Service-Oriented Enterprise Architecture for Enterprise Engineering. IEEE CS Press (2014)

A Dynamic Route-Exchanging Mechanism for Anticipatory Traffic Management

Ryo Kanamori[1] and Takayuki Ito[2]

[1] Nagoya University, Furo-cho, Chikusa-ku, Nagoya 464-8603, Japan
kanamori.ryo@nagoya-u.jp
[2] Nagoya Institute of Technology, Gokiso, Showa-ku, Nagoya 466-8555, Japan
ito.takayuki@nitech.ac.jp

Abstract. In this paper, we propose a dynamic route-exchanging mechanism based on anticipatory stigmergy and demonstrate its efficiency. Next-generation traffic management systems based on probe vehicle data have been attracting attention. Ito et al.[2] [3] [4] previously proposed a traffic management method based on anticipatory stigmergy that can search for an alternative route to avoid expected congestion by sharing the probe vehicles' expected locations in the near future, and they found that anticipatory stigmergy works well in particular experimental settings. On the other hand, Takahashi et al[6] identified two key issues: (1) The oscillation of congestion occurs because drivers do not know other drivers' decision making. This problem is well-known as the El Farol Bar Problem or the congestion game. (2) The saturation level of navigation systems could affect the performance of a dynamic route exchanging-mechanism. In this paper, we propose a new dynamic route-exchanging mechanism that can address the above two issues. In the basic procedure, each vehicle submits its intention about its near-future position (60 seconds). Then the traffic management center computes the near-future congestion information for each link. This information is anticipatory stigmergy. If there is an over-congested link after 60 seconds, the vehicles assumed to come to those links are allowed to negotiate with each other so that some of them will change their near-future routes. In this mechanism, vehicles automatically negotiate based on their rational judgment on the trade-off between travel time needed for passing the assigned route and the "concession coefficient" that represents how a driver can concede the way. The experimental results demonstrate that our new route-exchanging mechanism performs well for the efficiency of traffic flow when the saturation level of probe vehicles is greater than 70%.

Keywords: Anticipatory Stigmergy, Dynamic Route-exchanging Mechanism, and Multi-agent Traffic Simulation.

1 Introduction

In this paper, we propose a new dynamic route-exchanging mechanism based on automated negotiation among autonomic vehicles for next generation transportation systems, and validate its efficiency by using multiagent simulation. Recently, ITS (Intelligent Transportation Systems) have been focused to solve the traffic congestion problem.

H.K. Dam et al. (Eds.): PRIMA 2014, LNAI 8861, pp. 286–293, 2014.
© Springer International Publishing Switzerland 2014

ITS includes dynamic congestion pricing and real-time travel information providing based on the recent drastic evolution and spread of vehicle sensor systems and car navigation systems.

We have been working on building next generation traffic management system. In particular, we are focusing on shared information among semi-autonomic vehicles to solve and relief congestions in a city. These shared information is called "stigmergy"[1] that means indirect shared information for making a group or a society act and behave efficiently. In the real world, we utilize congestion information every day from the classic car-counting gates, where car-passage information are aggregated and estimated statistically, and inform them to the vehicle via radios, TVs, etc. This is called "long-term stigmergy". Also, recently, the probe vehicles that can have and share more dynamic car information emerges in the real world. For example, these probe cars can share the recent past information, like the past information in the most recent 60 seconds. This information is expected as the current advanced way to solve congestion problem in the real world. This is called "short-term stigmergy."

Further, Ito et al. have proposed "anticipatory stigmergy" that is shared **near-future** traffic information, and showed its possibility to efficiently solve congestion problem[2] [3] [4]. More concretely, they defined anticipatory stigmergy as a near-future congestion information in road networks. In particular, for generating anticipatory stigmergy, each vehicle submits its near future-position, like 60 seconds future position, where he/she is expected to be. In the real world, in the future, we believe that this will be possible because each vehicle will be equipped advanced car-navigation systems.

However, Takahashi et al. identified the following two important issues on their previous approaches[6]. (1) **oscillation of congestion** happens because drivers do not know the other drivers' decision making. This is a well-known problem as El Farol Bar problem or congestion games. (2) The **saturation level** (penetration level) of car-navigation systems could affect the performance of the dynamic route exchanging mechanism. When the saturation levels is very low, their mechanism itself cannot work. On the other hand, if the saturation level is very high, oscillation problem happens again. We have to find the adequate level of saturation of the navigation systems.

We propose a new route exchanging mechanism among vehicles to overcome oscillation problem. In our traffic management model, each vehicle submits its intention on its own near-future (60 seconds) position to the traffic manager that could be a facility or a device equipped on the road network. Then the manager computes the near-future (60 seconds) congestion for each link (road). This near-future congestion information is **anticipatory stigmergy**. If there is an over-congested link after 60 seconds, then the vehicles supposed to come to those links are allowed to negotiate with each other so that some of them will change their near future routes. In this mechanism, vehicles automatically negotiate based on their rational judgement on trade-off between "travel time" for passing the assigned route and "concession coefficient" that represents how a driver can concede or compromise their way. We validated that the proposed route-exchanging mechanism is effective for reducing the total travel times for vehicles and the total lost time by congestions.

In terms of (2)**saturation level of navigation systems**, we explicitly include the saturation ratio to estimate traffic volume based on the anticipatory stigmergy. For example, when the saturation level is 50%, this means only the half of entire vehicles have navigation systems, thus it is rational to estimate approximately that double of the estimated numbers of vehicles could exist on one certain link. To validate this, we conducted sensitivity analysis based on traffic simulations.

2   Traffic Management Based on Anticipatory Stigmergy

2.1   Past Stigmergy (Case 1)

In Case 1, vehicles manage past stigmergies that combines the long-term stigmergy and short-term stigmergy to search routes. The long-term stigmergy is all of the past travel time data of the vehicles while the short-term stigmergy is the travel time data in only the most recent 60 seconds.

$t_{past}(x)$ is the travel time of link x for a vehicle based on the past stigmergy.

$$t_{past}(x) = \omega \times t_{long}(x) + (1 - \omega) \times t_{short}(x) \tag{1}$$

where ω is the weight of the long-term stigmergy ($0 \leq \omega \leq 1$). Long term stigmergy updates for every 24 hours (1 day) and the weight set to 0.6 by our sensitivity analysis.

$t_{long}(x)$ is the travel time of link x for a vehicle based on the long term stigmergy. It is calculated from the average $ave_{long}(x)$ and the standard deviation $sd(x)$ of the entire past travel times for link x.

$$t_{long}(x) = ave_{long}(x) + \rho \times sd(x) \tag{2}$$

where ρ is the weight for standard deviation. We assume the long-term stigmergy is updated everyday and the weight for standard deviation ρ is 0.01 by our sensitivity analysis.

$t_{short}(x)$(Eq. (3)) is the travel time of link x for a vehicle based on the short term stigmergy that is travel time information in the most recent 60 seconds (unit-times).

$$t_{short}(x) = \begin{cases} ave_{short}(x) & (pv(x) > 0, x \in VA, \& cn = 1) \\ t_0(x) & (otherwise) \end{cases} \tag{3}$$

where $ave_{short}(x)$ is the average of travel time in the most recent 60 unit-times (seconds), VA means the vicinity area, $pv(x)$ is the passage volumes of the link, and $t_0(x)$ is free travel time which is the basic travel time if there is no vehicle passed in the 60 seconds. In detail, $t_0(x) = \lfloor |x|/v_{max}(x) \rfloor$, where $v_{max}(x)$ defines the maximum speed and $|x|$ is the distance of link x. If this vehicle is equipped a car navigation system that can handle stigmergies (means a probe car), $cn = 1$. Otherwise $cn = 0$.

$t_{short}(x)$ is updated every 60 unit-times (seconds). Each probe vehicle utilizes this short-term stigmergy information to search for new routes every 60 unit-times while traveling. Also, we do not include the standard deviation because it is statistically hard to get enough travel time data in the short time, i.e., in 60 unit-times.

We assume that each vehicle can gain the short-term stigmergy in only their vicinity because this stigmergy is very recent information. We define "the vicinity" as 2 links away from the vehicle (by the "manhattan" distance). Vehicles can not get the short-term stigmergy outside of their vicinity. Thus they use the free flow travel time as the short term stigmergy for outside of their vicinity.

2.2 Anticipatory Stigmergy (Case 2)

Anticipatory stigmergy is the near-future congestion information in road networks. By using the past stigmergy each vehicle submits the link where it moves on after 60 unit-times as its intention. The traffic manager gathers these intentions, and identifies expected congestion links. This congestion information is shared as anticipatory stigmergy. Then alternative routes (detour routes) are searched by the vehicles who will be on the estimated congestion links. Then, some of these vehicles are assigned to the alternative routes to avoid congestion.

The detailed procedure of routing based on anticipatory stigmergy described as the following steps.

(Step 1). Routes are provided to each vehicles based on the past stigmergy from a traffic manager.

(Step 2). Vehicles submit expected links, as an intention, to a traffic manager as to where they will be in the next 60 unit-times.

(Step 3). A traffic manager generates anticipatory stigmergy, and share it with the vehicles. Anticipatory stigmergy is information about the estimated travel times for all links in a road network. The estimated travel time for a link is calculated by using the submitted intentions by the link performance function defined by the American Bureau of Public Road (BPR)[5].

In Eq. (4), $t_{ant}(x)$ is a travel time of link x calculated by anticipatory stigmergies, i.e., intentions after 60 seconds.

$$t_{ant}(x) = \begin{cases} t_0(x)\left(1 + \alpha \left(\dfrac{Vol(x)/Sat}{\gamma \times Cap(x)}\right)^{\beta}\right) & (x \in VA) \\ t_0(x) & (otherwise) \end{cases} \tag{4}$$

where $0.0 < Sat < 1.0$ is the saturation levels of car-navigation systems, VA means the vicinity area, $Vol(x)$ is traffic volumes after 60 seconds, and $Cap(x)$ is the capacity of link x. $\alpha = 0.48$ and $\beta = 2.48$ are the parameters in reference to BPR function. γ is the adjustment parameter about traffic volume because of the limitation of the traffic simulator, i.e., cellular automaton in this study. We set $\gamma = 0.4$. $t_{ant}(x)$, is a free flow travel time if the traffic volume after 60 seconds is 0.

(Step 4). Vehicles search for the best route to their destination nodes based on the above link travel times with anticipatory stigmergies, $t_{ant}(x)$.

However, **oscillation of congestion** tends to occur if many vehicles select a similar route by anticipatory stigmergies. To overcome the oscillation, we propose a method to re-assign the different alternative routes to these vehicles to avoid congestion.

To identify "congested" link after 60 seconds, we define the threshold as the half amount of the capacity, $Cap(x)/2$, for that link. If the expected number of vehicles is more than this threshold, we identify this link will be congested. Some of the vehicles that are expected to come to this link will be re-assigned to the different alternative routes.

The different alternative routes are searched by the anticipatory stigmergy, and assign this alternative routes to the **randomly** selected vehicles that overflowed the capacity of that link. The number of the vehicles that is rerouted, $Reroute(x)$, is determined by $Reroute(x) = Vol(x)/Sat - \gamma \times Cap(x)$, where $Vol(x)$ is the traffic volume of link x after 60 seconds calculated based on past stigmergy, $Cap(x)$ is the capacity of link x, γ is the adjustment value of traffic volume, and $0 < Sat < 1.0$ is the saturation level of the navigation system. $Reroute(x)$ takes the saturation level into account because the estimated number of vehicles is largely affected by it. If we estimate 30 vehicles on a link with the saturation level 30%, then it would be rational to estimate it as that **at most** $30 \times 1/0.30 = 90$ vehicles will be there.

2.3   Exchanging Routes by Negotiation (Case 3)

In previous section, in Case 2, we divided the vehicles into two groups: one for alternative routes (called alternative-route-group) while the other for the original routes (original-route-group). In Case 2, the alternative-route-group is **forced** to select the alternative routes if congestion is expected to happen.

In Case 3, we propose a route-exchanging negotiation mechanism. When route assignment happens, if vehicle A in the alternative-route-group finds the alternative route is very detour for him/her, then vehicle is allowed to make a request to another vehicle in the original-route-group so that vehicle A can select the original route instead of the alternative route while another vehicle concedes to select the alternative route.

Figure 1 shows an example of our exchanging negotiation mechanism. Vehicles have original route (or) and alternative route (ar). The original routes are the route calculated by the past stigmergy. This is because this congestion itself was expected by the past stigmergy. The alternative route is calculated by the anticipatory stigmergy in this mechanism. While alternative-route-group selects "ar", original-route-group selects "or" as default.

Here, when vehicle 1 prefers or1 to ar1, and vehicle 3 prefers or3 to ar3, then vehicle 1 make a request to vehicle 3 to exchange their group. If vehicle 3 agrees the request, then they agreed to be exchanged. Finally, while vehicle 3 joins alternative-route group, vehicle 1 joins original-route-group. That means vehicle 1 goes to his original route while vehicle 3 goes to his alternative route. The probability, P_{req}, to make a request to exchange and the probability, P_{agree}, to agree the request are defined based on the logit model described below.

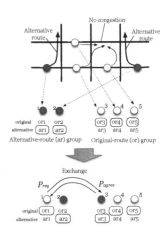

Fig. 1. The Flow of Negotiation

In order to model vehicle's judgement based on its driver's preference in exchanging negotiation, we employ the logit modelfor its basis. The logit model is one of the discrete choice models based on utility theory and it is applicable to travel behavior analysis and traffic planning.

The probability of making a request P_{req} is defined as equation (5).

$$P_{req} = \frac{exp(-\beta c(or))}{exp(-\beta c(or)) + exp(-\beta c(ar))}, \tag{5}$$

where $c(r)$ is the travel time on the route r. To calculate $c(r)$, we use the **past** stigmergy because we need to estimate more actual travel time for the route. $c(ar)$ represents the travel time for alternative route that is searched by the anticipatory stigmergy. $c(or)$ represents the travel time for original route that is searched by the past stigmergy.

The probability of making an agreement to exchange is given by equation (6).

$$P_{agree} = \frac{exp(-\beta c(ar) + p)}{exp(-\beta c(or)) + exp(-\beta c(ar) + p)}, \tag{6}$$

where p is a **concession coefficient** that represents driver's preference or strategy and affects this vehicle's acceptance of an exchanging request. For example, the coefficient would become higher while commuting, and lower while enjoying leisure time.

Vehicle i's utility for a route r can be defined as $U_i(r) = -\beta c(r) + \varepsilon$. β is a sensitivity parameter for the difference between alternative and original routes. If β is less, the vehicle does concede more. We set $\beta = 0.1$ after some sensitive analysis to show the effectiveness of our exchanging mechanism. ε is a random error term including several errors, e.g., measurement error and the other factors that can not be measured. We can assume that ε is defined as the widely used Gumbel distribution.

3   Traffic Simulator and Rad Network

There are many meso-simulation and micro-simulation systems as traffic simulators. In this paper, to treat each vehicle discretely (not continuously), we developed traffic simulation as a cellular automaton model, based on the popular rule, "Rule 184"[7]. The main aim of this traffic simulator is to clarify the effectiveness of our proposed mechanism to provide stigmergies and negotiation among vehicles to reduce congestion. *We do not intend to reproduce the actual travel time or actual vehicle behavior in the real world.* Thus these rules are simple. Elaboration of simulation itself is a future work. And we use a simple 9*9 grid road network and set 1000 vehicles (100 vehicles * 10 Origin-Destination) randomly.

4   Experimental Results

We compare the effectiveness of traffic flow, and verify the route-exchanging negotiation in Case 1 - 3. The following are the strategies for managing traffic congestion.

– Case1: Past stigmergy

– Case2: Anticipatory stigmergy
– Case3: Anticipatory stigmergy with route-exchanging negotiation mechanism

We conducted 500 days of simulation. OD information and the short term stigmergies are reset for each date. Long term stigmergies are accumulated in 500 days. In this analysis, we used the results of the last 100 days because the results are stable and converged in the last 100 days.

First, we assume 100% of the vehicles have a navigation device to send and receive stigmergy information (the saturation level is 100%).

4.1   Total Travel Time in All Cases

The total travel time is a typical measure to see the efficiency of the traffic flow. Figure 2 shows the averages in all cases.

While the total travel time in Case 1 is 615,182(sec × volume), the total travel time in Case 2 is 597,218(sec × volume) and more efficient. We confirmed statistical significance of 5 % between Case 1 and Case 2. Case 3, whose total travel time is 595,208 (sec × volume), outperformed Case 2. We confirmed statistical significance of 5 % between Case 1 and Case 3 as well. However, we cannot confirm statistical significance of 5 % between Case 2 and Case 3.

In summary, route assignment strategy based on anticipatory stigmergy (Case 2) can perform well in total travel time. In addition, negotiation mechanism (Case 3) for route assignment can perform more efficiently.

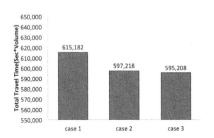

Fig. 2. Total Travel Time in All Cases

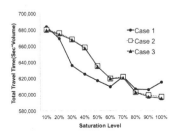

Fig. 3. Total Travel Time for Saturation Levels

4.2   Total Travel Time for Saturation Levels

So far we assumed 100% vehicles have a device, e.g., a car-navigation system, to send and receive information . In this section we investigate the saturation level of these devices. Figure 3 shows the result of total travel time by saturation levels in all cases.

When more than 70% vehicles have the device, case 2 and case 3 that utilize anticipatory stigmergy perform well. This is because our dynamic assignment strategy of anticipatory stigmergy can flexibly change its assignment weight with saturation levels. Especially, when more than 90% vehicles have the device, we confirm statistically significant difference of 5%.

When less than 60% vehicle have the device, case 1 performs well. Because there are many vehicles that cannot handle stigmergy make unpredicted congestion and even if some vehicles are assigned "detour" alternative route, he/she again faces with this unpredicted congestions. In addition, negotiation mechanism for route assignment works better than random assignment in all saturation levels although we cannot confirm statistically significant difference.

5 Conclusion

In this paper, we propose a dynamic route-exchanging mechanism based on anticipatory stigmergy and demonstrate its efficiency. Anticipatory stigmergy is the shared **near-future** traffic information. To avoid oscillation of congestions, we built a route-exchanging negotiation mechanism. Our experimental results demonstrated that the traffic flow efficiency was improved by assigning route based on our dynamic route-exchanging mechanism based on anticipatory stigmergy. One of future works is to include the uncertainty of the route selections in driver behaviors.

References

1. Dorigo, M., Gambardella, L.M.: Ant colony system: A cooperative learning approach to the traveling salesman problem pp. 53 – 66 (1997)
2. Ito, T., Kanamori, R., Takahashi, J., Maestre, I.M., de la Hoz, E.: The comparison of stigmergy strategies for decentralized traffic congestion control: Preliminary results. In: Anthony, P., Ishizuka, M., Lukose, D. (eds.) PRICAI 2012. LNCS, vol. 7458, pp. 146–156. Springer, Heidelberg (2012)
3. Kanamori, R., Takahashi, J., Ito, T.: Evaluation of anticipatory stigmergy strategies for traffic management. In: Proceedings of IEEE Vehicular Networking Conference (VNC), pp. 33–39 (2012)
4. Kanamori, R., Takahashi, J., Ito, T.: Evaluation of traffic management strategies with anticipatory stigmergy. Journal of Information Processing (2014)
5. Sheffi, Y.: Urban transportation networks: Equilibrium analysis with mathematical programming methods 1(1), 53–66 (1985)
6. Takahashi, J., Kanamori, R., Ito, T.: Stability evaluation of route assignment strategy by a foresight-route under a decentralized processing environment. In: WI/IAT2013, pp. 405–410 (2013)
7. Wolfram, S.: Theory and application of cellular automata. World Scientific, Singapore (1986)

Modelling Dynamic Normative Understanding in Agent Societies

Christopher K. Frantz[1], Martin K. Purvis[1], Bastin Tony Roy Savarimuthu[1], and Mariusz Nowostawski[2]

[1] Department of Information Science, University of Otago, New Zealand
{christopher.frantz,martin.purvis,tony.savarimuthu}@otago.ac.nz
[2] Faculty of Computer Science and Media Technology,
Gjøvik University College, Norway
mariusz.nowostawski@hig.no

Abstract. Agent-based Modelling offers strong prospects in the context of institutional modelling, which, from historical perspective, centres around the question of how far institutional instruments might have affected social and economic outcomes. To provide a richer representation of the institution formation process in the context of social simulation, we propose a norm generalisation process that uses an extended version of Crawford and Ostrom's institutional grammar and incorporates aspects from the area of social psychology. We believe that this approach offers a good compromise between generalisability and modelling detail. We briefly showcase this approach in the context of a scenario from the area of institutional economics to highlight its explanatory power.

Keywords: Norms, Institutions, Institutional Grammar, Norm Generalisation, Norm Synthesis, Dynamic Deontics, Maghribi Traders Coalition, Social Simulation, Agent-Based Modelling.

1 Introduction

Institutional modelling has received increasing attention in the area of multi-agent systems, and multi-agent-based simulation, such as in [9,1,20]. One central driver is the continued interest in explaining socio-economic development based on the institutional environment that either fostered or restrained economic development, which is a key theme of the area of New Institutional Economics [21]. Agent-based modelling is particularly useful in this context, since it can model human interaction on multiple levels of social organisation (micro, meso, macro).

In this connection our contribution concerns the development of a generalisable and accessible approach for the representation of institutions, here understood in their various forms, ranging from conventions, norms, to rules. In this work we augment an institutional representation structure, an extended version [6] of Crawford and Ostrom's institutional grammar [3], with a means of generalising norms from observed action experiences. By thus integrating 'structure' and 'process', we provide an integrated representation of social concepts

H.K. Dam et al. (Eds.): PRIMA 2014, LNAI 8861, pp. 294–310, 2014.

beyond the current precondition-deontic combination approach (see e.g. [14]). We illustrate the application of this mechanism using a specific scenario from the area of institutional economics.

In Section 2 we lay out the motivation in more detail. Section 3 provides a brief introduction of the institutional grammar, followed by the description of the norms generalisation process (Section 4). In Section 5 we apply the proposed mechanism to a simulation of our guiding scenario, concluding with a discussion and contextualisation of the contribution in Section 6.

2   Scenario Background and Motivation

To illustrate our present work, we employ a long-distance trading scenario metaphor inspired by the Maghribi Traders Coalition [11]. Under those arrangements, trade organisation was largely informal – traders delegated the transport and sale of goods to fellow traders in remote locations under the promise to reciprocate that service, an aspect that allowed them to expand the geographic range of their operations. Traders thus relied on mutual compliance; individuals that were suspected of embezzling profits, i.e. cheating, faced exclusion from trade.

In this society traders could at the same time adopt two roles: 1) *sender*, and 2) *operator*. Senders sent goods to other operators who then facilitated the actual sale and returned the realized profits to the sender.

We entertain a comparatively broad understanding of institutions [15,11], interpreting institutions as 'manifestations of social behaviour' that extend from conventions, via (informal) social norms, to (formal) rules. For this reason we seek to operationalise a general representation for institutions, such as that found in Crawford and Ostrom's Grammar of Institutions [3], which has been refined [6] to step beyond a descriptive perspective and support the modelling of emerging institutions. For our purposes the effectiveness of the 'grammar' lies in its human-readable interpretation, consideration of social structures (e.g. actors), as well as its cross-disciplinary applicability (see [19,18,9]). In the context of social simulation it can thus serve as an expressive interface between the experimenter and the observed artificial society. The present work's contribution is to augment this structural representation with a systematic process that describes how individuals can develop normative understanding based on generalised experience and observations.

3   Nested ADICO (nADICO)

The concept of Nested ADICO (nADICO) [6] builds on the essential purpose of the original institutional grammar [3] to represent conventions (or shared strategies[1]), norms and rules in the form of *institutional statements*. It consists

---

[1] A differentiation of 'shared strategies' beyond the notion introduced by Crawford and Ostrom [3] is discussed by Ghorbani et al. [8].

of five components (with the acronym ADICO), and is briefly explained in the following:[2]

- *A*ttributes (**A**) – describe the characteristics of individuals or groups of individuals that are subject to an institution;
- *D*eontics (**D**) – explicate whether the institutional statement is of prescriptive or permissive nature, originally based on deontic primitives (e.g. may, must, must not);
- A*I*m (**I**) – describes an action or outcome associated with the institutional statement;
- *C*onditions (**C**) – describe the circumstances under which a statement applies, which can include spatial, temporal and procedural aspects; and
- *O*r else (**O**) – describes consequences of non-compliance to a statement described by the above four components – 'Or else' itself can be a nested institutional statement.

This grammar allows for the expression of statements of varying nature and strength, representing different institution types, while allowing a straightforward transformation from natural language.

A convention, for example, can be adequately expressed using the components AIC, e.g.: **Traders (A) trade fair (I) when being observed (C).** Adding the *D*eontics component to the statement extends it to a norm statement: **Traders (A)** *must* **(D) trade fair (I) when being observed (C).** Finally, adding a consequence (*O*r else), constitutes a norm or a rule [6]:

> **Traders (A_0) must (D_0) trade fair (I_0) when being observed (C_0),** *or else observers (A_1) must (D_1) report this (I_1) in any case (C_1).*

Institutional statements can be *nested vertically* (as shown above), in which a consequential statement backs a statement it monitors (above: ADIC(ADIC)). Ideally this enables the modelling of comprehensive chains of responsibility. Beyond this, institutional statements can be *horizontally nested*, i.e. combined by logical operators that describe their co-occurrence (e.g. ADIC *and* ADIC) or alternative occurrence (inclusive or: ADIC *or* ADIC; exclusive or: ADIC *xor* ADIC). The formalised syntax is described in [6].

4   From Experiences to Institutions

Although conventions and norms surround us, we are often barely conscious of them and how they arise. Generally, norms are understood to be implicitly adopted on the basis of experiential [16] and social [2] learning in the contexts of existing institutions.

To follow this intuition concerning the subconscious development of such normative understanding, we employ a data-driven approach that utilizes the data structures we have described to facilitate agents' understanding of the normative environment involving a minimal amount of explicit reasoning. Although

---

[2] This elaboration is based on the extended grammar described in [6].

we present this model with respect to a specific problem, we believe that the proposed approach is generalisable and equips the modeller with a mechanism for norm representation that permits accessible inspection of simulations. Accordingly, we adopt a representation that has the descriptive power to capture instance-level actions as well as higher-level institutions (Section 4.1). Using this representation, we present a systematic process that describes the transition and derivation of institutional statements from individual observations (Section 4.2).

4.1 Action Representation

To put actions in a context for the purpose of instantiation, we can use the syntax of the grammar's AIC component that augments an action definition with the subject (*Attributes*) and context/conditions (*Conditions*). Utilising the term `act` to signify an individual action instance, an *action statement* is thus `act(attributes, aim, conditions)`, where `aim` represents the action definition.

Refining the *Attributes* component, we assume individuals to carry observable properties (attributes) that are equivalent to the social markers individuals display in real life, such as name, ethnic background, gender etc. We represent attributes as two sets, with the first set representing individual characteristics and the second highlighting group characteristics [12]. An example for the representation of attributes could thus be `attributes({id}, {role, ethnicity})`.

Furthermore, we need to specify a structured action specification in order to establish unambiguous symbolic references to an action and its properties. We define actions using a signifying term `a` and an associated set of properties `p`, the set of which depends on the nature of the action. Substituting the *aim* component of the institutional grammar, we can thus say `aim(a, p)`. Taking an example from our scenario, the central properties of the action 'send goods to trader' are the *object* that is dispatched ('goods'), as well as the destined *target* ('trader'). This *action definition* can thus be represented as `aim(send, {object, target})`, and instantiated as `aim(send, {goods, trader})`.

In addition we tailor the *Conditions* component to capture the context of action execution by allowing the specification of a potentially related preceding action (e.g. as a reaction to a previous action) as the first element, such as `conditions(act, *)`, along with potential further conditions.

Table 1 provides an overview of the refined component specifications.[3]

4.2 Generalisation

Individuals generally and unintentionally engage in processes of 'implicit social cognition' [10], one of which is the social generalisation process of 'stereotyping'. This process can lead to uncertainty reduction and efficiency enhancement, which is compatible with the purposes of institutions [15,22]. Stereotyping offers

---

[3] Note that as a matter of conciseness examples substitute the complete attributes specification of agents (i.e. including their social markers) with their name (e.g. Trader1).

Table 1. Component Specifications

Component	Structure	Example/Instance
Attributes	attributes(i, s), with i/s being sets of individual/social attributes	attributes({id}, {role})
Action Definition	aim(a, p), with a being a natural language action descriptor, and p being a set of action properties	aim(send, {object, target})
Conditions	conditions(act, c), with act being a preceding action, and c being a set of further conditions	act(Trader2, aim(trade, {goods}), conditions(act(Trader1, aim(send, {goods, Trader2}), *)))
Action Statement	act(attributes, aim, conditions)	act(Trader1, aim(send, {goods, Trader2}), *)

individuals the ability to develop predictors to anticipate another's behaviour and to call upon previously executed successful reactions.

We model such processes based on the collected action information by applying a set of steps outlined in Figure 1 and described in the following.

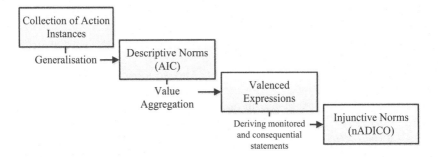

Fig. 1. Generalisation Process

Modelling subconscious generalisation processes shifts the perspective from the observation of individual behaviour instances to social behavioural regularities, closing the gap to what we perceive as institutions. We thus perform an aggregation of individual action statements to form generalised AIC statements, which we consider equivalent to observed conventions, or, in this case, *descriptive norms*. Operationally this is achieved by grouping the observed action statements based on their individual components, while keeping references to the action expressions constituting that respective AIC statement.

To explore this generalisation process, let us use a running example, a trade action instance. **Trader2** trades goods in the role of an **Operator**, after having been sent goods by another fellow trader **Trader1** (in the role of a **Sender**):

```
act(attributes({Trader2}, {Operator, Trader, Maghribi}),
    aim(trade, {goods}),
    conditions(act(attributes({Trader1}, {Sender, Trader, Maghribi}),
                   aim(send, {goods, attributes({Trader2}, {Operator, Trader, Maghribi})}),
                   conditions(*))))
```

Given the focal interest in actions, the totality of which express behavioural regularities, individual action statements are grouped based on the (decontextualised) action descriptor, i.e. the first element of an action statement's aim component. Referring to the running example this would be trade.

As a next step in the generalisation process, we consider the actor. Individuals base their generalisations on the social markers. In our example, the social marker with greatest relevance/salience in the context of trading is the role in which the individual operates (Sender/Operator). Ambiguous markers that describe supersets of the situationally relevant markers (here: Trader and Maghribi) are likewise maintained to serve for further generalisation (e.g. contrasting non-Maghribian traders from Maghribian ones, should such observation occur[4]) or to resolve conflicting statements.[5]

Finally, attributes components of actions held within the conditions component are likewise generalised to social markers, i.e. removing individual markers.

The generalisation process thus incurs the following steps:

1. Group all action statements (act) by action descriptor (aim component).
2. Group based on social markers by removing individual markers (attributes component).
3. Substitute all *preceding* action statements' attributes components (in conditions component) with social markers (i.e. remove individual markers as done in Step 2).

Assuming multiple statements showing the trading activity following the receipt of goods, we can express this as the generalised observation, or descriptive norm (aic), 'operators trade goods after having been sent goods by senders':

```
aic(attributes({Operator}),
    aim(trade, {goods}),
    conditions(aic(attributes({Sender}),
                   aim(send, {goods, attributes({Operator})}),
                   conditions(*))))
```

In order to develop more complex institutional statements beyond conventions or objectified descriptive norms, we need to assume that agents receive and associate feedback with individual action instances as part of their experiential learning process. Those then serve as input for the value aggregation process. The conceptualisation and implementation of feedback is domain/application-dependent and exemplified in Section 5.

4.3 Value Aggregation

The central purpose of the value aggregation process is to build up information used for an agent's overall understanding of a generalised convention. This is not

---

[4] Based on common marker subsets individuals could infer hierarchical conceptual relationships.

[5] For the following examples we will ignore the ambiguous markers.

to be confused with its attitude towards a convention, but instead represents the result of a cyclic internalisation and socialisation process which is based on experience and part of the agent's development of normative understanding. This aggregation operates on action instances grouped by the AIC statement. Table 2 shows simplified action instance representations for the previous generalisation, along with hypothetical feedback values.

Table 2. Exemplified action instances with valences

Simplified Action Example	Feedback
act(trader1, trade, ...)	30
act(trader2, trade, ...)	10
act(trader3, trade, ...)	−20
act(trader4, trade, ...)	20

For the aggregation we consider various *aggregation strategies*, possible approaches being the *summation of individual action feedback* to determine the *overall experience*; the *mean of feedback* represents a *rational conservative feedback expectation*; the *most extreme value* represents an *optimistic/pessimistic feedback expectation*.[6] The summation approach reflects the 'total experience', while the other measures discount feedback for a single action instance. Using the mean (in the example extract: 10) represents the rationally expected feedback. The aggregation based on the highest/lowest experience value, i.e. the individual's most extreme positive or negative experience (here: 30), puts emphasis on an individual's *most desired/feared* experience.

Ultimately, the aggregated value will be associated with the generalised AIC statement as a precursor for the development of nADICO statements. But, we first operationalise nADICO's *Deontics* component as a central mechanism to represent perceived duties, before deriving complete institutional statements.

4.4   Refining the Deontics Component

In contrast to the conventional characterisation of deontic primitives in discrete terms of prohibitions, permissions, and obligations, we apply a continuous notion of deontics, previously introduced as Dynamic Deontics [7], the essential intuitions of which are visualised in Figure 2.

In contrast to the discrete deontics understanding, a continuous representation of deontics can reflect the dynamic shifts between different deontics over time. Deontic terms, such as *must* and *may* are labels used for different deontic compartments along a deontic range, as shown in Figure 2. The tripartite nature of the deontic primitives demarks the midpoint and extremes of the deontic range, with intermediate compartments possibly labelled with terms[7] representing the

---

[6] One could introduce further aggregation mechanisms that include stronger weighting of recent or extreme values, or alternatively consider the variance of experiences.

[7] The choice of intermediate deontic terms for this example is not systematically grounded but follows the intuition of increasing prescriptiveness reaching from *may* to *must* and vice versa for proscriptions.

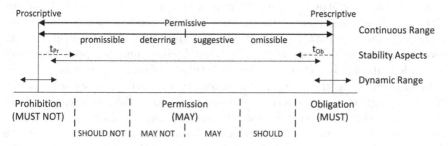

Fig. 2. Dynamic Deontic Range

gradual deontic notions of obligation and prohibition, such as the 'omissible' (obligations that can be foregone) or 'promissible' (prohibitions that can be ignored). The range itself is dynamic and determined by the individual's experience, a possible mapping being the direct association of the most positive and the most negative experiences with the respective ends of the deontic range. In the context of the current work, we operationalise this as the mean value across two memory instances holding sliding windows of memorized past highest and lowest aggregated values (see Subsection 4.3) for generalised action statements (see Subsection 4.2). Using the dynamically adjusting deontic compartments, the normative understanding of the individual, expressed as aggregated values, can be translated into semantically meaningful deontic labels.[8]

4.5   Deriving nADICO Expressions

To derive higher-level nADICO expressions from AIC statements, we revisit the developed action sequences that not only reflect an individual's actions but also multi-party actions. In addition the actors can be generalised based on their social markers, such as roles (e.g. sender of goods, recipient, etc.). Consequently agents cannot only derive behavioural conventions related to themselves, but, in principle, for any individual they observe, and further, predict individuals' behaviours based on existing social markers. This aspect is a precursor for applying cognitive empathy [4], such as the ability to perform perspective taking.

However, this mechanism requires the transformation of action sequences by *separating sequences into monitored statements and consequential statements* (see Section 3). The action sequences represent action/reaction pairs that suggest a 'because of', or 'on the grounds of' relationship. Using our example we would then arrive at the interpretation: "The operator trades goods *because* he has been sent goods by the sender.", which represents the descriptive norm perspective. However, to represent an injunctive perspective that highlights an individual's perception of its duties, we require the transformation into '*Or else*' relationships for cases in which the sequence's actors change (for example: '*Sender* sending goods', followed by '*Operator* trading goods.'). To reflect the injunctive nature

---

[8] A more comprehensive overview over concept and motivation is provided in [7].

of the 'Or else', we attach representations of perceived duty (deontics) and **invert** the derived consequential statement's deontic ('Senders *have to* send goods, or else Operators *will NOT* trade goods.'). Again, note that the deontic terms associated with the deontic range (*may, should, must*) may not precisely reflect this understanding, but they capture the intuition of such expression.

To proceed along these lines, it is necessary to distinguish separate action sequences originating in one's social environment. To do this, an agent identifies the first preceding statement whose attributes (i.e. generalised social markers) differ from the last statement's attributes. Using this approach, an agent can discriminate between actions and possible reactions. The aggregated value derived in the previous step can then be associated with the identified monitored statement's *Deontics* component.

To establish the deontic term's matching counterpart, the individual's existing deontic range facilitates the inversion of the aggregated value, the result of which is assigned to the consequential statement. For example, assuming a deontic range with midpoint value of 0, a value of 5 on a situational range – perhaps mapping to *should* – is inverted to its opposite scale value and deontic term (*should not*). Applying our running example, the corresponding nADICO statement reads:

```
adico(attributes({Sender}),
      deontics(5),
      aim(send, {goods, attributes({Operator})}),
      conditions(*),
      orElse(adic(attributes({Operator}),
                  deontics(-5),
                  aim(trade, {goods}),
                  conditions(*))))
```

Let us summarize the algorithmic steps for this approach:

1. Store last generalised action's *Attributes*.
2. Starting from the last generalised action, iterate through preceding generalised action statements (*previousAction* in *Conditions* component) until either finding a statement whose *Attributes* differ or no further preceding statement exists.
   - If statement with different *Attributes* is found, consider subsequence processed prior to current iteration as *consequential statement*; the tested statement and the remaining subsequence are assigned as *monitored statement*.
   - If no differing *Attributes* are found in preceding generalised action statements[a], treat first processed action statement (i.e. last action of action sequence) as *consequential statement*; the subsequence of preceding action statements is treated as *monitored statement*.
3. Assign aggregated value (see Subsection 4.3) to *Deontics* component of *monitored statement*.
4. If a *consequential statement* exists, invert the aggregated value (from Step 3) on the deontic range and assign it to the consequential statement's *Deontics* component.

---

[a] In this case all elementary actions of a sequence have been performed by agents of identical social markers. The last elementary action is then treated as previous actions' consequence.

Note that this derivation approach does not establish a consequential statement if no previous action has been observed, generating an injunctive norm without specified consequences.

At this stage, the derived nADICO statements provide the experimenter with a comprehensive insight into individuals' experience-based normative understanding. Moreover, the derived statements can be further generalised based on individual components, such as an overall normative understanding of actions (aims) by aggregating nADICO statements for specific actor perspectives (e.g. Operator, Sender), as alluded to in Subsection 4.2, or for a particular action.

We will explore this mechanism using the simulation scenario described at the outset of this article.

5   Simulating Normative Understanding within Maghribi Trader Society

To demonstrate how trading can develop normative understanding, we describe a model in which agents do so based on environmental feedback.

5.1   Model

Traders establish a maximum number ($maxRelationships$) of mutual trade relationships to other traders based on random requests, to which they then send goods. The receiver trades those goods at a profit that is determined by a random factor between $minProfit$ and $maxProfit$, with the market being represented by a random number generator. If initialised as cheater, the trader cheats with a probability $p_{cheating}$ and otherwise returns the profit to the original sender. Sending agents memorize the returned profits (as action feedback) in a memory holding a parametrised number of last entries, which they can query for specific individuals or across all their partners in order to gauge the correctness of the returned profit. In cases of presumed cheating, traders can fire the suspect and memorize it as a cheater. The interactions represent actions of the structure introduced in Subsection 4.1, with preceding actions stored in the *Conditions* component, successively building up action sequences that represent the comprehensive transactions between individual agents.

Naturally, the randomly generated profit (which we assume to be positive on average) introduces fuzziness into the decision-making of profit recipients (the original goods senders). To accommodate the fluctuation of returns, the sender's evaluation mechanism compares the operator's performance with its previous record. In the default strategy, operators are only fired if they produce negative profits and their mean previous returns are likewise negative. In all other cases agents are considered non-cheaters. To reflect the ongoing trade relationship, rewards are represented as the trade value of previous interactions with the rewarding party (i.e. the profits the other trader had generated for the service provider over time). If the operator's cheating was not detected, the embezzled fraction is added as part of his reward. In the case of firing, the inverted trade value of that partner is memorized along with the action sequence.

Agents can differentiate between private and public action sequences, with private action sequences containing additional actions, such as cheating (from the perspective of a cheating operator)[9] or suspected cheating (from the perspective of the original sender of the goods), which the agents memorize but do not share.

Based on their experience agents derive normative statements as outlined in the previous sections. Traders utilise the derived statements to guide their decisions whether to continue sending goods and to return profits, by aggregating them based on the given actions (e.g. sending goods, returning profit) across one's overall experience. Given our characterisation of norms as continua, traders have an individualised tolerance towards aggregated negative feedback (*defectionThreshold*), which is randomly determined at the time of initialisation and lies between zero and *maxDefectionThreshold*. Such tolerances ultimately limit market interactions and thus affect the overall economic performance.

Algorithm 1 outlines the agents' execution cycle; Algorithm 2 specifies agents' reactions to incoming requests.

Algorithm 1. Agent Execution Cycle

---

1 if $<$ *maxRelationships relationships to other traders* **then**
2 | Pick random trader this agent does not have relationship with
3 | and send relationship request;
4 | if *request is accepted* **then**
5 | | Add accepting trader to set of relationships;
6 if *agent has relationships to other traders* **then**
7 | Pick random fellow trader from set of relationships;
8 | if *normative understanding of action is above defectionThreshold* **then**
9 | | Send goods to selected trader and await return of profit;
10 | | if *profit $<$ 0* and *mean value of memorized past transactions from trader is $<$ 0* **then**
11 | | | Extend received action statement with action **cheat**;
12 | | | Memorize trader as cheater;
13 | | | Fire trader;
14 | | else
15 | | | Reward trader;
16 | | end
17 | | Memorize action statement in association with profit;
18 Derive nADICO statements from memory;

5.2 Evaluation

We initialise the simulation with the parameters outlined in Table 3 and use the number of performed transactions per round as a target variable to indicate overall economic performance.

---

[9] It would hardly be useful if an agent were to report his cheating to the goods' owner. Instead he would merely indicate that he traded the goods, but, depending on feedback, internalise if his cheating (in combination with trading) was successful.

Algorithm 2. Agent Reactions

---

1 Initialisation: Initialise agent as cheater with probability $p_{cheater}$;
2 Case 1: Receipt of relationship request
3 **if** *requester is not memorized as cheater and < maxRelationships relationships*
   then
4 | Accept request and add requester to relationships;
5 **else**
6 | Reject request;
7 **end**
8 Case 2: Receipt of trade request
9 Perform market transaction;
10 **if** *initialised as cheater* **then**
11 | Determine whether to cheat (based on $p_{cheating}$);
12 | **if** *cheating* **then**
13 | | Determine random fraction f of profit to embezzle ($0 \leq f \leq 1$);
14 | | Create private copy of action statement and add action **cheat**;
15 | | Memorize extended action sequence;
16 **if** *normative understanding of action is above defectionThreshold* **then**
17 | Return profit as part of publicly visible action statement (not indicating
18 | whether cheated or not);
19 Case 3: Receipt of firing notification
20 Remove sender from own relationships;
21 Mark sender as cheater;

Table 3. Simulation Parameters

Parameter	Value	Parameter	Value
Number of agents	100	$p_{cheater}$ (Fraction of cheaters)	0.2
maxRelationships	8	$p_{cheating}$	0.6
minProfit (Factor of goods' value)	0.8	*maxDefectionThreshold*	-100
maxProfit (Factor of goods' value)	1.3	Number of memory entries	100

Given the fuzziness in which traders determine cheating, the simulation parameters were refined after repeated operational runs to minimize the observation of false positives in the absence of cheating and to offer stable transaction levels, oscillating between 180 and 200 transactions per round (i.e. two transactions per trader per round – one as sender, one as operator). The generalised nADICO statements, along with deontic terms derived from the mapping of values can then be observed for individual agents as shown in Figure 3.

The statements show an overview of the agent's normative understanding, but also highlight potentially emerging conflicts, such as Statements 2 and 4, which are generalised based on the different reactions the agent experiences, in one case[10] indicating that it *must* return profit after he has been sent goods, traded and cheated, or otherwise not receive rewards. Given that he received a reward

---

[10] Read Statement 2 as (actions emphasized): 'Operators must *return profits* if they have *traded* goods they have been *sent* (by senders), and *cheated* while trading, or else senders will not *reward* them.'

for his trade (i.e. his cheating was not discovered), cheating appears to be a desirable action. Statement 4 shows generalisation based on the rare case that his cheating *was* discovered and sanctioned with dismissal (see the *O* component). Using the representation with dynamic deontics, different statements can be clearly prioritised: the higher deontic value in Statement 2 indicates that trading and cheating (see action sequence in conditions component) is more attractive, compared to mere trading shown in Statement 3 (Note the lower deontic value). Statements can likewise be integrated based on their common action sequence (e.g. by addition of deontic values). For example, Statements 2 and 4 (that have a common action sequence, but different consequences ('REWARD' vs. 'FIRE') and deontic values) can help explain why agents favour cheating (Statement 2) despite the (low) risk of being fired (Statement 4).

```
L0: A=A(*, [SENDER]), D=75.0 (MUST), I=I(SEND_GOODS, *), C=C(*),
    O=(L1: A=A(*, [OPERATOR]), D=-146.10054 (inv) (MUST NOT), I=I(RETURN_PROFIT, *), C=C({PREVIOUS_ACTION=   1
    A=A(*, [OPERATOR]), I=I(TRADE, *), C=C(*)})), O=(null))

L0: A=A(*, [OPERATOR]), D=79.25663 (MUST), I=I(RETURN_PROFIT, *), C=C({PREVIOUS_ACTION=
  (L0: A=A(*, [OPERATOR]), I=I(TRADE, *), C=C({PREVIOUS_ACTION=
  L0: A=A(*, [SENDER]), I=I(SEND_GOODS, *), C=C(*), O=(null)}), O=(null)) AND   2
  (L0: A=A(*, [OPERATOR]), I=I(CHEAT, *), C=C(*), O=(null)})),
    O=(L1: A=A(*, [SENDER]), D=-154.39249 (inv) (MUST NOT), I=I(REWARD, *), C=C(*), O=(null))

L0: A=A(*, [OPERATOR]), D=26.537308 (SHOULD), I=I(RETURN_PROFIT, *), C=C({PREVIOUS_ACTION=
  L0: A=A(*, [OPERATOR]), I=I(TRADE, *), C=C({PREVIOUS_ACTION=   3
  L0: A=A(*, [SENDER]), I=I(SEND_GOODS, *), C=C(*), O=(null)}), O=(null)}),
    O=(L1: A=A(*, [SENDER]), D=-51.694866 (inv) (SHOULD NOT), I=I(REWARD, *), C=C(*), O=(null))

L0: A=A(*, [OPERATOR]), D=-1.6361282 (INDIFFERENT), I=I(RETURN_PROFIT, *), C=C({PREVIOUS_ACTION=
  (L0: A=A(*, [OPERATOR]), I=I(TRADE, *), C=C({PREVIOUS_ACTION=   4
  L0: A=A(*, [SENDER]), I=I(SEND_GOODS, *), C=C(*), O=(null)}), O=(null)) AND
  (L0: A=A(*, [OPERATOR]), I=I(CHEAT, *), C=C(*), O=(null)})),
    O=(L1: A=A(*, [SENDER]), D=0.8398984 (inv) (INDIFFERENT), I=I(FIRE, *), C=C(*), O=(null))
```

Fig. 3. Situational nADICO Statements for individual agent

In order to gain a society-wide perspective on the normative landscape, we can analyse the distribution of individual normative understandings across the deontic range. We visualise this using a Kiviat-inspired chart that shows distributions across adjacent ordinally scaled values, such as deontic terms. Figure 4 shows monitored statements aggregated by leading attributes (i.e. acting role) and aim components at around 1,900 trading rounds.[11] At that stage traders are split whether or not it is worthwhile continuing to send goods (36 say *may* and 46 say *must not*) based on continuous cheating. Acting as operators, all traders maintain the understanding that processing received goods and returning them is worthwhile, indicating that they are generally rewarded. Only a subset of operators (the black series) perceives cheating as rewarding.

---

[11] Each statement is represented as a separate series. The axes' lengths are scaled relative to the deontic term with greatest support (here: 46).

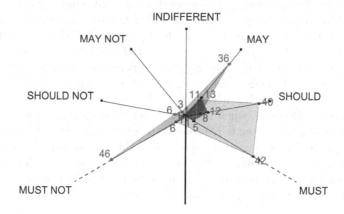

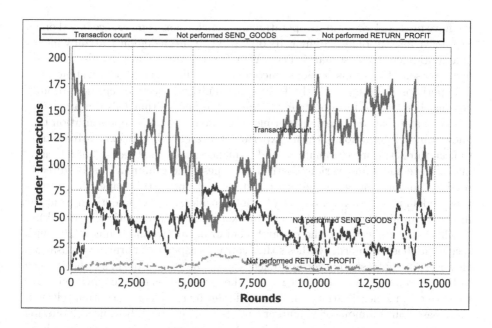

Fig. 4. Distribution of Normative Understanding after 1,900 rounds

Fig. 5. Number of trade interactions; defections from actions over time

To provide a dynamic perspective of this changing normative landscape over time, we provide a link to a video showing the evolution of the successive deontic charts (including a second chart focusing on cheaters) [5].

From Figure 5 we can observe an initially high commitment of traders to engage in trade interactions that starts to fluctuate once a sufficient degree of cheating is experienced. This is based on the understanding that sending goods is likely to be followed by cheating (Series 'SEND_GOODS'), and to a lesser extent, that returning goods honestly is sanctioned by firing (Series 'RETURN_PROFIT'). Trade is restored once those traders have only acted as operators for some time, erasing (by gradually forgetting) the negative experience associated with their operation as senders of goods. The parameter set explored here thus shows a borderline case between a well-functioning trader society and economic collapse caused by cheating. However, when higher numbers of traders also reject the returning of goods (e.g. at around 6,000 rounds), trading comes close to a collapse. The cheating probability is a central parameter in this simulation set, with lower values maintaining a functioning trade system, and values > 0.6 accelerating the oscillation even further. Increasing the number of traders, in contrast, reduces the amplitude of trade variations and thus increases economic stability.

6   Discussion and Outlook

We have provided a candidate operationalisation for norm emergence based on an expressive institutional grammar. Its operation has been demonstrated by means of a multi-agent trade scenario. The nADICO structure offers a detailed and unified representation of institutions, encompassing differentiated action structures, but, perhaps more importantly, fostering a multi-perspective representation of actions (here in the form of different roles). We believe that this grammar represents a suitable combination offering a) a human-readable representation that allows direct interaction with the experimenter, and b) highly expressive syntax that captures action combinations and sequences, action subjects, context, nesting of statements and various institution types. The grammar can be directly used, in conjunction with the process steps laid out in this paper, for normative modelling with a minimal set of prior specifications to be derived from the modelled application scenario (social markers, action specification, feedback).

This work fits well into the research field of normative modelling [1,20], with recent emphasis on norm synthesis that captures aspects of norm generalisation. However, in contrast to other approaches from the area of norm synthesis, such as [13,14], our approach does not require the specification of an explicit ontology to drive norm generalisation, but may well infer hierarchical conceptual relationships based on common social marker subsets (see Section 4.2) while still offering a richer syntax for norm representation. An important aspect of norm synthesis is the treatment of norm conflicts. Recent work on robust self-governing systems by Riveret et al. [17] relies on explicit concensus mechanisms to resolve norm conflicts. Our approach does not require such mechanisms. Instead, the numerical representation of 'oughtness' using the concept of Dynamic Deontics allows for a mathematical integration of conflicting perceived duties – recall the conflicting motivations to embezzle profits, with the carrot of being rewarded and the stick of being fired (Statements 2 and 4 in Figure 3).

Given our focus on the norm derivation process, the experimental model itself has not been explored to its full extent in this text. Nevertheless, the evaluation highlights the essential features of the generalisation process and showcases the interpretation of emerging norms. We also constrained the sensing capabilities for this scenario to experiential learning. However, the model itself is by no means limited to this type of learning, but could likewise incorporate social learning as well as direct communication. In fact, the action representation derived from the nADICO syntax (Section 4.1) can well serve as a message container for inter-agent communication, including (but not limited to) norm representation.

We believe that this modelling of norms is truthful to their actual nature. The approach assumes a consequentialist perspective in which we do not presume pre-imposed norms (though those may certainly exist and could be predefined), but drives normative understanding purely based on behaviouristic principles and without explicit sharing of norms. This supports their interpretation as shared implicit behavioural regularities, while maintaining an unambiguous representation that allows a flexible analysis based on arbitrary characteristics (e.g. for separate roles, specific actions, and different social groups/structures).

References

1. Andrighetto, G., Villatoro, D., Conte, R.: Norm internalization in artificial societies. AI Commun. 23(4), 325–339 (2010)
2. Bandura, A., Ross, D., Ross, S.A.: Transmission of aggression through imitation of aggressive models. J. of Abnormal and Social Psychology 63(3), 575–582 (1961)
3. Crawford, S.E., Ostrom, E.: A Grammar of Institutions. In: Understanding Institutional Diversity, ch. 5, pp. 137–174. Princeton University Press, Princeton (2005)
4. Decety, J., Grèzes, J.: The power of simulation: imagining one's own and other's behavior. Brain Research 1079(1), 4–14 (2006)
5. Frantz, C.: Video of Evolving Normative Understanding based on Dynamic Deontics, https://unitube.otago.ac.nz/view?m=zhQu6cTOdOj (accessed: September 2014)
6. Frantz, C., Purvis, M.K., Nowostawski, M., Savarimuthu, B.T.R.: nADICO: A Nested Grammar of Institutions. In: Boella, G., Elkind, E., Savarimuthu, B.T.R., Dignum, F., Purvis, M.K. (eds.) PRIMA 2013. LNCS, vol. 8291, pp. 429–436. Springer, Heidelberg (2013)
7. Frantz, C., Purvis, M.K., Nowostawski, M., Savarimuthu, B.T.R.: Modelling Institutions Using Dynamic Deontics. In: Balke, T., Dignum, F., van Riemsdijk, M.B., Chopra, A.K. (eds.) COIN 2013. LNCS, vol. 8386, pp. 211–233. Springer, Heidelberg (2014)
8. Ghorbani, A., Aldewereld, H., Dignum, V., Noriega, P.: Shared Strategies in Artificial Agent Societies. In: Aldewereld, H., Sichman, J.S. (eds.) COIN 2012. LNCS, vol. 7756, pp. 71–86. Springer, Heidelberg (2013)
9. Ghorbani, A., Bots, P., Dignum, V., Dijkema, G.: MAIA: a Framework for Developing Agent-Based Social Simulations. Journal of Artificial Societies and Social Simulation 16(2) (2013)

10. Greenwald, A.G., Banaji, M.R.: Implicit social cognition: attitudes, self-esteem, and stereotypes. Psychological Review 102, 4–27 (1995)
11. Greif, A.: Institutions and the Path to the Modern Economy. Cambridge University Press, New York (2006)
12. Haslam, S.A., Ellemers, N., Reicher, S.D., Reynolds, K.J., Schmitt, M.T.: The social identity perspective today: An overview of its defining ideas. In: Postmes, T., Branscombe, N.R. (eds.) Rediscovering Social Identity, pp. 341–356. Psychology Press (2010)
13. Morales, J., Lopez-Sanchez, M., Rodriguez-Aguilar, J.A., Wooldridge, M., Vasconcelos, W.: Automated synthesis of normative systems. In: AAMAS 2013 (2013)
14. Morales, J., Lopez-Sanchez, M., Rodriguez-Aguilar, J.A., Wooldridge, M., Vasconcelos, W.: Minimality and simplicity in the automated synthesis of normative systems. In: AAMAS (2014)
15. North, D.C.: Institutions, Institutional Change, and Economic Performance. Cambridge University Press, Cambridge (1990)
16. Parsons, T.: The Social System. Routledge, New York (1951)
17. Riveret, R., Artikis, A., Busquets, D., Pitt, J.: Self-governance by transfiguration: From learning to prescriptions. In: Cariani, F., Grossi, D., Meheus, J., Parent, X. (eds.) DEON 2014. LNCS, vol. 8554, pp. 177–191. Springer, Heidelberg (2014)
18. Siddiki, S., Weible, C.M., Basurto, X., Calanni, J.: Dissecting Policy Designs: An Application of the Institutional Grammar Tool. The Policy Studies Journal 39, 79–103 (2011)
19. Smajgl, A., Izquierdo, L.R., Huigen, M.: Modeling endogenous rule changes in an institutional context: The ADICO Sequence. Advances in Complex Systems 2(11), 199–215 (2008)
20. Villatoro, D., Andrighetto, G., Sabater-Mir, J., Conte, R.: Dynamic sanctioning for robust and cost-efficient norm compliance. In: IJCAI 2011, vol. 1, pp. 414–419. AAAI Press (2011)
21. Williamson, O.E.: Markets and Hierarchies, Analysis and Antitrust Implications: A Study in the Economics of Internal Organization. Free Press, New York (1975)
22. Williamson, O.E.: Transaction Cost Economics: How it works; Where it is headed. De Economist 146(1), 23–58 (1998)

Norms Assimilation in Heterogeneous Agent Community

Moamin A. Mahmoud[1], Mohd Sharifuddin Ahmad[1], Mohd Zaliman M. Yusoff[1],
and Aida Mustapha[2]

[1] Center for Agent Technology, College of Information Technology,
Universiti Tenaga Nasional, Kajang, Selangor, Malaysia
[2] Faculty of Computer Science and Information Technology
Universiti Tun Hussein Onn, Batu Pahat, Johor, Malaysia
{moamin,sharif,zaliman}@uniten.edu.my, aidam@uthm.edu.my

Abstract. This paper proposes a norms assimilation theory, in which a new agent attempts to assimilate with a social group's norms. This theory builds an approach to norm assimilation, analyzes the cases for an agent to decide to assimilate with a social group and develops a mathematical model to measure the assimilation cost and the agent's ability. Developing the norms assimilation theory is based on the agent's internal belief about its ability and its external belief about the assimilation cost of a number of social groups. From its belief about its ability and assimilation cost, it is able to decide whether to proceed or decline the assimilation with a specific social group or join another group.

Keywords: Norms, Social Norms, Normative Agent Systems, Norm Assimilation, Heterogeneous Agent Community.

1 Introduction

While empirical research on norms have been the subject of interest for many researchers, norms assimilation has not been discussed formally. Crudely put, norms assimilation is the process of joining and abiding by the rules and norms of a social group. Eguia [1] defined assimilation as "the process in which agents embrace new social norms, habits and customs, which is costly, but offers greater opportunities".

The problems of norms assimilation are attributed by the ability and capacity of an agent to assimilate in a heterogeneous community, which entails a number of social groups that adopt different social norms (in compliance and violation) and the motivation required for the agent to assimilate with a better-off group [1]. Accordingly, agents in heterogeneous communities are not joining other social groups randomly, but their decision is built upon their ability to assimilate norms of a desired social group.

This work aims to answer the question, how is norm assimilation practiced by agents in heterogeneous communities? The goal of norms assimilation can be achieved based on the social theory of assimilation that have been developed by Eguia [1], in which the decision to assimilate is influenced by two main elements which are the cost of assimilation and the ability of agents. Briefly, this paper aims to demonstrate the contribution of norm assimilation in establishing agents that are able to autonomously assimilate in heterogeneous communities.

H.K. Dam et al. (Eds.): PRIMA 2014, LNAI 8861, pp. 311–318, 2014.

The next section dwells upon the related work on norm assimilation. Section 3 details out the norm assimilation theory. In Section 4, we present the method of calculating the assimilation cost and agent's ability and Section 5 concludes the paper.

2   Related Work

The related research in this area are few and mainly limited to those proposed by social studies' researchers such as Eguia [1] and Konya [2] and similar research in Norm Internalization [3, 4]. Conte et al. [3] defined norm internalization as a mental process that acquires norms as inputs and presents them to the internalizing agent new goals as outputs.

Eguia [1] proposed a theory in norms assimilation, in which there are two types of agents; advantaged agents and disadvantaged agents and there are also two types of groups; better-off group and worse-off group. Any disadvantaged agents can choose to join the worse-off group without cost, or it can learn to enhance its ability to be able to assimilate with the better-off group but the enhancement is costly. He found that advantaged agents screen those who want to assimilate by imposing a difficult assimilation process such that the agents who assimilate are those whose ability is sufficiently high so that they generate a positive externality of the group. Members of the relatively worse-off group face an incentive to adopt the social norms of the better-off group and assimilate with it. The cost of assimilation is chosen by the better-off group to screen those who wish to assimilate.

Andrighetto et al. [4] presented an internalization module that has been integrated into EMIL-A agent architecture [5, 6]. The implemented experiments observed internalizer behavior (internalizer is the agent who has internalized the norm) in communities with different types of agents when a norm is salient and non-salient. The salient norm means providing information to people about the behavior and beliefs of the other individuals. Their results show that, a norm is salient EMIL-I-A and goes through all the internalization stages and when the norm is no more salient, it returns to its normative behavior.

We distinguish the difference between norm internalization and norm assimilation as follows. Conte et al. [3] defined norm internalization is a mental process, in other words, it is an internal process inside the agent's mind. While norm assimilation, according to Eguia [1], is the process of joining a social group, in other words, it is an external process between an agent and a social group. However, for an agent to assimilate with a social group, it might need to learn or internalize new norms. Consequently, norm internalization is a sub process of norm assimilation.

3   The Assimilation Theory

We develop an assimilation model based on an agent's internal belief about its ability and its external belief about the cost of assimilation with a specific social group. As shown in Figure 1, while the agent has its internal belief about its ability, it detects the various social groups' norms and calculates the cost of assimilation for each group.

Based on its ability and the cost, it then decides which social groups it should assimilate with.

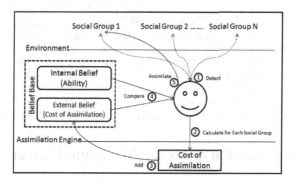

Fig. 1. The Assimilation Model

According to Eguia [10], the decision is influenced by two elements, one belongs to the agent's internal belief, which is the ability, and the other belongs to its external belief, which is the assimilation cost of a specific social group. The assimilation cost consists of the maximum and threshold costs [10]. We define these elements as follows:

Definition 1. The Ability, B, is the qualification and competence of an agent to assimilate the norms of a social group. The ability is considered prominent in this research because it represents an eligibility of an agent to join a group.

Definition 2. The Assimilation Cost, C, is the total effort and expenses incurred by an agent to assimilate with a social group. It consists of two types: the maximum and the threshold assimilation costs. In fact, the assimilation cost reflects how hard or easy for an agent to join a particular social group. It is considered prominent because it represents a social group constraint for any agent who wishes to join.

Definition 3. The Maximum Assimilation Cost, $C\mu$, is the highest cost imposed by a social group for assimilation. Any agent which is able to meet this cost is considered as optimal because it has the competence to practice all the required norms of a social group.

Definition 4. The Threshold Assimilation Cost, $C\tau$, is the minimum acceptable cost to assimilate with a specific group. The threshold cost differs from one group to another.

Based on these elements, agents or social groups can decide to accept or reject any assimilation. There are three cases to consider, two of which are favorable to the agent for assimilation. In the other case, the agent is not welcome to assimilate with the social group. Table 1 details out the cases. However, to present the different cases we assume that the Ability and Cost parameters are values.

Table 1. The different cases of assimilating a social group's norms

Case 1	Case 2	Case 3	
		Subcase 3.1	Subcase 3.2
The value of an agent's ability is greater than the value of threshold assimilation cost, we say that the agent α can assimilate σ, α(B) > σ(Cτ) ⇒ can (assimilate (α, σ))	The value of the agent's ability equals the value of threshold cost, we say that the agent α could assimilate σ, α(B) = σ(Cµ) ⇒ could (assimilate (α,σ))	The value agent's ability almost equals the threshold cost, we say the agent α could not assimilate σ, α(B) ≅ σ(Cτ) ⇒ could not (assimilate (α, σ))	The value agent's ability is less than the threshold assimilation cost, we say the agent α cannot assimilate σ, α(B) < σ(Cτ) ⇒ cannot (assimilate (α, σ))

4   The Formalization of Ability, Maximum Cost, and Threshold Cost

In this section, we present our method in evaluating B, Cµ, and Cτ. Since the elements of ability, maximum cost, and threshold cost deal with norms, the method begins from exploiting the types of norms. There are four types of norms that regulate an agent's behaviour which are convention, recommendation, obligation, and prohibition norms [7].

Definition 5. A Positive Effect Norm (Reward or Non-Penalty Type), χ, is a type of norm that brings reward or avoids penalty if an agent practices it, such as recommendation- and obligation-type norms.

Definition 6. A Negative Effect Norm (Penalty Type), ð, is a type of norm that brings penalty if an agent practices it, such as prohibition type of norms.

Definition 7. The Weight Parameter, φ, relies on the norm's type and norm's strength, π, of a social group. The Norm's Strength refers to the degree of enactment of, or the number of agents that practices a specific norm in a social group. As shown in Table 2, the weight parameter can have values of 1, 0, or -1 depending on the norm's type (η_κ), reward (χ), or penalty to agent (ð), and the norm's strength within the range $0 \leq \pi \leq 1$. According to Konya (2002), the majority is represented by ≥ 0.5 and minority by < 0.5 of population.

Table 2. The Weight Parameter

Positive Effect Norm	Negative Effect Norm
When the norm strength is more than or equal to 0.5 of population, then its Weight equals 1. But when its strength is less than 0.5, then its Weight equals 0	When the norm strength is less than or equal 0.5 then its Weight equals 0. But when its strength is more than 0.5, then its Weight equals -1
$\varphi = \begin{cases} 1 & \text{if } \pi(\eta_\kappa \in \chi) \geq 0.5 \\ 0 & \text{if } \pi(\eta_\kappa \in \chi) < 0.5 \end{cases}$ \qquad (1)	$\varphi = \begin{cases} 0 & \text{if } \pi(\eta_\kappa \in ð) \leq 0.5 \\ -1 & \text{if } \pi(\eta_\kappa \in ð) > 0.5 \end{cases}$ \qquad (2)

Definition 8. The Ability Parameter, ϕ, depends on the ability of an agent, α. As shown in Table 3, the parameter can have values of 1, 0, or -1 based on whether the agent adopts the positive effect norms, or avoids the negative effect norms.

Table 3. The Ability Parameter

Positive Effect Norm	Negative Effect Norm
When an agent, α, adopts it, then its Ability on assimilating η_κ equals 1. But when otherwise then its Ability on assimilating η_κ equals 0.	When an agent, α, does not adopt it, then its Ability on assimilating η_κ equals 0. But, when otherwise then its Ability on assimilating η_κ equals -1.
$\phi = \begin{cases} 1 & \text{if adopt}(\alpha, \eta_\kappa \leftarrow \chi) \\ 0 & \text{if} \neg \text{adopt}(\alpha, \eta_\kappa \leftarrow \chi) \end{cases}$ (3)	$\phi = \begin{cases} 0 & \text{if} \neg \text{adopt}(\alpha, \eta_\kappa \leftarrow \eth) \\ 1 & \text{if adopt}(\alpha, \eta_\kappa \leftarrow \eth) \end{cases}$ (4)

Definition 9. Conventions, Γ, are the type of norms that are adopted by every member of a social group. The weight of conventions is represented by the following formula,

$$\Gamma \in \chi \bigwedge \pi(\Gamma) > 0.5 \Rightarrow \varphi = 1 \tag{5}$$

Definition 10. Recommendation norms, Ω, are the type of norms that brings reward if an agent assimilates them otherwise, the agent is not penalized.

$$(\Omega \in \chi \bigwedge \pi(\Omega) \geq 0.5 \Rightarrow \varphi = 1) \bigvee (\Omega \in \chi \bigwedge \pi(\Omega) < 0.5 \Rightarrow \varphi = 0) \tag{6}$$

Definition 11. Obligation Norms, Π, are the type of norms that avoids penalty when an agent adopts them. Obligation norms are not optional and a social group's adoption of this norm type is based on the extent of applying penalty on violators.

$$(\Pi \in \chi \bigwedge \pi(\Pi) \geq 0.5 \Rightarrow \varphi = 1) \bigvee (\Pi \in \chi \bigwedge \pi(\Pi) < 0.5 \Rightarrow \varphi = 0) \tag{7}$$

Definition 12. Prohibition Norms, Ψ, are the type of norms that causes penalty when an agent adopts them. Prohibition norms are not optional and a social group's adoption of this norm type is based on the extent of applying penalty on violators.

$$(\Psi \in \eth \bigwedge \pi(\Psi) < 0.5 \Rightarrow \varphi = 0) \bigvee (\Psi \in \eth \bigwedge \pi(\Psi) \geq 0.5 \Rightarrow \varphi = -1) \tag{8}$$

Maximum Assimilation Cost. We define a formula for maximum assimilation cost, $C\mu$. Since $C\mu$ deals with the optimal assimilation, the formula of $C\mu$ must include the positive type norms (convention, recommendation, obligation) and exclude the negative type (prohibition) norms. If N is a set of norms that is adopted by a society, σ, then,

$$N = (\Gamma \cup \Omega \bigcup \Pi \bigcup \Psi) \tag{9}$$

This means that the set of norms, N, equals the union of all norms types (convention, recommendation, obligation, prohibition). Since the maximum cost deals with convention, recommendation, and obligation norms and exclude prohibition norms, then the maximum cost,

$$C\mu = \aleph \backslash \{\Psi\} \tag{10}$$

The weight, φ, for maximum cost always equals 1; hence we do not include it in the next formulas. If Γ is a set of convention norms, η_Γ; Ω is a set of recommendation norms, η_Ω; Π is a set of obligation norms, η_Π; and Ψ is a set of prohibition norms, η_Ψ,

$$\Gamma = \eta_{\Gamma 1}, \eta_{\Gamma 2}, ..., \eta_{\Gamma \kappa} \qquad \text{If } \mu_\Gamma \text{ is the cost of conventions, then,}$$

$$\mu_\Gamma = \{(\eta_{\Gamma 1}), (\eta_{\Gamma 2}), ..., (\eta_{\Gamma \kappa})\} \tag{11}$$

Similarly, for the other norms:

$$\Omega = \eta_{\Omega 1}, \eta_{\Omega 2}, ..., \eta_{\Omega \kappa} \qquad \text{If } \mu_\Omega \text{ is the cost of recommendation norms, then,}$$

$$\mu_\Omega = \{(\eta_{\Omega 1}), (\eta_{\Omega 2}), ..., (\eta_{\Omega \kappa})\} \tag{12}$$

$$\Pi = \eta_{\Pi 1}, \eta_{\Pi 2}, ..., \eta_{\Pi \kappa} \qquad \text{If } \mu_\Pi \text{ is the cost of obligation, then,}$$

$$\mu_\Pi = \{(\eta_{\Pi 1}), (\eta_{\Pi 2}), ..., (\eta_{\Pi \kappa})\} \tag{13}$$

$$\Psi = \eta_{\Psi 1}, \eta_{\Psi 2}, ..., \eta_{\Psi \kappa} \qquad \text{If } \mu_\Psi \text{ is the cost of prohibition, then,}$$

$$\mu_\Psi = \{(\eta_{\Psi 1}), (\eta_{\Psi 2}), ..., (\eta_{\Psi \kappa})\} \tag{14}$$

From Formulas (11), (12), (13), (14), we redefine Cμ in (10) as follows:

$$C\mu = (\mu_\Gamma \cup \mu_\Omega \cup \mu_\Pi \cup \mu_\Psi \setminus \mu_\Psi) \tag{15}$$

We remove μ_Ψ from Formula (15) to get the final formula of Cμ as follow,

$$C\mu = \bigcup \mu_\Gamma, \mu_\Omega, \mu_\Pi \tag{16}$$

The Threshold Assimilation Cost. Since Cτ represents the minimum assimilation cost, we include the cases that could be 0 based on the norm's strength. The weight, φ for obligation norms, η_Π, equals 1 when $\pi \geq 0.5$ or 0 when $\pi < 0.5$. Therefore, we include the weight parameter value within the formula of the threshold cost. The norm's strength is the prominent parameter which has a direct effect on the weight. If η_κ is any norms belong to the set N, then,

$$C\tau = N \setminus \{n \in N: \varphi(n) = 0\} \tag{17}$$

This means that the threshold cost equals the set of social group norms excluding the norms of weight equal 0 because their strengths are less than 0.5.

The threshold cost for Γ: The weight parameter is not included in the convention formula because it is always equal to 1 (norm strength > 0.5). From Formula 11,

$$\mu_\Gamma = \{(\eta_{\Gamma 1}), (\eta_{\Gamma 2}), ..., (\eta_{\Gamma \kappa})\}$$

The threshold cost for Ω: From Formula 12,

$$\mu_\Omega = \{(\eta_{\Omega 1}), (\eta_{\Omega 2}), ..., (\eta_{\Omega \kappa})\} \qquad \text{Adding φ becomes,}$$

$$\mu_{\varphi(\Omega)} = \{\varphi(\eta_{\Omega 1}), \varphi(\eta_{\Omega 2}), ..., \varphi(\eta_{\Omega \kappa})\} \tag{18}$$

The threshold cost for Π: From Formula 13,

$$\mu_\Pi = \{(\eta_{\Pi 1}), (\eta_{\Pi 2}), ..., (\eta_{\Pi \kappa})\} \text{Adding φ becomes,}$$

$$\mu_{\varphi(\Pi)} = \{\varphi(\eta_{\Pi 1}), \varphi(\eta_{\Pi 2}), ..., \varphi(\eta_{\Pi \kappa})\} \tag{19}$$

The value of φ can be 1 or 0; if the value is 1, the norm is included the in threshold cost (increasing the cost), but if the value is 0, the norm is not included in threshold cost.

The threshold cost for Ψ: From Formula 14,

$$\mu_\Psi = \{(\eta_{\Psi 1}), (\eta_{\Psi 2}), ..., (\eta_{\Psi \kappa})\} \qquad \text{Adding φ becomes,}$$

$$\mu_{\varphi(\Psi)} = \{\varphi(\eta_{\Psi 1}), \varphi(\eta_{\Psi 2}), ..., \varphi(\eta_{\Psi \kappa})\} \tag{20}$$

The value of φ can be 0 or -1; if the value is 0, the norm is not included in the threshold cost (increasing the cost because it is prohibition norm), but if the value is -1, the norm is included in the threshold cost (decreasing the cost). From (18), (19), (20) we redefine τ in (17) as follows:

$C\tau = (\mu_\Gamma \cup \mu_{\phi(\Omega)} \cup \mu_{\phi(\Pi)} \cup \mu_{\phi(\Psi)}) \setminus \{n \in N: \phi(n) = 0\}$, then

$$C\tau = \bigcup \mu_\Gamma, \mu_{\phi(\Omega)}, \mu_{\phi(\Pi)}, \mu_{\phi(\Psi)} \setminus \{n \in N: \phi(n) = 0\} \qquad (21)$$

The equation means that the threshold cost equals the union of all norms types but excluding the norms whose weight parameter, φ, equals 0. However, agents who meet the positive effects norms only is considered as fulfilling the threshold cost.

The Ability. Calculation is based on the formula of threshold assimilation cost, Cτ, and maximum assimilation cost, Cµ. When an agent detects the social group norms and calculates the maximum and threshold cost, it then calculates its ability based on what convention, recommendation and obligation norms to assimilate and what prohibition norms to avoid. Consequently,

$$B = N \setminus \{n \in N: \phi(n) = 0\} \qquad (22)$$

Each type of norms has an ability parameter, φ, for an assimilating agent, which is represented by (1, 0, -1). If the agent can assimilate Γ, Ω, and Π , then φ = 1, otherwise, φ = 0. If the agent can avoid Ψ, then φ = 0, otherwise, φ = −1. From Formula 22,

$\mu_\Gamma = \{(\eta_{\Gamma 1}), (\eta_{\Gamma 2}), \ldots\ldots, (\eta_{\Gamma\kappa})\}$ Adding the ability parameter φ becomes,

$$\mu_{\phi(\Gamma)} = \{\phi(\eta_{\Gamma 1}), \phi(\eta_{\Gamma 2}), \ldots\ldots, \phi(\eta_{\Gamma\kappa})\} \qquad (23)$$

Similarly, from Formula 12, 13, and14, adding the ability parameters to these formulas,

$$\mu_{\phi(\Omega)} = \{\phi(\eta_{\Omega 1}), \phi(\eta_{\Omega 2}), \ldots\ldots, \phi(\eta_{\Omega\kappa})\} \qquad (24)$$
$$\mu_{\phi(\Pi)} = \{\phi(\eta_{\Pi 1}), \phi(\eta_{\Pi 2}), \ldots\ldots, \phi(\eta_{\Pi\kappa})\} \qquad (25)$$
$$\mu_{\phi(\Psi)} = \{\phi(\eta_{\Psi 1}), \phi(\eta_{\Psi 2}), \ldots\ldots, \phi(\eta_{\Psi\kappa})\} \qquad (26)$$

From (23), (24), (25), (26), we redefine the ability as follows:

$B = (u_{\phi(\Gamma)} \cup u_{\phi(\Omega)} \cup u_{\phi(\Pi)} \cup u_{\phi(\Psi)}) \setminus \{n \in N: \phi(n) = 0\}$, then

$$B = \bigcup u_{\phi(\Gamma)}, u_{\phi(\Omega)}, u_{\phi(\Pi)}, u_{\phi(\Psi)} \setminus \{n \in N: \phi(n) = 0\} \qquad (27)$$

The equation means that the ability equals the union of all norms types excluding the norms of ability parameter equal 0. Since B,Cµ, Cτ are calculated based on the set of convention, recommendation, obligation, and prohibition norms, then from Case 1, Case 2, and Case 3, we can define the assimilation, S_Δ, as follows:

$$S_\Delta = \begin{cases} \text{If } C\tau \subseteq B \Rightarrow \text{can (assimilate } (\alpha, \sigma)) \\ \text{If } C\tau = B \Rightarrow \text{could (assimilate } (\alpha, \sigma)) \\ \text{If } \beta \subseteq C\tau \Rightarrow \begin{cases} \text{decide } (\sigma, \text{could not (assimilate } \alpha, \sigma))) \\ \text{decide } (\sigma, \text{cannot (assimilate } \alpha, \sigma \end{cases} \end{cases} \qquad (28)$$

5   Conclusion and Future Work

In this paper, we present a novel theory on norms assimilation in a heterogeneous community where there are a number of social groups practicing different norms. Any agent, which would like to join a social group, has to be able to assimilate their norms. The suggested assimilation approach is based on the internal and external agent's beliefs.

The study shows that an agent's decision (can assimilate; could assimilate; could not assimilate; cannot assimilate) is based on the ability of the agent and the threshold assimilation cost of a social group. A social group's strict compliance with its norms increases the threshold assimilation cost and attract prominent agents to assimilate and vice versa.

Since this work is in its theoretical stage, it only presents the conceptual underpinnings of pertinent issues in search and does not present the experimental results. Such outcome will be presented in our future work.

In addition, for our future work, we shall study the issue of norm assimilation based on morality of norms and an agent emotional state towards a particular group. In this work, we calculate the cost of assimilation based on the ability of agents to determine if they can or cannot assimilate. However, there is another case involving cost which is based on the morality of norms and the agent emotional state. Suppose an agent is able to assimilate a detected norm but the norm does not conform to its morality reference, or an agent is able to assimilate a detected norm for a social group but the agent has negative emotion towards the group. In this case, the agent has the option to accept or reject the assimilation not only basing on its ability, but also on the cost of breaking the norm's morality or resist its negative emotion.

References

1. Eguia, J.X.: A theory of discrimination and assimilation. New York University (2011)
2. Konya, I.: A dynamic model of cultural assimilation, Boston College Working Papers in Economics 546 (2002)
3. Conte, R., Andrighetto, G., Campenni, M.: Internalizing norms. A cognitive model of (social) norms' internalization. The International Journal of Agent Technologies and Systems (IJATS) 2(1), 63–73 (2010)
4. Andrighetto, G., Villatoro, D., Conte, R.: Norm internalization in artificial societies. AI Communications (2010b)
5. Campenni, M., Cecconi, G.A.F., Conte, R.: Normal = Normative? The Role of Intelligent Agents in Norm Innovation. In: Dagstuhl Seminar Proceedings - Normative Multi-Agent Systems. Dagstuhl, Germanu (2009)
6. Andrighetto, G., Conte, R., Turrini, P., Paolucci, M.: Emergence in the Loop: Simulating the two way dynamics of Norm Innovation. In: Normative Multi-agent Systems, in Dagstuhl Seminar Proceedings. Internationales Begegnungs-und Forschungszentrumfür Informatik (IBFI), Schloss Dagstuhl, Germany (2007)
7. Mahmoud, M.A., Ahmad, M.S., Yusoff, M.Z.M., Mustapha, A.: A Review of Norms and Normative Multiagent Systems. The Scientific World Journal, vol, Article ID 684587, 23 pages (2014), doi:10.1155/2014/684587

Computing a Payoff Division in the Least Core
for MC-nets Coalitional Games

Katsutoshi Hirayama[1], Kenta Hanada[1] Suguru Ueda[2], Makoto Yokoo[3],
and Atsushi Iwasaki[4]

[1] Kobe University, Japan
hirayama@maritime.kobe-u.ac.jp, kenta_hanada@stu.kobe-u.ac.jp,
[2] National Institute of Informatics, Japan
s-ueda@nii.ac.jp,
[3] Kyushu University, Japan
yokoo@inf.kyushu-u.ac.jp,
[4] University of Electro-Commnunications, Japan
iwasaki@is.uec.ac.jp

Abstract. MC-nets is a concise representation of the characteristic functions that
exploits a set of rules to compute payoffs. Given a MC-nets instance, the problem
of computing a payoff division in the least core, which is a generalization of the
core-non-emptiness problem that is known to be coNP-complete, is definitely a
hard computational problem. In fact, to the best of our knowledge, no algorithm
can actually compute such a payoff division for MC-nets instances with dozens of
agents. We propose a new algorithm for this problem, that exploits the constraint
generation technique to solve the linear programming problem that potentially
has a huge number of constraints. Our experimental results are striking since,
using 8 GB memory, our proposed algorithm can successfully compute a payoff
division in the least core for the instances with up to 100 agents, but the naive
algorithm fails due to a lack of memory for instances with 30 or more agents.

Keywords: coalitional games, least core, MC-nets, constraint generation.

1 Introduction

The computational issues of coalitional games are attracting much attention in multi-
agent systems [1]. Given an instance of a coalitional game, we face two fundamental
computational problems: the *coalition structure generation* problem and the *payoff division* problem. The coalition structure generation problem involves finding an optimal
partition (coalition structure) of agents to attain the maximum total sum of payoffs. On
the other hand, the payoff division problem seeks a reasonable division of payoffs to
the coalition members. This work focuses on the payoff division problem.

There are two well known solution concepts for the payoff division problem. One
is the *core* [3], which is the whole set of the *stable* payoff divisions over the agents
with which no subset S of the agents is willing to deviate to form another coalition of
S. The other is the *Shapley value* [10], which is computed by exploiting the *marginal
contribution* of individual agents to form coalitions.

H.K. Dam et al. (Eds.): PRIMA 2014, LNAI 8861, pp. 319–332, 2014.

To address the computational issues in coalitional games, the concise representations of characteristic functions are fundamental. Traditionally, a characteristic function has been considered a kind of "black-box" function. However, in the last decade, various concise representations have been proposed. Among them, the Synergy Coalition Group (SCG) [2] and Marginal Contribution Networks (MC-nets) [6] are arguably the most popular representations in the literature.

SCG explicitly describes the values of a characteristic function only for *synergy coalitions*, which produce synergy effects in payoffs. Given the payoff values for synergy coalitions, SCG allows the *core-non-emptiness* problem to be solved in a time polynomial based on the size of the representation [2]. However, it suffers from one serious drawback in that a NP-hard optimization problem has to be solved to get the payoffs of coalitions.

On the other hand, MC-nets uses a set of rules, each of which specifies a marginal contribution (increment/decrement in payoffs) when it is applied to a coalition. The condition part of each rule is generally described by a conjunction of literals, where the positive literals indicate the set of agents that must appear in a coalition and the negative literals indicate the set of agents that must not appear in a coalition. Compared to SCG, MC-nets has several advantages. First, computing the payoffs of coalitions is very fast. Second, it allows the Shapley value to be computed in time linear based on the size of the representation [6]. However, the core-non-emptiness problem in a grand coalition has been shown to be coNP-complete for MC-nets representation [4,8]. This indicates that the problem of computing a payoff division in the *least core*, which is a generalization of the core-non-emptiness problem, is NP-hard for the MC-nets representation. In fact, to the best of our knowledge, no algorithm can actually compute such a payoff division for MC-nets instances with dozens of agents. We believe this computational issue of the core is one of the major barriers to use MC-nets in practice.

Aiming to remove this barrier for the first time, we propose a new algorithm that computes a payoff division in the least core for MC-nets coalitional games. A naive approach to this problem generally suffers from a memory issue since it has to solve the linear programming (LP) problem in which the number of constraints grows exponentially by the number of agents. Our proposed algorithm exploits the *constraint generation* technique to alleviate this memory issue. A key technical contribution of this work lies in designing a *pricing problem* that identifies a missing constraint to be added to the current LP problem with a partial set of constraints. Our experimental results are striking since, using 8 GB memory, our proposed algorithm can successfully compute a payoff division in the least core for the MC-nets instances with up to 100 agents, but the naive algorithm fails due to a lack of memory for instances with 30 or more agents.

Indeed, applying the constraint generation technique, which is equivalent to the *column generation* technique in the dual formulation, to coalitional games is not new. Given the *weighted graph* representation of characteristic functions, Tombuş and Bilgiç solved the coalition structure generation problem by the column generation technique [11]. However, weighted graph representation is a special case of MC-nets that is not fully-expressive, which means that not every characteristic function can be described by it. Furthermore, they addressed the coalition structure generation problem, while we address the payoff division problem. Recently, Tran-Thanh *et.al.* proposed a new representation called the *coalitional skill vector* (CSV) and an algorithm using the constraint generation technique to find a payoff division in the least core for the games in CSV [12]. Although CSV itself is fully-expressive, the presented algorithm assumes a certain subclass of CSV instances where the goal set is convex. Namely, a different algorithm is required for CSV instances with non-convex goal sets. On the other hand, our algorithm finds a payoff division in the least core for the games in MC-nets that is fully-expressive. No restriction is made about the class of MC-nets instances that our algorithm can accept as its input.

The remainder of this paper is organized as follows. We first provide necessary background in Section 2, which includes the basics of coalitional games, the complementary slackness theorem of the LP problem, and MC-nets representation. Then we explain the details of the constraint generation technique in Section 3, which includes a necessary and sufficient condition for a payoff division obtained by solving the restricted problem to be in the least core (Theorem 2) and the concrete method to check this condition for MC-nets instances (Theorem 3). Next, we compare our algorithm with the naive algorithm, which solves a big LP problem produced straightforwardly from MC-nets rules in Section 4. Finally, we conclude this work in Section 5.

2 Preliminaries

2.1 Coalitional Game and Payoff Division

First we define the game.

Definition 1 (Coalitional Game (with Transferable Utility)). *An instance of a coalitional game is a pair (A, v), where A is a set of agents $1, 2, \ldots, n$ and $v : 2^A \to \Re$ is a characteristic function that returns a real-valued payoff for each possible set of agents (coalition). We assume that the payoff to a coalition can be freely redistributed among its members.*

Example 1. *Throughout this paper, we consider game (A, v), where $A = \{1, 2, 3, 4\}$ and v returns*

$$v(\{1, 4\}) = 1,$$
$$v(\{3\}) = v(\{1, 3\}) = v(\{3, 4\}) = v(\{1, 2, 4\}) = v(\{1, 2, 3, 4\}) = 3,$$
$$v(\{1, 3, 4\}) = 4,$$

and 0 for the other coalitions.

One commonly used assumption about a characteristic function is *super-additivity*. Characteristic function v is super-additive if for any two disjoint coalitions S_1 and S_2, $v(S_1 \cup S_2) \geq v(S_1) + v(S_2)$ holds. However, in this paper, we assume that v is not necessarily super-additive.

The following two problems are fundamental in coalitional games.

Definition 2 (Coalition Structure Generation Problem). *Given an instance (A, v) of a game, find optimal partition (coalition structure) CS^* of the agents that attains maximum total sum p_{max} of the payoffs.*

Definition 3 (Payoff Division Problem). *Given an instance of a game, find a reasonable division of the payoffs to the coalition members.*

Our focus is on the payoff division problem. We assume that the agents attain maximum total sum p_{max} of the payoffs by forming optimal coalition structure CS^*, which is then distributed among individual agents. Namely, the payoff obtained by forming an optimal coalition structure can be freely redistributed among the agents. Hereafter, we denote this payoff division problem by (A, v, p_{max}).

Example 2. *An optimal coalition structure of Example 1 is* $CS^* = \{\{1, 2, 4\}, \{3\}\}$ *that gives* $p_{max} = 6$ *as the maximum total sum of the payoffs. The payoff division problem requires us to find a reasonable division of* p_{max} *over the agents.*

To stabilize an optimal coalition structure, a payoff division in the *core* is of critical importance.

Definition 4 (Core). *Payoff division x is in the core of* (A, v, p_{max}) *if and only if the following conditions are met.*

$$\sum_{i \in S} x_i \geq v(S), \quad \forall S \subset A, S \neq \emptyset,$$
$$\sum_{i \in A} x_i = p_{max}.$$

However, the core can be empty, where for any payoff division x there exists at least one coalition with positive *excess*, which is defined by $v(S) - \sum_{i \in S} x_i$. The *least core* generalizes the core to deal with this situation.

Definition 5 (Least core). *Payoff division x is in the least core of* (A, v, p_{max}) *if and only if x is an optimal solution to the following LP problem.*

$$\begin{aligned}
\text{min. } & \varepsilon \\
\text{s.t. } & v(S) - \sum_{i \in S} x_i \leq \varepsilon, \quad \forall S \subset A, S \neq \emptyset, \\
& \sum_{i \in A} x_i = p_{max}.
\end{aligned} \tag{1}$$

Intuitively, the least core is the set of payoff divisions where the maximum excess over the coalitions (except the grand coalition) is minimized. We call this optimal value of (1) the *min-max excess*. The least core, which never becomes empty, is included in the core if it is non-empty.

Deciding if the core is non-empty (*core-non-emptiness*) is crucial in the payoff division problem. This problem is solved by checking whether the min-max excess is non-positive. The core is non-empty if and only if it is non-positive.

Example 3. *By solving (1) using the setting of Example 1, we get* $x = (3, 0, 3, 0)$ *in the least core that gives 0 as the min-max excess. Namely, the core is non-empty for this example.*

2.2 Complementary Slackness Theorem

The constraint generation technique is based on the *complementary slackness theorem* on the LP problem, which we describe below.

Theorem 1 (Complementary Slackness Theorem). *Assume the following primal LP problem:*

$$\text{min. } c^T x$$
$$\text{s.t. } A_1 x \geq b_1,$$
$$A_2 x = b_2,$$

and its dual LP problem:

$$\text{max. } y_1^T b_1 + y_2^T b_2$$
$$\text{s.t. } y_1^T A_1 + y_2^T A_2 \leq c^T,$$
$$y_1 \geq 0,$$

where T is a transpose. Both x^* and y^* are optimal solutions of the primal and the dual LP problems, respectively, if and only if the following four conditions are simultaneously met:

Primal Feasibility Condition. *x^* is a feasible solution to the primal LP problem.*
Dual Feasibility Condition. *y^* is a feasible solution to the dual LP problem.*
Primal Complementary Slackness Condition. *For each constraint of the dual LP problem, the constraint is tight on y^* or its corresponding primal variable has 0 on x^*.*
Dual Complementary Slackness Condition. *For each constraint of the primal LP problem, the constraint is tight on x^* or its corresponding dual variable has 0 on y^*.*

Proof: See a textbook like [5].

2.3 MC-nets

The basic idea of MC-nets is to use a set of rules, each of which specifies a marginal contribution (increment/decrement in payoffs) when it is applied to a coalition.

Definition 6 (MC-nets). *MC-nets is comprised of set R of rules, each rule r of which has a form $(P_r, N_r) \rightarrow v_r$, where P_r is the set of agents that must appear in a coalition, N_r is the set of agents that must not appear in a coalition ($P_r \cap N_r = \emptyset$), and v_r is a real number that will be added when rule r is applied to a coalition.*

When R_S is the set of rules that can be applied to coalition S, the payoff value of S is given by $v(S) = \sum_{r \in R_S} v_r$.

Example 4. *Assume that we have $A = \{1, 2, 3, 4\}$ and $R = \{r_1, r_2, r_3, r_4\}$, where*

$$r_1 : (\{1, 2\}, \emptyset) \rightarrow 2,$$
$$r_2 : (\{1, 2\}, \{4\}) \rightarrow -2,$$
$$r_3 : (\{1, 4\}, \emptyset) \rightarrow 1,$$
$$r_4 : (\{3\}, \{2\}) \rightarrow 3.$$

Since rules r_1 and r_3 can be applied to coalition $\{1, 2, 4\}$, we get $v(\{1, 2, 4\}) = 3$. In fact, these rules give exactly the same payoff value for any coalition as the characteristic function of Example 1.

MC-nets allows the Shapley value to be computed in time linear to the size of the representation [6]. However, in MC-nets, the core-non-emptiness problem on the grand coalition was first shown to be coNP-hard [6] and then proven to be coNP-complete [4,8]. Therefore, the problem of finding a payoff division in the least core for MC-nets coalitional games is computationally challenging since it belongs to the NP-hard problem.

3   Constraint Generation for MC-nets

We propose a new algorithm to compute a payoff division in the least core for our MC-nets coalitional games. A naive approach to this problem generally suffers from a memory issue since, as shown in Eq. (1), it entails the LP problem with a set of constraints that grows exponentially by the number of agents. The proposed algorithm exploits the constraint generation technique to alleviate this memory issue. This section provides details of constraint generation including its theoretical foundations.

3.1   Master Problem and Its Dual

Given a MC-nets instance, we need to solve the LP problem of Eq. (1). We call this LP problem the *master problem*, which is rewritten as follows.

$$
\begin{aligned}
&\text{min. } \varepsilon \\
&\text{s.t. } \sum_{i \in S} x_i + \varepsilon \geq v(S), \quad \forall S \subset A, S \neq \emptyset, \\
&\quad \sum_{i \in A} x_i = p_{max}.
\end{aligned}
\tag{2}
$$

The dual of this problem is called the *dual master problem* and is written as

$$
\begin{aligned}
&\text{max. } \sum_{S \subset A, S \neq \emptyset} v(S) y_S + p_{max} y_A \\
&\text{s.t. } \sum_{S \in \mathcal{CS}_i} y_S + y_A \leq 0, \quad \forall i \in A, \\
&\quad \sum_{S \subset A, S \neq \emptyset} y_S \leq 1, \\
&\quad y_S \geq 0, \quad \forall S \subset A, S \neq \emptyset,
\end{aligned}
\tag{3}
$$

where $\mathcal{CS}_i$ is the whole family of coalitions (except A) in which agent i appears. Their variables and constraints have the following one-to-one mapping:

$$
\begin{aligned}
x_i &\leftrightarrow \sum_{S \in \mathcal{CS}_i} y_S + y_A \leq 0, \quad i \in A, \\
\varepsilon &\leftrightarrow \sum_{S \subset A, S \neq \emptyset} y_S \leq 1, \\
y_S &\leftrightarrow \sum_{i \in S} x_i + \varepsilon \geq v(S), \quad \forall S \subset A, S \neq \emptyset, \\
y_A &\leftrightarrow \sum_{i \in A} x_i = p_{max}.
\end{aligned}
\tag{4}
$$

According to the complementary slackness theorem, values (x^*, ε^*) for the primal variables and values (y_S^*, y_A^*) for the dual variables are optimal if and only if the following conditions are simultaneously met:

Primal Feasibility Condition. (x^*, ε^*) is a feasible solution to Eq. (2).
Dual Feasibility Condition. (y_S^*, y_A^*) is a feasible solution to Eq. (3).

Primal Complementary Slackness Condition. For $\forall i \in A$, either $x_i^* = 0$ or $\sum_{S \in CS_i} y_S^* + y_A^* = 0$ holds. Furthermore, either $\varepsilon^* = 0$ or $\sum_{S \subset A, S \neq \emptyset} y_S^* = 1$ holds.

Dual Complementary Slackness Condition. For $\forall S \subset A, S \neq \emptyset$, either $y_S^* = 0$ or $\sum_{i \in S} x_i^* + \varepsilon^* = v(S)$ holds.

3.2 Restricted Master Problem and Its Dual

Since the master problem has a set of constraints that grows exponentially by the number of agents, we set a limit on its size and extract useful information about its optimality.

Assume we have family $\mathcal{T}$ of coalitions that covers all of the agents, which yields a limited number of constraints in Eq. (2). For example, $\mathcal{T}$ can be the whole family of individual coalitions. We get a *restricted* version of Eq. (2) that corresponds to $\mathcal{T}$:

$$\min. \; \varepsilon$$
$$\text{s.t.} \; \sum_{i \in S} x_i + \varepsilon \geq v(S), \quad \forall S \in \mathcal{T}, S \neq \emptyset, \tag{5}$$
$$\sum_{i \in A} x_i = p_{max},$$

which is called the *restricted master problem*. Its dual is formulated as

$$\max. \; \sum_{S \in \mathcal{T}, S \neq \emptyset} v(S) y_S + p_{max} y_A$$
$$\text{s.t.} \; \sum_{S \in \mathcal{CT}_i} y_S + y_A \leq 0, \quad \forall i \in A, \tag{6}$$
$$\sum_{S \in \mathcal{T}, S \neq \emptyset} y_S \leq 1,$$
$$y_S \geq 0, \quad \forall S \in \mathcal{T}, S \neq \emptyset,$$

which is called the *restricted dual master problem*. Note that $\mathcal{CT}_i$ is the family of coalitions in $\mathcal{T}$ in which agent i appears.

Example 5. *Suppose we have $\mathcal{T} = \{\{1\}, \{2\}, \{3\}, \{4\}\}$ as an initial family of coalitions in Example 1. The restricted master problem for $\mathcal{T}$ is*

$$\min. \; \varepsilon$$
$$\text{s.t.} \; x_1 + \varepsilon \geq 0,$$
$$x_2 + \varepsilon \geq 0,$$
$$x_3 + \varepsilon \geq 3,$$
$$x_4 + \varepsilon \geq 0,$$
$$x_1 + x_2 + x_3 + x_4 = 6,$$

where an optimal solution is $\hat{x} = (0.75, 0.75, 3.75, 0.75)$ and $\hat{\varepsilon} = -0.75$.

Let $(\hat{x}, \hat{\varepsilon})$ be an optimal solution to the restricted master problem of Eq. (5) and let $(\hat{y}_S, \hat{y}_A)$ be an optimal solution to the restricted dual master problem of Eq. (6). Since they are feasible, we obviously have

$$\sum_{i \in S} \hat{x}_i + \hat{\varepsilon} \geq v(S), \quad \forall S \in \mathcal{T}, S \neq \emptyset, \tag{7}$$
$$\sum_{i \in A} \hat{x}_i = p_{max},$$

which corresponds to the primal feasibility condition, and

$$\begin{aligned}
&\sum_{S \in CT_i} \hat{y}_S + \hat{y}_A \le 0, \quad \forall i \in A, \\
&\sum_{S \in T, S \ne \emptyset} \hat{y}_S \le 1, \\
&\hat{y}_S \ge 0, \quad \forall S \in T, S \ne \emptyset,
\end{aligned} \tag{8}$$

which corresponds to the dual feasibility condition. Furthermore, we obtain

$$\begin{aligned}
&\forall i \in A, \left(\hat{x}_i = 0 \right) \vee \left(\sum_{S \in CT_i} \hat{y}_S + \hat{y}_A = 0 \right), \\
&\left(\hat{\varepsilon} = 0 \right) \vee \left(\sum_{S \in T, S \ne \emptyset} \hat{y}_S = 1 \right),
\end{aligned} \tag{9}$$

as the primal complementary slackness condition and

$$\forall S \in T, S \ne \emptyset, \left(\hat{y}_S = 0 \right) \vee \left(\sum_{i \in S} \hat{x}_i + \hat{\varepsilon} = v(S) \right), \tag{10}$$

as the dual complementary slackness condition.

Note that dual variable y_S is defined only when coalition S is included in T. For the coalition excluded from T, we introduce a *virtual* dual variable with zero as its value. In other words, we create new values $(\tilde{x}, \tilde{\varepsilon})$ and $(\tilde{y}_S, \tilde{y}_A)$ from the optimal solutions $(\hat{x}, \hat{\varepsilon})$ and $(\hat{y}_S, \hat{y}_A)$ to the restricted problems, repectively, as

$$\begin{aligned}
\tilde{x}_i &\equiv \hat{x}_i, \quad \forall i \in A, \\
\tilde{\varepsilon} &\equiv \hat{\varepsilon}, \\
\tilde{y}_S &\equiv \hat{y}_S, \quad \forall S \in T, S \ne \emptyset, \\
\tilde{y}_S &\equiv 0, \quad \forall S \in 2^A - T - \{A\}, \\
\tilde{y}_A &\equiv \hat{y}_A.
\end{aligned} \tag{11}$$

With these new values, we can prove the following lemmas.

Lemma 1. $(\tilde{y}_S, \tilde{y}_A)$ *is a feasible solution to the dual master problem of Eq. (3).*

Proof: Considering Eq. (8) along with the fact that all of the virtual dual variables have zero as their values, all of the constraints in Eq. (3) are obviously satisfied by $(\tilde{y}_S, \tilde{y}_A)$. □

Lemma 2. $(\tilde{x}, \tilde{\varepsilon})$ *and* $(\tilde{y}_S, \tilde{y}_A)$ *satisfy the primal complementary slackness condition of the master problem.*

Proof: If $\tilde{x}_i \ne 0$, we get $\sum_{S \in CT_i} \hat{y}_S + \hat{y}_A = 0$ from Eq. (9). Since all of the virtual dual variables have zero as their values, we conclude that $\sum_{S \in CS_i} \tilde{y}_S + \tilde{y}_A = 0$. Similarly, if $\tilde{\varepsilon} \ne 0$, we also conclude that $\sum_{S \subset A, S \ne \emptyset} \tilde{y}_S = 1$. □

Lemma 3. $(\tilde{x}, \tilde{\varepsilon})$ *and* $(\tilde{y}_S, \tilde{y}_A)$ *satisfy the dual complementary slackness condition of the master problem.*

Proof: If $\tilde{y}_S \ne 0$, it is clear that we have $\hat{y}_S \ne 0$. Thus, from Eq. (10), we get $\sum_{i \in S} \hat{x}_i + \hat{\varepsilon} = v(S)$, which means $\sum_{i \in S} \tilde{x}_i + \tilde{\varepsilon} = v(S)$. □

We observed that the values created by Eq. (11) satisfy three of the four conditions of the master problem: dual feasibility, primal complementary slackness, and dual complementary slackness. Therefore, to argue that these values constitute an optimal solution to the master problem, we just verify whether the primal feasibility condition is met.

Theorem 2. *Optimal solution $(\hat{x}, \hat{\varepsilon})$ to the restricted master problem of Eq. (5) becomes an optimal solution to the master problem of Eq. (2) if and only if $(\hat{x}, \hat{\varepsilon})$ is feasible for Eq. (2).*

Proof: It is naturally deduced from Lemmas 1–3 and the complementary slackness theorem.   □

3.3 Pricing Problem to Check Primal Feasibility

The next goal is to check whether $(\hat{x}, \hat{\varepsilon})$ is feasible for Eq. (2). However, since the master problem has a set of constraints that grows exponentially by the number of agents, a clever method is required to check its feasibility for the master problem.

To develop such a method, we first rewrite the first inequality constraints of Eq. (2):

$$\sum_{i \in S} x_i - v(S) \geq -\varepsilon, \quad \forall S \subset A, S \neq \emptyset. \tag{12}$$

Given $(\hat{x}, \hat{\varepsilon})$, a key idea is to compute minimum value z^* of the left-hand-side of Eq. (12) over the whole family of coalitions. Namely, we compute

$$z^* = \min._{S \subset A, S \neq \emptyset} \sum_{i \in S} \hat{x}_i - v(S), \tag{13}$$

and then compare its minimum value to $-\hat{\varepsilon}$. We can conclude that $(\hat{x}, \hat{\varepsilon})$ is feasible for the master problem if and only if $z^* \geq -\hat{\varepsilon}$ holds.

On the other hand, assume we have a set of MC-nets rules. We can show that the above z^* can be computed directly from the MC-nets rules without expanding them to a table of characteristic function values.

Theorem 3. *Suppose we are given set R of MC-nets rules, each rule r of which has a form $(P_r, N_r) \rightarrow v_r$, and optimal solution $(\hat{x}, \hat{\varepsilon})$ to the restricted master problem. Denote R^+ as the set of rules whose values v_r are positive and R^- as the set of rules whose values v_r are negative. The value of z^*, which is defined by Eq. (13), is the optimal value of the following integer programming problem called the pricing problem:*

$$
\begin{aligned}
\min. \quad & \sum_{i \in A} \hat{x}_i \alpha_i - \sum_{r \in R} v_r \beta_r \\
\text{s.t.} \quad & \sum_{i \in P_r} \alpha_i + \sum_{i \in N_r} (1 - \alpha_i) \geq |P_r \cup N_r| \beta_r, \ \forall r \in R^+, \\
& \sum_{i \in P_r} (1 - \alpha_i) + \sum_{i \in N_r} \alpha_i \geq 1 - \beta_r, \ \forall r \in R^-, \\
& \sum_{i \in A} \alpha_i \leq |A| - 1, \\
& \sum_{i \in A} \alpha_i \geq 1, \\
& \alpha_i, \beta_r \in \{0, 1\}, \ \forall i \in A, \forall r \in R.
\end{aligned} \tag{14}
$$

Proof: In Eq. (14), α is a 0-1 vector that represents a coalition and β is also a 0-1 vector that represents the set of MC-nets rules applicable to that coalition. More precisely, given coalition S, α_i takes 1 if agent i is in S and 0 otherwise, while β_r takes 1 if rule r is applicable to S and 0 otherwise. A goal of this problem is to explore the space of α to identify the coalition that gives the minimum left-hand-side of Eq. (12). Assume we are given candidate coalition S that is represented by α. The first constraint of Eq.

(14) determines whether each positive-value rule r is applicable to S. In fact, the left-hand-side of the first constraint becomes $|P_r \cup N_r|$, which is the size of $P_r \cup N_r$, if r is applicable to S. This forces β_r to take one to reduce the objective by v_r. On the other hand, the second constraint of Eq. (14) determines whether each negative-value rule r is applicable to S. In fact, the left-hand-side of the second constraint becomes zero if r is applicable to S. This forces β_r to take one to increase the objective by $-v_r$. Thus, for candidate coalition S, the second term of the objective actually computes $-v(S)$ and the first term of the objective obviously computes $\sum_{i \in S} \hat{x}_i$. The third and fourth constraints of Eq. (14) just exclude a grand coalition and an empty coalition, respectively, from the space of α. Therefore, the optimal value of Eq. (14) is to agree with z^*. □

Note that by solving Eq. (14), we not only get z^* but also the coalition giving z^* in α. If $z^* \geq -\hat{\varepsilon}$, $(\hat{x}, \hat{\varepsilon})$ is feasible for the master problem of Eq. (2), which also means it is optimal to the master problem by Theorem 2. On the other hand, if $z^* < -\hat{\varepsilon}$, at least the coalition giving z^* should violate the potential constraint that does not appear in the current restricted master problem. In that case, we update the restricted master problem by adding a coalition of α to $\mathcal{T}$ to repeat this process until finding an optimal solution to the master problem.

Example 6. *Given the MC-nets rules in Example 4 and the restricted master problem in Example 5, the pricing problem is formulated as*

$$\min. \ 0.75\alpha_1 + 0.75\alpha_2 + 3.75\alpha_3 + 0.75\alpha_4 - 2\beta_1 + 2\beta_2 - \beta_3 - 3\beta_4$$
$$\text{s.t.} \ \ \alpha_1 + \alpha_2 \geq 2\beta_1,$$
$$(1 - \alpha_1) + (1 - \alpha_2) + \alpha_4 \geq 1 - \beta_2,$$
$$\alpha_1 + \alpha_4 \geq 2\beta_3,$$
$$\alpha_3 + (1 - \alpha_2) \geq 2\beta_4,$$
$$\alpha_1 + \alpha_2 + \alpha_3 + \alpha_4 \leq 3,$$
$$\alpha_1 + \alpha_2 + \alpha_3 + \alpha_4 \geq 1,$$
$$\alpha_i, \beta_r \in \{0, 1\}, \forall i \in \{1, 2, 3, 4\}, \forall r \in \{1, 2, 3, 4\},$$

where an optimal solution is $\alpha = (1, 1, 0, 1)$ and $\beta = (1, 0, 1, 0)$ that gives $z^* = -0.75$ as the optimal value. Since $z^* = -0.75 < 0.75 = -\hat{\varepsilon}$, the constraint on coalition $\{1, 2, 4\}$,

$$x_1 + x_2 + x_4 + \varepsilon \geq 3,$$

will be added to the restricted master problem in Example 5.

3.4 Algorithm for Finding the Least Core

To summarize the above, we got the following algorithm:

Step 1. Initialize $\mathcal{T}$ as the whole family of the individual coalitions;
Step 2. Find an optimal solution $(\hat{x}, \hat{\varepsilon})$ to the restricted master problem of Eq. (5);
Step 3. With the above $(\hat{x}, \hat{\varepsilon})$, get optimal value z^* and optimal solution α to the pricing problem of Eq. (14);
  Step 3.1. If $z^* \geq -\hat{\varepsilon}$, then terminate itself after reporting $\hat{x}$ as a payoff division in the least core and $\hat{\varepsilon}$ as the min-max excess;

Step 3.2. If $z^* < -\hat{\varepsilon}$, then go back to Step 2 after updating the restricted master problem of Eq. (5) by adding the coalition that corresponds to α to $\mathcal{T}$;

In updating the restricted master problem in Step 3.2, this algorithm adds a constraint that corresponds to α, which was violated under $\hat{x}$. Perhaps in the worst case, this algorithm may generate a whole set of constraints. However, in practice, it is much more likely that it will terminate before generating a whole set of constraints.

Example 7. *Let us continue Example 6. The updated restricted master problem is*

$$
\begin{aligned}
\min. \ & \varepsilon \\
\text{s.t.} \ & x_1 + \varepsilon \geq 0, \\
& x_2 + \varepsilon \geq 0, \\
& x_3 + \varepsilon \geq 3, \\
& x_4 + \varepsilon \geq 0, \\
& x_1 + x_2 + x_4 + \varepsilon \geq 3, \\
& x_1 + x_2 + x_3 + x_4 = 6,
\end{aligned}
$$

where an optimal solution is $\hat{x} = (3, 0, 3, 0)$ and $\hat{\varepsilon} = 0$. Hence, the pricing problem turns out to be

$$
\begin{aligned}
\min. \ & 3\alpha_1 + 0\alpha_2 + 3\alpha_3 + 0\alpha_4 - 2\beta_1 + 2\beta_2 - \beta_3 - 3\beta_4 \\
\text{s.t.} \ & \alpha_1 + \alpha_2 \geq 2\beta_1, \\
& (1 - \alpha_1) + (1 - \alpha_2) + \alpha_4 \geq 1 - \beta_2, \\
& \alpha_1 + \alpha_4 \geq 2\beta_3, \\
& \alpha_3 + (1 - \alpha_2) \geq 2\beta_4, \\
& \alpha_1 + \alpha_2 + \alpha_3 + \alpha_4 \leq 3, \\
& \alpha_1 + \alpha_2 + \alpha_3 + \alpha_4 \geq 1, \\
& \alpha_i, \beta_r \in \{0, 1\}, \ \forall i \in \{1, 2, 3, 4\}, \ \forall r \in \{1, 2, 3, 4\},
\end{aligned}
$$

where an optimal solution is $\alpha = (1, 1, 0, 1)$ and $\beta = (1, 0, 1, 0)$ that gives $z^* = 0$ as the optimal value. This time, since $z^* = 0 = 0 = -\hat{\varepsilon}$, the process can be terminated with $\hat{x} = (3, 0, 3, 0)$ as a payoff division in the least core and $\hat{\varepsilon} = 0$ as the min-max excess.

4   Evaluation

Since no algorithm has been proposed to compute a payoff division in the least core for MC-nets coalitional games, we compare our proposed algorithm with the naive algorithm, which naively solves the LP problem of Eq. (1) produced from the given MC-nets rules.

Each MC-nets instance was created using *decay distribution* under the CATS framework [9]. More specifically, it adheres to the following procedure. Starting from randomly selected individual coalition S, we repeatedly added one more agent with a probability of 0.55 until no agent was selected during an iteration or the grand coalition is formed. The value of $v(S)$ was randomly chosen to be a real number between 0 and $|S|$. We created a rule as $(S, \emptyset) \rightarrow v(S)$ to be modified by moving each agent in S from

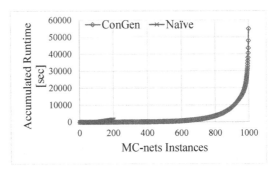

Fig. 1. Cactus plot for 1000 MC-nets instances

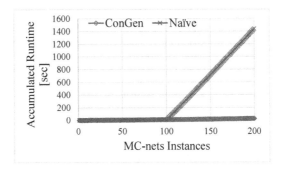

Fig. 2. Cactus plot for first 200 MC-nets instances

P_r to N_r with a probability of 0.2. Finally, we turned value $v(S)$ of each rule from positive to negative with a probability of 0.2. This method was also previously used [13] to generate MC-nets instances for the coalition structure generation problem. We set the number of rules $|R|$ equal to the number of agents $|A|$ and varied $|A|$ from 10 to 100 in steps of 10. We made 100 random instances for each number of $|A|$, which creates 1000 random instances in total.

In computing a payoff division in the least core for each MC-nets instance, we need p_{max}, which is the maximum total sum of the payoffs to form an optimal coalition structure. We assume that this value was computed prior to our algorithm by some method, such as *direct encoding* [13] or *weighted partial Max-SAT encoding* [7].

We used a machine that was equipped with Intel Core i7-4770 (3.5GHz, 4 cores, 32GB memory) and Windows 8.1 (64 bit). The source code was written in JAVA, which runs on a Java 1.7.0_25 runtime environment. We allowed a Java VM to use a maximum memory of 8 GB. To solve the LP and IP problems, we exploited CPLEX 12.5.1.

The results are shown in Fig. 1 with a *cactus plot*, where the x-axis indicates the problem instances and the y-axis indicates the accumulated runtime for an algorithm to find a payoff division in the least core. For each algorithm, the problem instances in the x-axis are sorted by increasing order of runtime. To make it easier to compare the

Table 1. Average number of generated constraints

#agents	20	40	60	80	100
ConGen	13.4	61.3	176.7	393.4	692.2
Naïve	$\approx 10^6$	$\approx 10^{12}$	$\approx 10^{18}$	$\approx 10^{24}$	$\approx 10^{30}$

performance of two algorithms, we give Fig. 2, where the plots at the first 200 instances in Fig. 1 are magnified. To solve the first 200 instances, the constraint generation algorithm (ConGen) consumed no more than 26 seconds, while the naive algorithm (Naïve) required more than 1400 seconds. Note that due to a lack of memory, Naïve failed to solve the remaining 800 instances, each of which involves 30 or more agents. The most time-consuming instance for ConGen was the one with 100 agents, which required 6997 seconds to identify a payoff division in the least core.

Table 1 shows the average number of generated constraints. For reference, we also show the rough estimate of the number of constraints that Naïve could deal with. The above most time-consuming instance caused ConGen to generate 6863 constraints, which was the largest number of constraints that were generated.

5 Conclusion

We presented a new algorithm to compute a payoff division in the least core for MC-nets instances. It exploits the constraint generation technique to solve the linear programming problem that potentially has a huge number of constraints. Although applying the constraint generation technique to coalitional games is not new, this is the very first algorithm that can actually compute a payoff division in the least core for MC-nets instances with up to 100 agents. This result is significant because it has been generally considered that the core issue is one of the major barriers to use MC-nets in practice. We believe that this work can be a first step toward removing this barrier to help increase the popularity of MC-nets as a way to represent a characteristic function.

References

1. Chalkiadakis, G., Elkind, E., Wooldridge, M.: Computational Aspects of Cooperative Game Theory. Morgan & Claypool Publishers (2011)
2. Conitzer, V., Sandholm, T.: Complexity of constructing solutions in the core based on synergies among coalitions. Artificial Intelligence 170, 607–619 (2006)
3. Gillies, D.: Some Theorems on n-Person Games. Ph.D. thesis, Princeton University (1953)
4. Greco, G., Malizia, E., Palopoli, L., Scarcello, F.: On the complexity of core, kernel, and bargaining set. Artificial Intelligence 175(12–13), 1877–1910 (2011)
5. Hillier, F.S., Lieberman, G.J.: Introduction to Operations Research, 9th edn. McGraw-Hill (2010)
6. Ieong, S., Shoham, Y.: Marginal contribution nets: A compact representation scheme for coalitional games. In: Proceedings of the 6th ACM Conference on Electronic Commerce (EC 2005), pp. 193–202 (2005)

 7. Liao, X., Koshimura, M., Fujita, H., Hasegawa, R.: Solving the coalition structure generation problem with MaxSAT. In: Proceedings of the 2012 IEEE 24th International Conference on Tools with Artificial Intelligence (ICTAI 2012), pp. 910–915 (2012)
 8. Malizia, E., Palopoli, L., Scarcello, F.: Infeasibility certificates and the complexity of the core in coalitional games. In: Proceedings of the 20th International Joint Conference on Artificial Intelligence (IJCAI 2007), pp. 1402–1407 (2007)
 9. Sandholm, T.: Algorithm for optimal winner determination in combinatorial auctions. Artificial Intelligence 135(1–2), 1–54 (2002)
10. Shapley, L.S.: A value for n-person games. In: Contributions to the Theory of Games, vol. 2. Princeton University Press (1953)
11. Tombuş, Ö., Bilgiç, T.: A column generation approach to the coalition formation problem in multi-agent systems. Computers & Operations Research 31, 1635–1653 (2004)
12. Tran-Thanh, L., Nguyen, T.D., Rahwan, T., Rogers, A., Jennings, N.R.: An efficient vector-based representation for coalitional games. In: Proceedings of the 23rd International Joint Conference on Artificial Intelligence (IJCAI 2013), pp. 383–389 (2013)
13. Ueda, S., Hasegawa, T., Hashimoto, N., Ohta, N., Iwasaki, A., Yokoo, M.: Handling negative value rules in MC-net-based coalition structure generation. In: Proceedings of the 11th International Conference on Autonomous Agents and Multiagent Systems (AAMAS 2012), pp. 795–802 (2012)

Marginal Contribution Stochastic Games for Dynamic Resource Allocation

Archie C. Chapman[1] and Pradeep Varakantham[2]

[1] School of Electrical and Information Engineering, University of Sydney, Australia
archie.chapman@sydney.edu.au
[2] School of Information Systems, Singapore Management University, Singapore
pradeepv@smu.edu.sg

Abstract. We develop a new formalism for solving team Markov decision processes (MDPs), called *marginal–contribution stochastic games* (MCSGs). In MCSGs, each agent's utility for a state transition is given by its *marginal contribution* to the team value function so that utilities differ between agents, and sparse interaction between them is naturally exploited. We prove that a MCSG admits a potential function and show that the locally optimal solutions, including the global optimum, correspond to the Nash equilibria of the game. We go on to show that any Nash equilibrium of a dynamic resource allocation problem with monotone submodular resource functions in MCSG form has a *price of anarchy* of $> 1/2$. Finally, we characterize a class of distributed algorithms for MCSGs.

Keywords: Potential games, sequential decision problems, distributed optimisation.

1 Introduction

Recent research into the control of large systems has focused much attention on multi–agent systems, because of their inherent distributed nature and robustness. In this context, two important research tasks are to develop distributed algorithms for solving team Markov decision problems (MDPs), and to derive bounds on solutions to problems with self–interested agents (e.g. price of anarchy). Although these lines of research consider similar problems. these two literatures have run largely in parallel.

This paper blends results and techniques from these literatures to derive a single model for *distributed planning* in team MDPs. We call this model *marginal contribution stochastic games* (MCSGs), and show that it guarantees convergence in a broad class of problems and spreads the computational load across the agents in the system, while providing price of stability and anarchy bounds on solution quality.

The agents' utilities, which drive their choice of policy, are given by their *marginal contributions* to the global value function. This utility design is the feature of the MCSG model that most differentiates it from existing methods and also results in two key benefits. First, by computing their marginal contributions, MCSGs admit a *potential function* over the joint policy space. This allows us to characterise an MCSG's Nash equilibria as local optima and a general distributed iterative approach to finding them.

H.K. Dam et al. (Eds.): PRIMA 2014, LNAI 8861, pp. 333–340, 2014.

The second major benefit of MCSGs, is that, under the natural condition that the reward function is is sub–modular, the NE of the system are guaranteed to be within a factor of $1/2$ of the system optimal (i.e. price of anarchy = $1/2$), and contain the optimal policy (i.e. price of stability = 1). This condition is satisfied in many resource allocation problems, such as target coverage, environmental monitoring and queueing systems.

Related Work: We build directly on: the joint equilibrium–based search for policies (JESP) algorithm [11,12], which uses iterative policy exchange but with a team game utility design; the multi–agent policy–iteration planning algorithm based on fictitious play (FP–PI) outlined in [4], for which there are limited convergence guarantees; and the overlapping potential game approximation (OPGA) for dynamic resource allocation games [2], which takes an ad–hoc approach to sequential decision–making. Our work complements sparse–interaction models such as TD–POMDPs [15], in that marginal contribution utilities can be applied directly to those abstractions. The idea of marginal contribution payments as incentives for an optimal joint action by a team is introduced by [5], and has been applied as a utility design principle in the context of artificial multi–agent systems [16]. Marginal contributions are applied specifically to submodular resource allocation games by [14], and to static resource allocation games in [8].

The paper progresses as follows: Section 2 reviews team MDPs and distributed resource allocation problems. MCSGs are described in Section 3 alongside the main theoretical results of the paper: pure NE existence and efficiency bounds. Section 4 discusses a class of iterative algorithms for solving MCSGs. Section 5 concludes.

2   Model

We begin with a recap of team Markov decision processes (MDPs) and stochastic games, before considering multi–agent resource allocation problems. Throughout, we adopt the following notation: $\mathbb{P}$ denotes the probability of an event, $\mathbb{R}$ the real numbers, $\mathcal{P}(X)$ the power set of X, and $\Delta(X)$ the set of all probability distributions over X.

2.1   Recap: Team MDPs and Stochastic Games

In general team MDPs, agents collectively optimise a global utility function.

Definition 1. *A* **Team MDP** *is represented using the tuple* $\langle \mathcal{S}, \mathcal{I}, \{\mathcal{A}^i\}_{i\in\mathcal{I}}, \mathcal{R}, \mathcal{T} \rangle$, *where* $S = \{s_1,\ldots,s_S\}$ *is the set of joint states;* $\mathcal{I} = \{1,\ldots,I\}$ *is the team of agents;* $\mathcal{A}^i$ *is the action set for each agent* $i \in \mathcal{I}$, *which is possibly state-dependent, such that the space of joint action profiles is given by* $\mathcal{A} = \times_{i\in\mathcal{I}}\mathcal{A}^i$; $\mathcal{R} : S \times \mathcal{A} \times S \to \mathbb{R}$ *is the global reward function; and* $\mathcal{T} : \mathcal{S} \times \mathcal{A} \to \Delta(\mathcal{S})$ *is the state transition function, which defines movements between the states. We write* $\mathcal{R}_{ss'}(a)$ *for the reward from joint action* $a \in \mathcal{A}$ *in state* s *leading to transition to state* s' *and* $\mathcal{T}_{ss'}(a) = \mathbb{P}(s^{t+1} = s'|s^t = s, a^t = a)$. *Collectively, the team aims to maximise the discounted sum of global rewards:*

$$R = \sum_{t=0}^{T} \gamma^t \mathcal{R}_t \qquad (1)$$

where $\mathcal{R}_t$ *is the team reward realised at timestep* t, $0 < \gamma \leq 1$ *is a discount factor, and* T *is the problem's duration; possibly with* $T = \infty$, *but in which case it must be that* $\gamma < 1$.

Different variants of team MDPs are characterised by how observable the global state is by the agents. Here we consider only the simplest variant, multi–agent MDPs. Generally, let Ω^i be a set of observations that i can make, with the probability of making an observation conditional on the underlying state of the problem: $\mathbb{P}(\Omega^i(t) = \omega^i) = \mathbb{P}(\Omega^i = \omega^i | a^t = a, s^{t+1} = s')$, which we denote by the observation function $O^i_{s'}(\omega^i)$.

Definition 2. *A **multi–agent MDP** (M–MDP) is a tuple,* $\langle \mathcal{S}, \mathcal{I}, \{\mathcal{A}^i, \Omega^i, O^i\}_{i \in \mathcal{I}}, \mathcal{R}, \mathcal{T} \rangle$ *in which, for every individual observation* $\omega^i \in \Omega^i$, *there is a state* $s \in \mathcal{S}$ *such that* $O^i_s(\omega^i) = 1;$[1] *that is, the agents have* individual full observability.

Since the state can be exactly recovered from individual observations, the *policy* of an agent i in an M–MDP is simply a map from states to actions, $\pi^i : \mathcal{S} \to \Delta(\mathcal{A}^i)$. The global *value* to the team for following a randomised joint policy profile $\pi = \{\pi^i\}_{i \in \mathcal{I}}$ starting from state s is given by:

$$V^\pi(s) = \sum_{a \in \mathcal{A}} \pi(a) \sum_{s' \in \mathcal{S}} \mathcal{T}_{ss'}(a) \left(\mathcal{R}_{ss'}(a) + \gamma V^\pi(s') \right) \tag{2}$$

An optimal policy, π^*, is one which maximises Eq. (2) over all states; that is $V^*(s) = \max_\pi V^\pi(s) \ \forall \, s \in \mathcal{S}$. A standard result in dynamic programming is that an optimal policy exists in deterministic policies for all finite MDPs.

We now introduce stochastic games, a general model of multi–agent interaction.

Definition 3. *A **stochastic game** (SG),* $\langle \mathcal{S}, \mathcal{I}, \{\mathcal{A}^i, r^i\}_{i \in \mathcal{I}}, \mathcal{T}, \rangle$ *comprises states* $\mathcal{S}$, *agents* $\mathcal{I}$ *each with actions* $\{\mathcal{A}^i\}_{i \in \mathcal{I}}$, *and a transition function* $\mathcal{T}$ *defined as in team MDPs, but where each agent has an* individual reward function $r^i : S \times A \to \mathbb{R}$, *which motivates its choice of policy. An agent's aim in a SG is to maximise the total discounted rewards it earns in the current state and all future states:*

$$R^i = \sum_{t=0}^{T} \gamma^t r^i_t \tag{3}$$

with $0 < \gamma \le 1$ *a discount factor, and* T *the game's duration.*

A policy (or *strategy*) for a SG $\pi^i : \mathcal{S} \to \Delta(A^i)$, is defined as for team MDP problems. The value to agent i for following a randomised policy π^i starting in state s, given the other agents' policies π^{-i}, is:[2]

$$U^i_{\pi^i}(s, \pi^{-i}) = \sum_{a^i \in A^i} \pi^i(a^i) \sum_{a^{-i} \in A^{-i}} \pi^{-i}(a^{-i}) \sum_{s'} \mathcal{T}_{ss'}(a^i, a^{-i}) \left(r^i_{ss'}(a^i, a^{-i}) + \gamma U^i_{\pi^i}(s', \pi^{-i}) \right) \tag{4}$$

where $r^i_{ss'}(a^i, a^{-i})$ is i's individual reward for taking action $a^i \in A^i$ in state s, when its opponents play joint action profile $a^{-i} \in A^{-i}$ in the same situation. Note that in this expression, π^{-i} can be considered part of the state from agent i's perspective.

Our next definition provides a solution concept that defines how the agents choose their policies. First, let $U^i_{\pi^*}(s, \pi^{-i})$ be the value of the policy that maximises Eq. (4); that is, an agent's optimal policy given its opponents' policy profile.

---

[1] Further variants (e.g. Dec–MDPs, Dec–POMDPs) are defined by generalising $O^i_{s'}(\omega^i)$; see [9].
[2] We use the notation $\pi = (\pi^i, \pi^{-i})$ to separately indicate i's component and i's opponents' component of a joint policy, and continue in the same manner for joint actions, rewards, etc.

Definition 4. *A **Nash equilibrium** (NE) in a SG, is a profile of policies, one for each agent, each of which simultaneously maximises Eq. (4) for all states; that is, π is a NE iff $\forall i \in \mathcal{I}$ and $\forall s \in \mathcal{S}$: $U^i_{\pi^i}(s, \pi^{-i}) = U^i_{\pi^*}(s, \pi^{-i})$.*

A common method for tackling team MDPs is to cast them as SGs in which every agent has the same reward function: $r^i_s(a) = \mathcal{R}_s(a) \ \forall i \in \mathcal{I}$. Theorem 4 of [13] shows that all SGs in this class have a pure NE (equilibria in which the agents' policies are deterministic). Our result in Section 3.1 generalises this result (Lemma 1).

2.2   Distributed Resource Allocation Problems

We are particularly interested in a subclass of team MDPs called (stochastic) distributed resource allocation problems, where agents need to allocate resources to tasks.

Definition 5. *A **distributed resource allocation** (DRA) game is a stochastic game with explicit resource and task sets, $\langle \mathcal{K}, \mathcal{M}, \{\mathcal{S}^m, \mathcal{R}^m, \mathcal{T}^m\}_{m \in \mathcal{M}}, I, \{\mathcal{S}^i, \mathcal{A}^i, \mathcal{R}^i\}_{i \in \mathcal{I}}, \mathcal{S}^0 \rangle$, consisting of the following. Let $\mathcal{K} = \{1, \ldots, K\}$ denote a set of resource types, and $\mathcal{M} = \{1, \ldots, M\}$ denote a set of tasks, with each task $m \in \mathcal{M}$ comprising a set of task states $\mathcal{S}^m$, a task reward function $\mathcal{R}^m : \mathcal{S}^m \times \mathbb{R}^K_+ \times \mathcal{S}^m \to \mathbb{R}$, and a task state transition function $\mathcal{T}^m : \mathcal{S}^m \times \mathcal{S}^0 \times \mathbb{R}^K_+ \to \Delta(\mathcal{S}^m)$. A team of agents $\mathcal{I} = \{1, \ldots, I\}$, is deployed to tackle the problem, with each agent $i \in \mathcal{I}$ comprising a set of agent states $\mathcal{S}^i$, describing its (varying) resource processing capacities, an agent action set $\mathcal{A}^i_{s^i}$, which may be state-dependent, giving a set of joint actions $\mathcal{A}_s = \times_{i \in \mathcal{I}} \mathcal{A}^i_{s^i}$, an agent state transition function $\mathcal{T}^i : \mathcal{S}^i \times \mathcal{A}^i \to \Delta(\mathcal{S}^m)$, and an agent reward function $r^i : \mathcal{S} \times \mathcal{A} \times \mathcal{S} \to \mathbb{R}$. The global problem is characterised by set of joint or global states $\mathcal{S} = \mathcal{S}^0 \times_{m \in \mathcal{M}} \mathcal{S}^m \times_{i \in \mathcal{I}} \mathcal{S}^i$, where $\mathcal{S}^0$ is an exogenous state variable. The global aim in a DRA problem is to maximise the discounted sum of global reward (complete as many tasks as possible):*

$$R = \sum_{t=0}^{T} \gamma \sum_{m \in \mathcal{M}} \mathcal{R}^m(t), \tag{5}$$

where $\mathcal{R}^m(t)$ is the reward task m realises at timestep t.

From the system designer's perspective, the goal is to construct agents' reward functions that align their individual incentives with the global goals of the system. Ideally, if the agents individually maximise their own total discounted reward,

$$R^i = \sum_{t=0}^{T} \gamma r^i(t), \tag{6}$$

then this should also produce a high quality solution to Eq. (5).

At each time–step, an agent i's action is to allocate its resources to different tasks, given the joint state of the tasks and the allocations of other agents. We assume that (i) an agent can allocate each resource type to at most one task at a time, and (ii) the null action $\emptyset^i$ is always available to an agent, which represents the agent's resource remaining idle. Thus, for each resource type k under its control, i has an action ground-set given by the set of tasks $\mathcal{M}$, and a set of allocations for all resource

$\mathcal{K}$ given by the power set $\times_{k\in\mathcal{K}}\mathcal{P}(M)$. However, the set of allocations available to i may be restricted, in that some subset of $\times_{k\in\mathcal{K}}\mathcal{P}(M)$ may not be feasible (e.g. due to physical constraints). Consequently, we define agent i's action set as $A^i = \{a^i \in \times_{k\in\mathcal{K}}\mathcal{P}(M) | a^i$ is a feasible allocation$\}$. Examples of typical restrictions are that: (i) agents have resource capacities, and cannot allocate more of a resource than its capacity, or (ii) an agent can allocate all of its resources to only one task at a time. An agent's policy, then, is a map of joint task states to a distribution over resource allocations, $\pi^i = \{\Delta(A^i)\}_{s\in\mathcal{S}}$.

The immediate task rewards and task state transitions depend on the total amount of resources allocated to them. At a given time–step, the total amount of each resource type allocated to a task under a pure action profile is:

$$x_k^m = \sum_{i\in\mathcal{I}} a_k^{i,m} \quad \forall k \in \mathcal{K}, \forall m \in \mathcal{M}. \tag{7}$$

Let $x^m = \{x_k^m\}_{k\in\mathcal{K}}$; the reward generated by the allocation is denoted $\mathcal{R}_{s^m s^{m'}}^m(x^m)$, and the transition probability $\mathcal{T}_{s^m s^{m'}}(x^m)$. These task rewards and transitions are *anonymous* functions; they do not depend on who supplies the resource. The global value to the team is the same as in team MDPs, but with rewards and transitions that can be factored:

$$V^\pi(s) = \sum_{a\in A} \pi(a) \sum_{m\in\mathcal{M}} \sum_{s^{m'}\in S^m} \mathcal{T}_{s^m s^{m'}}^m(x^m(a)) \left(\mathcal{R}_{s^m s^{m'}}^m(x^m(a)) + \gamma V^\pi(s^{m'})\right) \tag{8}$$

The DRA model we describe above is very general, and contains as subclasses several canonical team MDP problems, such as sensor coverage problems and multi–agent disaster response management.

3   MCSG Utility Design

In this section we describe the MCSG utility design, and state our main theoretical results. Specifically, we use a dynamic programming approach to prove the existence of pure NE in MCSGs, generalising [13]; and provide efficiency results that build on those regarding games with set function rewards from [14] and [8].

3.1   Existence of Pure Strategy NE

Agents in a team MDP jointly optimise the same global reward function, but this does not imply that in all team MDP representations, they must use Eq. (2) to compute individual utility. The only constraint for team MDP representations is that agents' individual utilities be aligned with the global value function. This condition is formalised by the following class of games and the associated lemma:

Definition 6. *A function* $\phi : A \times \mathcal{S} \to \mathbb{R}$ *is a* **potential** *for a SG if* $\forall i \in \mathcal{I}, \forall \pi^i, \tilde{a}^i \in A^i, \forall a^{-i} \in A^{-i}$ *and* $\forall s \in S$:

$$\phi(s, a^i, a^{-i}) - \phi(s, \tilde{a}^i, a^{-i}) = U_{a^i}^i(s, a^{-i}) - U_{\tilde{a}^i}^i(s, a^{-i}), \tag{9}$$

where $U_{a^i}^i(s, a^{-i})$ *is the value of policy* a^i *(in the dynamic programming sense) to agent* i *when the other agents play the deterministic policy* a^{-i}. *A SG that admits such a function is a* **stochastic potential game** *[10]*.

Lemma 1. *All SGs that admit a potential $\phi(a;s)$ possess a pure NE; all local maxima of $\phi(a;s)$ are pure NE.*

The argument follows that of Theorem 4 of [13] for common-interest SGs, but with $\phi(\cdot)$ taking the place of the common reward function, so the proof is omitted; while the existence and characterisation of pure NE are a consequence of Lemma 2.1 of [10].

In MCSGs, instead of using the global value function as the utility function that drives the agents' policy choice, an agent calculates its *marginal contribution* to Eq. (8). This involves computing $V^{0,\pi^{-i}}(s)$, which is the value, *sans i*, of the team of agents following π^{-i}. Agent i's marginal contribution to Eq. (8), denoted $U^{i,\pi^i}(s,\pi^{-i})$, is then computed by taking the difference of the value of state s if i contributes its component π^i of π and the value of s if i adopts its null action (i.e. as if i was excluded):

$$U^i_{\pi^i}(s,\pi^{-i}) = V^\pi(s) - V^{(0,\pi^{-i})}(s)$$
$$= V^\pi(s) - \sum_{a^{-i} \in \mathcal{A}^{-i}} \pi^{-i}_{a^{-i}}(s) \sum_{s^{m\prime} \in \mathcal{S}^m} \mathcal{T}_{s^m s^{m\prime}}(0,a^{-i})\left(\mathcal{R}^m_{s^m s^{m\prime}}(0,a^{-i}) + \gamma V^{(0,\pi^{-i})}(s^{m\prime})\right) \quad (10)$$

This is the marginal contribution of i to the system value for following π^i, given π^{-i}, which prescribes i's action as $\mathrm{argmax}_{\tilde\pi^i} mc^{i,\tilde\pi^i}(\pi^{-i},s)$. The expression in Eq. (10) gives rise to a potential game, with $V^\pi(s)$ from Eq. (8) as a potential function: for all $i \in N$ and for each pair of i's policies $\pi^i, \tilde\pi^i \in \{A^i\}_{s\in S}$, it can be shown that:

$$U^i_{\pi^i}(s,\pi^{-i}) - U^i_{\tilde\pi^i}(s,\pi^{-i}) = V^{(\pi^i,\pi^{-i})}(s) - V^{(\tilde\pi^i,\pi^{-i})}(s). \quad (11)$$

Thus Lemma 1 applies to MCSGs. We now discuss the efficiency of the NE in MCSGs.

3.2   Bounds on Solution Efficiency

The relevant measures of NE efficiency for MCSGs are the *price of stability* and *price of anarchy*, the ratio of the best and worst–case pure NE to the optimum, respectively.

Theorem 1. *In dynamic resource allocation problems in MCSG form, the ratio of the best NE to the optimum, is 1.*

Proof. Eq. (11) shows that any unilaterally improving change in policy also improves the global value. Thus $\pi^* \in NE$, because $\nexists \tilde\pi^i$ for which $V^*(s) - V^{\{\tilde\pi^i,\pi^{-i}\}}(s) < 0$.

In order to bound the price of anarchy, we must assume some additional conditions on the problem. Specifically, if the reward functions comprising the value function in Eq. (5) (and used in Eq. (8) and Eq. (10)) are non–decreasing submodular functions, then the price of anarchy of the locally optimal NE solutions can be bound.

Definition 7. *A set function $f : 2^{|Z|} \rightarrow \mathbb{R}$ in submodular if $f(X) + f(Y) \geq f(X \cup Y) + f(X \cap Y), \forall X,Y \subseteq Z$, and is non–decreasing if $f(X) \leq f(Y), \forall X \subseteq Y \subseteq Z$.*

Submodularity is preserved under positive linear combinations. Thus, if the global reward function is a separable set function and each resource function is non–decreasing and submodular, then so is the value function Eq. (8). Intuitively, this is because the marginal benefit that including an additional agent in the system decreases as the total number of agents increases.; or in other words, This property leads to the following.

Algorithm 1. MCSG iterative algorithmic framework

1:   **while** *true* **do**   ▷ For each time step
2:      $s \leftarrow CurrentState$ ▷ Get current state
3:      **while** *not converged* **do**   ▷ For each iteration, until actions converge to NE
4:         $z_k^{-i} \leftarrow B(\pi_{k-1}^{-i}, z_{k-1}^{-i}, s)$ ▷ Update beliefs
5:         $m \leftarrow ComputeMDP(b_k, s, T - t)$ ▷ Derive MDP using beliefs
6:         $\pi_k^i \leftarrow P(m)$ ▷ Find best–response policy
7:         $Communicate(\pi_k^i)$ ▷ Communicate policy
8:      $Act(\pi^i)$ ▷ Implement policy

Theorem 2. *In dynamic resource allocation problems with non–decreasing submodular task reward functions in MCSG form, the ratio of the worst–case NE to the optimum is bounded by* $1/2$.

This result is an application of the results of [14], as shown for static games by [8].

4   Iterative MCSG Algorithms

This section describe an iterative algorithmic framework with guaranteed convergence for MCSGs. Our focus on iterative approaches is in contradistinction to centralised computation of an optimal policy in M–MDPs, are in general NP-Complete. Moreover, in large and inherently distributed settings, communication latencies make both centralised computing and implementing such solutions more difficult again.

Specifically, we define a general class of distributed iterative procedures that can be used to solve MCSGs generally. Each agent runs a version of the algorithm given in Algorithm 1, given the utility function in Eq. (10) and taking as input on each iteration the other agents' policies. We call the generic procedure MCSG(B,P), and it alternates between *planning* a policy given beliefs (P, line 6) and sharing policies in order to *update beliefs* (B, line 4), with planning nested inside the belief update loop. For this procedure, the MCSG utility design acts to reduce the agents' computation and communication demands by only communicating with those agents that affect its marginal contribution, while still ensuring that the distributed iterative algorithm converges to a local optimum (i.e. a NE). This forms the belief updating component, whilst *local* planning uses these beliefs and the utility design to search an induced MDP which is smaller than the original problem and guarantees a coordinated outcome.

Theorem 3. *Let MCSG(B,P) comprise an optimal planning algorithm P and a belief update algorithm that converges in potential games B. Then MCSG(B,P) converges to a pure NE joint policy in any MCSG.*

Proof of this theorem depends on the optimality of the planning algorithms, and the convergence of the belief update algorithms when best or better–responses are played. Belief updating algorithms satisfying the above condition when best responses are played include: the family of *generalised weakened fictitious play processes* [1,3,6]; *adaptive play* and other finite memory *best–* and *better–reply processes* [17,18]; and *joint–strategy fictitious play* [7]. In practice, planning can be done using value iteration or policy iteration in the finite horizon case and point–based sampling techniques for infinite horizon problems.

5   Conclusions

In this short paper, we outlined the MCSG architecture, by showing how bounded–quality solutions to team MDPs can found using distributed iterative methods. We believe that, when used on representations with bounded worst–case performance, distributed iterative methods provide a promising approximation technique for large but sparse sequential decision making problems, and future work demonstrate this point.

Additionally, further work is required to explore the full scope of the MCSG architecture, including, e.g.: moving beyond submodular set functions and drawing on other price of anarchy bounds; extensions to systems with failures, partial–observability, or asynchronous operation; and applying reinforcement learning algorithms to MCSGs in place of optimal planners.

References

1. Brown, G.W.: Iterative solution of games by fictitious play. In: Koopmans, T.C. (ed.) Activity Analysis of Production and Allocation, New York, pp. 374–376 (1951)
2. Chapman, A.C., Micillo, R.A., Kota, R., Jennings, N.R.: Decentralised Dynamic Task Allocation Using Overlapping Potential Games. Computer Journal 53(9), 1462–1477 (2010)
3. Fudenberg, D., Levine, D.K.: The Theory of Learning in Games. MIT Press, Cambridge (1998)
4. Ganzfried, S., Sandholm, T.: Computing an approximate jam/fold equilibrium for 3-player no-limit Texas hold'em tournaments. In: Proc. of AAMAS 2008, pp. 919–926 (2008)
5. Groves, T.: Incentives in Teams. Econometrica 41(4), 617–631 (1973)
6. Leslie, D.S., Collins, E.J.: Generalised weakened fictitious play. Games and Economic Behavior 56, 285–298 (2006)
7. Marden, J.R., Arslan, G., Shamma, J.: Joint Strategy Fictitious Play With Inertia for Potential Games. IEEE Trans. Automatic Control 54(2), 208–220 (2009)
8. Marden, J.R., Wierman, A.: Distributed Welfare Games with Applications to Sensor Coverage. In: Proc. of IEEE CDC 2008, pp. 1708–1713 (2008)
9. Melo, F.S., Veloso, M.: Decentralized MDPs with Sparse Interactions. Artificial Intelligence 175, 1757–1789 (2011)
10. Monderer, D., Shapley, L.S.: Potential Games. Games and Economic Behavior 14, 124–143 (1996)
11. Nair, R., Tambe, M., Yokoo, M., Pynadath, D., Marsella, S.: Taming decentralized POMDPs: Towards efficient policy computation for multiagent settings. In: Proc. of IJCAI 2003, pp. 705–711 (2003)
12. Nair, R., Varakantham, P., Tambe, M., Yokoo, M.: Network Distributed POMDPs: A Synthesis of Distributed Constraint Optimization and POMDPs. In: Proc. of AAAI 2005 (2005)
13. Potters, J.A.M., Raghavan, T.E.S., Tijs, S.H.: Pure equilibrium strategies for stochastic games via potential functions. In: Advances in Dynamic Games and their Applications, pp. 433–444 (2009)
14. Vetta, A.: Nash Equilibria in Competitive Societies, with Applications to Facility Location, Traffic Routing and Auctions. In: Proc. of FOCS 2002, pp. 416–425 (2002)
15. Witwicki, S.J., Durfee, E.H.: Influence-based policy abstraction for weakly-coupled Dec-POMDPs. In: Proc. of ICAPS, pp. 185–192 (2010)
16. Wolpert, D.H., Tumer, K.: Optimal payoff functions for members of collectives. Advances in Complex Systems 4(2/3), 265–279 (2001)
17. Young, H.P.: The Evolution of Conventions. Econometrica 61, 57–84 (1993)
18. Young, H.P.: Strategic Learning and its Limits. Oxford University Press (2004)

Judgment Aggregation with Abstentions under Voters' Hierarchy

Guifei Jiang[1,2], Dongmo Zhang[1], and Laurent Perrussel[2]

[1] AIRG, University of Western Sydney, Australia
[2] IRIT, University of Toulouse, France

Abstract. Similar to Arrow's impossibility theorem for preference aggregation, judgment aggregation has also an intrinsic impossibility for generating consistent group judgment from individual judgments. Removing some of the pre-assumed conditions would mitigate the problem but may still lead to too restrictive solutions. It was proved that if completeness is removed but other plausible conditions are kept, the only possible aggregation functions are oligarchic, which means that the group judgment is purely determined by a certain subset of participating judges. Instead of further challenging the other conditions, this paper investigates how the judgment from each individual judge affects the group judgment in an oligarchic environment. We explore a set of intuitively demanded conditions under abstentions and design a feasible judgment aggregation rule based on the agents' hierarchy. We show this proposed aggregation rule satisfies the desirable conditions. More importantly, this rule is oligarchic with respect to a subset of agenda instead of the whole agenda due to its literal-based characteristics.

1 Introduction

Judgment aggregation is an interdisciplinary research topic in economics, philosophy, political science, law and recently in computer science [1–5]. It deals with the problem of how a group judgment on certain issues, represented in logical propositions, can be formed based on individuals' judgments on the same issues. Although most of voting rules for social choice, such as majority, two-thirds majority or unanimity, are applicable to judgment aggregation, their behaviour can be significantly different due to possible logical links among the propositions on which a collective decision has to be made. A well-known example is the so-called *doctrinal paradox* [6], which shows that the majority rule fails to guarantee consistent group judgments.

Suppose a court consisting of three judges has to reach a verdict in a breach-of-contract case. There are three propositions on which the court is required to make judgments:

p: The defendant was contractually obliged not to do a particular action.
q: The defendant did that action.
r: The defendant is liable for breach of contract.

H.K. Dam et al. (Eds.): PRIMA 2014, LNAI 8861, pp. 341–356, 2014.

According to legal doctrine, propositions p and q are jointly necessary and sufficient for proposition r, that is $p \wedge q \leftrightarrow r$. Now the three judges' judgments on the propositions are showed in Table 1.

Table 1. A doctrinal paradox

	p	q	r
Judge 1	T	T	T
Judge 2	T	F	F
Judge 3	F	T	F
Maj	T	T	F

If the three judges take a majority vote on proposition r which is regarded as the conclusion, the outcome is its rejection: a 'not liable' verdict. But if they take majority votes on each of p and q instead, then p and q are accepted and hence by the legal doctrine, r should be accepted as well: a 'liable' verdict. This specifically displays that the set of propositions $\{p, q, \neg r\}$ which is accepted by a majority is logically inconsistent relative to the constraint $p \wedge q \leftrightarrow r$. The problem generalizes well beyond this example and does not depend on the presence of any legal doctrine or exogenous constraints [7].

To illustrate a more general problem, consider any set of propositions with logical connections. Suppose a three-member committee has to make group judgments (acceptance/rejection) on three logically interconnected propositions:

p: We can afford a budget deficit.
$p \rightarrow q$: If we can afford a budget deficit, then we should spend more money on education.
q: We should spend more money on education.

The individual judgments on given propositions for each member are shown in Table 2.

Table 2. A discursive dilemma

	p	$p \rightarrow q$	q
1	T	T	T
2	T	F	F
3	F	T	F
Maj	T	T	F

Then each individual holds consistent judgments on the three propositions, and yet there are majorities for p, $p \rightarrow q$ and $\neg q$, a logically inconsistent set of propositions. The first is the demand that in aggregating judgment a group should be responsive to the views of members on each of judgments involved. The second is the demand that in aggregating judgment a group should reach a collective set of judgments that is itself rational. The paradox shows that the two demands are sometimes in conflict, so that a group that tries to aggregate judgment faces a dilemma. The fact that majority voting may generate inconsistent group judgments is called the *discursive dilemma* [3, 8, 9].

Naturally, the observation that majority voting may fail to produce consistent group judgments raises several questions. In particular, there are two fundamental questions: First, how general is the problem? Is it restricted to majority voting, or does it extend to other decision methods? Secondly, does it occur only in special situations, such as the breach-of-contract case, or does it arise more generally?

In response to these questions, a growing literature on the impossibility of consistent judgment aggregation under various conditions springs up. List and Pettit showed an impossibility result, similar to Arrow's impossibility theorem [10], that no aggregation rule can generate consistent group judgments if we require the rule to satisfy a set of "plausible" conditions [11]. However, such an impossibility result did not discourage the investigation of the possibility of judgment aggregation. None of the conditions on either aggregation rules or decision problems, is indefectible. By weakening or varying these conditions, a growing body of literature on judgment aggregation has emerged in recent years [12–16].

Among all the plausible conditions that lead to impossibility results on judgment aggregation, completeness as one of the rationality requirements has received criticism of being overly demanding in many real-world situations, where an individual may abstain on a decision issue, and the group judgment on some issue may be undetermined. In fact, if we give up completeness, we are able to circumvent impossibility [11, 17–20]. Among them, Gärdenfors has proved a representation theorem for judgment aggregation without completeness, which shows that under certain fairly natural conditions, the only possible aggregation rules are oligarchic. Dietrich and List (2008) have strengthened Gärdenfors' results and showed that by giving up completeness in favor of deductive closure, oligarchies instead of dictatorships are obtained. However, this by no means is a negative result. In fact, our previous work [21] demonstrates that with abstentions, oligarchic aggregation is no longer a single level determination but can also be a multiple-level democracy, which partially explains its pervasiveness in the real world.

Since in our society the hierarchy is one of the most basic organization forms and a hierarchical group may give individual members or subgroups the priority to determine the group judgments on certain propositions. However, such kind of expert rights has been rarely investigated in the current literature [22], let alone proposing a specific judgment aggregation rule to formally display how the hierarchical groups generate the group judgments. In [21] we deal with this issue by proposing a quasi-lexicographic judgment aggregation rule which works well over the limited agenda. It mainly focuses on the following two questions: How does the hierarchical group generate the group judgments? How can the non-oligarchs have the power to make the collective decision in an oligarchic environment?

In this paper, we continue this line of research and investigate the question of whether we can generate consistent group judgments when giving different agents different weights depending on their hierarchy on the propositions in question. We focus on judgment aggregation with abstentions under voter's hierarchy. Our contributions can be summarized in the following: First, we amend the "plausible" conditions in [21], which allows us to extend the set of propositions on which the quasi-lexicographic rule works well from a set of literals to logically interconnected formulas; Secondly, we propose a feasible literal-based aggregation rule for judgment aggregation with abstentions under voter's hierarchy, and show that it is neither dictatorial nor oligarchic over the whole set of agenda; Last but not least, to some extent, we circumvent the impossibility result in [23] by removing completeness from the requirements of both individual and collective levels.

The rest of this paper is structured as follows: In Section 2, we introduce the formal model of judgment aggregation with abstentions based on the formalisms in [11, 24]. In section 3, we list the conditions that sound natural in the context of abstentions and compare them with their counterparts in [19–21]. In Section 4, we propose a literal-based lexicographic judgment aggregation procedure and investigate its properties. In the last section, we conclude the paper with a discussion of further work.

2   The Model of Judgment Aggregation with Abstentions

We consider a finite set of individuals $N = \{1, 2, \ldots, n\}$ with $|N| \geq 2$. They are faced with a decision problem that requires group judgments on logically interconnected propositions represented by a logical language $\mathcal{L}$ with a set Φ_0 of atomic propositions and logical connectives $\{\neg, \vee, \wedge, \leftarrow, \leftrightarrow\}$. We assume that the underlying logic of the logical language is the classical propositional logic with standard syntax and semantics. The set of literals which are either propositional variables or negations of propositional variables, is denoted by $\mathcal{P}$, i.e., $\mathcal{P} = \{p, \neg p \mid p \in \Phi_0\}$.

Given a decision-making problem, the set of propositions on which judgments are to be made is called the *agenda*. Formally, the agenda is a finite non-empty subset $X \subseteq \mathcal{L}$ that is closed under negation, i.e., if $\varphi \in X$, then $\neg \varphi \in X$, and under propositional variables, i.e., for all $\varphi \in \mathcal{L}$, if $\varphi \in X$, then for all $p \in \Phi_0$ occur in φ, $p \in X$. Let $X_0 = X \cap \mathcal{P}$ be the set of literals included in the agenda. Consider the doctrinal paradox in Introduction as an example. In that situation, the agenda X is $\{p, q, p \wedge q, \neg p, \neg q, \neg(p \wedge q)\}$, and the set X_0 of literals in the agenda is $\{p, q, \neg p, \neg q\}$. Similar to [18], we assume that double negations in the agenda cancel each other. That is $X = \{\varphi, \neg \varphi : \varphi \in X^*\}$ where $X^* \subseteq \mathcal{L}$ is a set of unnegated propositions.

We represent each *individual judgment set* as a subset of the agenda, which represents all the propositions that this individual accepts. The individual i's judgment set is denoted by Φ_i, which is a subset of X. As we have mentioned in the previous section, we will not assume that each individual's judgment set must be complete. For each proposition $\varphi \in X$, it may happen that $\varphi \notin \Phi_i$ and $\neg\varphi \notin \Phi_i$. In this case, we say that individual i abstains from making a judgment on φ, denoted by $\varphi\#\Phi_i$. In other words, $\varphi\#\Phi_i$ if and only if $\varphi \notin \Phi_i$ and $\neg\varphi \notin \Phi_i$. We assume that each individual's judgment satisfies the following conditions:

(Individual Logical Closure). For every $\varphi \in X$, if $\Phi_i \models \varphi$, then $\varphi \in \Phi_i$.

(Individual Consistency). For every $\varphi \in X$, if $\varphi \in \Phi_i$, then $\neg\varphi \notin \Phi_i$.

The first condition requires that each individual judgment set is logically closed, that is for any φ in the agenda, if it is a logical consequence of an individual judgment set, then the individual accepts φ. The second condition specifies that each individual judgment set must be logical consistence, i.e., an individual cannot accept both φ and $\neg\varphi$ for every proposition φ in the agenda. Given each individual's judgment set Φ_i, the vector $(\Phi_i)_{i \in N}$ is called *a profile*. For instance, the individual judgment set of each judge in the doctrinal paradox is as follows: $\Phi_1 = \{p, q, p \wedge q\}$; $\Phi_2 = \{p, \neg q, \neg(p \wedge q)\}$; $\Phi_3 = \{\neg p, q, \neg(p \wedge q)\}$. They compose a profile.

Finally, an *(judgment) aggregation rule* is a function F that assigns to each admissible profile $(\Phi_i)_{i \in N}$ a single group judgment set $\Phi \subseteq X$, where $\varphi \in \Phi$ means that the group accepts φ. The set of admissible profiles is called the *domain* of F, denoted as $Dom(F)$. Note that we do not require the group judgments to be complete, which means that a group can also abstain from making a judgment on a proposition.

3 Conditions on Aggregation Rules

We now turn to investigating the conditions which are desirable to be put on an aggregation rule in terms of abstentions. Let F be an aggregation function. We first consider the following three conditions:

Universal Domain (UD). The domain of F includes all logically closed and consistent profiles $(\Phi_i)_{i \in N}$.

Collective Rationality (CR). *For all $\varphi \in X$ and for all $(\Phi_i)_{i \in N} \in Dom(F)$ $F((\Phi_i)_{i \in N}) \models \varphi$ implies $\varphi \in F((\Phi_i)_{i \in N})$, and $\varphi \in F((\Phi_i)_{i \in N})$ implies $\neg\varphi \notin F((\Phi_i)_{i \in N})$.* This requires the collective judgment set is logical closed and consistent.

Non-dictatorship (ND). *There is no $x \in N$ such that for all $\{\Phi_i\}_{i \in N} \in Dom(F)$, $F(\{\Phi_i\}_{i \in N}) = \Phi_x$.* This is a basic democratic requirement: no single individual should always determine the group judgment set.

The next condition is the counterpart of Unanimity with Abstentions in [21] which is restricted to literals.

Literal Unanimity with Abstentions (LU). *For every $\alpha \in \mathcal{P}$, if there is some $V \subseteq N$ such that $V \neq \emptyset$, $\forall i \in V.\alpha \in \Phi_i$ and $\forall j \in N\backslash V.\alpha\#\Phi_j$, then $\alpha \in F((\Phi_i)_{i \in N})$.* Intuitively, if a set of individuals agrees on a certain judgment on a literal α while all the others abstain from α, then this condition requires that $F((\Phi_i)_{i \in N})$ should accept α as well.

As we will see in the following example, this new condition plays a crucial role in extending the agenda set from a set of literals to a set of logically interconnected formulas without generating inconsistent aggregate results. On the other hand, it is neither an extension nor a restriction of Unanimity without abstentions, also called *Pareto optimality* in [20] and *Paretian condition* in [19], which is described as follows:

> *For every $\varphi \in X$, if $\varphi \in \Phi_i$ for every $i \in N$, then $\varphi \in F((\Phi_i)_{i \in N})$.*

The following proposition says that *non-dictatorship* can be derived from LU.

Proposition 1. *Every judgment aggregation rule satisfying literal unanimity with abstentions is non-dictatorial.*

Proof. Assume that F is dictatorial in some individual $a \in N$, then $N/\{a\} \neq \emptyset$. Take $\alpha \in X_0$ and define $\alpha \# \Phi_a$ and $\alpha \in \Phi_x$ for every $x \in N/\{a\}$. By literal unanimity with abstentions, $\alpha \in F((\Phi_i)_{i \in N})$, then $F((\Phi_i)_{i \in N}) \neq \Phi_a$, contradiction. $\square$

The following independence condition requires that the group judgment on each literal should depend only on individual judgments on that literal, which is a counterpart of Arrow's "independence of irrelevant alternative" [25]. With abstentions, this condition has two different versions:

Strong Literal Independence (LI^s). *For every $\alpha \in \mathcal{P}$ and every profiles $(\Phi_i)_{i \in N}$, $(\Phi'_i)_{i \in N} \in \mathrm{Dom}(F)$, if $\alpha \in \Phi_i \leftrightarrow \alpha \in \Phi'_i$ for every $i \in N$, then $\alpha \in F((\Phi_i)_{i \in N}) \leftrightarrow \alpha \in F((\Phi'_i)_{i \in N})$.*
Weak Literal Independence (LI). *For every $\alpha \in \mathcal{P}$ and every profiles $(\Phi_i)_{i \in N}$, $(\Phi'_i)_{i \in N} \in \mathrm{Dom}(F)$, if $\alpha \in \Phi_i \leftrightarrow \alpha \in \Phi'_i$ and $\neg\alpha \in \Phi_i \leftrightarrow \neg\alpha \in \Phi'_i$ for every $i \in N$, then $\alpha \in F((\Phi_i)_{i \in N}) \leftrightarrow \alpha \in F((\Phi'_i)_{i \in N})$.*

Note that these two versions are the same if we assume individual completeness. However, once we allow abstentions, these two versions become different and the strong version is intuitively too strong to be acceptable. Since in the profile even if all judges who abstain on α turn to rejecting α, no matter how big portion of these judges is, the strong version requires the group judgment on α to be the same so long as the same set of judges accepts α. The weak version solves the problem.

Similar conditions have been also discussed in the literature. It is not hard to see that the *strong (weak) literal Independence* condition strengthens the *independence of irrelevant propositional alternatives condition* in [23] to the set of literals under the provision of abstentions, while the weak independence condition amounts to reserving *the independent of irrelevant alternatives condition* in [19] to literals.

The following two conditions are two versions of the counterpart of the neutrality condition, which requires that literals should be treated in an even-handed way by the aggregation function.

Strong Literal Neutrality (LN^s). For every $\alpha, \beta \in \mathcal{P}$ and every profile $(\Phi_i)_{i \in N}$
$\in Dom(F)$, if $\alpha \in \Phi_i \leftrightarrow \beta \in \Phi_i$ for every $i \in N$, then $\alpha \in F((\Phi_i)_{i \in N}) \leftrightarrow \beta \in F((\Phi_i)_{i \in N})$.

Weak Literal Neutrality (LN). For every $\alpha, \beta \in \mathcal{P}$ and every profile $(\Phi_i)_{i \in N}$
$\in Dom(F)$, if $\alpha \in \Phi_i \leftrightarrow \beta \in \Phi_i$ and $\neg\alpha \in \Phi_i \leftrightarrow \neg\beta \in \Phi_i$ for every $i \in N$,
then $\alpha \in F((\Phi_i)_{i \in N}) \leftrightarrow \beta \in F((\Phi_i)_{i \in N})$.

Similarly, these two versions are the same if we assume individual completeness, and the strong version is intuitively too strong to be acceptable. Since in the profile even if all judges who abstain on α reject β, no matter how big portion of these judges is, the strong neutrality requires the group judgment on α and β to be the same so long as the set of judges accepting α and the set of judges accepting β are the same. The weak version solves the problem.

The last condition is the counterpart of Systematicity, introduced by List and Pettit (2002), which combines independency and neutrality: literals should be treated in an even-handed way by the aggregation function; the group judgment on each literal should depend exclusively on the pattern of individual judgment on that literal.

Strong Literal Systematicity (LS^s). *For every $\alpha, \beta \in \mathcal{P}$ and every profiles*
$(\Phi_i)_{i \in N}, (\Phi'_i)_{i \in N} \in \mathrm{Dom}(F)$, if for every $i \in N$, $\alpha \in \Phi_i \leftrightarrow \beta \in \Phi'_i$, then
$\alpha \in F((\Phi_i)_{i \in N}) \leftrightarrow \beta \in F((\Phi'_i)_{i \in N})$.

Weak Literal Systematicity (LS). *For every $\alpha, \beta \in \mathcal{P}$ and every profiles*
$(\Phi_i)_{i \in N}, (\Phi'_i)_{i \in N} \in \mathrm{Dom}(F)$, if for every $i \in N$, $\alpha \in \Phi_i \leftrightarrow \beta \in \Phi'_i$ and
$\neg\alpha \in \Phi_i \leftrightarrow \neg\beta \in \Phi'_i$, then $\alpha \in F((\Phi_i)_{i \in N}) \leftrightarrow \beta \in F((\Phi'_i)_{i \in N})$.

The reason why we reserve Independence, Neutrality and Systematicity to literals alone is based on the consideration that the problem of the doctrinal paradox and the discursive dilemma in Introduction comes from the requirement that the majority rule treats the compound formulas and propositional variables independently. Indeed *the principle of compositionality*, a fundamental presupposition of the semantics in most contemporary logics, denotes that the propositional variables are more primary than the compound formulas, since the truth of the later is determined by the truth of the former. For instance, in doctrinal paradox, the truth of the conjunctive formula $p \wedge q$ is determined by its constituents p and q. In this sense, we may say the judgments on p and q are the reasons to accept $p \wedge q$ or not, while the reason for whether p or q is accepted or not is beyond the expressivity of propositional logic. Of course in more powerful logic such as first-order logic, propositional variables are not primary atoms any more. In that more refined logic, once it presupposes the principle of compositionality, the new building blocks which replace propositional variables are the reasons for accepting propositional variables or not.

In the light of this thought, we take a reason-based perspective and apply the aggregation rule only to primary data whose reasons are beyond the expressivity power of the underlying logics, then use them to generate complex formulas within the underlying logic [23, 26]. Under abstentions, it is the literals instead of propositional variables that are primary data, since without completeness, we can not derive that p is rejected from that p is not accepted. It may be possible that p is abstained (neither accepted nor rejected). Therefore, we amount to reserving Independence, Neutrality and Systematicity to literals instead of propositional variables, which makes them more acceptable. For instance, one criticizes Systematicity (the independent part) being used for $p \lor q$, where p denotes "The government can afford a budget deficit", and q "Forbidding smoking should be legalized" on the ground that there are two propositions involved, and that the society should know how each individual feels about either proposition, and not just about their disjunction. There is no similar objection arising when Systematicity applies to either p or q [23].

Another advantage is that this provides a plausible solution for the paradoxes in Introduction. For instance, we may just apply the majority rule to literals and calculate p, q in the group judgment set; then use them to generate $p \land q$ in the group judgment set. According to this procedure, the group judgment set is $\{p, q, p \land q\}$ which is logically consistent.

In the following we denote *Universal Domain, Collective Rationality, Literal Unanimity with Abstentions* and *Weak Literal Systematicity* as UD, CR, LU and LS for short.

4   The Literal-Based Lexicographic Aggregation Rule

In this section, we improve the work [21] by proposing an aggregation rule for judgment aggregation with abstentions under voters' hierarchy that works well over a set of logically interconnected formulas instead of a set of literals.

As we have mentioned in the introduction, we assume that there is a hierarchy among all the individuals. In the real-world we can easily see such a hierarchy, for instance, the management structure of an enterprise, a democratic political regime or a community organisation. Members in different ranks may play different roles in collective decision-making.

Definition 1. *A hierarchy over the set N of individuals is a strict partial order $<$ over N that satisfies transitivity and asymmetry.*

It follows that there is no infinite ascending sequence $i_1 < i_2 < i_3 < \cdots$, where $i_n \in N$, which means all hierarchical chains of N must be "up-bounded" with at least one top leader. In this sense, we say $(N, <)$ is *well-prioritized*.

An aggregation rule determines which propositions are collectively accepted and which ones are collectively rejected. As we denoted, $X_0 = X \cap \mathcal{P}$ is the set of literals included in the agenda. We first define an aggregate procedure F for that a literal $\alpha \in X_0$ is collectively accepted, denoted by $\alpha \in F((\Phi_i)_{i \in N})$, as follows:

Definition 2. *For every $\alpha \in X_0$,*

$$\alpha \in F((\Phi_i)_{i \in N}) \text{ iff } \forall i \in N(\neg\alpha \notin \Phi_i \lor \exists j \in N(i < j \land \alpha \in \Phi_j)) \text{ and } \exists k \in N.\alpha \in \Phi_k \tag{1}$$

Intuitively, this aggregate procedure says that a literal α is accepted by a group if the following two conditions are both satisfied.

(1) for any individual if he rejects α, then there is an individual with higher hierarchy accepting α; and
(2) there is at least one individual accepting α.

We denote the set of collectively accepted literals by $F((\Phi_i)_{i \in N})_0$. Based on this concept, we define that any $\varphi \in X$ is collectively accepted as follows:

Definition 3. *For any $\varphi \in X$,*

$$\varphi \in F((\Phi_i)_{i \in N}) \text{ iff } F((\Phi_i)_{i \in N})_0 \models \varphi \tag{2}$$

This definition says that a proposition φ in the agenda X is collectively accepted if it is a logical consequence of the set of collectively accepted literals.

Similarly, a proposition $\varphi \in X$ is *collectively abstained* if neither itself nor its negation is collectively accepted. That is,

$$\varphi \# F((\Phi_i)_{i \in N}) \text{ iff } \varphi \notin F((\Phi_i)_{i \in N}) \text{ and } \neg\varphi \notin F((\Phi_i)_{i \in N}). \tag{3}$$

We call above defined judgment aggregation rule F *the literal-based lexicographic rule* since we just apply the lexicographic rule to the subset of literals in the agenda.

To demonstrate how this rule works, let us consider the following example.

Example 1. Suppose Ann, Bill and Tom have to make group judgments on three logically connected propositions as follows:

p: There is the elixir of life.
q: People can be immortal.
$p \to q$: If there is the elixir of life, then people can be immortal.

Ann thinks p is true and abstains on q and $p \to q$, Bill rejects q and abstains on p and $p \to q$, Tom accepts q and $p \to q$, and abstains on p. Their individual judgments are shown as follows:

Table 3.

	p	q	p→q
Ann	T	#	#
Bill	#	F	#
Tom	#	T	T

The hierarchy among them is Ann < Bill and Tom < Bill as illustrated below:

Fig. 1.

Note that individuals with the highest priority are written at the top of the diagram. We next apply the literal-based aggregation rule to generate the collective judgment set. The model of this aggregation situation is as follows:

- $N = \{Ann, Bill, Tom\}$ with Ann< Bill and Tom< Bill;
- $X = \{p, q, p \rightarrow q, \neg p, \neg q, \neg(p \rightarrow q)\}$ and $X_0 = \{p, q, \neg p, \neg q\}$.

The individual judgment sets for Ann, Bill and Tom are as follows:

- $p \in \Phi_{Ann}$, $q \# \Phi_{Ann}$, $p \rightarrow q \# \Phi_{Ann}$;
- $p \# \Phi_{Bill}$, $\neg q \in \Phi_{Bill}$, $p \rightarrow q \# \Phi_{Bill}$;
- $p \# \Phi_{Tom}$, $q \in \Phi_{Tom}$, $p \rightarrow q \in \Phi_{Tom}$.

We first calculate the group judgments on the set X_0 of literals by Definition 2.

- The collective accepts p, since all of them don't reject p, i.e., $\forall i \in N(\neg p \notin \Phi_i)$ holds, and Ann accepts p, i.e., $\exists j \in N(p \in \Phi_j)$ holds.
- The collective rejects q, since Bill with the highest priority rejects q, even though Tom accepts q.

Then the collective accepts p and rejects q, i.e., $F((\Phi_i)_{i \in N})_0 = \{p, \neg q\}$. And by Definition 3, the collective rejects $(p \rightarrow q)$, since $\{p, \neg q\} \models \neg(p \rightarrow q)$. Thus, the group judgment set is $\{p, \neg q, \neg(p \rightarrow q)\}$ by the literal-based lexicographic aggregation rule.

We would like to remind that the quasi-lexicographic rule in [21] fails to deal with this situation, since the agenda involves logically interconnected formula $p \rightarrow q$. If we apply that rule to this agenda, we could get an inconsistent aggregate result $\{p, \neg q, p \rightarrow q\}$.

Moreover, the literal-based lexicographic aggregation rule provides a plausible solution to the paradox in Introduction. Let's consider the discursive dilemma. We may take all the possible hierarchy among the three agents into consideration. One boss case: let $1 < 2 < 3$ be the hierarchy, then according to this rule the aggregate result is just the individual aggregate set of the first agent $\{p, q, p \rightarrow q\}$, which is consistent. Yet the cost of this case is that the first agent seems to be the dictator for this profile, which is a bit depressing. Two-boss case: let the priority order be $1 < 3$ and $1 < 2$, then in the virtue of this rule, they collectively reject q and abstain on p and $p \rightarrow q$. Three-boss (no boss or anonymity) case: according to this rule, p, q and $p \rightarrow q$ are all collectively abstained.

We next investigate the properties of the literal-based lexicographic rule F. The first proposition shows that the literal-based lexicographic rule F satisfies above desirable conditions UD, CR, LU and LS.

Theorem 1. *The literal-based lexicographic rule F satisfies conditions UD, CR, LU and LS.*

Proof. It is straightforward that F satisfies conditions UD according to the definition.

We next show F satisfies CR.

(Logical Closure) For any $\varphi \in X$ and for all $\{\Phi_i\}_{i \in N}$, assume $F(\{\Phi_i\}_{i \in N}) \models \varphi$. Since $F(\{\Phi_i\}_{i \in N})_0 \models F(\{\Phi_i\}_{i \in N})$ $(F(\{\Phi_i\}_{i \in N})_0 \models \psi$ for any $\psi \in F(\{\Phi_i\}_{i \in N}))$, so $F(\{\Phi_i\}_{i \in N})_0 \models \varphi$, so $\varphi \in F(\{\Phi_i\}_{i \in N})$ by Definition 3.

(Consistence) We first show for any $\alpha \in \mathcal{P}$, $\alpha \in F(\{\Phi_i\}_{i \in N})_0$ implies $\neg \alpha \notin F(\{\Phi_i\}_{i \in N})_0$. Suppose for a contradiction that for some $\beta \in \mathcal{P}$, $\beta \in F(\{\Phi_i\}_{i \in N})_0$ and $\neg \beta \in F(\{\Phi_i\}_{i \in N})_0$, then (i) $\forall i \in N(\neg \beta \notin \Phi_i \vee \exists j \in N(i < j \wedge \beta \in \Phi_j))$ and $\exists k \in N.\beta \in \Phi_k$; (ii) $\forall i \in N(\beta \notin \Phi_i \vee \exists j \in N(i < j \wedge \neg \beta \in \Phi_j))$ and $\exists k \in N.\neg \beta \in \Phi_k$. By (i), (ii) we can get an infinite ascending sequence $i_1, i_2, i_3, \cdots$, which is a contradiction with that $(N, <)$ is well-prioritized. Then $F(\{\Phi_i\}_{i \in N})_0$ is consistent, so by the Definition 3, $F(\{\Phi_i\}_{i \in N})$ is consistent as well.

For LU, assume for every $\alpha \in \mathcal{P}$, if there is some $V \subseteq N$ such that $V \neq \emptyset$, $\forall i \in V.\alpha \in \Phi_i$ and $\forall j \in N \setminus V.\alpha \# \Phi_j$, then by Definition 2, $\alpha \in F(\{\Phi_i\}_{i \in N})$.

For LS, given every $\alpha \in \mathcal{P}$, the individuals accepting α and these rejecting α are the same for every two profiles $(\Phi_i)_{i \in N}$, $(\Phi'_i)_{i \in N}$, then the aggregate results of α according to the Definition 2 are the same as well. Yet it is not the case for LS^s, for we could construct a counterexample: given a hierarchy on an agent set $N = \{1, 2, 3\}$ with $1 < 2$, $1 < 3$. For the profile $(\Phi_i)_{i \in N}$ where $\alpha \in \Phi_1$, $\alpha \# \Phi_2$ and $\alpha \# \Phi_3$, we have $\alpha \in F(\Phi_i)_{i \in N}$ by LU. Let individual $2, 3$ who abstain on it turn to rejecting α, while individual 1 still accepts α, we get a different profile $(\Phi'_i)_{i \in N}$, where $\alpha \in \Phi'_1$, $\neg \alpha \in \Phi'_2$ and $\neg \alpha \in \Phi'_3$, but $\alpha \notin F(\Phi'_i)_{i \in N}$. □

As we expected, F satisfies the four desirable conditions and thus is a feasible aggregation rule for hierarchical groups to generate group judgments. One may be surprised to find that as an 'unfair' aggregation rule, F is non-dictatorial by Proposition 1. On the other hand, this shows that *non-dictatorship* is a very weak condition imposed on judgment aggregation functions when abstention is allowable.

Gärdenfors and Dietrich *et al* have both showed that by giving up completeness, oligarchies instead of dictatorships are obtained [18, 20]. We investigate whether this proposed rule is oligarchic. The definition of an oligarchic rule is given as follows:

Definition 4. *An aggregation rule G satisfying UD is a weak oligarchy if there is a non-empty smallest subset $M \subseteq N$ such that for every profile $(\Phi_i)_{i \in N} \in Dom(G)$,*

$$\bigcap_{i \in M} \Phi_i \subseteq G((\Phi_i)_{i \in N}).$$

And an oligarchic rule G is strict if for every profile $(\Phi_i)_{i \in N} \in Dom(G)$,

$$\bigcap_{i \in M} \Phi_i = G((\Phi_i)_{i \in N}).$$

In this case, we call G to be weakly (strictly) oligarchic with respect to M.

That is, an aggregation rule satisfying universal domain is said to be weakly oligarchic if there is a non-empty smallest set M such that for any profile of individual judgment set, the group judgment set contains all the propositions if they are in every member's judgment set of M. Furthermore, we say an aggregation rule is strictly oligarchic if for any profile of individual judgment set, the group judgment set is exactly the set of propositions that are in every member's judgment set of M. Special cases of weak oligarchic aggregation rules are unanimous $(M = N)$, majority $(|M| > \frac{n}{2})$ and dictatorial $(M = \{i\})$ rules. Specifically, the unanimous and dictatorial rules are weakly and strictly oligarchic rules, majority rule is weakly but not strictly oligarchic. However, the literal-based lexicographic rule F is neither weakly oligarchic nor strictly oligarchic. Here is a simple counter-example.

Let the agent set $N = \{1,2\}$ with $<= \emptyset$, the agenda $X = \{p, q, p \rightarrow q, \neg p, \neg q, \neg(p \rightarrow q)\}$ and the set of literals in the agenda $X_0 = \{p, q, \neg p, \neg q\}$, the individual judgment set for each agent is as follows: $\Phi_1 = \{p, q, p \rightarrow q\}$, $\Phi_2 = \{\neg p, \neg q, p \rightarrow q\}$. Then $\Phi_1 \cap \Phi_2 = \{p \rightarrow q\}$, but according to the literal-based aggregation rule F, $p \# F(\Phi_1, \Phi_2)$, $q \# F(\Phi_1, \Phi_2)$ and $p \rightarrow q \# F(\Phi_1, \Phi_2)$. Thus, $\Phi_1 \cap \Phi_2 \not\subseteq F(\Phi_1, \Phi_2)$.

It may be a bit surprising to find that the literal-based aggregation rule is not oligarchic. In fact this does not violates the results in [18, 20] since their conditions imposed on the aggregation rules are more strengthened than ours. Specifically, the unanimity and systemacity conditions hold for all formulas while we restrict them to literals. On the other hand, our proposed rule is literal-based, and the compound formulas are dependent on the collective judgments on the literals instead of generating by this rule. That is, if a formula is a logical consequence of the collective literals, then it is in the collective set; otherwise, it is abstained. Therefore, Instead of the whole agenda, we need to consider the oligarchy notion with respect to the set of literals in the agenda on which the literal-based aggregation rule takes effect. This idea leads to a weak concept of an oligarchic aggregation rule as follows:

Definition 5. *An aggregation rule G satisfying UD is a weak oligarchy w.r.t X_0 if there is a non-empty smallest subset $M \subseteq N$ such that for every profile $(\Phi_i)_{i \in N} \in Dom(G)$,*

$$\{\varphi \in X \mid \bigcap_{i \in M} \Phi_i \cap X_0 \models \varphi\} \subseteq G((\Phi_i)_{i \in N}).$$

And an oligarchic rule G is strict w.r.t X_0 if for every profile $(\Phi_i)_{i \in N} \in Dom(G)$,

$$\{\varphi \in X \mid \bigcap_{i \in M} \Phi_i \cap X_0 \models \varphi\} = G((\Phi_i)_{i \in N}).$$

Intuitively, an aggregation rule satisfying universal domain is said to be weakly oligarchic w.r.t X_0 if there is a non-empty smallest set M such that for any profile of individual judgment set, the group judgment set contains all the consequences of literals that are in every member's judgment set of M. Similarly, an aggregation rule is strictly oligarchic w.r.t X_0 if for any profile of individual judgment set, the group judgment set is exactly the set of consequences of the literals that are in every member's judgment set of M.

We have the following proposition saying the literal-based lexicographic rule F is weakly oligarchic w.r.t X_0, but not strictly oligarchic w.r.t X_0.

Proposition 2. *The literal-based lexicographic rule F is weakly oligarchic w.r.t X_0, but not strictly oligarchic w.r.t X_0.*

Proof. Suppose F satisfies universal domain, it suffices to find a non-empty smallest set $M \subseteq N$, such that for every profile of individual judgment sets $(\Phi_i)_{i \in N}$, every $\varphi \in X$, if $\bigcap_{i \in M} \Phi_i \cap X_0 \models \varphi$, then $\varphi \in F((\Phi_i)_{i \in N})$. Let $O = Max_{\geq}(N) = \{i \in N : \nexists j \in N.i < j\}$. Since $(N, <)$ is well-prioritized and $|N| \geq 2$, so O must exist and be non-empty. Suppose for every profile of individual judgment sets $(\Phi_i)_{i \in N}$, every $i \in N$ and for all $\alpha \in X_0$, if $\alpha \in \bigcap_{i \in O} \Phi_i$, then according to Definition 2, $\alpha \in F((\Phi_i)_{i \in N})$. Then $\bigcap_{i \in O} \Phi_i \cap X_0 \subseteq F((\Phi_i)_{i \in N})_0$. Since $\bigcap_{i \in O} \Phi_i \cap X_0 \models \varphi$, so $F((\Phi_i)_{i \in N})_0 \models \varphi$, so $\varphi \in F((\Phi_i)_{i \in N})$ by Definition 3.

We next show O is the smallest one with $\{\varphi \in X \mid \bigcap_{i \in O} \Phi_i \cap X_0 \models \varphi\} \subseteq F((\Phi_i)_{i \in N})$. Suppose not, then there is some $A \subseteq N$ such that $A \subset O$ and $\{\varphi \in X \mid \bigcap_{i \in A} \Phi_i \cap X_0 \models \varphi\} \subseteq F((\Phi_i)_{i \in N})$, then there is some $a \in N$ such that $a \in O$ but $a \notin A$. Take some $\beta \in X_0$ and define $\beta \in \Phi_i$ for every $i \in N \backslash \{a\}$ and $\neg \beta \in \Phi_a$, then by Definition 2, $\beta \notin F((\Phi_i)_{i \in N})$, but $\beta \in \{\varphi \in X \mid \bigcap_{i \in A} \Phi_i \cap X_0 \models \varphi\}$, contradicting with assumption. Thus, O is just the required M.

It's easy to construct a profile such that $\bigcap_{i \in M} \Phi_i \cap X_0 \not\supseteq F((\Phi_i)_{i \in N})$ by LU. Take $\alpha \in X_0$ and define $\alpha \# \Phi_a$ for some $a \in M$ and $\alpha \in \Phi_x$ for every $x \in N/\{a\}$. By literal unanimity with abstentions, $\alpha \in F((\Phi_i)_{i \in N})$, but $\alpha \notin \bigcap_{i \in M} \Phi_i \cap X_0$. Thus F is not strictly oligarchic w.r.t X_0. □

On the one hand the literal-based lexicographic aggregation rule F satisfies all the desirable conditions given in Section 3; on the other hand, it is only oligarchic with respect to the subset of literals in the agenda not over the whole set of agenda due to its literal-base characteristics.

The last proposition of this section shows under which conditions two literal-based lexicographic rules are identical. We first introduce a helpful notation. For any $i \in N$ and any $\varphi, \psi \in X$, the individual i makes the same judgment on φ and ψ is denoted by $\Phi_i|_{\{\varphi\}} \Leftrightarrow \Phi_i|_{\{\psi\}}$, that is $\Phi_i|_{\{\varphi\}} \Leftrightarrow \Phi_i|_{\{\psi\}}$ is equivalent to $(\varphi \in \Phi_i$ iff $\psi \in \Phi_i)$ and $(\neg \varphi \in \Phi_i$ iff $\neg \psi \in \Phi_i)$.

Proposition 3. *Let $\{p\} \subseteq X \cap \Phi_0$, and f_1, f_2 be two literal-based lexicographic rules. If for all profiles of individual judgment sets $(\Phi_i)_{i \in N}$, $f_1((\Phi_i)_{i \in N})|_{\{p\}} \Leftrightarrow f_2((\Phi_i)_{i \in N})|_{\{p\}}$, then for all $\varphi \in X$, $f_1((\Phi_i)_{i \in N})|_{\{\varphi\}} \Leftrightarrow f_2((\Phi_i)_{i \in N})|_{\{\varphi\}}$.*

Proof. Take any $q \in X \cap \Phi_0$. Define the profile $(\Phi_i')_{i \in N}$ in terms of $(\Phi_i)_{i \in N}$ as follows: for all $i \in N$, $\Phi_i' = \Phi_i$ except at p where $\Phi_i'|_{\{p\}} \Leftrightarrow \Phi_i|_{\{q\}}$. Then

$$
\begin{aligned}
f_1((\Phi_i)_{i \in N})|_{\{q\}} &\Leftrightarrow f_1((\Phi_i|_{\{q\}})_{i \in N}) \text{ by LI} \\
&\Leftrightarrow f_1((\Phi_i'|_{\{p\}})_{i \in N}) \text{ by LS} \\
&\Leftrightarrow f_1((\Phi_i')_{i \in N})|_{\{p\}} \text{ by LI} \\
&\Leftrightarrow f_2((\Phi_i')_{i \in N})|_{\{p\}} \text{ by hypothesis} \\
&\Leftrightarrow f_2((\Phi_i'|_{\{p\}})_{i \in N}) \text{ by LI} \\
&\Leftrightarrow f_2((\Phi_i|_{\{q\}})_{i \in N}) \text{ by LS} \\
&\Leftrightarrow f_2((\Phi_i)_{i \in N})|_{\{q\}} \text{ by LI.}
\end{aligned}
$$

It is clear that $f_1((\Phi_i)_{i \in N}) \cap \Phi_0 = f_2((\Phi_i)_{i \in N}) \cap \Phi_0$.
Hence, $f_1((\Phi_i)_{i \in N}) = f_2((\Phi_i)_{i \in N})$.   □

This proposition says that if two literal-based lexicographic rules make a same judgment (acceptance, rejection and abstention) on a propositional variable in the agenda, then they make the same judgment on all the formulas in the agenda. In the other word, a literal-based lexicographic rule is determined by its responses to all the possible judgments (acceptance, rejection and abstention) on a fixed propositional variable in the agenda. This property paves the way to show a characterization result of the literal-based lexicographic rule. We leave this work for future.

5   Conclusion

In this paper, we have proposed a literal-based lexicographic rule which extends the set of agenda from a set of literals to a set of logically interconnected formulas [21] and further investigated the properties of this rule. It turns out that this proposed rule is neither dictatorial nor oligarchic in the standard sense. The reason for non-dictatorship is that, as proved in Proposition 1, we may take advantage of the abstention to show all individuals fail to play a role in collective decision-making on a particular proposition when they abstain from that proposition. This indicates that under the provision of abstentions, non-dictatorship is a rather weak condition imposed on the judgment aggregation rule. The reason for non-oligarchy is due to its literal-based characteristics. In fact, we may regard this proposed rule as a special case of premiss-based rule [27] where the set of premisses is the subset of literals in the agenda.

There are many directions for future investigations. Firstly, as a special kind of lexicographic rule, it is interesting to investigate a representation result for our proposed aggregation rule. The lexicographic rule has been extensively studies in preference aggregation, and [28] has proved that lexicographic rule is the only way of combining preference relations satisfying five natural conditions which are very close to Arrow's conditions. We expect to obtain a similar characterization result for our proposed rule. This work is under way;

Secondly, under the provision of abstentions, we have amended the commonly desirable conditions. It is natural to investigate some possibility results with respect to these amending conditions. In terms of the rationality requirements, this means that we drop the completeness condition. Comparing with the impossibility results, we get a possibility result which can be stated as: *there are non-dictatorial aggregation rules satisfying universal domain, collective rationality, literal unanimity with abstentions and weak literal systematicity*, which seems positive news to the result in [23]. However, it is not the case since we do not assume completeness at both individual and collective levels, which means that a judge can abstain from a proposition and the group judgment on a proposition can be undetermined.

In addition, with abstentions, the dictatorship in judgment aggregation can also vary in degrees [29]. It is highly interesting to investigate the possibility scope between rationality, dictatorship under a set of plausible conditions. Some work has been done in this direction [30].

Last but not least, since the universal and perfect aggregation rule does not exist, a plausible way is to boil down aggregation problems to three-sided matching questions between specific so-called degenerate rules, specific groups and specific agendas., which is a promising direction [22].

References

1. Dietrich, F., List, C.: Arrow's theorem in judgment aggregation. Social Choice and Welfare 29(1), 19–33 (2007)
2. Mongin, P.: Consistent bayesian aggregation. Journal of Economic Theory 66(2), 313–351 (1995)
3. Pigozzi, G.: Belief merging and the discursive dilemma: an argument-based account to paradoxes of judgment aggregation. Synthese 152(2), 285–298 (2006)
4. Wilson, R.: On the theory of aggregation. Journal of Economic Theory 10(1), 89–99 (1975)
5. Konieczny, S., Pérez, R.P.: Merging information under constraints: a logical framework. Journal of Logic and Computation 12(5), 773–808 (2002)
6. Kornhauser, L.A., Sager, L.G.: Unpacking the court. The Yale Law Journal 96(1), 82–117 (1986)
7. List, C.: The theory of judgment aggregation: an introductory review. Synthese 187(1), 179–207 (2012)
8. Pettit, P.: Deliberative democracy and the discursive dilemma. Philosophical Issues 11(1), 268–299 (2001)
9. Pivato, M.: The discursive dilemma and probabilistic judgement aggregation. Munich Personal RePEc Archive (2008)
10. Arrow, K.J.: A difficulty in the concept of social welfare. Journal of Political Economy 58, 328–346 (1950)
11. List, C., Pettit, P.: Aggregating sets of judgments: An impossibility result. Economics and Philosophy 18(01), 89–110 (2002)
12. Dietrich, F.: Judgment aggregation (im)possibility theorems. Journal of Economic Theory 126(1), 286–298 (2006)
13. List, C., Pettit, P.: Aggregating sets of judgments: Two impossibility results compared. Synthese 140(1-2), 207–235 (2004)
14. Mongin, P.: Factoring out the impossibility of logical aggregation. Journal of Economic Theory 141(1), 100–113 (2008)

15. Pauly, M., Van Hees, M.: Logical constraints on judgement aggregation. Journal of Philosophical logic 35(6), 569–585 (2006)
16. Van Hees, M.: The limits of epistemic democracy. Social Choice and Welfare 28(4), 649–666 (2007)
17. Dietrich, F., List, C.: Judgment aggregation with consistency alone. London School of Economics, Government Department, London, UK (2007)
18. Dietrich, F., List, C.: Judgment aggregation without full rationality. Social Choice and Welfare 31(1), 15–39 (2008)
19. Dokow, E., Holzman, R.: Aggregation of binary evaluations with abstentions. Journal of Economic Theory 145(2), 544–561 (2010)
20. Gärdenfors, P.: A representation theorem for voting with logical consequences. Economics and Philosophy 22(2), 181–190 (2006)
21. Jiang, G., Zhang, D., Tang, X.: Judgment aggregation with abstentions: A hierarchical approach. In: Grossi, D., Roy, O., Huang, H. (eds.) LORI. LNCS, vol. 8196, pp. 321–325. Springer, Heidelberg (2013)
22. Dietrich, F., List, C.: A liberal paradox for judgment aggregation. Social Choice and Welfare 31(1), 59–78 (2008)
23. Mongin, P.: Factoring out the impossibility of logical aggregation. Journal of Economic Theory 141(1), 100–113 (2008)
24. Dietrich, F.: A generalised model of judgment aggregation. Social Choice and Welfare 28(4), 529–565 (2007)
25. Arrow, K.J.: Social Choice and Individual Values. Cowles Foundation Monographs. Wiley, New York (1953, 1964)
26. Nehring, K., Puppe, C.: Consistent judgement aggregation: the truth-functional case. Social Choice and Welfare 31(1), 41–57 (2008)
27. Dietrich, F., Mongin, P.: The premiss-based approach to judgment aggregation. Journal of Economic Theory 145(2), 562–582 (2010)
28. Andréka, H., Ryan, M., Schobbens, P.Y.: Operators and laws for combining preference relations. Journal of Logic and Computation 12(1), 13–53 (2002)
29. Rossi, F., Venable, K.B., Walsh, T.: Aggregating preferences cannot be fair. Intelligenza Artificiale 2(1), 30–38 (2005)
30. Dietrich, F., List, C.: Propositionwise judgment aggregation: the general case. Social Choice and Welfare 40(4), 1067–1095 (2013)

A Social Trust Model Considering Trustees' Influence

Jian-Ping Mei [1], Han Yu [2], Yong Liu [2], Zhiqi Shen [2], and Chunyan Miao [2]

[1] College of Computer Science and Technology, Zhejiang University of Technology,
Hangzhou, China
[2] School of Computer Engineering, Nanyang Technological University, Singapore

Abstract. Online social networks can be viewed as multi-agent systems (MASs) built on top of social relationships. In these environments, relationships among agents are often formed through trust. Accurately estimating the degree of trust between agents is important in this case as social relationships are frequently leveraged to recommend products or services. Existing social trust models often utilize rating similarity between different agents to calculate how much they should trust each other. However, when a new truster enters the MAS and has not provided sufficient number of ratings, existing approaches cannot effectively advise the truster on which other agents can be trusted. To address this problem, we propose a social trust model that considers a trustee agent's influence in a social network. Evaluation based on the *Epinions* dataset shows that the proposed model significantly outperforms a state-of-the-art approach in social recommendation.

1 Introduction

Online social networking websites, such as *Epinions*[1], are becoming increasingly popular for people to share, organize and locate items of interest. It provides a platform for people to share their experience by disseminating their information or satisfaction on products or services to influence other people's opinions and decisions. Other than giving reviews and ratings to products, in the site of Epinions, users can also build up a list of trustworthy users, the idea of whom are most likely to be agreed or accepted. All the trust relationships form a trust network, i.e., a special social network where each edge represents a trust relationship. Once a trust relationship has been established, the ideas or behaviors of the trustee, i.e., the one who is trusted, could influence the behaviour of the truster, i.e., the one who trusts. Such an environment resembles an open multi-agent system (MAS) where potentially self-interested agents from diverse background need to establish trust between each other in order to leverage the information provided by other agents. Therefore, studies have been conducted to investigate how to design trust evaluation models that can use social network information to derive the degree of trust between agents [3].

---

[1] http://www.epinions.com

H.K. Dam et al. (Eds.): PRIMA 2014, LNAI 8861, pp. 357–364, 2014.
© Springer International Publishing Switzerland 2014

The most commonly used approach for calculating how much a *truster* agent should trust a particular *trustee* agent in social network settings is to compute the similarity between their past ratings [9,12]. It relies on the presumption that there are enough commonly rated items between any given pair of truster and trustee agents in order to produce accurate estimation of the trustee agent's trustworthiness. However, by analyzing the *Epinions* dataset in [14], we discovered that only about 7% of the users have rated at least one item together. This implies that the condition for similarity based social trust models to be effective may not always exist in practice. Furthermore, in the case where a new agent joins a social network, existing social trust models cannot effectively advise him on how much he should trust other agents based on rating similarities as he has not yet provided any rating.

To address this problem, we propose a social trust model that calculates the trustworthiness of a trustee agent based on its influence in the social network. The trust model is formulated based on evidence observed through analysis of real world rating and trusting behavior reflected by a large number of users in a real social network. Comparison with a state-of-the-art approach in social recommendation scenarios demonstrates the significant advantage of the proposed model.

2 Related Work

The concept of trust which is originally derived from social science has been introduced to computer science with diverse applicability in many decision making situations. Trust behavior shows the reliance on one person or entity from another. People usually trust others who have a good reputation or with an honourable title, e.g., experts in some area. Once a trust relationship has been established, the ideas or behaviors of the trustee, i.e., the one who is trusted, could influence the behaviour of the truster, i.e., the one who trusts. In the multi-agent systems, computational trust models have been developed to predict which agents are trustworthy [11].

Apart from research in multi-agent systems, online communities also make use of trust networks for recommendation. Recommender system is an important tool for finding the most relevant information from the vast amount of data we are facing today. In a typical recommender system, the similarity of rating profiles is used to define the neighbourhood of each user. This means a user and this user's neighbours have similar preference or interests reflected by observed rating profiles. However, when rating data is used merely, difficulties such as data sparsity and the "cold-start" problem may occur. To alleviate these problems and improve the recommendation accuracy, trust has been used in recommender systems as additional information to define neighbourhood.

The correlation between trust and ratings has been explored in many studies. In [10], the bidirectional interaction between trust and ratings was studied to explain the formation and evolution of online communities. In [1], it was shown that two users' rating similarity increases after a trust relation has been established between them. It has also been shown in [14] that rating similarity between users with a trust relation is higher on average than those without a trust relation.

Based on the assumption that a user and his neighbors give similar ratings, several studies proposed to make rating prediction based on a combination of the preference of "self" and "neighbor" [8,1,14]. The difference in these approaches lies in how they define the predicted rating in the objective function. In [8], both the user and his neighbors' ratings are estimated by Matrix Factorization (MF); in [1], a user's rating is predicted by MF while his neighbors' ratings are the observed ratings; and in [14], a user's rating is defined based on the user bias and the item bias, and ratings of the neighbors are the observed ratings. Although it is intuitive to directly use the neighbours' known ratings as part of the predicted ratings for a user, this is only effective when the neighbors have rated the same item, which is not true for many cases. In other words, for many users, none of his neighbors have rated the target item. Another difference in these approaches is the weight of trust. The work in [8] used equal weights for all the trust relationships while in [1] and [14], the strengths of trust relationships are formulated as unknown variables which are solved by minimizing the objective function.

Other than directly minimizing the rating difference on each item between a user and his neighbors, trust is also used as regularization in MF based method [5,9]. Neighborhood regularization aims to minimize the difference between the user's latent feature vector and the average of the neighbors' feature vectors; while pairwise regularization minimizes the difference of the feature vectors for each pair of users with a trust relationship. Neighorhood regularization is applied in [15] for circle-based recommendation, where the trust strengths between the same pair of users are different for items in different categories, and is dependent on the number of ratings the trustee made in that category.

There are also other studies on integrating trust into recommendation, such as the random walk based approach [4]. On the other hand, the correlation between trust and rating similarity has also been used for trust prediction [2,6,13].

3   Real World Rating and Trusting Behavior

We now perform analysis to understand the trustworthiness of agents in an online community where both ratings and trust relationships are available. Specifically, we are interested in two ways to measure the trustworthiness of an agent namely the *activeness* and the *influence*, which are defined based on rating data and trust data, respectively. Here *activeness* is simply defined as the number of ratings an agent has made. This method assumes that active agents are more trustworthy. The other way to measure an agent's trustworthiness is by his *influence* among all agents, which is calculated as the total number of trusters.

We analyze the *Epinions* dataset [14]. It contains 22,164 users who produced 912,441 ratings on 296,277 items. Among these users, 18097 users are involved in trust networks with 355,631 binary trust relations (e.g., a value of 1 indicates user u trusts user v, whereas a value of 0 indicates otherwise).

Table 1 compares two groups of trustees: 1) in the left column, it shows the top 10 *most active* trustees (i.e., those with the highest number of ratings) and the corresponding number of other agents who trust them; and 2) in the right column, it shows the top 10 *most trusted* trustees and their corresponding number of ratings. It can be observed that only three of the most active trustees are trusted by a large number of other agents, while 8 of the 10 most trusted trustee have provided only a small number of ratings.

Table 1. Trustees and ratings

ID	# Ratings	# trusters	ID	# trusters	# Ratings
6877	5337	15	716242	2016	25
2760	3131	1262	2760	1262	3131
19163	2496	0	7700	988	32
13658	2465	3	2425	971	760
2034	2453	177	9831	945	68
9262	2331	1	11288	879	46
16059	2328	5	19459	879	19
15827	2324	0	3906	863	48
557	2287	609	5550	841	15
7246	2059	0	16069	828	15

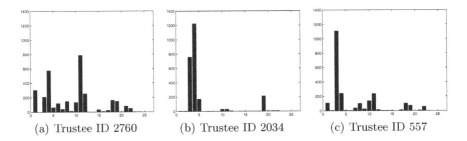

(a) Trustee ID 2760   (b) Trustee ID 2034   (c) Trustee ID 557

Fig. 1. Distribution of ratings

Figure 1 shows the rating distribution of the three most active and highly trusted trustees (i.e., user 2760, user 2034, and user 557) over different topics. The most trusted among the three - user 2760 - has provided a significant number of ratings across more diverse topics than users 2034 and 557. This makes it more likely for user 2760 to be known by others and build a larger trust network.

From the above analysis, it can be seen that simple *activeness* measured by the total number of ratings seems to be insufficient to reflect the trustworthiness as more factors such as the distribution of ratings and even the quality of comments also affect the formation of trust relationships. Differently, a trustee's *influence* as manifested by his binary trust network provides a more direct way for estimating his trustworthiness as the trust network is built by people who are able to consider a holistic set of factors when deciding whom to trust.

4   Trustee-Influence Based Trust for Recommendation

The original trust network is usually unweighted as existence rather than strength of trust relationships are often available. Since the degrees of trust between a user and users in this user's trust list are usually different, using equal weights for all trust relationships does not characterise the real trust data naturally and affects the effectiveness of the trust-integrated recommender systems.

Next, we propose a trust model based on trustee-influence and then incorporate it in recommendation methods.

4.1   Trust Model Based on Trustee-Influence

In a social network, the degree of incoming links is a basic way to measure the influence of the corresponding user in the network. When the social network is a trust network, the influence of each user is measured by the number of users that trust this user namely the number of trusters, which represents the reliableness or trustworthiness of this user.

Specifically, we propose a social trust model that takes a binary trust network around a trustee v as input to estimate the trustworthiness of v. Let I_v denote the influence of a trustee v, and it calculated as below

$$I_v = |\{u\}|v \in \mathcal{N}_u| \tag{1}$$

where $\mathcal{N}_u$ is the set of agents who are trusted by u. For a given binary trust relationship $u \to v$, the strength or weight of this trust relationship t_{uv} is given by

$$t_{uv} = I_v \tag{2}$$

which is only dependant on the trustee's influence and reflects the trustworthiness of v from the perspective of u. This is different from rating similarity, which is a function of both truster and trustee. According to our analysis in the previous section, influence defined above is a more preferred way to characterize trustworthiness compared to activeness calculated by rating data alone.

4.2   Trust Regularized Matrix Factorization

Recently, trust has been integrated into recommender systems as additional information to historical ratings to improve accuracy and deal with sparse rating data. The idea of trust-based recommendation is that people usually accept the idea of those who they trust even they have not shown similar interests according to the observed rating data.

Now we discuss how to make use of the trustee-influence based trust in a recommender system to improve rating prediction with the Matrix Factorization method. The problem is to predict unobserved rating $\hat{r}_{ui}$ with observed ratings $\mathbf{R}$ and trust $\mathbf{T}$. For each user u, we call u's trustees as u's neighbors. $\mathcal{N}_u$ represents the set of trustees of u, i.e., $v \in \mathcal{N}_u, \forall t_{uv} > 0$.

Matrix factorization (MF) is a popular model-based approach for rating prediction. The classic MF method factorizes the rating matrix $\mathbf{R}_{n_u \times n_i}$ into two lower ranked matrices $\mathbf{P}_{k \times n_u}$ and $\mathbf{Q}_{k \times n_i}$, where $\mathbf{P}$ is the user feature matrix, $\mathbf{Q}$ is the item feature matrix, and k is the number of latent features which is much smaller than n_u and n_i. A basic MF problem may be written as:

$$\min L_{MF} = \frac{1}{2} \sum_{u,i \in \mathcal{O}} (r_{ui} - \mathbf{p}_u^T \mathbf{q}_i)^2 + \frac{\lambda}{2} (\sum_u \|\mathbf{p}_u\|_2^2 + \sum_i \|\mathbf{q}_i\|_2^2) \tag{3}$$

In the above objective function, the first term is used to characterize the factorization quality. It is measured by the sum of squared errors between observed ratings and predicted ratings. To avoid over-fitting, regularization terms of both p and q are incorporated with parameter λ control the degree of regularization. The squared errors are only summed over those observed user-item pairs (i.e., $u, i \in \mathcal{O}$) where $\mathcal{O}$ is the set of observed ratings.

A pairwise regularized matrix factorization was proposed in [9] which constrains feature vectors of each pair of users with a trust relationship to be close. However, since the number of trust relationships of different users can vary significantly, proper normalization is necessary in order to ensure stable and robust performance. In this paper, we propose to use MF with Normalized Pairwise regularization (MF-NP). The objective function can be written as:

$$\min L_{MF-NP} = L_{MF} + \frac{\beta}{2} \sum_u \frac{\sum_{v \in \mathcal{N}_u} t_{uv} \|\mathbf{p}_u - \mathbf{p}_v\|^2}{\sum_{v \in \mathcal{N}_u} t_{uv}} \tag{4}$$

where β is the weight that controls the contribution of the regularization term.

Similar to MF, the solution for the user feature matrix $\mathbf{P}$ and the item feature matrix $\mathbf{Q}$ of MF-NP can be obtained with the gradient descent method using the following update equations:

$$\frac{\partial L_{MF-NP}}{\partial \mathbf{p}_u} = \sum_i d_{ui}(\mathbf{p}_u^T \mathbf{q}_i - r_{ui})\mathbf{q}_i + \lambda \mathbf{p}_u + \frac{\beta}{2} \frac{\partial H}{\partial \mathbf{p}_u} \tag{5}$$

$$\frac{\partial L_{MF-NP}}{\partial \mathbf{q}_i} = \sum_u d_{ui}(\mathbf{p}_u^T \mathbf{q}_i - r_{ui})\mathbf{p}_u + \lambda \mathbf{q}_i \tag{6}$$

where

$$\frac{\partial H_p(u)}{\partial \mathbf{p}_u} = 2 \frac{\sum_{v \in \mathcal{N}_u} t_{uv}(\mathbf{p}_u - \mathbf{p}_v)}{\sum_{v \in \mathcal{N}_u} t_{uv}} + 2 \frac{\sum_{w|u \in \mathcal{N}_w} t_{wu}(\mathbf{p}_u - \mathbf{p}_w)}{\sum_{w|u \in \mathcal{N}_w} t_{wu}} \tag{7}$$

and d_{ui} is the indicator that is equal to 1 if user u rated item i, and otherwise is equal to 0.

The first term of Eq. (7) considers u as a truster and the second term considers u as a trustee. This means that trust regularization not only affects the feature vector of users with neighbors or trustees, but also affects users without neighbors as long as they are trusted by others.

5 Experimental Evaluation

To evaluate the effectiveness of the proposed model, we design an experiment to study its performance in a social recommendation setting using the *Epinions* dataset. We select 80% of the ratings and all the trust relations as training data, and the remaining 20% of the ratings as testing data. Based on the dataset, we construct a new trust network with relationship strength representing the pairwise directional degree of trust calculated by the proposed model. This trust network is fed into the MF-NP that can take trust network as an input. We label this approach as MF-NP-I^t. It is then compared with the Matrix Factorization based recommendation approach (MF) [9] using the Root Mean Square Error (RMSE) and Mean Absolute Error (MAE) in rating predictions.

The results of the evaluation are shown in Table 2. K is the number of latent factors which affects the performance of the underlying recommendation approach. The rating prediction accuracy is improved by 2.00%, 1.66%, 1.91%, and 1.79% under various experiment configurations by using the proposed model. Although the improvement in accuracy seem small, such small improvement in RMSE terms have been shown to have a significant impact on the quality of the top few recommendations [7] (which are the recommendations most likely to influence the users). As reported in [7], when the performance improved from 0.9025 to 0.8870 with respect to RMSE (i.e, an improvement of 1.72%), it gains more than 50% relative improvement in terms of the top few recommendations. Therefore, the improvement brought about by the proposed model has significant implications in practice.

Table 2. Experiment results

	K=5		K=10	
	RSME	MAE	RSME	MAE
MF	1.111	0.841	1.100	0.837
MF-NP-I^t	1.089	0.827	1.079	0.822
Improvement	2.00%	1.66%	1.91%	1.79%

6 Conclusion and Future work

In this paper, we proposed a social trust model that can advise a truster on how much to trust a given trustee based solely on the trustee's influence in the social network. It complements existing social trust models by enabling agents who has insufficient commonly rated items for accurate similarity evaluation to determine how much to trust each other. The proposed model is applied to social recommendation and significantly outperforms a state-of-the-art approach.

In the future, more extensive experimental studies are needed for a comprehensively evaluation of the proposed method, especially to demonstrate its performance with different datasets of sufficient ratings and insufficient ratings. Another future work is to use both ratings and trust relationships to define trustworthiness so that the trust model is more comprehensive, more robust and less sensitive to data sparsity of either ratings or trust relationships.

References

1. Au Yeung, C.M., Iwata, T.: Strength of social influence in trust networks in product review sites. In: WSDM 2011, pp. 495–504 (2011)
2. Borzymek, P., Sydow, M., Wierzbicki, A.: Enriching Trust Prediction Model in Social Network with User Rating Similarity. In: CASoN, pp. 40–47 (2009)
3. Hang, C.-W., Wang, Y., Singh, M.P.: Operators for propagating trust and their evaluation in social networks. In: AAMAS, pp. 1025–1032 (2009)
4. Jamali, M., Ester, M.: Trustwalker: a random walk model for combining trust-based and item-based recommendation. In: KDD, pp. 397–406 (2009)
5. Jamali, M., Ester, M., Ester, M.: A matrix factorization technique with trust propagation for recommendation in social networks. In: RecSys, pp. 135–142 (2010)
6. Kim, Y.A., Phalak, R.: A trust prediction framework in rating-based experience sharing social networks without a web of trust. Inf. Sci. 191, 128–145 (2012)
7. Koren, Y.: Factorization meets the neighborhood: a multifaceted collaborative filtering model. In: KDD, pp. 426–434 (2008)
8. Ma, H., King, I., Lyu, M.R., Lyu, M.R.: Learning to recommend with social trust ensemble. In: SIGIR, pp. 203–210 (2009)
9. Ma, H., Zhou, D., Liu, C., Lyu, M.R., King, I.: Recommender systems with social regularization. In: WSDM, pp. 287–296 (2011)
10. Matsuo, Y., Yamamoto, H.: Community gravity: measuring bidirectional effects by trust and rating on online social networks. In: WWW, pp. 751–760 (2009)
11. Mui, L., Mohtashemi, M., Halberstadt, A.: A computational model of trust and reputation, pp. 188–196 (2002)
12. Salakhutdinov, R., Mnih, A.: Probabilistic matrix factorization. In: NIPS, pp. 1257–1264 (2008)
13. Tang, J., Gao, H., Hu, X., Liu, H.: Exploiting homophily effect for trust prediction. In: WSDM (2013)
14. Tang, J., Gao, H., Liu, H.: mTrust: discerning multi-faceted trust in a connected world. In: WSDM, pp. 93–102 (2012)
15. Yang, X., Steck, H., Liu, Y.: Circle-based recommendation in online social networks. In: KDD, pp. 1267–1275 (2012)

Continuous Approximation of a Discrete Situated and Reactive Multi-agent System: Contribution to Agent Parameterization

Simon Stuker[1], Françoise Adreit[1],
Jean-Marc Couveignes[2], and Marie-Pierre Gleizes[1]

[1]Institut de Recherche en Informatique de Toulouse,
Université Paul Sabatier - Toulouse III, France
[2]Institut de Mathématiques de Bordeaux,
Université de Bordeaux, France

Abstract. We propose a formal model for situated and reactive multi-agent systems based on correlated discrete random walks. In order to study this model, we construct a continuous approximation ending up on the Fokker-Planck equation. This result allows us to determine an optimal parameterization for the agents, with respect to the system's objective. Numerical simulations confirm the approach from two points of view, the validity of the continuous model and the optimality of the agents' parameterization.

Keywords: Modelling System Dynamics, Validation and Verification of Multi-Agent Systems, Multi-agent Simulation.

1 Introduction

Multi-agent systems offer an interesting approach for solving distributed problems. These problems can be industrial, like the optimal control of a heat engine [4] or resource management [2]. They can also be more academic, like constraint satisfaction problems [21] or constrained optimization of mathematical functions [18,15].

Although multi-agent solutions have proven to be efficient on difficult problems and may be methodically implemented[1], their formal validation is an important obstacle that has yet to be overcome. The main reason is that a multi-agent system can have a complex behaviour, meaning that it cannot be easily deduced from the agents' individual behaviour.

As a result, upon creation of a multi-agent system it is difficult to know if it turns out "functional", meaning that it fulfills its role. Furthermore the influence of the agents' parameters on the system's behaviour may be difficult to understand, and thus difficult to adjust if the system's performance is insufficient.

For these reasons, validating desired properties of the system and adjusting the agents' parameters are often done by experimentation. This step can be time-costly and offers only partial answers, of statistical order.

---

[1] By methods like TROPOS [6] or ADELFE [25].

H.K. Dam et al. (Eds.): PRIMA 2014, LNAI 8861, pp. 365–380, 2014.

In this article we focus on the formal establishment of basic dynamic properties of a restricted class of systems. We concentrate on systems of identical and situated agents. The objective we set for the agents is to have a desired distribution at equilibrium, given by a time-invariant function, that will be referred to as *resource*. Each individual moves randomly, according to some probabilities that depend on its local perceptions. The aim of our approach is to define and parameterize the agent's behaviour so that they position themselves, after some time, according to the target distribution.

This type of problem can be encountered in entomology, when an insect colony tries to harvest scattered food (if we ignore food repatriation), or in swarm robotics, when a group of medical robots needs to deploy in a critical situation where human victims are scattered in space.

We study long-term behaviours of such systems, and address two main questions:

1. Can we locally parameterize the agents so that the system achieves the objective?
2. Given some agent behaviour rule, can we predict their dynamics and measure their accomplishment?

Since discrete approaches have shown to be of limited use (see mentioned work in section 2) in the study of large complex systems, we study these questions by means of continuous approximations inspired by statistical physics.

Therefore, we approximate the system by two successive limits: the first (mean field) is valid when the number of agents goes to infinity, the second (continuity) is valid when the elementary time and space step tend to zero. The resulting approximated system is then studied using PDE results. The combination of these three steps provides satisfactory quantitative answers to questions 1 and 2.

After a brief presentation of related work (section 2), we propose a generic model for situated reactive multi-agent systems (section 3). We show that, under some specific hypotheses, the mathematical model can be approximated by an equation of which we can study some formal properties (section 4). Using this approximation, we manage to parameterize the agents' behaviour so that they collectively achieve the system's goal (section 5). Numerical simulations validate our approach (section 6). The article ends with a discussion of the stated results, and opens on some possible working directions (section 7).

2   Related Work

A vast literature focuses on the study of complex systems. Since multi-agent systems are endowed with some underlying objective, we divide related work in two classes: purely descriptive models, focused on the study of a given system, and control-type models, equipped with some utility function and the implicit task to maximize its value. These two classes of models are appropriate for question 2 and 1 respectively.

2.1   Descriptive Approaches

Interacting particle systems [20] model complex systems as a set of coupled random processes. The special case of Cellular automata and their application to multi-agent systems is studied in [29]. However, it is generally difficult to prove properties of these models.

A traditional population-based approach is to describe a system by the fraction of agents in each state, and its evolution by exchanges between those fractions. Well-known examples are the chemical rate equations and the Lotka-Volterra equation. Application to multi-agent systems without any formal derivations are found in [14,19]. In contrast, [17,1] provide general methods to derive these models from systems of individuals with "mean interaction".

Continuous spatial models close to the one used of this article are used in ecology to study social animal behaviours [26,16,7].

Our approach can be related to all the above works. Starting with a discrete system of random walkers with a given task, we derive some continuous model using a mean field result. However, our model also involves a global reward function that we want to maximize.

2.2   Control-Type Approaches

Markov Decision Processes [23] model stochastic systems equipped with some reward function that is to be maximized over time. This formalism is closely related to game theory [28] and its application to multi-agent systems is studied in [13,27]. However it seems difficult to use these methods for large systems, as the computational complexity increases rapidly with the number of agents [3].

Mean field methods have been used to solve optimal control problems on systems of identical individuals with global control [10,11,5] on small state spaces. Mean field games [12] can be seen as an extension of these methods to spatial systems.

In contrast to [10,11,5], we favour local control, and unlike mean field games we mainly focus on cooperative systems (where agents share identical interests) at equilibrium.

3   Formal Model

In this section we define the formal model that is used to study the class of problems we focus on. This model includes discrete time and state spaces. Agents are randomly distributed at the start, and follow discrete memoryless random walks from then on. Randomness of these movements has multiple motivations. Since agents are completely identical, a deterministic decision rule would lead to gregarious collective behaviour: all agents sharing identical information (e.g. global knowledge) move likewise, which is clearly a suboptimal behaviour. Furthermore, space exploration is often related to diffusion processes, which are mainly modeled by random walks.

3.1   System Description

The agents' **state space** is the unit circle $\mathcal{C}$, evenly divided in n_p positions (Fig. 1) and denoted

$$\mathcal{C}_\delta = \left\{ \frac{2k\pi}{n_p} \right\}_{k\in\{0,\dots,n_p-1\}} = \{k\delta\}_{k\in\{0,\dots,n_p-1\}}$$

where $\delta = \frac{2\pi}{n_p}$ is the spatial step, which will tend to 0 later, so that $\mathcal{C}_\delta \to \mathcal{C}$ (in the sense of Hausdorff's set convergence [22]).

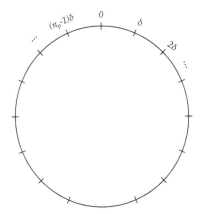

Fig. 1. Agents' positions

The periodic topology and compactness of this domain offer some theoretic advantages for the theorems of this article. Possible extensions are discussed in section 7.

Since agents are assumed to be identical, the system's state is completely described by the number of agents at each position. Let $(X_n(t))_{n=1}^N$ stand for the positions of the N agents at time t. The system's state is described by the *occupation density vector* $u^N(t) = \left(u^N(x,t)\right)_{x\in\mathcal{C}_\delta}$, where

$$u^N(x,t) = \frac{1}{N} \sum_{n=1}^N \mathbb{1}_{X_n(t)=x} \text{ with } \mathbb{1}_{X_n(t)=x} = \begin{cases} 1 \text{ if } X_n(t) = x \\ 0 \text{ else} \end{cases}.$$

Coordinate $u(x,t)$ is the proportion of agents located at position x. During a time interval τ, each agent may

- move by $-\delta$ with probability $p_{\delta,\tau}^N(x,u)$,
- move by $+\delta$ with probability $q_{\delta,\tau}^N(x,u)$,
- stay in place with probability $1 - p_{\delta,\tau}^N(x,u) - q_{\delta,\tau}^N(x,u)$.

These probabilities depend on the agent's current position and the density vector (Fig. 2).

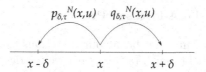

$$p_{\delta,\tau}{}^{N}(x,u) \qquad q_{\delta,\tau}{}^{N}(x,u)$$

$$x - \delta \qquad x \qquad x + \delta$$

Fig. 2. Agents' movements

At this stage we have defined a generic formal model describing the random movements of a set of agents[2]. The probabilities of the agents' movements have yet to be chosen. They will act as control parameters, and will be adjusted according to some objective function defined in the next paragraph.

3.2   Reward Function

In order to fit the system's goal in our model, we add a reward function r evaluating the system's success in its task (moving towards the resource).

Let f be the periodic function standing for the resource quantity at each point. This function is assumed to be time invariant, strictly positive and normalized so that $\int_{\mathcal{C}} f(x)dx = 1$. Reward function r defined by

$$r : (x, u) \mapsto u(x)\, e^{1 - \frac{u(x)}{f(x)}}$$

gives a local representation of the system's accomplishment in each length unit $[x, x + \delta[$ (Fig. 3).

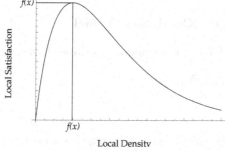

Fig. 3. Agents' reward function

The agents' presence at resources is increasingly rewarded, but overcrowding is punished exponentially. The system's global reward at time t is

$$R_\delta(t) = \sum_{x \in \mathcal{C}_\delta} r(x, u(x,t))\, \delta.$$

---

[2] Which is not limited to global dependence, since the probability $p_{\delta,\tau}^N(x,u)$ may depend only on the density of agents located at x.

Global reward R is bounded by the total amount of resources $\sum_{x \in \mathcal{C}_\delta} f(x)\,\delta$. Hence, the agents' optimal distribution is exactly the resource distribution.

3.3   Expression of the Addressed Problem

The objective is to find an agent behaviour (functions $p_{\delta,\tau}(x,u)$ and $q_{\delta,\tau}(x,u)$) yielding maximum global reward. In this paper we restrict the objective to some long-term reward $R(T)$ (with a large value for T)

$$\max_{p_{\delta,\tau},q_{\delta,\tau}} \mathbb{E}\left(R_\delta(T)\right),$$

where $\mathbb{E}$ stands for mathematical expectation over the possible system states.

It is a simple task to simulate the system for a given pair of functions $(p_{\delta,\tau},q_{\delta,\tau})$, and measure its reward. Formal study is however a bit more tricky, since the Markov chain $\left((X_n(t))_{n=1}^{N}\right)_t$ (or even $(u^n(t))_t$) describing the system's evolution has a state space that increases quickly with the number of agents. To mitigate this difficulty, we suggest a continuous approximation of this discrete model in the next section.

4   Approximation of the Discrete Model

The derivation of the continuous approximation is done according to the two steps described in section 1, and ends up in a partial differential equation known as the *Fokker-Planck equation*. We provide some interesting properties of this equation in a special case.

4.1   Derivation of the Continuous Model

The discrete system defined at section 3 has three characteristic dimensions:

- the number of agents N,
- the spatial step δ,
- the time step τ.

In this section we will make these values tend to some extreme values in order to obtain a limit model.

Statistical Limit. At first, we let the number of agents N tend to infinity. The idea behind this limit is the following: as the number of agents grows larger, the influence of each individual on the density becomes insignificant. As a consequence statistical fluctuations caused by the randomness of the movements have no impact on the system, which tends to behave in a deterministic way. In other words, agents observing the densities are interacting with a macroscopic (and deterministic) quantity on which they have no influence. This approach is known as *mean field theory* [17], and formalized by the following result:

Theorem 1 (Statistical Limit). *Suppose that, when $N \to \infty$ the initial distributions $u^N(0)$ converge almost surely to some limit $u(0)$, and that the probabilities $p^N_{\delta,\tau}(x,u)$, $q^N_{\delta,\tau}(x,u)$ converge uniformly in u to continuous functions $u \mapsto p_{\delta,\tau}(x,u)$, $u \mapsto q_{\delta,\tau}(x,u)$. Then, for each t, the function $u^N(t)$ converges almost surely to the vector $u(t)$ recursively defined by $u(x,0) = u_0(x)$ and*

$$u(x, t+\tau) = u(x,t)(1 - p_{\delta,\tau}(x,u) - q_{\delta,\tau}(x,u))$$
$$+ u(x-\delta, t)q_{\delta,\tau}(x-\delta, u) + u(x+\delta, t)p_{\delta,\tau}(x+\delta, u) \quad (1)$$

Relation (1) can be seen as a *balance equation*: agents located at x may

- come from the $x - \delta$, with probability $q_{\delta,\tau}(x - \delta, u)$,
- come from the $x + \delta$, with probability $p_{\delta,\tau}(x + \delta, u)$,
- have been immobile, with probability $1 - p_{\delta,\tau}(x, u) - q_{\delta,\tau}(x, u)$.

The macroscopic quantity $u(t)$, called *mean field*, is ruled by as many equations as positions (i.e. n_p) and may be difficult to study if n_p is large. This is why we carry out another approximation in the next section.

Spatiotemporal Limit. Consider a sufficiently smooth solution to (1), at least twice differentiable in t and once in x. A Taylor expansion of order 2 in δ, and of order 1 in t in (1) leaves, after simplification:

$$\tau \frac{\partial}{\partial t} u(x,t) + o(\tau) = -\delta \frac{\partial}{\partial x} ((p_{\delta,\tau}(x) - q_{\delta,\tau}(x))u(x,t))$$
$$+ \frac{\delta^2}{2} \frac{\partial^2}{\partial x^2} ((p_{\delta,\tau}(x) + q_{\delta,\tau}(x))u(x,t)) + o(\delta^2)$$

If both members are divided by τ and if $\delta, \tau \to 0$, so that $\frac{\delta^2}{\tau}$ is bounded $(0 < a < \frac{\delta^2}{\tau} < b < \infty)$, and if the limits below exist

$$c(x,u) = \lim_{\delta,\tau} \left(\frac{p_{\delta,\tau}(x,u) - q_{\delta,\tau}(x,u)}{\tau} \delta \right) \quad (2)$$

$$d(x,u) = \lim_{\delta,\tau} \left(\frac{p_{\delta,\tau}(x,u) + q_{\delta,\tau}(x,u)}{2\tau} \delta^2 \right), \quad (3)$$

we obtain the limit equation:

$$\frac{\partial u}{\partial t}(x,t) = -\frac{\partial}{\partial x} (c(x,u)u(x,t)) + \frac{\partial^2}{\partial x^2} (d(x,u)u(x,t)) \quad (4)$$

known as the *Fokker-Planck equation* [24]. Its convection term $-\frac{\partial}{\partial x}(c(x,u)u(x,t))$ accounts for macroscopic displacement, whereas *the diffusion term* $\frac{\partial^2}{\partial x^2}(d(x,u)u(x,t))$ accounts for dispersion.

    In a similar way, the *convection coefficient* c may be understood as the mean speed of individuals located at position x whereas the *diffusion coefficient* d quantifies the local tendency to leave position x.

Equations (2), (3) are commonly called *scaling conditions*. They show how the system's endogenous parameters need to scale with its characteristic dimensions if we want (4) to be a valid approximation.

Formulation of the Continuous Problem. The discrete model defined at section 3.2 has been approximated by the partial differential equation (4), which is parameterized by the coefficients c and d. By means of the scaling equations (2), (3) we translate[3] the optimal choice of the agents probabilities $p_{\delta,\tau}$ and $q_{\delta,\tau}$ into a continuous problem on c and d:

$$\max_{c,d} \int_C r\left(x, u(x, T)\right) dx$$

under the constraint given by equation (4). However it is not completely obvious that this formulation has really simplified our problem. Equation (4) may be difficult to solve according to the coefficients c and d, and may have solutions that have no physical sense[4]. The next section is devoted to a simple case where these difficulties do not appear.

4.2   Properties of the Linear Fokker-Planck Equation

A well-mastered special case of (4) is when the functions c and d depend only on x[5]. The corresponding Fokker-Planck equation is

$$\frac{\partial u}{\partial t} = -\frac{\partial}{\partial x}\left(c(x)u\right) + \frac{\partial^2}{\partial x^2}\left(d(x)u\right), \tag{5}$$

and is equipped with a boundary condition constraining solutions to be periodic. In order to show that equation (5) is a "good" representation of our system, we show that it has sufficiently regular solutions[6] that are density functions.

Theorem 2 (Well-Posedness of the Equation)

(i) *Suppose the coefficients c, d and the initial distribution u_0 infinitely differentiable, and d bounded from below: $d(x) \geq \epsilon > 0$.*
   Then equation (5) has a unique solution that is infinitely differentiable.

(ii) *If we suppose, in addition to the previous assumptions, that u_0 is positive and $\int_C u_0(x)dx = 1$, then the solution of (5) is positive and*

$$\int_C u(x,t)dx = 1, \forall t \geq 0.$$

Dynamics of the solutions of (5) are resumed by the following two theorems:

---

[3] In a non-bijective way: multiple probabilities $p_{\delta,\tau}$, $q_{\delta,\tau}$ may result in the same c, d.
[4] These *weak solutions* are purely mathematical objects with no concrete interpretation.
[5] In a situation where the agents only observe their position x.
[6] In particular, bounded and without discontinuities.

Theorem 3 (Existence of a Unique Stationary Distribution). *The stationary Fokker-Planck equation*

$$-\frac{\partial}{\partial x}\left(c(x)u_\infty(x)\right) + \frac{\partial^2}{\partial x^2}\left(d(x)u_\infty(x)\right) = 0$$

has a unique periodic solution u_∞ *so that* $\int_C u_\infty(x)dx = 1$, *which is positive.*

Thus, for each pair of coefficients c, d there is a unique stable distribution[7].

Theorem 4 (Convergence of Solutions). *Let* u *be a periodic solution of* (5). *There are two positive constants* A *and* B *such that*

$$\int_C |u(x,t) - u_\infty(x)|dx \le A\, e^{-Bt}$$

This provides a complete characterization of the solutions' dynamics: either the systems starts at the invariant distribution u_∞ and remains so indefinitely, or it starts at another distribution in which case it converges to u_∞ at exponential speed.

For now, we have made very few assumptions on the coefficients c and d. In the following section, we adjust them to maximize the system's performance.

5   Optimal Strategies

In this section, we establish two strategies with optimal long-term behaviour, with respect to the continuous formulation of the problem defined at section 3. Each of these strategies consists in a judicious choice of the coefficients c and d, and is interpreted in terms of agent behaviour.

5.1   A Resource-Dependent Strategy

We start off with the linear case (sect. 4.2). A simple way to maximize the system's global satisfaction is to identify the stationary solution u_∞ to the optimal distribution f. The results of the previous section then guarantee exponential convergence to the optimal distribution.

Replacing u_∞ by f in the stationary equation, we obtain

$$-\frac{d}{dx}\left(c(x)f(x)\right) + \frac{d^2}{dx^2}\left(d(x)f(x)\right) = 0.$$

This equation has an obvious solution:

$$c(x) = \frac{f'(x)}{f(x)} = \frac{d}{dx}\ln(f(x)),\ d(x) = 1,$$

where c is well defined, since f is assumed to be strictly positive.

---

[7] This does not imply that the agents are motionless, since movements may keep the global distribution unchanged.

This solution has an interesting meaning. Coefficients c and d correspond to a movement oriented towards the logarithmic gradient of resources. This fact can be related to the Weber-Fechner law [9] in psychophysics: *The intensity of a sensation varies as the logarithm of the stimulus*, translated in our case by: the agents move with an average speed proportional to the logarithmic derivative of their perception (the quantity of surrounding resources).

Even though this strategy is interesting, it has two flaws: agents only consider the amount of surrounding resources, and completely ignore each other, and local knowledge of the target distribution (the resource in this case) and its variations is required. This is why we suggest another strategy in the next section, based only on local and partial information.

5.2   A Strategy Based on Local Rewards

An interesting strategy, inspired by the previous one, is given by:

$$c(x, u) = \frac{\partial}{\partial x} \ln \left(r(x, u(x, t)) \right), \ d(x, u) = 1$$

with the reward function $r(x, u) = u(x)e^{1-\frac{u(x)}{f(x)}}$ defined at section 3.2. This means the agents move towards locations where local satisfaction is high. In agreement with Weber-Fechner's law, the intensity of these movements is given by the logarithmic derivative of the perception (i.e. local reward).

The corresponding Fokker-Planck equation is nonlinear, and the results of section 4.2 are of no use. We can however simplify its expression:

Proposition 1 (Simplification). *The nonlinear Fokker-Planck equation*

$$\frac{\partial u}{\partial t} = -\frac{\partial}{\partial x}\left(u \frac{\partial}{\partial x} \ln \left(r(x, u(x, t)) \right) \right) + \frac{\partial^2 u}{\partial x^2}$$

reduces to

$$\frac{\partial u}{\partial t} = \frac{\partial}{\partial x}\left[u \frac{\partial}{\partial x}\left(\frac{u}{f} \right) \right] \tag{6}$$

and show that this reduced equation has similar properties to the linear case. These properties are summed up by the following theorem:

Theorem 5. *Suppose that f is a strictly positive, periodic and regular function such that $\int_C f(x)dx = 1$.*

(i) *(Existence of regular solutions) If the initial condition u_0 is infinitely differentiable and strictly positive, equation (6) has a solution that is infinitely differentiable and strictly positive.*

(ii) *(Population size conservation) If the initial condition u_0 satisfies $\int_C u_0(x)dx = 1$, then for any regular solution u of (6):*

$$\int_C u(x, t)dx = 1, \forall t \geq 0$$

(iii) (Existence of a unique stationary solution) The stationary equation

$$\frac{\partial}{\partial x}\left[u_\infty \frac{\partial}{\partial x}\left(\frac{u_\infty}{f}\right)\right] = 0$$

has a unique positive periodic solution u_∞ so that $\int_C u_\infty(x)dx = 1$ and this solution is f.

(iv) (Convergence of solutions) Let u be a regular, positive and periodic solution of equation (6) so that $\int_C u(x,t)dx = 1$, $\forall t \geq 0$. There are two positive constants A and B such that

$$\int_C |u(x,t) - f(x)|dx \leq A\,e^{-Bt}.$$

Assertions (i) and (ii) show that equation (6) provides a satisfactory representation of our system. Assertions (iii) and (iv) show that solutions of equation (6) have desired long-term behaviour: they converge to the target distribution f at exponential speed.

We stress the fact that this section's strategy is only based on local satisfaction (and its spatial variations) and, in contrast to section 5.1, it involves agent interaction (through the local reward function).

6   Numerical Validation

In this section we validate the above theoretical results by numeric simulations, highlighting two main aspects: validity of the continuous approximation (section 4.1) and long-term optimality of the strategies (section 5).

6.1   Validation of the Continuous Model

We simulate all three models (discrete, mean field, continuous) for a given set of parameters and characteristic dimensions, and focus on the resource-dependent case (section 5.1).

For all the following simulations, the **resource** is distributed according to the function f proportional to $\cos\left(\frac{x-\pi}{2}\right)^{10} + 0.01$ and normalized so that $\int_C f(x)dx = 1$. It is displayed in hashed marks on every figure to show the objective.

The **discrete system** is shown on Fig. 4. The circle is evenly divided in $n_p = 20$ positions with spatial step $\delta = \frac{2\pi}{20} \simeq 0,3$. Time step τ is set to $\tau = 0,1$. The system contains $N = 500$ agents that are initialized according to independent uniform distributions on C_δ. Their movement probabilities are

$$p_{\delta,\tau}(x) = \frac{\tau}{2\delta^2}\left(2 + \frac{f(x+\delta) - f(x-\delta)}{2f(x)}\right)$$

$$q_{\delta,\tau}(x) = \frac{\tau}{2\delta^2}\left(2 - \frac{f(x+\delta) - f(x-\delta)}{2f(x)}\right) \quad (7)$$

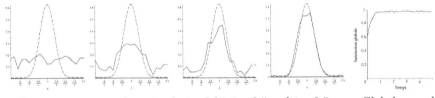

Discrete system at times $t = 0$, $t = 0.05$, $t = 0.5$ and $t = 2.5$ Global reward

Fig. 4. Dynamics of the discrete system

The **mean field**, shown on Fig. 5, is initialized according to the discrete uniform distribution $u_0 = (\frac{1}{20}, \ldots, \frac{1}{20})$ and evolves according to induction (1) in Theorem 1.

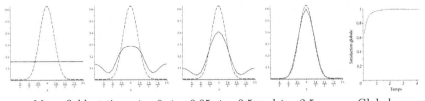

Mean field at times $t = 0$, $t = 0.05$, $t = 0.5$ and $t = 2.5$ Global reward

Fig. 5. Mean field dynamics

The **continuous system**, shown on figure 6, evolves according to the Fokker-Planck equation (4) with

$$c(x, u) = \frac{d}{dx} \ln (f(x)) \quad \text{and} \quad d(x, u) = 1$$

and is initialized as the uniform distribution on $\mathcal{C}$. Note that these coefficients c, d verify scaling conditions (2), (3) with the probabilities of the discrete system (7). We show numerical approximations obtained by the Crank-Nicholson method [8].

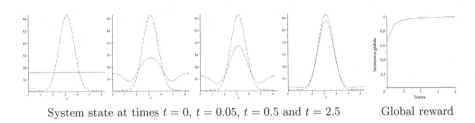

System state at times $t = 0$, $t = 0.05$, $t = 0.5$ and $t = 2.5$ Global reward

Fig. 6. Dynamics of the continuous system

Figures 4, 5, 6 show all three systems have similar dynamics and rewards. This confirms the validity of our approximation.

6.2   Validation of the Optimal Strategies

In order to show the optimality of the coefficients c and d found at section 5, we focus on the continuous system. The **resource** is distributed according to the function f defined at 6.1 and the **agents' initial distribution** u_0 is proportional to $\cos\left(\frac{x-3\pi}{2}\right)^{20}$ and normalized so that $\int_C u_0(x)dx = 1$. The functions f and u_0 are shown on each simulation in hashed lines.

The **resource-based strategy**, studied at paragraph 5.1 and displayed on Fig. 7, parameterizes the agents' movements as

$$c(x) = \frac{d}{dx}\ln\left(f(x)\right), \quad d(x) = 1.$$

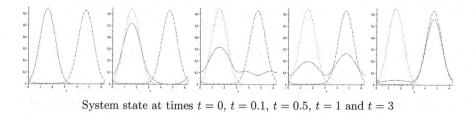

System state at times $t = 0$, $t = 0.1$, $t = 0.5$, $t = 1$ and $t = 3$

Global reward

Fig. 7. Dynamics and reward of the system for the resource-based strategy

The **reward-based strategy**, established at part 5.2 and displayed on Fig. 8, corresponds to the coefficients

$$c(u, x) = \frac{\partial}{\partial x}\ln\left(r(x, u(x, t))\right), d(u, x) = 1.$$

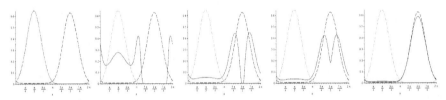

System state at times $t = 0$, $t = 0.02$, $t = 0.2$, $t = 0.3$ and $t = 1$

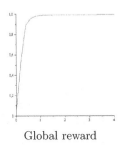

Global reward

Fig. 8. Dynamics and reward of the system for the reward-based strategy

Figures 7, 8 show that both suggested strategies have the anticipated dynamics, and converge to the optimal distribution. This fact is highlighted by the optimal reward that increases to its maximal value 1. Furthermore the reward-based strategy appears to converge faster, even though this might not be true in general.

The density curves of figures 7, 8 show that the this strategy favours convection, in particular at early stages, whereas the first strategy is more diffusive.

7   Conclusion and Perspectives

In this article we suggest a method to model and parameterize a situated reactive system of agents that we wish to move towards a given goal distribution. A continuous approximation leads to two strategies with optimal long-term behaviour:

- the first is based on local knowledge of the target distribution, and requires global control,
- the second is autonomous, and relies on local and individual perception of the reward function.

Numerical simulations validate our approach from two points of view: correctness of the approximation (section 6.1) and long-term optimality of the strategies (section 6.2).

Though the setting is very simple, the reasoning we used is easily extended to other types of domains. In this case it is necessary to ensure well-posedness of the limit equations with appropriate boundary conditions [24]. It is also possible to consider dynamic resources that move in space, exhaust over time or resources that are consumed by the agents. The explicit convergence bounds in theorems 4 and 7 allow a partial extension of our results to such situations if the resources evolve "slowly"[8].

Finally, another possible extension is to consider multiple agent populations, with mean field (density-dependent) interactions. In that case we obtain a system of coupled Fokker-Planck equations, with possible exchange terms between the populations. Examples found in literature [7,26,16], never involve objectives. Studying such systems with shared or diverging interests for each population is an interesting scope we plan to study in future work.

In regard to the optimal parameterizations, we limited this article to long-term global objectives. When facing cumulative rewards, it is necessary to study the limit of the corresponding MDP. The statistical limit towards some *mean field MDP* has been established by [10,5]. We expect the spatio-temporal limit to converge to a *mean field game* [12], whose connections to multi-agent systems have not yet been established.

References

1. Benaim, M., Le Boudec, J.Y.: A class of mean field interaction models for computer and communication systems. Performance Evaluation 65 (2008)
2. Benaouda, A., Zerhouni, N., Varnier, C.: Une approche multi-agents coopératifs pour la gestion des ressources matérielles dans un contexte multi-sites de e-manufacturing
3. Bernstein, D.S., Zilberstein, S., Immerman, N.: The complexity of decentralized control of markov decision processes. In: Proc. of the Sixteenth Conference on Uncertainty in Artificial Intelligence (2000)
4. Boes, J., Migeon, F., Gatto, F.: Self-Organizing Agents for an Adaptive Control of Heat Engines (short paper). In: International Conference on Informatics in Control, Automation and Robotics (ICINCO) (2013)
5. Bordenave, C., Anantharam, V.: Optimal control of interacting particle systems (June 2007), http://hal.archives-ouvertes.fr/hal-00397327
6. Bresciani, P., Perini, A., Giorgini, P., Giunchiglia, F., Mylopoulos, J.: Tropos: An agent-oriented software development methodology. JAAMAS 8(3) (2004)
7. Chen, X., Hambrock, R., Lou, Y.: Evolution of conditional dispersal: a reaction–diffusion–advection model. Journal of Mathematical Biology 57 (2008)
8. Fadugba, S.E., Edogbanya, O.H., Zelibe, S.C.: Crank Nicolson method for solving parabolic PDEs. Int. Journal of Applied Math. and Modeling IJA2M (2013)
9. Fechner, G.: Elemente der Psychophysik. No. Bd. 1 in Elemente der Psychophysik, Breitkopf und Härtel (1860)
10. Gast, N., Gaujal, B.: A mean field approach for optimization in particle systems and applications. ICST (Institute for Computer Sciences, Social-Informatics and Telecommunications Engineering) (2009)
11. Gast, N., Gaujal, B., Le Boudec, J.Y.: Mean field for markov decision processes: from discrete to continuous optimization. IEEE Transactions on Automatic Control (2012)

---

[8] With slower rate than the agents' convergence speed.

12. Guéant, O., Lasry, J.-M., Lions, P.-L.: Mean field games and applications. In: Paris-Princeton Lectures on Mathematical Finance (2011)
13. Guestrin, C., Koller, D., Parr, R.: Multiagent planning with factored MDPs. In: Neural Information Processing Systems (NIPS) (2001)
14. Ijspeert, A.J., Martinoli, A., Billard, A., Gambardella, L.M.: Collaboration through the exploitation of local interactions in autonomous collective robotics: The stick pulling experiment. Autonomous Robots 11 (2001)
15. Jorquera, T., Georgé, J.P., Gleizes, M.P., Régis, C.: A Natural Formalism and a MultiAgent Algorithm for Integrative Multidisciplinary Design Optimization. In: International Conference on Intelligent Agent Technology (IAT) (2013)
16. Jüngel, A.: Diffusive and nondiffusive population models. In: Mathematical Modeling of Collective Behavior in Socio-Economic and Life Sciences (2010)
17. Le Boudec, J.Y., McDonald, D., Mundinger, J.: A generic mean field convergence result for systems of interacting objects. In: Quantitative Evaluation of Systems (QEST). IEEE (2007)
18. Lepagnot, J., Nakib, A., Oulhadj, H., Siarry, P.: A new multiagent algorithm for dynamic continuous optimization. International Journal of Applied Metaheuristic Computing (IJAMC) (2010)
19. Lerman, K., Galstyan, A.: A general methodology for mathematical analysis of multi-agent systems. ISI-TR-529, USC Information Sciences Institute, Marina del Rey, CA (2001)
20. Liggett, T.M.: Particle Systems. Springer (1985)
21. Liu, J., Jing, H., Tang, Y.: Multi-agent oriented constraint satisfaction. Artificial Intelligence (2002)
22. Munkres, J.R.: Topology: a first course, vol. 23. Prentice-Hall, Englewood Cliffs (1975)
23. Puterman, M.L.: Markov decision processes: discrete stochastic dynamic programming. John Wiley & Sons (2009)
24. Risken, H.: Fokker-Planck Equation. Springer (1984)
25. Rougemaille, S., Arcangeli, J.-P., Gleizes, M.-P., Migeon, F.: ADELFE design, AMAS-ML in action. In: Artikis, A., Picard, G., Vercouter, L. (eds.) ESAW 2008. LNCS, vol. 5485, pp. 105–120. Springer, Heidelberg (2009)
26. Shigesada, N., Kawasaki, K., Teramoto, E.: Spatial segregation of interacting species. Journal of Theoretical Biology 79 (1979)
27. Shoham, Y., Leyton-Brown, K.: Multiagent systems: Algorithmic, game-theoretic, and logical foundations. Cambridge University Press (2009)
28. Spaan, M.T., Melo, F.S.: Interaction-driven markov games for decentralized multiagent planning under uncertainty. In: Proceedings of the 7th International Joint Conference on Autonomous Agents and Multiagent Systems, vol. 1 (2008)
29. Spicher, A., Fatès, N.A., Simonin, O., et al.: From reactive multi-agent models to cellular automata-illustration on a diffusion-limited aggregation model. In: Proceedings of ICAART 2009 (2009)

Appendix: References to Mathematical Proofs

Due to spatial constraints, this article cannot contain the proofs of the mentioned results. A document containing these proofs is provided at `ftp://ftp.irit.fr/IRIT/SMAC/DOCUMENTS/PUBLIS/PRIMA2014_Stuker_Proofs.pdf`.

A Preliminary Analysis of Interdependence in Multiagent Systems

Ronal Singh, Tim Miller, and Liz Sonenberg

University of Melbourne, Melbourne, Australia
ronals@student.unimelb.edu.au, {tmiller,l.sonenberg}@unimelb.edu.au

Abstract. Designers of human-agent systems use the term "interdependence," drawing on the work of organisational theorists and sociologists that is set in a human context. In this paper, we extend the agent systems analysis by semi-formally defining several types of task and agent interdependence that are introduced in the organisation theory literature. We illustrate how knowledge of different types of interdependence can assist designers in choosing appropriate coordination mechanisms between agents.

Keywords: interdependence, interdependence types, task interdependence, agent interdependence.

1 Introduction

To tackle the intricacies of designing agents capable of exhibiting collaboration with humans, Johnson et al. [4] propose the *Coactive Design Method*. This method allows designers to identify, analyse, implement and evaluate interdependence relationships between agents involved in joint activities. *Interdependence* has been highlighted as the central organising principle of Coactive Design Method, and has been defined as *"the set of complementary relationships that two or more parties rely on to manage...dependencies in joint activity"* [4]. This definition of interdependence builds on insights from earlier studies of human systems [10, 11, 12] that interdependence is more complex than simply mutual dependence: it is about relationships and includes consideration of the purpose of those relationships being to manage dependencies in joint activity. Interdependence relationships must be complementary, and help identify what common ground [6] should comprise.

While the Coactive Design Method explicitly considers interdependence as an organising principle, two additional fruitful contributions can be made in this area: (1) the extension of the concept of interdependence beyond *tasks*; and (2) a more rigorous analysis of interdependence. According to sociologists and organisational theorists [7, 8, 10, 11, 12] numerous types of interdependence exist, including interdependence between agents, tasks, and goals. This paper takes inspiration from these works. Similarly, we go further than the formalisms offered in [1, 9] for bilateral dependence. In this paper, we semi-formally define the concepts of task and agent interdependence. The more formal treatment provides a

H.K. Dam et al. (Eds.): PRIMA 2014, LNAI 8861, pp. 381–389, 2014.

more fine-grained analysis of different types of interdependence that can be used to assist designers in developing computational models of interdependence between humans and agents involved in joint activity. In the context of multi agent systems, coordination is the management of interaction between agents [5], and is also linked to the notion of agent autonomy [3]. One of the results of the studies performed by organisational theorists is that different types of interdependencies require different coordination mechanisms [12, 8]. Following the rigorous analysis of interdependence in this paper, we conjecture that a sound knowledge of the type of interdependency involved in various multi-agent scenarios will assist designers in the choice of appropriate coordination mechanisms.

The structure of this paper is as follows. Sections 2 and 3 discuss the different types of interdependence. In Section 4, we apply the formal definitions to a scenario discussed by Johnson et al. [4]. Section 5 compares our work with two closely related papers [1, 4], and Section 6 concludes the paper.

2   Task Interdependence

In this section, we present our formal definition of task interdependence.

We assume that agents are systems capable of autonomous *actions* on the environment. *Tasks*, which may require one or more actions, are performed to achieve goals. *Goals* represent the state of the environment that the agent wants to achieve. Task interdependence exists when the value generated from performing each task is different when the tasks are performed together versus when the tasks are performed separately [7].

Definition 1 (Task). The following grammar defines tasks:

$$t \quad ::= \quad act \quad | \quad t_1; t_2 \quad | \quad t_1 \parallel t_2 \quad | \quad t_1 \parallel\parallel t_2$$

in which act is an atomic action of an agent, $t_1; t_2$ represents sequential execution such that t_1 executes before t_2, $t_1 \parallel t_2$ represents interleaved execution, and $t_1 \parallel\parallel t_2$ represents true concurrent execution. The difference between interleaving and true concurrency is that in interleaving, actions cannot execute simultaneously, whereas in true concurrency, actions (and entire tasks) can execute simultaneously. We use the shorthand $t_1 \odot t_2$ to mean composition of t_1 and t_2 using any of the operators ;, $\parallel$, or $\parallel\parallel$, and the shorthand $\overline{t_1 \odot t_2}$ to mean the complement of (any composition *other than*) $t_1 \odot t_2$; for example, $\overline{t_1; t_2}$ means either $t_1 \parallel t_2$, $t_1 \parallel\parallel t_2$, or $t_2; t_1$. The operators $\parallel$ and $\parallel\parallel$ are commutative, so the complement $\overline{t_1 \parallel t_2}$ does not contain $t_2 \parallel t_1$, and similarly for $\parallel\parallel$. We consider the semantics of interleaved concurrency to be that of CSP [2]. For true concurrency, we consider the semantics to be that of independent actions [13].

Definition 2 (Task Value). The tangible value generated by executing a task (t) in some context (c) is measured by $\mathcal{V}_c(t)$.

Definition 3 (**Task Independence**). Tasks are independent if and only if the value generated by executing the composed tasks is the same as the sum of the value of each task in isolation. That is, we gain nothing by composing the two tasks. More formally:

$$TaskIndep(t_1, t_2) \Leftrightarrow \mathcal{V}_c(t_1) + \mathcal{V}_c(t_2) = \mathcal{V}_c(t_1 \odot t_2) \tag{1}$$

We can generalise this to $n \geq 2$ tasks:

$$TaskIndep(t_1, \ldots, t_n) \Leftrightarrow \mathcal{V}_c(t_1) + \mathcal{V}_c(t_2) = \mathcal{V}_c(t_1 \odot t_2) \ \wedge$$
$$\mathcal{V}_c(t_1) + \mathcal{V}_c(t_3) = \mathcal{V}_c(t_1 \odot t_3) \ \wedge \ \ldots \ \wedge \ \mathcal{V}_c(t_{n-1}) + \mathcal{V}_c(t_n) = \mathcal{V}_c(t_{n-1} \odot t_n) \tag{2}$$

which is equivalent to

$$TaskIndep(t_1, t_2) \wedge TaskIndep(t_1, t_3) \wedge \ldots \wedge TaskIndep(t_{n-1}, t_n)$$

Example 1 (Obstacle detection in human agent team (Independence)). One task required in the DARPA Robotics Challenge is obstacle detection [4]. Consider two tasks, *SenseObsHum* and *SenseObsRob*. The human detects obstacles via a user interface while the robot uses sensors. The two tasks are independent because the value of identifying an obstacle together is the same as both the human and robot identifying them independently. Given that the context c is detecting obstacles, independence is explained by applying Equation 1:

$$\mathcal{V}_c(SenseObsHum) + \mathcal{V}_c(SenseObsRob) = \mathcal{V}_c(SenseObsHum \odot SenseObsRob)$$

Definition 4 (Task Dependence). Composed execution of dependent tasks (using any composition operator) generates a value greater than independent execution of those tasks. If task t_2 is dependent on t_1 then formally:

$$TaskDep(t_1 \mid t_2) \Leftrightarrow \mathcal{V}_c(t_1 \odot t_2) > \mathcal{V}_c(t_1) + \mathcal{V}_c(t_2) \tag{3}$$

As with task independence, task dependence can be generalised to $n \geq 2$ tasks.

Definition 5 (Soft/Hard Task dependence). A soft (hard) task dependence is when a task is dependent on another task, but the value of executing the dependent task is non-zero (zero). Formally:

$$SoftTaskDep(t_1 \mid t_2) \Leftrightarrow TaskDep(t_1 \mid t_2) \wedge \mathcal{V}_c(t_2) > 0$$
$$HardTaskDep(t_1 \mid t_2) \Leftrightarrow TaskDep(t_1 \mid t_2) \wedge \mathcal{V}_c(t_2) = 0 \tag{4}$$

Definition 6 (Task Interdependence). Two tasks are interdependent if there is a two-way dependency between the tasks. Formally:

$$TaskInterdep(t_1, t_2) \Leftrightarrow TaskDep(t_1 \mid t_2) \wedge TaskDep(t_2 \mid t_1) \tag{5}$$

This can be generalised to $n \geq 2$ cases as is done for task independence.

Definition 6 captures the essence of interdependence but not the differences between the different *types of* interdependencies. Therefore, next we formalise several types of interdependencies, based on organisational theory [8].

2.1   Types of Task Interdependence

According to organisational theorists and sociologists [7, 8, 11], there are four types of task interdependence: sequential, reciprocal, team, and pooled. In the following sections, we formalise these definitions. We give definitions for pairs of tasks, but each is generalisable to $n \geq 2$, as done for independence.

Definition 7 (Reciprocal Task Interdependence). The value of reciprocally interdependent tasks is strictly greater than the value generated by any other composition. The notion of temporal lag between tasks is captured by the interleaved execution of the tasks. Formally:

$$TaskInterdep(t_1, t_2) \ \wedge \ \mathcal{V}_c(t_1 \parallel t_2) > \mathcal{V}_c(\overline{t_1 \parallel t_2}) \tag{6}$$

Example 2 (Writing a paper (Reciprocal Interdependence)). Consider one person writing a paper and another proof reading it and providing feedback, represented by the tasks *WritePaper* and *ReadPaper*. While these tasks can be executed sequentially, in many cases, more value is generated if the reader provides feedback on individual sections through the writing. But doing these truly concurrently would require the reader to read over the writer's shoulder, which is presumably not as valuable. Applying Equation 6:

$$\mathcal{V}_c(WritePaper \parallel ReadPaper) > \mathcal{V}_c(\overline{WritePaper \parallel ReadPaper})$$

Definition 8 (Team Task Interdependence). Team task interdependence exists for *joint activities* – that is, when agents must jointly execute one or more actions. There is no temporal lag between task executions, because tasks are executed simultaneously. For such tasks, the value of a truly concurrent composition is strictly greater than any other composition. Formally:

$$TaskInterdep(t_1, t_2) \ \wedge \ \mathcal{V}_c(t_1 \parallel\parallel t_2) > \mathcal{V}_c(\overline{t_1 \parallel\parallel t_2}) \tag{7}$$

Example 3 (Cooperative object transportation (Team Interdependence)).
Two robots are to move a table that is too heavy for one robot to move by itself. Consider two tasks *MoveEnd1* and *MoveEnd2*, where *MoveEnd1* means that one robot will lift and move the table at one of the two ends. Only true concurrent execution of the tasks will be able to move the table. Applying Equation 7:

$$\mathcal{V}_c(MoveEnd1 \parallel\parallel MoveEnd2) > \mathcal{V}_c(\overline{MoveEnd1 \parallel\parallel MoveEnd2})$$

Definition 9 (Sequential Task Interdependence). The value generated by sequential composition of two interdependent tasks is greater than any other composition. Formally:

$$TaskInterdep(t_1, t_2) \ \wedge \ \mathcal{V}_c(t_1; t_2) > \mathcal{V}_c(\overline{t_1; t_2}) \tag{8}$$

Note that this is not simply task dependence, because the value of performing the first task can be higher if the second task is performed; e.g. picking up a hose is only valuable if the hose is subsequently attached.

Definition 10 (Pooled Task Interdependence). Composition of tasks exhibiting pooled interdependence result in greater value than of executing the tasks independently. This is simply equivalent to the initial definition of interdependence, but with no constraint on how the tasks are composed. Each task contributes its share towards the group outcome, and failure of any task means that the goal will not be achieved. This is a *weak* form of interdependence.

3 Agent Interdependence

In the previous section, task interdependence is agnostic on who executes the task or who gains the value of the execution. In this section, we consider how *agents* can be independent, dependent, and interdependent. Throughout this section, we use the same grammar to define tasks, and $a_i.t_j$ to mean that agent a_i executes task t_j. The semantics remains the same, essentially ignoring the agent prefixes, which are just labels. This means that for composed tasks, if two agents a_1 and a_2 both execute the same action *act*, this is a synchronised event (they must execute together). We treat such synchronisations as *joint* actions.

According to Puranam et al. [7], *agent interdependence* results when *"...the reward to A from A's actions depends on the actions taken by B...".* We formalise the agent's reward using the notion of *utility*. We introduce *soft* and *hard* agent dependence and interdependence. Hard dependence means that the agent cannot complete its tasks independently (utility is zero), while for soft dependence, it can complete the task, but receives more utility if it works with other agents.

Definition 11 (Agent Utility). An agent's utility when executing a task t in a context c is defined as $\mathcal{U}_c^{a_i}(t)$. Each agent has their own utility function, which could be associated with measures such as how quickly the agent finishes a task.

Definition 12 (Agent Independence). Two agents, a_1 and a_2, are independent if each agent's utility is not affected by the actions of the other agent. Formally:

$$AgentIndep(a_1, a_2) \Leftrightarrow \forall t_1, t_2 : \mathcal{U}_c^{a_1}(a_1.t_1 \odot a_2.t_2) = \mathcal{U}_c^{a_1}(a_1.t_1) \wedge \\ \mathcal{U}_c^{a_2}(a_1.t_1 \odot a_2.t_2) = \mathcal{U}_c^{a_2}(a_2.t_2) \quad (9)$$

Definition 13 (Agent Dependence). Agent a_2 is dependent on a_1 for task t_2 if the utility of a_2 increases when agent a_1 executes a task t_1. Dependence is related to specific tasks; that is, it is possible to be dependent on another agent for some tasks, but not others. Formally:

$$AgentDep(a_1 \mid a_2, t_1, t_2) \Leftrightarrow \mathcal{U}_c^{a_2}(a_1.t_1 \odot a_2.t_2) > \mathcal{U}_c^{a_2}(a_2.t_2) \quad (10)$$

Agent dependence can also be defined for some unnamed task as:

$$AgentDep(a_1 \mid a_2) \Leftrightarrow \exists t_1, t_2 : AgentDep(a_1 \mid a_2, t_1, t_2) \quad (11)$$

Definition 14 (Soft/Hard Agent Dependence). Agent a_2 has a soft (hard) dependence on agent a_1 if the utility of a_2 at its task is non-zero (zero) and the utility of a_2 increases when agent a_1 executes one of its tasks. Formally:

$$SoftAgentDep(a_1 \mid a_2, t_1, t_2) \Leftrightarrow$$
$$AgentDep(a_1 \mid a_2) \wedge 0 < \mathcal{U}_c^{a_2}(a_2.(t_1 \odot t_2)) < \mathcal{U}_c^{a_2}(a_1.t_1 \odot a_2.t_2)$$
$$HardAgentDep(a_1 \mid a_2, t_1, t_2) \Leftrightarrow AgentDep(a_1 \mid a_2) \wedge \mathcal{U}_c^{a_2}(a_2.(t_1 \odot t_2)) = 0 \tag{12}$$

Definition 15 (Agent Interdependence). Agents a_2 and a_1 are interdependent if there is a two-way dependence between the agents. More formally:

$$AgentInterdep(a_1, a_2, t_1, t_2, t_3, t_4) \Leftrightarrow$$
$$AgentDep(a_1 \mid a_2, t_1, t_2) \wedge AgentDep(a_2 \mid a_1, t_3, t_4) \tag{13}$$

This definition demonstrates that agent interdependence is not merely task interdependence over utilities, because two pairs of dependent tasks between the agents is enough to establish interdependence. This is consistent with Puranum et al.'s view [7] that task interdependence is neither necessary nor sufficient to establish agent interdependence. As with agent dependence, we can omit the tasks t_1 to t_4 to avoid explicitly naming the tasks that are (inter)dependent.

Definition 16 (Soft/Hard Agent Interdependence). Soft (hard) agent interdependence between two agents exists when both agents have soft (hard) dependence on each other. Formally:

$$SoftAgentInterdep(a_1, a_2) \Leftrightarrow$$
$$SoftAgentDep(a_1 \mid a_2) \wedge SoftAgentDep(a_2 \mid a_1)$$
$$HardAgentInterdep(a_1, a_2) \Leftrightarrow$$
$$HardAgentDep(a_1 \mid a_2) \wedge HardAgentDep(a_2 \mid a_1) \tag{14}$$

Example 4 (Object transportation (Hard Agent Interdependence)). In Example 3, two robots (r_1 and r_2) moved a heavy table. Assume that the utility is: $\mathcal{U}_c^{a_i}(t) = total\_time$ and the context c is *object transportation*. The utilities of the individual tasks are zero because the robots can not move the table alone. When the two robots cooperatively move the table, the utility of each increases:

$$\mathcal{U}_c^{r_1}(r_1.MoveEnd1) = \mathcal{U}_c^{r_2}(r_2.MoveEnd2) = 0$$

$$\mathcal{U}_c^{r_1}(r_1.MoveEnd1 \mid\mid\mid r_2.MoveEnd2) > \mathcal{U}_c^{r_1}(r_1.(MoveEnd1 \odot MoveEnd2)) \wedge$$
$$\mathcal{U}_c^{r_2}(r_1.MoveEnd1 \mid\mid\mid r_2.MoveEnd2) > \mathcal{U}_c^{r_2}(r_2.(MoveEnd1 \odot MoveEnd2))$$

4   Example

One of the tasks in the DARPA Robotics Challenge was for the simulated robot to grasp a hose [4]. The robot and the operator each lacked the capability to correctly position the robot's hand for the robot to grasp the hose. Consider two tasks *PosHandOp* and *PosHandRb*, which represents the operator and the robot positioning the robot's hand respectively. The two tasks are interdependent because we need to execute both tasks to be able to grasp the hose. This follows that the agents are interdependent on each other.

The tasks could execute sequentially: the robot executes its task before the operator, and the tasks repeat until the robot's hand is positioned correctly. Alternatively, the tasks can be reciprocally executed such that while the robot tries to position its hand, the operator intervenes as necessary.

For a truly sequential execution of the tasks, the designer must program the robot to only receive operator command after the robot has positioned the hand. However, to enable reciprocal or interleaved execution, the designer needs to provision the robot to accept and execute commands from the operator as it is engaged in its task, and provide the necessary interfaces for the operator. The choice of the execution method depends on the objective of the designer. For example, if the objective is to minimise the temporal lag between the tasks, then reciprocal execution is appropriate. That is:

$$\mathcal{V}_c(PosHandOp \parallel PosHandRb) > \mathcal{V}_c(PosHandOp; PosHandRb)$$

As such, the robot should be designed to accept operator commands that override its own positioning tasks as it tries to position its hand.

The formalism provides designers with a more systematic and rigorous way to analyse the possibilities, and to weigh up different design decisions. Further, depending on the type of task interdependence, the designer may need to implement different coordination mechanisms between the agents.

5   Discussion

In this section, we discuss how our definitions align with two closely related papers: Castlefranchi et al.'s [1] formal definition of agent interdependence and Johnson et al.'s [4] informal work on task interdependence.

Castlefranchi at al. [1] formally define non-social and social dependence, and describe the complex patterns of dependence relationships, such as unilateral and bilateral dependence, AND-Dependence, and OR-Dependence. We go further than Castelfranchi et al.'s formal definitions of agent interdependence [1] by considering soft agent interdependence. In Castelfranchi et al.'s formalism, a dependence exists from agent a_1 to agent a_2 if and only if a_1 can only complete the task with a_2. By considering utility as the measure of task completion, we generalise agent interdependence, allowing us to capture Castelfranchi et al.'s notion of (inter)dependence as hard (inter)dependence (utility for a_1 is 0), as well as to consider a notion of soft (inter)dependence (utility for a_1 is non-zero, but less than the composed case). Castelfranchi et al. consider that bilateral dependence can either be mutual or reciprocal, differing based on whether the agents' goals are shared (mutual) or separate (reciprocal). We have also considered the treatment of *goal* interdependence, but our definitions and analysis are omitted from this paper for space reasons.

Johnson et al. [4] looked at numerous existing definitions of interdependence, including the work of sociologists [10], and we build on their final definition of task interdependence. We believe that their definitions of interdependence are equivalent to our formal definitions, including their notion of soft and hard interdependence, although their definitions are informal, so these equivalences are not straightforward to assess. However, they do not explicitly consider agent or goal interdependence.

6   Conclusion and Future Work

Existing literature [1, 4] makes a strong case that interdependence is an important concept for the design of human agent collaboration. In this paper, we claim that it is useful to consider the different types of interdependence, namely agent and task interdependence, and we provide semi-formal definitions of these. The example briefly illustrates how knowledge of the type of interdependence can assist designers in choosing an appropriate agent coordination mechanism. This indicates that there is a link between interdependence and coordination mechanisms, and support our view of the benefit to having a fine-grained understanding of interdependence.

Our motivation for this work is to build autonomous agents that can collaborate with humans in a natural way. In other work, we are analysing other types of interdependence, such as *goal* and *feedback* interdependence [8], which are crucial for agents that learn. We also plan to investigate appropriate coordination mechanisms for each type of interdependence, and to explore the relationships between the different interdependence types, for example, the relationship between agent and task interdependence.

References

[1] Castelfranchi, C., Miceli, M., Cesta, A.: Dependence relations among autonomous agents. In: Werner, E., Demazeau, Y. (eds.) Decentralized AI 3 - Proceedings of the Third European Workshop on Modelling Autonomous Agents and Multi-Agent Worlds (MAAMAW 1991), vol. (3), pp. 215–227 (1992)

[2] Hoare, C.: Communicating Sequential Processes. Prentice-Hall (1985)

[3] Johnson, M., Bradshaw, J., Feltovich, P., Jonker, C., Riemsdijk, B.V.: Autonomy and Interdependence in Human-Agent-Robot Teams. IEEE Intelligent Systems 27(2), 43–51 (2012)

[4] Johnson, M., Bradshaw, J., Feltovich, P., Jonker, C., Riemsdijk, M.B.V.: Coactive Design: Designing Support for Interdependence in Joint Activity. Journal of Human-Robot Interaction 3(1), 43–69 (2014)

[5] Parunak, H.V.D., Brueckner, S., Fleischer, M., Odell, J.: Co-x: Defining what agents do together. In: Proceedings of the AAMAS 2002, Workshop on Teamwork and Coalition Formation, pp. 62–69 (2002)

[6] Pfau, J., Miller, T., Sonenberg, L., Kashima, Y.: Logics of Common Ground (2014), http://people.eng.unimelb.edu.au/tmiller/pubs/logics-of-common-ground.pdf (under review)

[7] Puranam, P., Raveendran, M., Knudsen, T.: Organization Design: The Epistemic Interdependence Perspective. Acad. of Management Review 37(3), 419–440 (2012)

[8] Saavedra, R., Earley, P.C., Van Dyne, L.: Complex interdependence in task-performing groups. Journal of Applied Psychology 78(1), 61–72 (1993)

[9] Sichman, J.S.: DEPINT: Dependence-Based Coalition Formation in an Open Multi-Agent Scenario. JASSS 1(2) (1998)

[10] Thibaut, J.W., Kelley, H.H.: The social psychology of groups. John Wiley, Oxford (1959)

[11] Thompson, J.D.: Organizations in action. McGraw Hill, New York (1967)

[12] Van De Ven, A.H., Delbecq, A.L., Koenig, R.: Determinants of Coordination Modes within Organizations. American Soc. Review 41(2), 322–338 (1976)

[13] Winskel, G., Nielsen, M.: Models for concurrency. DAIMI Report Series 22(463) (1993)

Local Search Based Approximate Algorithm for Multi-Objective DCOPs

Maxime Wack[1], Tenda Okimoto[2], Maxime Clement[3], and Katsumi Inoue[4]

[1] Grenoble-INP: ESISAR, Valence, France
[2] Kobe University, Kobe, Japan
[3] The Graduate University for Advanced Studies, Tokyo, Japan
[4] National Institute of Informatics, Tokyo, Japan
{wack.max,forouhard}@gmail.com, tenda@maritime.kobe-u.ac.jp
inoue@nii.ac.jp

Abstract. Many real world optimization problems involve multiple criteria that should be considered separately and optimized simultaneously. A Multi-Objective Distributed Constraint Optimization Problem (MO-DCOP) is the extension of a mono-objective Distributed Constraint Optimization Problem (DCOP). A DCOP is a fundamental problem that can formalize various applications related to multi-agent cooperation. Solving an MO-DCOP is to find the Pareto front which is a set of cost vectors obtained by Pareto optimal solutions. In MO-DCOPs, even if a constraint graph has the simplest tree structure, the size of the Pareto front (the number of Pareto optimal solutions) is often exponential in the number of agents. Since finding all Pareto optimal solutions becomes easily intractable, it is important to consider fast but approximate algorithms. Various sophisticated algorithms have been developed for solving a DCOP and an MO-COP. However, there exists few works on an MO-DCOP. The Bounded Multi-Objective Max-Sum (B-MOMS) algorithm is the first and only existing approximate MO-DCOP algorithm. In this paper, we develop a novel approximate MO-DCOP algorithm called Distributed Iterated Pareto Local Search (DIPLS) and empirically show that DIPLS outperforms the state-of-the-art B-MOMS algorithm.

1 Introduction

A *Distributed Constraint Optimization Problem* (DCOP) [10, 16] is a fundamental problem that can formalize various applications related to multi-agent cooperation. A DCOP consists of a set of agents, each of which needs to decide the value assignment of its variables so that the sum of the resulting costs is minimized. Many application problems in multi-agent systems can be formalized as DCOPs, in particular, distributed resource allocation problems including meeting scheduling [6], sensor networks [5], and synchronization of traffic lights [4].

Many real world optimization problems involve multiple criteria that should be considered separately and optimized simultaneously. A *Multi-Objective Distributed Constraint Optimization Problem* (MO-DCOP) [1, 9, 12] is the extension of a mono-objective DCOP and a Multi-Objective Constraint Optimization

H.K. Dam et al. (Eds.): PRIMA 2014, LNAI 8861, pp. 390–406, 2014.
© Springer International Publishing Switzerland 2014

Problem (MO-COP) [7, 18, 19]. In MO-DCOPs, since trade-offs exist among objectives, there does not generally exist an ideal assignment, which minimizes all objectives simultaneously. Therefore, the "optimal" solution of an MO-DCOP is characterized by using the concept of *Pareto optimality*. An assignment is a Pareto optimal solution if there does not exist another assignment that weakly improves all of the objectives. Solving an MO-DCOP is to find the Pareto front which is a set of cost vectors obtained by all Pareto optimal solutions. Compared to DCOPs and MO-COPs, there exists few works on MO-DCOPs. The Bounded Multi-Objective Max-Sum (B-MOMS) algorithm [1] is the first and only existing approximate MO-DCOP algorithm which is an extension of the bounded max-sum algorithm [17] for solving a mono-objective DCOP. The B-MOMS works on a factor graph. It removes less important edges from a factor graph to make it cycle-free and obtains optimal solutions for the remaining cycle-free graph. A distributed search method with bounded cost vectors [9] is a complete algorithm which can guarantee to find all Pareto optimal solutions. This algorithm is a generalized ADOPT algorithm [10] that performs tree-search and partial dynamic programming. The Multi-Objective L_p-norm based Distributed Pseudo-tree Optimization Procedure (MO-DPOP$_{L_p}$) [12] is an incomplete algorithm which finds a subset of the Pareto front. The MO-DPOP$_{L_p}$ uses a widely used scalarization method and can guarantee to find a set of Pareto optimal solutions but not all.

Since finding all Pareto optimal solutions of MO-DCOPs becomes easily intractable for large-scale problem instances, it is important to consider fast but approximate algorithms. In MO-DCOPs, even if a constraint graph has the simplest tree structure, the number of all Pareto optimal solutions is often exponential (i.e. all assignments are Pareto optimal solutions in the worst case).

In this paper, we develop a novel approximate algorithm called *Distributed Iterated Pareto Local Search* (DIPLS) algorithm for solving an MO-DCOP. This algorithm is the extension of the well-known Pareto Local Search (PLS) [14], and we use it iteratively to generate an approximation of the Pareto front of an MO-DCOP. The PLS is the generalization of the hill-climbing method for optimization problems with multiple criteria. The DIPLS is the extension of this method for MO-DCOPs. In the experiments, we evaluate the performance of DIPLS with different problem settings and show that the local search technique is suitable for solving an MO-DCOP. We also compare DIPLS with the state-of-the-art approximate MO-DCOP algorithm B-MOMS, and empirically show that our proposed algorithm DIPLS outperforms the state-of-the-art B-MOMS.

About application domains of MO-DCOPs, we believe that sensor networks would be a promising area [11]. This problem is a kind of resource allocation problems which is a representative application problem for DCOPs. For example, consider a sensor network in a territory, where each sensor can sense a certain area in this territory. When we consider this problem with multiple criteria, e.g., data management, quality and quantity of observation data, and electrical consumption, this problem can be formalized as an MO-DCOP. Furthermore, when we consider a scheduling problem with several criteria, e.g., working hours, salary, and profit, it can be represented as an MO-DCOP. The other application

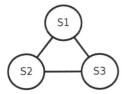

s_1	s_2	$cost$	s_2	s_3	$cost$	s_1	s_3	$cost$
a	a	5	a	a	0	a	a	1
a	b	7	a	b	2	a	b	1
b	a	10	b	a	0	b	a	0
b	b	12	b	b	2	b	b	3

Fig. 1. Example of mono-objective DCOP

problem for MO-DCOPs is wireless network of unmanned aerial vehicles [20]. Moreover, we believe that many DCOP application problems (concerned about "privacy") can be represented as MO-DCOPs by considering additional criteria.

The rest of the paper is organized as follows. In the next section, the formalizations of a DCOP and an MO-DCOP are introduced. The following section introduces a new approximate algorithm for MO-DCOPs. Afterwards, we compare our proposed algorithm with the state-of-the-art algorithm for MO-DCOPs. Just before the concluding section, some related works are discussed.

2   Preliminaries

In this section, we briefly describe the formalizations of Distributed Constraint Optimization Problems (DCOPs) and Multi-Objective Distributed Constraint Optimization Problems (MO-DCOPs) which is the extension of a DCOP.

2.1   Distributed Constraint Optimization Problem

A *Distributed Constraint Optimization Problem* (DCOP) [10, 16] is a fundamental problem that can formalize various applications related to multi-agent cooperation. In this paper, we assume all cost values are non-negative. Without loss of generality, we make the following assumptions for simplicity. Relaxing these assumptions to general cases is relatively straightforward:

- Each agent has exactly one variable.
- All constraints are binary.
- Each agent knows all constraints related to its variable.

A DCOP consists of a set of agents, each of which needs to decide the value assignment of its variables so that the sum of the resulting costs is minimized. This problem is defined by a set of agents S, a set of variables X, a set of constraint relations C, and a set of cost functions F. An agent i has its own variable x_i. A variable x_i takes its value from a finite, discrete domain D_i. A constraint relation (i, j) means there exists a constraint relation between x_i and x_j. For x_i and x_j, which have a constraint relation, the cost for an assignment

Table 1. Example of bi-objective DCOP

s_1	s_2	cost vector	s_2	s_3	cost vector	s_1	s_3	cost vector
a	a	(5,2)	a	a	(0,1)	a	a	(1,0)
a	b	(7,1)	a	b	(2,1)	a	b	(1,0)
b	a	(10,3)	b	a	(0,2)	b	a	(0,1)
b	b	(12,0)	b	b	(2,0)	b	b	(3,2)

$\{(x_i, d_i), (x_j, d_j)\}$ is defined by a cost function $f_{i,j}(d_i, d_j) : D_i \times D_j \to \mathbb{R}$. For a value assignment to all variables A, let us denote

$$R(A) = \sum_{(i,j)\in C, \{(x_i,d_i),(x_j,d_j)\}\subseteq A} f_{i,j}(d_i, d_j), \tag{1}$$

where $d_i \in D_i$ and $d_j \in D_j$. Then, an optimal assignment A^* is given as $\arg\min_A R(A)$, i.e., A^* is an assignment that minimizes the sum of the value of all cost functions. A DCOP can be represented using a constraint graph, in which a node corresponds to an agent and an edge represents a constraint.

Definition 1 (Total Ordering among Agents). *A total ordering among agents is a permutation of a sequence of agents* $\langle s_1, s_2, ..., s_n \rangle$*. We say agent* s_{i+1} *has higher priority than* s_i $(1 \leq i \leq n-1)$*.*

Example 1 (DCOP). Figure 1 shows a DCOP with three agents s_1, s_2 and s_3. Each agent/variable takes its value assignment from a discrete domain $\{a, b\}$. The table shows three cost tables among three agents. The optimal solution of this problem is $\{(s_1, a), (s_2, a), (s_3, a)\}$, and the optimal value is six.

2.2 Multi-objective Distributed Constraint Optimization Problem

A *Multi-Objective Distributed Constraint Optimization Problem* (MO-DCOP) [1, 9, 12] is the extension of a mono-objective DCOP. An MO-DCOP is defined with a set of agents S, a set of variables X, multi-objective constraints $C = \{C^1, ..., C^m\}$, i.e., a set of sets of constraint relations, and multi-objective functions $O = \{O^1, ..., O^m\}$, i.e., a set of sets of objective functions. For an objective l $(1 \leq l \leq m)$, a cost function $f_{i,j}^l : D_i \times D_j \to \mathbb{R}$, and a value assignment to all variables A, let us denote

$$R^l(A) = \sum_{(i,j)\in C^l, \{(x_i,d_i),(x_j,d_j)\}\subseteq A} f_{i,j}^l(d_i, d_j), \tag{2}$$

where $d_i \in D_i$ and $d_j \in D_j$. Then, the sum of the values of all cost functions for m objectives is defined by a cost vector, denoted $R(A) = (R^1(A), ..., R^m(A))$. Finding an assignment that minimizes all objective functions simultaneously is ideal. However, in general, since trade-offs exist among objectives, there does not exist such an ideal assignment. Therefore, the optimal solution of an MO-DCOP is characterized using the concept of *Pareto optimality*. Since this possible trade-off between objectives, the size of the Pareto front is exponential in the number of variables, i.e., every possible assignment can be Pareto optimal solution in the worst case. An MO-DCOP can be also represented using a constraint graph.

Definition 2 (Dominance). *For an MO-DCOP and two cost vectors $R(A)$ and $R(A')$, we call that $R(A)$ dominates $R(A')$, denoted by $R(A) \prec R(A')$, iff $R(A)$ is partially less than $R(A')$, i.e., it holds*

- $R^l(A) \leq R^l(A')$ *for all objectives l, and*
- *there exists at least one objective l', such that $R^{l'}(A) < R^{l'}(A')$.*

Definition 3 (Pareto Optimal Solution). *For an MO-DCOP, an assignment A is said to be the Pareto optimal solution, iff there does not exist another assignment A', such that $R(A') \prec R(A)$.*

Definition 4 (Pareto Front). *For an MO-DCOP, a set of cost vectors obtained by Pareto optimal solutions is said to be the Pareto front. Solving an MO-DCOP is to find the Pareto front.*

Example 2 (MO-DCOP). Table 1 shows a bi-objective DCOP, which is an extension of a DCOP in Figsure 1. Each agent takes its value from a discrete domain $\{a, b\}$. The Pareto optimal solutions of this problem are $\{\{(s_1, a), (s_2, a), (s_3, a)\}$ and $\{(s_1, a), (s_2, b), (s_3, b)\}\}$, and the Pareto front is $\{(6, 3), (10, 1)\}$.

2.3 Local Search

Local search algorithms are one of the most successful method for solving a wide variety of single objective optimization problems. However, it is really easy to adapt this notion to the multi-objective optimization problems. As in the first case, we use the same notion of neighborhood. But we need to redefine the criterion of acceptance for one solution. For the single-objective case, a solution is usually accepted if it is better than the current one, it is important to take into account several objectives. A simple approach may be to use the notion of dominance defined earlier. A solution is now accepted if and only if it is non dominated by another already discovered. All the solutions that are dominated by this new one are then deleted from the set of current solutions. Finally, the obtained set of non-dominated solutions is an approximation of the Pareto Front.

3   Distributed Iterated Pareto Local Search Algorithm

In this section, we develop a novel approximate algorithm called *Distributed Iterated Pareto Local Search* (DIPLS) algorithm for solving an MO-DCOP. This algorithm is the extension of the Pareto Local Search (PLS) [14], and we use it iteratively to generate an approximation of the Pareto front of an MO-DCOP. The PLS is the generalization of the hill-climbing method for optimization problems with multiple criteria. DIPLS is the distributed extension of this method.

Algorithm 1. Distributed Random Solution Generator for s_i

1: **Required** : a fixed total ordering on the agents: $\langle s_1, ..., s_n \rangle$
2: terminated: false
3: cpa_i: current partial solution
4: c_i: cost vector of cpa_i
5: **if** $i = 1$ **then**
6:     Assigns a random value and compute the cost c_1
7:     Send message $(PATH, cpa_1, c_1)$ to agent s_2
8:     Set terminated true
9: **end if**
10: **while** s_i not terminated **do**
11:     s_i receive message M
12:     **if** $M = (PATH, cpa_{i-1}, c_{i-1})$ **then**
13:         $cpa_i \leftarrow cpa_{i-1}$ // Update cpa
14:         Choose a random value and compute c_i of cpa_i
15:         **if** $(i \neq n)$ **then**
16:             Send message $(PATH, cpa_i, c_i)$ to s_{i+1}
17:         **else**
18:             $randomSol \leftarrow cpa_n$
19:         **end if**
20:         Set terminated true
21:     **end if**
22: **end while**
23: **Ensure** $randomSol$: a random solution.

The DIPLS uses local search approaches that have been already addressed in DCOPs [2, 3] and also been extended to Multi-Objective Optimization Problems (MOOP) [14, 21]. The basic idea of this algorithm is to try to evolve an initial population generated randomly by the agents, toward the Pareto front. The DIPLS has the following two phases:

Phase 1 : Generate the Initial solutions.
Phase 2 : Use a distributed PLS to evolve non-dominated solutions.

Let us describe phase 1. The initial solutions generation phase is trivial. The agents pick randomly some value for their variable. Then, each agent sends its value to its neighbors in the constraint graph and receives the assignments of its neighbors. The cost vector associated to the solution is computed. Algorithm 1 shows the pseudo-code to be executed by each agent in order to generate a random solution. This algorithm requires a total ordering on agents. Agents, starting by the first, choose randomly the value for their variable (lines 6 and 14) and pass around a single PATH message that includes the current partial assignment to the higher-priority agents and the current associated cost vector (lines 7 and 16). The algorithm stops once all agents assigned a value to their variable, and the process is repeated for each new random solution needed.

In phase 2, the obtained random solutions are iteratively evolved toward the Pareto front using a distributed iterated Pareto local search technique which is an extension of the local search algorithm to the distributed and multi-objective case. This algorithm uses the same notion of neighborhood as in the mono-

---

Algorithm 2. Distributed Pareto Local Search for s_i

1: **Require** a fixed total ordering on agents: $\langle s_1, ..., s_n \rangle$
2: *listRand*: a list of random solutions
3: *archive*: empty
4: terminated: false
5: **if** $i = n$ **then**
6:     *archive* $\leftarrow$ filter *listRand* by dominance
7:     Broadcast message $(ARCHIVE, archive)$
8: **end if**
9: **while** s_i is not terminated **do**
10:     s_i receives message M
11:     **if** $M = TERMINATE$ **then**
12:         Set terminated true
13:     **end if**
14:     **if** $M = (ARCHIVE, archive)$ **then**
15:         *neighbors* $\leftarrow$ createNeighbors($archive$)
16:         Send message $(MERGE, neighbors)$ to s_n
17:     **end if**
18:     **if** $M = (MERGE, neighbors)$ **then**
19:         Merge *archive* and *neighbors*
20:         **if** all merge messages received **then**
21:             Filter *archive* by dominance
22:             **if** new non-dominated solution in archive **then**
23:                 Broadcast message $(ARCHIVE, archive)$
24:             **else**
25:                 Broadcast message $(PF, archive)$ // Pareto front approximation
26:                 Broadcast message $(TERMINATE)$
27:             **end if**
28:         **end if**
29:     **end if**
30: **end while**
31: **Ensure** *archive*, a Pareto front approximation.

---

objective case. However, the acceptance criterion of the mono-objective local search algorithms needs to be changed to take into account several objectives. The pseudo-code of the distributed Pareto local search algorithm is given in Algorithm 2. This algorithm requires a total ordering on agents and the list of randomly generated solutions, and executes as follows : one agent, the controller (last agent), initially filters the list of random solutions by removing the dominated solutions and adds the non-dominated to an archive (line 6). It then broadcasts an ARCHIVE message that includes the archive (line 7). For each ARCHIVE message received (line 14), agents generates neighbors (line 15) and send MERGE messages including a list of generated neighbors to the controller. For each MERGE message received, the controller adds the received list of neighbors to the archive (line 18-19). After receiving MERGE messages from all the agents (line 20), the controller filters (by dominance) the archive (line 21) and if a new non-dominated solution has been added into the archive, it broadcasts an ARCHIVE message (line 22,23) and the process is repeated until no new non-dominated neighbor can be found starting from a solution of the archive.

Algorithm 3. Create neighbors for s_i

1: **Require** *archive*: a list of solutions
2: **for** each solution s_j in *archive* **do**
3:    $neighbor_j \leftarrow$ copy of s_j
4:    **for** each value v_k in s_i's domain **do**
5:       in $neighbor_j$, s_i assigns v_k to its variable and create $neighbor_{j,k}$
6:       Compute cost of $neighbor_{j,k}$
7:       Add $neighbor_{j,k}$ to $Neighbors_i$
8:    **end for**
9: **end for**
10: Filter by dominance $Neighbors_i$
11: **Ensure** $Neighbors_i$, the list of non-dominated neighbors of s_i.

The algorithm 3 presents the pseudo-code that allows an agent to generate neighbors when it receives an ARCHIVE message. For each solution in the archive, the agent assigns each domain value to its variable and computes the new corresponding cost vector. Each modification of the variable assignment leads to the creation of a neighbor which is added to a list of neighbors (line 1-9). At the end, the agent filters its list of neighbors by dominance and only the non-dominated neighbors will be send via the MERGE message to the controller.

Figure 2 shows the example of the behavior of DIPLS, how it finds the approximation of the Pareto front of an MO-DCOP. It starts with an initial set of solutions (Figure 2(a)). The square points on the figures represent the contents of the ARCHIVE messages sent by the controller to all the agents (Figure 2(b)), while the blue points represent the set of all the generated neighbors sent by each agent to the controller (MERGE messages) (Figure 2(c)). The algorithm is executed iteratively while a new non-dominated solution is found (Figure 2(d)-(e)). At the end, DIPLS provides an approximation of Pareto front (Figure 2(f)).

4   Experimental Evaluation

Experimental Setting

In this section, we compare the performances of DIPLS and the state-of-the-art approximate MO-DCOP algorithm B-MOMS. In our evaluations, we use the following problem instances: the domain size of each variable is two, and the cost values are randomly chosen from the range [0,100] for each objective. We solve bi-objective problem instances. Each data point in a graph represents an average of 100 problem instances. We generate random graphs varying the number of nodes and densities ($\delta \in [0.1, 1.0]$). The density is the constraint tightness of a problem instance by controlling the number of edges as follows. $|E| = \delta \times \frac{1}{2}|S|(|S| - 1)$, where $|S|$ is the number of agents. We implemented these algorithms in Java. All the experiments were carried out on 2.3GHz core with 4GB of RAM.

In order to evaluate the performances of DIPLS and B-MOMS, we define the following three metrics: Let PO be a set of all Pareto optimal solutions of an

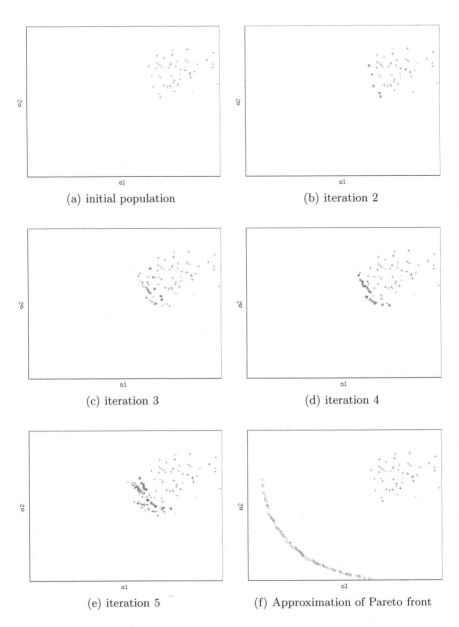

(a) initial population

(b) iteration 2

(c) iteration 3

(d) iteration 4

(e) iteration 5

(f) Approximation of Pareto front

Fig. 2. Behavior of DIPLS. By Algorithm 1, the agents pick randomly some value for their variable (a). The square points on the figures represent the contents of the ARCHIVE messages (b). The new cross points represent the set of all the generated neighbors (c). DIPLS executes (b) and (c) iteratively while a new non-dominated solution is found (d)-(e). At the end, it provides an approximation of Pareto front (f).

MO-DCOP and $\widetilde{PO}$ be an approximation of PO obtained by DIPLS and B-MOMS. The metric 1 represents the ratio of the Pareto optimal solutions over the set of obtained solutions by DIPLS and B-MOMS. The metric 2 shows the ratio of the obtained Pareto optimal solutions by DIPLS and B-MOMS over the whole set of Pareto optimal solutions of an MO-DCOP. The metric 3 is the required CPU runtime to compute $\widetilde{PO}$.

- Metric 1 $= \dfrac{|\widetilde{PO} \cap PO|}{|\widetilde{PO}|}$.

- Metric 2 $= \dfrac{|\widetilde{PO} \cap PO|}{|PO|}$.

- Metric 3 $=$ runtime to compute $\widetilde{PO}$.

In our experiments, we use the similar setting as in [1]. For metric 1 and 2, it is required to compute a set of all Pareto optimal solutions (PO). To compute the PO of an MO-DCOP, we use a brute-force optimal algorithm like [1]. Since finding all Pareto optimal solutions is exponential in the number of agents ($|S|$), we only report these three metrics for problem instances with $|S| \leq 16$. To go further, we show the quality solutions obtained by DIPLS for 3 and 4 objectives.

Experimental Results (Comparison with B-MOMS)

Figure 3 represents the results of metric 1 for constraint graphs with the density 0.1, 0.4, 0.7 and 1.0, varying the number of agents from 10 to 16. The line with

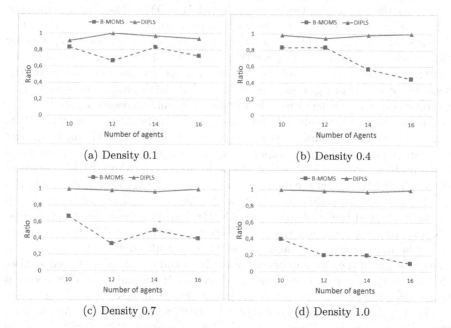

(a) Density 0.1   (b) Density 0.4

(c) Density 0.7   (d) Density 1.0

Fig. 3. Results of metric 1 for DIPLS and B-MOMS

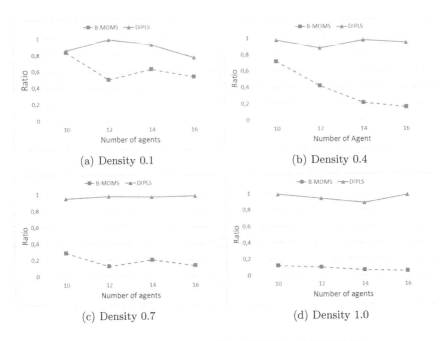

Fig. 4. Results of metric 2 for DIPLS and B-MOMS

triangle represents the results for our algorithm DIPLS and the line with square represents the results for the state-of-the-art B-MOMS. The x axis shows the number of agents/variables and the y axis represents the results of metric 1, i.e., the ratio of the Pareto optimal solutions over the set of obtained solutions by DIPLS and B-MOMS. We can see that over 90% of all obtained solutions by DIPLS are Pareto optimal solutions, and these results are independent on the densities of constraint graphs (Figure 3(a)-(d)). Additionally, the quality (i.e. the ratio) does not change when the number of agents increases for all densities. When the number of agents is 16 for the density 0.1, the ratio is 0.94 for DIPLS, while it is 0.98 for the density 1.0. On the other hand, for B-MOMS, by increasing the density of the constraint graph, i.e., by increasing the number of constraints in the problem, we can observe that the performances of B-MOMS become worse (Figure 3(a)-(d)). When the number of agents is 16 for the density 0.1, the ratio is 0.74 for B-MOMS, while it is 0.12 for the density 1.0. This can be explained by the number of removed edges in B-MOMS which increases for dense graphs. The experimental results reveal that DIPLS outperforms B-MOMS for metric 1. Furthermore, the performance of DIPLS is not affected by the density of a constraint graph (i.e. the number of constraints) and the number of agents. Also, the difference of the solution quality between DIPLS and B-MOMS becomes larger when the density of a constraint graph and the number of agents increase.

Figure 4 shows the results of metric 2 for DIPLS and B-MOMS. We obtained the similar results as in Figure 3, i.e., DIPLS outperforms B-MOMS for all cases (Figure 4 (a)-(d)). DIPLS can obtain more than 75% over the whole set of Pareto

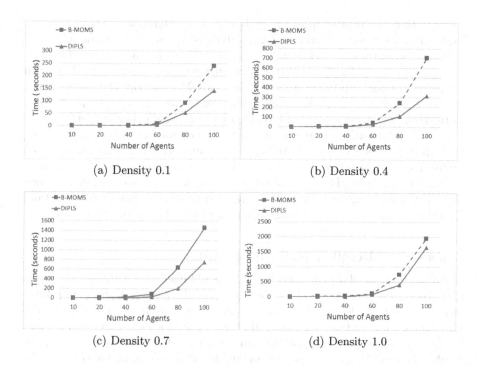

(a) Density 0.1

(b) Density 0.4

(c) Density 0.7

(d) Density 1.0

Fig. 5. Runtime of DIPLS and B-MOMS

optimal solutions for all cases. On the other hand, B-MOMS can obtain more than 50% of all Pareto optimal solutions for sparse graphs (i.e. constraint graph with low density). However, by increasing the density (i.e. Figure 4 (b)-(d)), the ratio becomes worse and the difference of the results between DIPLS and B-MOMS become larger. When the number of agents is 16 and the density is 0.1, the ratio for DIPLS is 0.77 and the ratio for B-MOMS is 0.54. In the case where density is equal to 0.4, the ratio obtained is 0.93 for DIPLS and 0.17 for B-MOMS. For the density 0.7, it is 0.98 for DIPLS and 0.15 for B-MOMS, and, finally, when the density is 1.0, it is 0.98 for DIPLS and 0.06 that for B-MOMS. The experimental results reveal that DIPLS can obtain more Pareto optimal solutions than B-MOMS. Also, the performance of DIPLS is not affected by the density of a constraint graph and the number of agents as in Figure 3.

Figure 5 shows the results of the average runtime in DIPLS and B-MOMS for constraint graphs with the density 0.1, 0.4, 0.7 and 1.0, varying the number of agents from 10 to 100. In Figure 5(a), the average runtime of DIPLS and B-MOMS increases significantly when the number of agents is upper than 60. We can see the similar results for all densities (see (a)-(d)). Also, when the number of agents is large (more than 60 agents), the average runtime of DIPLS is shorter compared to those for B-MOMS. Additionally, in case the number of agents is smaller than 60, we can see that both results are almost same for most cases, and they are independent from the density. The experimental results for metric

3 reveal that the average runtime in DIPLS is shorter compared to those in B-MOMS for large-scale and complex (high density) problem instances.

In summary, these experimental results reveal that (i) the quality of the obtained solutions by DIPLS is better compared with B-MOMS, (ii) DIPLS can obtain more Pareto optimal solutions than B-MOMS, and (iii) the required runtime of DIPLS is shorter. Also, the differences of these results (i)-(iii) become more significant when we increase the density and the number of agents.

Let us consider why our algorithm DIPLS can obtain better results compared to B-MOMS. This is because B-MOMS obtains an optimal solution for a relaxed problem, i.e., it looses the informations of the original problem by removing some constraints, while DIPLS does not relax the original problem (we never remove the constraints from the graph). If the relaxed problem is not so different from the original problem, the both algorithms can find a better solution quickly.

Experimental Results (Quality Solutions)

In this section, we show the quality solutions obtained by DIPLS for three and four objectives. Table 2 represents the results of the metrics 1 and 2 with three objectives, and Table 3 shows those for four objectives. In both tables, we also show the runtime and the number of all Pareto optimal solutions denoted #POS. In Table 2, we can see that DIPLS can obtain good quality solutions, i.e. the results of metric 1 and 2 are more than 90% for all densities, and also the results are independent on the number of agents (see (a)-(d)). In Table 3, we can see the similar results as in Table 2, i.e., all results of metric 1 and 2 exceed 90% for all cases. These experimental results reveal that the quality solutions obtained by DIPLS do not change by increasing the number of objectives. Furthermore, we observed that the number of Pareto optimal solutions increases when we

Table 2. Results of DIPLS for MO-DCOPs with 3 objectives

(a) Density 0.1

#agents	metrics1	metrics2	Runtime	#POS
10	1.0	0.988	0.008	20
11	1.0	0.997	0.018	39
12	0.999	0.966	0.030	59
13	1.0	1.0	0.057	85
14	1.0	0.970	0.073	90
15	1.0	0.970	0.093	80
16	0.998	0.991	0.410	192

(b) Density 0.4

#agents	metrics1	metrics2	Runtime	#POS
10	1.0	0.989	0.010	13
11	1.0	1.0	0.037	66
12	1.0	0.994	0.035	55
13	1.0	0.986	0.037	41
14	0.974	0.915	0.065	55
15	1.0	0.996	0.167	114
16	0.997	0.997	0.323	161

(c) Density 0.7

#agents	metrics1	metrics2	Runtime	#POS
10	1.0	1.0	0.021	28
11	1.0	0.990	0.028	41
12	1.0	0.995	0.032	31
13	1.0	0.964	0.060	42
14	1.0	0.990	0.254	146
15	1.0	0.965	0.156	83
16	0.998	0.982	0.315	129

(d) Density 1.0

#agents	metrics1	metrics2	Runtime	#POS
10	1.0	1.0	0.025	31
11	1.0	1.0	0.064	74
12	1.0	0.994	0.072	64
13	1.0	0.992	0.120	83
14	1.0	0.985	0.113	64
15	1.0	0.958	0.126	55
16	1.0	1.0	0.430	40

Table 3. Results of DIPLS for MO-DCOPs with 4 objectives

(a) Density 0.1

#agents	metrics1	metrics2	Runtime	#POS
10	1.0	1.0	0.089	190
11	1.0	0.978	0.104	46
12	1.0	0.998	0.069	119
13	1.0	1.0	0.109	147
14	1.0	1.0	0.194	187
15	1.0	1.0	1.576	538
16	1.0	0.998	2.322	572

(b) Density 0.4

#agents	metrics1	metrics2	Runtime	#POS
10	1.0	1.0	0.045	100
11	1.0	1.0	0.153	208
12	1.0	1.0	0.499	364
13	1.0	1.0	0.220	194
14	1.0	0.990	0.119	107
15	1.0	0.999	1.962	594
16	1.0	0.992	1.585	459

(c) Density 0.7

#agents	metrics1	metrics2	Runtime	#POS
10	0.999	0.996	0.043	61
11	1.0	1.0	0.228	208
12	1.0	0.998	0.086	86
13	1.0	1.0	0.140	117
14	1.0	0.993	0.295	178
15	1.0	0.991	0.286	147
16	0.999	0.995	1.268	370

(d) Density 1.0

#agents	metrics1	metrics2	Runtime	#POS
10	1.0	1.0	0.082	111
11	1.0	1.0	0.113	119
12	1.0	1.0	0.388	269
13	1.0	0.999	0.664	319
14	1.0	0.990	0.444	213
15	1.0	0.999	1.637	450
16	1.0	0.999	2.890	577

increase the number of objectives. In Table 2 (a), when the number of agents is 16, the number of Pareto optimal solutions ($\#POS$) is 192, while $\#POS$ is 572 for four objectives (Table 3 (a)). In Table 2 (d), in case the number of agents is 16, $\#POS$ is 40, while $\#POS$ is 577 for 4 objectives (Table 3 (d)). The runtime of our algorithm increases, when the number of objectives increases. In Table 2 (a), when the number of agents is 16, the runtime is 0.4, while it is 2.3 for four objectives (Table 3 (a)). In Table 2 (d), in case the number of agents is 16, the runtime is 0.4, while it is 2.8 for four objectives (Table 3 (d)). We consider that this is because the runtime depends on the number of Pareto optimal solutions. For the relationship between the number of objectives and the quality solution, and also the runtime, we will analyze more detailed in our future work.

5 Related Works

The Bounded Multi-Objective Max-Sum (B-MOMS) algorithm [1] is the first and only existing approximate MO-DCOP algorithm which is an extension of the bounded max-sum algorithm [17] for solving a mono-objective DCOPs. The B-MOMS works on a factor graph. It considers the importance of edges and removes less important edges from a factor graph to make it cycle-free, and obtain optimal solutions for the remaining cycle-free graph. For approximate algorithms, providing the bound of a solution is one of the important issues. The B-MOMS can provide the bound of a solution a posteriori, i.e., the error bound is obtained only after we actually run the algorithm and obtain an approximate solution. Having a priori bound, i.e., the error bound is obtained before actually running the algorithm, is desirable, but a posteriori bound is usually more accurate. Compared to B-MOMS, DIPLS cannot guarantee the quality bound.

Various approximate algorithms have been developed for solving a MO-COP, e.g., Multi-Objective Mini-Bucket Elimination (MO-MBE) [18], Multi-objective Best- First AND/OR search algorithm (MO-AOBF) [8], and Multiobjective A* search algorithm (MOA*) [15]. MO-MBE computes a set of lower bounds of MO-COPs. MO-AOBF and MOA* compute a relaxed Pareto front using ϵ-dominance [13]. Most of these approximate algorithms are extension of the representative search and inference based mono-objective COP algorithms. DIPLS is the local search based algorithm, and our experimental results reveal that the local search technique is suitable for solving a MO-DCOP. We consider that this is because of the huge number of Pareto optimal solutions, i.e., small local change has a big chance to obtain the Pareto optimal solution in MO-DCOPs.

6   Conclusion

Many real world optimization problems involve multiple criteria that should be considered separately and optimized simultaneously. An MO-DCOP is a DCOP which involves multiple criteria. In MO-DCOPs, since finding all Pareto optimal solutions is not realistic, it is important to consider fast but approximate algorithms. In this paper, we developed a novel approximate algorithm called Distributed Iterated Pareto Local Search (DIPLS) algorithm. DIPLS use PLS iteratively to generate an approximation of the Pareto front of an MO-DCOP. In the experiments, we evaluated the performance of DIPLS with different problem settings. We compared DIPLS with the state-of-the-art approximate algorithm B-MOMS and empirically showed that DIPLS outperforms B-MOMS. Our experimental results reveal that (i) the quality of the obtained solutions by DIPLS is better compared with B-MOMS, (ii) DIPLS can obtain more Pareto optimal solutions than B-MOMS, and (iii) the required runtime of DIPLS is shorter. Our future works include developing an approximate algorithm which can provide the bound of a solution a priori and a posteriori. Also, we will extend approximate DCOP algorithms for solving an MO-DCOP, and compare the performances of these algorithms with DIPLS. Furthermore, we intend to apply DIPLS on challenging real world problems, e.g., sensor network and scheduling problems.

References

[1] Fave, F.D., Stranders, R., Rogers, A., Jennings, N.: Bounded decentralised coordination over multiple objectives. In: Proceedings of the 10th International Conference on Autonomous Agents and Multiagent Systems, pp. 371–378 (2011)

[2] Fitzpatrick, S., Meertens, L.: An experimental assessment of a stochastic, anytime, decentralized, soft colourer for sparse graphs. In: Steinhöfel, K. (ed.) SAGA 2001. LNCS, vol. 2264, pp. 49–64. Springer, Heidelberg (2001)

[3] Hirayama, K., Yokoo, M.: The distributed breakout algorithms. Artificial Intelligence 161(1-2), 89–115 (2005)

[4] Junges, R., Bazzan, A.: Evaluating the performance of DCOP algorithms in a real world, dynamic problem. In: Proceedings of the 7th International Conference on Autonomous Agents and Multiagent Systems, pp. 599–606 (2008)

[5] Lesser, V., Ortiz, C., Tambe, M. (eds.): Distributed Sensor Networks: A Multiagent Perspective (Edited book), May 2003. Kluwer Academic Publishers (2003)

[6] Maheswaran, R., Tambe, M., Bowring, E., Pearce, J., Varakantham, P.: Taking dcop to the real world: efficient complete solutions for distributed multi-event scheduling. In: Proceedings of the 3rd International Conference on Autonomous Agents and Multiagent Systems, pp. 310–317 (2004)

[7] Marinescu, R.: Exploiting problem decomposition in multi-objective constraint optimization. In: Gent, I.P. (ed.) CP 2009. LNCS, vol. 5732, pp. 592–607. Springer, Heidelberg (2009)

[8] Marinescu, R.: Best-first vs. depth-first and/or search for multi-objective constraint optimization. In: Proceedings of the 22nd IEEE International Conference on Tools with Artificial Intelligence, pp. 439–446 (2010)

[9] Matsui, T., Silaghi, M., Hirayama, K., Yokoo, M., Matsuo, H.: Distributed search method with bounded cost vectors on multiple objective dCOPs. In: Rahwan, I., Wobcke, W., Sen, S., Sugawara, T. (eds.) PRIMA 2012. LNCS, vol. 7455, pp. 137–152. Springer, Heidelberg (2012)

[10] Modi, P., Shen, W., Tambe, M., Yokoo, M.: ADOPT: asynchronous distributed constraint optimization with quality guarantees. Artificial Intelligence 161(1-2), 149–180 (2005)

[11] Okimoto, T., Ribeiro, T., Clement, M., Inoue, K.: Modeling and algorithm for dynamic multi-objective weighted constraint satisfaction problem. In: Proceedings of the 6th International Conference on Agents and Artificial Intelligence, pp. 420–427 (2014)

[12] Okimoto, T., Schwind, N., Clement, M., Inoue, K.: Lp-norm based algorithm for multi-objective distributed constraint optimization. In: Proceedings of the 13th International Conference on Autonomous Agents and Multiagent Systems, pp. 1427–1428 (2014)

[13] Papadimitriou, C.H., Yannakakis, M.: On the approximability of trade-offs and optimal access of web sources. In: Proceedings of the 41st Annual Symposium on Foundations of Computer Science, pp. 86–92 (2000)

[14] Paquete, L., Chiarandini, M., Stutzle, T.: Pareto local optimum sets in the bi-objective traveling salesman problem: An experimental study. In: Metaheuristics for Multiobjective Optimisation. Lecture Notes in Economics and Mathematical Systems, pp. 177–200. Springer (2004)

[15] Perny, P., Spanjaard, O.: Near admissible algorithms for multiobjective search. In: Proceedings of the 18th European Conference on Artificial Intelligence, pp. 490–494 (2008)

[16] Petcu, A., Faltings, B.: A scalable method for multiagent constraint optimization. In: Proceedings of the 19th International Joint Conference on Artificial Intelligence, pp. 266–271 (2005)

[17] Rogers, A., Farinelli, A., Stranders, R., Jennings, N.: Bounded approximate decentralised coordination via the max-sum algorithm. Artificial Intelligence 175(2), 730–759 (2011)

[18] Rollon, E., Larrosa, J.: Bucket elimination for multiobjective optimization problems. Journal of Heuristics 12(4-5), 307–328 (2006)

[19] Rollon, E., Larrosa, J.: Multi-objective russian doll search. In: Proceedings of the 22nd AAAI Conference on Artificial Intelligence, pp. 249–254 (2007)

[20] Sivakumar, A., Tan, C.: UAV swarm coordination using cooperative control for establishing a wireless communications backbone. In: Proceedings of the 9th International Conference on Autonomous Agents and Multiagent Systems, pp. 1157–1164 (2010)

[21] Thibaut, L., Jacques, T.: Two-phase pareto local search for the biobjective traveling salesman problem. Journal of Heuristics 16(3), 475–510 (2010)

Multi-objective Distributed Constraint Optimization Using Semi-rings

Graham Billiau[1], Chee Fon Chang[2], and Aditya Ghose[1]

[1] Decision Systems Lab, University of Wollongong, NSW, Australia
[2] Centre for Oncology Informatics, University of Wollongong, NSW, Australia
{gdb339,cfchang,aditya}@uow.edu.au

Abstract. In this paper, we extend the Support Based Distributed Optimization (SBDO) algorithm to support problems which do not have a total pre-order over the set of solutions. This is the case in common real life problems that have multiple objective functions. In particular, decision support problems. These disparate objectives are not well supported by existing Distributed Constraint Optimization Problem (DCOP) techniques, which assume a single cost or utility function. As a result, existing Distributed COP techniques (with some recent exceptions) require that all agents subscribe to a common objective function and are therefore unsuitable for settings where agents have distinct, competing objectives. This makes existing constraint optimization technologies unsuitable for many decision support roles, where the decision maker wishes to observe the different trade-offs before making a decision.

1 Introduction

Optimization problems with multiple competing objective functions are common in real life, where human decision makers have to balance objectives such as time, cost and quality. These problems are even more prevalent in multi-agent settings such as supply chain optimization, optimal transport planning or group decision support, where each agent may have different objectives. Despite how common these problems are, most current Distributed Constraint Optimization Problem (DCOP) techniques assume that all agents subscribe to the same objective function (an exception being [1]). While it is possible to combine various quantitative objectives into a single utility value using approaches such as a weighted sum, each weighting results in an alternate Constraint Optimization Problem (COP) and hence potentially transforming into a different "optimal" solution. For decision support systems, a single solution is not sufficient. The decision maker needs to see all the pareto-optimal solutions. They can then use their human judgment and additional knowledge to discriminate between the options presented.

On the other hand, evolutionary algorithms are well-recognized for their ability to solve multi-objective optimization problems. Many evolutionary techniques require all relevant knowledge to be centralized, which violates the assumptions of DCOPs. Several other evolutionary techniques permit distributed solving,

H.K. Dam et al. (Eds.): PRIMA 2014, LNAI 8861, pp. 407–422, 2014.
© Springer International Publishing Switzerland 2014

though they assume that each node in the system possesses complete knowledge of the problem [2].

Our approach is to extend an existing DCOP algorithm (SBDO [3]) to support multiple objective functions. This allows us to maintain the distributed nature of the problem and the advantages of the DCOP approach such as autonomy, privacy and fault tolerance. We are also able to find a good approximation of the pareto-frontier, which offers a rich repertoire of possible solutions and allows context-specific trade-offs to be made.

There exists several approaches that enable DCOP solvers to solve problems with many objective functions. The first approach, adopted in [4] involves transforming all but one of the objective functions into hard constraints by setting a threshold. These approaches are not acceptable as it does not offer the opportunity to explore the space of alternative trade-offs over the pareto-frontier (instead, a single solution is computed - the optimal one with respect to the single remaining objective). Which solution is returned, and how good it is with respect to the human decision makers extra knowledge depends on which objective is retained and the thresholds specified for the other objectives. This often requires a trial and error approach, where many different choices of objective and thresholds are made so the decision maker has a reasonable choice. Secondly, an extension to the max-sum algorithm, the Bounded Multi-Objective Max Sum (B-MUMS) algorithm [1] has been developed to solve problems with many objective functions. Fave et al. [1] proposed the use of an array of real numbers to represent the cost/utility of each solution, hence B-MUMS only supports valued constraints. Another approach, presented by Matsui et al. [5], utilizes bounded cost vectors to represent utilities. This approach also only supports valued constraints. Our interest is in the greater expressive power and flexibility that is gained by using semirings (such as the ability to handle qualitative specifications of preference).

In section 2, we present the definition of a DCOP utilizing semirings. The semirings are used to store the cost/utility values of a solution. Semirings are an abstract algebraic structure containing a set of values, a comparison operator and an aggregation operator. By using semirings instead of a specific representation (such as the reals or the integers), any ordering over the solutions can be represented. We exploit this property to represent problems which do not have a total pre-order over the solutions. This allows many types of problems to be represented such as multi-objective problems and problems with qualitative valuations. Semirings have been used previously to characterise many different Constraint Satisfaction Problems (CSPs). C-semirings have been proposed by Bistarelli et al. [6] and have been shown to represent many of the different types of CSPs. A c-semiring is defined as follows:

Definition 1. *A c-semiring [6] is a tuple $\mathcal{V} = \langle V, \oplus, \otimes, \bot, \top \rangle$ satisfying (for all $\alpha \in V$):*

- *V is a set of abstract values with $\bot, \top \in V$.*
- *$\oplus$ is defined over possibly infinite sets as follows:*
  - *$\forall v \in \mathcal{V}, \oplus(\{v\}) = v$*

- $\oplus(\emptyset) = \perp$ *and* $\oplus(\mathcal{V}) = \top$
- $\oplus(\bigcup v_i, i \in S) = \oplus(\{\oplus(v_i), i \in S\})$ *for all sets of indices* S
- $\otimes$ *is a commutative, associative and closed binary operator on* V *with* $\top$ *as unit element* $(\alpha \otimes \top = \alpha)$ *and* $\perp$ *as absorbing element* $(\alpha \otimes \perp = \perp)$.
- $\otimes$ *distributes over* $\oplus$ *(i.e.,* $\alpha \otimes (\beta \oplus \gamma) = (\alpha \otimes \beta) \oplus (\alpha \otimes \gamma)$*).*

In section 3, we extend the SBDO [3] algorithm to Support Based Distributed Optimization with Semirings (SBDOsr). The design of SBDO avoids a hierarchy of agents (during construction) as used by most other DCOP solvers. Instead, each agent has an equal standing to the other agents, and communicates by sending arguments to their neighbours. The loose structure between agents and the redundant information each agent stores means that the entire system is robust and resilient to fault or changes, whether from a change to the problem or a failure of some of the agents. While SBDO is complete with respect to hard constraints, the loose structure means SBDO is not complete with respect to valued constraints.

In section 4, we present an empirical evaluation of the SBDOsr algorithm which suggests that the approach is effective in practice.

2   Semiring-Based DCOP

2.1   Idempotent Semirings

In this section, we present an idempotent semiring as the algebraic structure used to compare different solutions to a given SDCOP. We propose the use of an idempotent semiring instead of a c-semiring as proposed by Bistraelli et al. [6] because we believe that a c-semiring is too restrictive. Specifically, a c-semiring does not support optimization problems where the objective is to maximize a value. Note that an idempotent semiring is a generalization of a c-semiring.

Definition 2. *An* **idempotent semiring** *is a tuple* $\mathcal{V} = \langle V, \oplus, \otimes, \perp \rangle$ *satisfying the following conditions:*

- V *is a set of abstract values.*
- $\oplus$ *is a commutative, associative, idempotent and closed operator over* V.
- $\otimes$ *is an associative and closed operator over* V.
- $\otimes$ *left and right distributes over* $\oplus$.
- $\perp \in \mathcal{V}$ *is the absorbing element for the* $\otimes$ *operator.*

The idempotent property of the $\oplus$ operator can be used to obtain a partial order $\preceq_V$ over the set of abstract values V. Such a partial order is defined as: $\forall(v_1, v_2 \in V), v_1 \leq_V v_2$ iff $v_1 \oplus v_2 = v_1$ (intuitively, $v_1 \leq_V v_2$ denotes that v_1 is at least as preferred as v_2). The $\oplus$ operator enables comparisons between two semiring values while the $\otimes$ operator allows us to aggregate two semiring values.

The idempotent semiring structure is capable of representing all the different constraint schemes. As a c-semiring is an idempotent semiring, all constraint schemes that can be represented as c-semirings can be represented as idempotent semirings. Bistarelli et al.[6] has shown that classic, fuzzy, probabilistic, weighted and set based constraints are all instances of a c-semiring. Valued constraints with a maximization objective are not an instance of a c-semiring, but can be represented by the idempotent semiring $\langle \Re, \max, +, -\infty \rangle$.

Multiple idempotent semirings may be combined into a single idempotent semiring in a similar fashion to that proposed by Bistarelli et al.[6] for c-semirings. The semirings in question are capable of evaluations on multiple heterogeneous scales - both qualitative and quantitative. We leverage this property in handling multi-objective DCOPs. The following definition formalizes the composition of idempotent semirings.

Definition 3. *Given n idempotent semirings $S_i = \langle V_i, \oplus_i, \otimes_i, \perp_i, \rangle$ for $i = 1, \ldots, n$ we define the structure $Comp(S_1, \ldots, S_n) = \langle \langle V_1, \ldots, V_n \rangle, \oplus, \otimes, \langle \perp_1, \ldots, \perp_n \rangle \rangle$ where $\oplus$ and $\otimes$ are defined as follows: Given $\langle a_1, \ldots, a_n \rangle$ and $\langle b_1, \ldots, b_n \rangle$ such that $a_i, b_i \in V_i$ for $i = 1, \ldots, n$, $\langle a_1, \ldots, a_n \rangle \oplus \langle b_1, \ldots, b_n \rangle = \langle a_1 \oplus_1 b_1, \ldots, a_n \oplus_n b_n \rangle$ and $\langle a_1, \ldots, a_n \rangle \otimes \langle b_1, \ldots, b_n \rangle = \langle a_1 \otimes_1 b_1, \ldots, a_n \otimes_n b_n \rangle$.*

Theorem 1. *If $S_i = \langle V_i, \oplus_i, \otimes_i, \perp \rangle$ for $i = 1, \ldots, n$ are all idempotent semirings, then $Comp(S_1, \ldots, S_n)$ is an idempotent semiring.*

Proof. From definition 3, The combined semiring uses the $\oplus$ and $\otimes$ operators from the component semirings directly, so the properties that hold for the component semirings also hold for the combined semiring.

2.2 Constraint Optimization Problems

To support multi-objective problems, we have replaced the real numbers which are normally used to measure the cost or utility of a solution with an idempotent semiring. The idempotent semiring could itself describe an objective function which does not have a total pre-order, or it could be a collection of idempotent semirings combined to form a new idempotent semiring. By combining different idempotent semirings as per definition 2, it is possible to mix different constraint types in the same problem.

Definition 4. *A Semiring-Based Distributed Constraint Optimization Problem is a tuple $SDCOP = \langle \mathcal{A}, \mathcal{X}, \mathcal{D}, \mathcal{V}, \mathcal{S}, \mathcal{C} \rangle$ where*

- *$\mathcal{A}$ is a non-empty set of agents. Each agent $A \in \mathcal{A}$ is a set of variables $A \subseteq \mathcal{X}$ that the agent owns.*
- *$\mathcal{X}$ is a set of variables.*
- *$\mathcal{D}$ is a set of domains.*
- *$\mathcal{V} = \langle V, \oplus, \otimes, \perp \rangle$ is an idempotent semiring utilized to evaluate variable assignments.*
- *$\mathcal{C}$ is a non-empty set of constraints.*

Each constraint returns a value from the set of values in the idempotent semiring, which allows all the common types of DCOPs to be represented.

For classic satisfaction problems the semiring $\langle \{\text{True}, \text{False}\}, \vee, \wedge, \text{False} \rangle$ is suitable to represent the result of the constraints. For valued constraint optimization problems the semiring $\langle \Re, \min, +, \infty \rangle$ is suitable for minimization problems and $\langle \Re, \max, +, -\infty \rangle$ is suitable for maximization problems. In the case that there are multiple objective functions, each objective is represented by its own idempotent semiring which are combined using $Comb()$. Combining the different objectives in this way naturally leads to a search for a pareto-optimal solution, as there is no ordering specified between the objectives, though one can be added if desired.

3   Semi-ring Support Based Distributed Optimisation

The same as in SBDO, most communication is in the form of proposal messages. These messages are inspired by formal argumentation, where the notion of an argument is used to encode viewpoints and attack to describe conflict between arguments. A proposal message contains the values an agent has selected for its variables and the context in which the decision was made.

Definition 5. *An* **assignment** *is a triple* $\langle a, v, u \rangle$ *where* a *is an agent in the SDCOP,* v *is a set of variable-value pairs, and* u *is the utility of this assignment returned by the agents local constraints.* v *must contain a variable-value pair for every variable in* W_a *for which another agent has read privileges.*

Definition 6. *Given a SDCOP* $= \langle \mathcal{A}, \mathcal{X}, \mathcal{D}, \mathcal{V}, \mathcal{C} \rangle$, *a* **proposal** *is a pair* $\langle VA, SCE \rangle$. *Where VA (variable assignments) is a sequence* $\langle ass_1, \ldots, ass_n \rangle$ *of assignments such that the sequence of agents forms a simple path through the neighbourhood graph and there are no conflicting assignments. SCE (shared constraint evaluations) is a set of evaluations of shared constraints. A shared constraint can only be evaluated if an assignment to every variable involved in the constraint is included in VA. Each evaluation is a tuple* $\langle o, u \rangle$ *where* o *is a shared objective and* u *is the utility returned by the objective function* o *given the assignments in VA.*

As an example, consider the two agents A and B, who share a constraint O, as well as having their own local constraints. When A first creates a proposal it simply contains an assignment to A, $\langle \langle \langle A, \{\langle a, 1 \rangle\} \rangle, 3 \rangle \rangle, \{\} \rangle$. Later when B extends the proposal, B then has enough information to evaluate the shared objective, producing $\langle \langle \langle A, \{\langle a, 1 \rangle\}, 3 \rangle, \langle B, \{\langle b, 2 \rangle\}, 2 \rangle \rangle, \{\langle O, 10 \rangle\} \rangle$.

As the idempotent semirings we are using to represent the utility of a partial solution generalise the concepts of 'constraint' and 'objective' used in SBDO, it is no longer necessary to differentiate between them. So the concept of 'objective' has been removed from SBDOsr. Instead the semiring associated with a constraint defines if it's a hard constraint, valued constraint, objective, etc.

The sequence of variable assignments indicates the order in which this proposal has been constructed and is required both to store the utility of the solution and for the generation of nogoods. The set of shared constraint evaluations is required to record the utility of constraints shared by more than one agent.

If the utility of the shared constraints is combined with the local constraints they might be double counted when cycles form. Note that in situations where privacy is important, the assignment to a variable only needs to be disclosed if another agent has a constraint involving this variable.

The utility of an assignment can be determined by evaluating the applicable functions in $\mathcal{C}$ and aggregating them using $\otimes$. The total utility of an proposal is determined by applying the aggregation ($\otimes$) operator over the utility of each assignment and evaluation. As such a proposal encodes a partial solution to the problem as well as the relative utility of the partial solution. When a proposal is considered as an argument the first $n - 1$ assignments form the justification and the last assignment is the conclusion.

The utility value provides a partial order over the the proposals (partial solutions). Comparison between proposals can be performed by first applying the $\otimes$ operator over the utility of each assignment and evaluation to determine its utility value and then the $\oplus$ operator to determine which proposal is better. Whenever we refer to one proposal being better than another in this paper it is with respect to this induced ordering.

The counterpart of a proposal is a nogood. A nogood represents a partial solution that violates at least one constraint and should never be reconsidered or included in the final solution. This inconsistency is discovered when the utility of an isgood is $\perp$. Nogoods with justifications [7] are used as these allow us to guarantee that all the hard constraints are satisfied (as shown in [8]) as well as allowing obsolete nogoods to be identified after the constraints that the nogood violated are removed from the problem. For our purposes, a nogood with justification (originally defined in [7]) is treated as follows:

Definition 7. *Given an SDCOP $\langle \mathcal{A}, \mathcal{X}, \mathcal{D}, \mathcal{V}, \mathcal{C} \rangle$, a **nogood** is a pair $\langle P, C \rangle$ where P is a set of variable-value pairs representing a partial solution and $C \subseteq \mathcal{C}$ is the set of constraints that provides the **justification** for the nogood, such that the combination of s and C is inconsistent (results in $\perp$). As such a nogood represents a partial solution that is proven to not be part of any global solution.*

*A **minimal nogood** is a nogood $n = \langle P, C \rangle$ such that there does not exist a nogood $n' = \langle P', C \rangle$ where $P' \subset P$ or a nogood $n'' = \langle P, C' \rangle$ where $C' \subset C$.*

In static environments, detecting that the network has reached a quiescent state is sufficient to detect termination. This can be achieved by taking a consistent global snapshot [9]. The algorithm will also terminate if it detects that there is no solution to the problem, by generating the empty nogood. Otherwise, due to the dynamic nature of the input problem, the algorithm will only terminate when instructed to by an outside entity. Detecting that the network of agents has reached a quiescent state, or detecting that the problem is over-constrained are in themselves insufficient as terminating criteria, since new inputs from the environment, in the form of added or deleted variables/constraints might invalidate them.

Algorithm 1: send_nogood(I)

---

begin

   Let N be a nogood derived from I

   Send N to A

   Delete I

Algorithm 2: process remove-nogood message

---

begin

   Let C be the constraint referenced

   for *Each received nogood N* **do**

      if *N is in the remove-nogood message* **then**

         Delete N from nogoods

         delete N from the remove-nogood message

   if *counter $\neq$ 0* **then**

      Add the remove-nogood message to removed-constraints

   `receive remove constraint(C)`

3.1 Algorithm

Due to space constraints we only discuss the parts of SBDOsr that are changed when generalising SBDO to use the SDCOP formulation. For a full discussion of SBDO readers are directed to Billiau et al. 2010 [3].

The core of SBDO is very simple (alg. 5). First the agent reads any messages it has received from other agents and updates its knowledge. If it has received a proposed solution from another agent that is inconstant, it responds with a nogood message. Second it chooses a new assignment for all variables for which it has write privileges. Third the agent sends a message to each of its neighbours, informing them of any change to its proposal. Finally the agent waits until it receives new messages.

All agents continue in this fashion until all their proposals are consistent. When this happens all agents will no longer send any new messages, as their proposed solution doesn't change. If deployed in a static environment termination can be detected by taking a consistent global snapshot [9]. Otherwise they continue to wait until they are informed that the environment has changed, or they are requested to terminate.

Because there is no ordering defined over the agents, this algorithm can very easily adapt to changes in the problem, such as adding or removing constraints. It also degrades gracefully when agents fail, making the overall system fault tolerant.

In order to generalise SBDO to support SDCOP, agents have been adapted to maintain more than one proposed solution at a time. This allows the algorithm to find many pareto-optimal solutions. Changing the agent's view from a single

---

Algorithm 3: process remove-constraint message

---

begin

  Let C be the removed constraint

  for *Each neighbour A* **do**

    for *Each nogood N sent to A* **do**

      Let obsolete = {}

      if *N contains C as part of its justification* **then**

        Add N to obsolete

        Delete N from sent-nogoods

    if $|obsolete| > 0$ **then**

      Let M be a new remove-constraint message with C and nogoods

      Send M to A

  for *Each received nogood N* **do**

    if *N contains C as part of its justification* **then**

      Mark N as obsolete

Algorithm 4: update_view()

---

begin

  Let A be a valid assignment to all local variables, chosen greedily

  Choose support and A such that all the following hold:

    − view is recv(support) extended by A

    − **for** *All received proposals I* **do**

  view $\prec$ I or I is consistent with A

---

proposal to a set of proposals requires changes to the way the agent's view is created as well as how proposals are sent to other agents. After these changes the information an agents γ stores is:

- support. The agent that γ is using as the basis for almost all decisions it makes. The support's beliefs about the world (its view) are considered to be facts.
- view. This is a set of proposal consisting of the proposals received from support with an assignment to γ's variables appended. This represents the γ's current beliefs about the world, or its world view.
- recv(A). This is a mapping from an agent α to the last set of proposals received from α. This stores the other agents most recent arguments.
- nogoods. This is an unbounded multi-set of all current nogoods received. It contains pairs $\langle sender, nogood \rangle$.
- sent(A). This is a mapping from an agent α to the last set of proposals sent to α. This stores the arguments most recently sent to the agents neighbours.

Algorithm 5: main()

---

begin
  while *Not Terminated* **do**
    for *All received nogoods N* **do**
      if *this nogood is obsolete* **then**
        decrement counter on the removed-constraint message
        if *counter = zero* **then**
          delete constraint-removed message
      else
        Add N to nogoods
        for *All neighbours A* **do**
          if *There is no valid assignment to myself wrt* recv(A) **then**
            send_nogood(A)

    for *All received environment messages* **do**
      Process message
    for *All received sets of proposals S_i* **do**
      Let A be the agent who sent I
      Set recv(A) to I
      for *Each proposal I in S_i* **do**
        if *There is no valid assignment to myself wrt I* **then**
          send_nogood(A)

    Set view to the non-dominated sub-set of all consistent extensions to all received proposals
    for *All neighbours A* **do**
      Set proposed_proposals to an empty set
      for *Each proposal I in* view **do**
        if *I is part of a cycle* **then**
          if *I is dominated by an proposal in* recv(A) **then**
            Postpone this proposal
          else
            Add I to proposed_proposals
        else
          Set preferred such that it meets the criteria
          Set I' to a tail of I, such that the length of I is min(max_length, preferred)
          add I' to proposed_proposals
      if *proposed_proposals $\neq$* sent(A) **then**
        Set sent(A) to proposed_proposals
        Send proposed_proposals to A
  Wait until at least one message has been received

- sent-nogoods. This is an unbounded set of all nogoods sent by γ. It contains pairs ⟨destination, nogood⟩.
- removed-constraints. An unbounded set of known obsolete nogoods. This stores references to all the nogoods that are known to be obsolete, but have not yet been deleted.
- constraints. A set of all constraints γ knows. It must include all of an agent's local constraints and all constraints this agent shares with other agents.

As with SBDO, each agent must first update its view based on its current support (alg. 4), as new information may have made its current view obsolete. After updating its view, it must select one of its neighbours as its support. The approach used in SBDO is to choose the neighbour that has sent the best proposal as this agent's support, which clearly does not apply to SBDOsr. Instead the agent that has sent the largest number of non-dominated proposals is chosen as this agent's support. Specifically, all proposals this agent knows of, i.e. those it has received from its neighbours and those it has generated as its current view, are considered. Out of those proposals, the set of non-dominated proposals is computed. If the largest number of non-dominated proposals originated from this agent's view, then this agents support does not change. Otherwise this agent changes its support to the agent which sent the largest number of non-dominated proposals. If there is a tie for the largest number of non-dominated proposals it is broken by considering the following criteria, in lexicographical order:

1. Largest number of proposals received from each source.
2. Largest total length of received proposals from a specific source.
3. Consistent random choice. i.e. if the set of proposals A is preferred over the set of proposals B, A will always be preferred over B[1].

In the case of SBDO, where there is at most one proposal from each source, there is normally only one proposal in the non-dominated set. It is possible for two (or more) proposals with equal utility to form the non-dominated set. When this happens the tie breaking procedure is equivalent in this and in SBDO.

If this agent's support has changed, then it must re-compute its view (alg. 4). To generate its view this agent extends the proposals it has received from its support. For each proposal it has received from its support, this agent computes the set of non-dominated proposals which can be generated by extending the received proposal with an assignment to this agent.

Once the agent has selected values for its own variables, it must inform its neighbours (alg. 5) The procedure in SBDO for updating an agent's neighbours assumes that one proposal has been sent to and received from each neighbour. It must be generalised for sending sets of proposals, taking care to ensure the properties required for the proof of termination and completeness still hold. These are the postponement of some proposals that are involved in a cycle, must send a new proposal if this agent (A) is in conflict with the destination agent and should not send a new message if the content has not changed since the last message.

---

[1] Hash functions can provide a suitable comparison.

As with SBDO, each proposal is treated individually, then the proposals that will be sent to this neighbour are grouped and sent in one message. Cycle elimination is the same as in SBDO, if there are two consecutive assignments in the proposal which were generated by this agent and the destination agent respectively, then this proposal is part of a cycle. If the proposal is dominated by one of the proposals previously sent to the destination agent, then it must not be sent at this time. Otherwise the entire proposal should be sent. If the proposal is not part of a cycle, the next consideration is how much of the proposal to send to the destination agent. The proposal must be long enough to meet the following criteria:

1. If one of the proposals previously sent to the destination agent is a sub-proposal of this proposal, then this proposal is an update. In which case the length of the newly sent proposal should be the length of the previously sent proposal +1.
2. It must contain enough assignments to evaluate shared objectives/constraints. Specifically, if there exists a constraint/objective involving at least the destination agent B and an agent C in this agents' view (which might be A), then the proposal must contain the assignment to C.
3. If the assignment to A is not consistent with any proposal received from B, then A should send a counter-proposal that is more preferred than the conflicting proposal.
4. The proposal should be equal to or longer than the shortest proposal previously sent to B.

It is not always possible to send a proposal of the desired length, as the length of the sent proposal is limited by the length of the proposal in view. Once the correct length of the proposal has been decided a new proposal is created by taking the n most recent assignments and all valid shared assignments from the proposal in view. Once all proposals in view have been considered the new proposals are checked against the proposals previously sent to this agent. If any of them have changed a proposal message is sent to the destination agent containing all of the proposals.

The procedure for determining the length of each proposal to send is the same as in SBDO. The previous proposal that it is compared against changes, as there will normally be more than one candidate previous proposal. The main change is that an update message is not sent only when the set of proposals is the same as the previously sent. When a proposal is postponed, the previous version of the proposal must be sent with the new update message, rather than not be sent.

The changes made to the procedure for sending updates to an agent's neighbours invalidate the proof of termination for SBDO. Specifically the change from sending a single proposal to a set of proposals makes lemma 2 from Billiau et al. 2010 [3] not applicable. Here we present a generalisation of that lemma for sets of proposals.

Lemma 1. *If no new nogoods are generated, then eventually the utility of view will become stable for each agent.*

Proof. Let $W_i \subseteq \mathcal{X}$ be the set of agents whose view dominates $i \in \mathcal{Z}$ of the possible solutions to the problem. An agent's view v dominates a solution s iff there exists a proposal $p \in v$ such that the utility of p is greater than or equal to the utility of s (not less than or incomparable). We will prove that any decrease in $|W_i|$ must be preceded by an increase in $|W_j|$, where $j < i$.

First, we note that an agent will never willingly reduce the number of solutions its view dominates, as per the proposal ordering and the requirements of update_view(). So, in the usual case, $|W_i|$ will be monotonically increasing, for all i. However, in limited circumstances an agent may receive a weaker proposal from its support, and so the number of solutions its view dominates could be forced to decrease. Such events are rare, but they can occur whenever a cycle of supporting agents is formed. Let us assume that some agent v receives a worse proposal I from its current support, and so v is forced to choose a view which dominates less solutions. Let i number of solutions v's old view dominates, and j be the number of solutions v's new view dominates, respectively. The new, worse view for v will obviously decrease each $|W_k|$, where $j < k \leq i$.

However, for v to have received the worse proposal I, some agent w must have formed a cycle by changing its support. Note that w will only have selected a new support if it could increase the number of solutions its view dominates, as per the proposal ordering and the requirements of update_view(). Also note that the newly-formed cycle cannot have a total utility of more than j, else there would have been no reason to reduce the number of solutions v's view dominates. Therefore, the number of solutions w's new view dominates must then be less than or equal to j, but is certainly more than it's old view.

So, if an agent v is forced to reduce the number of solutions its view dominates, then there must be some preceding agent w which increased the number of solutions its view dominates. Further, w's new view is guaranteed to dominate no more solutions than v's new view. Therefore, the term $|W_1|.|W_2|.|W_3|....$ must increase lexicographically over time. As the term is bounded above, we can conclude that the utility of view must eventually become stable for each agent.

3.2 Example

As an example of how SBDOsr works consider the following simple graph colouring problem. Note that while SDCOP requires the constraints to be encoded as functions returning semiring values, for ease of understanding we will discuss the problem in terms of hard and valued constraints. There are three agents, Γ, Δ and Θ, each of which have write privileges for one variable, γ, δ and θ respectively. Each variable can take one of three 'colours', 0, 1 and 2. Neighbouring variables share a valued constraint of colour difference, maximize the difference between the values assigned to each agent. Each variable also has a unary valued constraint of colour affinity, minimize the distance between its value and an ideal value. The ideal value is 0, 1 and 1 for γ, δ and θ respectively.

When the algorithm starts each agent has received no other proposals to build upon. So all of them choose an assignment based on the colour affinity constraint. Γ adopts the proposal $\langle\langle\langle\Gamma, \{\langle\gamma, 0\rangle\}, (0, 2)\rangle\rangle, \{\}\rangle$, Δ adopts the proposal

$\langle\langle\langle\Delta, \{\langle\delta, 1\rangle\}, (0, 2)\rangle\rangle, \{\}\rangle$ and Θ adopts the proposal $\langle\langle\langle\Theta, \{\langle\theta, 1\rangle\}, (0, 2)\rangle\rangle, \{\}\rangle$. Each agent then sends their choice to each of the other agents.

Now we concentrate only on Θ. The reasoning for the other agents is similar. None of the proposals Θ has dominate any of the others, and each of itself, Δ and Γ have supplied one non-dominated proposal, and all proposals are of length 1. As such Θ randomly chooses Γ as its support and extends each of Γ's proposals to find the following non-dominated proposals:

- $\langle\langle\langle\Gamma, \{\langle\gamma, 0\rangle\}, (0, 2)\rangle, \langle\Theta, \{\langle\theta, 2\rangle\}, (0, 0)\rangle\rangle, \{\langle(\gamma, \theta), (2, 0)\rangle\}\rangle$ with a utility of $(2, 2)$
- $\langle\langle\langle\Gamma, \{\langle\gamma, 0\rangle\}, (0, 2)\rangle, \langle\Theta, \{\langle\theta, 1\rangle\}, (0, 1)\rangle\rangle, \{\langle(\gamma, \theta), (1, 0)\rangle\}\rangle$ with a utility of $(1, 3)$

As the first proposal found is new, only the front of it, $\langle\langle\langle\Theta, \{\langle\theta, 2\rangle\}, (0, 0)\rangle\rangle, \{\}\rangle$, is sent to the other agents, while the entirety of the second proposal is sent.

In Θ's next cycle it receives the following proposals from Γ and Δ:

- $\langle\langle\langle\Delta, \{\langle\delta, 1\rangle\}, (0, 1)\rangle, \langle\Gamma, \{\langle\gamma, 0\rangle\}, (0, 2)\rangle\rangle, \{\langle(\gamma, \delta), (1, 0)\rangle\}\rangle$ with a utility of $(1, 3)$
- $\langle\langle\langle\Theta, \{\langle\theta, 1\rangle\}, (0, 2)\rangle, \langle\Delta, \{\langle\delta, 1\rangle\}, (0, 2)\rangle\rangle, \{\langle(\delta, \theta), (0, 0)\rangle\}\rangle$ with a utility of $(0, 4)$
- $\langle\langle\langle\Delta, \{\langle\delta, 0\rangle\}, (0, 0)\rangle\rangle, \{\}\rangle$ with a utility of $(0, 0)$, (because it is a new assignment it starts at length one)
- $\langle\langle\langle\Delta, \{\langle\delta, 2\rangle\}, (0, 0)\rangle\rangle, \{\}\rangle$ with a utility of $(0, 0)$

Θ then decides to retain Γ as its support because the largest number of non-dominated proposals are from Θ's view (Δ and Θ supply one each). Next Θ extends the proposal received from Γ to get:

- $\langle\langle\langle\Delta, \{\langle\delta, 1\rangle\}, (0, 1)\rangle, \langle\Gamma, \{\langle\gamma, 0\rangle\}, (0, 2)\rangle, \langle\Theta, \{\langle\theta, 1\rangle\}, (0, 1)\rangle\rangle,$
  $\{\langle(\gamma, \delta), (1, 0)\rangle, \langle(\gamma, \theta), (1, 0)\rangle, \langle(\delta, \theta), (0, 0)\rangle\}\rangle$ with a utility of $(2, 4)$
- $\langle\langle\langle\Delta, \{\langle\delta, 1\rangle\}, (0, 1)\rangle, \langle\Gamma, \{\langle\gamma, 0\rangle\}, (0, 2)\rangle, \langle\Theta, \{\langle\theta, 2\rangle\}, (0, 0)\rangle\rangle,$
  $\{\langle(\gamma, \delta), (1, 0)\rangle, \langle(\gamma, \theta), (2, 0)\rangle, \langle(\delta, \theta), (1, 0)\rangle\}\rangle$ with a utility of $(4, 3)$

Again Θ then informs Δ and Γ of the solutions it has chosen.

As these two proposals represent the optimal solutions for this problem execution continues for one more cycle, as Δ and Γ accept them as the optimal solutions.

4   Results

We ran a set of experiments to evaluate SBDOsr. To do so, we implemented SBDOsr in C++[2] and ran tests on a set of graph colouring problems. The tests were run on an Intel Xeon X3450 CPU with 8GB of RAM.

At this time there is only one other published algorithm that is capable of solving problems with many objective functions, B-MUMS [1]. We do not compare SBDOsr with B-MUMS as B-MUMS does not support hard constraints, as are used in our experiments, and only returns one solution[3].

---

[2] Source code available from http://www.geeksinthegong.net/svn/sbdo/trunk/.

[3] We acknowledge that B-MUMS could easily be modified to return many solutions, as it finds them during processing.

In our test problem there is a one to one mapping from agents to variables and each variable can take a value from the domain $\{0, 1, 2, 3, 4\}$. Each variable is identified by a unique integer. There are three constraints between each pair of neighbouring variables. The first is a hard constraint that neighbouring variables must not have the same value. The second is a valued constraint to maximize the distance between the two values, given that the values wrap around i.e. the distance between 0 and 4 is 1. The third is a valued constraint where the variable with the higher identifier should be assigned a larger value. Finally, every variable has a unary valued constraint to minimize the distance between the variables value and an ideal value, being the variables identifier modulo 5.

For our tests, we varied the number of variables in each problem and the number of constraints. The parameter for the graph connectedness varies linearly between 0, where the constraints form a spanning tree over the variables, and 1, which is a fully connected graph. We used a number of variables from the set $\{4, 5, 6, 7, 8, 9, 10, 15, 20, 25\}$, a number of constraints from the set $\{0.0, 0.1, 0.2, 0.3. 0.4\}$, and randomly generated five problems for each pair of parameters. Each problem was solved five times and the performance averaged to give the results presented here. Individual runs were terminated after half an hour of wall clock time.

We present the performance of SBDOsr based on five metrics, and the standard deviation for each metric:

1. (Terminate) Time for the algorithm to terminate.
2. (Aggregate) Time to aggregate the partial solutions.
3. (number of solutions) Total number of solutions found.
4. (solution quality) The average of the minimum euclidean distance from the utility of each non-optimal solution to the utility of an optimal solution. Formally:
$$\text{quality} = \frac{\sum_{n \in N} \min\left(f\left(n, o_1\right), \ldots, f\left(n, o_x\right)\right)}{|N|}$$

where $f(x, y)$ is the euclidean distance between x and y, S is the set of the utilities of the solutions found by SBDOsr, O is the set of utilities of the optimal solutions and $N = S/O$.

5. (Proportion) The proportion of optimal solutions found. Formally:

$$\text{proportion} = \frac{|O \cap S|}{|O|}$$

Note that the set of optimal solutions must be known to compute metrics four and five. We used exhaustive search to find all the optimal solutions for problems with up to ten variables, it proved to be infeasable to solve bigger problems using exhaustive search.

Because each agent only has a local view of the problem a post-processing step is required to combine all the partial solutions into complete solutions. Whether this step is required depends on the problem being solved, decision support applications will require complete solutions, but some things like autonomous robots may be able to function using only local knowledge. It also depends on how many solutions are desired, for these experiments we extracted all pareto-optimal solutions found by SBDOsr. Because of this we have presented the time required for the algorithm to terminate and the time to aggregate the partial solutions into global solutions separately.

Table 1. Performance of SBDOsr. See text for description of metrics.

variables	Terminate (s)	Aggregate (s)	number of solutions	solution quality	Proportion
4	0.15 (0.13)	0.01 (0.00)	9.66 (5.20)	0.13 (0.13)	0.46 (0.26)
5	0.20 (0.12)	0.01 (0.01)	11.38 (6.33)	0.22 (0.32)	0.49 (0.26)
6	0.35 (0.33)	0.02 (0.01)	13.58 (6.11)	0.25 (0.29)	0.52 (0.24)
7	0.76 (0.83)	0.04 (0.04)	17.54 (10.18)	0.23 (0.27)	0.47 (0.24)
8	1.87 (3.24)	0.05 (0.04)	21.87 (14.65)	0.35 (0.34)	0.38 (0.24)
9	3.68 (5.54)	0.15 (0.24)	31.63 (24.70)	0.38 (0.33)	0.35 (0.24)
10	6.02 (8.33)	0.16 (0.20)	30.27 (17.72)	0.50 (0.33)	0.25 (0.21)
15	125.10 (233.45)	5.43 (20.17)	52.47 (66.61)	-	-
20	287.72 (259.97)	64.67 (184.73)	76.44 (189.77)	-	-
25	433.88 (548.73)	269.87 (546.00)	50.00 (158.81)	-	-

The performance of SBDOsr is shown in Table 1. The number of constraints in the problem had very little effect on the performance, so we have not reported those results here. As expected, the number of variables in the problem has a large impact on the performance. Both the time required for the algorithm to terminate and the number of solutions found when the algorithm does terminate increases exponentially with the number of variables. Further the time required to aggregate all solutions is dependant on the number of solutions, so it also rises exponentially.

The standard deviations show that the performance of SBDOsr is highly unstable, often the standard deviation is greater than the mean. This is due to the highly non-deterministic nature of the SBDOsr algorithm. The order in which agents act introduces a search bias. This bias determines which solutions are found and how much effort is required to terminate.

The proportion of optimal solutions that SBDOsr finds drops off as the number of variables increases. While the average distance from each non-optimal, found solution to an optimal solution remains constant, representing a change to the assignment to one variable by about one unit. This shows that while the number of points discovered on the actual pareto-front drops off as the number of variables increases, the solutions found remain close to the actual pareto-front.

In the process of solving these problems, SBDOsr generates a large number of nogoods. As our implementation of SBDOsr only has relatively simple code for searching and checking nogoods, this represents a significant performance bottleneck and contributes to the time required for the larger problems.

5   Conclusion

We have presented a modified SBDO to support problems with multiple objectives, or in general, any DCOP problem where there does not exist a total pre-order over the set of solutions. In order to represent these problems, we propose a new definition of a DCOP using an idempotent semiring to measure the cost/utility of a solution. The SBDO algorithm was then modified to use this new definition. To solve problems of this form, each agent maintains multiple candidate solutions simultaneously. The partial solutions maintained by each agent can then be combined into a set of complete solutions.

Empirical evaluation shows that the algorithm finds a good approximation of the pareto-frontier, however the post-processing step to combine each agent's partial solutions into complete solutions requires significant computational effort, and is currently done centrally. While this is a weakness of this approach, in situations such as autonomous robot control where complete solutions are not required for the agents to act, such a weakness is acceptable.

References

1. Fave, F.M.D., Stranders, R., Rogers, A., Jennings, N.R.: Bounded Decentralised Coordination over Multiple Objectives. In: AAMAS, pp. 371–378 (2011)
2. Alba, E., Troya, J.M.: A survey of parallel distributed genetic algorithms. Complexity 4(4), 31–52 (1999)
3. Billiau, G., Chang, C.F., Ghose, A.: SBDO: A new robust approach to dynamic distributed constraint optimisation. In: Desai, N., Liu, A., Winikoff, M. (eds.) PRIMA 2010. LNCS, vol. 7057, pp. 11–26. Springer, Heidelberg (2012)
4. Bowring, E., Tambe, M., Yokoo, M.: Multiply-constrained distributed constraint optimization. In: Nakashima, H., Wellman, M.P., Weiss, G., Stone, P. (eds.) AAMAS, pp. 1413–1420. ACM (2006)
5. Matsui, T., Silaghi, M., Hirayama, K., Yokoo, M., Matsuo, H.: Distributed Search Method with Bounded Cost Vectors on Multiple Objective DCOPs. In: Rahwan, I., Wobcke, W., Sen, S., Sugawara, T. (eds.) PRIMA 2012. LNCS, vol. 7455, pp. 137–152. Springer, Heidelberg (2012)
6. Bistarelli, S., Montanari, U., Rossi, F.: Semiring-based constraint satisfaction and optimization. J. ACM 44(2), 201–236 (1997)
7. Schiex, T., Verfaillie, G.: Nogood Recording for Static and Dynamic Constraint Satisfaction Problem. International Journal of Artifical Intelligence Tools 3(2), 187–207 (1994)
8. Harvey, P., Chang, C.F., Ghose, A.: Support-based distributed search: a new approach for multiagent constraint processing. In: AAMAS 2006, pp. 377–383. ACM (2006)
9. Chandy, K.M., Lamport, L.: Distributed Snapshots: Determining global states of distributed systems. ACM Transactions on Computer Systems 3(1), 63–75 (1985)

Leximin Multiple Objective Optimization for Preferences of Agents

Toshihiro Matsui[1], Marius Silaghi[2], Katsutoshi Hirayama[3],
Makoto Yokoo[4], and Hiroshi Matsuo[1]

[1] Nagoya Institute of Technology, Gokiso-cho Showa-ku, Nagoya 466-8555, Japan
{matsui.t,matsuo}@nitech.ac.jp
[2] Florida Institute of Technology, Melbourne, FL 32901, USA
msilaghi@fit.edu
[3] Kobe University, 5-1-1 Fukaeminami-machi Higashinada-ku, Kobe 658-0022, Japan
hirayama@maritime.kobe-u.ac.jp
[4] Kyushu University, 744 Motooka Nishi-ku, Fukuoka 819-0395, Japan
yokoo@is.kyushu-u.ac.jp

Abstract. We address a variation of Multiple Objective Distributed Constraint
Optimization Problems (MODCOPs). In the conventional MODCOPs, a few objectives are globally defined and agents cooperate to find the Pareto optimal solution. On the other hand, in several practical problems, the share of each agent is
important. Such shares are represented as preference values of agents. This class
of problems is defined as the MODCOP on the preferences of agents. Particularly,
we focus on the optimization problems based on the leximin ordering (Leximin
AMODCOPs), which improves the equality among agents. The solution methods
based on pseudo trees are applied to the Leximin AMODCOPs.

Keywords: leximin, preference, multiple objectives, Distributed Constraint Optimization, multiagent, cooperation

1 Introduction

The Distributed Constraint Optimization Problem (DCOP) [3,10,15,21] lies at the foundations of multiagent cooperation. With DCOPs, the optimization in distributed resource allocation uses the representation of a single objective function. The Multiple
Objective Distributed Constraint Optimization Problem (MODCOP) [2] is an extension
of the DCOP framework, where agents cooperatively have to optimize simultaneously
multiple objective functions. For the case of multiple objectives, evaluation values are
defined as vectors of objective values. Agents cooperate to find the Pareto optimal solution. In [2], a bounded Max-Sum algorithm for MODCOPs has been proposed. A
solution method based on tree-search and dynamic programming has also been applied
to MODCOPs [7]. In conventional MODCOPs, a few objectives are globally defined
for the whole system. However, such models do not capture the interests of each agent.
In several practical problems, the share of each agent is important. Such shares are represented as preference values of agents. This point of view recently has been addressed

H.K. Dam et al. (Eds.): PRIMA 2014, LNAI 8861, pp. 423–438, 2014.

in the context of DCOPs which are designed for dedicated resource allocation problems [12,6,13,14]. These problems define multiple objective functions, optimizing the preferences for all the agents.

In this work, we address a class of MODCOPs on the preferences of agents. Particularly, we focus on problems where the importance of objective functions is based on the leximin ordering (referred to as Leximin AMODCOPs). Since the optimization based on the leximin ordering improves the equality among agents, this class of problems is important. The solution methods based on pseudo trees are applied to the Leximin AMODCOPs. Also, the investigated search methods employ the concept of boundaries of the sorted vectors.

2   Preliminary

2.1   Distributed Constraint Optimization Problem

A Distributed Constraint Optimization Problem (DCOP) is defined as follows.

Definition 1 (Distributed Constraint Optimization Problem). *A Distributed Constraint Optimization Problem is defined by* (A, X, D, F) *where* A *is a set of agents,* X *is a set of variables,* D *is a set of domains of variables, and* F *is a set of objective functions. Variable* $x_i \in X$ *represents a state of agent* $i \in A$. *Domain* $D_i \in D$ *is a discrete finite set of values for* x_i. *An objective function* $f_{i,j}(x_i, x_j) \in F$ *defines a utility extracted for each pair of assignments to* x_i *and* x_j. *The objective value of assignment* $\{(x_i, d_i), (x_j, d_j)\}$ *is defined by the binary function* $f_{i,j} : D_i \times D_j \rightarrow \mathbb{R}$. *For an assignment* $\mathcal{A}$ *of variables, the global objective function* $F(\mathcal{A})$ *is defined as* $F(\mathcal{A}) = \sum_{f_{i,j} \in F} f_{i,j}(\mathcal{A}_{|x_i}, \mathcal{A}_{|x_j})$. *The value of* x_i *is controlled by agent* i. *Agent* i *locally knows the objective functions that relate to* x_i *in the initial state. The goal is to find a global optimal assignment* $\mathcal{A}^*$ *that maximizes the global objective value.*

The computation to find the optimal solution is a distributed algorithm. We assume that each pair of agents has a communication route on an overlay network. For the sake of simplicity, we assume that all the objective functions are binary. Also, the state of each agent is represented by only one variable. However, the proposal can be generalized for n-ary functions and agent states represented by multiple variables.

2.2   Multiple Objective Problem

Multiple objective DCOP [2] (MODCOP) is a generalization of the DCOP framework. With MODCOPs, multiple objective functions are defined over the variables. The objective functions are simultaneously optimized based on appropriate criteria. The tuple with the values of all the objective functions for a given assignment is called *objective vector*.

Definition 2 (Objective vector). *An objective vector* $\mathbf{v}$ *is defined as* $[v_0, \cdots, v_K]$. *Here,* v_k *is an objective value. The Vector* $\mathbf{F}(X)$ *of objective functions is defined as* $[F^0(X^0), \cdots, F^K(X^K)]$, *where* X^k *is the subset of* X *on which* F^k *is defined.* $F^k(X^k)$ *is an objective function for objective* k. *For assignment* $\mathcal{A}$, *the vector* $\mathbf{F}(\mathcal{A})$

of the functions returns an objective vector $[v_0, \cdots, v_K]$. *Here,* $v_k = F^k(\mathcal{A}^k)$ *for each objective* k.

Objective vectors are compared based on Pareto dominance. For maximization problems, the dominance between two vectors is defined as follows: Vector $\mathbf{v}$ dominates $\mathbf{v}'$ if and only if $\mathbf{v} \geq \mathbf{v}'$, and $v_k > v'_k$ for at least one objective k. Similarly, Pareto optimality on the assignments is defined as follows: Assignment $\mathcal{A}^*$ is Pareto optimal if and only if there is no other assignment $\mathcal{A}$, such that $\mathbf{F}(\mathcal{A}) \geq \mathbf{F}(\mathcal{A}^*)$, and $F^k(\mathcal{A}) > F^k(\mathcal{A}^*)$ for at least one objective k. In previous studies of MODCOPs [2], each objective function $f_{i,j}(x_i, x_j)$ in the original DCOPs is extended to a vector $[f^0_{i,j}(x_i, x_j), \cdots, f^K_{i,j}(x_i, x_j)]$. $F^k(\mathcal{A}^k)$ is therefore defined as $\sum_{f^k_{i,j} \in F^k} f^k_{i,j}(\mathcal{A}^k_{|x_i}, \mathcal{A}^k_{|x_j})$ for each objective k. Also, all the objectives are evaluated for the same assignment. Namely, $\mathcal{A}^0 = \mathcal{A}^1 = \cdots = \mathcal{A}^K$. Multiple objective problems generally have a set of Pareto optimal solutions that form a Pareto front. With an appropriate social welfare that defines an order on objective vectors, traditional solution methods for single objective problems find a Pareto optimal solution.

2.3 Social Welfare

There are several criteria of social welfare [17] and scalarization methods [5]. A well-known social welfare function is defined as the summation $\sum_{k=0}^{K} F^k(\mathcal{A}^k)$ of objectives. The maximization of this summation ensures Pareto optimality. This summation is a 'utilitarian' criterion since it represents the total value of the objectives while it does not capture the equality on these objectives. On the other hand, the minimization $\min_{k=0}^{K} F^k(\mathcal{A}^k)$ on objectives emphasizes the objective of the worst value. Although the maximization of the minimum objective (maximin) reduces the worst complaint among all the objectives, the optimal assignment on the maximin is not Pareto (but weak Pareto) optimal. To improve maximin, the summation welfare function is additionally employed. A social welfare is defined as a vector $[\min_{k=0}^{K} F^k(\mathcal{A}^k), \sum_{k=0}^{K} F^k(\mathcal{A}^k)]$ with an appropriate definition of dominance. When the maximization on the minimization part dominates that on the summation part, it can be considered as a (partial) lexicographical ordering that yields the Pareto optimal solution, similar to the lexicographic weighted Tchebycheff method [5].

Another social welfare, called *leximin* [11,1], is defined with a lexicographic order on objective vectors whose values are sorted in ascending order.

Definition 3 (Sorted vector). *A sorted vector based on vector* $\mathbf{v}$ *is the vector where all the values of* $\mathbf{v}$ *are sorted in ascending order.*

Definition 4 (Leximin). *Let* $\mathbf{v}$ *and* $\mathbf{v}'$ *denote vectors of the same length* $K + 1$. *Let* $[v_0, \cdots, v_K]$ *and* $[v'_0, \cdots, v'_K]$ *denote sorted vectors of* $\mathbf{v}$ *and* $\mathbf{v}'$, *respectively. Also, let* $\prec_{leximin}$ *denote the relation of the leximin ordering.* $\mathbf{v} \prec_{leximin} \mathbf{v}'$ *if and only if* $\exists t, \forall t' < t, v_{t'} = v'_{t'} \wedge v_t < v'_t$.

The maximization on the leximin ordering ensures Pareto optimality. The leximin is an 'egalitarian' criterion since it reduces the inequality on objectives. It is also considered as an improved version of maximin similar to a variation with the summation.

The above property of the leximin is important for the preferences of agents. Further we focus on the leximin social welfare.

2.4   Preferences of Agents

While previous studies address MODCOPs [2,7], their goal is to optimize a few global objectives. Agents cooperate with each other to optimize those global objectives. On the other hand, in practical resource allocation problems, such as power supply networks, each agent has a strong interest for its share of the result. Hence there is the need for a more appropriate model where the objectives represent the preferences of agents. This class of problems has two key characteristics: 1) Each agent individually has its set of objective functions whose aggregated value represents its preferences, while several agents are related since subsets of their variables are in the scope of the same function. 2) The problem is a MODCOP where a solution is characterized by an objective vector consisting of objective values that are individually aggregated for different agents.

In [6], a resource constrained DCOP, which is designed for resource allocation on power supply networks, is extended to a MODCOP on the preferences of agents. In that study, min-max as well as min-max with the additional summation was introduced for minimizing problems. In addition, to reduce inequality among agents, a few first methods that consider the variance of objective values were shown. A general representation of the objectives of individual agents has been proposed as Asymmetric DCOP (ADCOP) [4]. In the ADCOP, two different objective functions are asymmetrically defined for a pair of two agents. Here, each objective function represents the valuation for one of the agents. Several classes of ADCOPs with multiple objectives for individual agents have been proposed in [12,13,14]. We focus on a class of ADCOPs optimizing the leximin social welfare. Since the leximin is known to reduce the inequality among agents, it helps define an important class of MODCOPs on preferences of agents.

3   Leximin Multiple Objective Optimization on Preferences of Agents

3.1   Problem Definition

A Leximin MODCOP on preferences of agents (Leximin AMODCOP) is defined as follows.

Definition 5 (Leximin MODCOP on preferences of agents). *A leximin MODCOP on preferences of agents is defined by* (A, X, D, F), *where* A, X *and* D *are similarly defined as for the DCOP in Definition 1. Agent* $i \in A$ *has its local problem defined on* $X_i \subseteq X$. *Here,* $\exists (i, j), i \neq j \wedge X_i \cap X_j \neq \emptyset$. *F is a set of objective functions* $f_i(X_i)$. *The function* $f_i(X_i) : D_{i_0} \times \cdots \times D_{i_k} \to \mathbb{R}$ *represents the objective value for agent* i *based on the variables in* $X_i = \{x_{i_0}, \cdots, x_{i_k}\}$. *For an assignment* $\mathcal{A}$ *of variables, the global objective function* $\mathbf{F}(\mathcal{A})$ *is defined as* $[f_0(\mathcal{A}_0), \cdots, f_{|A|-1}(\mathcal{A}_{|A|-1})]$. *Here,* $\mathcal{A}_i$ *denotes the projection of the assignment* $\mathcal{A}$ *on* X_i. *The goal is to find the assignment* $\mathcal{A}^*$ *that maximizes the global objective function based on the leximin ordering.*

As shown in Definition 5, each agent i has a function $f_i(X_i)$ that represents i's local problem. In a simple case, the local problem is defined as a part of an ADCOP where $f_i(X_i)$ is the summation of the corresponding functions in the ADCOP. In an ADCOP, variable x_i of agent i relates to other variables by objective functions. When x_i relates to x_j, agent i evaluates an objective function $f_{i,j}(x_i, x_j)$. On the other hand, j evaluates another function $f_{j,i}(x_j, x_i)$. Based on this ADCOP, a local problem is represented as $f_i(X_i) = \sum_{j \in Nbr_i} f_{i,j}(x_i, x_j)$ for agent i, aggregating objective functions among i and its neighborhood agents Nbr_i. While we will discuss our solution methods based on this ADCOP for the sake of simplicity, we address several motivated domains below.

Example 1 (Resource allocation on a power supply network). In a resource allocation problem on a power supply network [9,6], each agent represents a node of the network. An agent i has several input links, output links and its resource. Given the amount $x_{i,j}^l$ of transferred resource on each input/output link (i, j) and x_i^r of its own resource, the total amount must satisfy resource constraint c_i : $\sum_{x_{j,i}^l \in X_i^{in}} x_{j,i}^l = x_i^r + \sum_{x_{i,k}^l \in X_i^{out}} x_{i,k}^l$. Here, X_i^{in} and X_i^{out} corresponds to input and output links, respectively. In addition, agent i has an objective function $f_i^r(x_i^r)$ of its own resource use x_i^r. Using a sufficiently small objective value for the violation of hard constraint c_i, this problem is represented by $f_i(X_i)$ for agent i, where X_i consists of $\{x_r^i\} \cup X_i^{in} \cup X_i^{out}$. The value of $f_i(X_i)$ is $f_i^r(x_i^r)$ if assignments for X_i satisfy c_i. Otherwise, $f_i(X_i)$ takes the sufficiently small value. Each agent desires to improve its local objective value under the resource constraints and preferences of other agents.

Example 2 (Variation of Coalition Structure Generation). A Coalition Structure Generation problem is represented as a DCOP [18]. An agent i has two variables x_i and x_i^g. x_i^g represents a group to which agent i belongs. x_i represents i's decision. Depending on x_i^g, utility values that relate to x_i are defined as follows. $f_{i,j}^v(x_i, x_j, x_i^g, x_j^g) = v_{i,j}(x_i, x_j)$ if $x_i^g \neq$ 'alone' $\wedge x_i^g = x_j^g$. Otherwise, $f_{i,j}^v(x_i, x_j, x_i^g, x_j^g) = 0$. $f_i^v(x_i, x_i^g) = v_i(x_i)$ if $x_i^g =$ 'alone'. Otherwise, $f_i^v(x_i, x_i^g) = 0$. Based on this DCOP, a local problem is represented as $f_i(X_i) = f_i^v(x_i, x_i^g) + \sum_{j \in Nbr_i} f_{i,j}^v(x_i, x_j, x_i^g, x_j^g)$ for agent i aggregating utility functions among i and its neighborhood agents Nbr_i.

4   Solution Method Based on Pseudo Tree

4.1   Pseudo Tree for Local Problems

Several solution methods for DCOPs are based on pseudo trees on constraint networks [10,15]. A pseudo tree of the problem is a depiction of its constraint network (adding directions to edges and levels for the nodes), based on a spanning tree in which there are no edges between different sub-trees of the corresponding spanning tree. Such pseudo trees can be generated using several algorithms, including the depth-first traversal on the constraint network. Edges of the spanning tree are called tree-edges while other edges are called back-edges. Based on the pseudo tree, the following notations are defined for each agent i: parent agent (p_i), set of child agents (Ch_i), the set of lower neighborhood agents, i.e. the child and pseudo child nodes $(Nbrs_i^l)$, and the set

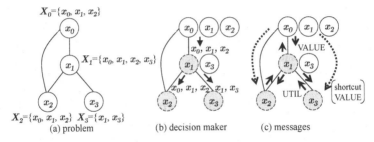

$X_0 = \{x_0, x_1, x_2\}$

$X_1 = \{x_0, x_1, x_2, x_3\}$

$X_2 = \{x_0, x_1, x_2\}$ $X_3 = \{x_1, x_3\}$

(a) problem   (b) decision maker   (c) messages

Fig. 1. Pseudo tree for local problems

of upper neighborhood agents, i.e. the parent and pseudo parent nodes ($Nbrs_i^u$). A partial order on a set of agents is defined based on the tree edges of a pseudo tree. The priorities induced by this order are used for breaking ties during decision making.

Figure 1(a) shows a pseudo tree for a problem. In the figure, four nodes represent agents/variables while four edges represent functions. In our problem, each edge stands for a pair of two asymmetric objective functions. Since an objective function is evaluated by only one related agent, each agent has to evaluate all the related objective functions. Namely, each agent has to manage all the assignments for its local problem. Therefore, the value of a variable x_i is decided by the highest neighborhood agent whose variable relates to the variable x_i with an edge. Hence a modification of pseudo trees is necessary. Figure 1(b) shows the pseudo tree modified from (a). The priority on decisions of assignments is represented as shown in (b).

To set up the data structures need for this pseudo tree, agent i computes the following information. XX_i^{upr}: A set of pairs of variables to compute the related agent in the highest level of the pseudo tree. X_i^{dcd}: The set of variables whose values are determined by agent i. X_i^{sep}: The set of *separator* variables that are shared between the sub-tree rooted at i and another part of the problem. Except at the root agent in the pseudo tree, the information is recursively computed as follows.

$$XX_i^{upr} = \bigcup_{h \in Nbrs_i^u} \{(x_i, x_h)\} \cup \{(x_a, x_b) | (x_a, x_b) \in \bigcup_{j \in Ch_i} XX_j^{upr} \wedge x_b \neq x_i\} \quad (1)$$

$$X_i^{dcd} = \{x_a | (x_a, x_i) \in \bigcup_{j \in Ch_i} XX_j^{upr} \wedge \nexists b, (x_a, x_b) \in XX_i^{upr}\} \quad (2)$$

$$X_i^{sep} = \left(\bigcup_{h \in Nbrs_i^u} \{x_h\} \cup \bigcup_{j \in Ch_i} X_j^{sep} \right) \setminus X_i^{dcd} \quad (3)$$

Equation (1) enables defining the agent assigning x_i as the highest placed agent in the set of those having a relation with some node in the sub-tree rooted as x_i (upper neighbors of i and upper neighbors of variables in sub-trees defined by its children, and found above i). Equation (2) defines the variables assigned by agent i as the lower neighbors of x_i in sub-trees defined by children, and which do not have upper neighbors above i. Equation (3) defines the separator variables as those in the upper neighbors of

x_i and its sub-tree, and of that are not controlled by agent i or its children. Note that $x_i \in X_i^{sep}$ and $x_i \notin X_i^{dcd}$, unlike the standard definition of separators on pseudo trees.

On the other hand, in the root agent, $XX_i^{upr} = \emptyset$, $X_i^{dcd} = \{x_a | (x_a, x_i) \in \bigcup_{j \in Ch_i} XX_j^{upr}\}$ and $X_i^{sep} = \emptyset$. Note that the root agent also determines the value of its own variable. The actual computation is performed as a distributed processing, after the preprocessing of generating a pseudo tree. Each non-root agent i sends XX_i^{upr}, X_i^{dcd} and X_i^{sep} to its parent agent p_i in a bottom-up manner.

4.2 Computation of the Optimal Objective Vector

We apply a computation of the optimal objective value, which is employed in the solution method DPOP [15], to the Leximin AMODCOP. The computation is performed on the modified pseudo tree shown in Subsection 4.1. For the aggregation of objective values, we define an addition on vectors that is different from the common definition. The addition is the operator concatenating all the values.

Definition 6 (Addition on vectors). *Let* $\mathbf{v}$ *and* $\mathbf{v}'$ *denote vectors* $[v_0, \cdots, v_K]$ *and* $[v'_0, \cdots, v'_{K'}]$. *The addition* $\mathbf{v} \oplus \mathbf{v}'$ *of the two vectors gives a vector* $\mathbf{v}'' = [v''_0, \cdots v''_{K+K'+1}]$ *where each value in* $\mathbf{v}''$ *is a distinct value in* $\mathbf{v}$ *or* $\mathbf{v}'$. *Namely,* $\mathbf{v}''$ *consists of all values in* $\mathbf{v}$ *and* $\mathbf{v}'$. *As a normalization, the values in* $\mathbf{v}''$ *are sorted in ascending order.*

The computation of the optimal objective vector is recursively defined. The optimal objective vector $g_i^*(\mathcal{A}_i^{sep})$ for assignment $\mathcal{A}_i^{sep}$ of variables X_i^{sep} whose values are determined by i's ancestor nodes and parent node is represented as follows.

$$g_i^*(\mathcal{A}_i^{sep}) = \max_{\mathcal{A}_i^{dcd} \text{ for } X_i^{dcd}} g_i(\mathcal{A}_i^{sep} \cup \mathcal{A}_i^{dcd}) \tag{4}$$

$$g_i(\mathcal{A}) = [f_i(\mathcal{A}_{|X_i})] \oplus \bigoplus_{j \in Ch_i, \mathcal{A}_j^{sep} \subseteq \mathcal{A}} g_j^*(\mathcal{A}_j^{sep}) \tag{5}$$

Here, $\mathcal{A}_i^{dcd}$ denotes an assignment of the variables in X_i^{dcd} whose values are determined by i. The operator $\oplus$ denotes aggregation of objective values. While the summation operator is used in common DCOPs, we aggregate objective vectors using the operator shown in Definition 6. Similarly, max denotes the maximization on the leximin ordering. This computation is a dynamic programming based on the following proposition.

Proposition 1 (Invariance on leximin relation). *Let* $\mathbf{v}$ *and* $\mathbf{v}'$ *denote vectors of the same length. Also, let* $\mathbf{v}''$ *denote another vector. If* $\mathbf{v} \prec_{leximin} \mathbf{v}'$, *then* $\mathbf{v} \oplus \mathbf{v}'' \prec_{leximin} \mathbf{v}' \oplus \mathbf{v}''$.

Proof. Let $[v_0, \cdots, v_K]$ and $[v'_0, \cdots, v'_K]$ denote values in the sorted vectors of $\mathbf{v}$ and $\mathbf{v}'$, respectively. From the definition of leximin, there is a value t such that $\forall t' < t, v_{t'} = v'_{t'} \wedge v_t < v'_t$. Let t'' denote the value such that $v_{t''} < v_t \wedge v_{t''+1} = v_t$. Namely, $v_{t''}$ is the value just before the sequence of values equal to v_t. Note that $t'' + 1 \leq t$. In the case of $t = 0$, the value of t'' is generalized using -1. Consider the values in the sorted vectors of $\mathbf{v} \oplus \mathbf{v}''$ and $\mathbf{v}' \oplus \mathbf{v}''$. When vector $\mathbf{v}''$ contains k values smaller than v_t, then there are $t'' + k$ such values in both sorted vectors of $\mathbf{v} \oplus \mathbf{v}''$ and $\mathbf{v}' \oplus \mathbf{v}''$. Namely, the sequences of values less than v_t are the same in both of the sorted vectors. When vector $\mathbf{v}''$ contains k' values equal to v_t, $\mathbf{v} \oplus \mathbf{v}''$ contains a sequence of at least $(t - t'') + k'$ values equal to v_t. On the other hand, $\mathbf{v}' \oplus \mathbf{v}''$ contains a sequence of $(t - 1 - t'') + k'$ values equal to v_t. The above property also holds in the cases where $k = 0$ and/or $k' = 0$. Now, we can conclude that the sequences of the first $(t'' + k) + (t - 1 - t'') + k'$ values are the same in both sorted vectors of $\mathbf{v} \oplus \mathbf{v}''$ and $\mathbf{v}' \oplus \mathbf{v}''$, while the next values are the value equal to v_t and a value greater than v_t, respectively. Therefore, $\mathbf{v} \oplus \mathbf{v}'' \prec_{leximin} \mathbf{v}' \oplus \mathbf{v}''$.

The maximization in Expression (4) compares objective vectors for the same assignment $\mathcal{A}_i^{sep}$ that will produce the same partial objective vector. The above computation therefore correctly calculates the globally optimal objective vector.

After the computation of the optimal objective vector, the root agent i determine its optimal assignment $\mathcal{A}_i^{dcd*}$ such that $g_i(\emptyset \cup \mathcal{A}_i^{dcd*}) = g_i^*(\emptyset)$. $\mathcal{A}_j^{sep*} \subseteq \mathcal{A}_i^{dcd*}$ is then computed for each child $j \in Ch_i$. Similarly, non-root agent i computes $\mathcal{A}_i^{dcd*}$ such that $g_i(\mathcal{A}_i^{sep*} \cup \mathcal{A}_i^{dcd*}) = g_i^*(\mathcal{A}_i^{sep*})$, and $\mathcal{A}_j^{sep*} \subseteq \mathcal{A}_i^{sep*} \cup \mathcal{A}_i^{dcd*}$ for each child $j \in Ch_i$. The protocol of the modified version of DPOP is basically the same as the original one. The DPOP employs two types of messages UTIL and VALUE shown in Figure 1(c). After the processing of the modified pseudo tree, agents compute the optimal objective vector. In this computation, UTIL messages are propagated in a bottom-up manner. Each agent i sends $g_i^*(\mathcal{A}_i^{sep})$ to its parent p_i using UTIL message. Then the optimal assignment is computed propagating VALUE messages in a top-down manner. Each agent i sends $\mathcal{A}_j^{sep*}$ to its child agents $j \in Ch_i$ using VALUE message. The protocol of DPOP is quite simple. However, the size of UTIL messages and memory use to store $g_i^*(\mathcal{A}_i^{sep})$ of all the assignments exponentially increases with the size $|X_i^{sep}|$ of i's separator.

4.3   Search Method

We apply solution methods based on tree search and partial dynamic programming to the Leximin AMODCOPs. The methods are variations of ADOPT [10,20,6], therefore needing less memory and employing messages of relatively smaller size. First, we show a simple search method, which is basically a time division of DPOP. While this method employs messages named VALUE and UTIL shown in Figure 1(c), they are different from those of DPOP. Similar to DPOP, the method consists of two phases of computations.

In the first phase, the optimal objective vector is computed in a manner of tree search. The root agent i chooses an assignment $\mathcal{A}_{i,j}^{dcd}$ for variables in $X_i^{dcd} \cap X_j^{sep}$ for its child $j \in Ch_i$. Then the root agent sends the current assignment $\mathcal{A}_j^{sep} = \mathcal{A}_{i,j}^{dcd}$ to its child node j using a VALUE message. When non-root agent i receives $\mathcal{A}_i^{sep}$ from its parent p_i, agent i chooses an assignment $\mathcal{A}_{i,j}^{dcd}$ for variables in $X_i^{dcd} \cap X_j^{sep}$ for its child j. Agent i then sends $\mathcal{A}_j^{sep} \subseteq \mathcal{A}_i^{sep} \cup \mathcal{A}_{i,j}^{dcd}$ for variables in X_j^{sep} to its child j. Namely, an assignment is expanded for all children of a node in a pseudo tree, in the same time. The current assignment $\mathcal{A}_i^{sep}$ is called *current context*. In the root agent, the current context is always $\emptyset$.

For the current context $\mathcal{A}_i^{sep}$, each agent computes $g_i^*(\mathcal{A}_i^{sep})$. Then $g_i^*(\mathcal{A}_i^{sep})$ is sent to i's parent p_i using a UTIL message. When agent i receives $g_j^*(\mathcal{A}_j^{sep})$ from its child j, $g_i^*(\mathcal{A}_j^{sep})$ is stored in the agent, if $\mathcal{A}_j^{sep}$ is compatible with $\mathcal{A}_i^{sep}$. When the current context changes to new assignment $\mathcal{A}^{sep\prime}_i$, objective vector $g_j^*(\mathcal{A}_j^{sep})$ whose $\mathcal{A}_j^{sep}$ is incompatible with $\mathcal{A}^{sep\prime}_i$ is deleted.

While the computation of $g_i^*(\mathcal{A}_i^{sep})$ is based on Equations (4) and (5), the computation is generalized to the case where agent i has not received $g_j^*(\mathcal{A}_j^{sep})$ from child j. In such cases, the lower and upper limit values of unknown objective values are introduced. With the limit values, the objective values are separated into lower and upper bound values. For the leximin ordering, we define the upper and lower bounds of objective vectors.

Definition 7 (Boundaries of unknown vector). *For an objective vector* $\mathbf{v}$ *of K unknown values, lower bound* $\mathbf{v}^\perp$ *and upper bound* $\mathbf{v}^\top$ *are vectors of K values, whose values are* $-\infty$ *and* ∞, *respectively.*

These boundaries are obviously reasonable since they are the minimum vector and the maximum vector on the leximin ordering. Operators $\oplus$ and $\prec_{leximin}$ are applied to the boundaries of vectors without any modifications. For a vector $\mathbf{v} = [v_0, \cdots, v_K]$ and the lower bound $\mathbf{v}'^\perp = [-\infty, \cdots, -\infty]$ of unknown vector $\mathbf{v}'$, the vector $\mathbf{v} \oplus \mathbf{v}'^\perp$ consists of $-\infty, \cdots, -\infty$ and $v_0, \cdots, v_K$. Similarly, $\mathbf{v} \oplus \mathbf{v}'^\top$ consists of $v_0, \cdots, v_K$ and $\infty, \cdots, \infty$. We consider these vectors as $(\mathbf{v} \oplus \mathbf{v}')^\perp$ and $(\mathbf{v} \oplus \mathbf{v}')^\top$, respectively.

Proposition 2 (Lower bound of partially unknown vector). *Let* $\mathbf{v}^\perp$ *denote a vector whose values are* $v_0, \cdots, v_K$ *and K' values of* $-\infty$. *For any vector* $\mathbf{v}$ *whose values are* $v_0, \cdots, v_K$ *and K' values greater than* $-\infty$, $\mathbf{v}^\perp \prec_{leximin} \mathbf{v}$.

Proof. While the first value in the sorted vector of $\mathbf{v}^\perp$ is $-\infty$, that of $\mathbf{v}$ is greater than $-\infty$. Therefore, $\mathbf{v}^\perp \prec_{leximin} \mathbf{v}$.

Proposition 3 (Upper bound of partially unknown vector). *Let* $\mathbf{v}^\top$ *denote a vector whose values are* $v_0, \cdots, v_K$ *and K' values of* ∞. *For any vector* $\mathbf{v}$ *whose values are* $v_0, \cdots, v_K$ *and K' values less than* ∞, $\mathbf{v} \prec_{leximin} \mathbf{v}^\top$.

Proof. Consider a vector $\mathbf{v}^{\top[v_0']}$ where one of values ∞ in $\mathbf{v}^\top$ is replaced by a value v_0' less than ∞. Both sorted vectors of $\mathbf{v}^{\top[v_0']}$ and $\mathbf{v}^\top$ contain the same sequence of k values less than v_0', since v_0' does not affect this sequence. When $\mathbf{v}^\top$ contains k' values of v_0', $\mathbf{v}^{\top[v_0']}$ contains $k' + 1$ values of v_0'. We can conclude that the sequences of the first $k + k'$ values are the same in both sorted vectors of $\mathbf{v}^{\top[v_0']}$ and $\mathbf{v}^\top$, while the next values are the value equal to v_0' and a value greater than v_0', respectively. Therefore, $\mathbf{v}^{\top[v_0']} \prec_{leximin} \mathbf{v}^\top$. Consider a vector $\mathbf{v}^{\top[v_0', v_1']}$ where one of values ∞ in $\mathbf{v}^{\top[v_0']}$ is replaced by a value v_1' less than ∞. Similar to $\mathbf{v}^{\top[v_0']} \prec_{leximin} \mathbf{v}^\top$, we can conclude $\mathbf{v}^{\top[v_0', v_1']} \prec_{leximin} \mathbf{v}^{\top[v_0']}$. Based on the mathematical induction, we can conclude that $\mathbf{v} = \mathbf{v}^{\top[v_0', \cdots v_{K'-1}']} \prec_{leximin} \cdots \prec_{leximin} \mathbf{v}^{\top[v_0']} \prec_{leximin} \mathbf{v}^\top$ for any combination $[v_0', \cdots v_{K'-1}']$ of values that replace the values of ∞ in $\mathbf{v}^\top$.

In addition, with a bottom-up preprocessing, the lower and upper limit values for each function $f_i(X_i)$ can be aggregated to vectors of limit values instead of the vectors of $-\infty$ and ∞.

$g_i^*(\mathcal{A}_i^{sep})$ is extended to a pair of $g_i^{*\perp}(\mathcal{A}_i^{sep})$ and $g_i^{*\top}(\mathcal{A}_i^{sep})$ that are simultaneously computed. To introduce the boundaries, an agent has to know the number of descendants of each sub-tree rooted at each child. The information of the descendants is additionally computed in the preprocessing. When the number of descendants for a child j is dcd_j, $g_j^{*\perp}(\mathcal{A}_j^{sep})$ for unknown $g_j^*(\mathcal{A}_j^{sep})$ is a vector of dcd_j values of $-\infty$. Similarly, $g_j^{*\top}(\mathcal{A}_j^{sep})$ is a vector of dcd_j values of ∞.

Based on the boundaries, agents complete the tree search for sub problems. When $g_j^{*\perp}(\mathcal{A}_j^{sep}) = g_j^{*\top}(\mathcal{A}_j^{sep})$ for child $j \in Ch_i$, agent i completes the tree search for the assignment $\mathcal{A}_j^{sep}$. Then i chooses another assignment $\mathcal{A}_j^{sep'}$ such that $g_j^{*\perp}(\mathcal{A}_j^{sep'}) \prec_{leximin} g_j^{*\top}(\mathcal{A}_j^{sep'})$. While there are several search strategies on the assignments, we employ a depth-first search based on the pseudo tree.

Now, a UTIL message carries a pair of vectors for the both boundaries. Since the boundaries are narrowed with the true objective values that are propagated in a bottom-up manner on the pseudo tree, agents repeatedly send UTIL messages. When agent i receives new vectors of $g_j^{*\perp}(\mathcal{A}_j^{sep})$ and $g_j^{*\top}(\mathcal{A}_j^{sep})$ from child $j \in Ch_i$, those vectors update the previous vectors. While $g_j^{*\perp}(\mathcal{A}_j^{sep})$ is maximized, $g_j^{*\top}(\mathcal{A}_j^{sep})$ is minimized with the new vectors based on the leximin ordering.

When $g_i^{*\perp}(\emptyset) = g_i^{*\top}(\emptyset)$ in the root agent i, agent i compute the optimal assignment $\mathcal{A}_i^{dcd*}$ such that $g_i^{\perp}(\emptyset \cup \mathcal{A}_i^{dcd*}) = g_i^{\top}(\emptyset \cup \mathcal{A}_i^{dcd*}) = g_i^{*\perp}(\emptyset) = g_i^{*\top}(\emptyset)$. $\mathcal{A}_j^{sep*} \subseteq \mathcal{A}_i^{dcd*}$ is then sent to each child $j \in Ch_i$ using a VALUE message with a flag of the termination. When $g_i^{*\perp}(\mathcal{A}_i^{sep*}) = g_i^{*\top}(\mathcal{A}_i^{sep*})$ in non-root agent i, the agent similarly computes the optimal assignment $\mathcal{A}_i^{dcd*}$ such that $g_i^{\perp}(\mathcal{A}_i^{sep*} \cup \mathcal{A}_i^{dcd*}) = g_i^{\top}(\mathcal{A}_i^{sep*} \cup \mathcal{A}_i^{dcd*}) = g_i^{*\perp}(\mathcal{A}_i^{sep*}) = g_i^{*\top}(\mathcal{A}_i^{sep*})$, and $\mathcal{A}_j^{sep*} \subseteq \mathcal{A}_i^{sep*} \cup \mathcal{A}_i^{dcd*}$ for each child $j \in Ch_i$ under $\mathcal{A}_i^{sep*}$. As a result, all the agents determine their optimal assignment.

4.4 Pruning

Next, we introduce the pruning based on the global lower bound of objective vectors. The global lower bound is $g_r^{*\perp}(\emptyset)$ in the root agent r. $g_r^{*\perp}(\emptyset)$ is propagated in a top-down manner using VALUE messages. An assignment $\mathcal{A}_j^{sep}$ for agent j is pruned if $g_r^{*\perp}(\emptyset) \not\prec_{leximin} g_j^{*\top}(\mathcal{A}_j^{sep})$. However, the length of $g_j^{*\top}(\mathcal{A}_j^{sep})$ is the number of agents in the sub-tree rooted at j while the length of $g_r^{*\perp}(\emptyset)$ equals the number of all the agents $|A|$. In this case, $\prec_{leximin}$ is applied as follows. Since $g_j^{*\top}(\mathcal{A}_j^{sep})$ is an upper bound, unknown objective values are represented by ∞. Therefore, with padding of ∞, $g_j^{*\top}(\mathcal{A}_j^{sep})$ and $g_r^{*\perp}(\emptyset)$ can be compared as the same length of vectors. Let $g_j^{*\top\top}(\mathcal{A}_j^{sep})$ denote the vector $g_j^{*\top}(\mathcal{A}_j^{sep})$ with the padding of ∞. In actual computation, the padding can be omitted since the sequence of ∞ is the last part of vectors. When $g_j^{*\perp}(\mathcal{A}_j^{sep}) = g_j^{*\top}(\mathcal{A}_j^{sep}) \vee g_r^{*\perp}(\emptyset) \not\prec_{leximin} g_j^{*\top\top}(\mathcal{A}_j^{sep})$ for child $j \in Ch_i$, agent i completes the tree search for the assignment $\mathcal{A}_j^{sep}$.

Moreover, to improve effects of the pruning, the upper bound for other parts of the problem is introduced. Namely, for each child agent $j \in Ch_i$, agent i computes the upper bound of objective vector $h_j^{+\top}(\mathcal{A}_j^{sep})$ for sub-trees except one rooted at j.

$$h_j^{+\top}(\mathcal{A}_j^{sep}) = h_i^{+\top}(\mathcal{A}_i^{sep}) \oplus \max_{\mathcal{A}_i^{dcd'} \text{ for } X_i^{dcd} \setminus X_j^{sep}} h_i^{\top}(\mathcal{A}_i^{sep} \cup \mathcal{A}_i^{dcd'} \cup \mathcal{A}_j^{sep}) \quad (6)$$

$$h_i^\top(\mathcal{A}) = [\delta_i(\mathcal{A})] \oplus \bigoplus_{j \in Ch_i \setminus \{j\}, \mathcal{A}_j^{sep} \subseteq \mathcal{A}} g_j^{*\top}(\mathcal{A}_j^{sep}) \qquad (7)$$

Note that the maximization in Equation (6) is not the maximization of objective values but the selection of the widest boundary. Since $\mathcal{A}_j^{sep}$ is a part of an assignment for $X_i^{sep} \cup X_j^{dcd}$, there are several assignments compatible with $\mathcal{A}_j^{sep}$. For such compatible assignments, the widest boundary prevents an over estimation. $h_j^{+\top}(\mathcal{A}_j^{sep})$ is sent from agent i to its child j using VALUE messages. When $g_j^{*\perp}(\mathcal{A}_j^{sep}) = g_j^{*\top}(\mathcal{A}_j^{sep}) \vee g_r^{*\perp}(\emptyset) \nprec_{leximin} h_j^{+\top}(\mathcal{A}_j^{sep}) \oplus g_j^{*\top}(\mathcal{A}_j^{sep})$ for child $j \in Ch_i$, agent i completes the tree search for the assignment $\mathcal{A}_j^{sep}$.

4.5 Shortcut VALUE Messages for Modified Pseudo Tree

In several search methods [10,20], additional VALUE messages are sent from ancestor agents to descendant agents taking shortcut paths. The shortcut VALUE messages directly carry assignments to deep levels of the pseudo tree. Then the assignments are propagated in a bottom-up manner using extended UTIL messages to update contexts. In our solution methods, the shortcut messages are particularly important to reduce the delay in updating the contexts since the decision makers of most variables are the agents in higher levels of the pseudo tree. In the conventional methods, the paths of shortcut VALUE messages are back edges. On the other hand, in our cases, back edges may not directly connect the decision maker and the deepest agent which relate to the same variable. In the example of Figure 1(c), the root agent sends x_0, x_1 and x_2 to the agent of x_2, and sends x_1 to the agent of x_3, respectively. Note that the root agent and the agent of x_3 are not directly connected. Therefore, we compute the deepest related agent for each variable in a bottom-up preprocessing, which is integrated to the preprocessing. The information on the deepest agent is stored in the corresponding decision maker. Agent i knows a set Sc_i of agents, to which shortcut VALUE messages are sent. For each agent $k \in Sc_i$, i computes $\mathcal{A}_k^{sc}$ containing assignments for k based on $\mathcal{A}_j^{sep}$, where child $j \in Ch_i$ is an ancestor of k. In addition, we employ timestamps based on the logical clock of the assignment for each variable, to compare the freshness of the assignment.

4.6 Pseudo Code of Search Method

Algorithm 1 shows the pseudo code of the search method for agent i. Here $^i*$ denotes agent i's copy of $*$. Also, $*^{\perp/\top}$ denotes a pair of $*^\perp$ and $*^\top$. $\overrightarrow{-\infty}$ and $\overrightarrow{\infty}$ denote the vectors consisting of $-\infty$ and ∞, respectively. The length of these vectors is the same as the length of the vectors to be assigned. After the initialization (lines 2-4), agents repeatedly receive messages and maintain their status (lines 5-8). Note that the message passing is initiated by the root agent when it first enters the Maintenance state (line 8). When an agent receives a message, the agent updates its status based on the type of messages (lines 9-19). Then the agent maintains other data structures (lines 21-23). The root agent updates the global lower bound $^ig^{*\perp}(\emptyset)$ (line 21). If the termination condition is achieved, the agent determines its optimal assignment (line 22-23). Based on the updated status, messages are sent to other agents (line 24-29).

Algorithm 1. Distributed search for leximin AMODCOP (agent i)

```
1  Main:
2    if p_i = null then { A_i^{sep} ← ∅. h_i^{+⊤}(A_i^{sep}) ← [ ]. ptrm_i ← true. }
3    else { A_i^{sep} ← null. ptrm_i ← false. }
4    {}^i g_r^{*⊥}(∅) = −∞⃗. trm_i ← false.
5    forever do {
6      until receive loop exits do
7        | if ¬trm_i then { receive a message. } else { purge all messages. }
8      if A_i^{sep} ≠ null ∧ ¬trm_i then Maintenance. }
9  Receive(VALUE, A, g, h, trm):
10   update A_i^{sep} by A. if A_i^{sep}=A then { h_i^{+⊤}(A_i^{sep}) ← h. } else { h_i^{+⊤}(A_i^{sep}) ← ∞⃗. }
11   {}^i g_r^{*⊥}(∅) ← g. ptrm_i ← trm. Consistent. return.
12 Receive(VALUE, A):
13   if A_i^{sep} ≠ null then {
14     update A_i^{sep} by A. if A_i^{sep} is updated then h_i^{+⊤}(A_i^{sep}) ← ∞⃗.
15     Consistent. } return.
16 Receive(UTIL, A, g^{⊥/⊤}):
17   update A_i^{sep} by A. if A_i^{sep} is updated then h_i^{+⊤}(A_i^{sep}) ← ∞⃗.
18   if A_i^{sep} is compatible with A then store/update {}^i g_j^{*⊥/⊤}(A) by g^{⊥/⊤}.
19   Consistent. return.
20 Maintenance:
21   if p_i = null ∧ {}^i g_r^{*⊥}(∅) ≺_{leximin} g_i^{*⊥}(∅) then {}^i g_r^{*⊥}(∅) ← g_i^{*⊥}(∅).
22   if ptrm_i ∧ g_i^{*⊥}(A_i^{sep}) = g_i^{*⊤}(A_i^{sep}) then {
23     | determine A_i^{*dcd} corresponding to the termination condition. trm_i ← true. }
24   foreach j ∈ Ch_i do {
25     | if trm_i then { determine A_j^{sep} from A_i^{*dcd}. } else { choose A_j^{sep} with a strategy. }
26     send (VALUE, A_j^{sep}, {}^i g_r^{*⊥}(∅), h_j^{+⊤}(A_j^{sep}), trm_i) to j. }
27   foreach k ∈ Sc_i do {
28     | determine A_k^{sc} from A_j^{sep} of k's ancestor j. send (VALUE, A_k^{sc}) to j. }
29   if ¬ptrm_i then send (UTIL, A_i^{sep}, g_i^{*⊥/⊤}(A_i^{sep})) to p_i.
30   return.
31 Consistent:
32   foreach A incompatible with A_i^{sep} do delete {}^i g_j^{*⊥/⊤}(A).
33   return.
```

4.7 Representation of Objective Vectors

In the whole computation of objective vectors, sorted vector can be employed. With the sorted vectors, the objective values of individual agents are not directly identified. The length of the objective vectors is upper bounded by the number of agents $|A|$. On the other hand, the sorted vector is compressed with run-length encoding, as a sequence of pairs $(objective\ value,\ length)$. This reduces both the size of the representation and the computation of $\prec_{leximin}$, when there are a number of the same objective values.

4.8 Correctness and Complexity

The both of the extended DPOP and the search method are variations of the previous solution methods [10,15] while we use a representation without any subtraction. Therefore, their correctness is proven with the same reasoning as for the previous methods, replacing the assignment concept with the proposed vectors (since we proved above that it satisfies the same additive properties). We have addressed how the computation is extended to Leximin AMODCOPs. Propositions 1, 2 and 3 shows that the monotonicity in the computation resembles the conventional solution methods based on addition. The properties on the computational/communication complexity of the proposed methods are also the same as those of the previous methods. On the other hand, the modified pseudo tree implicitly increases the induced width [15], which is $\prod_{x_i \in X_i^{sep}} |D_i|$ for agent i. The worst case of the basic tree search is as follows. 1) The tree is a single sequence of agents. 2) The decision maker is only the root node. 3) The evaluation is only made in the single leaf node. 4) No pruning works. Therefore, the maximum number of message cycles is $2(|A| - 1) \prod_{x_j \in X} |D_j|$. However, this is an inherent property of the AMODCOPs. One can address large size problems using approximation methods. The maximum length of objective vector is the same as the number of agent $|A|$. With the representation using pairs of a value and its length, the size of the representation is between 2 and $2|A|$. This representation can be implemented with several tree structures, including Red-Blacks, tree whose major operations are performed in $O(\log n)$ time. The size of messages increases since their scalar values are replaced by the vectors.

5 Evaluation

The proposed method was experimentally evaluated. In our experiments with Leximin AMODCOPs (see Subsection 3.1) each problem consists of n ternary variables and c pairs of asymmetric objective functions. The constraint network is randomly generated by first creating a spanning trees and then adding additional edges. For each assignment, the objective function $f_{i,j}(x_i, x_j)$ returns an integer value w from $[0, 1]$ or $[0, 10]$ based on a uniform distribution. Note that we treat the aggregated function $f_i(X_i)$ as a black-box which cannot be decomposed. For each type of problem, the results are averaged over 25 instances. As the first experiment, we focused on the effects of search methods on the modified pseudo trees and the leximin ordering. The following solution methods were evaluated. b: the basic search method shown in Subsection 4.3. gl: b with the pruning based on the global lower bound shown in Subsection 4.4. glou: bl with the upper bound for other part of the problem shown in Subsection 4.4. glousv: glou with shortcut VALUE messages shown in Subsection 4.5. lvb, lvgl, lvglou, lvglousv: solution methods with the vectors of lower and upper limit values for each function $f_i(X_i)$ addressed in Subsection 4.3 [1]. The experiments were performed using simulation programs based on message cycles. In each message cycle, each agent receives messages from its message queue. Then the agent updates its status and sends messages if necessary. A simulation is interrupted after a number of 50000 cycles. Additionally, the number of non-concurrently performed operations (ncops) relating to objective functions and assignments is also evaluated. While it resembles ncccs [8], we also consider several operations that involve a (partial) assignment.

---

[1] In this case, to avoid over estimation, we modified the condition of the pruning in the second phase using a flag. Agent i completes the tree search for the assignment $\mathcal{A}_j^{sep}$ when $g_j^{*\perp}(\mathcal{A}_j^{sep}) = g_j^{*\top}(\mathcal{A}_j^{sep}) \vee h_j^{+\top}(\mathcal{A}_j^{sep}) \oplus g_j^{*\top}(\mathcal{A}_j^{sep}) \prec_{leximin} g_r^{*\perp}(\emptyset)$ for child $j \in Ch_i$.

Table 1. Number of iterations ($w = [0, 10]$) (trm.: number of completed instances)

n, c	10, 9			10, 12			10, 15			20, 19			20, 22			40, 39		
alg.	msg. cyc.	ncop. (10^3)	trm.	msg. cyc.	ncop. (10^3)	trm.	msg. cyc.	ncop. (10^3)	trm.	msg. cyc.	ncop. (10^3)	trm.	msg. cyc.	ncop. (10^3)	trm.	msg. cyc.	ncop. (10^3)	trm.
b	781	125	25	16312	6582	22	42125	45183	8	12092	1535	23	38866	16147	11	38499	8303	9
gl	660	118	25	6617	4349	25	28349	36721	18	8413	1320	23	29768	12341	16	35431	7847	11
glou	332	300	25	3169	4622	25	20553	42786	23	3602	3930	25	19774	25064	21	19922	28369	19
glousv	212	268	25	2140	5268	25	17692	52776	24	1561	3068	25	12813	25179	24	11267	22692	24
lvb	511	96	25	15584	6342	23	41998	44905	8	9295	1314	24	37743	15529	13	33538	8009	13
lvgl	434	92	25	6001	4206	25	25216	36259	19	5903	1095	24	27612	11706	19	30150	7372	15
lvglou	214	231	25	2473	4409	25	16461	41398	25	1046	2829	25	7645	18228	25	12305	23290	23
lvglousv	146	216	25	1787	5065	25	13970	51438	25	605	2465	25	4758	19189	25	4974	17074	25

Table 2. Size of pseudo tree (no dcd.: $|X_i^{dcd}| = 0$)

n, c	max. depth	max. $\|Ch_i\|$	max. $\|X_i^{sep}\|$	max. $\|X_i\|$	max. $\|X_i^{dcd}\|$	#agent no dcd.	max. $\|Sc_i\|$
10, 9	5	4	2	5	5	4	5
10, 12	6	2	5	5	5	6	5
10, 15	7	2	7	6	6	6	6
20, 19	8	4	2	5	5	9	5
20, 22	9	3	5	6	6	10	6
40, 39	11	5	2	6	6	17	6

Table 3. Size of vector

w	[0, 1]						[0, 10]					
n, c	20, 22			40, 39			20, 22			40, 39		
alg.	len.	sz.	2sz.	len.	sz.	2sz.	len.	sz.	2sz.	len.	sz.	2sz.
lvb	5	2	4	4	2	4	5	4	8	4	3	7
lvgl	9	3	5	15	2	5	9	6	13	15	7	14
lvglou	11	3	6	20	3	6	11	7	15	20	9	19
lvglousv	10	3	6	20	3	6	11	7	14	20	9	18

Table 1 shows the number of iterations. The efficient methods reduce the number of message cycles. Particularly, glou is effective since it prunes branches with full information of boundaries. Although glou employs the limit values $-\infty$ and ∞, the pruning works. The effect comes from the property that leximin partially compares values in two vectors. In addition, the lower and upper limit values for each function $f_i(X_i)$ are effective in the case of trees and less effective for cyclic networks. This reveals the need for better bounding methods, as available with conventional DCOP solvers. Such methods are, however, domain specific since the decomposition of $f_i(X_i)$ and the identification of the preferences of the agents will be necessary. Advanced methods need more ncops than basic methods. Also, the additional shortcut VALUE messages are necessary, similar to ADOPT [10,20]. Therefore, there are several trade-offs between computation and communication. On the other hand, there are opportunities to reduce ncops in our implementation. Table 2 shows the size of the pseudo trees. There are a number of agents with an empty X_i^{dcd}. These agents only evaluate their objective values. While there are opportunities to reduce this redundancy by revealing the objective functions of the agents, it will also be domain specific. Table 3 shows the size of the vectors. The actual size (2sz.) of the representation of the vectors is relatively smaller than the length (len.) of the vectors in the case of $w = [0, 1]$. In these results, the computation of leximin is reduced since the number of pairs (sz.) to be enumerated is less than the length of vectors. Table 4 shows the comparison between leximin (max-leximin) and other optimization criteria. The other optimization criteria are summation (max-sum), maximin (max-min), and maximin with additional summation (max-LWT). These criteria were also applied to the solvers based on pseudo trees, similar to the previous solvers [6]. Each cell shows the number of cases of dominance ($\prec$ or $\succ$) or tie (=). On the summation of objective values, max-sum and max-LWT are never dominated by max-leximin. Max-leximin, max-min and max-LWT give the same minimum objective value. For max-sum and

Table 4. Comparison between max-leximin and other optimization criteria ($w = [0, 10]$)

comparison	sum									min									max								
optimization	max-sum			max-min			max-LWT			max-sum			max-min			max-LWT			max-sum			max-min			max-LWT		
n, c	≺	=	≻	≺	=	≻	≺	=	≻	≺	=	≻	≺	=	≻	≺	=	≻	≺	=	≻	≺	=	≻	≺	=	≻
10, 15	24	1	0	3	3	19	19	6	0	0	6	19	0	25	0	0	25	0	21	2	2	14	3	8	18	7	0
20, 22	25	0	0	2	0	23	23	2	0	0	2	23	0	25	0	0	25	0	23	2	0	11	3	11	18	6	1
40, 39	25	0	0	0	0	25	24	1	0	0	0	25	0	25	0	0	25	0	22	1	2	10	3	12	18	5	2

comparison	variance									leximin									Pareto								
optimization	max-sum			max-min			max-LWT			max-sum			max-min			max-LWT			max-sum			max-min			max-LWT		
n, c	≺	=	≻	≺	=	≻	≺	=	≻	≺	=	≻	≺	=	≻	≺	=	≻	≺	=	≻	≺	=	≻	≺	=	≻
10, 15	24	1	0	14	2	9	20	5	0	0	1	24	0	2	23	0	5	20	0	25	0	0	22	3	0	25	0
20, 22	25	0	0	11	0	14	24	1	0	0	0	25	0	0	25	0	1	24	0	25	0	0	24	1	0	25	0
40, 39	25	0	0	12	0	13	24	0	1	0	0	25	0	0	25	0	0	25	0	25	0	0	25	0	0	25	0

max-LWT, max-leximin relatively decreases the variance of objective values. Max-min is not Pareto optimal while the other criteria are Pareto optimal.

6   Related Works and Discussions

In ADCOP [4], each value of a function is defined by a pair of values that correspond to different directions on an edge of a constraint graph. Therefore, an agent has its local view based on the direction of connected edges. However, its optimal solution corresponds to the maximum summation over all functions and directions. In [12,13,14,6], resource allocation problems similar to ones in this study have been addressed. On the other hand, we addressed an extension of ADCOPs based on the leximin social welfare. While Theil based social welfare has been addressed in [12], that solution method is a local search. In our proposed search methods, the high induced width exponentially increases the number of search iterations. For addressing this issue, a promising direction is to investigate more aggressive modifications of graphs [19]. Also, there are opportunities to approximate the problems [16,2]. While existing efficient techniques including forward-bounding may improve the efficiency of solution methods [13], it needs several assumptions such that each preference function is additive and can be decomposed to sub-functions in exchange for the privacy of the agents. While several solution methods for a centralized constraint optimization problem on the leximin ordering have been proposed, for example [1], they are dedicated extensions of centralized solvers.

7   Conclusions

In this work, we presented a multiple objective DCOP that considers preferences of agents, and its solution method based on the leximin ordering on multiple objectives. Our future work will include improvements to reduce redundant computations, evaluations in practical domains, and analysis on various types of problems.

References

1. Bouveret, S., Lemaître, M.: Computing leximin-optimal solutions in constraint networks. Artificial Intelligence 173(2), 343–364 (2009)

2. Delle Fave, F.M., Stranders, R., Rogers, A., Jennings, N.R.: Bounded decentralised coordination over multiple objectives. In: 10th International Conference on Autonomous Agents and Multiagent Systems, vol. 1, pp. 371–378 (2011)
3. Farinelli, A., Rogers, A., Petcu, A., Jennings, N.R.: Decentralised coordination of low-power embedded devices using the max-sum algorithm. In: 7th International Joint Conference on Autonomous Agents and Multiagent Systems, pp. 639–646 (2008)
4. Grinshpoun, T., Grubshtein, A., Zivan, R., Netzer, A., Meisels, A.: Asymmetric distributed constraint optimization problems. Journal of Artificial Intelligence Research 47, 613–647 (2013)
5. Marler, R.T., Arora, J.S.: Survey of multi-objective optimization methods for engineering. Structural and Multidisciplinary Optimization 26, 369–395 (2004)
6. Matsui, T., Matsuo, H.: Considering equality on distributed constraint optimization problem for resource supply network. In: 2012 IEEE/WIC/ACM International Joint Conferences on Web Intelligence and Intelligent Agent Technology, vol. 2, pp. 25–32 (2012)
7. Matsui, T., Silaghi, M., Hirayama, K., Yokoo, M., Matsuo, H.: Distributed search method with bounded cost vectors on multiple objective dCOPs. In: Rahwan, I., Wobcke, W., Sen, S., Sugawara, T. (eds.) PRIMA 2012. LNCS, vol. 7455, pp. 137–152. Springer, Heidelberg (2012)
8. Meisels, A., Kaplansky, E., Razgon, I., Zivan, R.: Comparing performance of distributed constraints processing algorithms. In: 3rd International Workshop on Distributed Constraint Reasoning (2002)
9. Miller, S., Ramchurn, S.D., Rogers, A.: Optimal decentralised dispatch of embedded generation in the smart grid. In: 11th International Conference on Autonomous Agents and Multiagent Systems, vol. 1, pp. 281–288 (2012)
10. Modi, P.J., Shen, W., Tambe, M., Yokoo, M.: Adopt: Asynchronous distributed constraint optimization with quality guarantees. Artificial Intelligence 161(1-2), 149–180 (2005)
11. Moulin, H.: Axioms of Cooperative Decision Making. Cambridge University Press, Cambridge (1988)
12. Netzer, A., Meisels, A.: SOCIAL DCOP - Social Choice in Distributed Constraints Optimization. In: 5th International Symposium on Intelligent Distributed Computing, pp. 35–47 (2011)
13. Netzer, A., Meisels, A.: Distributed Envy Minimization for Resource Allocation. In: 5th International Conference on Agents and Artificial Intelligence, vol. 1, pp. 15–24 (2013)
14. Netzer, A., Meisels, A.: Distributed Local Search for Minimizing Envy. In: 2013 IEEE/WIC/ACM International Conference on Intelligent Agent Technology, pp. 53–58 (2013)
15. Petcu, A., Faltings, B.: A scalable method for multiagent constraint optimization. In: IJCAI 2005, pp. 266–271 (2005)
16. Rogers, A., Farinelli, A., Stranders, R., Jennings, N.R.: Bounded approximate decentralised coordination via the Max-Sum algorithm. Artificial Intelligence 175(2), 730–759 (2011)
17. Sen, A.K.: Choice, Welfare and Measurement. Harvard University Press (1997)
18. Ueda, S., Iwasaki, A., Yokoo, M., Silaghi, M., Hirayama, K., Matsui, T.: Coalition structure generation based on distributed constraint optimization (2010)
19. Vinyals, M., Rodriguez-Aguilar, J.A., Cerquides, J.: Constructing a unifying theory of dynamic programming dcop algorithms via the generalized distributive law. Autonomous Agents and Multi-Agent Systems 22(3), 439–464 (2011)
20. Yeoh, W., Felner, A., Koenig, S.: Bnb-adopt: an asynchronous branch-and-bound dcop algorithm. In: 7th International Joint Conference on Autonomous Agents and Multiagent Systems, Estoril, Portugal, pp. 591–598 (2008)
21. Zivan, R.: Anytime local search for distributed constraint optimization. In: AAAI 2008, pp. 393–398 (2008)

Compromising Adjustment Based on Conflict Mode for Multi-times Bilateral Closed Nonlinear Negotiations

Katsuhide Fujita

Faculty of Engineering, Tokyo University of Agriculture and Technology
Naka-cho, Koganei-shi, Tokyo, Japan
katfuji@cc.tuat.ac.jp

Abstract. Bilateral multi-issue closed negotiation is an important class for real-life negotiations. Usually, negotiation problems have constraints such as a complex and unknown opponent's utility in real time, or time discounting. In the class of negotiation with some constraints, the effective automated negotiation agents can adjust their behavior depending on the characteristics of their opponents and negotiation scenarios. Recently, the attention of this study has focused on the nonlinear utility functions. In nonlinear utility functions, most of the negotiation strategies for linear utility functions can't adopt to the scenarios of nonlinear utility functions.

In this paper, we propose an automated agent that estimates the opponent's strategies based on the past negotiation sessions. Our agent tries to compromise to the estimated maximum utility of the opponent by the end of the negotiation. In addition, our agent can adjust the speed of compromise by judging the opponent's Thomas-Kilmann Conflict Mode and search for the pareto frontier using past negotiation sessions. In the experiments, we demonstrate that the proposed agent has better outcomes and greater search technique for the pareto frontier than existing agents. Additionally, we demonstrate the change of the utility in multi-times negotiation for analyzing the learning strategies in the nonlinear preferences.

1 Introduction

Negotiation is an important process in forming alliances and reaching trade agreements. Research in the field of negotiation originates in various disciplines including economics, social science, game theory and artificial intelligence (e.g. [6,16]). Automated agents can be used side-by-side with a human negotiator embarking on an important negotiation task. They can alleviate some of the effort required of people during negotiations and also assist people that are less qualified in the negotiation process. There may even be situations in which automated negotiators can replace the human negotiators. Another possibility is for people to use these agents as a training tool, prior to actually performing the task. Thus, success in developing an automated agent with negotiation capabilities has great advantages and implications.

H.K. Dam et al. (Eds.): PRIMA 2014, LNAI 8861, pp. 439–454, 2014.
© Springer International Publishing Switzerland 2014

Motivated by the challenges of bilateral negotiations between automated agents, the automated negotiating agents competition (ANAC) was organized [11]. The purpose of the competition is to facilitate research in the area of bilateral multi-issue closed negotiation. The setup at ANAC is a realistic model including time discounting, closed negotiations, alternative offering protocol, and so on. By analyzing the results of ANAC, the stream of the strategies of automated negotiations and important factors for developing the competition have been shown [2]. Also, some effective automated negotiating agents have been proposed through the competitions [3,13].

Recently, for automated negotiation agents in bilateral multi-issue closed negotiation, attention has focused on interleaving learning with negotiation strategies from past negotiation sessions. By analyzing the past negotiation sessions, agents can adapt to domains over time and use them to negotiate better with future opponents. However, some outstanding issues regarding them remain, such as effective use of past negotiation sessions. In particular, the way of understanding the opponent's strategy and negotiation scenarios from the past sessions is unclear. In other words, it is still an open and interesting problem to design more efficient automated negotiation strategies against a variety of negotiating opponents in different negotiation domains by utilizing the past negotiation sessions. Another key point in achieving automated negotiation in real life is the nonlinearity of the utility functions. Many real-world negotiation problems assume the multiple nonlinear utility function. When an automated negotiation strategy covers the linear function effectively, it is not always possible or desirable in the nonlinear situations [15].

In this paper, we propose an adaptive strategy based on the past negotiation sessions by adjusting the speed of compromising depending on the opponent's strategy, automatically. For judging the opponent's strategy, we need to characterize the opponents in terms of some global style, such as negotiation styles or a known conflict-handling style. One important style is the Thomas-Kilmann Conflict Mode Instrument (TKI) [14,20]. The TKI is designed to measure a person's behavior in a conflict situation based on the concerns of two people appearing to be incompatible. The proposed agent tries to compromise speedily when the opponent is cooperative and passive. By employing this strategy, our agent achieves an agreement in the earlier stage compared with existing negotiating agents. If agents achieve an agreement in the earlier stage, agents can gain more utility because the time-discounted factor decreases the total utility. In addition, our agent has an effective search strategy for finding the pareto optimal bids. The main idea of this strategy was proposed by Fujita [8,9], however, which focused on the linear utility functions only. This paper focuses on the nonlinear utility function, which is close to the negotiation in the real life.

In the experiments, we demonstrate that the proposed agent outperforms the other agents that participated in the final round of ANAC-2014. We also compare the performance of our agent with that of the state-of-the-art negotiation agents. By analyzing the results, it is clear that our agent can obtain higher mean utilities against a variety of opponents in the earlier steps in the nonlinear domains.

The remainder of the paper is organized as follows. First, we describe related works. Second, we show the negotiation environments and our proposed agent's basic strategy. Third, we propose a way of adjusting the compromising speed, and a search method for finding pareto optimal bids. Then, we demonstrate the overall results of tournaments among top-4 finalist in ANAC-2014 and some experimental analysis. Finally, we present our conclusions.

2   Related Works

This paper focuses on research in the area of bilateral multi-issue closed negotiation, which is an important class of real-life negotiations. Closed negotiation means that opponents do not reveal their preferences to each other. Negotiating agents designed using a heuristic approach require extensive evaluation, typically through simulations and empirical analysis, since it is usually impossible to predict precisely how the system and the constituent agents will behave in a wide variety of circumstances. Motivated by the challenges of bilateral negotiations between people and automated agents, the automated negotiating agents competition (ANAC) was organized in 2010 [1]. The purpose of the competition is to facilitate research in the area of bilateral multi-issue closed negotiation. The declared goals of the competition are (1) to encourage the design of practical negotiation agents that can proficiently negotiate against unknown opponents and in a variety of circumstances, (2) to provide a benchmark for objectively evaluating different negotiation strategies, (3) to explore different learning and adaptation strategies and opponent models, (4) to collect state-of-the-art negotiating agents and negotiation scenarios, and make them available to the wider research community. The competition was based on the GENIUS environment, which is a General Environment for Negotiation with Intelligent multi-purpose Usage Simulation [17]. By analyzing the results of ANAC, the stream of the strategies of ANAC and important factors for developing the competition have been shown. Baarslag et al. present an in-depth analysis and the key insights gained from ANAC 2011 [2]. This paper mainly analyzes the different strategies using classifications of agents with respect to their concession behavior against a set of standard benchmark strategies and empirical game theory (EGT) to investigate the robustness of the strategies. It also shows that the most adaptive negotiation strategies, while robust across different opponents, are not necessarily the ones that win the competition. Furthermore, our EGT analysis highlights the importance of considering metrics.

Chen and Weiss proposed a negotiation approach called OMAC, which learns an opponent's strategy in order to predict future utilities of counter-offers by means of discrete wavelet decomposition and cubic smoothing splines [4]. They also present a negotiation strategy called EMAR for this kind of environment that relies on a combination of Empirical Mode Decomposition (EMD) and Autoregressive Moving Average (ARMA) [5]. EMAR enables a negotiating agent to acquire an opponent model and to use this model for adjusting its target utility in real time on the basis of an adaptive concession-making mechanism.

Hao and Leung proposed a negotiation strategy named ABiNeS, which was introduced for negotiations in complex environments [12]. ABiNeS adjusts the time to stop exploiting the negotiating partner and also employs a reinforcement-learning approach to improve the acceptance probability of its proposals. Williams et al. proposed a novel negotiating agent based on Gaussian Processes in multi-issue automated negotiation against unknown opponents [25]. Pan et al. [19] addresses the problem of finding win-win outcome in multi-attribute negotiation based on an evolutionary method. This paper presents a negotiation model that can find win-win solutions of multiple attributes, and needs not to reveal negotiating agents private utility functions to their opponents or a third-party mediator. This paper tackles on the multi-issue negotiation with the nonlinear utility functions, however, it doesn't assume the multiple "times" negotiations as our paper focusing.

Kawaguchi et al. proposed a strategy for compromising the estimated maximum value based on estimated maximum utility [13]. These papers have been important contributions for bilateral multi-issue closed negotiation; however, they don't deal with multi-times negotiation with learning and reusing the past negotiation sessions. After that, Fujita [8,9] proposed the compromising strategy with adjusting the speed of making agreements using the Conflict Mode, and focused on the multi-times negotiations. However, these strategies focused on the linear utility function, only. In the real life, most utility functions are nonlinear because of the complexity of the preferences structures. Most existing negotiation protocols, though well-suited for linear utility functions, work poorly when applied to nonlinear problems because of the complexity of utility domain, multiple optima, and interdependency between issues. However, the negotiation strategy based on the compromising strategy by Fujita can adopt the nonlinear situation. In this paper, we demonstrate that the novel negotiation strategy based on the compromising strategy is effective in the nonlinear domains, not only the linear domain.

Recently, some studies have focused on the divided parts of negotiating strategies in the alternative offering protocol: proposals, responses, and opponent modeling. Effective strategies can be achieved by combinations of these strong strategies depending on the opponent's strategies and negotiation environments. Many of the sophisticated agent strategies that currently exist are comprised of a fixed set of modules. Therefore, the studies for proposing the negotiation strategies focusing on the modules are important and influential. Baarslag et al. focus on the acceptance dilemma: accepting the current offer may be suboptimal, as better offers may still be presented [3]. On the other hand, accepting too late may prevent an agreement from being reached, resulting in a break off with no gain for either party. This paper proposed new acceptance conditions and investigated correlations between the properties of the negotiation environment and the efficacy of acceptance conditions.

3   Negotiation Environments

The interaction between negotiating parties is regulated by a *negotiation protocol* that defines the rules of how and when proposals can be exchanged. The competition used the alternating-offers protocol for bilateral negotiation as proposed in [21,22], in which the negotiating parties exchange offers in turns. The alternating-offers protocol conforms with our criterion to have simple rules. It is widely studied in the literature, both in game-theoretic and heuristic settings of negotiation[7,6,16,18].

For example, *Agents A* and *B* take turns in the negotiation. One of the two agents is picked at random to start. When it is the turn of agent X (X being A or B), that agent is informed about the action taken by the opponent. In negotiation, the two parties take turns in selecting the next negotiation action. The possible actions are:

Accept: It indicates that the agent accepts the opponent's last bid.
Offer: It indicates that the agent proposes a new bid.
End Negotiation: It indicates that the agent terminates the entire negotiation, resulting in the lowest possible score for both agents.

If the action was an *Offer*, agent X is subsequently asked to determine its next action and the turn taking goes to the next round. If it is not an *Offer*, the negotiation has finished. The turn taking stops and the final score (utility of the last bid) is determined for each of the agents, as follows:

- The action of agent X is an Accept. This action is possible only if the opponent actually did a bid. The last bid of the opponent is taken, and the utility of that bid is determined in the utility spaces of agents A and B.
- The action is returned an EndNegotiation. The score of both agents is set to the lowest score.

The parties negotiate over *issues*, and every issue has an associated range of alternatives or *values*. A negotiation outcome consists of a mapping of every issue to a value, and the set Ω of all possible outcomes is called the negotiation *domain*. The domain is common knowledge to the negotiating parties and stays fixed during a single negotiation session. Both parties have certain preferences prescribed by a *preference profile* over Ω. These preferences can be modeled by means of a utility function U that maps a possible outcome $\omega \in \Omega$ to a real-valued number in the range $[0, 1]$. In contrast to the domain, the preference profile of the players is private information.

An agent's utility function, in the formulation, is described in terms of constraints. There are l constraints, $c_k \in C$. Each constraint represents a region in the contract space with one or more dimensions and an associated utility value. In addition, c_k has value $v_a(c_k, s)$ if and only if it is satisfied by contract s. Every agent has its own, typically unique, set of constraints. An agent's utility for contract s is defined as the weighted sum of the utility for all the constraints it satisfies, i.e., as $u_a(s) = \sum_{c_k \in C, s \in x(c_k)} v_a(c_k, s)$, where $x(c_k)$ is a set of possible contracts (solutions) of c_k. This expression produces a "bumpy" nonlinear

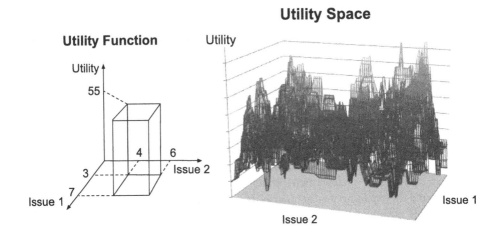

Fig. 1. Example of a nonlinear utility space

utility function with high points where many constraints are satisfied and lower regions where few or no constraints are satisfied. This represents a crucial departure from previous efforts on multi-issue negotiation, where contract utility is calculated as the weighted sum of the utilities for individual issues, producing utility functions shaped like flat hyperplanes with a single optimum.

Figure 1 shows an example of a utility space generated via a collection of binary constraints involving Issues 1 and 2. In addition, the number of terms is two. The example, which has a value of 55, holds if the value for Issue 1 is in the range $[3, 7]$ and the value for Issue 2 is in the range $[4, 6]$. The utility function is highly nonlinear with many hills and valleys. This constraint-based utility function representation allows us to capture the issue interdependencies common in real-world negotiations. The constraint in Figure 1, for example, captures the fact that a value of 4 is desirable for issue 1 if issue 2 has the value 4, 5 or 6. Note, however, that this representation is also capable of capturing linear utility functions as a special case (they can be captured as a series of unary constraints). A negotiation protocol for complex contracts can, therefore, handle linear contract negotiations.

A negotiation lasts a predefined time in seconds (*deadline*). The time line is normalized, i.e.: time $t \in [0, 1]$, where $t = 0$ represents the start of the negotiation and $t = 1$ represents the deadline. Apart from a deadline, a scenario may also feature discount factors. Discount factors decrease the utility of the bids under negotiation as time passes. Let d in $[0, 1]$ be the discount factor. Let t in $[0, 1]$ be the current normalized time, as defined by the timeline. We compute the discounted utility U_D^t of an outcome ω from the undiscounted utility function U as follows:

$$U_D^t(\omega) = U(\omega) \cdot d^t \qquad (1)$$

At $t = 1$, the original utility is multiplied by the discount factor. Furthermore, if $d = 1$, the utility is not affected by time, and such a scenario is considered to be undiscounted.

In addition, automated negotiation agents have had the concept introduced that an agent can save and load information for each preference profile. This means that an agent can learn from previous negotiations, against the same opponent or multiple opponents, to improve its competence when having a specific preference profile. By analyzing the past negotiation sessions, agents can estimate the opponent's utility function based on exchanging bids. For example, the bids an opponent proposes many times in the early stage might be the effective bids for the opponents. The last bid proposed by the opponent might be the lowest utility for agreeing with the bid. The information an agent can save and load for each preference profile and opponent is as follows: Offered bids, received bids,[1] and exchange sequence of the bids. Therefore, we need to predict or analyze the opponent's utility of bids to utilize the past negotiation sessions.

4 Negotiating Agent with Compromise Strategy

This section shows the compromising strategies [13] based on our proposed strategies.

4.1 Opponent Modeling in Basic Strategy

Our agent estimates the alternatives the opponent will offer in the future based on the opponent's offers. In particular, we estimate them using the values mapping the opponent's bids to our own utility function. The agent works at compromising to the estimated optimal agreement point.

Concretely, our behavior is decided based on the following equations (2), (3).

$$emax(t) = \mu(t) + (1 - \mu(t))d(t) \tag{2}$$
$$target(t) = 1 - (1 - emax(t))t^{\alpha} \tag{3}$$

$emax(t)$ means the estimated maximum utility of a bid the opponent will propose in the future. $emax(t)$ is calculated by $\mu(t)$ (the mean of the opponent's offers in our utility space), $d(t)$ (the deviation of the opponent's offers in our utility space. In other words, it means the width of the opponent's offers in our utility space) when the timeline is t.

We can see how favorable the opponent's offer is based on the deviation $(d(t))$ and the mean $(\mu(t))$.

If we assume that the opponent's offer is generated based on uniform distribution $[\alpha, \alpha + d(t)]$, the deviation is calculated using the continuous probability distribution as follows.

$$\sigma^2(t) = \frac{1}{n}\sum_{i=0}^{n} x_i^2 - \mu^2 = \frac{d^2(t)}{12} \tag{4}$$

---

[1] Bids don't include the utility information.

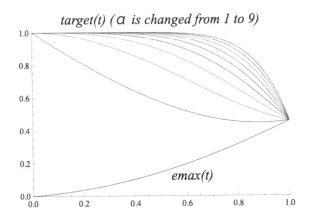

target(t) (a is changed from 1 to 9)

Fig. 2. $target(t)$ when $emax(t)$ is $\mu(t) = \frac{1}{10}t$ $d(t) = \frac{2}{5}t^2$

Therefore, $d(t)$ is described as follows.

$$d(t) = \sqrt{12}\sigma(t) \tag{5}$$

We consider the means as the weights for the following reason. When the mean of the opponent's action is located at the center of the domain of the utility, $emax(t)$ is the mean plus half of the width of the opponent's offers. However, it is possible to move only in the high direction when the mean of the utility value is low, and the action can be expanded only in the low direction when the mean is high. Therefore, an accurate estimation is made by introducing the weights.

$target(t)$ is a measure of proposing a bid when time is t, and α is a coefficient for adjusting the speed of compromise. It is effective to search for the opponent's utility information by repeating the proposal to each other as long as time allows. On the other hand, our utility value is required to be as high as possible. Our bids are the higher utility for the opponent at the first stage, and approach asymptotically to $emax(t)$ as the number of negotiation rounds increases.

Figure 2 is an example of $target(t)$ when α is changed from 1 to 9. $emax(t)$ is $\mu(t) = \frac{1}{10}t$, $d(t) = \frac{2}{5}t^2$.

4.2   Proposal and Response Opponent's Bids

First, we show the method of selecting the bids from our utility space. Our agent searches for alternatives whose utility is $target(t)$ by changing the starting points randomly by iteratively deepening the depth-first search method. Next, we show the decision of whether to accept the opponent's offer. Our agent judges whether to accept it based on $target(t)$ and the mean of the opponent's offers. Equation (6) defines the probability of acceptance.

$$P = \frac{t^5}{5} + (Offer - emax(t)) + (Offer - target(t)) \tag{6}$$

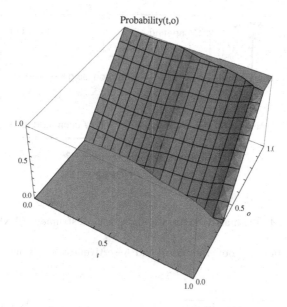

Fig. 3. Acceptance probability space

Acceptance probability P is calculated using t, $Offer$, $target(t)$ and the estimated maximum value $emax(t)$. $Offer$ is the utility of the opponent's bid in our utility space. Figure 3 shows the acceptance probability space when $emax(t)$ is $\mu(t) = \frac{1}{10}t$, $d(t) = \frac{2}{5}t^2$. The horizontal axis is time t and the vertical axis is a utility value o of the opponent's offer. As figure showing, the acceptance probability becomes higher as the time t and the α is larger.

5   Strategy Adaptation and Efficient Search Technique based on Past Negotiation Sessions

The compromising strategy described in the previous section has following issues:

1. Determination of α adjusting the speed of compromising isn't easy.
2. It doesn't always find the pareto optimal bids in searching bids.

To solve these issues, we propose two strategies using past negotiation sessions.

5.1   Strategy Adaptation Using Past Negotiations

An opponent's strategy is predictable based on earlier encounters or an experience profile, and can be characterized in terms of some global style, such as the negotiation styles[23,24], or a known conflict-handling style. One important style is the Thomas-Kilmann Conflict Mode Instrument (TKI) [14,20]. The TKI

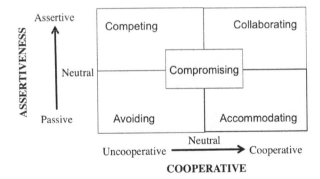

Fig. 4. Thomas-Kilmann Conflict Mode Instrument (TKI)

Table 1. Estimation of Cooperativeness and Assertiveness based on Past Negotiation Sessions

Condition	Cooperativeness
$u(bid_t) > \mu_h$	Uncooperative
$u(bid_t) = \mu_h$	Neutral
$u(bid_t) < \mu_h$	Cooperative

Condition	Assertiveness
$\sigma^2(t) > \sigma_h^2$	Passive
$\sigma^2(t) = \sigma_h^2$	Neutral
$\sigma^2(t) < \sigma_h^2$	Assertive

is designed to measure a person's behavior in conflict situations. "Conflict situations" are those in which the concerns of two people appear to be incompatible. In this situation, an individual's behavior has two dimensions: (1) assertiveness, the extent to which the person attempts to satisfy his own concerns, and (2) cooperativeness, the extent to which the person attempts to satisfy the other person's concerns. These two basic dimensions of behavior define five different modes for responding to conflict situations: Competing, Accommodating, Avoiding, Collaborating, and Compromising as Figure 4 shows.

The left side of Table 1 shows the relationships between the condition and cooperativeness, and the right side of Table 1 shows the relationship between the condition and assertiveness. When bid_t (opponent's bid in time t) is higher than μ_h (mean of the bids from past negotiation sessions), our agent regards the opponent as uncooperative. On the other hand, when bid_t is lower than μ_h, our agent regards the opponent as cooperative. In addition, our agent evaluates the assertiveness by comparing between the variance of proposals in the session and that in past negotiation sessions. Usually, assertive agents tend to propose the same bids because they try to push through their proposals by proposing many times. In other words, it is hard for our agent to make win-win agreements when the opponent's bids are dispread. On the other hand, passive agents tend to propose various bids because they change their proposals by searching for win-win agreements. In other words, our agent can make an agreement when

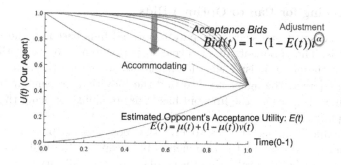

Fig. 5. Adjustment of Speed of Compromising

the opponent's bids are spread. Considering the above theory, our agent tries to compromise more and more when the opponent is cooperative and passive, which means the opponent is "accommodating" or "compromising" (yellow box in figure 4) in the TKI. For judging the opponent's TKI, we employ the past negotiation sessions.

Figure 5 shows the concept of adjusting the speed of compromising in this paper. As equation (3) in the previous section shows, the speed of compromising is decided by α in $target(t)$. α is set as a higher value at the first stage, and α is decreased when the opponent is "accommodating" or "compromising." By introducing this adjustment algorithm, our agent can adjust its strategy from hardheaded to cooperative more and more when the opponent tries to make agreement. When there is a discount factor, our agent can make an agreement in the early stage by employing the adjustment of α, despite that the existing compromising strategy makes an agreement just before the finish. In addition, our agent can prevent poor compromising because it considers the opponent's strategy and situation.

The detailed algorithm of adapting the agent's strategies based on past negotiation sessions is as follows:

1. Our agent sets α in $target(t)$ to the highest value.
2. It calculates the mean (μ_h) and variance (σ_h^2) of the opponent's bids from past negotiation sessions in appropriate domains.
3. It calculates the utility of offered bid in time t ($u(bid_t)$) and the variance of offered bids from 0 to t ($\sigma^2(t)$).
4. It compares between μ_h and $u(bid_t)$ to judge the cooperativeness.
5. It compares between σ_h^2 and $\sigma^2(t)$ to judge the assertiveness.
6. It updates the α in $target(t)$ based on the following equation when the opponent is "accommodating" or "compromising":

$$\alpha' = \alpha - \epsilon \qquad (7)$$

(α' is a renewed coefficient for adjusting the speed of compromise, ϵ is a constant for adjusting the α.)

5.2   Searching for Pareto Optimal Bids

The proposed agent can search for pareto optimal bids based on the similarity between bids. The opponents don't reveal their preferences to each other in the negotiation; therefore, it isn't easy for agents to search for the pareto optimal bids. In this paper, the agent tries to find the bids that are similar to the opponent's first bid because the first bid has high possibility of being the best bid for the opponent.

In this paper, our agent tries to find the most similar bids using the following equation. v_0 means the opponent's bid proposed the first time, and v_x means the target bid for evaluating the similarity. The similarity between v_0 and $v_x(sim(v_0, v_x))$ is defined as follows:

$$sim(v_0, v_x) = \sum_{i=1}^{m} w_i \cdot bool(v_0, v_i) \tag{8}$$

$(bool(v_0, v_i)$: if$(v_0 == v_i)$ then return 1 else return 0$)$

Our agent searches for the bids in which the utility is the same as $target(t)$ and $sim(v_0, v_x)$ is highest using the Genetic Algorithm (GA). In the large-size nonlinear utility function, Genetic Algorithm is effective to search the optimal bids [10]. GA is a search technique inspired by evolutionary biology, using such techniques as inheritance, mutation, selection, and crossover. Initially many individual contracts are randomly generated to form an initial population. After that, at each step, a proportion of the existing population is selected, based on their 'fitness' (i.e. utility values). Crossover and mutation is then applied to these selections to generate the next generation of contracts. This process is repeated until a termination condition has been reached. We employ a basic crossover method in which two parent individuals were combined to produce two children (one-point crossover). The fitness function is our agents' utility. 500 iterations were conducted. Mutations happened at very small probability. In a mutation, one of the issues in a contract vector was randomly chosen and changed.

6   Experimental Analysis

The performance of our proposed agent is evaluated with GENIUS (General Environment for Negotiation with Intelligent multipurpose Usage Simulation [17]), which is also used as a competition platform for ANAC.

First, we evaluated our agent by comparing with four state-of-the-art agents submitted in ANAC-2014 (AgentM, E2Agent, Gangster, and Whale Agent[2]). These four agents are the top-4 in ANAC-2014 social utility categories, in other words, they are effective and state-of-the-art agents to get the high social utility in the nonlinear utility functions. They are implemented by negotiation experts from different research groups.

---

[2] All the agents and the domains that participated in the final round of ANAC-2014 will be available in the newest GENIUS.

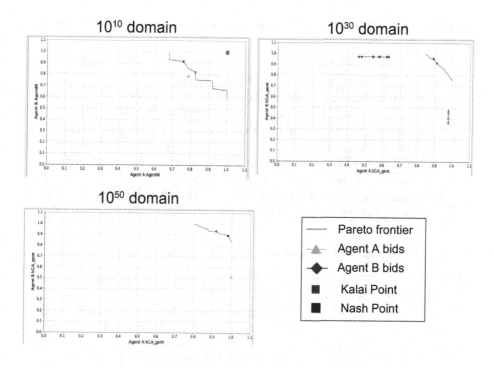

Fig. 6. Pareto-front lines of three domains

The three domains were selected from archives of ANAC-2014. All domains are nonlinear and complex written in the previous session with the discounted factor $(= 0.5)$. The size of the domains are $10^{10}, 10^{30}, and \, 10^{50}$. Each constraint in these domains are related to 1 to 5 issues. The properties of the scenarios in the experiment can also be observed in the shape of the outcome space of each scenario, as presented graphically in Figure 6 in three domains. The horizontal axis means the agent A's utility and vertical axis means the agent B's utility in each figure. The three scenarios contained broadly similar characteristics such as the shapes of the pareto frontier and so on. In all domains, the discount factor and the reservation value are set to 0.5 and 0, respectively.

For each pair of agents, under each utility function, we ran a total of 20 negotiations (including the exchange of preference profiles). The maximum negotiation time of each negotiation session is set to 3 minutes and normalized into the range of $[0, 1]$. Table 2 shows mean scores over all the scores achieved by each agent (against Our Agent) and variances.

As Table 2 shows, our agent has won by a big margin in the 10^{10} domain and 10^{30} domain. Considering the variance among the domains, our agent had advantages compared with other agents. Some reasons for this are as follows. First, we try to improve the speed of making agreements by adjusting $emax(t)$. In addition, our agent tries to compromise positively when the opponent is cooperative. Agents couldn't learn from the past negotiation sessions in the past

Table 2. Individual utility of each agent against our agent in different negotiation domains

Agent	10^{10} domain		10^{30} domain		10^{50} domain	
	Mean	Variance	Mean	Variance	Mean	Variance
OurAgent	**0.663584**	**0.156852**	**0.706638**	**0.015634**	**0.692816**	**0.033247**
AgentM	0.557693	0.109715	0.709559	0.016246	0.704370	0.033600
OurAgent	**0.476070**	**0.012932**	**0.151085**	**0.036328**	**0.301058**	**0.025424**
E2Agent	0.400251	0.009068	0.133538	0.030307	0.369168	0.044595
OurAgent	**0.649159**	**0.000864**	**0.512566**	**0.001171**	**0.522964**	**0.002968**
WhaleAgent	0.529163	0.000262	0.395057	0.001024	0.467015	0.002817
OurAgent	**0.391714**	**0.029468**	**0.225447**	**0.035972**	**0.241957**	**0.033713**
Gangster	0.365660	0.033716	0.207486	0.040348	0.259846	0.048887

Table 3. Number of bidding of each agent in different negotiation domains

Agent	10^{10} domain		10^{30} domain		10^{50} domain	
	Mean	Variance	Mean	Variance	Mean	Variance
OurAgent	**1103.08**	**0.01269**	**218.725**	**0.077873652**	**172.99**	**0.062145433**
AgentM	2801.45	0.04489	725.445	0.229121191	359.87	0.127683156
E2Agent	7328.41	0.05302	4029.3	0.569168861	2608.315	0.419727844
WhaleAgent	5895.90	0.02576	2399.035	0.326968808	1478.17	0.06857048
Gangster	7417.49	0.00887	1111.18	0.158211808	1541.155	0.24386606

ANAC; therefore, they tried to find effective agreements by eliciting the opponent's utility in the negotiation session. In other words, agents won the utility decreased by the discount factor because they needed to continue many rounds to get enough of the opponent's utility information. On the other hand, our agent tries to make agreements in the early stage using the past negotiation sessions when the opponent looks cooperative. Second, our agent could propose pareto optimal bids many times. If agents could offer the pareto optimal bids, the offers are effective and easy for making win-win agreements. Therefore, our agent could find better agreements by the effective search technique. However, our agent can't win in the large size domain such as the 10^{50} domain. The improvements of this issues are one of the important future work.

We also compare the negotiation efficiency of our proposed agent with top four state-of-the-art negotiation agents that entered the final round of ANAC-2014 in the social utility category. For each pair of agents, under each utility function, we ran a total of 20 negotiations (including the exchange of preference profiles). Table 3 shows the mean number of bidding for each agent in each domain. Our agent tries to improve the speed of making agreements by adjusting α in $emax(t)$, and compromises positively when the opponent is cooperative. The results of mean number of bidding outperformed compared with other agents in Table 3, definitely.

7   Conclusion

This paper focused on bilateral multi-issue closed "nonlinear" negotiation, which is an important class of real-life negotiations. This paper proposed a novel agent that estimates the alternatives the opponent offers based on past negotiation sessions. In addition, our agent could adjust the speed of compromising using the past negotiation sessions. We demonstrated that the proposed method results in good outcomes.

In our possible future works, we will prove the amount of past negotiation sessions for judging the opponent's TKI mode. In learning technology (especially real-time learning), cold start problems are important. For proposing and analyzing this issue, we will demonstrate experimentally or prove in theory the amount of past negotiation sessions. In addition, we will prove the timing of changing the strategy in theory. By getting the payoff table every time, the optimal timing of adjusting the agent's strategy can be calculated.

References

1. Aydogan, R., Baarslag, T., Fujita, K., Ito, T., Jonker, C.: The fifth international automated negotiating agents competition, (anac 2014) (2014), http://www.itolab.nitech.ac.jp/ANAC2014/
2. Baarslag, T., Fujita, K., Gerding, E., Hindriks, K., Ito, T., Jennings, N.R., Jonker, C., Kraus, S., Lin, R., Robu, V., Williams, C.: Evaluating practical negotiating agents: Results and analysis of the 2011 international competition. Artificial Intelligence Journal (AIJ) 198, 73–103 (2013)
3. Baarslag, T., Hindriks, K.: Accepting optimally in automated negotiation with incomplete information. In: Proceedings of the 2013 International Conference on Autonomous Agents and Multi-Agent Systems (AAMAS 2013), pp. 715–722 (2013)
4. Chen, S., Weiss, G.: An efficient and adaptive approach to negotiation in complex environments. In: Proceedings of the 19th European Conference on Artificial Intelligence (ECAI 2012), vol. 242, pp. 228–233 (2012)
5. Chen, S., Weiss, G.: An efficient automated negotiation strategy for complex environments. Engineering Applications of Artificial Intelligence (2013)
6. Faratin, P., Sierra, C., Jennings, N.R.: Using similarity criteria to make issue trade-offs in automated negotiations. Artificial Intelligence 142, 205–237 (2002)
7. Fatima, S.S., Wooldridge, M., Jennings, N.R.: Multi-issue negotiation under time constraints. In: Proceedings of the First International Joint Conference on Autonomous Agents and Multiagent Systems (AAMAS 2002), New York, NY, USA, pp. 143–150 (2002)
8. Fujita, K.: Automated strategy adaptation for multi-times bilateral closed negotiations. In: Proceedings of the 13th International Conference on Autonomous Agents and Multiagent Systems (AAMAS 2014), pp. 1509–1510 (2014)
9. Fujita, K.: Compromising strategy based on conflict mode for multi-times bilateral closed negotiations. In: Proceedings of the Seventh International Workshop on Agent-based Complex Automated Negotiations (ACAN 2014) (2014)
10. Fujita, K., Ito, T., Klein, M.: A secure and fair protocol that addresses weaknesses of the nash bargaining solution in nonlinear negotiation. Group Decision and Negotiation 21(1), 29–47 (2012), http://dx.doi.org/10.1007/s10726-010-9194-6

11. Gal, K., Ito, T., Jonker, C., Kraus, S., Hindriks, K., Lin, R., Baarslag, T.: The forth international automated negotiating agents competition (anac2013) (2013), http://www.itolab.nitech.ac.jp/ANAC2013/
12. Hao, J., Leung, H.-F.: Abines: An adaptive bilateral negotiating strategy over multiple items. In: 2012 IEEE/WIC/ACM International Conferences on Intelligent Agent Technology (IAT 2012), vol. 2, pp. 95–102 (2012)
13. Kawaguchi, S., Fujita, K., Ito, T.: Compromising strategy based on estimated maximum utility for automated negotiation agents competition (anac-10). In: 24th International Conference on Industrial Engineering and Other Applications of Applied Intelligent Systems (IEA/AIE 2011), pp. 501–510 (2011)
14. Kilmann, R.H., Thomas, K.W.: Developing a forced-choice measure of conflict-handling behavior: The mode instrument. Engineering Applications of Artificial Intelligence 37(2), 309–325 (1977)
15. Klein, M., Faratin, P., Sayama, H., Bar-Yam, Y.: Negotiating complex contracts. Group Decision and Negotiation 12(2), 58–73 (2003)
16. Kraus, S.: Strategic Negotiation in Multiagent Environments. MIT Press (2001)
17. Lin, R., Kraus, S., Baarslag, T., Tykhonov, D., Hindriks, K., Jonker, C.M.: Genius: An integrated environment for supporting the design of generic automated negotiators. Computational Intelligence (2012)
18. Osborne, M.J., Rubinstein, A.: Bargaining and Markets (Economic Theory, Econometrics, and Mathematical Economics). Academic Press (April 1990)
19. Pan, L., Luo, X., Meng, X., Miao, C., He, M., Guo, X.: A two-stage win-win multiattribute negotiation model: Optimization and then concession. Computational Intelligence 29(4), 577–626 (2013)
20. Pruitt, D.G.: Trends in the scientific study of negotiation and mediation. Negotiation Journal 2(3), 237–244 (1986)
21. Rubinstein, A.: Perfect equilibrium in a bargaining model. Econometrica 50(1), 97–109 (1982)
22. Rubinstein, A.: A bargaining model with incomplete information about time preferences. Econometrica 53(5), 1151–1172 (1985)
23. Shell, G.R.: Bargaining for Advantage: Negotiation Strategies for Reasonable People. Penguin Books (2006)
24. Thompson, L.: Mind and heart of the negotiator, 2nd edn. The Prentice Hall Press (2000)
25. Williams, C.R., Robu, V., Gerding, E.H., Jennings, N.R.: Using gaussian processes to optimise concession in complex negotiations against unknown opponents. In: Proceedings of the 22nd International Joint Conference on Artificial Intelligence (IJCAI 2011), pp. 432–438 (2011)

Autonomous Strategy Determination with Learning of Environments in Multi-agent Continuous Cleaning

Ayumi Sugiyama and Toshiharu Sugawara

Department of Computer Science and Eng., Waseda University, Tokyo 1698555, Japan
sugi.ayumi@ruri.waseda.jp, sugawara@waseda.jp

Abstract. With the development of robot technology, we can expect self-propelled robots working in large areas where coordinated and collaborative behaviors by multiple robots are necessary. Thus, the learning appropriate strategy for coordination and cooperation in multiple autonomous agents is an important issue. However, conventional methods assumed that agents was given knowledge about the environment. This paper proposes a method of autonomous strategy learning for multiple agents coordination integrated with learning where are easy to become dirty in the environments using examples of continuous cleaning tasks. We found that agents with the proposed method could operate as effectively as those with the conventional method and we found that the proposed method often outperformed it in complex areas by splitting up in their works.

1 Introduction

Coordination by multiple autonomous robots have attracted attention in multi-agent systems. Recent technological advances in robotics and computer sciences have enabled robots to coordinate activities in a wide range of applications such as cleaning, security patrolling in homes/common areas. In particular, coordination enables agents, which are programs to control robot behavior, to complete tasks in large areas that cannot be covered with a single agent. We have addressed the issue of continuous cooperation problem, such as continuous cleaning and security patrols, as one of the higher autonomy problems by agents.

A number of studies on cleaning and patrolling by single and multiple robots have been conducted along this line. In particular, there have been two approaches to cooperative operations. The first is to segment an area into subareas, each of which is allocated to one or a few agents to operate there ([1], [3], [5]). The second approach is that the area is not divided but agents generate their own routes to effectively clean/monitor the environments ([6], [7], [9]). We have focused on the second approach, especially Yoneda et al.'s method [9] that assumed limited battery and autonomous behavior. However, they assumed that environmental knowledge about where are easy to become dirty was provided to agents in advance, although such knowledge is often unknown in real situations.

Therefore, we have extended the method in [9] by incorporating it with learning to identify the locations that are easy to become dirty, in order to apply it to real world systems. Agents gradually learn the probability of dirt accumulation at each location from the amount of vacuumed dirt using the variable learning rate according to the lengths of the observation intervals.

H.K. Dam et al. (Eds.): PRIMA 2014, LNAI 8861, pp. 455–462, 2014.

2   Model and Problem Definition

2.1   Assumptions

Our method is an extension of the *adaptive meta-target decision strategy* (AMTDS) proposed in [9]. We will introduce three assumptions that were also assumed in AMTDS. First, agents know their own and others' locations. For example, we can consider a system that consists of a number of agents equipped with indicators (such as infrared emission/reflecting devices) on the top and a receiver installed on the ceiling that identified their locations and periodically broadcast these data to all agents. Second, agents have a map (graph) of the environment. Finally, multiple agents can be at the same node. Of course, such a map and collision avoidance function are required, but we focus on autonomous learning of strategy in this paper and introduced these assumptions by relying on studies on these topics (e.g., [8], [2], [4]),

2.2   Models of Agent and Environment

An environment for agents to clean is described by graph $G = (V, E)$, where $V = \{v_1, \dots\}$ is the set of nodes to clean and E is the set of edges (paths) along which agents can traverse. We introduce discrete time with units called *ticks*. Without loss of generality, we can set the length of any edge to one, by adding a number of dummy nodes to G where no dirt has accumulated. Thus, agents can move one of the neighboring nodes and clean it every tick.

Let $A = \{1, \dots, n\}$ be a set of agents. The ease of dirt accumulation is represented by probabilities $\{P_v | v \in V, 0 \le P_v \le 1\}$. Thus, the amount of dust at time t on node $v \in V$, $L_t(v)$, is updated as

$$L_t(v) \leftarrow \begin{cases} L_{t-1}(v) + 1 & \text{(if dust occurs with probability } P_v) \\ L_{t-1}(v) & \text{(otherwise).} \end{cases} \tag{1}$$

However, if an agent has visited v at t, then the agent vacuums dirt up, so $L_t(v) = 0$. The higher P_v means that node v is easier to become dirty. Thus, we can express uniform or biased environments using these probabilities. Because the actual values of P_v (for $\forall v \in V$) are unknown to agent $i \in A$, i has to estimate P_v. The estimated probability of P_v is denoted by P_v^i and its initial value is set to zero. Agent i learns P_v^i during its cleaning tasks as described in Section 3. Note that AMTDS assumed that the probabilities of dirt accumulation in the environment were given to all agents. This correspond to the situation where $P_v^i = P_v$ for $\forall v \in V$ and $\forall i \in A$.

Agents have their own rechargeable batteries and have to visit their charging base, v_{base}^i. Because the description of battery in agents is identical to that used in [9], we omit it due to the limitation of page length.

2.3   Performance Measure

A continuous cleaning task is requested to decrease the amount of dirt remaining in the environment, and dirt should be cleaned up as soon as possible. Hence, we use the cumulative existence duration of dirt at certain intervals between time t_s and t_e as the performance measure to evaluate our proposed method. This is defined as

$$D_{t_s,t_e} = \sum_{v \in V} \sum_{t=t_s+1}^{t_e} L_t(v), \tag{2}$$

where $t_s < t_e$. The smaller D_{t_s,t_e} indicates the better system performance.

3 Proposed Method

The proposed method, like AMTDS [9], determines the appropriate path planning strategy from the set of strategies agents know, S, by reinforcement learning. Agent i decides strategy according to the Q-values with the ε-greedy learning strategy. we denote the Q-value for strategy s as $Q^i(s)$ where $s \in S$.

$Q^i(s)$ is updated by a reward u_t that is the average amount of vacuumed dirt on the way to the target from deciding the strategy. Then Q-value of s, $Q^i(s)$ is updated as

$$Q^i(s) \leftarrow (1-\alpha)Q^i(s) + \alpha \cdot u_t, \tag{3}$$

where α is learning parameter $(0 < \alpha \leq 1)$.

The proposed method also enables agents to learn probabilities of dirt accumulation in the environment. After agent i has vacuumed up dirt at node v at time t, it calculates the interval, $I_t^i(v)$, between the most recent time when any agent cleaned node v and the current time:

$$I_t^i(v) = t - t_{visit}^v. \tag{4}$$

Then, the estimated probability of dirt accumulation from the most recent observation can be calculated by $L_t(v)/I_t^i(v)$. However, the reliability of this value heavily depends on the length of the interval, $I_t^i(v)$, so agents take into account this reliability to calculate the estimated probability, P_v^i, as:

$$P_v^i \leftarrow (1 - \alpha(I_t^i(v)))P_v^i + \alpha(I_t^i(v))\frac{L_t(v)}{I_t^i(v)}, \tag{5}$$

where $\alpha(k)$ $(0 < \alpha(k) \leq \alpha_{max})$ is the learning rate function, which is monotonically increasing. The learning rate function is defined as:

$$\alpha(k) = \max(\alpha_{ini} \cdot k, \alpha_{max}), \tag{6}$$

where α_{ini} $(0 < \alpha_{ini} \ll 1)$ is the base learning rate. We also introduce the upper bound, α_{max}, to avoid ignoring the past value. The proposed method is called *AMTDS with learning of dirt accumulation probabilities* (AMTDS/LD), after this.

4 Path Planning Strategies

We use the set of path planning strategies, S, that are identical to those in [9] in the experiments below because we clarify difference of AMTDS and our proposed method. We briefly explain these strategies. Agents create the plans for their paths in two stages: target decision and path generation. Agent i with AMTDS and AMTDS/LD selects one of the following target decision strategies to select the next target node, v_{tar}^i.

Random Selection : Agent i randomly selects the next target node from V.

Probabilistic Greedy Selection (PGS) : Agent i estimate $L_t(v)$ from the learned probability of dirt accumulation as:

$$EL_t^i(v) = P_v^i \cdot (t - t_{visit}^v),$$

where t_{visit}^v is the most recent time when an agent visited v (agents can know such a time due to the assumptions in Section 2.1. Agent i randomly select one v_{tar}^i from the first N_g nodes according to the values of $EL_t^i(v)$.

Repulsive Selection (RS) : Let V_{rep}^i be the set of N_{rep} nodes that i randomly selected from V. Then, i decides v_{tar}^i as the farthest node from other agents in V_{rep}^i.

Balanced Neighbor-Preferential Selection (BNPS) : The basic idea behind the *balanced neighbor-preferential selection* strategy is that, if agent i decides that there are *dirty nodes* in the neighborhood according to the values of $EL_t^i(v)$, i selects nearby nodes as v_{tar}^i, but otherwise selects farther dirtier distant nodes based on the PGS method.

We use one path generation strategy called the *gradual path generation* (GPG), which first generates the shortest path but if there are dirty nodes near the path, agents visit there to clean them. The details of method is omitted here [9]. Set of strategies S can be defined as R, RS, PGS, BNPS.

Finally, we want to point out that PGS and BNPS use knowledge on dirt accumulation, i.e. , P_v^i for $(v \in V)$ and R and RS do not. Also note that agents have different values of P_v^i because they are individually learned through their task operations.

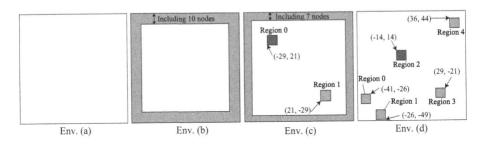

Fig. 1. Environments used in our experiments

5   Experiments

5.1   Experimental Environments

We examined how our proposed method could improve performance. We set the number of agents $|A|$ to 20 and adopted AMTDS or AMTDS/LD to select the path planning strategies from S. Environment $G = (V, E)$ is the 101×101 grid space and node $v \in V$ is expressed as (x, y) whose ranges were $-50 \le x, y \le 50$. Initially, all agents started cleaning from their charging base, $v_{base}^i = v_{base} = (0, 0)$, where agents could always charge their batteries.

Table 1. Parameters in target decision strategies

Target Decision Strategy	Parameter	Value
PGS	N_g	5
RS	N_{rep}	100
AMTDS	α	0.1
	ε	0.05
AMTDS/LD	α_{ini}	0.00001
	α_{max}	0.1

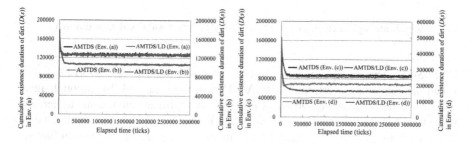

Fig. 2. Improvement in $D(s)$ over time

We prepared four environments that had different probabilities of dust accumulation, as outlined in Figs. 1. Env. (a) is a uniform environment and the probability of node v was randomly defined as $P_v = 0.0$ or $P_v = 5.0 \times 10^{-6}$ at the beginning of each experimental trial. In the other environments, we set P_v for $v \in V$ as:

$$P_v = \begin{cases} 10^{-3} \text{ (if } v \text{ is in a red region)} \\ 10^{-4} \text{ (if } v \text{ is in an orange region} \\ 10^{-6} \text{ (otherwise).} \end{cases} \tag{7}$$

In Envs. (c) and (d), we labelled block regions such as *Region 1*, and *Region 2*. *Region N* (where N is a positive integer) will also be denoted by R_N after this.

Agents could continuously operate up to 900 ticks and required 2700 ticks for a full charge if the battery was flat, making the maximum cycle of operation and charge 3600 ticks [9]. We obtained D_{t_s,t_e} every 3600 ticks to measure performance. Thus D_{t_s,t_e} can be expressed as $D_{t,t+3600}$ and for simplicity, when agents adopted strategy s, $D_{t,t+3600}$ has been denoted by $D(s)$ if there is no confusion, where s = AMTDS, or AMTDS/LD. The parameter values used in the target decision strategies are listed in Table 1. Other initial parameter values are identical to those used in [9]. The initial value of P_v^i for $v \in V$ is set to zero. The experimental results given below are the averages of twenty independent trials based on different random seeds.

5.2 Experimental Results

We investigated how performance had improved over time and compared it with that with AMTDS. Figures 2 plot how $D(s)$ was improved when agents used AMTDS or

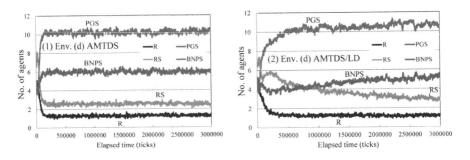

Fig. 3. Strategies selected by agents with AMTDS and AMTDS/LD in Env. (d)

AMTDS/LD. These graphs indicate that the proposed method, AMTDS/LD, demonstrated the comparable performance to AMTDS in Envs. (a) and (b), although agents with AMTDS/LD had no data about the probabilities of dirt accumulation. Furthermore, AMTDS/LD slightly outperformed AMTDS in Envs. (c) and (d). In particular, the improvement ratio of D is significant (21.3%, by expressing as a percentage) in Env. (d). This seems a counter-intuitive result (we will discuss this later).

We also compared the transition in how many agents adopted individual strategies — this structure of strategies is referred as the *strategy regime structure* — in both method. The results in Env. (d) are plotted in Figs. 3. We show the results of Env. (d) that is one of the set environment but we could observe the similar features in the strategy regime structures in other environments. First, the final regime structures with AMTDS/LD were almost identical to those with AMTDS in all the environments. Because the probabilities of dirt accumulation were gradually learned over time, their regime structures also gradually converged to appropriate ones.

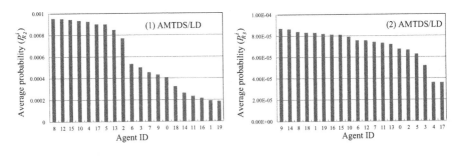

Fig. 4. Learned probabilities of dirt accumulation if R_2 and R_3 are in Env. (d)

Second, at the beginning of the experiments (before 100000 ticks), the number of agents that adopted the RS strategy temporally increased in all environments when they adopted AMTDS/LD. When the learning of dirt accumulation was insufficient, agents believed that the environments were almost uniform. Hence, PGS and BNPS strategies that relied on knowledge of dirt accumulation did not work well, and the RS strategy that made agents operate separately could perform relatively better. Of course, in Env. (d), agents with the RS strategy gradually decreased (whereas they retained large numbers with the RS strategy in other environments where it was the majority strategy in the final regimes).

Finally, if we compare these graphs with those in Figs. 2, we find that the entire performance, $D(\text{AMTDS/LD})$, seems to be stable after 50000 ticks, but their strategy regime structures are still internally varying after that. Because the appropriate strategy is mutually affected by other agents' strategies, it takes more time to converge to stable structures.

5.3   Analysis of Improved Performance in Env. (d)

We could observe better performance with AMTDS/LD than that with AMTDS in Envs. (c) and (d), as shown in Figs. 2. We tried to identify the reason for this phenomenon from additional data. Figs. 4 plots the average probabilities of dirt accumulation in block regions, R_2 and R_3, in Env. (d), where we define:

$$P_{R_N}^i = \sum_{v \in R_N} P_v^i / |R_N|$$

and $|R_N|$ is the number of nodes in region R_N. Note that in these figures, agent IDs are sorted in descending order by $P_{R_N}^i$. Note that these graphs were the result in one of twenty trials but similar characteristics could be observed in other trials.

Figures 4 indicate that all agents did not accurately identify the values of $P_{R_N}^i$; some identified them as less than the half value of P_{R_N} $(= \sum_{v \in R_N} / |R_N|)$ for R_2 and R_3. These differences in their learned probabilities resulted in differences in their movements. Note that when agents adopted AMTDS, agents have same information of probability of dirt accumulation. However, because agents with AMTDS/LD had different learned probabilities of dirt accumulation, those having high probabilities of $P_{R_2}^i$ visited R_2 much more frequently. This phenomenon was also observed for regions R_3. Another important observation is that agents with AMTDS/LD that had high values of $P_{R_3}^i$ (they visited R_3 more frequently) had relatively small values of $P_{R_2}^i$.

These experimental results suggested an important feature; they split up in working — division of labor —, although agents did not intentionally communicate with one another to determine the place they worked. In the beginning, they were likely to use the RS strategy as previously mentioned. Thereafter, they learned that the regions were dirtier and returned to visit there frequently. Of course, they sometimes visited other dirty regions, but as the regions were likely to have been cleaned by other agents (who frequently visited there), other agents might have identified that the regions were not so dirty. As a result, each agent differently identified one or a few dirtier regions. Such a division of labor improved overall performance by avoiding agents bustling everywhere ineffectively. We think that such easy-to-dirty regions appear everywhere in actual environments, such as regions under tables/desks and near intakes/vents of air conditioners. Thus, the improvements found here are important phenomena for actual applications.

6   Conclusion

We extended the method of appropriately selecting target decision strategies that proposed in [9], so that agents could perform continuous cleaning tasks without knowledge about areas that were easy to dirty in advance. Agents learned such knowledge through actual cleaning tasks while learning what appropriate planning strategies were for their coordinated tasks. We experimentally evaluated the proposed method, AMTDS/LD, and found that agents could clean their environments as well as that with AMTDS, which is the conventional method. We also found that in certain environments, AMTDS/LD could outperform AMTDS although it did not require knowledge. We then investigated why such a phenomenon occurred using the experimental results.

We intend to introduce communication capabilities to agents in our settings and investigate how they can improve system performance. Such outcomes could not only to be applied cleaning tasks but also to security patrolling and collecting tasks.

References

1. Ahmadi, M., Stone, P.: A multi-robot system for continuous area sweeping tasks. In: Proc. of the 2006 IEEE Int. Conf. on Robotics and Automation, pp. 1724–1729 (2006)
2. Dinnissen, P., Givigi, S., Schwartz, H.: Map merging of multi-robot slam using reinforcement learning. In: Proc. of 2012 IEEE Int. Conf. on Systems, Man, and Cybernetics (SMC), pp. 53–60 (2012)
3. Elor, Y., Bruckstein, A.M.: Multi-a(ge)nt graph patrolling and partitioning. In: Proc. of the 2009 IEEE/WIC/ACM International Joint Conf. on Web Intelligence and Intelligent Agent Technologies, pp. 52–57 (2009)
4. Hennes, D., Claes, D., Meeussen, W., Tuyls, K.: Multi-robot collision avoidance with localization uncertainty. In: Proc. of the 11th Int. Conf. on Autonomous Agents and Multiagent Systems, AAMAS 2012, vol. 1, pp. 147–154 (2012)
5. Kato, C., Sugawara, T.: Decentralized area partitioning for a cooperative cleaning task. In: Boella, G., Elkind, E., Savarimuthu, B.T.R., Dignum, F., Purvis, M.K. (eds.) PRIMA 2013. LNCS, vol. 8291, pp. 470–477. Springer, Heidelberg (2013)
6. Kurabayashi, D., Ota, J., Arai, T., Yoshida, E.: Cooperative sweeping by multiple mobile robots. In: Proc. of 1996 IEEE International Conf. on Robotics and Automation, vol. 2, pp. 1744–1749 (April 1996)
7. Sampaio, P., Ramalho, G., Tedesco, P.: The gravitational strategy for the timed patrolling. In: Proc. of 2010 22nd IEEE Int. Conf. on Tools with Artificial Intelligence (ICTAI), pp. 113–120 (2010)
8. Wolf, D., Sukhatme, G.: Mobile robot simultaneous localization and mapping in dynamic environments. Autonomous Robots 19(1), 53–65 (2005)
9. Yoneda, K., Kato, C., Sugawara, T.: Autonomous learning of target decision strategies without communications for continuous coordinated cleaning tasks. In: Proc. of 2013 IEEE/WIC/ACM Int. Joint Conf. on Web Intelligence and Intelligent Agent Technologies, vol. 2, pp. 216–223 (November 2013)

Author Index